Lonely Planet Publications
Melbourne · Oakland · London

W9-AVI-465

Steve Fallon &
Annabel Hart

Paris

The Top Five

1 Champs-Élysées
Broad, famous, crowded and even a bit daggy (p130)

2 The Louvre
The world's richest museum with something for everyone (p100)

3 Notre Dame
Sacred (medieval statues) and profane (gargoyles, tourists – p111)

4 Montmartre
The Paris of story, song, legends and lies (p148)

5 Eiffel Tower
The Paris icon, most beautiful from below looking up (p127)

Introducing Paris

Paris is the world's most seductive city, with art, beauty and romance everywhere. But, to the unfamiliar, it can be intimidating. Paris has more familiar landmarks than any other city in the world. As a result, visitors often arrive with all sorts of expectations: grand vistas, intellectual discussions, romance along the Seine, sexy cabaret revues...

You'll find all those things here, make no mistake about that. But another approach is to set aside your preconceptions of Paris and explore the city's avenues and backstreets as if the tip of the Eiffel Tower and the spire of Notre Dame weren't about to pop into view at any moment.

It is not hyperbole to say that Paris is the most beautiful, the most romantic city in the world. A lot of people who have come before you have not hesitated to say so, in prose or poetry or song. Indeed, Paris has just about exhausted the superlatives that can be reasonably applied to any city. Sacré Coeur, the Seine, the av des Champs-Élysées – at sunrise, at sunset, at night, in the sun, in the rain – have all been painted, sung about and described, as have the Seine and the subtle (and not-so-subtle) differences between the Left and Right Banks. What artists, singers and writers have rarely been able to capture, though, is the sheer magic of strolling along the city's broad avenues, which lead from impressive public buildings and museums to parks, gardens and esplanades. But it's no longer the living museum or Gallic theme park it may have seemed a generation ago. Today Paris is a welcoming, fun and increasingly cosmopolitan city to visit.

Parisians believe they have savoir-vivre – the art of knowing how to live well – and indeed you'll find that Paris is a sensory feast. It's a city to gaze at, with its wide boulevards, impressive monuments, great works of art and magical lights. It's a city to taste, with its great cheese, chocolate, wine, breads and *charcuterie* (cured, smoked or processed meat products). It's a city to hear, whether you like opera, jazz or world music.

It's a city to smell: perfume boutiques, cafés with fresh coffee and croissants, chestnuts roasting on an open fire in winter. It's a city to feel: the wind in your face as you cycle along the Seine, the *frisson* of fear and pleasure as you peer out from the top of the Eiffel Tower or the Grande Arche de la Défense.

Above all, it's a city to discover. By all means read *Paris* – it's designed to whet your appetite and to guide you when you arrive – and visit as many of the sights and museums as time allows; they're part of the Paris package. But remember: what you hold in your hand is a guidebook not a handbook. Leave *Paris* in your hotel or packed away in your rucksack from time to time, and go out and find your own Paris. Jump on the metro or a bus and get off at a place you've never heard of. Wander through a neighbourhood where French mixes easily with Arabic, Bengali or Vietnamese, poke your head into little shops, invite yourself to play *basket* (basketball)

LOWDOWN

Grand crème on a Champs-Élysées café terrace €4.50

Length of the av des Champs-Élysées 1910m

Metro/bus ticket €1.40 (€10.70 for 10)

Metro stations 372

Markets 19 (covered), 62 (open)

No-no Summoning the waiter by shouting '*Garçon!*' (Boy!)

Percentage of polled visitors who say they intend to return to Paris 97.8%

Population 2.144 million (Paris proper), 11.3 million (greater Paris)

Three-star double room €100 to €150

Time it would take to see everything in the Louvre 9 months

Time zone Central European Time (GMT + 1 hour)

in a park or just lounge on a café terrace with a glass of wine and watch Paris pass by. It won't be long before you fall in love with your very own Paris and discover that it is enchanting almost everywhere, at any time, even 'in the summer, when it sizzles' and 'in the winter, when it drizzles' as Cole Porter put it in *I Love Paris*. And, like a good meal, it excites, it satisfies and the memory lingers. Like us, you'll dine out on the memories for many years to come.

STEVE'S TOP PARIS DAY

If it's Sunday morning and this is Paris, I'm going to sacrifice my 'greasy morning' (*grasse matinée,* a lie-in) and get myself to the closest *marché découvert* (open-air market) which, seeing as I'm staying with my mate at her *belle époque* flat near place de la République, is Marché Bastille, a hop, skip and four metro stops south on the orange (number 5) or purple (number 8) line. I've just realised I'm fresh out of essentials like truffle oil and those huge Breton crabs called *tourteaux* that taste of the very sea itself and I must stock up. Having made my purchases, I'll no longer be in such a hurry so I'll wend my way through medieval Marais, stopping for a *grand crème* (coffee with cream) and a *pain au chocolat* at Ma Bourgogne in the scrumptious place des Vosges. The landmark bridge Pont de Sully leads to my favourite island, Île St-Louis, but once I reach the Île de la Cité, I'll eschew Notre Dame in favour of the smaller, more delicate Ste-Chapelle and its stained glass. Before lunch (somewhere on the rue Montorgueil) I'll window-shop at the boutiques of rue Étienne Marcel or have another look at the antique clothes for sale in the Galerie de Montpensier. Though close by, the Louvre is just too daunting for a postprandial visit; instead I'll rent a bike from Fat Tire Bike Tours and cruise along the car-free (it's Sunday!) banks of the Seine. If I feel culturally peckish, I'll make my way to the Musée Guimet and have a zen-like kip (AKA nap) in the annexe's peaceful Japanese garden. As far as I'm concerned, any corner café works for an *apéro* (apéritif), but since I'm having dinner at Le Chansonnier near the Gare de l'Est, I head for Chez Wolf, for mixers, mirth and Motown.

City Life

City Life

PARIS TODAY

It was as *horribilis* an *annus* as any in recent memory. Rioters were running ragged through the streets again, and Paris was burning for the second time in four months. This time, however, a very different kettle of fish was on the boil.

The riots that broke out in October and November 2005 were – in Paris at least – restricted to the *banlieues* (suburbs), with their faceless *cités*, the enormous housing estates or projects encircling the capital, and dispossessed population of mostly Blacks and Muslims. This and the subsequent torture and murder of 23-year-old Jewish Parisian Ilan Halimi by a suspected Palestinian Muslim gang had many a *Libération*-reading liberal navel-gazing on issues of race and racism. Parisians began to talk about and debate ethnic origin and affirmative action (what the French called 'positive discrimination'). But this remained a problem 'out there'.

The trouble became more central – both literally and figuratively – in March 2006 after parliament passed the controversial Contrat de Première Embauche (CPE; First Employment Contract; p21) bill. Some 64 of the nation's 84 universities went on strike, workers and students mobilised and 1.5 million protesters took to the streets nationwide. In Paris, demonstrators torched cars and clashed with police, who responded with tear gas and water cannons.

It certainly had not been a very good year for the national leadership – or that of the capital for that matter. In May 2005, in what was seen as a massive protest vote against President Jacques Chirac, 55% of the electorate voted against the EU constitution (p68) – though it must be said that 66% of Parisians voted in favour of it. And just over a month later, Paris mayor Bertrand Delanoë, the man who could usually not put a wrong foot forward, was dealt a major blow when the IOC awarded the 2012 Olympic Games not to the all-round favourite candidate – Paris – but to London and the perfidious *Anglo-Saxons* (p18). Then in the autumn greater Paris was gripped by three weeks of some of the worst violence since WWII, which thankfully saw no deaths but 3000 arrests and millions of euros in property damage. And just

Café scene on Rue Mouffetard (p52)

when tourism seemed to be getting back on its feet (p160)…

Both Paris municipal and French national elections are scheduled for the spring of 2007. While the blond-haired boy Delanoë will doubtless remain right where he is at the Hôtel de Ville it is unlikely that Chirac will still be in resident at the Palais de l'Élysée by the time half the year is over. The heir apparent is Prime Minister Dominique de Villepin, the president's loyal henchman who has never been elected to public office, though the get-tough Interior Minister Nicolas 'Sarko' Sarkozy, who famously fanned the flames during the race riots by calling the rioters *racaille* (rabble or riffraff) and whose loyalties to Chirac

HOT CONVERSATION TOPICS

- Food – fooding and fuelling, restaurants and recipes
- Property prices – is La Goutte d'Or the next *bobo* (bohemian bourgeois) target?
- Riots – is it yesterday (ie 1968) once more, shoobedoo la la?
- Roadworks – won't Paris look great when it's finished?
- Ségo or Sarko? – is France ready for a Mme La Présidente?
- Sex – all the dirty details (and – blush – in mixed company)

seem to blow with the prevailing wind, stands a much better chance of winning. Watching from the wings was Socialist Ségalène 'Ségo' Royal, perhaps the left's only hope of ending a dozen years of right-wing incumbency. Blessed with a classy face and an even classier name, Royal is one of the country's most intelligent and popular politicians, and one poll had her winning 57% of the vote if the elections were held the following day.

And along with topics like riots and Royal are the other perennial Parisian problems such as litter – notably cigarette butts and dog droppings (p23) – and the in-your-face billboards in the metro and elsewhere, featuring half-naked women being used to sell cars and watches, that are routinely defaced by *les antipublicistes* (those against advertising). Heroes to some, vandals to others, along with food, wine and women (or men), they'll keep Paris talking. And debating. And bickering.

CITY CALENDAR

Innumerable festivals, cultural and sporting events and trade shows take place in Paris throughout the year; weekly details appear in *Pariscope* and *L'Officiel des Spectacles* and the more colourful entertainment magazine *Zurban* (p258). You can also find them listed under 'What's On' on the website of the **Office de Tourisme et de Congrès de Paris** (Paris Convention & Visitors Bureau; www.parisinfo.com).

The following abbreviated list gives you a taste of what to expect throughout the year. To ensure that your trip does not coincide with a public holiday, when *everything* will be shut, see p377.

JANUARY & FEBRUARY
GRANDE PARADE DE PARIS
www.parisparade.com
The city's New Year's Day parade originated in Montmartre but may take place in different venues (eg under the Eiffel Tower, in Chantilly, along the Grands Boulevards) from year to year. Check the website for details.

LOUIS XVI COMMEMORATIVE MASS
☎ 01 44 32 18 00; www.monum.fr
On the Sunday closest to 21 January, royalists and right-wingers attend a mass at the Chapelle Expiatoire (p133) marking the execution by guillotine of King Louis XVI in 1793.

PARIS, CAPITALE DE LA CREATION
www.pariscapitaledelacreation.com
Prêt-à-Porter, the ready-to-wear fashion salon that is held twice a year in January or February and again in September, joins forces with 16 other trade shows dealing with every possible aspect of fashion – as well as interior design – to create this blockbuster of an exposition which is a must for fashion buffs. Held jointly at Parc des Expositions at Porte de Versailles in the 15e arrondissement (metro Porte de Versailles), southwest of the city centre, and Parc des Expositions, Paris-Nord Villepinte, to the north of the fashion capital.

CHINESE NEW YEAR
www.paris.fr
Dragon parades and other festivities are held late January/early February in two Chinatowns: the smaller, more authentic one in the 3e, taking in rue du Temple, rue au Maire and rue de Turbigo (metro Temple or Arts et Métiers), and the flashier one in the 13e in between porte de Choisy, porte d'Ivry and blvd Masséna (metro Porte de Choisy, Port d'Ivry or Tolbiac).

SALON INTERNATIONAL DE L'AGRICULTURE
www.salon-agriculture.com
A 10-day international agricultural fair with lots to eat and drink, including dishes and wine from all over France, is held at the Parc des Expositions at Porte de Versailles in the 15e (metro Porte de Versailles) from late February to early March.

MARCH-MAY
PRINTEMPS DU CINÉMA
www.printempsducinema.com in French
Cinemas across Paris offer filmgoers a unique entry fee of €3.50 over three days (usually Sunday, Monday and Tuesday) sometime around 21 March.

BANLIEUES BLEUES
www.banlieuesbleues.org
The 'Suburban Blues' jazz and blues festival (with world, soul, funk, and rhythm and blues thrown in for good measure) is held over five weeks in March and April in the suburbs of Paris, including St-Denis (p157), and attracts some big-name talent.

MARATHON INTERNATIONAL DE PARIS
www.parismarathon.com
The Paris International Marathon, held in early April, starts on the av des Champs-Élysées, 8e, and finishes on av Foch, in the 16e. The Semi-Marathon de Paris is a half-marathon held in early March; see the website for map and registration details.

FOIRE DU TRÔNE
www.foiredutrone.com in French
This huge funfair, with 350 attractions spread over 10 hectares, is held on the pelouse de

Reuilly of the Bois de Vincennes (metro Porte Dorée) for eight weeks during April and May.

FOIRE DE PARIS
www.foiredeparis.fr
This huge modern-living fair, including crafts, gadgets and widgets, and food and wine, is held in late April/early May at the Parc des Expositions at Porte de Versailles in the 15e (metro Porte de Versailles).

ATELIERS D'ARTISTES DE BELLEVILLE: LES PORTES OUVERTES
www.ateliers-artistes-belleville.org in French
Some 200 painters, sculptors and other artists in Belleville (metro Belleville) in the 10e open their studio doors to visitors over four days (Friday to Monday) in mid-May.

INTERNATIONAUX DE FRANCE DE TENNIS
www.frenchopen.org
The glitzy French Open tennis tournament takes place from late May to mid-June at Stade Roland Garros (metro Porte d'Auteuil) at the southern edge of the Bois de Boulogne in the 16e.

JUNE-AUGUST
FÊTE DE LA MUSIQUE
www.fetedelamusique.fr in French
This national music festival welcoming in summer on the evening of 21 June caters to a great diversity of tastes (including jazz, reggae and classical) and features staged and impromptu live performances all over the city and the nation.

GAY PRIDE MARCH
www.gaypride.fr in French
This colourful Saturday-afternoon parade in late June through the Marais to Bastille celebrates Gay Pride Day, with various bars and clubs sponsoring floats, and participants in some pretty outrageous costumes.

FOIRE ST-GERMAIN
www.foiresaintgermain.org in French
This month-long festival of concerts and theatre from early June to early July takes place on the place St-Sulpice, 6e (metro St-Sulpice) and various other venues in the quartier St-Germain.

Contents

Published by Lonely Planet Publications Pty Ltd
ABN 36 005 607 983

Australia Head Office, Locked Bag 1, Footscray,
Victoria 3011, ☎ 03 8379 8000, fax 03 8379 8111,
talk2us@lonelyplanet.com.au

USA 150 Linden St, Oakland, CA 94607,
☎ 510 893 8555, toll free 800 275 8555,
fax 510 893 8572, info@lonelyplanet.com

UK 72–82 Rosebery Ave, Clerkenwell, London,
EC1R 4RW, ☎ 020 7841 9000, fax 020 7841 9001,
go@lonelyplanet.co.uk

© Lonely Planet 2006
Photographs © Jean-Bernard Carillet and as listed
(p397) 2006

Printed by SNP Security Printing Pte Ltd, Singapore

The Authors

Steve Fallon

Steve, who's worked on every edition of *Paris* and *France* other than the first, was surrounded by things French from a young age when his neighbour's (and best friend's) mother in Boston thought it would be a 'bunny day' (or was that a *bonne idée*?) to rock them in the same cradle. Convinced that Parisians were seriously devoid of a sense of humour after he and said best friend dropped water-filled condoms on the heads of passers-by from a 5e arrondissement hotel balcony at age 16, he nevertheless went back to the 'City of Light' five years later to complete a degree in French at the Sorbonne. Based in East London, Steve will be just one Underground stop away from Paris when Eurostar trains begin departing from Stratford. Steve wrote the front chapters, along with Sights, Walking Tours, Eating, Sleeping and the Directory for this book.

Annabel Hart

Annabel left her hometown of Melbourne in 2000 with a backpack and a handful of French grammar, planning to stay in France for three months. Six years later she's still struggling to tear herself away from the city that has become a second home. Most of her first years in Paris were spent doing freelance writing, travelling and learning slang in bars. She more recently completed a Masters in International Relations in Paris and a stint in Thailand working in sustainable development. Annabel has contributed to various LP guides as well as many in-house projects. Her travels have taken her through Europe, Southeast Asia, Australia, New Zealand and bits of the USA. Annabel wrote the Entertainment, Drinking, Activities, Shopping, Excursions and Transport chapters for this book.

PHOTOGRAPHER
Jean-Bernard Carillet

A Paris-based author and photographer, Jean-Bernard's photos have appeared in many Lonely Planet guides, including *Best of Brussels* and *Naples & the Amalfi Coast*. When not in the tropics or markets in Eastern Africa, he heads for eastern France, southern Belgium and the Ruhr in Germany to capture the industrial wasteland. He was all too happy to photograph from his doorstep and rediscover his city. As a true-blue Parisian, he confirms that Paris is the City of Light.

PARIS JAZZ FESTIVAL
www.parcfloraldeparis.com
There are free jazz concerts every Saturday and Sunday afternoon in June and July in the Parc Floral de Paris (metro Château de Vincennes).

LA COURSE DES GARÇONS ET SERVEUSES DE CAFÉ
☎ 01 42 96 60 75
A Sunday-afternoon 8km foot race starting and finishing at the Hôtel de Ville (metro Hôtel de Ville) in the Marais in June, with some 500 wait staff each carrying a small, circular tray with glasses and a bottle. Breaking – or even spilling – anything results in disqualification.

LA GOUTTE D'OR EN FÊTE
www.gouttedorenfete.org in French
This week-long world-music festival (featuring raï, reggae and rap) is held at square Léon, 18e (metro Barbès Rochechouart or Château Rouge) from late June to early July.

BASTILLE DAY (14 JULY)
Paris is *the* place to be on France's national day. Late on the night of the 13th, *bals des sapeurs-pompiers* (dances sponsored by Paris' firefighters, who are considered sex symbols in France) are held at fire stations around the city. At 10am on the 14th, there's a military and fire-brigade parade along av des Champs-Élysées, accompanied by a fly-past of fighter aircraft and helicopters. In the evening, a huge display of *feux d'artifice* (fireworks) is held at around 11pm on the Champ de Mars, 7e.

TOUR DE FRANCE
www.letour.fr
The last stage of this prestigious cycling event finishes with a race up av des Champs-Élysées on the 3rd or 4th Sunday of July, as it has done since 1975.

PARIS PLAGE
www.paris.fr
'Paris Beach', one of the most inspired and successful city recreational events in the world, is now copycatted in cities across Europe from Berlin to Budapest. It sees 3km of embankment from the quai Henri IV at the Pont de Sully (metro Sully Morland) in the 4e to the quai des Tuileries (metro Tuileries) below the Louvre in the 1er transformed for four weeks from mid-July to mid-August into three sand and pebble beaches with sun beds, umbrellas, atomisers and plastic palm trees – there's even a 38m paddling pool for kids. It's open from 7am to midnight Saturday to Thursday and to 4am on Friday.

PARIS CINÉMA
www.pariscinema.org
This relatively new two-week festival in late July/early August sees rare and restored films screened in selected cinemas across Paris.

SEPTEMBER
JAZZ À LA VILLETTE
www.villette.com
This super 10-day jazz festival in early September has sessions in Parc de la Villette, at the Cité de la Musique and in surrounding bars.

FESTIVAL D'AUTOMNE
www.festival-automne.com
The Autumn Festival of arts has painting, music, dance and theatre at venues throughout the city from mid-September to December.

Hôtel de Ville (p107) with carousel in foreground

- Fête des Vendanges de Montmartre – lots of noise for a bunch of old (and some say sour) grapes
- Gay Pride March – feathers and beads and participants in and out of same
- La Course des Garçons et Serveuses de Café – the fastest service you'll ever see in or out of Paris
- Louis XVI Commemorative Mass – wrong- and right-wing sob-fest for aristocrats, pretenders and hangers-on
- Paris Plage – the next best thing to the seaside along France's smallest beach

EUROPEAN HERITAGE DAYS

www.journeesdupatrimoine.culture.fr
As elsewhere in Europe on the third weekend in September, Paris opens doors to buildings (embassies, government ministries, corporate offices – even the Palais de l'Élysée) normally shut tight to outsiders.

OCTOBER
NUIT BLANCHE

www.paris.fr
'White Night' is when Paris 'does' New York and becomes 'the city that doesn't sleep at all', with museums across town joining bars and clubs and staying open till the very wee hours.

FÊTE DES VENDANGES DE MONTMARTRE

www.fetedesvendangesdemontmartre.com
This festival is held over the second weekend in October following the harvesting of

grapes from the Close du Montmartre (p174), with costumes, speeches and a parade.

FOIRE INTERNATIONALE D'ART CONTEMPORAIN

www.fiac-online.com
This huge contemporary art fair held over five days in late October with some 160 galleries represented has moved back to central Paris and now takes place at the Louvre and the Grand Palais.

DECEMBER
JUMPING INTERNATIONAL DE PARIS

www.salon-cheval.com
This annual showjumping tournament features the world's most celebrated jumpers at the Palais Omnisports de Paris-Bercy in the 12e arrondissement (metro Bercy) in early December. The annual International Showjumping Competition forms part of the Salon du Cheval at the Parc des Expositions at Porte de Versailles in the 15e (metro Porte de Versailles) with some of the best showjumpers in the world testing their limits.

CHRISTMAS EVE MASS

Mass is celebrated at midnight on Christmas Eve at many Paris churches, including Notre Dame, but get there by 11pm to find a place.

NEW YEAR'S EVE

Blvd St-Michel (5e), place de la Bastille (11e), the Eiffel Tower (7e) and especially av des Champs-Élysées (8e) are the places to be to welcome in the new year.

CULTURE
IDENTITY

According to the 2005 census, the population of central Paris is 2.144 million, while the greater metropolitan area – in effect, the Île de France – has 11.3 million inhabitants, or about 18.5% of France's total population of 60.7 million. The largest arrondissement (district), the 15e, is the most populous with more than 231,000 people, while the 1er, the third-smallest district, is the least populous with just under 17,000 people. Large working-class arrondissements such as the 19e and the 20e are growing rapidly.

France has had waves of immigration, particularly from its former colonies (p170) for centuries. The number of official immigrants in central Paris is just under 400,000 or 18.5% of the city's population; the figure would be much higher – possibly four times that number – if the number of those living clandestinely and in the greater metropolitan region was known. Of these official immigrants, 29% come from a North African country,

28% come from an EU member-state, 15% from Sub-Saharan Africa, 17% from Asia and 7% from a non-EU country.

Immigrants from Morocco, Tunisia and Algeria, each a French colony until the 1950s and 1960s, have been settling and working in France since the beginning of the 20th century, especially in the districts of Belleville in the 19e and 20e and in the neighbourhood known as La Goutte d'Or in the 18e. French-born North Africans are often called *beurs,* which is a nonpejorative Verlan term (p20) and is used frequently by the media and second-generation North Africans themselves.

The majority of black Sub-Saharan Africans in Paris hail from Mali as well as from Senegal, the Côte d'Ivoire, Cameroon, Mauritania, Congo, Guinea, Togo and Benin. Among the first immigrants were Senegalese soldiers who had fought for the French during WWI. They moved into the 18e, which remains the heart of African Paris. Students and intellectuals arrived from Africa in the 1940s and 1950s, and immigration was actively promoted during this time to boost France's workforce.

Many of the ethnic Chinese in Paris hail from the former French colonies of Indochina. Large waves of Asians arrived in France at the end of the First Indochina War in 1954; to escape the Khmer Rouge and Pathet Lao regimes in Cambodia and Laos in the 1970s; and as a result of the exodus of the Vietnamese boat people that continued well into the 1980s. The events in Tiananmen Square in 1989 prompted the flight of many Chinese; a relatively large number have arrived from mainland China in recent years. But Chinese immigration is nothing new; Chinese from the Zhejiang province have been settling in Paris since the 1920s, mainly in the 3e, 13e, 19e and 20e arrondissements.

Immigrants from India, Pakistan, Bangladesh and Sri Lanka, as well as from the former French colonies of Madagascar and Mauritius and the overseas *département* (department or, loosely, county) of Réunion, often appear to share a common culture, but each group is quite distinct and has its own network in Paris. Many immigrants from this region tend to work in and around the 10e; others commute from the suburbs.

Jews have come to live and work in Paris since the Middle Ages, and today Ashkenazi Jews (from Germany and Eastern Europe) tend to live in the Marais, while Sephardic Jews (of Spanish, Portuguese and North African descent) live in Belleville. In the latter, so-called 'Tunes' have managed to recreate something of the Tunisia they left behind in the 1950s. Other Jews work around rue du Sentier, 2e, the heart of Paris' rag trade.

The Portuguese presence in Paris dates back to the late 19th century. Political refugees were fleeing Portugal up until the revolution of 1974, but the majority of Portuguese living in greater Paris are workers who helped build the new suburbs. Turks and Kurds started arriving in the late 1960s and number around 45,000 in the greater Paris region. They, too, commonly live in the suburbs and commute into the city.

SEINE-FUL PURSUITS

The Seine is more than just Paris' dividing line (p22) and its dustless highway; it is a source of great amusement all year-round. The river's Oscar-winning role comes in July and August, when 3km of its banks are transformed into Paris Plage (p11), a bitch of a 'beach' with real sand and fake trees. But the river banks can be just as much fun at the weekend during the rest of the year. As part of the city's 'Paris Respire' (Paris Breathes) program, most roads running along the Seine are closed on Sundays and public holidays between mid-March and mid-December. Strollers, cyclists and skaters repossess the quays and some of the three-dozen bridges spanning the river. The banks between the Pont Alexandre III (Map pp426–7) and the Pont d'Austerlitz (Map pp446–7) have been listed as a Unesco World Heritage Site since 1991, but the choicest spots for sunning, picnicking and maybe even a little romancing are the delightful Square du Vert Gallant, 1er (metro Pont Neuf), the little park at the tip of the Île de la Cité named after that rake Henri IV (p113) and the Quai St-Bernard, 5e, just opposite the Jardin des Plantes. Here you'll find the **Musée de Sculpture de Plein Air** (Open-Air Sculpture Museum; Map pp444–5; ☎ 01 43 26 91 90; square Tino Rossi, 5e; admission free; ⏱ 24hr; Ⓜ Quai de la Rapée); a sandwich beneath a César or a baguette beside a Brancusi is a pretty classy way to see the Seine up close short of actually getting on it by joining a cruise (p96). Something to look forward to is the Métro Fluvial, now on the drawing board and scheduled for 2008. This 'River Metro' would run for 25km from Vitry-Port à l'Anglais in the east to Barrage de Suresnes in the west and make 35 stops (most of them on the Left Bank) along the way.

Paris has long been a haven for intellectuals in search of freedom of expression. Many of the Paris-based Greeks arrived during the dictatorship of the colonels (1967–74); exiles from South America settled in the city for similar reasons. Many of the 4500-odd Lebanese immigrants fled the civil war that began there in 1975.

Russians have emigrated to Paris throughout the 20th century. Immigration from Poland and other Eastern and central European countries has also figured largely. In inner Paris there are now some 10,500 immigrants from the former Yugoslavia.

Of course this influx of immigrants over the years has changed Parisians' tastes in many things, including the obvious, and, like the Indian curry and Turkish kebabs of London, in recent years ethnic food has become as Parisian as onion soup. The *nems* and *pâtés impérials* (spring or egg rolls) and *pho* (soup noodles with beef) of Vietnam, the couscous and tajines of North Africa, the *boudin antillais* (West Indian blood pudding) from the Caribbean and the *yassa* (meat or fish grilled in onion and lemon sauce) of Senegal are all eaten with – or perhaps without – relish throughout the capital. Indian (p219) and Japanese (p179) are also very popular non-French cuisines in Paris. You'll find a fair few *cacher* (kosher) restaurants of varying quality in the Marais (p183), blvd de Belleville, 20e, (p222) and the areas around rue Richer, rue Cadet and rue Geoffroy Marie, 9e, off the Grands Boulevards (p216).

Those who may think that Paris is multiracial heaven should think again. Racism does exist here, and the incidence of racist acts of violence have been high in recent years, particularly in Paris' crowded suburbs (see p8).

Like all French people, Parisians have a very strong sense of national identity based on their history, language, culture and pursuit of the finer things in life. But not only do a large number of Parisians believe that they live in the most civilised country in the world, they are also convinced that they are in the most civilised city in that country. Once you accept that fact, you're halfway to understanding in what high esteem most Parisians hold themselves.

Though outsiders sometimes see them as *coincé* – uptight, inhibited, chauvinistic – the average Parisian sees himself as open-minded and cultured. While the former is debatable, there is no excuse not to be the latter in Paris, where the sheer number of museums, cinemas, exhibitions, concerts and so on effect everyday life and, it must be said, conversation over an *apéro* (predinner drink). It's always safer to discuss the exhibition you stood in the queue for an hour to catch or the art film you saw last night than politics, race or religion.

Anything between 83% and 88% of French people are nominally Roman Catholic but, although most have been baptised, very few ever attend church or receive the sacraments.

Couple reading by fountain in Jardin du Palais Royal (p103)

TOP FIVE BOOKS ABOUT PARISIANS & THE FRENCH

- *An Englishman in Paris: L'Éducation Continentale,* Michael Sadler (2003) – rollicking, *very* funny (mis)adventures of a self-proclaimed Francophile teacher in the City of Light with a preface from Peter Mayle.
- *Culture Shock France,* Sally Adamson Taylor (2005) – subtitled 'A Survival Guide to Customs and Etiquette', this was the first (and remains the very best) introductory handbook to France and its culture, Parisians and their peculiarities.
- *The Last Time I Saw Paris,* Elliot Paul (2001) – a superb classic work by an American expat that looks back on the working-class Paris of the interwar years in a series of interwoven episodes.
- *Paris in Mind,* Jennifer Lee (2003) – an anthology of essays and excerpts by 29 American writers – from Edith Wharton and James Baldwin to David Sedaris and Dave Barry (who discusses how to pronounce the French 'r').
- *Sixty Million Frenchmen Can't Be Wrong,* Jean-Benoit Nadeau and Julie Barlow (2003) – a Paris-based Canadian journalist couple explains the essence of what it means to be French and how they got to be the way they are.

In Paris an estimated 300,000 to 350,000 Catholics are regular worshippers. *Conversion,* such as that experienced by the poet Paul Claudel (1868–1955) and the novelist Henry de Montherlant (1896–1972), thus actually means 're-conversion' in English. The Catholic Church in France is generally very progressive and ecumenically minded. Cardinal Jean-Marie Lustiger, archbishop of Paris since 1981, was born in Paris in 1926 to Jewish immigrants from Poland. He converted to Catholicism at age 14. His mother died in the Nazi extermination camp Auschwitz in 1942. France's Protestants, who were severely persecuted during much of the 16th and 17th centuries, make up only about 2% of the population (about 1.2 million) nationwide. They are largely concentrated in Alsace, the Jura, the southeastern part of the Massif Central, along the Atlantic coast and, of course, in Paris, with an estimated 40,000 followers.

Between five and six million French citizens and residents – 8% to 10% of the population – are nominally Muslim, and they now make up the country's second-largest religious group. The vast majority are immigrants (or their offspring) who arrived from North Africa starting in the 1950s. In Paris between 45,000 and 90,000 people regularly practice Islam.

There has been a Jewish community in France for most of the time since the Roman period. During the Middle Ages, the community suffered persecution and there were a number of mass expulsions. French Jews, the first in Europe to achieve emancipation, were granted full citizenship in 1790–91. Since 1808, the French Jewish community has had an umbrella organisation known as the **Consistoire** (www.consistoire.org), based in Paris. The country's Jewish community, which now numbers upwards of 700,000 – the largest in Europe, with between 150,000 and 200,000 in Paris – grew substantially during the 1960s as a result of immigration from Algeria, Tunisia and Morocco.

LIFESTYLE

As long as there has been a Paris, visitors have complained that its citizens can be bitchy, arrogant, full of attitude and as prickly as hedgehogs. If you do encounter some irritability, remember that the more tourists a city attracts – and Paris, as the first- or second-most popular destination in Europe (depending on who is doing the counting), gets more than its fair share – the less patience locals tend to have for them. At the same time, there are certain peculiarities about Parisians that do make them both frustrating and endearing to outsiders. Though it is difficult – and dangerous – to generalise about a greater metropolitan area of more than 11 million people, we're going to give it a try.

Parisians may, indeed, have a very strong sense of their own identity but, surprising as it sounds, they tend to be somewhat shy with strangers. They will be more than willing to help, however, if approached in a friendly, polite manner and with a word or two of even imperfect French. Etiquette is extremely important here and to be *'correcte'* – a catch-all word that can mean everything from acting properly to being honest – is all-important. To do (or *not* to do, as the case may be) certain things is considered extremely boorish. It is not rocket science, but there are pitfalls for the uninitiated.

In Paris, one does not smile at a passer-by or in general acknowledge a stranger's existence; this is considered unnecessary – even idiotic. However, if there is a 'relationship' involved – even one as simple as buyer and seller – you should greet people with a simple 'Bonjour, madam/monsieur'. This is always your first 'in' in Paris. People who know each other well greet one another with *bises* (kisses) on the cheek. Close male friends and relations always did this in the south of France, but it is becoming increasingly common nowadays among younger and educated 21st-century Parisians who don't give a toss that older males consider it *pédérastique* (queer). The usual ritual is one glancing peck on each cheek, but some people go for three (or even four) kisses. People who don't kiss each other will almost always shake hands when meeting up. People always stand up when meeting one another for the first time, including women with women.

An important distinction is made in French between *tu* and *vous*, which both mean 'you'. *Tu* is only used when addressing people you know very well, children or animals. When addressing an adult who is not a personal friend, *vous* should be used until the person invites you to use *tu*. In general, younger people insist less on this distinction, and they may use *tu* from the beginning of an acquaintanceship (but never with an elder).

In general people tend to meet outside when they socialise. Invitations to a private home are not frequent – though this is changing somewhat among a younger, modern, well-travelled generation – and if you do get one consider it as something of a privilege as a foreigner. Along with the address, be sure to get the entry code to the *porte cochère* (literally the 'carriage gate', or street door) of the apartment building (p97) as the individual door bells will be inside. Bring some sort of gift, but not wine unless it's a bottle of chilled Champagne: the wine your host has chosen will be an expression of his or her tastes and hospitality. Flowers are always a good idea, but *chrysanthèmes* (chrysanthemums) are only brought to cemeteries, *œillets* (carnations) are said to bring bad luck and red roses are reserved for lovers and yellow roses suggest cuckoldry. Flowers are usually presented in odd-numbered bunches (eg seven not a half-dozen and 11 not a dozen but certainly not 13!). It is impossible to overdress for a Parisian *soirée* (evening out). Both women and men take tremendous care of how they groom and dress themselves; smart casual is always the safest way to go.

After what might seem a cool start, warmed up no doubt when predinner drinks are served, a meal with French friends will be fuelled by chat, *badinage* (light-hearted banter) and much gesticulation. Parisians are great conversationalists and love debating everything from the best restaurant in the *quartier* (quarter) to subjects of great intellectual import. Like most French people, they are competitive and will try to win you over to their side (or at least their way of thinking). And they can't stand being bored; you will know when they are. As designer Coco Chanel allegedly once advised 'Flee boredom – it's fattening'. Use humour – Parisians can be among the funniest people anywhere – but charm is always preferential to mere jokes.

Any number of topics are deemed acceptable for discussion at a Parisian table – politics, religion, films, sports, food and wine, even sex – and people here love a good *engueulade* (a bicker, but let's call it a debate). Some subjects, though, are generally avoided among people who are not close friends or are meeting for the first time. Obvious 'taboo' topics are money (especially salaries and the price of things) and age, but family, considered a very private matter here, is generally off limits in the early stages. And never ask for or expect a 'tour' of the house or apartment. A polite way of getting rid of guests, by the way, is to offer *tisane* (herbal tea) – a sign recognised by most that it's time to say *bonne nuit* (good night). For detailed information on how to conduct yourself *à table* see p51.

The French are generally more relaxed about the discussion of sexual relations than many English-speaking visitors might be accustomed to. Marital fidelity is not quite the precious stone here that it is elsewhere, as we all know from those old B&W French films. Most people here are genuinely bemused by the American 'political correctness' of the past 20 years and the fuss made in the UK over sex scandals involving politicians. Flirting is an accepted part of daily relationships, even at work. Having a family is not always a bar to sexual license here.

It is sometimes said here that France treats its children as adults until they reach puberty – at which time they revert to being children again; childhood here is not an age of innocence but one of ignorance, which must be corrected and disciplined. You'll see

DUMPED? HOW TO GET OVER IT IN PARIS *Donna Wheeler*

Walk the streets with La Ritournelle on your iPod Current French darling Sebastien Tellier's flippy lyrics, brittle melodies and soaring cinematic tangents will give you the perfect soundtrack for aimless, abject wandering and staring into the Seine contemplating what went wrong.

Stare at Camille Claudel's sculptures at the Rodin Museum Claudel's work at the Musée Rodin (p126) is impassioned, fluid and frighteningly prescient of her fate. And it beats Rodin's (love-rat, idea-stealer) hands down. Heartbreak, madness, incarceration – weep for her, vow it won't happen to you. Plus the garden is a treat.

Buy and read books by those who know how you feel Jean Rhys' *Quartet* or James Baldwin's *Giovanni's Room* are a good place to start. Shakespeare & Company (p291) – the most famous English bookshop in the city – is a gorgeous living cliché and open late (but avoid the American college boys posing as Ethan Hawke).

Visit Marcel Duchamp's Urinal at the Pompidou Centre Toilet. Absurd. Men. Perhaps the perpetually pervy old Marcel's not right for you at the moment. Just thank god the Bride Stripped Bare lives in Philadelphia.

Contemplate Manet's Olympia at the Musee d'Orsay Once scandalous for its Titian-quoting, second-empire, pornography-evoking subject matter, *Olympia* is today oddly cheering. With her galling gaze and jewels aplenty, it's obvious she was only ever in it for the Manet.

Shop for clothes, shop for shoes, just shop The *grands magasins* have gone to *les chiens,* so head to the sublimely simple **APC** (☎ 01 42 22 12 77; 3 rue de Fleurus, 6e ⌚ 11am-8pm Tue-Sun). Pick out a new-you outfit then trot across the road to the **Magasin General** (☎ 01 45 48 72 42; 4 rue de Fleurus, 6e ⌚ 11am-8pm Tue-Sun) to peruse the CDs, kooky ephemera and local talent.

Eat cake You will live to regret gorging on frites all day, but you do deserve a sweet, solitary afternoon at **Sadaharu Aoki's patisserie** (Map pp434–5; 35 rue de Vaugirard, 6e). No need to share the violet macaroons, *mâcha* éclairs and tarts with caramel *au sel de Guérande*.

Buy a new perfume Smell is the key conjurer of memory, so purge the old. L'Artisan Parfumeur (p288) creates unusual, liminal scents just right for new beginnings. Eschew Tea for Two, opt for the Passage d'Enfer (gates of hell) or Méchant Loup (bad, crazy wolf).

French contemporary art and you – back on the scene With its raw, seemingly abandoned space and its perpetual state of reinvention, Palais de Tokyo (p129) could be your metaphor. And yes, it's open till midnight, with those cute, clued-up 'mediators' waiting to talk performance, installation and music.

Visit Liberty Leading the People and know you're over it Liberty is beautiful, bare-breasted, looks good in yellow and she's got a gun. Share in her violent, ecstatic 1830 moment you'll be reminded that Romantic has nothing whatsoever to do with wan promises and wilting flowers. M Delacroix, *merci*.

Overcome heartbreak with a strong dose of Parisian beauty...

a fair few *petits hommes* (little men) and *petites dames* (little ladies) dining decorously on the town with their parents. Things are lightening (and loosening) up here as they are everywhere in the Western world, and you probably won't hear a parent sternly tell his or her rambunctious child *'Ne bouges pas de table, s'il te plaît'* (Don't move from the table, please) as you would a few years ago. But then again you just might.

TOP FIVE FOR CHILDREN

- Canal or river boat cruise (p95)
- Cité des Enfants (Children's Village; Cité des Sciences et de l'Industrie; p150)
- Jardin du Luxembourg (p119)
- Musée des Arts et Métiers (p109)
- Palais de la Découverte (p131)

By their very nature French people do not take seriously laws they consider stupid or intrusive; whether others feel the same is another matter. Laws banning smoking in public places in Paris do exist, but not everyone pays attention to them. Diners will often light up in the nonsmoking sections of restaurants (which is usually no more than 70cm away from the smoking section, in any case) and the waiter will sometimes bring them an ashtray if asked. Parisians, big smokers in general, light up between courses both at home and when dining out.

Education is everything here and there is a great emphasis on learning and logical thought. Unlike in what the French call *le monde Anglo-Saxon* (the English-speaking world; which has nothing to do with people as such – former South African president Nelson Mandela and US secretary of state Condoleezza Rice are both 'Anglo-Saxons' to the French), in France certificates and diplomas take precedence over experience. Where you were educated and what grades you received at the end of your course is all-important.

The French education system has long been highly centralised. Its high standards have produced great intellectuals and almost universal literacy, but equal opportunities are still not available to people of all classes (though education is compulsory for all until the age of 16).

Most children attend a primary school and then the *lycée* (secondary school), with some three quarters of students sitting the matriculation exam called the Baccalauréat (or Bac). The passing mark for a Bac is 10 out of 20. The success rate in mainland France is just under 80%.

The largest university, of which there are 84 in France, is the University of Paris system, which was decentralised and split into 13 autonomous universities and colleges after the violent student protests of 1968 (p68), one of which is the prestigious Sorbonne. About one-third of all tertiary students in France study in Paris.

Some of the most able and ambitious young people do not attend the overcrowded universities, however. About 5% of students are enrolled in the country's 140 prestigious *grandes écoles,* institutions offering training in such fields as business management, engineering and the applied sciences. The 26,000 students who graduate each year do not pay tuition and even receive salaries, but they must work as civil servants after graduation – for up to 10 years in some cases. An overwhelming proportion of students come from highly educated, well-to-do families and end up in top positions in the public sector, the traditionally less prestigious private sector and politics. Thus education produces a meritocratic elite who all recognise and know one another and are nicknamed *'bon chic bon genre'* (BCBG; 'good style, good attitude') for their style, taste and, of course, dosh.

SPORT

Parisians love spectator sports and in addition to such international sports as football, rugby and tennis, they're mad for cycling, horse racing and showjumping. Depending on what time of year you visit, you can catch all types of matches and events (see p274).

Le foot (football), by far the most popular sport here, acquired an even larger following after the national team won the 1998 World Cup at home, beating the reigning champions and tournament favourite, Brazil, 3-0 in a one-sided final. Footballer Zinedine Zidane was immediately catapulted to the status of national hero, the first Frenchman of North African origin to reach such dizzying heights. France went on to win the 2000 European

Championships, defeating Italy in the final in spectacular style, but everything went pear-shaped in the first round of the 2002 World Cup when Senegal beat France 1-0, and again in the quarter-finals of the 2004 European championships when Greece, the eventual winners, beat France by the same score. In 2006 France made it to the final but was defeated by Italy on penalties.

Rugby has always had a strong following in the southwest of France with the favourite teams being Toulouse, Montauban and St-Godens though it has gained tremendously in popularity in Paris recently following the repeat successes of its own team, **Stade Français CASG** (www.stade.fr), on the field. Some say it is the team's too-hot-to-handle (!) calendar that has increased their, er, exposure among hitherto nonfans but in fact it's been heavily discounted tickets that have filled the 80,000-seat Stade de France to near capacity. The Stade de France and nine other grounds in France will host the lion's share of matches of the 2007 Rugby World Cup.

The glitziest annual sporting event in Paris is the French Open, the second of the four Grand Slam tennis tournaments, held at the Stade Roland Garros in the Bois de Boulogne from late May to mid-June. The following month, tens of thousands of spectators gather along the av des Champs-Élysées to watch the final stage of the prestigious Tour de France cycling race.

Gambling on various sporting events, including horse racing, is also popular.

MEDIA

The main national daily newspapers are *Le Figaro* (centre-right; aimed at professionals, businesspeople and the bourgeoisie), *Le Monde* (centre-left; popular with professionals and intellectuals), *France Soir* (right-wing; working and middle-class), *Libération* (left-wing; popular with students and intellectuals) and *L'Humanité* (communist; working-class and intellectuals). The capital's own daily is *Le Parisien* (centre; working class) and is easy to read if you have basic French. *L'Équipe* is a daily devoted exclusively to sport.

News weeklies with commentary include the comprehensive, left-leaning *Le Nouvel Observateur* and the more conservative *L'Express*. For investigative journalism blended with satire, pick up *Le Canard Enchaîné* (assuming your French is of a certain level). *Paris Match* is a gossipy, picture-heavy weekly with a penchant for royalty and film stars.

Public radio is grouped under the umbrella of Radio France, which broadcasts via a network of 53 radio stations, including national stations France Inter, the flagship talk station; the very highbrow France Culture; France Musique, which broadcasts over 1000 concerts each year; Radio Bleu, the station for over-50s listeners; and France Info, a 24-hour news station that broadcasts headlines in French every few minutes and can be heard in Paris at 105.5 MHz FM. FIP has a wide range of music – from hip-hop and chanson to world and jazz – while Le Mouv' is bubblegum pop.

Radio France Internationale (RFI), France's voice abroad since 1931, broadcasts in 17 languages (including English) and can be reached in Paris at 738 kHz AM.

Among the private radio networks, RTL (104.3 MHz FM) is the leading general-interest station with over eight million listeners. The droves of FM pop-music stations include Hot Mix, Zone 80 and Nostalgie, most of which follow the breakfast-time format with phone-ins and wisecracking DJs. Hard-core clubbers turn the dial to Radio Nova at 101.5 MHz FM for the latest on the nightclub scene, Radio FG (98.2 MHz FM) for house, techno, garage and trance, and Paris Jazz (88.2, 98.1 MHz FM) for jazz and blues. Paris Live Radio (963 kHz AM) is an English-language station with news, music, community information and so on.

By law, at least 40% of musical variety broadcasts must consist of songs in French, and stations can be fined if they don't comply. This helps explain why so many English-language hits are re-recorded in French – not always very successfully.

Half of France's six major national TV channels are public: France 2 and France 3 are general-interest stations designed to complement each other: the former focuses on news, entertainment and education, while the latter broadcasts regional programmes and news. France 5 targets its audience with documentaries (eg a daily health program) and cartoons for the kids. Arte is a highbrow cultural channel.

The major private stations are the Franco-German TF1 and M6. The former focuses on entertainment – *télé-réalité* (reality shows) is a big deal here – and sport; with about one-third of all French viewers, it is the most popular station in France. M6 lures a youngish audience with its menu of drama, music and news programmes. Canal+ is a pay channel that shows lots of films, both foreign and French – which isn't surprising, as it's the chief sponsor of the French cinema industry.

LANGUAGE

Respect for the French language is one of the most important aspects of claiming French nationality, and the concept of *la francophonie*, linking the common interests where French is spoken, is supported by both the government and the people. Modern French developed from the *langue d'oïl*, a group of dialects spoken north of the River Loire that grew out of the vernacular Latin used during the late Gallo-Roman period. The *langue d'oïl* – particularly the

Experience 'la vie germanopratin' (p117)

francien dialect spoken in the Île de France around today's Paris – eventually displaced the *langue d'oc*, the dialects spoken in the south of the country.

Standard French is taught and spoken in schools, but its various accents and subdialects are an important source of identity in certain regions. In addition, some languages belonging to peoples long since subjected to French rule have been preserved. These include Flemish in the far north; Alsatian on the German border; Breton, a Celtic tongue, in Brittany; Basque, a language unrelated to any other, in the Basque Country; Catalan, the official language of nearby Andorra and the Spanish autonomous republic of Catalonia, in Roussillon; Provençal in Provence; and Corsican, closely related to Tuscan Italian, on the island of Corsica.

French was *the* international language of culture and diplomacy until WWI, and the French are sensitive to its decline in importance and the hegemony of English, especially since the advent of the Internet. It is impossible to separate a French person from his or her language, and it is one of the things they love most about their own culture. Your best bet is always to approach people politely in French, even if the only words you know are *'Pardon, parlez-vous anglais?'* (Excuse me, do you speak English?).

For more on what to say and how to say it *en français*, see p392. Lonely Planet also publishes the more comprehensive *French Phrasebook*.

SPEAKA DA LINGO

Verlan, a kind of French Pig Latin has been the lingua franca of choice among the *branché* (hip) street-smart of Paris for almost two decades now. It's really just a linguistic sleight of hand, and its very name is illustrative of how it works. *L'envers* means 'reverse' in French, right? Well, twist it around – take the 'vers' and have it precede the 'l'en' and you get *verlan* – more or less. Of course that's the easy bit; shorter words – 'meuf' for *femme* (woman), 'keum' for *mec* (guy), 'teuf' for *fête* (party), 'keuf' for *flic* (cop) and 'auch' for *chaud* (hot; as in cool) are a bit trickier to recognise.

In recent years the language has started to go mainstream and a few words of verlan – for example *beur* – have entered the lexicography (if not dictionary) of standard French. Of course, the whole idea of verlan was for it to be a secret language – a kind of Cockney slang – for youths, drug users and criminals to communicate freely in front of parents, the police etc. The next step was obvious: re-verlan words already in the lingo. Thus *beur* becomes *reub* and *keuf* is *feuk*.

ECONOMY & COSTS

If greater Paris were a country, its economy would rank as one of the world's largest. The 617,000 companies employing 5.4 million people in Île de France contribute to the region's €430-million GDP. That number of pharmaceutical manufacturers, software developers, publishers and civil servants produce only slightly less than Russia and Brazil, and more than the whole of Switzerland. The service industries employ the most people (65%) while tourism accounts for more than 10% of the workforce. Not surprisingly only 0.2% of Parisians are involved in agriculture or the fishing industry.

The metropolitan area is home to global industrial companies, including familiar names like carmaker Renault and Sanofi Aventis, the world's third-largest drug maker. As most industry is located outside the Périphérique (p22), about the only factories you're likely to see during your visit are those lining the highway from Charles de Gaulle airport. As a result, 50% of Parisians commute out of – rather than into – the city every day to work.

That is, those who have a job to commute to do. Unemployment hovers just under 10% nationally and for youths who live in the dire housing estates surrounding the city, the figure reaches almost 23%. The government's attempts to reduce the numbers of jobless youth through its controversial CPE plan, which it claims will fall by 20%, was stymied in early 2006 when a million workers and students took to the streets in protest. They argued that the law, which would allow companies with more than 20 employees to fire workers under 26 within the first two years of employment with no severance pay, encouraged a regular turnover of cut-rate staff and did not allow young people to build careers.

To a certain extent the government's ability to boost employment through training and aid is crimped: it simply doesn't have the money. First and foremost is the need to reduce debt, which was at €1.1 trillion in 2005 (or about 66% of GDP). The country was also in danger of breaching EU rules regulating national debt if it didn't cut its spending. The national public deficit rose to 3.6% of GDP in 2004, which was above the 3% limit, but is expected to drop to 2.6% in 2007.

To fill the national coffers, France was also planning to flog the family silver, hoping to raise as much as €30 billion by selling stakes in state-owned companies such as Aéroports de Paris, the company that manages Charles de Gaulle and Orly airports. It's not the first time: in recent years it has sold shares in power companies Gaz de France and Électricité de France.

HOW MUCH?

An hour's car parking From €2 (street), €4 (garage)

Average seat at the opera €60

Cinema ticket €5 to €9.50 (adult)

Copy of Le Monde €1.20 (€2 weekend edition)

Cup of coffee at a café bar From €1.20

Entry to the Louvre €8.50 (adult)

Litre of Vittel bottled water From €1.40 (supermarket), €1.30 (corner shop)

Pint of Kronenbourg beer From €6 (€4.50 at happy hour)

Pop music CD €15 to €22

Street snack From €2 (crepe or *galette*)

GOVERNMENT & POLITICS

NATIONAL GOVERNMENT

France is a republic with a written constitution adopted by referendum in September 1958 and adapted seven times since, most notably in 1962 when a referendum was organised calling for the election of the president by direct universal suffrage; in 1993 when immigration laws were tightened; in 2000 when the president's term was reduced from seven to five years; and in 2003 when parliament approved amendments allowing for the devolution of wide powers to the regions and departments.

As the capital city, Paris is home to almost all the national offices of state, including, of course, the Parlement (parliament), which is divided into two houses: the Assemblée

Nationale (National Assembly) and Sénat (Senate). The 577 deputies of the National Assembly are directly elected in single-member constituencies for terms lasting five years (next election: 2007). The 321 members of the rather powerless Senate, who serve for nine years, are indirectly elected by thirds every three years. The president of the republic is directly elected for a term lasting five years and can stand for re-election.

Executive power is shared by the president and the Conseil des Ministres (Council of Ministers), whose members – including the prime minister – are appointed by the president but are responsible to parliament. The president serves as commander-in-chief of the armed forces and theoretically makes all major policy decisions.

LOCAL GOVERNMENT

Paris is run by the *maire* (mayor), who is elected by the 163 members of the Conseil de Paris (Council of Paris). They serve terms of six years (next election: 2007). The mayor has 18 *adjoints* (deputy mayors), whose offices are in the Hôtel de Ville (City Hall).

The first mayor of Paris to be elected with real powers was Jacques Chirac in 1977; from 1871 until that year, the mayor was nominated by the national government as the capital was considered a dangerous and revolutionary hotbed. After the 1995 election of Chirac as national president, the Council of Paris elected Jean Tiberi as mayor, a man who was very close to the president and from the same party. In May 2001, Bertrand Delanoë, a socialist with support from the Green Party, became Paris' – and a European capital's – first openly gay mayor. The mayor has many powers, but they do not include control of the police, which is handled by the Préfet de Police (Chief of Police), part of the Ministère de l'Intérieur (Ministry of the Interior). Delanoë continues to enjoy widespread popularity, particularly for his efforts to make Paris more liveable by promoting bicycles and buses, reducing the number of cars on the road and creating a more approachable and responsible city administration.

Paris is a *département* – Ville de Paris; No 75 – as well as a city and the mayor is the head of both. The city is divided into 20 arrondissements and each has its own *maire d'arrondissement* (mayor of the arrondissement) and *conseil d'arrondissement* (council of the arrondissement), who are also elected for six-year terms. They have very limited powers, principally administering local cultural activities and sporting events.

ENVIRONMENT

CLIMATE

As the old song says, Paris is lovely in springtime – though winterlike relapses and heavy rains are not uncommon in the otherwise beautiful month of April. The best months are probably May and June – but early, before the hordes descend. Autumn is also pleasant – some people say the best months to visit are September and October – but of course the days are getting shorter and in October hotels are booked solid by businesspeople attending conferences and trade shows. In winter Paris has all sorts of cultural events going on, while in summer the weather is warm – sometimes sizzling. In any case, in August Parisians flee for the beaches to the west and south, and many restaurateurs and café owners lock up and leave town too. It's true that you will find more places open in August than even a decade ago, but it still can feel like a ghost town in certain districts. For more information in Paris' climate, see p373.

THE LAND

The city of Paris – the capital of both France and the historic Île de France region – measures approximately 9.5km (north to south) by 11km (west to east), not including the Bois de Boulogne and the Bois de Vincennes; its total area is 105 sq km. Within central Paris – which Parisians call *intra-muros* (Latin for 'within the walls') – the Right Bank is north of the Seine, while the Left Bank is south of the river (banks are designated left or right according to the flow of a river).

Paris is a relatively easy city to negotiate. The ring road, known as the Périphérique, makes an irregularly shaped oval containing the entire central area. The Seine cuts an arc across the oval, and the terrain is so flat that the 126m-high Butte de Montmartre (Montmartre Hill) to the north is clearly visible for some distance.

Paris is divided neatly into two by the Seine and also into 20 arrondissements, which spiral clockwise from the centre in a logical fashion. City addresses *always* include the number of the arrondissement, as streets with the same name exist in different districts. In this book, arrondissement numbers are given after the street address using the notation generally used by the French: 1er for *premier* (1st), 2e for *deuxième* (2nd), 3e for *troisième* (3rd) and so on. On some signs or commercial maps, you will see the variations 2ème, 3ème etc.

There is almost always a metro station within 500m of wherever you are in Paris so all offices, museums, hotels, restaurants and so on included in this book have the nearest metro or RER (a network of suburban lines) station given immediately after the contact details. Metro stations generally have a *plan du quartier* (map of the neighbourhood) on the wall near the exit(s).

GREEN PARIS

For a densely populated urban centre inhabited for more than two millennia, Paris is a surprisingly healthy and clean city. Thanks mainly to Baron Haussmann (p76), who radically reshaped the city in the second half of the 19th century, a small army of street sweepers brush litter into the gutters from where it is hosed into sewers, and a city ordinance requires residents to have the façades of their buildings cleaned every 10 years.

These days, despite the city's excellent (and cheap) public transport system, Haussmann's wide boulevards are usually choked with traffic, and air pollution is undoubtedly the city's major environmental hazard. But things are improving on that score; the city leadership, which came to power in coalition with the Green Party, has restricted traffic on some roads at certain times and created lanes only for buses, taxis and bicycles.

Though upwards of 90,000 trees (mostly plane trees and horse chestnuts) line the avenues and boulevards of Paris, the city can often feel excessively built-up. Yet there are more than 400 parks to choose from – some not much bigger than a beach blanket, others the size of a small village. Over the past decade or so, the city government has spent a small fortune transforming vacant lots and derelict industrial land into new parks. Some of the better ones are Parc de Bercy (Map p449) and the unique Promenade Plantée (Map pp444–5), the 'planted walkway' above the Viaduc des Arts, both in the 12e; the Jardin de l'Atlantique (Map pp434–5), behind the Gare Montparnasse, and Parc André Citroën (Map pp434–5) on the banks of the Seine, both in the 15e; Parc de la Villette (Map pp422–3) and Parc des Buttes-Chaumont (Map pp428–9), both in the 19e; and Parc de Belleville (Map pp428–9), 20e.

In just about every park in Paris, regardless of the size, you'll see a signboard illustrating and explaining the trees, flowers and other plants of the city. Most are rich in birdlife, including magpies, jays, great and blue tits, and even woodpeckers. In winter, seagulls are

REMEMBRANCE OF DOGS PAST & PRESENT

The Paris municipality spends €11 million each year to keep the city's pavements free of *la pollution canine,* and the technology it employs – most notably the distinktive [sic] *moto-crottes* (motorised pooper-scooters) driven by so-called *chevaliers du trottoir* (knights of the pavement/sidewalk) – is undeniably impressive. But it would seem that repeated campaigns to get people to clean up after their pooches, which now number 200,000 and produce 16 tonnes of dog dirt a year, have had only limited success, with just 60% of dog owners admitting to doing so. Evidence to this effect takes the form of 'souvenirs' left by recently walked poodles and other breeds, often found smeared along the pavement by daydreaming strollers, one assumes, or guidebook writers absorbed in jotting down something important. And it gets more serious than that: some 650 people are admitted to hospital each year after slipping on a *crotte.* Until Parisians – and their beloved canines – change their dirty ways, the word on the street remains the same: watch your step.

sometimes seen on the Seine, and a few hardy ducks also brave the river's often swift-flowing waters. Believe it or not, there are crayfish in the city's canals and the Seine is teeming with roach, carp, bleak, pike and pike-perch.

If you want to keep Paris clean, leave your car at home and resist the temptation to rent one unless you're touring around the Île de France (p335). Instead, bring or rent a bike (p276), enjoy the city on foot – Paris is an eminently walkable city (p160) – or use the public transport system, which is cheap and extremely efficient. For further tips on how you can reduce your impact on the environment, contact **Les Amis de la Nature** (☎ 01 42 85 29 84; www.amisnature-pariscentre.org in French; 18 rue Victor Massé, 9e) or the **World Wildlife Fund France** (☎ 01 55 25 84 84; www.wwf.fr in French; 1 carrefour de Longchamp, 16e). In theory Parisians can be fined up to €183 for littering but we've never heard of anyone having to pay up. Don't be nonplussed if you see locals drop paper wrappings or other detritus along the side of the pavement, however; the gutters in every quarter of Paris are washed and swept out daily and Parisians are encouraged to use them if litter bins are not available.

TOP FIVE PARKS

- Bois de Boulogne (p153)
- Jardin du Luxembourg (p119)
- Parc des Buttes-Chaumont (p152)
- Parc Floral de Paris (p153)
- Parc de La Villette (p152)

Arts & Architecture

Arts & Architecture

Paris is a bottomless well when it comes to the arts. There are philharmonic orchestras, ballet and opera troupes, theatre companies and copious cinemas from which to choose your art form. And its museums are among the richest in the world, with artwork representing the best of every historical period and school from the Romans to postmodernism. Generous government funding allows local venues to attract top international performers, and the number of international arts festivals hosted here seems to grow each year.

At the same time, the French capital is a treasure trove of architectural styles: from Roman arenas and Gothic cathedrals to postmodernist cubes and glass pyramids that not only look great but serve a function.

LITERATURE

Literature is something that matters deeply to French people, and it is an important focus in their sense of identity. Problem is, nowadays there are no schools or clear literary trends emerging, some authors are impossible to read and, relatively speaking, little contemporary literature finds its way into English translation. Much French writing today tends to focus in a rather nihilistic way on what the nation has lost in recent decades (such as identity, international prestige etc), particularly in the work of Michel Houellebecq, who rose to national prominence in 1998 with his *Les Particules Élémentaires* (Atomised). And accessibility? In 2002 the winner of the Prix Goncourt (Goncourt Prize; see boxed text, below) – *Les Ombres Errantes* by Pascal Quignard – was denounced even by some of the prestigious prize's judges as 'elitist', 'over-erudite' and 'inaccessible' to the average reader.

Such novels do not help the traveller get into the head of Paris, to see and feel how the city thinks and works. For now perhaps it is better to stick with the classics of French literature or even those writers who are more descriptive and thus accessible. The *roman policier* (detective novel), for example, has always been a great favourite with the French, and among its greatest exponents has been Belgian-born Georges Simenon, author of the Inspector Maigret novels. *La Nuit du Carrefour* (Maigret at the Crossroads) portrays Montmartre at its 1930s sleaziest and seediest best. And then there are the works of all those foreigners, such as Gertrude Stein, George Orwell and Dan Brown (see boxed text, p28).

Going back in time, in the history of early medieval French literature Paris does not figure largely, though the dalliances of Pierre Abélard (1079–1142), a wandering scholar who found his way to Paris after having clashed with yet another theologian in the provinces, and his paramour Héloïse (1101–64), the daughter of Canon Fulbert, took place in the

---

AND THE WINNER IS...

Like the UK's Mann Booker or the Pulitzer in the USA, the Prix Goncourt (Goncourt Prize) is the most highly respected and coveted literary prize in France, awarded annually since 1903 to the best volume of imaginative work in prose published during that year. In the event of a tie, novels are to be given preference over collections of short stories or sketches. The winner is awarded by the 10-strong Académie Goncourt each March at the Drouant restaurant in the 2e arrondissement. Though the prize comes with a purse of less than €10, it guarantees much media attention and soaring sales.

Among the writers who have won the Prix Goncourt in the past and are still read are Marcel Proust (1919), Julien Gracq (1951), Simone de Beauvoir (1954) and Marguerite Duras (1984). Winners in recent years:

2002 Pascal Quignard *Les Ombres Errantes* (Wandering Shadows)
2003 Jacques-Pierre Amette *La Maîtresse de Brecht* (Brecht's Mistress)
2004 Laurent Gaudé *Le Soleil des Scorta* (The House of Scorta)
2005 François Weyergans *Trois Jours chez Ma Mère* (Three Days at My Mother's)

capital. When Héloïse gave birth to a son, Fulbert had Abélard castrated and then packed off Héloïse to a nunnery. Despite their confinement, the pair of star-crossed lovers, to the great benefit of French literature, continued to exchange passionate, poetic letters until the death of Abélard.

François Villon, considered the finest poet – in any language – of the late Middle Ages, received the equivalent of a Master of Arts degree from the Sorbonne before he turned 20 years of age. Involved in a series of brawls, robberies and generally illicit escapades, 'Master Villon' (as he became known) was sentenced to be hanged in 1462 for stabbing a lawyer. However, the sentence was commuted to banishment from Paris for 10 years, and he disappeared forever. As well as a long police record, Villon left behind a body of poems charged with a highly personal lyricism, among them the *Ballade des Pendus* (Ballad of the Hanged Men), in which he writes his own epitaph, and the *Ballade des Femmes du Temps Jadis,* which was translated by the English poet and painter Dante Gabriel Rossetti as the 'Ballad of Dead Ladies'.

The great landmarks of French Renaissance literature are the works of François Rabelais, La Pléiade and Michel de Montaigne. The exuberant narratives of the erstwhile monk Rabelais blend coarse humour with erudition in a vast *œuvre* that seems to include every kind of person, occupation and jargon to be found in the France of the mid-16th century. Rabelais had friends in high places in Paris, including Archbishop Jean du Bellay, whom he accompanied to Rome on two occasions. But some of Rabelais' friends and associates fell afoul with the clergy, including his publisher Étienne Dolet. After being convicted of heresy and blasphemy in 1546, Dolet was hanged and then burned at place Maubert in the 5e arrondissement.

During the 17th century, François de Malherbe, court poet under Henri IV, brought a new rigour to the treatment of rhythm in literature. One of his better-known works is his sycophantic *Ode* (1600) to Marie de Médici. Transported by the perfection of Malherbe's verses, Jean de La Fontaine went on to write his charming *Fables* in the manner of Aesop – though he fell afoul of the Académie Française (French Academy) in the process. The mood of classical tragedy permeates *La Princesse de Clèves* by Marie de La Fayette, which is widely regarded as the precursor of the modern psychological novel.

The literature of the 18th century is dominated by philosophers, among them Voltaire (François-Marie Arouet) and Jean-Jacques Rousseau. Voltaire's political writings, arguing that society is fundamentally opposed to nature, had a profound and lasting influence on the century, and he is buried in the Panthéon. Rousseau's sensitivity to landscape and its moods anticipate romanticism, and the insistence on his own singularity in *Les Confessions* made it the first modern autobiography. He, too, is buried in the Panthéon.

The 19th century brought Victor Hugo, as much acclaimed for his poetry as for his novels, who lived on the place des Vosges before fleeing to the Channel Islands during the Second Empire. *Les Misérables* (1862) describes life among the poor and marginalised of Paris during the first half of the 19th century; the 20-page flight of the central character, Jean Valjean, through the sewers of the capital is memorable. *Notre Dame de Paris* (The Hunchback of Notre Dame; 1831), a medieval romance and tragedy revolving around the life of the celebrated cathedral, made Hugo the key figure of French romanticism.

In fact, *Notre Dame de Paris* also served another purpose. Hugo's evocation of the colourful and intense life of the medieval city was seen by some as a plea for the preservation of Gothic Paris and its decaying

Exterior of the Panthéon (p117)

PARIS: THE VIEW FROM THE OUTSIDE

- *The Autobiography of Alice B Toklas,* Gertrude Stein (1933) – autobiographical account of the author's years in Paris written through the eyes and ears of her secretary and long-term lover, Toklas. Includes much about their salon at 27 rue de Fleurus (near Luxembourg Gardens) and her friendship with Henri Matisse, Pablo Picasso, Georges Braque, Ernest Hemingway and others.
- *Birds of America,* Mary McCarthy (1971) – philosophical novel about a young man (and his over-indulgent mother) who makes his way to Paris.
- *Black Elk in Paris,* Kate Horsley (2006) – *The New World* (as in the film) *à la française,* this is the dreamy, dark and sexually tense story of Native American mystic and healer Black Elk's sojourn in 19th-century Paris.
- *The Da Vinci Code,* Dan Brown (2003) – Best-selling cliffhanger about the genealogy of Jesus partly set in Paris. See boxed text, p160, for more on this controversial novel.
- *Le Divorce,* Diane Johnson (1997) – expatriate society and French manners in 1990s Paris through the eyes of a young American woman embroiled in her sister's divorce.
- *Down and Out in Paris and London,* George Orwell (1940) – intriguing account of a time spent working as a *plongeur* (dishwasher) in Paris and living with tramps in both cities in the early 1930s.
- *Giovanni's Room,* James Baldwin (1956) – poignant account of a young American in Paris who falls in love with an Italian bartender, and his struggle with his sexuality.
- *The Life of Samuel Johnson,* James Boswell (1791) – milestone biography of Johnson includes account of travels to Paris in the autumn of 1775.
- *A Moveable Feast,* Ernest Hemingway (1961) – celebrated American novelist's humorous and sometimes bitchy reminiscences of bohemian life in Paris in the late 1920s.
- *Murder Without Pity,* Steve Haberman (2004) – page-turner about the grandson of a French Nazi investigating the murder of a suspected member of the far right.
- *Our Lady,* Dale Gershwin (1999) – a story of intrigue and eroticism with a (literally) running narrator who takes the reader on a plot-filled tour of Paris.
- *Satori in Paris,* Jack Kerouac (1966) – sometimes entertaining (eg the scene in the Montparnasse gangster bar) but often intensely irritating account of this American beat writer's last trip to France.
- *Scarlet Pimpernel,* Baroness Orczy (1905) – adventure story set during the French Revolution in which the foppish young English protagonist turns out to be the daring rescuer of aristocrats in distress.
- *Shakespeare and Company,* Sylvia Beach (1960) – recollections of the proprietor of Paris' most famous literary bookshop between the wars.
- *A Tale of Two Cities,* Charles Dickens (1859) – Paris and London are the settings for the greatest novel ever written about the French Revolution.
- *Tropic of Cancer & Quiet Days in Clichy,* Henry Miller – steamy novels set in Paris, which were published in France in the 1930s but banned under obscenity laws in the UK and USA until the 1960s.

architecture. Indeed, the condition of Notre Dame in the early 19th century was so bad that artists, politicians and writers, including Hugo, beseeched King Louis-Philippe to rectify the situation. Hugo was appointed to the new Commission for Monuments and the Arts, on which he sat for 10 years. In 1845 the Gothic revivalist architect Eugène Viollet-le-Duc began his renovation of Notre Dame, during which he added, among other things, the steeple and the gargoyles. The work continued for almost two decades.

Other influential 19th-century novelists include Stendhal (Marie-Henri Beyle), Honoré de Balzac, Amandine Aurore-Lucile-Dupin (better known as George Sand) and, of course, Alexandre Dumas, who wrote the swashbuckling adventures *Le Compte de Monte Cristo* (The Count of Monte Cristo) and *Les Trois Mousquetaires* (The Three Musketeers). The latter tells the story of d'Artagnan (based on the historical personage Charles de Baatz d'Artagnan, 1623–73), who arrives in Paris as a young Gascon determined to become one of the guardsmen of Louis XIII.

In 1857 two landmarks of French literature were published: *Madame Bovary* by Gustave Flaubert and *Les Fleurs du Mal* by Charles Baudelaire. Both writers were tried for the supposed immorality of their works. Flaubert won his case, and his novel was distributed without censorship. Baudelaire, who moonlighted as a translator in Paris (he introduced the works of the American writer Edgar Allan Poe to Europe in editions that have since become classics of the French language), was obliged to cut several poems from his work, and he died an early and painful death, practically unknown. Flaubert's second–most popular novel, *L'Éducation Sentimentale* (Sentimental Education), presents a vivid picture of life among Parisian dilettantes, intellectuals and revolutionaries during the decline and fall of Louis-Philippe's monarchy and the February Revolution of 1848.

The aim of Émile Zola, who came to Paris with his close friend Paul Cézanne in 1858, was to convert novel-writing from an art to a science by the application of experimentation. His theory may now seem naive, but his work influenced most significant French writers of the late 19th century and is reflected in much 20th-century fiction as well. His novel *Nana* tells the decadent tale of a young woman who resorts to prostitution to survive the Paris of the Second Empire.

Paul Verlaine and Stéphane Mallarmé created the symbolist movement, which strove to express states of mind rather than simply detail daily reality. Arthur Rimbaud, apart from crowding an extraordinary amount of rugged, exotic travel into his 37 years and having a tempestuous sexual relationship with Verlaine, produced two enduring pieces of work: *Illuminations* and *Une Saison en Enfer* (A Season in Hell). Rimbaud stopped writing and left Europe for Africa in 1874, never to return. Verlaine died at 39 rue Descartes (5e) in 1896.

Marcel Proust dominated the early 20th century with his giant seven-volume novel *À la Recherche du Temps Perdu* (Remembrance of Things Past), which is largely autobiographical and explores in evocative detail the true meaning of past experience recovered from the unconscious by 'involuntary memory'. In 1907 Proust moved from the family home near av des Champs-Élysées to the apartment on blvd Haussmann that's famous for its cork-lined bedroom (on display at the Musée Carnavalet in the Marais – see p107) from which he almost never stirred. André Gide found his voice in the celebration of gay sensuality and, later, left-wing politics. *Les Faux-Monnayeurs* (The Counterfeiters) exposes the hypocrisy and self-deception with which people try to avoid sincerity.

André Breton led the group of French surrealists and wrote its three manifestos, although the first use of the word 'surrealist' is attributed to the poet Guillaume Apollinaire, a fellow traveller of surrealism who was killed in action in WWI. As a poet, Breton was overshadowed by Paul Éluard and Louis Aragon, whose most famous surrealist novel was *Le Paysan de Paris* (Nightwalker). Colette (Sidonie-Gabriel Colette) enjoyed tweaking the nose of conventionally moral readers with titillating novels that detailed the amorous exploits of such heroines as the schoolgirl Claudine. One of her most interesting works, *Paris de Ma Fenêtre* (Paris from My Window), concerned the German occupation of Paris. Her view, by the way, was from 9 rue de Beaujolais in the 1er, overlooking the Jardin du Palais Royal.

After WWII, existentialism developed as a significant literary movement around Jean-Paul Sartre (see boxed text, p32), Simone de Beauvoir and Albert Camus, who worked and conversed in the cafés around the Église St-Germain des Prés. All three stressed the importance of the writer's political engagement. *L'Âge de Raison* (The Age of Reason), the first volume of Sartre's trilogy *Les Chemins de la Liberté* (The Roads to Freedom), is a superb Parisian novel; the subsequent volumes recall Paris immediately before and during WWII. De Beauvoir, author of the ground-breaking study *Le Deuxième Sexe* (The Second Sex), had a profound influence on feminist thinking. Camus' novel *L'Étranger* (The Stranger) reveals that the absurd is the condition of modern man, who feels himself a stranger – more accurately in French, an 'outsider' – in his world.

In the late 1950s certain novelists began to look for new ways of organising narrative. The so-called *nouveau roman* (new novel) refers to the works of Nathalie Sarraute, Alain Robbe-Grillet, Boris Vian, Julien Gracq, Michel Butor and others. However, these writers never formed a close-knit group, and their experiments took them in divergent directions. Today the *nouveau roman* is very much out of favour in France.

Mention must also be made of *Histoire d'O* (Story of O), the highly erotic sadomasochistic novel written by Dominique Aury under a pseudonym in 1954. It sold more copies than any other contemporary French novel outside France.

In 1980 Marguerite Yourcenar, best known for her memorable historical novels such as *Mémoires d'Hadrien* (Hadrian's Memoirs), became the first woman to be elected to the Académie Française.

Detail of Arc de Triomphe (p130)

Marguerite Duras came to the notice of a larger public when she won the prestigious Prix Goncourt (see boxed text, p26) for her novel *L'Amant* (The Lover) in 1984. She also wrote the screenplay of *Hiroshima Mon Amour,* described by one critic as part *nouveau roman,* part Mills & Boon.

Philippe Sollers was one of the editors of *Tel Quel,* a highbrow, then left-wing, Paris-based review that was very influential in the 1960s and early 1970s. His 1960s novels were highly experimental, but with *Femmes* (Women) he returned to a conventional narrative style.

Another editor of *Tel Quel* was Julia Kristeva, best known for her theoretical writings on literature and psychoanalysis. In recent years she has turned her hand to fiction, and *Les Samuraï,* (The Samurai; 1990) a fictionalised account of the heady days of *Tel Quel,* is an interesting document on the life of the Paris intelligentsia. Roland Barthes and Michel Foucault are other authors and philosophers associated with the 1960s and '70s.

So-called accessible contemporary authors who enjoy a wide following include Patrick Modiano, Yann Queffélec, Pascal Quignard, Denis Tillinac and Nicole de Buron, a very popular mainstream humour writer whose books, including *Docteur, Puis-Je Vous Voir avant Six Mois?* (Doctor, Can I See You within Six Months?) and *Chéri, Tu M'écoutes?* (My Dear, You Hear Me?), sell in the hundreds of thousands. Fred Vargas is a popular writer of crime fiction.

More-serious authors whose careers and works are closely scrutinised by the literary establishment and the well-read include Jean Echenoz, Nina Bouraoui, Jean-Philippe Toussaint, Annie Ernaux and Erik Orsenna.

PHILOSOPHY

France may be one of the few countries in the world to require its secondary-school students to demonstrate a solid mastery of philosophical concepts before pursuing an academic career. Forced to expostulate upon such brain ticklers as 'Can demands for justice be separated from demands for liberty?' (discuss) or 'Do passions prevent us from doing our duty?' (elaborate) in order to receive a *baccalauréat* (school-leaving certificate), many people here develop a lifelong passion for philosophical discourse. Most French towns of any size have at least one bar or café that will sponsor a regular *'philocafé'* in which anyone may contribute their ideas on a particular philosophical question; in Paris the most popular *philocafés* is at Café des Phares (p241), which goes into debate from 11am to 1pm on Sunday.

Left Bank philosophers Bernard-Henri Levy, Jean-François Revel, André Glucksmann and the late Marc Sautet, who founded the Café des Phares and died in 1998 at the age of 51, have achieved a level of celebrity normally reserved for film stars. Even politicians are expected to show a philosophical bent. President Jacques Chirac has opined that 'Poetry is a necessity for daily living', and in 2003 then Foreign (now Prime) Minister Dominique de Villepin quietly published *Éloge des Voleurs de Feu* (Elegy to the Fire Thieves), an 824-page critique and homage to such 'Promethean rebels' as Villon and Rimbaud (p29) in French poetry. It was his third work in as many years.

René Descartes, who lived in the first half of the 17th century, was the founder of modern philosophy and one of the greatest thinkers since Aristotle. After making important contributions to analytical geometry and algebra, Descartes sought to establish certainty from a position of absolute doubt. Descartes' famed phrase 'Cogito, ergo sum' (I think, therefore I exist/am) is the basis of modern philosophical thought. His method and systems of thought came to be known as Cartesianism. In positing that there is an external reality that can be grasped through reason, Descartes rendered possible the development of modern science.

Blaise Pascal, a contemporary of Descartes, was also a mathematician, but addressed the absurdity of the human predicament in a manner that foreshadowed the existentialists. Pascal's central concern was in reconciling his religious devotion – he was a convert to Jansenist Catholicism and ended his days at Port Royal, an abbey near Versailles – with his scientific background. Thus, in *Pensées* (Thoughts) he put forth 'Pascal's Razor', which stated that the most logical approach is to believe in God. If God does not exist, one has lost nothing; if God does exist one has assured oneself of a favourable afterlife.

MY DEAR DIARY

A genre virtually unknown in the literature of the English-speaking world but boasting a massive following in France is the so-called *carnet de voyage* (travel notebook). Call it an illustrated journal or diary or even a blog with pictures, a *carnet de voyage* doesn't really have to be about travel at all; some of the most interesting and/or successful ones published in recent years have dealt with the Israel–Palestine conflict and the *cour d'assises* (the French equivalent of the crown court). But the vast majority do deal with wandering and discovery.

Carnets de voyage share two essential ingredients. They always contain descriptive text and they have illustrations – be they line drawings, sketches, watercolours or even photographs (or a combination thereof) – of the subject matter. The idea is for the artist and writer (one and the same person, or a pair) to witness and comment on places and people as they go about their everyday lives. They are thus humanistic, deeply personal observations of the world.

Proto-*carnets de voyage* date back as far as the mid-13th century and the Frenchman Villard de Honnecourt, who left behind approximately 250 architectural drawings of cathedrals, monasteries and abbeys. The first illustrated journal is usually ascribed to the 15th-century Italian Renaissance painter Antonio Pisano, better known as Pisanello. Artists in search of realism would study perspective in Tuscany using Piero de la Francesca's mathematical notebooks, and those interested in anatomy would study Leonardo da Vinci's sketches. The sketchbooks kept by Albrecht Dürer as he crossed the Alps into Italy to learn more about perspective is an early example of a *carnet de voyage*.

Artists played key roles during the 'age of discovery', especially on voyages to the New World. For example, in 1585 John White accompanied Sir Richard Grenville and Ralph Lane on their expedition to the English colony at Roanoke in North Carolina, visiting and sketching Indian settlements as far north as the Chesapeake Bay. In 1698, engineer Duplessis travelled to the Galapagos Islands off the west coast of South America, keeping a very precise diary containing ethnological accounts and maps of his travels. In the following century Captain James Cook was accompanied by scientists as well as up to six artists on his three voyages to the South Pacific over a dozen years. The French Geographical Society, founded in 1821, actively encouraged voyages of discovery by awarding special prizes. Explorers brought back testimonies, maps and drawings. Above all, these drawings were destined for scientific use.

Photography gave birth to a new way of translating reality, but the artistic drawing as an expression did not suffer. Scientists continued to favour drawing, especially for purposes of reproduction, and travelling artists began to turn away from photographic reality and instead experiment with style. Photography changed nothing for Paul Gauguin, for example, arguably the most important artist-traveller. His notes and drawings of Tahiti would eventually be published as *Noa Noa*, believed to be the first modern *carnet de voyage*.

Among the major publishers of *carnets de voyage* in France are award-winning Jalan Publications (contact@jalan .fr) with *Alger, Israël Palestine* and *Cour d'Assises*; Éditions Glénat (www.glenat.com) with *Erythrée* and *Mali sur Les Rives du Niger*; and Éditions Albin Michel (www.albin-michel.fr) with *Saint-Louis de Sénégal*. The Internet is an excellent source if you just want a taste of what the books look and feel like; check out http://carnetsdevoyage.blog.expedia .fr (in French).

Because the *carnet de voyage* is essentially a French genre, almost all of the information you encounter will be in French. One of the few exceptions to this over recent years is American Craig Thompson's appropriately named *Carnet De Voyage* (2004), which depicts, through text and drawings, his journeys through Europe and Morocco in May 2004. While his illustrations and cultural observations were highly praised, what came though loudest and most clear was the author's voice and the astonishing journey that was taking place within the author himself. That is the essence of a *carnet de voyage*.

As one of the major thinkers of the 18th century (the Age of Enlightenment), Jean-Jacques Rousseau addressed the relationship of the individual to society. His 1762 work *Le Contrat Social* (The Social Contract) laid the foundations for modern democracy by arguing that sovereignty resides with the people who express their will through majority vote. Liberty is an inalienable 'natural' right that cannot be exchanged for civil peace.

In the late 19th century Henri Bergson abandoned reason as a tool towards discovering the truth, arguing that direct intuition is deeper than intellect. He developed the concept of *élan vital* (creative impulse), a spirit of energy and life that moves all living things, as the heart of evolution – not Darwin's theory of natural selection. His thoughts about the subjective experience of time greatly influenced his brother-in-law, Marcel Proust, and the latter's *À la Recherche du Temps Perdu* (Remembrance of Things Past; p29).

The 20th century's most famous French thinker was Jean-Paul Sartre, the quintessential Parisian intellectual who was born in Paris in 1905 and died there in 1980. For most people he embodied an obscure idea known as existentialism. It's one of the great 'isms' of popular culture, but even philosophers have trouble explaining what existentialism really means. The word derives from Sartre's statement, 'Existence takes priority over essence', meaning that man must create himself because there is no eternal 'natural self' or 'meaning of life'. Realising that there is no meaning of life provokes 'existential dread' and 'alienation'.

A woman must also create herself, according to philosopher Simone de Beauvoir, who applied existentialist concepts to the predicament of females in French society. There is no essential 'female' or 'male' nature, she opined in her seminal work *Le Deuxième Sexe* (The Second Sex), published in 1949. According to Beauvoir, women's status as the perpetual 'other' relegates them to remaining 'objects' of the subjective male gaze.

Sartre and de Beauvoir were strong advocates of communism until 1956 and the Soviet invasion of Hungary. Disillusionment with communism and with the political engagement implied by existentialism led a new generation towards the social science called structuralism. Coined by the anthropologist Claude Levi-Strauss, who died in 2004 at the age of 95, structuralists believe that sociological, psychological and linguistic structures shape individuals. Individuals do not shape themselves as the existentialists believe. Beginning as a scientific method for studying differences between cultures, structuralism soon came

EXISTENCE VS ESSENCE

Jean-Paul Sartre never used the term existentialism in his early defining works, but it came to represent a body of thought that he, in part, inherited from German philosopher Edmund Husserl. It was also adopted by a Parisian café clique of writers, dramatists and intellectuals, which included his lifelong companion, Simone de Beauvoir, and even painters and musicians. Sartre's intellectual influences were German philosophers, in particular Martin Heidegger and Friedrich Nietzsche, and he was also influenced by Dane Søren Kierkegaard.

Sartre was an atheist, and the 'loss of God' was a phrase he used often. In the 1930s he wrote a series of analyses of human self-awareness that culminated in his most important philosophical work, *L'Être et le Néant* (Being and Nothingness; 1943). The central idea of this long and complex book is to distinguish between objective things and human consciousness, and to assert that consciousness is a 'non-thing'. Consciousness is made real by taking a point of view on things, on 'being'. He claimed that we are 'condemned to be free' and that even in indecision we choose not to choose, thus making freedom inescapable.

For all its lofty language and convoluted philosophical argument, *Being and Nothingness* is a treatise on a fairly simple way of life that embraces one's own autonomy and seeks to maximise one's choices (or one's awareness of those choices). Many accept Sartre's message as a positive one, but for him this heightened human awareness was characterised by emptiness, boredom and negativity.

Sartre's many literary works, essays, plays and political writings were charged with his philosophical ideas, and his first published novel, *La Nausée* (Nausea; 1938), introduced many themes common in his later philosophical works. *Huis Clos* (No Exit; 1944), his most popular play, is an allegorical and unnerving story about three people who find themselves in a room together with no way out and includes Sartre's famous words, 'Hell is other people'. Oddly, few people read Sartre nowadays and, when reference is made to existentialism in French literature, the work of Albert Camus – who refuted much of that philosophy – is cited.

to represent a rejection of all the universal ideas – reason, progress, democracy – that had held sway since the Age of Enlightenment.

As a poststructuralist, Michel Foucault rejected the idea that it was possible to step outside the 'discursive practices' that claim to reveal knowledge and arrive at an ultimate truth. The search for knowledge cannot be separated from the power relationships that lie at the heart of every social and political relationship.

Jacques Derrida, first published in the influential *Tel Quel* (p30) in the 1960s, and the director of studies at Paris' École des Hautes Études en Science Sociales when he died in 2004, introduced the concept of deconstructionism. This concept suggests that outside language there is nothing to which we can refer directly, since all language is indicative only of itself (*il n'y a pas de hors-texte* – there is no subtext). So knowledge outside of language is literally unthinkable; it is not a natural reflection of the world. Each text allows for multiple interpretations, making it impossible to find certainty in textual analysis. Deconstructionism posed an obvious paradox: how can one use language to claim that language is meaningless?

In recent years French philosophers have turned back to political commitment and moral philosophy. Bernard-Henri Levy was an outspoken critic of the war in Bosnia and made several films on the subject in the 1990s. Along with revolutionary intellectual and 'friend of Che' Régis Debray and other noteworthy thinkers, Levy was a contributor to Prime Minister Dominique de Villepin's *Toward A New World* (2004), a series of essays on the war in Iraq, the UN and Europe in the 21st century. André Glucksmann's *Ouest contre Ouest* (West against West), published in 2003, looked at the Iraq war and the paradox that those groups for and against the war both claimed to be inspired by the same principles. Jean-François Revel, who died in early 2006, had become the self-appointed spokesman of Europe's antipathy toward Bush America.

PAINTING

Voltaire wrote that French painting began with Nicolas Poussin, the greatest representative of 17th-century classicism who frequently set scenes from ancient Rome, classical mythology and the Bible in ordered landscapes bathed in golden light.

In the 18th century Jean-Baptiste Chardin brought the humbler domesticity of the Dutch masters to French art. In 1785 the public reacted with enthusiasm to two large paintings with clear republican messages: *The Oath of the Horatii* and *Brutus Condemning His Son* by Jacques Louis David. David became one of the leaders of the French Revolution, and a virtual dictator in matters of art, where he advocated a precise, severe classicism. He was made official state painter by Napoleon Bonaparte, glorifying him as general, first consul and then emperor, and is best remembered for his *Death of Mara,* depicting the Jacobin propagandist lying dead in his bath.

Jean-Auguste-Dominique Ingres, David's most gifted pupil in Paris, continued in the neoclassical tradition. The historical pictures to which he devoted most of his life *(Oedipus and the Sphinx)* are now generally regarded as inferior to his portraits. The name of Ingres, who played the violin for enjoyment, lives on in the phrase *violon d'Ingres,* which means 'hobby' in French.

The gripping *Raft of the Medusa* by Théodore Géricault is on the threshold of romanticism; if Géricault had not died at a young age – he was 33 – he would probably have become a leader of the movement, along with his friend Eugène Delacroix. Delacroix's most famous – if not best – work, perhaps, is *Liberty Leading the People,* which commemorates the July Revolution of 1830 (p77).

The members of the Barbizon School brought about a parallel transformation of landscape painting. The school derived its name from a village near the Forêt de Fontainebleau (Forest of Fontainebleau; p345), where Camille Corot and Jean-François Millet, among others, gathered to paint in the open air. Corot is best known for his landscapes *(The Bridge at Nantes, Chartres Cathedral)*; Millet took many of his subjects from peasant life *(The Gleaners)* and had a great influence on Van Gogh.

Millet anticipated the realist programme of Gustave Courbet, a prominent member of the Paris Commune (he was accused of – and imprisoned for – destroying the Vendôme

Column), whose paintings show the drudgery of manual labour and dignity of ordinary life *(Funeral at Ornans, The Angelus)*.

Édouard Manet used realism to depict the life of the Parisian middle classes, yet he included in his pictures numerous references to the old masters. His *Déjeuner sur l'Herbe* and *Olympia* both were considered scandalous, largely because they broke with the traditional treatment of their subject matter.

Impressionism, initially a term of derision, was taken from the title of an 1874 experimental painting by Claude Monet, *Impression: Soleil Levant* (Impression: Sunrise). Monet was the leading figure of the school, which counted among its members Alfred Sisley, Camille Pissarro, Berthe Morisot and Pierre-Auguste Renoir. The impressionists' main aim was to capture the effects of fleeting light, painting almost universally *en plein air* (in the open air) – and light came to dominate the content of their painting.

Edgar Degas was a fellow traveller of impressionism, but he favoured his studio to the open air, preferring to paint at the racecourse *(At the Races)* and in ballet studios *(The Dance Class)*. Henri de Toulouse-Lautrec was a great admirer of Degas, but chose subjects one or two notches below: people in the bistros, brothels and music halls of Montmartre (eg *Au Moulin Rouge*). He is best known for his posters and lithographs, in which the distortion of the figures is both satirical and decorative.

Paul Cézanne is celebrated for his still lifes and landscapes depicting the south of France, though he spent many years in Paris after breaking with the impressionists. The name of Paul Gauguin immediately conjures up studies of Tahitian and Breton women. Both painters are usually referred to as postimpressionists, something of a catch-all term for the diverse styles that flowed from impressionism.

In the late 19th century Gauguin worked for a time in Arles in Provence with the

> ## TOP FIVE ART & SCULPTURE MUSEUMS
>
> - Musée Atelier Zadkine (p120)
> - Musée d'Art Moderne de la Ville de Paris (p128)
> - Musée d'Orsay (p124)
> - Musée du Louvre (p100)
> - Musée Rodin (p126)

Dutch-born Vincent Van Gogh, who spent most of his painting life in France and died in the town of Auvers-sur-Oise (p357) north of Paris in 1890. A brilliant, innovative artist, Van Gogh produced haunting self-portraits and landscapes in which colour assumes an expressive and emotive quality.

Van Gogh's later technique paralleled pointillism, developed by Georges Seurat, who applied paint in small dots or uniform brush strokes of unmixed colour, producing fine mosaics of warm and cool tones in such tableaux as *Une Baignade*. Henri Rousseau was a contemporary of the postimpressionists but his 'naive' art was totally unaffected by them. His dreamlike pictures of the Paris suburbs and of jungle and desert scenes – eg *The Snake Charmer* – have had a lasting influence on 20th-century art.

Gustave Moreau was a member of the symbolist school. His eerie treatment of mythological subjects can be seen in his old studio, which is now the Musée National Gustave Moreau (p150) in the 9e. Fauvism took its name from the slur of a critic who compared the exhibitors at the 1905 Salon d'Automne (Autumn Salon) with *fauves* (beasts) because of their radical use of intensely bright colours. Among these 'beastly' painters were Henri Matisse, André Derain and Maurice de Vlaminck.

Cubism was effectively launched in 1907 with *Les Demoiselles d'Avignon* by the Spanish prodigy Pablo Picasso. Cubism, as developed by Picasso, Georges Braque and Juan Gris, deconstructed the subject into a system of intersecting planes and presented various aspects simultaneously. A good example is Braque's *Houses at L'Estaque*.

In the 1920s and 1930s the École de Paris (School of Paris) was formed by a group of expressionists, mostly foreign born, including Amedeo Modigliani from Italy, Foujita from Japan and Marc Chagall from Russia, whose works combined fantasy and folklore.

Dada, both a literary and artistic movement of revolt, started in Zürich in 1915. In Paris, one of the key Dadaists was Marcel Duchamp, whose *Mona Lisa* adorned with moustache and goatee epitomises the spirit of the movement. Surrealism, an offshoot of Dada, flourished between the wars. Drawing on the theories of Sigmund Freud, it attempted to reunite the conscious and unconscious realms, to permeate everyday life with fantasies and dreams. Among the most important proponents of this style in Paris were Chagall, as well as René Magritte, André Masson, Max Ernst, André Breton and Piet Mondrian. The most influential, however, was the Spanish-born artist Salvador Dalí, who arrived in the French capital in 1929 and painted some of his most seminal works (eg *Sleep, Paranoia*) while residing here (see Dalí Espace Montmartre, p149).

World War II ended Paris' role as the world's artistic capital. Many artists left France, and though some returned after the war, the city never regained its old magnetism, with New York and then London picking up the baton. A few postwar Parisian artists are noteworthy, however, including Nicolas de Staël, Jean Fautrier, Bernard Buffet and Robert Combas. Popular installation artists include Christian Boltanski and Xavier Veilhan.

SCULPTURE

By the 14th century, sculpture was increasingly commissioned for the tombs of the nobility. In Renaissance Paris, Pierre Bontemps decorated the beautiful tomb of François I at the Basilique de St-Denis (p157), and Jean Goujon created the Fontaine des Innocents in central Paris (see Forum des Halles, p100). The baroque style is exemplified by Guillaume Coustou's *Horses of Marly* at the entrance to the av des Champs-Élysées.

In the 19th century, memorial statues in public places came to replace sculpted tombs. One of the best artists in the new mode was François Rude, who sculpted the Maréchal Ney statue (Map pp444–5), *Maréchal under Napoleon,* outside the Closerie des Lilas, and the relief on the Arc de Triomphe. Another sculptor was Jean-Baptiste Carpeaux, who began as a romantic, but whose work – such as *The Dance* on the Palais Garnier and his fountain in the Jardin du Luxembourg – look back to the warmth and gaiety of the baroque era. At the end of the 19th century Auguste Rodin's work overcame the conflict between neoclassicism and romanticism; his sumptuous bronze and marble figures of men and women did much to revitalise sculpture as an expressive medium. One of Rodin's most gifted pupils was Camille Claudel, whose work can be seen along with that of Rodin in the Musée Rodin (p126).

Braque and Picasso experimented with sculpture, and in the spirit of Dada, Marcel Duchamp exhibited 'found objects', one of which was a urinal, which he mounted, signed and titled *Fountain* in 1917.

One of the most influential sculptors to emerge before WWII was the Romanian-born (and Paris-based) sculptor Constantin Brancusi, whose work can be seen in the Atelier Brancusi outside the Centre Pompidou (p99). After the war César Baldaccini – known as César to the world – used iron and scrap metal to create his imaginary insects and animals, later graduating to pliable plastics. Among his best-known works are the *Centaur* statue (Map pp434–5) of the mythological half-horse, half-man with disproportionate gonads the size of grapefruits in the 6e, and the statuette handed to actors at the Césars

Sculptures at Gallery of Kings, Musée National du Moyen Age (p116)

(French cinema's equivalent to the Oscars). Two sculptors who lived and worked most of their adult lives in Paris and each have a museum devoted to their life and work are Ossip Zadkine (p120) and Antoine Bourdelle (p122).

In 1936 France put forward a bill providing for 'the creation of monumental decorations in public buildings' by allotting 1% of all building costs to public art, but this did not really get off the ground for another half-century when Daniel Buren's *Les Deux Plateaux* sculpture (p103) was commissioned at Palais Royal. The whole concept mushroomed, and artwork appeared throughout La Défense, Parc de la Villette (eg *Bicyclette Ensevelie;* 1990) and even in the metro (see boxed text, p104). In addition, Paris counts some 120 commissioned murals, including a fine set of wall paintings (Map pp428–9) by a group of four artists at 52 rue de Belleville, 20e, and one by Robert Combas (Map pp436–7) at 3 rue des Haudriettes, 3e.

MUSIC

In the 17th and 18th centuries French baroque music influenced much of Europe's musical output. Composers François Couperin and Jean Philippe Rameau were two major players during this period.

France produced and cultivated a number of musical luminaries in the 19th century. Among these were Hector Berlioz, Charles Gounod, César Franck, Camille Saint-Saëns and Georges Bizet. Berlioz was the founder of modern orchestration, while Franck's organ compositions sparked a musical renaissance in France that would go on to produce such greats as Gabriel Fauré, and the impressionists Maurice Ravel and Claude Debussy. The latter's adaptations of poems are among the greatest contributions to the world of music.

More-recent classical composers include Olivier Messiaen, the chief organist for decades at the Église de la Trinité in the 9e, who (until his death in 1992 at the age of 84) combined modern, almost mystical music with natural sounds such as birdsong. His student, the radical Pierre Boulez, includes computer-generated sound in his compositions.

Jazz hit Paris with a bang in the 1920s and has remained popular ever since. France's contribution to the world of jazz has been great, including the violinist Stéphane Grapelli and the legendary three-fingered Roma guitarist Django Reinhardt.

The most popular form of indigenous music is the *chanson française,* with a tradition going back to the troubadours of the Middle Ages. 'French songs' have always emphasised lyrics over music and rhythm, which may explain the enormous success of rap in France in the 1990s, especially of groups like MC Solaar, NTM and I Am. The *chanson* tradition, celebrated by street singers such as Lucienne Delisle and Dahlia, was revived from the 1930s onwards by the likes of Édith Piaf and Charles Trénet. In the 1950s singers such as Georges Brassens, Léo Ferré, Claude Nougaro, Jacques Brel and Barbara became national stars; a big revival is taking place now called *la nouvelle chanson française.* Among the most exciting performers of this old-fashioned, slightly wordy genre are Vincent Delerm, Bénabar, Jeanne Cherhal, Camille and a group called Les Têtes Raides. The music of balladeer/folk

---

TOP FIVE CDS

- *Anthologie Serge Gainsbourg* – three-CD anthology includes the metro man's most famous tracks, including 'Le Poinçonneur des Lilas' and 'Je t'aime…Moi Non Plus' in duet with Brigitte Bardot.
- *Édith Piaf: Live at the Paris Olympia* – a collation of live recordings made in the 1950s and '60s, this album contains 20 of the belle of Belleville's classics, including 'Milord', 'Hymne à l'Amour' and, of course, 'Non, Je Ne Regrette Rien'.
- *Georges Brassens: Le Disque d'Or* – everything you need to know about one of France's greatest performers (and the inspiration for Jacques Brel) is in this 21-track double helping.
- *Luaka Bop Présente Cuisine Non-Stop* – there's something for everyone in David Byrne's homage to *la nouvelle chanson française,* with Arthur H coming over all Serge Gainsbourg on 'Naïve Derviche', and Têtes Raides light and breezy on 'Un P'tit Air'.
- *M: Le Tour de M* – everybody's favourite sing-along gives a little Prince and a titch of Zappa, and even gives Brel a nod with 'Au Suivant' in this double CD with two-dozen tracks.

singer Serge Gainsbourg – very charming, very sexy and very French – remains enormously popular a decade and a half after his death.

France was among the first countries to 'discover' *sono mondiale* (world music). You'll hear everything from Algerian *raï* (type of Algerian popular music) to North African music (Khaled, Cheb Mami, Racid Taha) and Senegalese *mbalax* (Youssou N'Dour) to West Indian *zouk* (Kassav, Zouk Machine), and Cuban salsa and Brazilian music. In the late 1980s, Mano Negra and Les Négresses Vertes were two bands that combined many of these elements – often with brilliant results. Magic System from Côte d'Ivoire has helped popularise *zouglou* (a kind of West African rap and dance music) with its album *Premier Gaou,* and Congolese Koffi Olomide still packs the halls. A truly world band is the Afro-Cuban Africando, whose members hailed from West Africa, Cuba, Puerto Rico (via New York) and Vietnam.

In recent years a distinctly urban and highly exportable Parisian sound has developed, often mixing computer-enhanced Chicago blues and Detroit techno with 1960s lounge music and vintage tracks from the likes of Gainsbourg and Brassens. Among those playing now are Parisian duo Daft Punk, who adapt first-wave acid house and techno to their younger roots in pop, indie rock and hip-hop, and the very distinctive M, Arthur H and Manu Chao, whose music is simple guitar and lyrics – plain and straightforward. Despite their problems (the lead singer, Bertrand Cantat, was imprisoned for the murder of his girlfriend), Noir Désir is *the* sound of French rock. Worth noting is rocker Nosfell who sings in his very own invented language called Klokobetz. It's a long way from the *yéyé* (imitative rock) of the 1960s as sung by Johnny Halliday. For reviews of music venues around Paris, see p259.

CINEMA

Parisians go to the cinema once a week, on average – the 5pm *séance* (performance) on Sunday afternoon is a very popular time. They also take films, especially French films (of which about 160 are produced annually), very seriously. Parisians always prefer to watch foreign films in their original language with French subtitles.

France's place in film history was firmly ensured when the Lumière brothers from Lyon invented 'moving pictures' and organised the world's first paying public film-screening – a series of two-minute reels – in Paris' Grand Café on the blvd des Capucines (9e) in December 1895.

In the 1920s and 1930s avant-garde directors, such as René Clair, Marcel Carné and the intensely productive Jean Renoir, son of the artist, searched for new forms and subjects.

In the late 1950s a large group of young directors arrived on the scene with a new genre, the so-called *nouvelle vague* (new wave). This group included Jean-Luc Godard, François Truffaut, Claude Chabrol, Eric Rohmer, Jacques Rivette, Louis Malle and Alain Resnais. This disparate group of directors believed in the primacy of the film maker, giving rise to the term *film d'auteur* (loosely, 'art-house film').

Many films followed, among them Alain Resnais' *Hiroshima Mon Amour* (Hiroshima My Love) and *L'Année Dernière à Marienbad* (Last Year at Marienbad), and Luis Buñuel's *Belle de Jour.* François Truffaut's *Les Quatre Cents Coups* (The 400 Blows) was partly based on his own rebellious adolescence. Jean-Luc Godard made such films as *À Bout de Souffle* (Breathless), *Alphaville* and *Pierrot le Fou,* which showed even less concern for sequence and narrative. The new wave continued until the 1970s, by which time it had lost its experimental edge.

Of the directors of the 1950s and 1960s who were not part of this school, one of the most notable was Jacques Tati, who made many comic films based around the charming, bumbling figure of Monsieur Hulot and his struggles to adapt to the modern age. The best examples are *Les Vacances de M Hulot* (Mr Hulot's Holiday) and *Mon Oncle* (My Uncle).

The most successful directors of the 1980s and 1990s included Jean-Jacques Beineix, who made *Diva* and *Betty Blue,* Jean-Luc Besson, who shot *Subway* and *The Big Blue,* and Léos Carax *(Boy Meets Girl).*

Light social comedies, such as *Trois Hommes et un Couffin* (Three Men and a Cradle) by Coline Serreau, *La Vie Est un Long Fleuve Tranquille* (Life is a Long Quiet River) by Étienne Chatiliez, and Jean-Pierre Jeunet's *Le Fabuleux Destin d'Amélie Poulain* (Amelie), have been among the biggest hits in France in recent years.

Matthieu Kassovitz's award-winning *La Haine* (Hate), apparently inspired by *Meanstreets, Taxi Driver* and *Do the Right Thing,* examined the prejudice and violence among young French-born Algerians. Alain Resnais' *On Connaît la Chanson* (Same Old Song), based on the life of the late British TV playwright Dennis Potter, received international acclaim and six Césars in 1997.

Other well-regarded directors active today include Bertrand Blier (*Trop Belle pour Toi;* Too Beautiful for You), Cédric Klapisch (*Un Air de Famille;* Family Relations), German-born Dominik Moll (*Harry, un Ami qui Vous Veut du Bien;* With a Friend like Harry), Agnès Jaoul (*Le Gout des Autres;* The Taste of Others), Yves Lavandier (*Oui, Mais...;* Yes, But...) and Catherine Breillat (*À Ma Sœur;* Fat Girl).

Among the most popular and/or biggest-grossing French films at home and abroad in recent years have been Christophe Barratier's *Les Choristes* (The Chorus) about a new teacher at a strict boarding school who affects the students' lives through music; *De Battre Mon Cœur S'est Arrêté* (The Beat My Heart Skipped) by Jacques Audiard, a film noir about a violent rent collector turned classical pianist confronting his own life and that of his criminal father; Michael Haneke's suspenseful *Caché* (Hidden) about a TV book reviewer and his wife receiving videos and alarming drawings of themselves from an unknown (and unseen) person or persons; and the unexpected success of 2005 called *La Marche de l'Empereur* (March of the Penguins), a documentary about penguins by Louis Jaquet that had film-goers gaga over the tuxedoed critters.

DANCE

Ballet as we know it today originated in Italy but was brought to France in the late 16th century by Catherine de Médici. The first *ballet comique de la reine* (dramatic ballet) was performed at an aristocratic wedding at the court in Paris in 1581. It combined music, dance and poetic recitations (usually in praise of the monarchy) and was performed by male courtiers with women of the court forming the corps de ballet. Louis XIV so enjoyed the spectacles that he danced many leading roles himself at Versailles. In 1661 he founded the Académie Royale de Danse (Royal Dance Academy), from which modern ballet developed.

By the end of the 18th century, choreographers such as Jean-Georges Noverre had become more important than musicians, poets and the dancers themselves. In the early 19th century, romantic ballets, such as *Giselle* and *Les Sylphides,* were better attended than the opera. Between 1945 and '55 Roland Petit created such innovative ballets as *Turangalila,* with music composed by Olivier Messiaen, and *Le Jeune Homme et la Mort.* Maurice Béjart shocked with his *Symphonie pour un Homme Seul* (which was danced in black in 1955), *Le Sacre du Printemps* (The Rite of Spring) and *Le Marteau sans Maître,* with music by Pierre Boulez.

Today French dance seems to be moving in a new, more personal direction with such performers as Caroline Marcadé, Maguy Martin, Laurent Hilaire and Aurélie Dupont. Choreographers include the likes of Odile Duboc, Jean-Claude Gallotta, Jean-François Duroure and

TOP FIVE PARIS FILMS

- *À Bout de Souffle* (Breathless; France, 1959) – Jean-Luc Goddard's first feature is a carefree, fast-paced B&W celebration of Paris – from av des Champs-Élysées to the cafés of the Left Bank.
- *Last Tango in Paris* (USA, 1972) – in Bernardo Bertolucci's classic, Marlon Brando gives the performance of his career portraying a grief-stricken American in Paris who tries to find salvation in anonymous, sadomasochistic sex.
- *La Haine* (Hate; France, 1995) – Matthieu Kassovitz's incendiary B&W film examines the racism, social repression and violence among Parisian *beurs* (young French-born Algerians).
- *Le Fabuleux Destin d'Amélie Poulain* (Amelie; France, 2001) – one of the most popular French films internationally in years, Jean-Pierre Jeunet's feel-good story of a winsome young Parisian do-gooder named Amelie takes viewers on a colourful tour of Pigalle, Notre Dame, train stations and, above all, Montmartre.
- *Les Quatre Cents Coups* (The 400 Blows; France, 1959) – based on the French idiom *faire les quatre cents coups* (to raise hell), François Truffaut's first film is the semiautobiographical story of a downtrodden and neglected Parisian teenage boy who turns to outward rebellion.

the wunderkind of French choreography, Philippe Decouflé, who (among other things) masterminded the opening gala of the 2006 FIFA World Cup in Berlin.

THEATRE

France's first important dramatist was Alexandre Hardy, who appeared in Paris in 1597 and published almost three dozen plays over a relatively short period. Though few of his plays have withstood the test of time, Hardy was an innovator who helped bridge the gap between the French theatre of the Middle Ages and Renaissance and that of the 17th century.

During the golden age of French drama the most popular playwright was Molière, who (like William Shakespeare) started his career as an actor. Plays such as *Tartuffe,* a satire on the corruption of the aristocracy,

Notre Dame viewed from behind (p111)

won him the enmity of both the state and the church – and a ban – but are now staples of the classical repertoire. Playwrights Pierre Corneille and Jean Racine, in contrast, drew their subjects from history and classical mythology. Racine's *Phèdre,* for instance, taken from Euripides, is a story of incest and suicide among the descendants of the Greek gods, while Corneille's tragedy *Horace* is derived from Livy.

Theatre in France didn't really come into its own again until the postwar period of the 20th century with the arrival of two foreigners, both proponents of the so-called Theatre of the Absurd who wrote in French. Works by Irish-born Samuel Beckett, such as *En Attendant Godot* (Waiting for Godot; 1952), are bleak and point to the meaninglessness of life but are also richly humorous. The plays of Eugène Ionesco – eg *La Cantatrice Chauve* (The Bald Soprano; 1948) – are equally dark and satirical, and are ultimately compassionate.

Plays performed in Paris are – for obvious reasons – performed largely in French but more and more mainstream theatres are projecting English-language subtitles on screens. For information on theatres that host English-speaking troupes and/or stage plays in languages other than French, see p269.

ARCHITECTURE

Traditionally, Parisians have not been as intransigent as, say, Londoners, in accepting changes to their cityscape, nor as unshocked by the new as New Yorkers seem to be. But then Paris never had as great a fire as did London (1666), which offered architects a tabula rasa on which to redesign and build a modern city, or the green field that was New York in the late 18th century.

It took disease, clogged streets, an antiquated sewage system, a lack of open spaces and one Baron Georges-Eugène Haussmann (p76) to move Paris from the Middle Ages into a modern age, and few town planners anywhere in the world have had as great an impact on the city of their birth as he did on his.

Haussmann's 19th century transformation of Paris was a huge undertaking – Parisians endured years of 'flying dust, noise, and falling plaster and beams', as one contemporary observer wrote; entire areas of the city (eg the labyrinthlike Île de la Cité) were razed and hundreds of thousands of (mostly poor) people displaced. Even worse – or better, depending on your outlook – it brought to a head the *vieux* (old) Paris versus *nouveau* (new) Paris, a debate in which writer Victor Hugo played a key role (p27) and which continues to this day.

In 1967 stringent town-planning regulations in Paris, which had been on the books since Haussmann's day, were eased and buildings were allowed to 'soar' to 37m. However, they had to be set back from the road so as not to block the light. But this change allowed the erection of high-rise buildings, which broke up the continuity of many streets. A decade later new restrictions required that buildings again be aligned along the road and that their height be in proportion to the width of the street. In some central areas that means buildings cannot go higher than 18m.

At first glance, much of the architecture of Paris may appear to be the same – six- or seven-storey apartment blocks in the style of the Second Empire (1852–70) lining grand boulevards and interspersed with leafy squares. That is, in effect, exactly what Haussmann had in mind when he oversaw the construction of a new city in the middle of the 19th century. But Paris is a lot less homogeneous than that.

GALLO-ROMAN

Classical architecture is characterised both by its elegance and its grandeur. The Romans' use and adaptation of the classical Greek orders (Doric, Ionic and Corinthian) influenced Western architecture for millennia. The Romans were the first to use bricks and cement to build vaults, arches and domes. The emphasis was on impressive public buildings, aqueducts, triumphal arches, temples, fortifications, marketplaces, amphitheatres and bathhouses, some examples of which can be found in Paris. The Romans also established regular street grids.

From the mid–1st century BC the Romans turned a small Gallic settlement of wattle and daub huts on the Île de la Cité into a provincial capital called Lutetia (Lutèce in French). A temple to Jupiter was erected on the site where the Cathédrale de Notre Dame de Paris (p111) now stands, and the Roman town spread to the south bank, with rue St-Jacques as the main north–south axis. A forum stood at the corner of today's rue Soufflot, near today's Panthéon and the Jardin du Luxembourg.

Traces of Roman Paris can be seen in the residential foundations and dwellings in the Crypte Archéologique (p112) under the square in front of Notre Dame; in the partially reconstructed Arènes de Lutèce (p114); and in the *frigidarium* (cooling room) and other remains of Roman baths dating from around AD 200 at the Musée National du Moyen Age (p116).

The Musée National du Moyen Age also contains the so-called Pillier des Nautes (Boatsmen's Pillar), one of the most valuable legacies of the Gallo-Roman period. It is a 2.5m-high monument dedicated to Jupiter and was erected by the boatmen's guild during the reign of Tiberius (AD 14–37) on the Île de la Cité. What makes it so important is that it is lined with *bas-reliefs* of both Roman (eg Jupiter, Venus, Mercury, Mars) and Gallic (eg Esus, Cernunnos, Smertrios) deities, suggesting that while the Gauls had submitted to Roman authority, part of their ancient Celtic culture survived alongside as late as the 1st century AD. The boat remains the symbol of Paris, and the city's Latin motto is *'Fluctuat Nec Mergitur'* (Tosses but Does Not Sink).

MEROVINGIAN & CAROLINGIAN

Although quite a few churches were built in Paris during the Merovingian and Carolingian periods (6th to 10th centuries), very little of them remain.

When the Merovingian ruler Clovis I made Paris his seat in the early 6th century, he established an abbey dedicated to Sts Peter and Paul on the south bank of the Seine. All that remains of this once great abbey (later named in honour of Paris' patron, Sainte Geneviève, and demolished in 1802) is the Tour Clovis (Map pp444–5), a heavily restored Romanesque tower within the grounds of the prestigious Lycée Henri IV just east of the Panthéon.

Clovis' son and successor, Childeric II, founded the Abbey of St-Germain des Prés; the Merovingian kings were buried here during the 6th and 7th centuries, but their tombs were emptied and destroyed during the French Revolution. The dynasty's most productive ruler, Dagobert, established an abbey at St-Denis north of Paris, which would soon become the richest and most important monastery in France. Archaeological excavations in the crypt of the 12th-century Basilique de St-Denis (p157) have uncovered extensive tombs from both the Merovingian and Carolingian periods. The oldest of these dates from around AD 570.

40

ROMANESQUE

A religious revival in the 11th century led to the construction of a large number of *roman* (Romanesque) churches, so-called because their architects adopted many architectural elements (eg vaulting) from Gallo-Roman buildings still standing at the time. Romanesque buildings typically have round arches, heavy walls, few windows that let in very little light, and a lack of ornamentation that borders on the austere. Chateaux built during this era tended to be massive, heavily fortified structures that afforded few luxuries to their inhabitants.

No civic buildings or churches in Paris are entirely Romanesque in style, but a few have important representative elements. The Église St-Germain des Prés (p118), built in the 11th century on the site of the Merovingian ruler Childeric's 6th-century abbey, has been altered many times over the centuries, but the Romanesque bell tower over the west entrance has changed little since 1000. There are also some decorated capitals (the upper part of the supporting columns) in the nave dating from this time. The choir, apse and truncated bell tower of the Église St-Nicholas des Champs (Map pp428–9), just south of the Musée des Arts et Métiers, are Romanesque dating from about 1130. The Église St-Germain L'Auxerrois (p99) was built in a mixture of Gothic and Renaissance styles between the 13th and 16th centuries on a site used for Christian worship since about AD 500. But the square belfry that rises from next to the south transept arm is Romanesque in style.

The choir and ambulatory of the Basilique de St-Denis (p157) have features illustrating the transition from Romanesque to Gothic while the magnificent 13th-century Cathédrale Notre Dame at Chartres (p352) is crowned by two soaring spires – one Romanesque and the other Gothic. The west entrance to the cathedral, known as the Portail Royal (Royal Portal), is adorned with statues whose features are elongated in the Romanesque style. The other main Romanesque feature of the cathedral at Chartres is the Clocher Vieux (Old Bell Tower), which was begun in the 1140s. At 105m, it is the tallest Romanesque steeple still standing. Also in Chartres is the empty shell of the Collégiale St-André, a Romanesque collegiate church dating from the 12th century.

GOTHIC

The Gothic style originated in the mid-12th century in northern France, where great wealth attracted the finest architects, engineers and artisans. Gothic structures are characterised by ribbed vaults carved with great precision, pointed arches, slender verticals, chapels (often built or endowed by the wealthy or by guilds), galleries and arcades along the nave and chancel, refined decoration and large stained-glass windows. If you look closely at certain Gothic buildings, however, you'll notice minor asymmetrical elements. These elements were introduced to avoid monotony, in accordance with standard Gothic practice.

The world's first Gothic building was the Basilique de St-Denis (p157), which combined various late Romanesque elements to create a new kind of structural support in which each arch counteracted and complemented the next. Begun in around 1135, the basilica served as a model for many other 12th-century French cathedrals, including Notre Dame de Paris and the cathedral at Chartres. Gothic technology – and the width and height it made possible – subsequently spread to the rest of Western Europe.

Cathedrals built in the early Gothic style, which lasted until about 1230, were majestic but lacked the lightness and airiness of later works. Since the stained-glass windows could not support the roof, thick stone buttresses were placed between them. It was soon discovered that reducing the bulk of the buttresses and adding outer piers to carry the thrust created a lighter building without compromising structural integrity.

This discovery gave rise to flying buttresses, which helped lift the Gothic style to its greatest achievements between 1230 and 1300. During this period, when French architecture dominated the European scene for the first time, High Gothic masterpieces such as the seminal cathedral at Chartres were decorated with ornate tracery (the delicate stone rib-work on stained-glass windows) and huge, colourful rose windows.

In the 14th century, the Rayonnant – Radiant – Gothic style, which was named after the radiating tracery of the rose windows, developed, with interiors becoming even lighter thanks to broader windows and more-translucent stained glass. One of the most influential Rayonnant buildings was the Ste-Chapelle (p113), whose stained glass forms a curtain of glazing on the 1st floor. The two transept façades of the Cathédrale de Notre Dame de Paris (p111) and the vaulted Salle des Gens d'Armes (Cavalrymen's Hall) in the Conciergerie (p112), the largest surviving medieval hall in Europe, are other fine examples of the Rayonnant Gothic style.

By the 15th century, decorative extravagance led to what is now called Flamboyant Gothic, so named because the wavy stone carving made the towers appear to be blazing or flaming (*flamboyant*). Beautifully lacy examples of Flamboyant architecture include the Clocher Neuf (New Bell Tower) at Chartres' Cathédrale Notre Dame (p352), the Église St-Séverin (Map pp436–7) and the Tour St-Jacques (p105), a 52m tower which is all that remains of the Église St-Jacques la Boucherie from the early 16th century. Inside the Église St-Eustache (p99), there's some outstanding Flamboyant Gothic archwork holding up the ceiling of the chancel. Several *hôtels particuliers* (private mansions) were also built in this style, including the Hôtel de Cluny, now the Musée National du Moyen Age (p116) and the Hôtel de Sens (p162).

RENAISSANCE

The Renaissance, which began in Italy in the early 15th century, set out to realise a 'rebirth' of classical Greek and Roman culture. It had its first impact on France at the end of the 15th century, when Charles VIII began a series of invasions of Italy, returning with some new ideas.

During what is now called the Early Renaissance period, a variety of classical components and decorative motifs (columns, tunnel vaults, round arches, domes etc) were blended with the rich decoration of Flamboyant Gothic. The Early Renaissance style of architecture is best exemplified in Paris by the Église St-Eustache (p99) on the Right Bank and Église St-Étienne du Mont (p114) on the Left Bank.

Mannerism, which followed Early Renaissance, began around 1530, when François I, who had been so deeply impressed by what he had seen in Italy that he brought Leonardo da Vinci back with him in 1516, hired Italian architects and artists – many of them disciples of Michelangelo or Raphael – to design and decorate his new Château de Fontainebleau (p343). Over the following decades French architects who had studied in Italy took over from their Italian colleagues. In 1546 Pierre Lescot designed the richly decorated southwestern corner of the Cour Carrée of the Musée du Louvre (p100). The Petit Château at the Château de Chantilly (p347) was built about a decade later. The Marais remains the best area for spotting reminders of the Renaissance in Paris proper, with some fine *hôtels particuliers* from this era such as Hôtel Carnavalet, housing part of the Musée Carnavalet (p107) and Hôtel Lamoignon (p162).

Because French Renaissance architecture was very much the province of the aristocracy and designed by imported artists, the middle classes – resentful French artisans among them – remained loyal to the indigenous Gothic style, and Gothic churches continued to be built in Paris throughout the 1500s. The Mannerist style lasted until the early 17th century.

BAROQUE

During the baroque period – which lasted from the tail end of the 16th to the late 18th centuries – painting, sculpture and classical architecture were integrated to create structures and interiors of great subtlety, refinement and elegance. With the advent of the baroque, architecture became more pictorial, with the painted ceilings in churches illustrating the Passion of Christ and infinity to the faithful, and palaces invoking the power and order of the state. Baroque architecture in Paris bears little resemblance to that of the capital cities of Catholic central and southern Europe. Here, as in the Protestant countries of northern Europe, baroque architecture was meant to appeal to the intellect – not the senses. As a result it was more geometric, formal and ordered.

Salomon de Brosse, who designed Paris' Palais du Luxembourg (see Jardin du Luxembourg, p119) in 1615, set the stage for two of France's most prominent early baroque architects: François Mansart, designer of the Église Notre Dame du Val-de-Grâce (Map pp444–5), and his young rival Louis Le Vau, the architect of the Château de Vaux-le-Vicomte (p347), which served as a model for Louis XIV's palace at Versailles. Baroque elements are particularly evident in the lavish interiors of the Château de Versailles (p340), such as the Galerie des Glaces (Hall of Mirrors). Jules Hardouin-Mansart, Le Vau's successor at Versailles, also designed the landmark Église du Dôme (p124), considered the finest church built in France during the 17th century.

Other fine examples of French baroque are the Église St-Louis en l'Île (p114), built between 1664 and 1726; the Chapelle de la Sorbonne (p117); the Palais Royal (p103); and the 17th-century Hôtel de Sully (p106), with its inner courtyard decorated with allegorical figures. The Cathédrale St-Louis in Versailles (p339) fuses elements of baroque and neoclassicism.

Streetlight on place de l'Hôtel de Ville (p107)

Rococo

Rococo, a derivation of late baroque, was popular during the Enlightenment (1700–80). The word comes from the French *rocaille* ('loose pebbles'), which, together with shells, were used to decorate inside walls and other surfaces. In Paris, rococo was confined almost exclusively to the interiors of private residences and had a minimal impact on churches and civic buildings, which continued to follow the conventional rules of baroque classicism. Rococo interiors, such as the oval rooms of the Archives Nationales (p106), were lighter, smoother and airier than their baroque predecessors, and favoured pastels over vivid colours.

NEOCLASSICISM

Neoclassical architecture, which emerged in about 1740 and remained popular in Paris until well into the 19th century, had its roots in the renewed interest in classical forms. Although it was, in part, a reaction against baroque and its adjunct, rococo, with emphases on decoration and illusion, neoclassicism was more profoundly a search for order, reason and serenity through the adoption of the forms and conventions of Graeco-Roman antiquity: columns, simple geometric forms and traditional ornamentation.

Among the earliest examples of this style in Paris are the Italianate façade of the Église St-Sulpice (p118), designed in 1733 by Giovanni Servandoni, which took inspiration from Christopher Wren's Cathedral of St Paul in London, and the Petit Trianon at Versailles (p338), designed by Jacques-Ange Gabriel for Louis XV in 1761. The domed building housing the Institut de France (p118) is a masterpiece of early French neoclassical architecture, but France's greatest neoclassical architect of the 18th century was Jacques-Germain Soufflot, who designed the Panthéon (p117).

Neoclassicism really came into its own, however, under Napoleon, who used it extensively for monumental architecture intended to embody the grandeur of imperial France and its capital. Well-known Paris sights designed (though not necessarily completed) under the First Empire (1804–14) include the Arc de Triomphe (p130); the Arc de Triomphe du Carrousel (p98); the Église de la Madeleine (p132); the Bourse de Commerce (p98); and the Assemblée Nationale (p124) in the Palais Bourbon.

BUILDING INSPIRATION

For the most part, skyscrapers and other tall buildings are restricted to La Défense, but that doesn't mean other parts of Paris are bereft of interesting and inspired new buildings. Some of our favourites:

1er arrondissement

Marché de St-Honoré (Map pp426–7; place du Marché St-Honoré; (M) Tuileries or Opéra) This monumental glass hall (Ricardo Bofill, 1996) of offices and shops replaces an unsightly parking garage (now underground) and evokes the wonderful *passages couverts* (covered shopping arcades) that begin a short distance to the northeast (p167).

Immeuble des Bons Enfants (Map pp436–7; 182 rue St-Honoré; (M) Palais Royal-Musée du Louvre) The new home (Francis Soler and Frédéric Druot, 2004) of the Ministère de la Culture et de la Communication (Ministry of Culture & Communication) is actually two separate and disparate buildings 'linked' by a metallic net of what can only be described as tracery that allows in light and also allows the diversity of the existing buildings to be seen.

7e arrondissement

Musée du Quai Branly (Map pp434–5; www.quaibranly.fr; quai Branly; (M) Pont de l'Alma) Jean Nouvel's glass, wood and sod structure, which combines the collection of the erstwhile Musée National des Arts d'Afrique et d'Océanie in the Bois de Vincennes and some items from the Musée de l'Homme (p129), takes advantage of its experimental garden designed by Gilles Clément and is virtually a vertical garden.

9e arrondissement

Drouot (p300) We like this zany structure (Jean-Jacques Fernier and André Biro, 1980), a rebuild of the mid-19th-century Hôtel Drouot, for its 1970s retro design.

10e arrondissement

Crèche (Map pp428–9; 8ter rue des Récollets; (M) Gare de l'Est) This day nursery (Marc Younan, 2002) of wood and resin in the garden of the Couvent des Récollets looks like a jumbled pile of gold- and mustard-coloured building blocks. A central glass atrium functions as a 'village square'.

12e arrondissement

Direction de l'Action Sociale Building (Map pp446–7; 94-96 quai de la Rapée; (M) Quai de la Rapée) The headquarters of Social Action (Aymeric Zublena, 1991) is unabashed in proclaiming the power of the state, with an enormous central square within and vast glass-and-metal gates. When the gates are closed the square turns into an antechamber worthy of a palace.

Cinémathèque Française (Map pp446–7; 51 rue de Bercy; (M) Bercy) The former American Centre (Frank Gehry, 1994), from the incomparable American architect of Bilbao's Guggenheim Museum, is a fascinating building of creamy stone that looks, from some angles, as though it is falling in on itself.

14e arrondissement

Fondation Cartier pour l'Art Contemporain (Map pp434–5; 261 blvd Raspail; (M) Raspail) As with his Musée du Quai Branly (see earlier in this list), Master Nouvel set to 'conceal' the Cartier Foundation for Contemporary Arts when he designed it in 1993. In some ways the structure (lots of glass and what looks like scaffolding) appears at once both incomplete and invisible.

19e arrondissement

Les Orgues de Flandre (Map pp428–9; 67-107 av de Flandre & 14-24 rue Archereau; (M) Riquet) As outlandish a structure as you'll find anywhere, these two enormous housing estates opposite one another are known as 'The Organs of Flanders' due to their resemblance to that musical instrument and their street address. Storeys are stacked at oblique angles and the structures appear to be swaying, though they are firmly anchored at the end of a small park south of blvd Périphérique.

Neoclassicism remained very much in vogue in Paris, though in slightly different forms, until late into the 19th century. It even spilled into the 20th century, such as in the Palais de Chaillot (p129), which was built for the World Exhibition of 1937. Two architects (associated with Paris' École des Beaux-Arts, the most important centre of architectural education in Europe in the 19th century) who best exemplify this late period of classicism are Jacques-Ignace Hittorff, who designed the Gare du Nord in 1861, and Louis Duc, responsible for the Palais de Justice (p113). The work of both men influenced a generation of architects, including Henri Deglane and Victor Laloux, who were both involved in designing the Grand Palais (p131) and the Gare d'Orsay, now the Musée d'Orsay (p124), for the World Exhibition in 1889 (held to commemorate the centenary of the French Revolution). The Eiffel Tower (p127), which at first faced massive opposition from Paris' artistic and literary elite, was also opened for the 1889 World Exhibition. Two years previously the dramatist Alexandre Dumas *fils* (the son rather than the father of the same name) and the short-story writer Guy de Maupassant signed a petition protesting against the construction of a 'gigantic black factory chimney'; when the tower was complete Maupassant frequented the restaurant at its base, claiming it was the only place where he could not see the 'monstrosity'.

The climax of 19th-century classicism in Paris, however, is thought to be the Palais Garnier (p135), designed by Charles Garnier to house the opera and to showcase the splendour of Napoleon III's France. It was one of the crowning glories of the urban redevelopment plans of Baron Haussmann.

ART NOUVEAU

Gothic Revival, a style of architecture extremely popular in London and especially in New York between the late 18th and mid-19th centuries, never caught on in Paris as it did in those cities; much of that style was confined to restorations by architect Eugène Emmanuel Viollet-le-Duc at Ste-Chapelle (p113), Cathédrale de Notre Dame de Paris (p111) and the Église St-Germain L'Auxerrois (p99). However, Art Nouveau, which emerged in Europe and the USA in the second half of the 19th century under various names (Jugendstil, Sezessionstil, Stile Liberty) caught on quickly in Paris, and its influence lasted until about 1910.

Art Nouveau was characterised by sinuous curves and flowing, asymmetrical forms reminiscent of tendrilous vines, water lilies, the patterns on insect wings and the flowering boughs of trees. Influenced by the arrival of exotic *objets d'art* from Japan, its French name came from a Paris gallery that featured works in the 'new art' style.

Art Nouveau had a profound impact on all the applied arts, including interior design, glasswork, wrought-iron work, furniture-making and graphics. It combined a variety of materials – including iron, brick, glass and ceramics – in ways never seen before. Paris is still graced by Hector Guimard's Art Nouveau metro entrances (see p104). There are some fine Art Nouveau interiors in the Musée d'Orsay (p124), an Art Nouveau glass roof over the Grand Palais (p131) and, on rue Pavée in the Marais, a synagogue designed by Guimard (p110). The city's main department stores, including Le Bon Marché (p293) and Galeries Lafayette (p300), also have elements of this style throughout their interiors.

MODERN

France's best-known 20th-century architect, Charles-Édouard Jeanneret (better known as Le Corbusier), was born in Switzerland but settled in Paris in 1917 at the age of 30. A radical modernist, he tried to adapt buildings to their functions in industrialised society without ignoring the human element. Not everyone thinks he was particularly successful in this endeavour, however.

Most of Le Corbusier's work was done outside Paris though he did design several private residences and the Pavillon Suisse, a dormitory for Swiss students at the Cité Universitaire (Map pp422–3; metro Cité Universitaire) in the southeastern 14e bordering the blvd Périphérique. Perhaps most interesting – and frightening – are Le Corbusier's plans for Paris that never left the drawing board. Called Plan Voisin (Neighbour Project; 1925), it envisaged wide boulevards linking the Gare Montparnasse with the Seine and lined with skyscrapers. The project would have required bulldozing much of the Latin Quarter.

Until 1968, French architects were still being trained almost exclusively at the conformist École de Beaux-Arts, which certainly shows in most of the early structures erected in the skyscraper district of La Défense (p155). It can also be seen in buildings such as the Unesco building, erected in 1958 southwest of the École Militaire in the 7e, and the unspeakable, 210m-tall Tour Montparnasse (1973; p123), whose architects, in our opinion, should have been frogmarched to the place de la Concorde and guillotined.

CONTEMPORARY

France owes many of its most attractive and successful contemporary buildings in Paris to the narcissism of its presidents. For centuries France's leaders have sought to immortalise themselves by erecting huge public edifices – known as *grands projets* – in the capital, and the recent past has been no different. The late President Georges Pompidou commissioned the once reviled but now beloved Centre Beaubourg (Renzo Piano and Richard Rogers, 1977), later renamed the Centre Pompidou (p98), in which the architects – in order to keep the exhibition halls as spacious and uncluttered as possible – put the building's insides outside (a very radical concept at the time).

Pompidou's successor, Valéry Giscard d'Estaing, was instrumental in transforming the derelict Gare d'Orsay train station into the glorious Musée d'Orsay (p124), a design carried out by the Italian architect Gaeltana Aulenti in 1986. But François Mitterrand, with his decided preference for the modern, surpassed them both with a dozen or so monumental projects in Paris.

Since the early 1980s, Paris has seen the construction of such structures as IM Pei's controversial Grande Pyramide (1989; see Musée du Louvre, p100), a glass pyramid that serves as the main entrance to the hitherto sacrosanct – and untouchable – Louvre and an architectural cause célèbre in the late 1980s; the city's second opera house, the tile-clad Opéra Bastille (1989; p109) designed by Canadian Carlos Ott; the monumental Grande Arche de la Défense (p156) by Danish architect Johan-Otto von Sprekelsen, which opened in 1989; the delightful Conservatoire National Supérieur de Musique et de Danse (1990; p263) and Cité de la Musique (1994; p150), designed by Christian de Portzamparc and serving as a sort of gateway from the city to the whimsical Parc de la Villette; the twinned Grandes Serres (Great Greenhouses; Map pp422–3) built by Patrick Berger in 1992 at the main entrance to the Parc André Citroën; the Ministère de l'Économie et des Finances (Map pp446–7) designed by Paul Chemetov and Borja Huidobro in 1990, with its striking 'pier' overhanging the Seine in Bercy; and the four glass towers of Dominique Perrault's Bibliothèque Nationale de France (National Library of France; p147), which opened in 1995.

One of the most beautiful and successful of the late-20th-century modern buildings in Paris is the Institut du Monde Arabe (p115), a highly praised structure that opened in 1987 and successfully mixes modern and traditional Arab and Western elements. It was designed by Jean Nouvel, France's leading and arguably most talented architect.

However, not everything new, different and/or monumental that has appeared in the past two decades has been a government undertaking. The vast majority of the buildings in La Défense (p155), Paris' skyscraper district on the Seine to the west of the city centre, are privately owned and house some 1500 companies, including the head offices of more than a dozen of France's top corporations. Unfortunately, most of the skyscrapers here are impersonal and forgettable 'lipstick tubes' and 'upended shoeboxes', with a few notable exceptions.

Those wanting to learn more about Paris' contemporary architecture should visit the **Pavillon de l'Arsenal** (Map pp440–1; ☎ 01 42 76 33 97; www.pavillon-arsenal.com; 21 blvd Morland, 4e; admission free; 🕑 10.30am-6.30pm Tue-Sat, 11am-7pm Sun; Ⓜ Sully Morland), which is the city's town-planning and architectural centre. It has a permanent collection called 'Paris: The Making of a City' and rotating exhibits. Two excellent books on the subject include the introductory *Paris: Architecture & Design* (teNeues), edited by Christian van Uffelen, and the much more serious (and bilingual) *Guide de l'Architecture Moderne á Paris/Guide to Modern Architecture in Paris* (Éditions Alternatives) by Hervé Martin, which also includes architectural walking tours of the city.

Food

Food

No other cuisine (with the arguable exception of Chinese) comes close to that of the French for freshness of ingredients, natural flavours and refined (and very often complex) cooking methods. It is the West's most important and influential style of cooking.

The very word 'cuisine', of course, is French in origin – the English 'cooking style' just cannot handle all the nuances – while 'French' conjures up a sophisticated, cultured people who know their arts, including gastronomy. While there is only some truth to that notion (not *every* French man, woman and child is a walking *Larousse Gastronomique,* the seminal encyclopedia of French gastronomy), eating well is still of prime importance to most people here, and they continue to spend an inordinate amount of time thinking about, talking about and consuming food.

Do not think for a moment, though, that this national obsession with things culinary and a familiarity with the complexities of *haute cuisine* (high cuisine) means that eating out or dining in a private home here has to be a ceremonious or even formal occasion, one full of pitfalls for the uninitiated. Indeed, contrary to a commonly held Anglo-Saxon belief, the French (and that includes Parisians) can be among the kindest, most generous and open people anywhere. Approach their food and wine with half the enthusiasm that they themselves do, and you will be warmly received, tutored, encouraged and well fed.

HISTORY

Up to the Middle Ages, dining – at least for the wealthier classes and the court in Paris – essentially meant sitting around a large table, sawing off hunks of meat with small knives. Peasants and the urban poor subsisted on bread or dumplings made of rye flour and whatever *companaticum* (Latin for 'that which goes with bread') was available in the cauldron forever on the boil over the hearth. Even by the time the first French-language cookbook was published by Charles V's head chef, Guillaume Tirel (or Taillevent), in about 1375, menus consisted almost entirely of 'soups' (actually sodden pieces of bread, or 'sops', boiled in a thickened stock), and meat and poultry heavy with the taste of herbs and spices, including new ones, such as ginger, cinnamon and cloves, first introduced into Spain by the Moors. The book's very title, *Le Viander de Taillevent,* would suggest a carnivorous diet, but at that time *viande* (meat) simply meant 'food'.

The 16th century was something of a watershed for French cuisine. When Catherine de Médici, future consort to François' son, Henri II, arrived in Paris in 1533, she brought with her a team of Florentine chefs and pastry cooks adept in the subtleties of Italian Renaissance cooking. They introduced such delicacies as aspics, truffles, *quenelles* (dumplings), artichokes, macaroons and puddings to the French court. Catherine's cousin, Marie de Médici, brought even more chefs to Paris when she married Henri IV in 1600. The French cooks, increasingly aware of their rising social status, took the Italians' recipes and sophisticated cooking styles on board, and the rest – to the eternal gratitude of epicures everywhere – is history.

France and its capital enjoyed an era of order and prosperity under Henri's rule, who is famously credited with having wished all of his subjects to have a *poule au pot* (chicken in the pot) every Sunday. Later in the century the sweet tooth of Louis XIV (1643–1715) launched the custom of eating desserts, once reserved for feast days and other celebrations, at the end of a meal.

The most decisive influence on French cuisine at this time, however, was the work of chef François-Pierre de la Varenne, who learned his trade in Marie de Médici's kitchens. La Varenne's cookbook, *Le Cuisinier François* (1652), was a gastronomic landmark for many reasons. It was the first to give instructions for preparing vegetables; it introduced soups in the modern sense, with the 'soup' being more important than the sops it contained; and it discarded bread and breadcrumbs as thickening agents in favour of *roux,* a much more versatile mixture of flour and fat. Most importantly, La Varenne downplayed the use of spices, preferring to serve meat in its natural juices sharpened with vinegar or lemon juice. A basic tenet of French cuisine was thus born: to enhance the natural flavours of food in cooking and not to disguise it with heavy seasonings.

The 18th century, the so-called Grand Siècle (Great Century) of reason, brought little enlightenment to the French table apart from dishes and sauces named after lords and other royalty by their sycophantic chefs. This was the century when newfangled foodstuffs from the New World – the tomato, corn, bean, red pepper and especially the potato so integral today in French cuisine – gained currency, and when the fork became a standard part of the table setting. Most important was the new trend to serve dishes in a logical order rather than heaping them in a pyramid on the table all at the same time.

This century also saw the birth of the restaurant as we know it today. In 1765 a certain Monsieur A Boulanger opened a small business in rue Bailleul in the 1er, just off rue de Rivoli, selling soups, broths and, later, the crowd-pleasing sheep's trotters in a white sauce. Above the door he hung a sign to advertise these *restaurants* ('restoratives', from the verb *se restaurer,* 'to feed oneself'). Before that time not everyone cooked at home every day of the year. Hostelries and inns existed, but they only served guests set meals at set times and prices from the *table d'hôte* (host's table) and cafés only offered drinks. Monsieur Boulanger's restaurant is thought to have been the first public place where diners could order a meal from a menu that offered a range of dishes.

During the French Revolution and the Reign of Terror that followed, the ovens in the kitchens of the great aristocratic households went cold, and their chefs were driven in tumbrels to the guillotine. But a new avenue soon opened to those who managed to escape execution: employment in the kitchens of the hundreds of restaurants opening to the public in Paris. By 1804 Paris counted some 500 restaurants. A typical menu at that time included 12 soups, two dozen hors d'oeuvre, between 12 and 30 dishes of beef, veal, mutton, fowl and game, 24 fish dishes, 12 types of pâtisserie (pastries) and 50 desserts.

The first and most important of these new chefs was Marie-Antoine Carême (1784–1833), who set out to establish 'order and taste' in French gastronomy and became personal chef to such luminaries as French statesman Talleyrand, England's Prince Regent and Russia's Tsar Alexander I. But to most English speakers, the name Georges-August Escoffier (1846–1935) is more synonymous with *haute cuisine.* Escoffier, nicknamed 'the king of chefs and the chef of kings', was a reformer who simplified or discarded decorations and garnishes, shortened menus and streamlined food preparation in kitchens, having taken his cue from Prosper Montagné, one of the great French chefs of all time and author of *Larousse Gastronomique.*

The most important development in French gastronomy in the 20th century was the arrival of *nouvelle cuisine* (new cuisine), a reaction against Escoffier's *grande cuisine* (great cuisine). This low-fat style of cooking eliminated many sauces in favour of stock reductions, prepared dishes in such a way as to emphasise the inherent textures and colours of the ingredients, and served them artistically on large plates. *Nouvelle cuisine* made a big

BOUNTY FROM THE ISLAND OF FRANCE

The *maraîchers* (market gardeners) of the Île de France encircling Paris traditionally supplied the capital with fresh produce. Today, while the Île de France is less important agriculturally and encompasses the eight *départements* that make up the urbanised Région Parisienne (Parisian Region), the green and gentle 'Island of France' has clung to many of the products it knows best.

A list of fruits and vegetables from the region reads like a map of the RER: *asperges d'Argenteuil* (Argenteuil asparagus), *carottes de Crécy* (Crécy carrots), *cerises de Montmorency* (Montmorency cherries), *fraises de Palaiseau* (Palaiseau strawberries), *pétales de roses de Provins* (Provins rose petals, used to make jam), *tomates de Montlhéry* (Montlhéry tomatoes), *champignons de Paris* (Paris mushrooms grown *for* not *in* the capital) and so on. A dish served *à la parisienne* then is a combination of vegetables along with potato balls that have been sautéed in butter, glazed in meat drippings and sprinkled with parsley.

splash in the diet-conscious 1970s and '80s, when it was also know as *cuisine minceur* (lean cuisine), and its proponents, including chefs Paul Bocuse, Jean and Pierre Troisgros and Michel Guérard, became the new saints of the grazing faithful from Paris to Perth.

By the turn of the millennium, however, this revolutionary new style of cooking had fallen out of favour and in a 2003 article the *New York Times* accused French chefs of resting on their laurels and French cuisine of having 'congealed into complacency'. French chefs – including Pierre Gagnaire (p214) rose to the bait in no time, arguing that French cuisine remained both modern and dynamic. 'There have been considerable developments in recent years in so many directions, which reveal an unparalleled vigour in French cooking', said Gagnaire. At the same time, he said, French cuisine had kept to its traditions and did not seek to be sensational. And that could very well be its secret.

CULTURE

When it comes to food, Paris has everything and nothing. As the culinary centre of the most aggressively gastronomic country in the world, it has more 'generic French', regional and ethnic restaurants, fine food shops and markets than any other place in the country. But *la cuisine parisienne* (Parisian cuisine) is a poor relation of that extended family known as *la cuisine des provinces* (provincial cuisine). That's because those greedy country cousins have consumed most of what was once on Paris' own plate. Today very few dishes are associated with the capital as such, though certain side dishes bear the names of some of its suburbs (boxed text, p49).

Since the time of the French Revolution, the cuisines of the capital and the surrounding Île de France have been basically indistinguishable from the cooking of France in general. Dishes associated with the regions are few – *vol-au-vent*, the 'flight in the wind' that is a light pastry shell filled with chicken or fish in a creamy sauce; *potage Saint Germain*, a thick green pea soup; *gâteau Paris-Brest*, a ring-shaped cake filled with *praline* (butter cream) and topped with flaked almonds and icing sugar; and the humble onion soup and pig's trotters described so intimately in Ernest Hemingway's *The Sun Also Rises*. Deep-frying potatoes (ie *frites*) and other dishes has always been a Parisian speciality as well.

At the same time, a lot of dishes have been created in Paris that seem to have flown the coop and settle elsewhere. The 'Breton' *homard à l'américaine* (lobster chunks simmered in white wine and tomatoes) was created in Paris. *Sole normande*, a dish of sole caught off the Norman coast and cooked with shrimps in a white cream sauce, was first made in the Île de France. Even *crêpes Suzette*, those thin pancakes served with liberal doses of orange-flavoured brandy and usually associated with Brittany, were first served in Paris with Grand Marnier made at Neauphle-le-Château, just southwest of Paris.

Most people in Paris buy a good part of their food from a series of small neighbourhood shops, each with its own speciality (p64), though like everywhere more and more people are relying on supermarkets and hypermarkets these days. At first, having to go to four shops and stand in four queues to fill the fridge (or assemble a picnic) may seem rather a waste of time, but the whole ritual is an important part of the way many Parisians live their daily lives.

Neighbourhood markets are equally a part of life here. If on a Saturday morning you notice throngs of basket-toting people passing you by with great determination, and others, laden down with bags, going the opposite direction in a more relaxed pace, then by all means follow the crowds as you have stumbled upon the most Parisian of weekend pastimes: shopping at the *marché alimentaire* (street food market). There is no better way to be mistaken for a native; forsake that day at the Louvre, grab a basket and load up on fresh provisions.

The city's *marchés découverts* (open-air markets) – some five dozen of which pop up in public squares around the city two or three times a week – are usually open from about 7am or 8am to 1pm or 2pm, depending on the time of year. The 19 *marchés couverts* (covered markets) keep more regular hours: 8am to 1pm and 3.30pm or 4pm to 7pm or 7.30pm from Tuesday to Saturday and till lunch time on Sunday. Completing the picture are numerous independent *rues commerçantes*, pedestrian streets where the shops set up outdoor stalls.

Oysters at L'Écailler du Bistrot (p228)

To find out when there's a market near you, check the list on p52, enquire at your hotel or hostel or ask anyone who lives in the neighbourhood.

To foreigners, food markets in the capital are the most delightful of all Parisian stereotypes. They offer the usual French standbys plus more – fresh vegetables and fruit, meat, bread, pastries and cakes, dozens of cheeses, prepared meats and other dishes, foie gras, nuts, fish, flowers and, of course, organic produce – all painstakingly arrayed in colour-coordinated displays beneath chalkboards with the prices marked in that characteristic French scrawl. Tradespeople and peddlers ply basket- and chair-repair services, Oriental carpets, sewing machines and kitchen utensils. Children sell €2 bunches of fragrant purple lilacs in spring. A Paris market fulfils every fantasy we have entertained about the City of Light.

But markets are far more than a cute picture postcard or simply a remembrance of France past. They are very much a symbol of Paris present and an integral part of modern life. Touring them gives you a look at a cross-section of the wildly diverse group of peoples that make up Paris today.

Dependable quality is ensured by the intimate relationship of the vendors and their repeat customers. Truck-garden culture brings fresh produce that reflect the seasons in a way that supermarkets, with mass-produced fruits and vegetables available year-round, cannot. The sometimes-daunting number of competing stands allows you to pick and choose for quality and price. The flourishing immigrant populations are bringing new blood to the old tradition with booming ethnic markets as well.

ETIQUETTE

The French invented *etiquette* (from *estique*, the daily rules for soldiers). That said, it's actually not easy to cause offence at a French table, and manners here have more to do with common sense than learned behaviour. Still, there are subtle differences in the way French people handle themselves while eating that are worth pointing out. Attitudes are more relaxed in a private home than in a top-class restaurant, of course, but even those distinctions are becoming somewhat blurred.

A French table will be set for all courses at restaurants (not always at home), with two forks, two knives and a large spoon for soup or dessert. When diners finish each course, they cross their knife and fork (not lay them side by side) face down on the plate to be cleared away. If there's only one knife and fork at your setting, you should place the cutlery back on the table after each course.

At a dinner party courses may not be served in the order to which you are accustomed; salad may follow the main course, for example, and cheese always precedes dessert (boxed

IN THE MARKET FOR EVERYTHING

The following is a list of Paris markets selected according to the variety of their produce, their ethnicity and the neighbourhood. They are *la crème de la crème*.

Marché aux Enfants Rouges (Map pp440–1; 39 rue de Bretagne, 3e; 9am-2pm & 4-8pm Tue-Fri, 9am-8pm Sat, 9am-2pm Sun; Filles du Calvaire) This covered market south of place de la République has both ethnic (Italian, North African etc) stalls as well as French ones.

Marché Bastille (Map pp440–1; blvd Richard Lenoir, 11e; 7am-2pm Tue, 7am-2.30pm Sun; Bastille or Richard Lenoir) Stretching as far north as the Richard Lenoir metro station, this is arguably the best open-air market in Paris with a lot more ethnic food stalls now in attendance than ever before.

Marché Batignolles-Clichy (Map pp426–7; blvd des Batignolles btwn rue des Batignolles & rue Puteaux, 8e & 17e; 9am-2pm Sat; Place de Clichy or Rome) This is one of the several *marchés biologiques* (organic markets) in Paris that are becoming increasingly popular.

Marché Beauvau (Map pp446–7; place d'Aligre, 12e; 8.30am-1pm & 4-7.30pm Tue-Sat, 8.30am-1.30pm Sun; Ledru Rollin) This covered market remains a colourful Arab and North African enclave close to the Bastille.

Marché Belleville (Map pp428–9; blvd de Belleville btwn rue Jean-Pierre Timbaud & rue du Faubourg du Temple, 11e & 20e; 7am-1.30pm Tue & Fri; Belleville or Couronne) This market offers a fascinating (and easy) entry into the large, vibrant ethnic communities of the *quartiers de l'est* (eastern neighbourhoods), home to African, Middle Eastern and Asian immigrants as well as artists and students.

Marché Brancusi (Map pp434–5; place Constantin Brancusi, 14e; 9am-2pm Sat; Gaîté) This weekly open-air market specialises in organic produce.

Marché Grenelle (Map pp434–5; blvd de Grenelle btwn rue de Lourmel & rue du Commerce, 15e; 7am-2.30pm Wed, 7am-3pm Sun; La Motte-Picquet Grenelle) Arranged below an elevated railway and surrounded by stately Haussmann boulevards and Art Nouveau apartment blocks, the Grenelle market attracts a posh clientele.

Marché Maubert (Map pp444–5; place Maubert, 5e; 7am-2.30pm Tue & Thu, 7am-3pm Sat; Maubert Mutualité) This market, spread over a small triangle of intersecting streets, reigns over St-Germain des Prés, the poshest part of the bohemian 5e.

Marché Monge (Map pp444–5, place Monge, 5e; 7am-2pm Wed & Fri, 7am-2.30pm Sun; Place Monge) This is one of the better open-air neighbourhood markets on the Left Bank.

Marché Président Wilson (Map pp426–7; av du Président Wilson btwn rue Debrousse & place d'Iéna, 16e; 7am-2.30pm Wed, 7am-3pm Sat; Iéna or Alma Marceau) This upscale market attracts a well-heeled crowd from the 16e.

Marché Raspail (Map pp434–5; blvd Raspail btwn rue de Rennes & rue du Cherche Midi, 6e; 8am-1.30pm Tue & Sun; Rennes) This traditional open-air market north of Rennes metro station features organic produce on Sunday.

Marché St-Charles (Map pp434–5; rue St-Charles btwn rue de Javel & rond-point St-Charles, 15e; 8am-1pm Tue & Fri; Charles Michels) This market may appear somewhat far-flung off in the western 15e, but shoppers will go any distance for its quality produce, including organic goods.

Marché St-Quentin (Map pp428–9; 85 blvd de Magenta, 10e; 8.30am-1pm & 4-7.30pm Tue-Sat, 8.30am-1pm Sun; Gare de l'Est) This iron-and-glass covered market, built in 1866, is a maze of corridors lined mostly with gourmet and upmarket food stalls.

Rue Cler (Map pp434–5; rue Cler, 7e; 7am or 8am-7pm or 7.30pm Tue-Sat, 8am-noon Sun; École Militaire) This commercial street in the 7e is a breath of fresh air in a sometimes stuffy *quartier* and can almost feel like a party at the weekend when the whole neighbourhood turns out en masse.

Rue Montorgueil (Map pp428–9; rue Montorgueil btwn rue de Turbigo & rue Réaumur, 2e; 8am-7.30pm Tue-Sat, 8am-noon Sun; Les Halles or Sentier) This *rue commerçante* is the closest market to Paris' 700-year-old wholesale market, Les Halles, which was moved from this area to Rungis in 1969 so expect a fair number of nostalgia-seekers.

Rue Mouffetard (Map pp444–5; rue Mouffetard around rue de l'Arbalète, 5e; 8am-7.30pm Tue-Sat, 8am-noon Sun; Censier Daubenton) Rue Mouffetard is the city's most photogenic commercial market street and it's the place where Parisians send tourists (travellers go to Marché Bastille).

Rue Poncelet & Rue Bayen (Map pp426–7; rue Poncelet & rue Bayen, 17e; 9am-1pm & 4-7.30pm Tue-Sat, 8am-1pm Sun; Ternes) This *rue commerçante* caters to the flush denizens of the 16e and 17e arrondissements.

text, p54). A separate plate for bread may or may not be provided. If it is missing, rest the slice on the edge of the main plate or on the tablecloth itself. It is quite acceptable – in fact, encouraged – to sop up sauces and juices with slices of bread but generally you should use a fork – not your hands – to do so.

You will not be expected to know the intricacies of how to cut different types of cheese but at least try to remember the basic rules (see p54 for details). If there are wine glasses of varying sizes at each place setting, the larger one (or ones) will be for red wine (and water), the smaller one for white wine. In general it's better to wait for the host to pour the wine rather than helping yourself, but this depends on your relationship and the tone of the evening. Tasting the wine in restaurants and pouring it at home have traditionally been male tasks, but these days many women will happily serve and more enlightened *sommeliers* (wine waiters) will ask which one of a male/female couple would prefer to try the wine.

HOW PARISIANS EAT

French people do not eat in the clatter/clutter style of the Chinese or with the exuberance and sheer gusto of, say, the Italians. A meal is an artistic and sensual delight to most people here, something to be savoured and enjoyed with a certain amount of style and savoir-vivre.

In general, the very first and very last morsel a Parisian consumes on an average day is on the sweet rather than the savoury side – eating habits that are quite different from, say, the English and most Asians.

Breakfast

What the French call *petit déjeuner* is not every Anglo-Saxon's cup of tea. For many, a crois-sant with butter and jam, and a cup of milky coffee do not a breakfast make. Masters of the kitchen throughout the rest of the day, French chefs don't seem up to it in the morning. But there's reason to their meanness; the whole idea not to fill up – *petit déjeuner* means 'little lunch' and the real *déjeuner* (lunch) is just around the corner!

In the Continental style, people here traditionally start the day with a bread roll or a bit of baguette left over from the night before eaten with butter and jam and followed by a *café au lait* (coffee with lots of hot milk), a small black coffee or even a hot chocolate. Some people also eat cereal, toast, fruit and even yoghurt in the morning – something they never did in the past. Commuters will often eschew breakfast at home altogether, opting for a quick coffee and a sweet roll at a train station kiosk or at their desk in the office.

Contrary to what many foreigners think, Parisians do not eat croissants every day but usually reserve these for a treat at the weekend, when they may also choose brioches (small roll or cake sometimes flavoured with nuts, currants or candied fruits), *pains au chocolat* (chocolate-filled brioche) or other *viennoiserie* (baked goods).

Lunch & Dinner

Many Parisians still consider *déjeuner* (lunch) to be the main meal of the day. Restaurants generally serve it between noon and 2.30pm to 3pm and *dîner* (dinner or supper) from 7.30pm to sometime between 10pm and midnight. With the exception of brasseries, cafés and fast-food places, very few restaurants are open between lunch and dinner. The vast majority of restaurants close on Sunday; in August, when most Parisians flee for the beaches or the mountains, many restaurateurs lock up and leave town along with their customers.

As the pace of life is as hectic here as it is elsewhere in the industrialised world nowadays, the two-hour midday meal has become increasingly rare, at least during the week. Dinner, however, is still turned into an elaborate affair whenever time and finances permit. A fully fledged traditional French meal at home is an awesome event, often comprising six distinct *plats* (courses). They are always served with wine – red, white or rosé, depending on what you're eating. A meal in a restaurant almost never consists of more than three courses: the *entrée* (starter or first course), the *plat principal* (main course) and dessert or cheese.

STAPLES & SPECIALITIES

Every nation or culture has its own staples dictated by climate, geography and tradition. French cuisine has long stood apart for its great use of a variety of foods – beef, lamb, pork, poultry, fish and shellfish, cereals, vegetables and legumes – but its three most important staples are bread, cheese and *charcuterie* (cured, smoked or processed meat products). And as for regional specialities, well, *tout est possible* (the sky's the limit).

STAPLES

The complete list of French staples might include everything from cereals, grains and pulses to jams and honeys but we'll restrict ourselves to the 'holy trinity' of the French kitchen.

Bread

Nothing is more French than *pain* (bread). More than 80% of all French people eat it at every meal, and it comes in infinite varieties. One bakery – there are some 1260 in Paris – we happened to pass listed no fewer than 28 types.

All bakeries have *baguettes* (and the somewhat similar *flûtes*), which are long, thin and crusty loaves weighing 250g, and wider loaves of what are simply called *pains*. A *pain,* which weighs 400g, is softer on the inside and has a less crispy crust than a baguette. Both types are at their best if eaten within four hours of baking; if you're not very hungry, ask for a half a loaf: a *demi baguette* or a *demi pain*. A *ficelle* is a thinner, crustier 200g version of a baguette – not unlike a very thick breadstick, really.

Bread has experienced a renaissance here in recent years, and most bakeries also carry heavier, more expensive breads made with all sorts of grains and cereals; you will also find loaves studded with nuts, raisins or herbs. These heavier breads keep much longer than baguettes and standard white-flour breads.

Bread is baked at various times during the day, so it's available fresh as early as 6am and also in the afternoon. Most bakeries close for one day a week.

> ### THE ORDER OF THINGS
>
> At a traditional French meal – be it lunch starting at around 1pm or dinner at about 8.30pm – courses are served as follows:
> - *Apéritif* – a predinner drink
> - *Hors-d'œuvre* – appetisers; cold and/or warm snacks served before the start of the meal
> - *Entrée* – first course or starter
> - *Plat principal* – main course
> - *Salade* – salad, usually a relatively simple green one with dressing
> - *Fromage* – cheese
> - *Dessert* – pudding
> - *Fruit* – sometimes served in place of dessert
> - *Café* – coffee, almost always drunk black
> - *Digestif* – digestive; an after-dinner drink

Cheese

France has nearly 500 varieties of *fromage* (cheese) made of cow's, goat's or ewe's milk. Bear in mind that there are just five basic types (p56), which can be raw, pasteurised or *petit-lait* ('little milk'; the whey left over after the milk fats and solids have been curdled with rennet, an enzyme derived from the stomach of a calf or young goat).

When cutting cheese at the table, remember that a small circular cheese such as a Camembert is cut in wedges like a pie. If a larger cheese (eg a Brie) has been bought already sliced into a wedge shape, cut from the tip to the rind; cutting off the top is considered rude. Slice cheeses whose middle is the best part (eg the blue or veined cheeses) in such a way as to take your fair share of the rind. A flat piece of semi-hard cheese like Emmental is usually just cut horizontally in hunks.

Wine and cheese are often a match made in heaven. It's a matter of taste, but in general, strong, pungent cheeses require a young, full-bodied red or a sweet wine, while soft cheeses with a refined flavour call for more quality and age in the wine. Some classic pairings include: Alsatian Gewürztraminer and Munster; Côtes du Rhone red with Roquefort; Côte d'Or (Burgundy) red and Brie or Camembert; and mature Bordeaux with Emmental or Cantal.

Charcuterie

Traditionally *charcuterie* is made only from pork, though a number of other meats – from beef and veal to chicken and goose – are now used in making sausages, blood puddings, hams, and other cured and salted meats. Pâtés, terrines and *rillettes* are essentially *charcuterie* and are prepared in many different ways.

The difference between a pâté and a terrine is academic: a pâté is removed from its container and sliced before it is served or sold, while a terrine is sliced from the container itself. *Rillettes,* on the other hand, is potted meat (pork, goose, duck or rabbit) or even fish that is not ground, chopped or sliced but shredded with two forks, seasoned, mixed with fat and spread cold like pâté over bread or toast.

While every region in France produces standard *charcuterie* favourites as well as its own specialities, Alsace, Lyon and the Auvergne produce the best sausages, and Périgord and the north of France some of the most popular pâtés. Some very popular types of *charcuterie* are *andouillette* (soft raw sausage made from the pig's small intestines that is grilled and eaten with onions and potatoes), *boudin noir* (blood sausage or pudding made with pig's blood, onions and spices, and usually eaten hot with stewed apples and potatoes), *jambon* (ham, either smoked or salt-cured), *saucisse* (usually a small fresh sausage that is boiled or grilled before eating), *saucisson* (usually a large salami eaten cold) and *saucisson sec* (air-dried salami).

REGIONAL SPECIALITIES

There are all sorts of reasons for the amazing variety of France's regional cuisine. Climatic and geographical factors have been particularly important: the hot south tends to favour olive oil, garlic and tomatoes, while the cooler, pastoral northern regions prefer cream and butter. Coastal areas specialise in mussels, oysters and saltwater fish, while those near lakes and rivers make full use of the freshwater fish available.

Diverse though it may be, French cuisine is typified by certain regions, most notably by Normandy, Burgundy, Périgord, Lyon and, to a lesser extent, Alsace, Provence and the Loire region and, still further down the influencial-regions list, the Auvergne, Languedoc, the Basque Country and Corsica. The first four types of regional cuisine can be found in restaurants throughout Paris, while Alsatian *choucroute* (sauerkraut with sausage and other prepared meats) is the dish of choice at the capital's many brasseries. *La cuisine provençale* (Provence cooking) can be somewhat elusive in Paris, though many seafood restaurants claim to do an authentic bouillabaisse (fish soup). Cuisine of the Loire region has made more contributions to what can generically be called French food than any other. Dishes from the last five regions appear on menus from time to time while certain food products can be bought from speciality shops.

Normandy

Cream, apples and seafood are the three essentials of Normandy cuisine. Specialities include such delicacies as *moules à la crème normande* (mussels in a cream sauce with a dash of cider) and *canard à la Rouennaise* ('Rouen-style duck'; duck

Cheese on display in rue Mouffetard

stuffed with its liver and served with a red-wine sauce), preferably interrupted by a *trou normand* (literally meaning 'Norman hole'; a glass of Calvados) to allow room for more courses.

Burgundy

The 'trinity' of the Burgundy kitchen is beef, red wine and mustard. *Bœuf bourguignon* (beef marinated and cooked in young red wine with mushrooms, onions, carrots and bacon) combines the first two; Dijon, the Burgundian capital, has been synonymous with mustard for centuries.

Périgord

This southwest region is famous for its truffles and its poultry, especially the ducks and geese whose fattened livers are turned into *pâté de foie gras* (duck or goose liver pâté), which is sometimes flavoured with cognac and truffles. *Confit de canard* and *confit d'oie* are duck or goose joints cooked very slowly in their own fat. The preserved fowl is then left to stand for some months before being eaten.

Lyon

Many people consider France's third-largest city to be France's *temple de gastronomie* (gastronomic temple), and Paris has many Lyonnaise restaurants. Typical *charcuteries* are *saucisson de Lyon*, which feature in Lyon's trademark dish, *saucisson aux pommes* (sausage with potatoes). Another speciality is the *quenelle*, a poached dumpling made of freshwater fish (usually pike) and served with a *sauce Nantua*, a sauce made with cream and a paste made from freshwater crayfish.

THE FIVE BASIC CHEESE TYPES

The choice on offer at a *fromagerie* (cheese shop) can be overwhelming, but *fromagers* (cheese merchants) always allow you to sample what's on offer before you buy, and are usually very generous with their guidance and pairing advice. The following list divides French cheeses into five main groups as they are usually divided in a *fromagerie* and recommends several types to try.

Fromage à pâte demi-dure 'Semi-hard cheese' means uncooked, pressed cheese. Among the finest are Tomme de Savoie made from either raw or pasteurised cow's milk; Cantal, a cow's milk cheese from Auvergne that tastes something like cheddar; Saint Nectaire, a strong-smelling pressed cheese that has both a strong and complex taste; and Ossau-Iraty, a ewe's milk cheese made in the Basque Country.

Fromage à pâte dure 'Hard cheese' is always cooked and pressed in France. Among the most popular are: Beaufort, a grainy cow's milk cheese with a slightly fruity taste from Rhône-Alpes; Comté, a cheese made with raw cow's milk in Franche-Comté; Emmental, a cow's milk cheese made all over France; and Mimolette, an Edam-like bright orange cheese from Lille that can be aged for as long as 36 months.

Fromage à pâte molle 'Soft cheese' is moulded or rind-washed. Camembert, a classic moulded cheese from Normandy that for many is synonymous with 'French cheese', and the refined Brie de Meaux are both made from raw cow's milk; Munster from Alsace and the strong Époisses de Bourgogne are rind-washed, fine-textured cheeses.

Fromage à pâte persillée 'Marbled' or 'blue cheese' is so called because the veins often resemble *persille* (parsley). Roquefort is a ewe's milk veined cheese that is to many the king of French cheeses. Fourme d'Ambert is a very mild cow's milk cheese from Rhône-Alpes. Bleu du Haut Jura (also called Bleu de Gex) is a mild blue-veined mountain cheese.

Fromage de chèvre 'Goat's milk cheese' is usually creamy and both sweet and a little salty when fresh, but hardens and gets much saltier as it matures. Among the best varieties are: Sainte Maure de Touraine, a creamy, mild cheese from the Loire region; Crottin de Chavignol, a classic though saltier variety from Burgundy; Cabécou de Rocamadour from Midi-Pyrénées, often served warm with salad or marinated in oil and rosemary; and Saint Marcellin, a soft white cheese from Lyon.

Alsace

A classic dish of this meaty cuisine is *choucroute alsacienne* (or *choucroute garnie*), which is sauerkraut flavoured with juniper berries and served hot with sausages, bacon, pork and/or ham knuckle. You should drink chilled Riesling or Alsatian Pinot Noir with *choucroute* – not beer – and follow it with a *tarte alsacienne*, a scrumptious custard tart made with local fruits like *mirabelles* (sweet yellow plums) or *quetsches* (a variety of purple plums).

Provence

The Roman legacy of olives, wheat and wine remain the triumvirate of *la cuisine provençale*, and many dishes are prepared with olive oil and generous amounts of garlic. Provence's most famous dish is bouillabaisse, a chowder made with at least three kinds of fresh fish, cooked for 10 minutes or so in broth with onions, tomatoes, saffron and various herbs, and eaten as a main course with toasted bread and *rouille*, a spicy mayonnaise of olive oil, garlic and chilli peppers.

Loire Region

The cuisine of the Loire region, refined in the kitchens of the region's chateaux from the 16th century onwards, ultimately became the cuisine of France as a whole; *rillettes, coq au vin* (chicken stewed in wine with mushrooms, bacon, onion, garlic and herbs), basic *beurre blanc* sauce (emulsified white sauce made of a vinegar and white wine reduction blended with softened butter and shallots) and *tarte Tatin* (caramelised upside-down apple pie) are all specialities from this area. The Loire region is also known for its *pruneaux de Tours,* prunes dried from luscious Damson plums and used in poultry, pork or veal dishes.

Other Regions

AUVERGNE

This *rude* (that is, 'rugged' or 'harsh') region of the Massif Central specialises in *charcuterie*, and its celebrated *salaisons d'Auvergne* (salt-cured meats) are sold and consumed throughout France. Specialities of the Auvergne include *lentilles vertes du Puy aux saucisses fumées* (smoked pork sausages with green Puy lentils).

LANGUEDOC

No dish is more evocative of Languedoc than *cassoulet*, a casserole or stew with beans and meat. There are at least three major varieties but a favourite is the cassoulet from Toulouse, which adds *saucisse de Toulouse*, a fat, mild-tasting pork sausage. France's most famous blue cheese is made at Roquefort, also in Languedoc.

BASQUE COUNTRY

Among the essential ingredients of Basque cooking are the deep-red chillies that add the extra bite to many of the region's dishes, including its signature *jambon de Bayonne*, the locally prepared Bayonne ham. Basques love their cakes and pastries but the most popular of all is *gâteau basque*, a relatively simple layer cake that is filled with cream or cherry jam.

CORSICA

The hills and mountains of the rugged island of Corsica have always been ideal for raising stock and the dense Corsican underbrush called the *maquis* is made up of shrubs mixed with wild herbs. These raw materials come together to create such trademark Corsican dishes as *stufatu*, a fragrant mutton stew, *premonata*, beef braised with juniper berries, and *lonzo aux haricots blancs*, a Corsican sausage cooked with white beans, white wine and herbs.

DRINKS

ALCOHOLIC DRINKS

Although alcohol consumption has dropped by 30% in less than two decades – the stereotypical Frenchman no longer starts the day with a shot of red wine in order to *tuer le ver* (kill the worm) followed by a small, black coffee – France still ranks 5th in the world in the boozing stakes behind Luxembourg, Portugal, Ireland and Germany. The average French person consumes 10.9L of pure alcohol a year, compared to 8.2L in the UK and 6.3L in the USA.

Wine

Grapes and the art of winemaking were introduced to Gaul by the Romans. In the Middle Ages important vineyards developed around monasteries as the monks needed wine to celebrate Mass. Large-scale wine production later moved closer to the ports (eg Bordeaux) from where it could be exported.

In the middle of the 19th century phylloxera aphids were accidentally brought to Europe from the USA. The pests ate through the roots of Europe's grapevines, destroying some 10,000 sq km of vineyards in France alone. European wine production appeared to be doomed until root stocks resistant to phylloxera were brought from California and original cuttings grafted onto them.

Winemaking is a complicated chemical process, but ultimately the taste and quality of the wine depend on four key factors: the varietal (type) or blend of grape(s), the climate, the soil and the art of the *vigneron* (winemaker).

Some viticulturists have honed their skills and techniques to such a degree that their wine is known as a *grand cru* (literally 'great growth'). If this wine has been produced in a year of optimum climatic conditions, it becomes a *millésime* (vintage) wine. *Grands crus* are aged first in small oak barrels and then in bottles, sometimes for 20 years or more, before they develop their full taste and aroma. These are the memorable (and pricey) bottles that wine experts talk about with such passion.

Wine has been the 'totem' drink of France for centuries but, frankly, all is not well in the French wine industry at the start of the 21st. Today the nation counts just over 10,000 sq km of vineyards – half of the amount under cultivation in 1950. While less *vin de table* (table wine) and *vin de pays* (country wine) and more quality wines are being

Le Dôme restaurant (p186)

produced – there will always be a market for the latter – wine consumption here has dropped by 10% since 1999 and is expected to fall another 7% by 2008 as young people continue to reach for alcopops and beer. At the same time, exports to the USA, France's second-biggest wine market after the UK, have fallen steadily for several years due for the most part to the strength of the euro and American's preference for big, in-your-face New World wines, including Australian and New Zealand imports.

There are dozens of wine-producing regions throughout France, but the seven principal ones are Alsace, Bordeaux, Burgundy, Champagne, Languedoc-Roussillon, the Loire Valley and the Rhône. Areas such as Burgundy comprise many well-known districts, including Chablis, Beaujolais and Mâcon, while Bordeaux encompasses Médoc, St-Émilion and Sauternes – to name just a few of its many subregions.

With the exception of Alsatian ones, wines in France are named after the location of the vineyard rather than the grape varietal.

ALSACE

Alsace produces almost exclusively white wines – mostly varieties produced nowhere else in France – that are known for their clean, fresh taste and compatibility with the often heavy local cuisine (p57). The vineyards closest to Strasbourg produce light red wines from Pinot Noir grapes that are not dissimilar to rosé and best served chilled.

Alsace's four most important varietal wines are riesling, known for its subtlety; the more pungent and highly regarded Gewürztraminer; the robust, high alcohol Pinot Gris; and muscat d'alsace, which is not as sweet as that made with muscat grapes grown further south.

BORDEAUX

Britons have had a taste for the full-bodied red wines of Bordeaux, known as clarets in the UK, since the mid-12th century when King Henry II, who controlled the region through marriage, tried to gain the favour of the locals by granting them tax-free trade status with England. Thus began a roaring business in wine exporting that continues to this day.

The reds of Bordeaux, which produces more fine wine than any other region in the world, are often described as well balanced, a quality achieved by blending several grape varieties. The grapes predominantly used are Merlot, Cabernet Sauvignon and Cabernet Franc. Bordeaux's foremost wine-growing areas are Médoc, Pomerol, St-Émilion and Graves. The sweet whites of its Sauternes area are arguably the world's finest dessert wines.

BURGUNDY

Burgundy developed its reputation for viticulture during the reign of Charlemagne, when monks first began to make wine here.

Burgundy's red wines are produced with Pinot Noir grapes; the best vintages need 10 to 20 years to age. White wine is made from the Chardonnay grape. The five main wine-growing areas of Burgundy are Chablis, Côte d'Or, Côte Chalonnais, Mâcon and Beaujolais, which alone produces 13 different types of light Gamay-based red wine.

CHAMPAGNE

Champagne is made from the red Pinot Noir, the black Pinot Meunier or the white Chardonnay grape. Each vine is vigorously pruned and trained to produce a small quantity of high-quality grapes. Indeed, to maintain exclusivity (and price), the amount of champagne that can be produced each year is limited to between 160 and 220 million bottles depending on the year. Most of it is consumed in France and the UK followed by the USA, Germany, Japan and now China.

Making champagne – carried out by innumerable *maisons* (houses) – is a long, complex process. There are two fermentation processes, the first in casks and the second after the wine has been bottled and had sugar and yeast added. The bottles are aged in cellars for between two and five years (sometimes longer), depending on the *cuvée* (vintage).

If the final product is labelled *brut*, it is extra dry, with only 1.5% sugar content. *Extra-sec* means it's very dry (but not as dry as *brut*), *sec* is dry and *demi-sec* is slightly sweet. The sweetest champagne is labelled *doux*.

Some of the most famous champagne houses are Dom Pérignon, Moët et Chandon, Veuve Cliquot, Mercier, Mumm, Krugg, Laurent-Perrier, Piper-Heidsieck and Taittinger.

LANGUEDOC

This region is the country's most productive wine-growing area, with up to 40% of France's wine – mainly cheap red *vin de table* – produced here. About 3000 sq km of the region is 'under vine', which represents just under a third of France's total.

In addition to the well-known Fitou label, the area's other quality wines are Coteaux du Languedoc, Faugères, Corbières and Minervois. The region also produces about 70% of France's *vin de pays* from a particular named village or region, most of which is labelled Vin de Pays d'Oc.

LOIRE REGION

The Loire Valley's 750 sq km of vineyards rank the region as the third-largest area in France for the production of quality wines but, while fertile, the vineyards are small, and winemakers are used to selling directly to Parisians who take day trips to buy their favourite wines. Although sunny, the climate is moist and not all grape varieties are grown here.

The most common grapes are the Muscadet, Cabernet Franc and Chenin Blanc varieties. Wines tend to be light and delicate. The most celebrated areas are Pouilly-Fumé, Vouvray, Sancerre, Bourgueil, Chinon and Saumur.

RHÔNE REGION

The Rhône region is divided up into northern and southern areas. The different soil, climate, topography and grapes used means there is a dramatic difference in the wines produced by each area.

Set on steep hills beside the river, the northern vineyards make red wines from the ruby-red Syrah grape exclusively; the aromatic Viognier grape is the most popular for white wines. The south is better known for the quantity rather than quality of the wine it produces. The Grenache grape, which ages well when blended, is used in the reds, while the whites use the Ugni Blanc grape.

Apéritifs & Digestifs

Meals are often preceded by an appetite-stirring apéritif, such as *kir* (white wine sweetened with cassis or blackcurrant syrup), *kir royale* (champagne with cassis), *pineau* (cognac and grape juice) or just a glass of champagne. *Pastis,* a 90-proof, anise-flavoured alcoholic drink that turns cloudy when you add water, is especially popular at cafés in the warmer months.

After-dinner drinks *(digestifs)* are sometimes ordered along with coffee. France's most famous brandies are Cognac and Armagnac, both of which are made from grapes in the regions of those names. *Eaux de vie,* literally 'waters of life', can be made with grape skins and the pulp left over after being pressed for wine (Marc de champagne, Marc de Bourgogne), apples (Calvados), pears (poire William), as well as plums *(eau de vie de prune)* and raspberries *(eau de vie de framboise).*

Beer & Cider

The *bière à la pression* (draft beer) served by the *demi* (half-pint) in bars and cafés across Paris is usually one of the national brands, such as Kronenbourg, 33 or Pelforth, and is totally forgettable. Alsace, with its close cultural ties to Germany, produces some excellent local beers (eg Bière de Scharrach, Schutzenberger Jubilator and Fischer d'Alsace, a hoppy brew from Schiltigheim), and northern France, close to Belgium and the Netherlands, has its own great beers, including Saint Sylvestre 3 Monts, Terken Brune and Grain d'Orge made from barley.

Cidre (apple cider) is made in many parts of France, including Savoy, Picardy and the Basque Country, but its real home is Normandy and Brittany.

NONALCOHOLIC DRINKS

The most popular nonalcoholic beverages consumed in Paris are coffee and mineral water, with fruit juices, squashes, soft drinks and tea trailing far behind.

Water & Mineral Water

All tap water in Paris is safe to drink, so there is no need to buy bottled water. Parisians don't agree, however, and less than 1% of the water consumed by a typical Parisian household each day is actually drunk. Tap water that is not drinkable (eg at most public fountains and on trains) will usually have a sign reading *'eau non potable'*.

At a restaurant if you prefer tap water rather than some pricey bottled water, make sure you ask for *de l'eau* (some water), *une carafe d'eau* (a jug of water) or *de l'eau du robinet* (tap water). Otherwise you'll most likely get bottled *eau de source* (spring water) or *eau minérale* (mineral water), which comes *plate* (flat or still) like Évian, Vittel and Volvic, or *gazeuse* (fizzy or sparkling), such as Badoit and Perrier.

Coffee

The most ubiquitous form of coffee in Paris is espresso, made by a machine that forces steam through ground coffee beans. A small espresso, served without milk, is called *un café noir*, *un express* or simply *un café*. You can also ask for a *grand* (large) version.

Café crème is espresso with steamed milk or cream. *Café au lait* is lots of hot milk with a little coffee served in a large cup or, sometimes, a bowl. A small *café crème* is a *petit crème*. A *noisette* (literally 'hazelnut') is an espresso with just a dash of milk. Decaffeinated coffee is *café décaféiné*.

Tea & Hot Chocolate

The French have never taken to *thé* (tea) the way the British have, and there's a slightly snobbish, Anglophile association attached to it here. Some people consider it medicinal and drink *thé noir* (black tea) only when they are feeling unwell.

Tea is usually served *nature* (plain) or *au citron* (with lemon) and never with milk. *Tisanes* (herbal teas) are widely available.

Chocolat chaud (hot chocolate), available at most cafés, varies greatly and can be excellent or verging on the undrinkable.

Squashes & Soft Drinks

All the international brands of soft drinks are available in Paris, as well as many overly sweet, fizzy local ones like Orangina in its iconic light-bulb-shaped bottle and the 7UP-like Pschitt.

One popular and inexpensive café drink is *sirop* (fruit syrup or cordial) served *à l'eau* (mixed with water), with soda or with a carbonated mineral water such as Perrier – basically a squash. A *citron pressé* is a glass of iced water (either flat or carbonated) with freshly squeezed lemon juice and sugar. Parisians are not overly fond of drinking very cold things – they're rather into 'cool' – so you'll probably have to ask for ice cubes *(des glaçons)*.

CELEBRATING WITH FOOD

It may sound silly but food itself makes French people celebrate and, hey, any excuse for a party. There are birthdays and engagements and weddings and christenings and, like everywhere, special holidays.

One tradition that is very much alive is *le jour des rois* (day of the kings), which falls on 6 January and marks the feast of the Épiphanie (Epiphany), when the Three Wise Men called on the Infant Jesus. A *galette des rois* (literally 'kings' cake'; a puff pastry tart with frangipane cream), which has a little dried *fève* bean (or plastic or silver figurine) hidden inside and is topped with a gold paper crow, is placed on the table. The youngest person in the room goes under the table and calls out which member of the party should get each slice. The person who gets the bean is named king or queen, dons the crown and chooses his or her consort. This tradition is popular not just at home among families but also at offices and dinner parties.

At Chandeleur (Candlemas, marking the Feast of the Purification of the Virgin Mary) on 2 February, family and friends gather together in their kitchens to make *crêpes de la Chandeleur* (sweet pancakes).

Pâques (Easter) is marked as elsewhere with *œufs au chocolat* (chocolate eggs) – here filled with candy fish and chickens – and there is always an egg hunt for the kids. The traditional meal at Easter lunch is *agneau* (lamb) or *jambon de Pâques* (Easter ham), which – like hot-cross buns in Britain – seems to be available throughout the year nowadays.

After the *dinde aux marrons* (turkey stuffed with chestnuts) eaten at lunch on Noël (Christmas), a *bûche de Noël*, a 'Yule log' of chocolate and cream or ice cream, is served. A friend still reminisces about the little *champignons en meringue* (meringue mushrooms) topping the log that she and her sister would fight over.

WHERE TO EAT & DRINK

There are a vast number of eateries in Paris where you can get breakfast or brunch, a full lunch or dinner, and a snack between meals. Most have defined roles, though some definitions are less strict nowadays and some are even becoming a bit blurred.

AUBERGE

In the provinces, an *auberge* (inn), which may also appear as an *auberge de campagne* or *auberge du terroir* (country inn), is just that: a restaurant serving traditional country fare attached to a rural inn or small hotel. If you see the word attached to an eatery in Paris, they're usually just being cute.

BAR

A *bar* or *bar américain* (cocktail bar) is an establishment dedicated to elbow-bending and rarely serves food beyond sandwiches or snacks. A *bar à vins* is a wine bar, which may or may not serve full meals at lunch and dinner. A *bar à huîtres* is an oyster bar.

BISTRO

A bistro (sometimes spelled *bistrot*) is not clearly defined in Paris. It can be simply a pub or bar serving snacks and light pub meals, or a fully fledged restaurant.

BRASSERIE

Unlike the vast majority of restaurants in Paris, brasseries – which can look very much like cafés – serve full meals from morning till late at night. The featured dishes almost always include *choucroute* and sausages because the brasserie, which actually means 'brewery' in French, originated in Alsace. Most Parisians go to a brasserie as much for the lively atmosphere and the convenience as for the food.

BUFFET

A *buffet* (or *buvette*) is a kiosk usually found at train stations and airports selling drinks, filled baguettes and snacks.

CAFÉ

Cafés are an important focal point for social life in Paris, and sitting in a café to read, write, talk with friends or just daydream is an integral part of many people's day-to-day existence here. Many Parisians see café-sitting – like shopping at outdoor markets – as a way of keeping in touch with their neighbourhood and maximising their chances of running into friends and acquaintances.

The main focus here, of course, is coffee (p61), and only basic food is available at most cafés. Common options include a baguette filled with Camembert or pâté with *cornichons* (gherkins), a *croque-monsieur* (grilled ham and cheese sandwich) or a *croque-madame* (a *croque-monsieur* topped with a fried egg).

Three factors determine how much you'll pay in a café: where the café is situated, where you are sitting within the café, and what time of day it is. Progressively more expensive tariffs apply at the *comptoir* or *zinc* (counter), in the *salle* (inside seating area) and on the *terrasse* (pavement terrace), the best vantage point from which to see and be seen. A café on a major boulevard, such as blvd du Montparnasse or the av des Champs-Élysées, will charge considerably more than a place that fronts a quiet side street in the 3e. The price of drinks usually goes up at night (generally after 8pm).

Ordering a cup of coffee (or anything else, for that matter) earns you the right to occupy the seat for as long as you like. You will never feel pressured to order something else.

You usually run a tab at a café and pay the *addition* (bill or check) right before you leave. However, if your waiter is going off duty, you may be asked to pay up at the end of his or her shift.

CAFÉTÉRIA

Paris has several chains of *cafétérias* (caféteria restaurants), including Flunch, that offer a decent and cheap (two-course menus below €8) selection of dishes that you can see before ordering, a factor that can make life easier if you're travelling with kids.

CREPERIE

Creperies (sometimes seen as *galetteries*) specialise in crepes, ultrathin pancakes cooked on a flat surface and then folded or rolled over a filling. Sometimes the word *crêpe* is used to refer only to sweet crepes made with *farine de froment* (wheat flour), whereas a savoury crepe, more accurately a *galette,* is made with *farine de sarrasin* (buckwheat flour), and filled with cheese, mushrooms, eggs and the like.

RESTAURANT

The restaurant, the French word for 'restorative', comes in many guises and price ranges in Paris – from ultrabudget *restaurants universitaires* (canteens or refectories, p64) to three-star Michelin *restaurants gastronomiques* (gourmet restaurants).

Menu board at Chartier (p218)

An important distinction between a brasserie and a restaurant is that while the former serves food throughout the day, a restaurant is usually open only for lunch and dinner (p53). Almost all restaurants close for at least 1½ days (ie a full day and either one lunch or dinner period) each week, and this schedule is usually posted on the front door. Chain restaurants are usually open throughout the day, seven days a week.

Restaurants generally also post a *carte* (menu) outside, so you can decide before going in whether the selection and prices are to your liking and/or budget. Most offer at least one fixed-price, multicourse meal known in French as a *menu, menu à prix fixe* or *menu du jour* (daily menu). A *menu* (not to be confused with a *carte*) almost always costs much less than ordering à la carte (off the menu).

When you order a *menu*, you usually get to choose an entrée, such as salad, pâté or soup; a main dish (several meat, poultry or fish dishes, including the *plat du jour*, or 'the daily special', are generally on offer); and one or more final courses (usually cheese or dessert). In some places, you may also be able to order a *formule*, which usually has fewer choices but allows you to pick two of three courses – an entrée and a main course, say, or a main course and a dessert.

Boissons (drinks), including wine, cost extra unless the menu says *boisson comprise* (drink included), in which case you may get a beer or a glass of mineral water. If the *menu* has *vin compris* (wine included), you'll probably be served a 250mL *pichet* (jug) of house red or white. The waiter will always ask if you would like coffee to end the meal, but this will almost always cost extra.

Restaurant meals in Paris are almost always served with bread, which is rarely accompanied by butter. If you run out of bread in your basket, don't be afraid to ask the waiter for more *('Pourrais-je avoir encore du pain, s'il vous plaît')*.

RESTAURANT LIBRE-SERVICE

A *restaurant libre-service* is a self-service restaurant not unlike a *cafétéria*.

RESTAURANT RAPIDE

A *restaurant rapide* is a fast-food restaurant, be it imported (McDonald's, Pizza Hut and KFC, with branches all over Paris) or home-grown ones such as Quick.

RESTAURANT UNIVERSITAIRE

The University of Paris system has some 17 *restaurants universitaires* (canteens or refectories) subsidised by the Ministry of Education and operated by the Centre Régional des Œuvres Universitaires et Scolaires, better known as CROUS (p178). They serve very cheap meals (typically under €5 for visiting students or €7 for nonstudents).

SALON DE THÉ

A *salon de thé* (tearoom) is a trendy, somewhat pricey establishment that offers quiches, salads, cakes, tarts, pies and pastries, in addition, of course, to black and herbal teas.

SELF-CATERING

The number of specialised food shops in Paris is legion and Parisians patronise them regularly. Since each *commerçant* (shopkeeper) specialises in purveying only one type of food, he or she can almost always provide all sorts of useful tips: which round of Camembert is ripe, which wine will complement a certain food, which type of pot to cook rabbit in and so on. In any case, most products for sale at *charcuteries* (delicatessens), patisseries and *traiteurs* or *charcuteries-traiteurs* (delicatessens/caterers) are clearly marked and labelled.

As these stores are geared to people buying small quantities of fresh food each day, it's perfectly acceptable to purchase only meal-size amounts: a few *tranches* (slices) of meat to

TOP FIVE BAKERIES

Boulangerie de Monge (Map pp444–5; ☎ 01 43 37 54 20; www.leboulangerdemonge.com; 123 rue Monge, 5e; ⏰ 7.30am-8.30pm Tue-Sun; Ⓜ Censier Daubenton)

Boulangerie Kayser (Map pp444–5; ☎ 01 44 07 01 42; www.maison-kayser.com; 8 rue Monge, 5e; ⏰ 7am-8.30pm Mon & Wed-Mon; Ⓜ Maubert Mutualité)

Boulangerie-Pâtisserie Secco (Map pp434–5; ☎ 01 43 17 35 20; 20 rue Jean Nicot, 7e; ⏰ 9.30am-8.30pm Tue-Sat; Ⓜ La Tour Maubourg)

La Fournée d'Augustine (Map pp422–3; ☎ 01 45 43 42 45; 96 rue Raymond-Losserand, 14e; ⏰ 7.30am-8pm; Ⓜ Pernety)

Poilâne (www.poilane.fr) 6e branch (Map pp434–5; ☎ 01 45 48 42 59; 8 rue du Cherche Midi, 6e; ⏰ 7.15am-8.15pm Mon-Sat; Ⓜ Sèvres Babylone); 15e branch (Map pp434–5; ☎ 01 45 79 11 49; 49 blvd de Grenelle; Ⓜ Dupleix)

make a sandwich, perhaps, or a *petit bout* (small hunk) of sausage. You can also request just enough for *une/deux personne(s)* (one/two persons). If you want a bit more, ask for *encore un petit peu*, and if you are being given too much, say *'C'est trop'*.

Fresh bread is baked and sold at *boulangeries*; mouth-watering pastries are available at patisseries; a *fromagerie* can supply you with cheese that is *fait* (ripe) to the exact degree that you request; a *charcuterie* offers sliced meat, pâtés and so on; and fresh fruit and vegetables are sold at *épiceries* (greengrocers), supermarkets and open-air markets.

A *boucherie* is a general butcher, but for specialised poultry you have to go to a *marchand de volaille*. A *boucherie chevaline*, easily identifiable by the gilded horse's head above the entrance, sells horse meat, which some people prefer to beef or mutton. Fresh fish and seafood are available from a *poissonnerie*.

Paris' neighbourhood food markets offer the freshest and best quality fruit, vegetables, cheese, prepared salads and so on at the lowest prices. For a list of the best ones see p52. Note that many food shops are closed on Sunday afternoon and all day Monday.

Bear in mind that when buying fruit and vegetables anywhere except at supermarkets, you should not touch the produce unless invited to do so. Indicate to the shopkeeper what you want and they will choose for you. This is food, after all, something near and dear to every French person.

VEGETARIANS & VEGANS

Vegetarians and vegans make up a small minority in a society where *viande* (meat) once also meant 'food', and they are not very well catered for; specialised vegetarian restaurants are few and far between. In fact, the vegetarian establishments that do exist in Paris often look more like laid-back cafés than restaurants. On the bright side, more and more restaurants are offering vegetarian choices on their set menus and *produits biologiques* (organic products) are all the rage nowadays, even among carnivores. Other options include *saladeries*, casual restaurants that serve a long list of *salades composées* (mixed salads).

Many restaurants now have at least one or two vegetarian dish on the menu, though it may be one of the starters/first courses. Unfortunately, very few set menus include vegetarian options. The best – perhaps only – way for vegetarians to assemble a real meal is by ordering one or more side dishes.

Strict vegetarians and vegans should note that most French cheeses are made with rennet, an enzyme derived from the stomach of a calf or young goat, and that some red wines (especially Bordeaux) are clarified with the albumin of egg whites.

The trade of *produits sans chimiques* (products without additives) or *produits biologiques*, usually abbreviated to *bio* is carefully government-regulated and very much on the increase in France (though many stalwart traditionalists still regard them with suspicion).

KOSHER

There has been a Jewish community in France for most of the time since the Roman period and French Jews were the first in Europe to be granted full citizenship (1790). But from the look of things most don't keep *cacher* (kosher) or eat out very often; the only places where you'll find kosher (mostly Ashkenazic) restaurants of any number are clustered in the Marais either on or just off rue des Rosiers, 4e. For Sephardic kosher food head for the North African–Jewish restaurants on rue Richer, rue Cadet and rue Geoffroy Marie just south of the Cadet metro stop in the 9e or the handful along blvd de Belleville in the 20th arrondissement.

CHILDREN

Quite a few Parisian restaurants offer a *menu enfant* (children's set menu), usually available for children under 12. Some restaurants have high chairs and baby seats and offer features of interest for parents with children, including an enclosed area or terrace allowing games. *Cafétérias* (p63) are a good place to bring kids if you just want to feed and water them fast and cheaply.

Baby food is readily available in grocery shops and supermarkets throughout Paris, and the vast majority of goods in jars are produced by Nestlé. In typically French fashion, some of the products sound, well, good enough to eat: *petits légumes au bœuf* (baby vegetables with beef), *coquillettes jambon à la tomate* (pasta shells with ham in tomato sauce), *jardinière de légumes* (mixed vegetables) and so on. Nestlé also produces Le P'tit Menu with the meat and vegetable 'courses' in separate trays and Le P'tit Goûter with three kinds of strained fruit.

For *lait biologique* (organic formula) or *lait infantile* (baby milk) choose Babybio with the teddy bear on the label.

QUICK EATS

Though Parisians may *grignoter entre les repas* (snack or eat between meals), they do not seem to go in for street food; hot dogs stands and noodle carts are nowhere to be seen and snacking in public is considered somewhat gauche. You may encounter a crepe-maker on a busy street corner in Bastille, Marais or the Latin Quarter, or someone selling roasted *châtaignes* (chestnuts) in autumn and winter, but generally people will duck into a café for *un truc à grignoter* (something to nibble on) or a patisserie for a slice of something sweet to be eaten on the trot. Food shop window displays in Paris, among the most attractive and tempting in the world, certainly have something to do with this; patisseries, *traiteurs* and *confiseries* (sweet shops or candy stores) arrange their wares in such a way as to pull in the crowds. And they succeed every time.

History

History

With around 11 million inhabitants, the greater metropolitan area of Paris is home to more than 18% of France's total population. Since before the Revolution, Paris has been what urban planners like to call a 'hypertrophic city' – the enlarged 'head' of a nation-state's 'body'. The urban area of the next biggest city – Marseilles – is barely a third of the size of central Paris.

As the capital city, Paris is the administrative, business and cultural centre; virtually everything of importance in the republic starts, finishes or is currently taking place here. And as the French traditionally express it: *'Quand Paris éternue, la France s'enrhume'* (When Paris sneezes, France catches cold). But having said that, there have been conscious efforts – going back at least four decades – by governments to decentralise Paris' role, and during that time the population – and thus to a certain extent the city's authority – has actually shrunk. The pivotal year was 1968, a watershed not just in France but throughout Western Europe.

THE RECENT PAST

There is no underestimating the effect the student riots of 1968 had on France and the French people, and on the way they govern themselves today. After stability was restored the government made a number of immediate changes, including the decentralisation of the higher education system, and reforms (eg lowering the voting age to 18, an abortion law and workers' self-management) continued through the 1970s, creating, in effect, the modern society that is France today.

President Charles de Gaulle resigned in 1969 and was succeeded by the Gaullist leader Georges Pompidou, who was in turn replaced by Valéry Giscard d'Estaing in 1974. François Mitterrand, long-time head of the Partie Socialiste (PS), was elected president in 1981 and, as the business community had feared, immediately set out to nationalise privately owned banks, large industrial groups and various other parts of the economy. However, during the mid-1980s Mitterrand followed a generally moderate economic policy and in 1988, aged 69, he was re-elected for a second seven-year term.

In the 1986 parliamentary elections the right-wing opposition led by Jacques Chirac, mayor of Paris since 1977, received a majority in the National Assembly; for the next two years Mitterrand was forced to work with a prime minister and cabinet from the opposition, an unprecedented arrangement known as *cohabitation*.

In the May 1995 presidential elections Chirac enjoyed a comfortable victory (Mitterrand, who would die in January 1996, decided not to run again because of failing health). In his first few months in office Chirac received high marks for his direct words and actions in matters relating to the European Union (EU) and the war in Bosnia. His cabinet choices, including the selection of 'whiz kid' foreign minister Alain Juppé as prime minister, were well received. But Chirac's decision to resume nuclear testing on the French Polynesian island of Mururoa and a nearby atoll was met with outrage in France and abroad. On the home front, Chirac's moves to restrict welfare payments (designed to bring France closer to meeting the criteria for the European Monetary Union; EMU) led to the largest protests since 1968. For three weeks in late 1995 Paris was crippled by public-sector strikes, battering the economy.

In 1997 Chirac took a big gamble and called an early parliamentary election for June. The move backfired. Chirac remained president but his party, the Rassemblement Pour la République (RPR; Rally for the Republic), lost support, and a coalition of Socialists, Com-

3rd century BC	52 BC
Celtic Gauls called Parisii arrive in what is now Paris and settle on Île de la Cité	Roman legions crush Celtic Gauls and establish the town of Lutetia

MITHRA & THE GREAT SACRIFICE

Mithraism, the worship of the god Mithra, originated in Persia. As Roman rule extended into Asia, the religion became extremely popular with traders, imperial slaves and mercenaries of the Roman army and spread rapidly throughout the empire in the 2nd and 3rd centuries AD. In fact, Mithraism was the principal rival of Christianity until Constantine came to the throne in the 4th century.

Mithraism was a mysterious religion with its devotees sworn to secrecy. What little is known of Mithra, the god of justice and social contract, has been deduced from reliefs and icons found in sanctuaries and temples, particularly in Eastern and Central European countries. Most of these portray Mithra clad in a Persian-style cap and tunic, sacrificing a white bull in front of Sol, the sun god. Grain and grapes sprout from the bull's blood, and animals sprout from its semen. The reliefs and icons also show Sol's wife Luna (the moon) beginning her cycle, signifying the birth of time.

Mithraism and Christianity were close competitors partly because of the striking similarity in many of their rituals. Both involve the birth of a deity on 25 December; shepherds; death and resurrection; and a form of baptism. Devotees knelt when they worshipped and a common meal – a 'communion' of bread and water – was a regular feature of both liturgies.

munists and Greens came to power. Lionel Jospin, a former minister of education in the Mitterrand government (who, most notably, promised the French people a shorter working week for the same pay), became prime minister. France had once again entered into a period of *cohabitation* – with Chirac on the other side this time around.

For the most part Jospin and his government continued to enjoy the electorate's approval, thanks largely to a recovery in economic growth and the introduction of a 35-hour working week, which created thousands of (primarily part-time) jobs. But this period of *cohabitation,* the longest-lasting government in the history of the Fifth Republic, ended in May 2002 when Chirac was returned to the presidency for a second five-year term with 82% of the vote. This reflected less Chirac's popularity than the fear of Jean-Marie Le Pen, leader of the right-wing Front National, who had garnered nearly 17% of the first round of voting against Chirac's 20%.

Chirac appointed Jean-Pierre Raffarin, a popular regional politician, as prime minister and pledged to lower taxes with declining revenues from a sluggish economy. But in May 2005 the electorate handed Chirac an embarrassing defeat when it overwhelmingly rejected, by referendum, the international treaty that was to create a constitution for the EU. Several days later Raffarin was replaced by Foreign Minister Dominique de Villepin. Since then the government has had to weather one storm after another (p8).

FROM THE BEGINNING

Paris has a timeless quality, a condition that can often be deceiving. And while the cobbled backstreets of Montmartre, the terraced cafés of Montparnasse, the iconic structure of the Eiffel Tower and the placid waters of the Seine may all have some visitors believing that the city has been here since time immemorial, that's hardly the case.

THE GAULS & THE ROMANS

The early history of the Celts is murky, but it is thought that they originated somewhere in the eastern part of central Europe around the 2nd millennium BC and began to migrate across the continent, arriving in France sometime in the 7th century BC. In the 3rd century a group of Celtic Gauls called the Parisii (believed to mean 'boat men') set up a few wattle-and-daub huts on what is now the Île de la Cité and engaged in fishing and trading.

Centuries of conflict between the Gauls and Romans ended in 52 BC, when Julius Caesar's legions crushed a Celtic revolt led by Vercingétorix on the Mons Lutetius (now

845–86	1163
Paris repeatedly raided by Vikings but French are ultimately victorious	Construction of Notre Dame Cathedral begins and continues for a century and a half

the site of the) and took control of the territory. The settlement on the Seine prospered as the Roman town of Lutetia (from the Latin for 'midwater dwelling'), counted some 10,000 inhabitants by the 3rd century AD.

The Great Migrations, beginning around the middle of the 3rd century AD with raids by the Franks (AD 253) and then by the Alemanii from the east, left the settlement on the south bank scorched and pillaged, and its inhabitants fled to the Île de la Cité, which was subsequently fortified with stone walls. Christianity (as well as Mithraism; see boxed text, p69) had been introduced early in the previous century, and the first church, probably made of wood, was built on the western part of the island.

THE MEROVINGIANS & CAROLINGIANS

The Romans occupied what would become known as Paris (after its first settlers) from AD 212 to the late 5th century. It was at this time that a second wave of Franks and other Germanic groups under Merovius from the north and northeast overran the territory. Merovius' grandson, Clovis I, converted to Christianity, making Paris his seat in 508. Childeric II, Clovis' son and successor, founded the Abbey of St-Germain des Prés in 558, and the dynasty's most productive ruler, Dagobert, established an abbey at St-Denis. This abbey soon became the richest, most important monastery in France and was, for a time, the final resting place of its kings.

The militaristic rulers of the Carolingian dynasty, beginning with Charles Martel (688–741) – the Hammer – were almost permanently away fighting wars in the east, and Paris languished, controlled mostly by the counts of Paris. When Charles Martel's grandson, Charlemagne (768–814), moved his capital to Aix-la-Chapelle (today's Aachen in Germany), Paris' fate was sealed. Basically a group of separate villages with its centre on the island, Paris was badly defended throughout the second half of the 9th century and suffered a succession of raids by the 'Norsemen' (Vikings); the siege of 885–86 by Siegfried the Saxon lasted 10 months but ended with a victory by the French.

THE MIDDLE AGES

The counts of Paris, whose powers had increased as the Carolingians feuded among themselves, elected one of their own, Hugh Capet, as king at Senlis (p350) in 987. He made Paris the royal seat and resided in the renovated palace of the Roman governor on the Île de la Cité (the site of the present Palais de Justice). Under Capetian rule, which would last for the next 800 years, Paris prospered as a centre of politics, commerce, trade, religion and culture. By the time Hugh Capet had assumed the throne, the Norsemen (or Normans, descendants of the Vikings) were in control of northern and western French territory. In 1066 they mounted a successful invasion of England, the so-called Norman Conquest, from their base in today's Normandy. This would lead to almost 300 years of conflict between the Normans and the Capetians.

Paris' strategic river-side position ensured its importance throughout the Middle Ages, although settlement remained centred on the Île de la Cité, with the *rive gauche* (left bank) to the south given over to fields and vineyards; the Marais area on the *rive droite* (right bank) to the north was a waterlogged marsh. The first guilds were established in the 11th century, and rapidly grew in importance; in the mid-12th century the ship merchants' guild bought the principal river port, by today's Hôtel de Ville (city hall), from the crown.

This was a time of frenetic building activity in Paris. Abbot Suger, both confessor and minister to several Capetian kings, was one of the powerhouses of this period, and in 1136 he commissioned the basilica at St-Denis (p157). Less than three decades later, work started on the cathedral of Notre Dame, the greatest creation of medieval Paris, under Maurice de Sully, the bishop of Paris. At the same time Philippe-Auguste (r 1180–1223) expanded the city wall, adding 25 gates and hundreds of protective towers.

1337–1453	1429
The Hundred Years' War between France and England	French forces under Joan of Arc defeat the English near Orléans; Joan captured and burned at the stake three years later

The swampy Marais was drained and settlement moved to the north (or right) bank of the Seine, which would become the mercantile centre, especially around place de Grève (today's place de l'Hôtel de Ville). The food markets at Les Halles first came into existence in 1183, the beautiful Ste-Chapelle on the Île de la Cité was consecrated in 1248 and the Louvre began its existence as a river-side fortress in the 13th century. In a bid to do something about the city's horrible traffic congestion and stinking excrement (the population numbered about 200,000 by the year 1200), Philippe-Auguste paved four of Paris' main streets for the first time since the Roman occupation, using metre-square sandstone blocks. By 1292 Paris counted 352 streets, 10 squares and 11 crossroads.

Meanwhile, the area south of the Seine – today's Left Bank – was developing as the centre of European learning and erudition, particularly in the area known as the Latin Quarter, where students and their teachers communicated in that language exclusively. The ill-fated lovers Pierre Abélard and Héloïse (p26) wrote the finest poetry and their treatises on philosophy, and Thomas Aquinas taught at the new University of Paris (founded under papal protection in about 1215). About 30 other colleges were established, including the Sorbonne, founded in 1253 by Robert de Sorbon, confessor to Louis IX.

In 1337 some three centuries of hostility between the Capetians and the Anglo-Normans degenerated into the Hundred Years' War, which would be fought on and off until 1453. The Black Death (1348–49) killed about a third of Paris' population (an estimated 80,000 souls) but only briefly interrupted the fighting. Paris would not see its population reach 200,000 again until the beginning of the 16th century.

The Hundred Years' War and the plague, along with the development of free, independent cities elsewhere in Europe, brought political tension and open insurrection to Paris. In 1355, the provost of the merchants, a wealthy draper named Étienne Marcel, allied himself with peasants revolting against the dauphin (the future Charles V) and seized Paris in a bid to limit the power of the throne and secure a city charter. But the dauphin's supporters recaptured it within two years, and Marcel and his followers were executed at place de Grève. Charles then completed the right-bank city wall begun by Marcel and turned the Louvre into a sumptuous palace for himself.

Musée du Louvre (p100)

1589	1635
Henry IV, the first Bourbon king, ascends the throne after renouncing Protestantism	Cardinal Richelieu founds the Académie Française, the first and best known of France's five academies of arts and sciences

After the French forces were defeated by the English at Agincourt in 1415, Paris was once again embroiled in revolt. The dukes of Burgundy, allied with the English, occupied the capital in 1420. Two years later John Plantagenet, duke of Bedford, was installed as regent of France for the English king, Henry VI, who was then an infant. Henry was crowned king of France at Notre Dame less than 10 years later, but Paris was almost continuously under siege from the French for much of that time.

In 1429 a 17-year-old peasant girl known to history as Jeanne d'Arc (Joan of Arc) persuaded the French pretender Charles VII that she'd received a divine mission from God to expel the English from France and bring about Charles' coronation. She rallied French troops and defeated the English at Patay, north of Orléans, and Charles was crowned at Reims. But Joan of Arc failed to take Paris. In 1430 she was captured by the Burgundians and sold to the English. She was convicted of witchcraft and heresy by a tribunal of French ecclesiastics and burned at the stake two years later at Rouen.

Charles VII returned to Paris in 1436 ending more than 16 years of occupation, but the English were not entirely driven from French territory (with the exception of Calais) until 1453. The occupation had left Paris a disaster zone. Conditions improved while the restored monarchy moved to consolidate its power under Louis XI (r 1461–83), the first Renaissance king under whose reign the city's first printing press was installed at the Sorbonne (1463). Churches were rehabilitated or built in the Flamboyant Gothic style (see p42) and a number of *hôtels particuliers* (private mansions) such as the Hôtel de Cluny (now the Musée National du Moyen Age) and the Hôtel de Sens (now the Bibliothèque Forney; see p162) were erected.

THE RENAISSANCE

The culture of the Italian Renaissance (French for 'rebirth') arrived in full swing in France in the early 16th century, during the reign of François I (1515–47), partly because of a series of indecisive French military operations in Italy. For the first time, the French aristocracy was exposed to Renaissance ideas of scientific and geographical scholarship and discovery as well as the value of secular over religious life. The population of Paris at the start of François' reign was 170,000 – still almost 20% less than it had been some three centuries before, when the Black Death had decimated the population.

Writers such as François Rabelais, Clément Marot and Pierre de Ronsard were influential at this time, as were the architectural disciples of Michelangelo and Raphael. Evidence of this architectural influence can be seen in François I's chateau at Fontainebleau (p343) and the Petit Château at Chantilly (p347). In the city itself, a prime example of the period is the Pont Neuf (new bridge), which is, in fact, the oldest bridge in Paris. This new architecture was meant to reflect the splendour of the monarchy, which was fast moving towards absolutism, and of Paris as the capital of a powerful centralised state. But all this grandeur and show of strength was not enough to stem the tide of Protestantism that was flowing into France.

THE REFORMATION

By the 1530s the position of the Protestant Reformation sweeping across Europe had been strengthened in France by the ideas of John Calvin, a Frenchman exiled to Geneva. The edict of January 1562, which afforded the Protestants certain rights, was met by violent opposition from ultra-Catholic nobles whose fidelity to their faith was mixed with a desire to strengthen their power bases in the provinces. Paris remained very much a Catholic stronghold, and executions by burning at the stake (39 took place between 1547 and 1550) in place de Grève continued apace up to the outbreak of religious civil war.

The Wars of Religion (1562–98) involved three groups: the Huguenots (French Protestants supported by the English), the Catholic League and the Catholic king. The fighting severely weakened the position of the monarchy and brought the kingdom of France

1682	14 July 1789
Louis XIV moves his court from the Palais des Tuileries in Paris to Versailles	French Revolution begins with the storming of the Bastille

close to disintegration. The most grievous event took place in Paris on 23 and 24 August 1572, when some 3000 Huguenots who had come to Paris to celebrate the wedding of the Protestant Henri of Navarre (the future Henri IV) were slaughtered in what is now called the St Bartholomew's Day Massacre. On 7 May 1588, on the 'Day of the Barricades', the Catholic League rose up against Henri III and forced him to flee the Louvre; he was assassinated the following year.

Henri III was succeeded by Henri IV (r 1589–1610), who inaugurated the Bourbon dynasty and was a Huguenot when he ascended the throne. Catholic Paris refused to allow its new Protestant king entry into the city, and a siege of the capital continued for almost five years. Only when Henri embraced Catholicism at St-Denis did the capital welcome him. In 1598 he promulgated the Edict of Nantes, which guaranteed the Huguenots religious freedom as well as many civil and political rights, but this was not universally accepted.

Henri consolidated the monarchy's power and began to rebuild Paris (the population of which was now about 450,000) after more than 30 years of fighting. The magnificent place Royale (today's place des Vosges in the Marais) and place Dauphine at the western end of the Île de la Cité are prime examples of the new era of town planning. But Henri's rule ended as abruptly and violently as that of his predecessor. In 1610 he was assassinated by a Catholic fanatic named François Ravaillac when his coach became stuck in traffic along rue de la Ferronnerie in the Marais. Ravaillac was executed by an irate mob of Parisians (who were mightily sick of religious turmoil by this time) by being quartered – after a thorough scalding.

At nine years of age, Henri IV's son, the future Louis XIII, was too young to assume the throne, so his mother, Marie de Médici, was named regent. She set about building the magnificent Palais du Luxembourg and its enormous gardens for herself just outside the city wall. Louis XIII ascended the throne in 1617 but throughout most of his undistinguished reign he remained under the control of Cardinal Richelieu, his ruthless chief minister. Richelieu is best known for his untiring efforts to establish an all-powerful monarchy in France, opening the door to the absolutism of Louis XIV, and French supremacy in Europe. Under Louis XIII's reign two uninhabited islets in the Seine were joined to form the Île de Saint Louis, and Richelieu commissioned a number of palaces and churches, including the Palais Royal and the Église Notre Dame du Val-de-Grâce.

LOUIS XIV & THE ANCIEN RÉGIME

Le Roi Soleil (the Sun King) – Louis XIV – ascended the throne in 1643 at the tender age of five. His mother, Anne of Austria, was appointed regent, and Cardinal Mazarin, a protégé of Richelieu, was named chief minister. One of the decisive events of Louis XIV's early reign was the War of the Fronde (1648–53), a rebellion by the bourgeoisie and some of the nobility who were opposed to taxation and the increasing power of the monarchy. The revolt forced the royal court to flee Paris for a time.

When Mazarin died in 1661, Louis XIV assumed absolute power until his own death in 1715. Throughout his long reign, characterised by 'glitter and gloom' as one historian has put it, Louis sought to project the power of the French monarchy – bolstered by claims of divine right – both at home and abroad. He involved France in a long series of costly, almost continuous wars with Holland, Austria and England, which gained France territory but terrified its neighbours and nearly bankrupted the treasury. State taxation to fill the coffers caused widespread poverty and vagrancy in Paris, which was by then a city of almost 600,000 people.

But Louis was able to quash the ambitious, feuding aristocracy and create the first truly centralised French state, elements of which can still be seen in France today. While he did pour huge sums of money into building his extravagant palace at Versailles, by doing so he was able to sidestep the endless intrigues of the capital. And by turning his nobles into courtiers, Louis forced them to compete with one another for royal favour, reducing them to ineffectual sycophants.

1799	1815
Napoleon Bonaparte seizes control of government in a coup d'état	Napoleon defeated by the British and Prussians at Waterloo and sent into exile

Arch of Notre Dame (p111)

Louis mercilessly persecuted his Protestant subjects, whom he considered a threat to the unity of the state and thus his power. In 1685 he revoked the Edict of Nantes, which had guaranteed the Huguenots freedom of conscience.

It was Louis XIV who said '*Après moi, le déluge*' (After me, the flood); in hindsight his words were more than prophetic. His grandson and successor, Louis XV (r 1715–74), was an oafish, incompetent buffoon, and grew to be universally despised. However, Louis XV's regent, Philippe of Orléans, did move the court from Versailles back to Paris; in the Age of Enlightenment, the French capital had become, in effect, the centre of Europe.

As the 18th century progressed, new economic and social circumstances rendered the *ancien régime* (old order) dangerously out of step with the needs of the country and its capital. The regime was further weakened by the antiestablishment and anticlerical ideas of the Enlightenment, whose leading lights included Voltaire (François-Marie Arouet), Jean-Jacques Rousseau and Denis Diderot. But entrenched vested interests, a cumbersome power structure and royal lassitude prevented change from starting until the 1770s, by which time the monarchy's moment had passed.

The Seven Years' War (1756–63) was one of a series of ruinous military engagements pursued by Louis XV. It led to the loss of France's flourishing colonies in Canada, the West Indies and India. It was in part to avenge these losses that Louis XVI sided with the colonists in the American War of Independence (1775–83). But the Seven Years' War cost France a fortune and, more disastrously for the monarchy, it helped to disseminate at home the radical democratic ideas that were thrust upon the world stage by the American Revolution.

THE FRENCH REVOLUTION & THE FIRST REPUBLIC

By the late 1780s, the indecisive Louis XVI (r 1774–93) and his dominating queen, Marie-Antoinette, known to her subjects disparagingly as *l'Autrichienne* (the Austrian), had managed to alienate virtually every segment of society – from the enlightened bourgeoisie to the conservatives – and the king became increasingly isolated as unrest and dissatisfaction reached boiling point. When he tried to neutralise the power of the more reform-minded delegates at a meeting of the États-Généraux (States-General) at the Jeu de Paume in Versailles from May to June 1789 (see boxed text, p338), the

1830	1848
Charles X overthrown in July Revolution	King Louis-Philippe ousted and Second Republic established

masses – spurred on by the oratory and inflammatory tracts circulating at places like the Café de Foy (p168) at Palais Royal – took to the streets of Paris. On 14 July, a mob raided the armoury at the Hôtel des Invalides for rifles, seizing 32,000 muskets, and then stormed the prison at Bastille – the ultimate symbol of the despotic *ancien régime*. The French Revolution had begun.

At first, the Revolution was in the hands of moderate republicans called the Girondins. France was declared a constitutional monarchy and various reforms were introduced, including the adoption of the *Déclaration des Droits de l'Homme and du Citoyen* (Declaration of the Rights of Man and of the Citizen). This document set forth the principles of the Revolution in a preamble and 17 articles, and was modelled after the American Declaration of Independence. A forward-thinking document called *Les Droits des Femmes* (The Rights of Women) was also published. But as the masses armed themselves against the external threat to the new government – posed by Austria, Prussia and the exiled French nobles – patriotism and nationalism mixed with radical fervour and then popularised and radicalised the Revolution. It was not long before the Girondins lost out to the extremist Jacobins, led by Maximilien Robespierre, Georges-Jacques Danton and Jean-Paul Marat. The Jacobins abolished the monarchy and declared the First Republic in September 1792 after Louis XVI proved unreliable as a constitutional monarch. The Assemblée Nationale (National Assembly) was replaced by an elected Revolutionary Convention.

In January 1793 Louis XVI, who had tried to flee the country with his family but only got as far as Varennes, was tried as 'Louis Capet' (as all kings since Hugh Capet were declared to have ruled illegally), convicted of 'conspiring against the liberty of the nation' and guillotined at place de la Révolution, today's place de la Concorde. His consort, Marie-Antoinette, was executed in October of the same year.

In March 1793 the Jacobins set up the notorious Committee of Public Safety to deal with national defence and to apprehend and try 'traitors'. This body had dictatorial control over the city and the country during the so-called Reign of Terror (September 1793 to July 1794), which saw most religious freedoms revoked and churches closed to worship and desecrated. Paris during the Reign of Terror was not unlike Moscow under Joseph Stalin.

Jacobin propagandist Marat was assassinated in his bathtub by the Girondin Charlotte Corday in July 1793 and by autumn the Reign of Terror was in full swing; by mid-1794 some 2500 people had been beheaded in Paris and more than 14,500 executed elsewhere in France. In the end, the Revolution turned on itself, 'devouring its own children' in the words of an intimate of Robespierre, Jacobin Louis Antoine Léon de Saint-Just. Robespierre sent Danton to the guillotine; Saint-Just and Robespierre eventually met the same fate. Paris celebrated for days afterwards.

A DATE WITH THE REVOLUTION

Along with standardising France's – and, later, most of the world's – system of weights and measures with the metric system, the Revolutionary government adopted a new, 'more rational' calendar from which all 'superstitious' associations (eg saints' days and mythology) were removed. Year 1 began on 22 September 1792, the day the First Republic was proclaimed. The names of the 12 months – Vendémiaire, Brumaire, Frimaire, Nivôse, Pluviôse, Ventôse, Germinal, Floréal, Prairial, Messidor, Thermidor and Fructidor – were chosen according to the seasons. The autumn months, for instance, were Vendémiaire, derived from *vendange* (grape harvest); Brumaire, derived from *brume* (mist or fog); and Frimaire, derived from *frimas* (wintry weather). In turn, each month was divided into three 10-day 'weeks' called *décades*, the last day of which was a rest day. The five remaining days of the year were used to celebrate Virtue, Genius, Labour, Opinion and Rewards. While the republican calendar worked well in theory, it caused no end of confusion for France in its communications and trade abroad because the months and days kept changing in relation to those of the Gregorian calendar. The revolutionary calendar was abandoned and the old system was restored in France in 1806 by Napoleon Bonaparte.

1852–70	1889
Second Empire under Napoleon III; Haussmann redesigns Paris	Eiffel Tower completed for *Exposition Universelle* (World Exhibitions) and is vilified in the press and on the street

After the Reign of Terror faded, a five-man delegation of moderate republicans led by Paul Barras, who had ordered the arrests of Robespierre and Saint-Just, set itself up to rule the republic as the Directoire (Directory). On 5 October 1795 (or 13 Vendémiaire in year 6 – see boxed text, p75 for an explanation), a group of royalist *jeunesse dorée* (gilded youth) bent on overthrowing the Directory was intercepted in front of the Église St-Roch on rue St-Honoré. They were met by loyalist forces led by a young Corsican general named Napoleon Bonaparte, who fired into the crowd. For this 'whiff of grapeshot' Napoleon was put in command of the French forces in Italy, where he was particularly successful in the campaign against Austria. His victories would soon turn him into an independent political force.

NAPOLEON & THE FIRST EMPIRE

The post-Revolutionary government led by the five-man Directory was far from stable, and when Napoleon returned to Paris in 1799 he found a chaotic republic in which few citizens had any faith. In November, when it appeared that the Jacobins were again on the ascendancy in the legislature, Napoleon tricked the delegates into leaving Paris for St-Cloud to the southwest ('for their own protection'), overthrew the discredited Directory and assumed power himself.

At first, Napoleon took the post of First Consul, chosen by popular vote. In 1802 a referendum declared him 'Consul for Life' and his birthday became a national holiday. By December 1804, when he crowned himself 'Emperor of the French' in the presence of Pope Pius VII at Notre Dame, the scope and nature of Napoleon's ambitions were obvious to all. But to consolidate and legitimise his authority Napoleon needed more victories on the battlefield. So began a seemingly endless series of wars and victories by which France would come to control most of Europe.

In 1812 Napoleon invaded Russia in an attempt to do away with his last major rival on the Continent, Tsar Alexander I. Although his Grande Armée managed to capture Moscow, it was wiped out by the brutal Russian winter; of the 600,000 soldiers mobilised, only 90,000 – a mere 15% – returned. Prussia and Napoleon's other adversaries quickly recovered from their earlier defeats, and less than two years after the fiasco in Russia the Prussians, backed by Russia, Austria and Britain, entered Paris. Napoleon abdicated and was exiled to the island of Elba off the coast of Italy. The Senate then formally deposed him as emperor.

At the Congress of Vienna (1814–15), the victorious allies restored the House of Bourbon to the French throne, installing Louis XVI's brother as Louis XVIII (Louis XVI's second son, Charles, had been declared Louis XVII by monarchists in exile but he died while under arrest by the Revolutionary government). But in February 1815 Napoleon escaped from Elba, landed in southern France and gathered a large army as he marched

HOUSING BARON HAUSSMANN

Few town planners anywhere in the world have had as great an impact on the city of their birth as did Baron Georges-Eugène Haussmann (1809–91) on Paris. As Prefect of the Seine département under Napoleon III between 1853 and 1870, Haussmann and his staff of engineers and architects completely rebuilt huge swaths of Paris. He is best known (and most bitterly attacked) for having demolished much of medieval Paris, replacing the chaotic narrow streets – easy to barricade in an uprising – with the handsome, arrow-straight thoroughfares for which the city is celebrated. He also revolutionised Paris' water supply and sewerage systems and laid out many of the city's loveliest parks, including large areas of the Bois de Boulogne (Map pp422–3) and Bois de Vincennes (Map pp422–3) as well as the Parc des Buttes Chaumont (Map ppp428–9) and Parc de Montsouris (Map pp422–3). The 12 avenues leading out from the Arc de Triomphe, for example, were also his work.

1918	1940
Armistice ending WWI signed at Fôret de Compiègne near Paris	Germany begins four-year occupation of Paris

towards Paris. On 1 June he reclaimed the throne at celebrations held at the Champs de Mars. But his reign came to an end just three weeks later when his forces were defeated by the Prussians and British under the Duke of Wellington at Waterloo in Belgium. Napoleon was exiled again, this time to the remote South Atlantic island of St Helena, where he died in 1821.

Although reactionary in some ways – he re-established slavery in France's colonies, for example – Napoleon instituted a number of important reforms, including a reorganisation of the judicial system; the promulgation of a new legal code, the Code Napoléon (or civil code), which forms the basis of the French legal system to this day; and the establishment of a new educational system. More importantly, he preserved the essence of the changes brought about by the Revolution. Napoleon is therefore remembered by many French people as the nation's greatest hero.

Few of Napoleon's grand architectural plans for Paris were completed, but the Arc de Triomphe, Arc de Triomphe du Carrousel, La Madeleine, Pont des Arts, rue de Rivoli and some buildings within the Louvre complex as well as the Canal St-Martin all date from this period.

THE RESTORATION & THE SECOND REPUBLIC

The reign of 'the gouty old gentleman' Louis XVIII (1814–24) was dominated by the struggle between extreme monarchists who wanted a return to the *ancien régime,* liberals who saw the changes wrought by the Revolution as irreversible, and the radicals of the working-class neighbourhoods of Paris (by 1817 the population of Paris stood at 715,000). Louis' successor, the reactionary Charles X (r 1824–30), handled this struggle with great incompetence and was overthrown in the so-called July Revolution of 1830 when a motley group of revolutionaries seized the Hôtel de Ville. The Colonne de Juillet in the centre of the place de la Bastille honours those killed in the street battles that accompanied the revolution; they are buried in vaults under the column.

Louis-Philippe (r 1830–48), an ostensibly constitutional monarch of bourgeois sympathies and tastes, was then chosen by parliament to head what became known as the July Monarchy. His tenure was marked by inflation, corruption and rising unemployment and was overthrown in the February Revolution of 1848, in whose wake the Second Republic was established. The population of Paris had reached one million by 1844.

FROM THE SECOND REPUBLIC TO THE SECOND EMPIRE

In presidential elections held in 1848, Napoleon's inept nephew, the German-accented Louis Napoleon Bonaparte, was overwhelmingly elected. Legislative deadlock caused Louis Napoleon to lead a coup d'état in 1851, after which he was proclaimed Emperor Napoleon III (Bonaparte had conferred the title Napoleon II on his son upon his abdication in 1814, but the latter never ruled). A plebiscite overwhelmingly approved the motion (7.8 million in favour and 250,000 against), and he moved into the Palais des Tuileries.

The Second Empire lasted from 1852 until 1870. During this period France enjoyed significant economic growth, and Paris was transformed by Baron Georges-Eugène Haussmann (see boxed text, opposite) into the modern city it now is. The city's first department stores were also built at this time – the now defunct La Ville de Paris in 1834 followed by Le Bon Marché in 1852 – as were the *passages couverts,* Paris' delightful covered shopping arcades (p167).

Like his uncle before him, Napoleon III embroiled France in a number of costly conflicts, including the disastrous Crimean War (1854–56). In 1870 Otto von Bismarck goaded Napoleon III into declaring war on Prussia. Within months the thoroughly unprepared French army was defeated and the emperor taken prisoner. When news of the debacle reached Paris the masses took to the streets and demanded that a republic be declared.

25 August 1944	1958
Spearheaded by Free French units, Allied forces liberate Paris	De Gaulle returns to power and forms the Fifth Republic

THE THIRD REPUBLIC & THE BELLE ÉPOQUE

The Third Republic began as a provisional government of national defence in September 1870. The Prussians were, at the time, advancing on Paris and would subsequently lay siege to the capital, forcing starving Parisians to bake bread partially with sawdust and consume most of the animals on display in the Ménagerie at the Jardin des Plantes. In January 1871 the government negotiated an armistice with the Prussians, who demanded that National Assembly elections be held immediately. The republicans, who had called on the nation to continue to resist the Prussians and were overwhelmingly supported by Parisians, lost to the monarchists, who had campaigned on a peace platform.

As expected, the monarchist-controlled assembly ratified the Treaty of Frankfurt (1871). However, when ordinary Parisians heard of its harsh terms – a huge war indemnity, cession of the provinces of Alsace and Lorraine and the occupation of Paris by 30,000 Prussian troops – they revolted against the government.

Following the withdrawal of Prussian troops on 18 March 1871, an insurrectionary government, known to history as the Paris Commune, was established and its supporters, the Communards, seized control of the capital (the legitimate government had fled to Versailles). In late May, after the Communards had tried to burn the centre of the city, the Versailles government launched an offensive on the Commune known as *La Semaine Sanglante* (Bloody Week) in which several thousand rebels were killed. After a mop-up of the Parc des Buttes Chaumont, the last of the Communard insurgents – cornered by government forces in the Cimetière du Père Lachaise – fought a hopeless, all-night battle among the tombstones. In the morning, the 147 survivors were lined up against what is now known as the Mur des Fédérés (Wall of the Federalists). They were then shot, and buried in a mass grave. A further 20,000 or so Communards, mostly working class, were rounded up throughout the city and executed. As many as 13,000 were jailed or transported to Devil's Island penal colony off French Guyana in South America.

Karl Marx, in his *The Civil War in France*, interpreted the Communard insurrection as the first great proletarian uprising against the bourgeoisie, and socialists came to see its victims as martyrs of the class struggle. Among the buildings destroyed in the fighting were the original Hôtel de Ville, the Palais des Tuileries and the Cours des Comptes (site of the present-day Musée d'Orsay). Both Ste-Chapelle and Notre Dame were slated to be torched but those in charge apparently had a change of heart at the last minute.

Despite this disastrous start, the Third Republic ushered in the glittering *belle époque* ('beautiful age'), with Art Nouveau architecture, a whole field of artistic 'isms' from impressionism onwards and advances in science and engineering, including the construction

TOP FIVE BOOKS ON PARIS' HISTORY

- *A Traveller's History of Paris*, Robert Cole (2003) – at just over 300 pages, this book is hardly the most in-depth treatment of Parisian history but as an introductory text it's easy to read, often insightful and sometimes witty.
- *Is Paris Burning?* Larry Collins & Dominique Lapierre (1965) – this is a tense and very intelligent reportage of the last days of the Nazi occupation of Paris.
- *Paris: The Biography of a City*, Colin Jones (2005) – although written by a University of Warwick professor this one-volume history is not at all academic. Instead, it's rather chatty, and goes into much detail on the physical remains of history as the author walks the reader through the centuries and the city.
- *The Flâneur: A Stroll Through the Paradoxes of Paris*, Edmund White (2001) – doyen of American literature and long-term resident (and *flâneur* – 'stroller') of Paris, White notices things rarely noticed by others – veritable footnotes of footnotes – in this loving portrait of his adopted city.
- *The Seven Ages of Paris: Portrait of a City*, Alistair Horne (2002) – this superb, very idiosyncratic 'biography' of Paris divides the city's history into seven ages – from the 13th-century reign of Philippe-Auguste to President Charles de Gaulle's retirement in 1969.

1968	1989
Student-led riots result in de Gaulle's resignation the following year	Opéra Bastille opens to mark bicentennial of French Revolution; IM Pei's Grande Pyramide is unveiled at the Louvre

Architectural detail of the Panthéon (p117)

of the first metro line, which opened in 1900. *Expositions universelles* (world exhibitions) were held in Paris in 1889 – showcasing the then maligned Eiffel Tower – and again in 1900 in the purpose-built Petit Palais. The Paris of nightclubs and artistic cafés made its first appearance around this time, and Montmartre became a magnet for artists, writers, pimps and prostitutes (see p172).

But France was consumed with a desire for revenge after its defeat by Germany, and jingoistic nationalism, scandals and accusations were the order of the day. The most serious crisis – morally and politically – of the Third Republic, however, was the infamous Dreyfus Affair. This began in 1894 when a Jewish army captain named Alfred Dreyfus was accused of betraying military secrets to Germany – he was then court-martialled and sentenced to life imprisonment on Devil's Island. Liberal politicians, artists and writers, including the novelist Émile Zola who penned his celebrated 'J'accuse!' (I Accuse) open letter in support of the captain, succeeded in having the case reopened – despite bitter opposition from the army command, right-wing politicians and many Catholic groups – and Dreyfus was vindicated in 1900. When he died in 1935 Dreyfus was laid to rest in the Cimetière de Montparnasse. The Dreyfus affair discredited the army and the Catholic Church in France. This resulted in more-rigorous civilian control of the military and, in 1905, the legal separation of Church and State.

WWI & THE INTERWAR YEARS

Central to France's entry into WWI was the desire to regain the provinces of Alsace and Lorraine, lost to Germany in 1871. Indeed, Raymond Poincaré, president of the Third Republic from 1913 to 1920 and later prime minister, was a native of Lorraine and a firm supporter of war with Germany. But when the heir to the Austrian throne, Archduke Franz Ferdinand, was assassinated by a Bosnian Serb in Sarajevo on 28 June 1914, Germany and Austria-Hungary – precipitating what would erupt into the first-ever global war – jumped the gun. Within a month, they had declared war on Russia *and* France.

1992	1998
Disneyland Resort Paris (then Euro-Disney) opens at Marne-la-Vallée east of Paris	France beats Brazil to win the World Cup at the Stade de France in St-Denis

By early September German troops had reached the River Marne, just 15km east of Paris, and the government moved to Bordeaux. But Marshal Joffre's troops, transported to the front by Parisian taxicabs, brought about the 'Miracle of the Marne', and Paris was safe within a month. In November 1918 the armistice was finally signed in a railway carriage in a clearing of the Forêt de Compiègne, 82km northeast of Paris.

The defeat of Austria-Hungary and Germany in WWI, which regained Alsace and Lorraine for France, was achieved at an unimaginable human cost. Of the eight million French men who were called to arms, 1.3 million were killed and almost one million crippled. In other words, two of every 10 Frenchmen aged between 20 and 45 years of age were killed in WWI. At the Battle of Verdun (1916) alone, the French, led by General Philippe Pétain, and the Germans each lost about 400,000 men.

The 1920s and '30s saw Paris as a centre of the avant-garde, with artists pushing into new fields of cubism and surrealism, Le Corbusier rewriting the textbook for architecture, foreign writers such as Ernest Hemingway and James Joyce drawn by the city's liberal atmosphere (see p164), and nightlife establishing a cutting-edge reputation for everything from jazz clubs to striptease.

France's efforts to promote a separatist movement in the Rhineland, and its occupation of the Ruhr in 1923 to enforce German reparations payments, proved disastrous. But it did lead to almost a decade of accommodation and compromise with Germany over border guarantees, and to Germany's admission to the League of Nations. The naming of Adolf Hitler as German chancellor in 1933, however, would put an end to all that.

WWII & THE OCCUPATION

During most of the 1930s, the French, like the British, had done their best to appease Hitler. However, two days after the German invasion of Poland on 1 September 1939, Britain and France declared war on Germany. For the first nine months Parisians joked about le drôle de guerre – what Britons called 'the phoney war' – in which nothing happened. But the battle for France began in earnest in May 1940 and by 14 June France had capitulated. Paris was occupied, and almost half the population of just under five million fled the city by car, by bicycle or on foot. The British expeditionary force sent to help the French barely managed to avoid capture by retreating to Dunkirk, described so vividly in Ian McEwan's *Atonement* (2001), and crossing the English Channel in small boats. The Maginot Line, a supposedly impregnable wall of fortifications along the Franco-German border, had proved useless – the German armoured divisions simply outflanked it by going through Belgium.

The Germans divided France into a zone under direct German rule (along the western coast and the north, including Paris), and into a puppet-state based in the spa town of Vichy and led by General Philippe Pétain, the ageing WWI hero of the Battle of Verdun. Pétain's collaborationist government, whose leaders and supporters assumed that the Nazis were Europe's new masters and had to be accommodated, as well as French police forces in German-occupied areas (including Paris) helped the Nazis round up 160,000 French Jews and others for deportation to concentration and extermination camps in Germany and Poland.

After the fall of Paris, General Charles de Gaulle, France's undersecretary of war, fled to London. In a radio broadcast on 18 June 1940, he appealed to French patriots to continue resisting the Germans. He set up a French government-in-exile and established the Forces Françaises Libres (Free French Forces), a military force dedicated to fighting the Germans.

The underground movement known as the Résistance (Resistance), whose active members never amounted to more than about 5% of the French population, engaged in such activities as sabotaging railways, collecting intelligence for the Allies, helping Allied airmen who had been shot down and publishing anti-German leaflets. The other 95% of the popula-

2000	2001
Length of the presidential term reduced from seven to five years	Socialist Bertrand Delanoë becomes Paris' – and a European capital's – first openly gay mayor

tion were either collaborators, such as the film stars Maurice Chevalier and Arletty, and the designer Coco Chanel, or did nothing whatsoever to resist or help victims.

The liberation of France began with the Allied landings in Normandy on D-day (*Jour-J* in French): 6 June 1944. On 15 August Allied forces also landed in southern France. After a brief insurrection by the Resistance, Paris was liberated on 25 August by an Allied force spearheaded by Free French units – these units were sent in ahead of the Americans so that the French would have the honour of liberating the capital the following day. Hitler, who visited Paris in June 1940 and loved it, ordered that the city be torched toward the end of the war. It was an order that, gratefully, had not been obeyed.

THE FOURTH REPUBLIC

De Gaulle returned to Paris and set up a provisional government, but in January 1946 he resigned as president, wrongly believing that the move would provoke a popular outcry for his return. A few months later, a new constitution was approved by referendum. De Gaulle formed his own party (Rassemblement du Peuple Français) and spent the next 13 years in opposition.

The Fourth Republic was a period that saw unstable coalition cabinets follow one another with bewildering speed (on average, one every six months), and economic recovery that was helped immeasurably by massive American aid. The war to reassert French colonial control over Indochina ended in 1954 with France's disastrous defeat at Dien Bien Phu in Vietnam. France also tried to suppress an uprising by Arab nationalists in Algeria, where over one million French settlers lived.

THE FIFTH REPUBLIC

The Fourth Republic came to an end in 1958, when extreme right-wingers, furious at what they saw as defeatism rather than tough action in dealing with the uprising in Algeria, began conspiring to overthrow the government. De Gaulle was brought back to power to prevent a military coup and possible civil war. He soon drafted a new constitution that ushered in the Fifth Republic and gave considerable powers to the president at the expense of the National Assembly.

The Fifth Republic was rocked in 1961 by an attempted coup staged in Algiers by a group of right-wing military officers. When it failed, the Organisation de l'Armée Secrète (OAS) – a group of French *colons* (colonists) and sympathisers opposed to Algerian independence – turned to terrorism, trying several times to assassinate de Gaulle and nearly succeeding in August 1962 in the Parisian suburb of Petit Clamart. The book and film *The Day of the Jackal* portrayed a fictional OAS attempt on de Gaulle's life.

In 1962, after more than 12,000 died as a result of this 'civil war', de Gaulle negotiated an end to the war in Algeria. Some 750,000 *pied-noir* ('black feet'), as Algerian-born French people are known in France, flooded into France and the capital. Meanwhile, almost all of the other French colonies and protectorates in Africa had demanded and achieved independence. Shrewdly, the French government began a program of economic and military aid to its former colonies to bolster France's waning importance internationally and to create a bloc of French-speaking nations – *la Francophonie* – in the Third World.

Paris retained its position as a creative and intellectual centre, particularly in philosophy and film-making, and the 1960s saw large parts of the Marais beautifully restored. But the loss of the colonies, the surge in immigration, economic difficulties, and an increase in unemployment weakened de Gaulle's government.

In March 1968 a large demonstration in Paris against the war in Vietnam was led by student Daniel 'Dany the Red' Cohn-Bendit, today co-president of the Green/Free European Alliance Group in the European Parliament. This gave impetus to the student movement, and protests were staged throughout the spring. A seemingly insignificant incident in May

2002	2003
President Jacques Chirac overwhelmingly defeats Front National leader Jean-Marie Le Pen to win second term	Hundreds of (mostly elderly) Parisians die from complications arising from an unusually hot summer

1968, in which police broke up yet another in a long series of demonstrations by students of the University of Paris, sparked a violent reaction on the streets of the capital; students occupied the Sorbonne and barricades were erected in the Latin Quarter. Workers joined in the protests and six million people across France participated in a general strike that virtually paralysed the country and the city. It was a period of much creativity and new ideas with slogans appearing everywhere such as *'L'Imagination au Pouvoir'* (Put Imagination in Power) and *'Sous les Pavés, la Plage'* (Under the Cobblestones, the Beach), a reference to Parisians' favoured material for building barricades and what they could expect to find beneath them.

The alliance between workers and students couldn't last long. While the former wanted to reap greater benefits from the consumer market, the latter wanted (or at least said they wanted) to destroy it – and were called 'fascist *provocateurs*' and 'mindless anarchists' by the French Communist leadership. De Gaulle took advantage of this division and appealed to people's fear of anarchy – if not civil war. Just as Paris and the rest of France seemed on the brink of revolution, 100,000 Gaullists demonstrated on the av des Champs-Élysées in support of the government and stability was restored.

2004	2005
France bans the wearing of Muslim headscarves and other religious symbols in schools	French electorate rejects European Union Constitution; Parisian suburbs and cities around France wracked by rioting by Arab and African youths

1 *Peruse the books and posters for sale on the banks of the Seine (p165)* 2 *In-line skaters, cyclists and pedestrians enjoy pollution-free sorties along river-side quais* 3 *Sunrise on the banks of the Seine* 4 *One of the many Seine bridges*

1 *Painting within L'Atelier de Joël Robouchon (p211)* 2 *Detail of sculpture at Musée Rodin (p126)* 3 *Graffiti on a market truck* 4 *Mosaic detail on Mosquée de Paris (p116)*

1 *Painting at Le Chansonnier restaurant (p220)* 2 *Statue inside Musée d'Orsay (p124)* 3 *Statue in front of Eiffel Tower (p127)* 4 *Exterior of Palais Garnier (p271)*

1 *Woman drinking at Le Clown Bar (p223)* 2 *A violin outside Sacré Cœur (p148), Montmartre* 3 *Family fun near Canal St-Martin (p13*

1 *Buskers on rue Mouffetard (p52), one of Paris' most popular market streets* 2 *Costumed participants in the Gay Pride March (p10)* 3 *Two men catch some sleep on the Champs-Élysées (p130)* 4 *Relaxing in a café on rue Mouffetard*

1 *Children playing in Place des Vosges (p110)* **2** *Musicians beside Canal St-Martin (p13...)* **3** *Mechanical Fountain, Cent... Pompidou (p98)*

1 *Ride at Jardin d'Acclimatation (p154)* 2 *Sculpture in Jardin du Luxembourg (p119)* 3 *Costumed street entertainer* 4 *Picnickers with Eiffel Tower (p127) in the distance*

1 *Ice-skating (p278) at Place de l'Hôtel de Ville* **2** *Rue Foyatier behind Basilique du Sacré Cœur (p148)* **3** *Sailing toy boat in Jardin des Tuileries (p100)* **4** *Cyclists on the Champs-Élysées (p130)*

Sights

Sights

The central part of Paris – what Parisians call *intra-muros* (Latin for 'within the walls') – is a compact, easily negotiated city. Some 20 arrondissements (city districts) spiral clockwise more or less from the centre and are important locators; their numbers are always included in addresses given on business cards, advertisements, the Internet and in this guide.

Unlike numbered districts or postcodes in some other cities, Paris' arrondissements usually have distinct personalities: the 1er has plenty of sights but few residents, the 5e is studenty, the 7e full of ministries and embassies, the 10e has traditionally been working class but is becoming a trendy district in which to live, the 15e is huge and the 16e is a bastion of the very well-heeled. But such profiles are not always so cut-and-dried, and the lay of the land becomes much clearer to visitors when they see the city as composed of about two-dozen named *quartiers* (quarters or neighbourhoods).

This guide starts in the heart of the Right Bank north of the Seine, in the area around the **Louvre** and **Les Halles**, which largely takes in the 1er but also part of the 2e and the westernmost edge of the 4e. Next come the **Marais** (4e and 3e) and the contiguous **Bastille** (11e) districts to the east and southeast.

The two islands in the Seine – the **Île de la Cité** and the **Île St-Louis** – are neither fish nor fowl when it comes to the question of Right or Left Bank but they do belong to an arrondissement. Most of the former is in the 1er and all of the latter is in the 4e.

We encounter the Left Bank in the **Latin Quarter**, traditional centre of learning in Paris, and the leafy **Jardin des Plantes** to the east of it (both 5e). The 6e, to the west and southwest, is both a frenetic district of sights, shops, galleries and cafés (**St-Germain** and **Odéon**) and a tranquil park and residential neighbourhood (**Luxembourg**). To the south is **Montparnasse** in the 14e, once

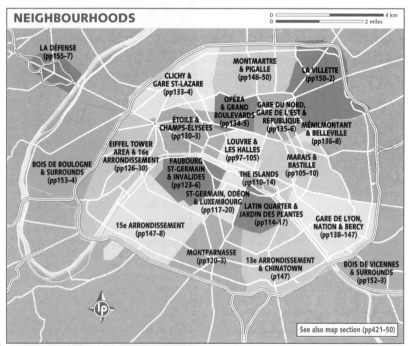

the centre of nightlife in Paris and now known for its massive commuter train station and unsightly landmark, the **Tour Montparnasse**. **Faubourg St-Germain** and **Les Invalides** to the north in the 7e are important for their sights but also as the locations of many branches of government, including the **Assemblée Nationale** (Parliament), embassies and cultural centres. To the west is the **Eiffel Tower** and, across the Seine on the Right Bank, the posh **16e arrondissement**, a district of broad, tree-lined avenues, grand apartment blocks and small but exquisite museums.

To the east and still on the Right Bank is the 8e, which includes what many visitors consider to be the quintessential Parisian sights: **Étoile**, with its landmark **Arc de Triomphe**, and the wide boulevard known as the **Champs-Élysées**. At the end of this grand avenue is **Concorde** and to the north of that **Madeleine**, two very important – and very different – *places* (squares). Above the 8e is the schizophrenic 17e, with its beautiful, Haussmann-era buildings beyond the **Gare St-Lazare** and the working-class neighbourhoods of **Clichy**. To the east is the 9e, where you'll find the city's original **Opéra** and the **Grands Boulevards**.

The 10e, hosting both the **Gare du Nord** and the **Gare de l'Est**, is the city's rail hub. It also has some wonderful residential districts around the **Canal St-Martin** (p136). **République** gets a toe-hold in to the 10e to the south but most of this enormous and chaotic square is in the 3e. Below that is the *branché* (trendy) district of **Ménilmontant**, awash in alternative bars, cafés and restaurants especially along rue Oberkampf in the northern 11e, and to the east, the solidly working-class neighbourhood of **Belleville** (20e), where Édith Piaf was born, socialism once thrived and Paris' first immigrants from North Africa settled.

The 12e contains three very different districts: the **Gare de Lyon** to the northwest, the huge square-cum-roundabout called **Nation** to the east and, to the south, the redeveloped area of **Bercy**, its old wine warehouses having been turned into a wining and dining 'theme park' popular with suburbanites. Across the Seine is the **13e arrondissement**, home to the grandiose **Bibliothèque Nationale de France** and **Chinatown**, and currently undergoing massive redevelopment. The **15e arrondissement**, the largest and most populous but arguably least interesting district to tourists, is to the west.

To the north in the 18e is **Montmartre**, the Paris of myth and films, and **Pigalle**, the naughty red-light district that looks pretty tame when compared with its equivalents in London or New York. **La Villette**, with its lovely park, canal and cutting-edge museums and other attractions in the far-flung 19e arrondissement of the northeast, is the last district of major importance *intra-muros*. 'Outside the walls', however, are at least four areas of particular interest to visitors: the **Bois de Vincennes** and **Bois de Boulogne**, Paris' 'lungs' and recreational centres to the east and the west; **La Défense**, the futuristic business and residential district at the end of metro line No 1 to the northwest of Étoile; and **St-Denis**, to the north on metro line 13, where France's kings were laid to rest for well over a millennium and where there is an important 12th-century cathedral.

ITINERARIES

If you want a general overview of Paris before striking out on your own, take one of the organised tours described later in this chapter (p94). At least you'll be sure to see what the French call *les incontournables* (the unmissables) even on a very brief visit. The 'jump-on/jump-off' bus tours are particularly useful for this purpose though the Batobus (p365) is another option in all but the coldest months.

Failing that, you can always go up to look down. Paris is a relatively flat city and the views are excellent from the Eiffel Tower, the Centre Pompidou, Sacré Cœur, the Tour Montparnasse, Parc de Belleville and the Grande Arche de la Défense. The highest point in Paris, by the way, is the elevated Télégraphe metro station on line 11. Those who are not making their first visit to Paris or anyone who wants to see a smaller section of the city in greater detail should follow any of the five walking tours described in the Walking Tours chapter starting on p160.

Opening hours for Paris' museums and other attractions can vary wildly; closing times for parks, in particular, may vary according to the season. In this chapter, we have indicated seasonal opening and closing times with a span. Thus '9am-5.30pm to 9.30pm' indicates that the venue in question may close any time between 5.30pm and 9.30pm, according to the time of year.

One Day

Those with just – would you believe? – one day in Paris should join a morning tour to get an idea of the lay of the land and then concentrate on the most Parisian of sights and attractions: **Notre Dame** (p110), the **Louvre** (p100), the **Eiffel Tower** (p127) and the **Arc de Triomphe** (p130). In the late afternoon have a coffee or a pastis on the **av des Champs-Élysées** (p131) and then make your way to **Montmartre** (p148) for dinner.

Two Days

If you have two days to spare in the City of Light, you could also take in such sights as the **Musée d'Orsay** (p124), **Ste-Chapelle** (p113), **Conciergerie** (p112), **Musée National du Moyen Age** (p116) and/or the **Musée Rodin** (p126). Have brunch on the **place des Vosges** (p110) and enjoy a night of mirth and gaiety in the **Marais** (p105).

Three Days

With another day to look around the city, you should consider a **cruise** (opposite) along the Seine or the Canal St-Martin and visit some place further afield – the **Cimetière du Père Lachaise** (p137), say, or the **Parc de la Villette** (p152). Take in a concert, opera or ballet at the **Palais Garnier** (p271) or **Opéra Bastille** (p271) or a play at the **Comédie Française** (p269), and go on a bar and club crawl along rue Oberkampf in **Ménilmontant** (p136).

One Week

If you have one week here you can see a good many of the major sights listed in this chapter, including places 'outside the walls' such as **La Défense** (p155) and **St-Denis** (p157), and leave Paris for a day or two on an **excursion** (p335): Vaux-le-Vicomte can be easily combined with Fontainebleau, Senlis with Chantilly and, if you travel hard and fast, Chartres with Versailles.

ORGANISED TOURS

If you can't be bothered making your own way around Paris or don't have the time, consider a tour by air, bus, boat or bicycle or on foot. There's no reason to feel sheepish or embarrassed about taking a guided tour – even one of those super-touristy ones in eight languages. They are an excellent way to learn the contours of a new city, and even experienced guidebook writers have been known to join them from time to time. Most useful, though, are the buses and other conveyances that allow you to disembark when and where you want and board the next one that suits you. They usually offer little or no commentary aside from calling out the stop names but offer the most freedom to do what you want.

Couch potatoes, head for **Explore Paris!** (Map pp426–7; ☎ 01 42 66 62 06; www .exploreparis.fr in French; 11bis rue Scribe, 9e; Ⓜ Auber or Opéra; adult/student & 6-17 yr/family €10/6/26, under 6 yr free; Ⓨ 9am-7.45pm), which includes **Paris Story**, a 50-minute audiovisual romp through Paris' 2000-year history on the hour, with headset commentary in 13 languages; **Paris Miniature**,

an interactive model of Paris; and **Paris Experience**, with video clips and Internet access.

Air

BALLON EUTELSAT Map pp434-5
☎ 01 44 26 20 00; www.aeroparis.com in French; Parc André Citroën, 2 rue de la Montagne de la Fage, 15e; Mon-Fri adult/3-11 yr/12-17 yr €10/5/9, Sat & Sun €12/6/10, under 3 yr free; Ⓨ 9am-5.30pm to 9.30pm (seasonal); Ⓜ Balard or Lourmel
This hot-air balloon in the Parc André Citroën in southwestern Paris lifts you 150m off the ground and offers fabulous views of Paris and the Seine but do not expect to get very far; the helium-filled balloon remains firmly tethered to the ground. Be sure to call in advance; the balloon does not ascend in windy conditions.

PARIS HÉLICOPTÈRE Map p334
☎ 01 48 35 90 44, 01 45 54 95 11; www.paris -helicoptere.com; €122-149; Ⓨ 9am-6pm Sun
This outfit at Aéroport du Bourget, northeast of central Paris, offers an 80km circuit over the city every Sunday lasting 25 minutes for

Bateaux-Mouches river cruise (p96)

€122 and a longer one that includes Versailles for €149. Book 10 to 15 days ahead. You can reach Le Bourget by RER line B3 or B5 or by RATP bus 350 from Gare du Nord, Gare de l'Est or Porte de la Chapelle, or bus 152 from Porte de la Villette.

Bicycle

FAT TIRE BIKE TOURS Map pp434-5
☎ 01 56 58 10 54; www.fattirebiketoursparis.com; 24 rue Edgar Faure, 15e; ☒ office 9am-7pm; Ⓜ La Motte-Picquet Grenelle
Fat Tire Bike Tours offers day tours of the city (adult/student €24/22; four hours), starting at 11am daily from March to November, with an additional departure at 3pm from mid-May to July. Night bicycle tours (adult/student €28/26) depart at 7pm on Sunday, Tuesday and Thursday in March and November and at the same time daily from April to October. A day and night combination tour costs €48/44.

Participants can meet at the Fat Tire Bike Tours office, where you can store bags, log on to the Internet and get tourist information, but tours actually depart from av Gustave Eiffel, 7e, just opposite the Eiffel Tower's South Pillar at the start of the Champ de Mars. Costs include the bicycle and, if necessary, rain gear.

The same company runs City Segway Tours (www.citysegwaytours.com) which, though not on bicycles, involve two-wheeled, electric-powered conveyances. Segway tours

(€70), which follow an abbreviated route of the bike tours and last four hours, depart at 10.30am from mid-February to mid-December and at 6.30pm April to October. You must book these tours in advance.

GEPETTO & VÉLOS Map pp444-5
☎ 01 43 54 19 95; www.gepetto-et-velos.com in French; 59 rue du Cardinal Lemoine, 5e; €25; ☒ 9am-1pm & 2-7.30pm Tue-Sat, 9.30am-1pm & 2-7pm Sun; Ⓜ Cardinal Lemoine
Bike tours lasting three hours from this cycle shop include guide, bicycle and insurance. There is also a Latin Quarter branch (☒ 01 43 37 16 17; 46 rue Daubenton, 5e; ☒ 9am-1pm & 2-7.30pm Tue-Sat; Ⓜ Censier Daubenton).

MAISON ROUE LIBRE Map pp436-7
☎ 0 810 44 15 34; www.rouelibre.fr; Forum des Halles, 1 passage Mondétour, 1er; adult/under 26 yr €25/20, with own bike €15; ☒ 9am-7pm Feb-Nov, 10am-6pm Dec & Jan; Ⓜ Les Halles
This RATP-sponsored outfit has 20 different bike tours from 12km to 26km lasting from three to eight hours. Tours operate on certain weekend days throughout the year starting at 10am or 2pm. Consult the website for exact details. The Bastille branch (Map pp440-1; ☎ 0 810 44 15 34; 37 blvd Bourdon, 4e; Ⓜ Bastille) keeps the same hours.

Boat
Be it on what Parisians call the Seine – *la ligne de vie de Paris* (the lifeline of Paris) or the rejuvenated canals to the northeast, a boat cruise is the most relaxing way to watch the city glide by.

CANAL CRUISES
CANAUXRAMA Map pp440-1 & Map pp428-9
☎ 01 42 39 15 00; www.canauxrama.com; Bassin de la Villette, 13 quai de la Loire, 19e; Mon-Fri adult/6-12 yr/student & senior €14/8/11, under 6 yr free, admission after noon Sat & Sun €14; ☒ Mar-Nov; Ⓜ Jaurès or Bastille
Barges run from Port de Plaisance de Paris-Arsenal, 12e, opposite 50 blvd de la Bastille, to Parc de la Villette, 19e, along charming Canal St-Martin and Canal de l'Ourcq. Departures are at 9.45am and 2.30pm from Port de Plaisance de Paris-Arsenal during the season and, in summer only, at 9.45am and 2.45pm from Bassin de la Villette.

PARIS CANAL CROISIÈRES Map pp428-9

☎ 01 42 40 96 97; www.pariscanal.com; Bassin de la Villette, 19-21 quai de la Loire, 19e; adult/4-11yr/senior & 12-25 yr €16/9/13, under 4 yr free; ☺ mid-Mar–mid-Nov; Ⓜ Jaurès or Musée d'Orsay
This outfit has 2½-hour cruises from quai Anatole France (7e), northwest of Musée d'Orsay, at 9.30am and departing from Parc de la Villette for the return trip at 2.30pm.

RIVER CRUISES
BATEAUX-MOUCHES Map pp426-7

☎ 01 42 25 96 10; www.bateauxmouches.com in French; Port de la Conférence, 8e; adult/senior & 4-12 yr €8/4, under 4 yr free; ☺ mid-Mar–mid-Nov; Ⓜ Alma Marceau
On the Right Bank just east of Pont de l'Alma, the most famous river-boat company in Paris runs 1000-seat tour boats, still the largest on the Seine. Cruises (70 minutes) run at 11am, 2.30pm, 4pm, 6pm and 9pm mid-March to mid-November, with additional winter cruises available, depending on demand. Commentary is in six languages.

BATEAUX PARISIENS Map pp434-5

☎ 01 46 99 43 13; www.bateauxparisiens .com; Port de la Bourdonnais, 7e; adult/3-11 yr €9.50/4.50, under 3 yr free; ☺ every ½hr 10am-10.30pm Apr-Sep, hourly 10am-10pm Oct-Mar; Ⓜ Pont de l'Alma
From its base northwest of the Eiffel Tower, Bateaux Parisiens runs one-hour river circuits with recorded commentary in 13 different languages.

LA MARINA DE PARIS Map pp434-5

☎ 01 43 43 40 30; www.marinadebercy.com; port de Solferino, quai Anatole France, 7e; Ⓜ Musée d'Orsay
This company offers lunch cruises at 12.15pm (€49) and dinner cruises at 6.15pm (€59) and 9pm (€89). They last about 2¼ hours and a menu for those under 12 (€39) is available at all meals.

VEDETTES DU PONT NEUF Map pp436-7

☎ 01 46 33 98 38; www.pontneuf.net; square du Vert Galant, 1er; adult/4-12 yr €10/5; ☺ every ½hr 10am-noon, 1.30-8pm & 9-10.30pm Mar-Oct; Ⓜ Pont Neuf
Vedettes du Pont Neuf, whose home dock is at the far western tip of the Île de la Cité

(1er), has one-hour boat excursions year-round. From November to February there are 12 departures from 10.30am to 10pm Monday to Thursday and 14 departures until 10.30pm Friday to Sunday.

Bus
BALABUS

☎ 0 892 68 77 14 in French, 0 892 68 41 14 in English; www.ratp.fr; €1.40 or 1 metro/bus ticket; ☺ departures 12.30-8pm Sun Apr-Sep
In season this RATP bus designed for tourists follows a 50-minute route from Gare de Lyon (Map pp446–7) to La Défense (Map p155), passing many of central Paris' most famous sights.

CITYRAMA Map pp426-7

☎ 01 44 55 61 00; www.graylineparis.com; 2 rue des Pyramides, 1er; adult/4-11 yr €17/8.50; ☺ tours 10 & 11.30am, 1.30 & 3.30pm Apr-Oct, 10 & 11.30am, 2pm Nov-Mar; Ⓜ Tuileries
Located just opposite the western end of the Louvre, Cityrama runs 1½-hour tours of the city, accompanied by taped commentaries in 16 languages, between three and four times a day year-round.

L'OPEN TOUR Map pp426-7

☎ 01 42 66 56 56; www.paris-opentour.com; 13 rue Auber, 9e; 1 day adult/4-11 yr €25/12, 2 consecutive days €28/12; Ⓜ Havre Caumartin or Opéra
L'Open Tour runs open-deck buses along four circuits (central Paris, 2¼ hours; Montmartre–Grands Boulevards, 1¼ hours; Bastille–Bercy, one hour; and Montparnasse–St-Germain, one hour) daily year-round. You can jump on and off at more than 50 stops. On the 'Grand Tour' of central Paris, with some 20 stops on both sides of the river between Notre Dame and the Eiffel Tower, buses depart every 10 to 15 minutes from 9.20am to 8pm April to October and every 25 to 30 minutes from 9.30am to 6pm November to March. Holders of the **Paris Visite card** (p369) pay €21 for a one-day pass.

Walking
If your French is up to scratch, the sky's the limit on specialised and themed walking tours available in Paris. Both *Pariscope* and *Officiel des Spectacles* (p258) list a number of themed walks (usually €10) each week

under the heading 'Conférences' or 'Visites Conférences'. They are almost always informative and entertaining, particularly those run by **Paris Passé, Présent** (☎ 01 42 58 95 99) and **Écoute du Passé** (☎ 01 42 80 25 20).

PARIS WALKS

☎ 01 48 09 21 40; www.paris-walks.com; adult/under 15 yr/student under 21 from €10/5/8
This long-established and well-received outfit has tours in English of several different districts, including Montmartre at 10.30am on Sunday and Wednesday (leaving from metro Abbesses, Map p432) and the Marais at 10.30am on Tuesday and 2.30pm on Sunday (departing from metro St-Paul, Map pp436–7). There are other tours focusing on people and themes, eg Hemingway, Medieval Paris, fashion, the French Revolution and, of course, the Da Vinci Code (p160).

LOUVRE & LES HALLES

Drinking p239; Eating p179; Shopping p283; Sleeping p309

The fascinating and complex **1er arrondissement** contains some of the most important sights in Paris for visitors. And while there are some who frown on the area's wild side, it remains a place where history and culture embrace on the banks of the Seine.

Sculptures merge with trees, grassy lawns, flowers, pools and fountains, while casual strollers lose themselves in the lovely promenade stretching from the gardens of the Tuileries to the square courtyard of the Louvre. A few metres away, under the arcades of the rue de Rivoli, the pace quickens with bustling shops and chaotic traffic. Parallel to rue de Rivoli, rue St-Honoré runs from place Vendôme to Les Halles, leaving in its wake the Comédie Française and the manicured gardens of the Palais Royal. Opulent, affected, but anxious to please, this street combines classic style with new trends, and tasteful colours and pure lines with a quiet atmosphere.

The Forum des Halles and rue St-Denis seem kilometres away but are already visible, soliciting unwary passers-by with bright lights and jostling crowds. The mostly pedestrian zone between the Centre Pompidou and the Forum des Halles (with rue Étienne Marcel to the north and rue de Rivoli to the south) is filled with people day and night, just as it was for the 850-odd years when part of it served as Paris' main *halles* (marketplace).

The Bourse (Stock Exchange) is the financial heart of the **2e arrondissement** to the north, the Sentier district the centre of the city's rag trade and the Opéra its ode to music and dance. From rue de la Paix, where glittering jewellery shops display their wares, to blvd Poissonnière and blvd de Bonne Nouvelle, where stalls and fast-food outlets advertise with garish neon signs, this arrondissement is a real hotchpotch.

Banks and insurance agencies have head offices in solid, elegant 19th-century buildings here, and business and finance types in smart suits abound. The surrounds and atmosphere change as soon as you hit rue d'Aboukir or rue du Sentier. Retail and wholesale outlets and clothing workshops are alive to the sound of haggling.

This arrondissement is a busy place during the week, its neighbourhoods divided

Sights

LOUVRE & LES HALLES

FINDING YOURSELF IN PARIS

In Paris, when a building is put up in a location where they've run out of consecutive street numbers, a new address is formed by fusing the number of an adjacent building with the notation *bis* (twice), *ter* (thrice) or even *quater* (four times). Therefore, the street numbers 17bis and 89ter are the equivalent of 17a and 89b in English.

The *portes cochères* (street doors) of most apartment buildings in Paris can be opened only if someone has given you the *digicode* (entry code), which is usually alphanumeric (eg 26A10) and changed periodically; the days of the concierges, who would vet every caller before allowing them in, are well and truly over. In some buildings the *digicode* device is deactivated during the day but to get in (or out) you still have to push a button (usually marked *porte*) to release the electric catch.

The doors of many apartments are unmarked: the occupants' names are nowhere in sight and there isn't even an apartment number. To know which door to knock on, you'll usually be given cryptic instructions, such as *cinquième étage, premier à gauche* (5th floor, first on the left) or *troisième étage, droite droite* (3rd floor, turn right twice).

In France (and in this book), the 1st floor is the floor above the *rez-de-chaussée* (ground floor).

by a thin line; you only need cross the street to find yourself in an area characterised by a completely different look, feel and rhythm. On weekends, most of the hustle and bustle is in the areas around rue Étienne Marcel.

ARC DE TRIOMPHE DU CARROUSEL
Map pp436-7

place du Carrousel, 1er; M **Palais Royal-Musée du Louvre**
Erected by Napoleon to celebrate his battlefield successes of 1805, this triumphal arch, which is set in the Jardin du Carrousel at the eastern end of the Jardin des Tuileries, was once crowned by the ancient Greek sculpture called *The Horses of St Mark's,* 'borrowed' from the portico of St Mark's in Venice by Napoleon but returned after his defeat at Waterloo in 1815. The replacement quadriga (the two-wheeled chariot drawn by four horses on the top) was added in 1828 and celebrates the return of the Bourbons to the French throne after Napoleon's downfall. The sides of the arch are adorned with depictions of Napoleonic victories and eight pink marble columns, atop each of which stands a soldier of the emperor's Grande Armée.

BOURSE DE COMMERCE Map pp436-7
☎ **01 55 65 55 65; 2 rue de Viarmes, 1er; admission free;** ⏱ **9am-6pm Mon-Fri;** M **Les Halles**
At one time the city's grain market, the circular Trade Exchange was capped with a

copper dome in 1811. The murals running along internal walls bellow the galleries show French trade and industry through the ages. They were painted in 1889 and restored in 1998.

CABINET DES MÉDAILLES ET MONNAIES Map pp428-9
☎ **01 53 79 53 79; www.bnf.fr; 58 rue de Richelieu, 2e; admission free;** ⏱ **1-5.45pm Mon-Fri, 1-4.45pm Sat, noon-6pm Sun;** M **Bourse**
Housed in the original home of the Bibliothèque Nationale de France before it moved to its high-tech headquarters in the 13e arrondissement more than a decade ago is this enormous hoard of coins, medals and tokens numbering more than 500,000. There's also an important collection of antiques, including items confiscated during the French Revolution from Ste-Chapelle and the abbey at St-Denis, including the so-called Dagobert's Throne, dating from the 7th century, on which French kings were once crowned.

CENTRE POMPIDOU Map pp436-7
☎ **01 44 78 12 33; www.centrepompidou.fr; place Georges Pompidou, 4e;** M **Rambuteau**
The Centre National d'Art et de Culture Georges Pompidou (Georges Pompidou National Centre of Art & Culture) is the most successful cultural centre in the world. An €85 million renovation completed at the start of the new millennium gave the cen-

Île St-Louis

tre a new look, expanded exhibition space and created a new cinema, audiovisual centre, dance and theatre venues and a posh restaurant – and succeeded in bringing in even bigger crowds.

The Centre Pompidou, also known as the Centre Beaubourg, has amazed and delighted visitors since it was inaugurated in 1977, not just for its outstanding collection of modern art but for its radical architectural statement (p39). But it all began to look somewhat *démodé* by the late 1990s, hence the refit.

The **Forum du Centre Pompidou** (admission free; 🕐 11am-10pm Wed-Mon), the open space at ground level, has temporary exhibits and information desks. The 4th and 5th floors of the centre exhibit a fraction of the 50,000-plus works of the **Musée National d'Art Moderne** (MNAM; National Museum of Modern Art; adult/senior & 18-25 yr €10/8, under 18 yr free, 1st Sun of the month free; 🕐 11am-9pm Wed-Mon), France's national collection of art dating from 1905 onward, and including the work of the Surrealists and Cubists as well as pop art and contemporary works.

The huge **Bibliothèque Publique d'Information** (BPI; 🕿 01 44 78 12 33; www.bpi.fr in French; 🕐 noon-10pm Mon & Wed-Fri, 11am-10pm Sat & Sun), entered from rue du Renard, takes up part of the 1st as well as the entire 2nd and 3rd floors of the centre. The 6th floor has two galleries for **temporary exhibitions** (usually now included in the entrance fee) and a restaurant from the trendy Costes stable called **Georges** (🕿 01 44 78 47 99; 🕐 noon-2am) with panoramic views of Paris, which is perhaps best visited for a mid-afternoon drink. There are **cinemas** (adult/senior & 18-25 yr €5.50/3.50) and other entertainment venues on the 1st floor and in the basement.

West of the centre, **Place Georges Pompidou** and the nearby pedestrian streets attract buskers, musicians, jugglers and mime artists, and can be a lot of fun. South of the centre on place Igor Stravinsky, the fanciful **mechanical fountains** (Map pp436–7) of skeletons, dragons, treble clefs and a big pair of ruby-red lips, created by Jean Tinguely and Niki de St-Phalle, are a positive delight.

The **Atelier Brancusi** (Map pp436–7; 55 rue Rambuteau, 4e; 🕐 2-6pm Wed-Mon), across place Georges Pompidou to the west of the main building, was designed by Renzo Piano and contains almost 140 examples of the work of Romanian-born sculptor Constantin

Brancusi (1876–1957) as well as drawings, paintings and glass photographic plates. A MNAM ticket allows entry.

The **Défenseur du Temps** (Defender of Time; Map pp436–7; 8 rue Bernard de Clairvaux; 🕐 9am-10pm), a mechanical clock erected in 1979 whose protagonist does battle on the hour with the elements (air, water and earth in the form of a phoenix, crab and dragon), is a block north of the Centre Pompidou just off rue Brantôme (3e), in a development known as Quartier de l'Horloge. Particularly lively combat takes place at noon, 6pm and 10pm when our hero is attacked by all three 'villains'.

ÉGLISE ST-EUSTACHE Map pp436-7

🕿 01 42 36 31 05; www.saint-eustache.org in French; 2 impasse St-Eustache, 1er; 🕐 9am-7.30pm; Ⓜ Les Halles

This majestic church, one of the most beautiful in Paris, is just north of the gardens next to the Forum des Halles. Constructed between 1532 and 1640, St-Eustache is primarily Gothic, though a neoclassical façade was added on the western side in the mid-18th century. Inside, there are some exceptional Flamboyant Gothic arches holding up the ceiling of the chancel, though most of the ornamentation is Renaissance and classical. Above the western entrance, the gargantuan organ with 101 stops and 8000 pipes dating from 1854 is used for concerts (long a tradition here) and at Sunday Mass (11am and 6pm). There's a 'free' audioguide available, though a donation of €3 is suggested.

ÉGLISE ST-GERMAIN L'AUXERROIS
Map pp436-7

🕿 01 42 60 13 96; 2 place du Louvre, 1er; 🕐 8am-8pm; Ⓜ Louvre-Rivoli or Pont Neuf

Built between the 13th and 16th centuries in a mixture of Gothic and Renaissance styles and with similar dimensions and ground plans to those of Notre Dame, this once royal parish church stands on a site at the eastern end of the Louvre that has been used for Christian worship since about AD 500. After being mutilated in the 18th century by churchmen intent on 'modernisation', and damaged during the Revolution, the church was restored by the Gothic Revivalist architect Eugène Viollet-le-Duc in the mid-19th century. It boasts some fine stained glass.

FORUM DES HALLES Map pp436-7

☎ 01 44 76 96 56; 1 rue Pierre Lescaut, 1er; Ⓜ Les Halles or Châtelet les Halles

Les Halles, the city's main wholesale food market, occupied the area just south of the Église St-Eustache from the early 12th century until 1969, when it was moved lox, stock and lettuce leaf to the southern suburb of Rungis near Orly. In its place, this unspeakably ugly, four-level underground shopping centre was constructed in the glass-and-chrome style of the early 1970s.

Inside the Forum des Halles is the **Pavillon des Arts** (☎ 01 42 33 82 50; 101 rue Rambuteau, 1er; adult/14-26 yr/senior & student €5.40/2.50/4, under 14 yr free; Ⓨ 11.30am-6.30pm Tue-Sun), with temporary exhibits and a popular rooftop **garden** with a rather stunning sculpture by Henri de Miller (1953–99) called *Listen,* an oversized human head with its ear to the ground. In the warmer months, street musicians, fire-eaters and other performers display their talents here, especially at **place Jean du Bellay**, which is adorned by a multitiered Renaissance fountain, the **Fontaine des Innocents** (1549). It is named after the Cimetière des Innocents, a cemetery formerly on this site from which two million skeletons were disinterred after the Revolution, and transferred to the **Catacombes** (p121), south of the Cimetière du Montparnasse in the 14e. A block south of the fountain is **rue de la Ferronnerie**, where erstwhile Huguenot Henri IV was stabbed to death in 1610 by a Catholic fanatic, while passing house No 11 in his carriage.

JARDIN DES TUILERIES Map pp426-7 & Map pp434-5

☎ 01 40 20 90 43; Ⓨ 7am-9pm late Mar-late Sep, 7.30am-7.30pm late Sep-late Mar; Ⓜ Tuileries or Concorde

The formal, 28-hectare Tuileries Garden, which begins just west of the Jardin du Carrousel, was laid out in its present form, more or less, in the mid-17th century by André Le Nôtre, who also created the gardens at **Vaux-le-Vicomte** (p347) and **Versailles** (p336). The Tuileries soon became the most fashionable spot in Paris for parading about in one's finery; today it is a favourite of joggers and forms part of the Banks of the Seine World Heritage Site as listed by Unesco in 1991.

The **Voie Triomphale** (Triumphal Way), also called the Axe Historique (Historic Axis), the western continuation of the Tuiler-

ies' east–west axis, follows the av des Champs-Élysées to the Arc de Triomphe and, ultimately, to the Grande Arche in the skyscraper district of **La Défense** (p155).

JEU DE PAUME Map pp426-7

☎ 01 47 03 12 52; www.jeudepaume.org; 1 place de la Concorde, 1er; adult/senior, student & 13-18 yr €6/3; Ⓨ noon-9pm Tue, noon-7pm Wed-Fri, 10am-7pm Sat & Sun; Ⓜ Concorde

The Galerie du Jeu de Paume – Site Concorde (Jeu de Paume National Gallery at Concorde) is housed in an erstwhile *jeu de paume* (real, or royal, tennis court), built in 1861 during the reign of Napoleon III, in the northwestern corner of the Jardin des Tuileries. Once the home of a good part of France's national collection of impressionist art, which is now housed across the Seine in the **Musée d'Orsay** (p124), the two-storey Jeu de Paume now stages innovative exhibitions of contemporary art. A new branch of the gallery, the **Jeu de Paume – Site Sully** (p106) in the Hôtel de Sully in the Marais concentrates on top-notch photography. A joint ticket to both galleries costs €8 for adults and €4 for seniors, students and 13- to 18-year-olds.

MUSÉE DU LOUVRE Map pp436-7

☎ 01 40 20 53 17; www.louvre.fr; permanent collections/permanent collections & temporary exhibits €8.50/13, after 6pm Wed & Fri €6/11, permanent collections free for under 18 yr & after 6pm Fri for under 26 yr, 1st Sun of the month free; Ⓨ 9am-6pm Mon, Thu, Sat & Sun, 9am-9.45pm Wed & Fri; Ⓜ Palais Royal-Musée du Louvre

The vast Palais du Louvre was constructed as a fortress by Philippe-Auguste in the early 13th century and rebuilt in the mid-16th century for use as a royal residence. The Revolutionary Convention turned it into a national museum in 1793.

The paintings, sculptures and artefacts on display in the Louvre Museum have been assembled by French governments over the past five centuries. Among them are works of art and artisanship from all over Europe and collections of Assyrian, Etruscan, Greek, Coptic and Islamic art and antiquities. The Louvre's *raison d'être* is to present Western art from the Middle Ages to about the year 1848 (at which point the Musée d'Orsay across the river takes over) as well as the works of ancient civilisations that formed the starting point for Western art, but in recent years it has acquired, and begun to exhibit, other important collections as well.

When the museum opened in the late 18th century it contained 2500 paintings and *objets d'art;* today some 35,000 are on display. The 'Grand Louvre' project inaugurated by the late President Mitterrand in 1989 doubled the museum's exhibition space, and new and renovated galleries have opened in recent years devoted to *objets d'art* such as Sèvres porcelain and the crown jewels of Louis XV (Room 66, 1st floor, Apollo Gallery, Sully Wing), as well as primitive art collected from Africa, Asia, Australasia and the Americas (Rooms 1 to 8, ground floor, Denon Wing), which is in the process of being moved to the new Musée du Quai Branly.

Daunted by the richness and sheer size of the place (the side facing the Seine is 700m long and it is said that it would take nine months to see – well, glance at – every piece of art here), both local people and visitors often find the prospect of an afternoon at a smaller museum far more inviting, meaning the Louvre may be the most actively avoided museum in the world. (Although judging from the number of visitors clutching *The Da Vinci Code*, p160, under their arms, it's gained a new lease of life in recent years, and not necessarily for the right reasons.) Eventually, most people do their duty and come, but many leave overwhelmed, unfulfilled, exhausted and frustrated at having got lost on their way to Da Vinci's *La Joconde,* better known as *Mona Lisa* (Room 6, 1st floor, Salle de la Joconde, Denon Wing; below). Since it takes several serious visits to get anything more than a brief glimpse of the works on offer, your best bet – after checking out a few you really want to see – is to choose a particular period or section of the Louvre and pretend that the rest is in another museum somewhere across town.

The most famous works from antiquity include the *Seated Scribe* (Room 22, 1st floor, Sully Wing), the *Code of Hammurabi* (Room 3, ground floor, Richelieu Wing) and that armless duo, the *Venus de Milo* (Room 12, ground floor, Sully Wing) and the *Winged Victory of Samothrace* (opposite Room 1, 1st floor, Denon Wing). From the Renaissance, don't miss Michelangelo's *The Dying Slave* (ground floor, Michelangelo Gallery, Denon Wing) and works by Raphael, Botticelli and Titian (Denon Wing, 1st floor). French masterpieces of the 19th century include Ingres' *The Turkish Bath* (Room 60, 2nd floor, Sully Wing), Géricault's *The Raft of the Medusa* (Room 77, 1st floor, Denon Wing) and works by Corot, Delacroix and Fragonard (2nd floor, Denon Wing).

The main entrance and ticket windows in the Cour Napoléon are covered by the 21m-high **Grande Pyramide**, a glass pyramid designed by the Chinese-born American architect IM Pei. You can avoid the queues outside the pyramid or at the Porte des Lions entrance by entering the Louvre complex via the Carrousel du Louvre entrance (Map pp436–7), at 99 rue de Rivoli, or by following the 'Musée du Louvre' exit from

LOUVRE & LES HALLES

MONA LISA: COLD, LONELY & LOVELY

Are you warm, are you real, Mona Lisa
Or just a cold and lonely, lovely work of art?

Jay Livingston & Ray Evans 1950

So much has been written, most recently (and most widely read) by Dan Brown in his best-selling *The Da Vinci Code* (p160), about the painting the French call *La Joconde* and the Italians *La Gioconda* yet so little has been known of the lady behind that enigmatic smile. For centuries admirers speculated on everything from the possibility that the subject was mourning the death of a loved one to that she might have been in love – or in bed – with her portraitist.

Mona (actually *monna* in Italian) is a contraction of *madonna* while Gioconda is the feminine form of the surname Giocondo. With the emergence of several clues in recent years, it is almost certain that the subject was Lisa Gherardini (1479–1539?), the 24-year-old wife of Florentine merchant Franceso del Giocondo and that the painting was done between 1503 and 1507. At the same time, tests done in 2005 with 'emotion recognition' computer software suggest that the smile on 'Madam Lisa' is at least 83% happy. And one other point remains unequivocally certain despite occasional suggestions to the contrary: she was not the lover of Leonardo, who preferred his *Vitruvian Man* to his *Mona*.

Sculpture outside Église St-Eustache (p99)

the Palais Royal–Musée du Louvre metro station. Those in the know buy their tickets in advance from the ticket machines in the Carrousel du Louvre, online or by ringing ☎ 0 892 68 36 22 or 0 825 34 63 46, or from the *billeteries* (ticket offices) of **Fnac** (p259) for an extra €1.50 or so, and walk straight in without queuing. Tickets are valid for the whole day, so you can come and go as you please. They are also valid for the **Musée National Eugène Delacroix** (p120) on the day.

The Louvre is divided into four sections: the Sully, Denon and Richelieu Wings and Hall Napoléon. **Sully** creates the four sides of the Cour Carrée (literally 'square courtyard') at the eastern end of the complex. **Denon** stretches along the Seine to the south; **Richelieu** is the northern wing along rue de Rivoli.

The split-level public area under the Grande Pyramide is known as the **Hall Napoléon** (🕑 9am-10pm Wed-Mon). The hall has an exhibit on the history of the Louvre, a bookshop, a restaurant, a café, auditoriums for concerts, lectures and films, and **CyberLouvre** (🕑 10am-4.45pm Wed-Mon), an Internet research centre with online access to some 20,000 works of art. The centrepiece of the **Carrousel du Louvre** (☎ 01 40 20 67 30; 99 rue de Rivoli, 1er; 🕑 8.30am-11pm), the shopping centre that runs underground from the pyramid to the **Arc de Triomphe du Carrousel** (p98), is a **pyramide inversée** (inverted glass pyramid), also created by Pei.

Free English-language maps of the complex (titled *Louvre Plan/Information*) can be obtained from the information desk in the centre of the Hall Napoléon. Excellent publications to guide you if you are doing the Louvre on your own are *Destination Louvre: A Guided Tour* (€7.50), *Visit the Louvre: a Guide to the Masterpieces* (€8) and the hefty, 475-page *Guide to the Louvre* (€17). An attractive and useful memento is the DVD entitled *Louvre: The Visit* (€26). All are available from the museum bookshop.

English-language **guided tours** (🕑 01 40 20 52 63) lasting 1½ hours depart from the area under the Grande Pyramide, marked 'Acceuil des Groupes' (Groups Welcome), at 11am, 2pm and 3.45pm Monday to Saturday. Tickets cost €5 in addition to the cost of admission. Groups are limited to 30 people, so it's a good idea to sign up at least 30 minutes before departure time.

Self-paced audioguide tours in six languages with 1½ hours of commentary can be rented for €5 under the pyramid at the entrance to each wing.

MUSÉE DU LOUVRE: OTHER MUSEUMS Map pp436-7

The Palais du Louvre contains three other museums run by the **Union Centrale des Arts Décoratifs** (UCAD; ☎ 01 44 55 57 50; www.ucad .fr in French; 107 rue de Rivoli, 1er; adult/18-25 yr €6/4.50, under 18 free; 🕑 11am-6pm Tue, Thu & Fri, 11am-9pm Wed, 10am-6pm Sat & Sun; Ⓜ Palais Royal-Musée du Louvre) in the Rohan Wing of the Louvre, which were revamped or created under the Grand Louvre project. Admission includes entry to all three museums.

The **Musée des Arts Décoratifs** (Applied Arts Museum) on the 3rd floor displays furniture, jewellery and such *objets d'art* as ceramics and glassware from the Middle Ages and the Renaissance through the Art Nouveau and Art Deco periods to modern times. Some sections may be closed as the museum is undergoing extensive renovations.

The **Musée de la Publicité** (Advertising Museum), which shares the 3rd floor, has some 100,000 posters dating as far back as the 13th century, and innumerable promotional materials touting everything from 19th-century elixirs and early radio advertisements to Air France and electronic publicity. Only certain items are on exhibit at any one time; most of the rest of the space is given over to special exhibitions.

The **Musée de la Mode et du Textile** (Museum of Fashion & Textiles) on the 1st and 2nd floors has some 16,000 costumes dating from the 16th century till today, including *haute couture* creations by the likes of Dior and Chanel. Most of the outfits are warehoused, however, and only displayed during unusual themed exhibitions.

ORANGERIE Map pp426-7

☎ 01 42 97 49 21; www.musee-orangerie.fr; Jardin des Tuileries, 1er; ⏰ 12.30-7pm Wed-Mon, 12.30-10pm Fri; Ⓜ Concorde

The **Musée de l'Orangerie** (Orangerie Museum) in the southwestern corner of the Jardin des Tuileries is, with the Jeu de Paume, all that remains of the once palatial Palais des Tuileries, which was razed during the **Paris Commune** (p78) in 1871. It reopened in May 2006 after extensive renovations and exhibits important impressionist works, including a series of Monet's *Decorations des Nymphéas* (Water Lilies) in two huge oval rooms purpose-built on the artist's instructions, as well as paintings by Cézanne, Matisse, Picasso, Renoir, Sisley, Soutine and Utrillo.

PALAIS ROYAL Map pp436-7

place du Palais Royal, 1er; Ⓜ Palais Royal-Musée du Louvre

The Royal Palace, which accommodated a young Louis XIV for a time in the 1640s, lies to the north of place du Palais Royal and the Louvre. Construction was begun in the 17th century by Cardinal Richelieu, though most

of the present neoclassical complex dates from the latter part of the 18th century. It now contains the governmental **Conseil d'État** (State Council) and is closed to the public.

The colonnaded building facing place André Malraux is the **Comédie Française** (p269), founded in 1680 and the world's oldest national theatre.

Just north of the palace is the **Jardin du Palais Royal** (Map pp428-9 & Map pp436-7; ⏰ 7.30am-10.15pm Apr & May, 7am-11pm Jun-Aug, 7am-9.30pm Sep, 7.30am-8.30pm Oct-Mar), a lovely park surrounded by two arcades. Nowadays **Galerie de Valois** on the eastern side shelters designer fashion shops, art galleries and jewellers, though Guillaumot Graveur, an engraver's at Nos 151 to 154, has been trading here since 1785. **Galerie de Montpensier** on the western side has a few old shops remaining, selling things like colourful Légion d'Honneur-style medals (shops No 6 to 8) and lead toy soldiers (shops No 13 to 15). **Le Grand Véfour** (p180), one of Paris' oldest and most illustrious restaurants, is at the northern end of the park. At the southern end there's a controversial **sculpture** of black-and-white striped columns of various heights by Daniel Buren. It was started in 1986, interrupted by irate Parisians and finished – following the intervention of the Ministry of Culture and Communication – in 1995. The story goes (invented by Buren?) that if you toss a coin and it lands on one of the columns your wish will come true. Don't miss the zany Palais Royal-Musée du Louvre **metro entrance** (p104) on the place du Palais Royal.

PLACE VENDÔME Map pp426-7

Ⓜ Tuileries or Opéra

This octagonal square, and the arcaded and colonnaded buildings around it, was built between 1687 and 1721. In March 1796, Napoleon married Josephine, Viscountess Beauharnais, in the building that's at No 3 in the southwest corner. Today, the buildings around the square house the posh

Sights

LOUVRE & LES HALLES

TOP FIVE: LOUVRE & LES HALLES

- Centre Pompidou (p98)
- Église St-Eustache (p99)
- Jardin des Tuileries (p100)
- Musée du Louvre (p100)
- Palais Royal (left)

ART IN THE METRO

Art cannot just be seen in the many museums and art galleries of Paris, it is all around you – even in metro stations. Few underground railway systems are as convenient, as reasonably priced or, the better stations at least, as elegant as the Paris Métropolitain. About 175 metro stations were given a face-lift to mark the centenary of the world-famous metro system in 2000. This upgrade resulted in their lighting being improved, permanent decorations being spruced up and/or rearranged and new ones being added. And the work has continued apace at still more stations ever since.

Line 14 – the so-called 'Météor' between Bibliothèque and Madeleine stations – is a particularly arty one, especially on the way down to the platforms, where there is art projected on the walls at different levels. At varying times, other stations and lines might have temporary exhibitions (such as the comic-strip theme throughout the stations on line 4 between Porte d'Orléans and Porte de Clignancourt that was showing at the time of researching this guide).

The following list is just a sample of the most interesting stations from an artistic perspective. The specific platform is mentioned for those stations served by more than one line.

Abbesses (Map p432; line 12) The noodle-like pale-green metalwork and glass canopy of the station entrance is one of the finest examples of the work of Hector Guimard (1867–1942), the celebrated French Art Nouveau architect whose signature style once graced most metro stations. For a complete list of the metro stations that retain entrances designed by Guimard see www.parisinconnu.com.

Arts et Métiers (Map pp428–9; line 11 platform) The copper panelling, portholes and mechanisms of this station recall Jules Verne, Captain Nemo and the nearby Musée des Arts et Métiers.

Bastille (Map pp440–1; line 5 platform) A large ceramic fresco features scenes taken from newspaper engravings published during the Revolution.

Bibliothèque (Map p449; line 14) This enormous station – all screens, steel and glass, and the terminus of the high-speed Météor line that opened in 1998 – resembles a hi-tech cathedral.

Bonne Nouvelle (Map pp428–9; platforms on lines 8 & 9) The theme here is cinema.

Carrefour Pleyel (line 13) This station just south of St-Denis (Map p157) and named in honour of composer and piano-maker Ignace Joseph Pleyel (1757–1831) is reconfigured as a 'contemporary musical instrument', with the rumble of the trains the 'music' and, no doubt, commuters the 'picks'.

Champs-Élysées Clemenceau (Map pp426–7; transfer corridor between lines 1 & 13) The elegant frescoes in blue, enamelled faïence recall Portuguese *azulejos* tiles and so they should: they were installed as part of a cultural exchange between Paris and Lisbon.

Cluny-La Sorbonne (Map pp436–7; line 10 platform) A large ceramic mosaic replicates the signatures of intellectuals, artists and scientists from the Latin Quarter through history.

Concorde (Map pp426–7; line 12 platform) On the walls of the station what look like children's building blocks in white and blue ceramic are 45,000 tiles that spell out the text of the *Déclaration des Droits de l'Homme et du Citoyen* (Declaration of the Rights of Man and of the Citizen), the document setting forth the principles of the French Revolution.

Europe (Map pp426–7; line 3) What else should be the focus but Europe? Displays are changed regularly but in the past it's been very hi-tech, with more TV screens than an electronics superstore broadcasting programs from across the Continent and the British Isles in languages from Greek to Finnish.

Louvre-Rivoli (Map pp436–7; line 1 platform & corridor) Statues, bas-reliefs and photographs offer a small taste of what to expect at the Musée du Louvre above ground.

Palais Royal-Musée du Louvre (Map pp436–7) The zany entrance on the place du Palais Royal (a kind of back-to-the-future look at the Guimard entrances), designed by young artist Jean-Michel Othoniel, is made up of 800 red, blue, amber and violet glass balls and resembles a crown.

Parmentier (Map pp428–9; line 3) The theme in this station is agricultural crops, particularly the potato since it was the station's namesake, Antoine-Auguste Parmentier (1737–1817), who brought the potato into fashion in France. Today, any dish with the word *parmentier* has potatoes in some form in it.

Pont Neuf (Map pp436–7; line 7) With the old mint and the Musée de la Monnaie de Paris just above, the focus here is on medals and coins.

Hôtel Ritz Paris (p323) and some of the city's most fashionable boutiques. The **Ministère de la Justice** (Ministry of Justice; Map pp426–7) has been at Nos 11 to 13 since 1815.

In the centre, the 43.5m-tall **Colonne Vendôme** (Vendôme Column) consists of a stone core wrapped in a 160m-long bronze spiral that's made from 1250 Austrian and Russian cannons captured by Napoleon at the Battle of Austerlitz in 1805. The 425 bas-reliefs on the spiral celebrate Napoleon's victories between 1805 and 1807. The statue on top depicts Napoleon as a Roman emperor.

TOUR JEAN SANS PEUR Map pp436-7
☎ 01 40 26 20 28; www.tourjeansanspeur.com in French; 20 rue Étienne Marcel, 2e; adult/student & 7-18 yr €5/3; ☺ 1.30-6pm Wed, Sat & Sun Apr-Oct, 1.30-6pm Tue-Sun Nov-Mar; Ⓜ Étienne Marcel
The Gothic, 29m-high Tower of John the Fearless was built as part of a splendid mansion by the duke of Bourgogne in the early 15th century so he could hide at the very top, safe from his enemies. It is one of the very few examples of feudal military architecture extant in Paris. Visitors can ascend the 140 steps of the spiral staircase to the turret on top.

TOUR ST-JACQUES Map pp436-7
square de la Tour St-Jacques, 4e; Ⓜ Châtelet
The Flamboyant Gothic 52m-high St James Tower just north of place du Châtelet is all that remains of the Église St-Jacques la Boucherie, which was built by the powerful butchers' guild in 1523 as a starting point for pilgrims setting out for the shrine of St James at Santiago de Compostela in Spain. It was demolished by the Directory in 1797 but the bell tower was spared so it could be used to drop globules of molten lead in the manufacture of shot. The tower is topped by a meteorological station and is not open to the public.

MARAIS & BASTILLE
Drinking p240; Eating p183; Shopping p286; Sleeping p309

The Marais, the area of the Right Bank directly north of Île St-Louis, was exactly what its name in French implies – 'marsh' or 'swamp' – until the 13th century, when it was put to agricultural use. In the early 17th century, Henri IV built the place Royale (today's place des Vosges), turning the area into Paris' most fashionable residential district and attracting wealthy aristocrats who then erected their own luxurious private mansions and less expensive *pavillons* (smaller houses).

When the aristocracy moved out of Paris to Versailles and Faubourg St-Germain during the late 17th and the 18th centuries, the Marais and its town houses passed into the hands of ordinary Parisians. The 110-hectare area was given a major face-lift in the late 1960s and early '70s.

Centuries of history are inscribed on the façades and pediments of the **4e arrondissement** and in the narrow streets, alleys, porches and courtyards; today the Marais is one of the few neighbourhoods of Paris that still has most of its pre-Revolution architecture intact. These include the house at 3 rue Volta (Map pp436–7) in the 3e arrondissement, parts of which date back to 1292; the one at 51 rue de Montmorency (Map pp436–7) in the 3e dating back to 1407; and the half-timbered 16th-century building at 11 and 13 rue François Miron (Map pp436–7) in the 4e.

Though the Marais has become a coveted trendy address in recent years, it remains home to a long-established Jewish community and is the centre of Paris' gay life. At night the short walk from Beaubourg to the place des Vosges is intoxicating. The historic Jewish quarter – the so-called Pletzl – starts in rue des Rosiers then continues along rue Ste-Croix la Bretonnerie to rue du Temple; you'll also find a lot of gay and lesbian bars and restaurants in this area. Re-entering the urban bustle as rue St-Antoine becomes rue de Rivoli, the small, dark streets of the Marais seem like a distant memory. But you only have to cross the street at rue St-Paul or rue du Pont Louis-Philippe to experience something of the bourgeois and bohemian tranquillity of the Marais of the past.

The **3e arrondissement** contains a small corner of the Marais that has managed to remain friendly and picturesque. Noisy during the week, calm and languid on weekends, the opulent renovations of its period homes and the dictates of fashion haven't yet destroyed its soul. Rue du Temple and rue de Turenne move to the rhythm of clothing workshops, artisans and wholesalers. The tempo picks up along rue de Turbigo, rue

Detail of Institut du Monde Arabe (p115)

Réaumur and blvd de Sébastopol, and is perfectly offset by the place de la République. Business calls at all hours and the blvd du Temple, blvd des Filles du Calvaire and blvd Beaumarchais barely manage to contain the hive of activity. Properties on rue des Archives, rue Charlot, rue de Saintonge and rue de Bretagne require neither artifice nor restoration to reveal their lovely bas-reliefs, balustrades, courtyards and vaulted cellars. Suddenly, the tempo takes on an elegant nonchalance. The Musée Picasso and the Musée Carnavalet appear, and the Archives Nationales makes its presence felt.

After years as a run-down immigrant neighbourhood notorious for its high crime rate, the Bastille area has undergone a fair degree of gentrification, largely due to the opening of the Opéra Bastille back in 1989. The courtyards and alleyways of the **11e arrondissement** used to belong to artisans and labourers. When you went into a building or entered a cul-de-sac off rue du Faubourg St-Antoine, rue de Charonne or rue de la Roquette, you'd find workshops, factories and warehouses. The area thrived with cabinet makers, joiners, gilders, dressmakers and lace makers – a whole range of crafts, each with its characteristic activities and sounds. Today most of that's gone, replaced with artists and their lofts. But the old spirit lives on in some hidden parts of the 11e, and the areas to the east of place de la Bastille in particular retain their lively atmosphere and ethnicity.

ARCHIVES NATIONALES Map pp436-7

☎ 01 40 27 60 96; www.archivesnationales. culture.gouv.fr; 60 rue des Francs Bourgeois, 3e; Ⓜ Rambuteau

France's National Archives are housed in the Soubise wing of the impressive, early-18th-century Hôtel de Rohan-Soubise, which also contains the **Musée de l'Histoire de France** (Museum of French History; ☎ 01 40 27 60 96; 87 rue Vieille du Temple, 3e; adult/senior & 18-25 yr €3/2.30, under 18 yr free, 1st Sun of the month free; ⊗ 10am-12.30pm & 2-5.30pm Mon & Wed-Fri, 2-5.30pm Sat & Sun; Ⓜ Rambuteau or St-Paul), which has been undergoing ambitious renovations for some time but opens up part of its collection year-round. Here you'll find antique furniture and 18th-century paintings but primarily documents – everything from medieval incunabula and letters written by Joan of Arc to the wills of Louis XIV and Napoleon. The ceiling and walls of the interior are extravagantly painted and gilded in the rococo style; look out for the Monkey Cabinet, a simian-filled room painted by Christophe Huet in 1745.

ÉGLISE NOTRE DAME DE L'ESPÉRANCE Map pp440-1

☎ 01 40 21 49 39; 47 rue de la Roquette, 11e; ⊗ 8am-6.30pm; Ⓜ Bastille

If you're in the area (or feeling a bit guilty about that late night) head for the wonderful Church of Our Lady of Hope designed by Bruno Legrand in 1997. Startling both for its modern design and size (it stands 20m tall and is 11m wide), the interior is filled with all sorts of interesting elements and features, including Nicolas Alquin's *Croix d'Espérance* (Cross of Hope) made of an 18th-century oak beam and three gold squares representing the Trinity, and calligrapher Franck Lalou's fragments of the Gospel etched onto glass of the façade facing rue de la Roquette.

HÔTEL DE SULLY Map pp440-1

62 rue St-Antoine, 4e; Ⓜ St-Paul

This aristocratic mansion dating from the early 17th century was given a major face-lift in 1973. Today it houses the headquarters of the **Centre des Monuments Nationaux** (Monum; ☎ 01 44 61 20 00; www.monum .fr; ⊗ 9am-12.45pm & 2-6pm Mon-Thu,

9am-12.45pm & 2-5pm Fri), the body responsible for many of France's historical monuments (with lots of brochures and information available), as well as the **Jeu de Paume – Site Sully** (☎ 01 47 03 12 52; www .jeudepaume.org; adult/senior, student & 13-18 yr €5/2.5; ☼ noon-7pm Tue-Fri, 10am-7pm Sat & Sun), a branch of the more famous **Galerie de Jeu de Paume** (p100), with excellent rotating photographic exhibits. Visiting both galleries costs €8/4. The **Hôtel de Sully bookshop** (p289) is excellent, and the two **Renaissance-style courtyards** (p160) are worth the trip alone.

HÔTEL DE VILLE Map pp436-7
☎ 0 820 007 575, 01 42 76 50 49; www.paris.fr; place de l'Hôtel de Ville, 4e; Ⓜ Hôtel de Ville
After having been gutted during the Paris Commune of 1871, Paris' city hall was rebuilt in luxurious neo-Renaissance style from 1874 to 1882. The ornate façade is decorated with 108 statues of noteworthy Parisians. There's a **Salon d'Accueil** (Reception Hall; 29 rue de Rivoli, 4e; ☼ 10am-7pm Mon-Sat), which dispenses information and brochures and is used for temporary (and very popular) exhibitions, usually with a Paris theme.

The Hôtel de Ville faces majestic **place de l'Hôtel de Ville**, used since the Middle Ages for many of Paris' celebrations, rebellions, book-burnings and public executions. Known as place de Grève (Strand Sq) until 1830, it was in centuries past a favourite gathering place of the unemployed, which is why a strike is called *une grève* in French to thi_ day.

MAISON EUROPÉENNE DE LA PHOTOGRAPHIE Map pp436-7
☎ 01 44 78 75 00; www.mep-fr.org in French; 5-7 rue de Fourcy, 4e; adult/senior & 9-25 yr €6/3, under 9 free, 5-8pm Wed free; ☼ 11am-8pm Wed-Sun; Ⓜ St-Paul or Pont Marie
The European House of Photography, housed in the rather overwrought Hôtel Hénault de Cantorbe (which dates from the early 18th century, though you'd hardly know it now), has cutting-edge temporary exhibits (usually retrospectives on single photographers), as well as an enormous permanent collection on the history of photography and its connections with France. There are frequent showings of short films and documentaries on week-end afternoons.

MUSÉE CARNAVALET Map pp440-1
☎ 01 44 59 58 58; www.v1.paris.fr/musees /musee_carnavalet in French; 23 rue de Sévigné, 3e; temporary exhibits adult/14-25 yr/senior & student €7/3.50/5.50, permanent collections free, under 14 yr free; ☼ 10am-6pm Tue-Sun; Ⓜ St-Paul or Chemin Vert
This museum, subtitled Musée de l'Histoire de Paris (Paris History Museum), is housed in two *hôtels particuliers* (private mansions): the mid-16th-century, Renaissance-style Hôtel Carnavalet, home to the letter writer Madame de Sévigné from 1677 to 1696, and the Hôtel Le Peletier de St-Fargeau, which dates from the late 17th century.

AVOIDING MUSEUM FATIGUE

Warm-up exercises, half-hour breathers, a portable seat, bottled water and an energy-providing snack… It might sound as if you're preparing for a trek in the Alps, but these are some of the recommendations for tackling Paris' 140-odd museums. And with almost 30 major ones free of charge on at least one day of the week, the temptation to see more and more is greater than ever.

Take the Louvre: encompassing some 40 sq hectares, it has seven enormous departments spread over 60,000 sq metres of gallery space and almost 6 million visitors a year, all elbowing each other to see what they want to see in a limited amount of time. It's hardly surprising that many people feel worn out almost before they've entered the Cour Napoléon.

To avoid museum fatigue wear comfortable shoes and make use of the cloakrooms. Be aware that standing still and walking slowly promote tiredness; sit down as often as you can. Reflecting on the material and forming associations with it causes information to move from your short- to long-term memory; your experiences will thus amount to more than a series of visual 'bites'.

Tracking and timing studies suggest that museum-goers spend no more than 10 seconds viewing an exhibit and another 10 seconds reading the label as they try to take in as much as they can before succumbing to exhaustion. Your best bet in a large museum is to choose a particular period or section and forget the rest on this visit. Joining a guided tour of the highlights is another way to avoid museum fatigue.

The artefacts on display in the museum's sublime rooms chart the history of Paris from the Gallo-Roman period, in the museum's Orangerie section, to the 20th century. Some of the nation's most important documents, paintings and other objects from the French Revolution are here (Rooms 101 to 113), as is Fouquet's stunning Art Nouveau jewellery shop from the rue Royale (Room 142) and Marcel Proust's cork-lined bedroom from his apartment on blvd Haussmann (Room 147), where he wrote most of the 7350-page literary cycle *À la Recherche du Temps Perdu (Remembrance of Things Past)*.

MUSÉE COGNACQ-JAY Map pp436-7

☎ 01 40 27 07 21; www.paris.fr/musees/cognacq_jay in French; 8 rue Elzévir, 3e; permanent collections free; ⏰ 10am-6pm Tue-Sun; Ⓜ St-Paul or Chemin Vert

This museum in the Hôtel de Donon brings together oil paintings, pastels, sculpture, *objets d'art,* jewellery, porcelain and furniture from the 18th century. The displays were assembled by Ernest Cognacq (1839–1928), founder of La Samaritaine department store (now undergoing a five-year renovation) and his wife Louise Jay. Although Cognacq appreciated little of his collection, boasting to all who would listen that he had never visited the Louvre and was only acquiring collecting for the status of it all, the artwork and *objets d'art* give a pretty good idea of upper-class tastes during the Age of Enlightenment.

MUSÉE D'ART ET D'HISTOIRE DU JUDAÏSME Map pp436-7

☎ 01 53 01 86 60; www.mahj.org; 71 rue du Temple, 3e; adult/student & 18-26 yr €6.80/4.50, under 18 yr free; ⏰ 11am-6pm Mon-Fri, 10am-6pm Sun; Ⓜ Rambuteau

The Museum of the Art & History of Judaism is in the sumptuous 17th-century Hôtel de St-Aignan. The museum was formed by combining the crafts, paintings and ritual objects from Eastern Europe and North Africa of the Musée d'Art Juif (Jewish Art Museum) in Montmartre with medieval Jewish artefacts from the **Musée National du Moyen Age** (p116).

The museum traces the evolution of Jewish communities from the Middle Ages to the present, with particular emphasis on the history of the Jews in France but also communities in other parts of Europe and North Africa. Highlights include documents relating to the Dreyfus Affair and works by Chagall, Modigliani and Soutine. The admission fee includes an audioguide. Temporary exhibits cost an extra €5.40/4 and a combined ticket is €8.50/6.

MUSÉE DE LA CHASSE ET DE LA NATURE Map pp436-7

☎ 01 53 01 92 40; www.chassenature.org; Hôtel Guénégaud, 60 rue des Archives, 3e; adult/5-16 yr/senior & student €4.60/1/2.30; ⏰ 11am-6pm Tue-Sun; Ⓜ Rambuteau or Hôtel de Ville

The Hunting and Nature Museum may sound like an oxymoron to the politically correct, but in France, where hunting is a very big deal, to show your love for nature is to go out and shoot something – or so it would seem. The delightful Hôtel Guénégaud, dating from 1651, is positively crammed with weapons, paintings, *objets d'art* related to hunting and, of course, lots and lots of trophies – horns, antlers, you name it – adorning the walls.

MUSÉE DE LA CURIOSITÉ ET DE LA MAGIE Map pp436-7

☎ 01 42 72 13 26; www.museedelamagie.com in French; 11 rue St-Paul, 4e; adult/3-12 yr €7/5; ⏰ 2-7pm Wed, Sat & Sun, 2-7pm Wed-Sun Easter & Christmas school holidays; Ⓜ St-Paul

The Museum of Curiosity & Magic in the 16th-century *caves* (cellars) of the house of the Marquis de Sade examines the ancient arts of magic, optical illusion and sleight of hand, with regular magic shows (last one at 6pm) included. But some visitors feel that the displays – optical illusions and wind-up toys – and very basic magic tricks do not justify the very high admission fee. An audioguide costs €3.

MUSÉE DE LA POUPÉE Map pp436-7

☎ 01 42 72 73 11; www.museedelapoupeeparis.com; impasse Berthaud, 3e; adult/aged 3-18 yr/senior & student €6/3/4; ⏰ 10am-6pm Tue-Sun; Ⓜ Rambuteau

Frightening to some – all those beady eyes staring out at you – the Doll Museum is more for adults than for children. There are around 500 of the lifeless creatures, dating back to 1800, all arranged in scenes representing Paris through the centuries. There are also temporary exhibitions (think Barbie and Cindy and 'France's best plush animals') as well as a 'hospital' for antique dolls.

MÉMORIAL DE LA SHOAH Map pp436-7

☎ 01 42 77 44 72; www.memorialdelashoah.org; 17 rue Geoffroy-l'Asnier, 4e; admission free; ☷ 10am-6pm Sun-Wed & Sat, 10am-10pm Thu; Ⓜ St-Paul

Established in 1956, the Memorial to the Unknown Jewish Martyr has metamorphosed into the Memorial of the Holocaust and documentation centre after a lengthy renovation. The permanent collection and temporary exhibits relate to the Holocaust and the German occupation of parts of France and Paris during WWII; the film clips of contemporary footage and interviews are heart-rending and the displays instructive and easy to follow. The actual memorial to the victims of the 'Shoah', a Hebrew word meaning 'catastrophe' and synonymous in France with the Holocaust, stands at the entrance and there is a wall inscribed with the names of 76,000 men, women and children deported from France to Nazi extermination camps. A plaque on the wall of the building opposite on allée des Justes, 4e, recalls that as many as 500 of the 11,000 Jewish children deported by the Germans between 1942 and 1944 lived in the 4e.

MUSÉE DES ARTS ET MÉTIERS

Map pp428-9

☎ 01 53 01 82 00; www.arts-et-metiers.net in French; 60 rue de Réaumur, 3e; adult/student & 18-26 yr €6.50/4.50, under 18 free; ☷ 10am-6pm Tue & Wed, Fri-Sun, 10am-9.30pm Thu; Ⓜ Arts et Métiers

The Arts & Crafts Museum, the oldest museum of science and technology in Europe, is a must for anyone with an interest in how things work. Housed in the 18th-century priory of St-Martin des Champs, some 80,000 instruments, machines and working models from the 18th to 20th centuries are displayed across three floors. Taking pride of place is Foucault's original pendulum, which he introduced to the world in 1855 with the words: 'Come and see the world turn'. There's lots of workshops and other activities here for children. An audioguide is €2.50.

MUSÉE PICASSO Map pp440-1

☎ 01 42 71 25 21; www.musee-picasso.fr; 5 rue de Thorigny, 3e; adult/18-25 yr €6.70/5.20 Wed-Sat & Mon, admission Sun €5.20, under 18 yr free, 1st Sun of the month free; ☷ 9.30am-6pm Wed-Mon Apr-Sep, 9.30am-5.30pm Wed-Mon Oct-Mar; Ⓜ St-Paul or Chemin Vert

The Picasso Museum, housed in the stunning Hôtel Aubert de Fontenay (1656), forms one of Paris' best-loved art collections. It includes more than 3500 of the *grand maître*'s (great master) engravings, paintings, ceramic works, drawings and sculptures, which the heirs of Pablo Picasso (1881–1973) donated to the French government in lieu of inheritance taxes. Among the collection is his *Girl with Bare Feet*, painted when Picasso was only 14. You can also see part of Picasso's personal art collection, which includes works by Braque, Cézanne, Matisse, Modigliani, Degas and Rousseau.

OPÉRA BASTILLE Map pp440-1

☎ 0 892 899 090; www.opera-de-paris.fr in French; 2-6 place de la Bastille, 12e; Ⓜ Bastille

Paris' giant 'second' opera house, designed by the Canadian architect Carlos Ott, was inaugurated on 14 July 1989, the 200th anniversary of the storming of the Bastille. There are 1¼-hour **guided tours** (☎ 01 40 01 19 70; adult/under 19 yr/ senior & student €11/6/9) of the building, which generally depart at 1.15pm from Monday to Saturday. Tickets go on sale just 15 minutes before departure at the **box office** (130 rue de Lyon, 12e; ☷ 10.30am-6.30pm Mon-Sat).

Sights

MARAIS & BASTILLE

TOP FIVE: MARAIS & BASTILLE

- Hôtel de Sully (p106)
- Mémorial de la Shoah (p109)
- Musée Picasso (p109)
- Place des Vosges (below)
- Opéra Bastille (p109)

PLACE DE LA BASTILLE Map pp440-1
Ⓜ Bastille

The Bastille, built during the 14th century as a fortified royal residence, is the most famous monument in Paris that no longer exists. The notorious prison – the quintessential symbol of royal despotism – was demolished shortly after a mob stormed it on 14 July 1789 and freed a total of just seven prisoners. The site where it once stood, place de la Bastille (11e and 12e), is now a very busy traffic roundabout.

In the centre of the square is the 52m-high Colonne de Juillet (July Column), whose shaft of greenish bronze is topped by a gilded and winged figure of Liberty. It was erected in 1833 as a memorial to those killed in the street battles that accompanied the July Revolution of 1830 – they are buried in vaults under the column – and was later consecrated as a memorial to the victims of the February Revolution of 1848.

PLACE DES VOSGES Map pp440-1
Ⓜ St-Paul or Bastille

Inaugurated in 1612 as place Royale, Place des Vosges (4e) is an ensemble of 36 symmetrical houses with ground-floor arcades, steep slate roofs and large dormer windows arranged around a large square. Only the earliest houses were built of brick; to save time, the rest were given timber frames and faced with plaster, which was later painted to resemble brick. Duels were once fought in the elegant park in the centre. The square received its present name in 1800 to honour the Vosges département (administrative division), the first in France to pay its taxes. Today, the arcades around Place des Vosges are occupied by upmarket art galleries, pricey antique shops and elegant places to sip tea.

The author Victor Hugo lived in an apartment on the 3rd floor of the square's Hôtel de Rohan-Guéménée from 1832 to 1848, moving here a year after the publication of Notre Dame de Paris (The Hunchback of

Notre Dame) and completing Ruy Blas while in residence here. The Maison de Victor Hugo (Victor Hugo House; ☎ 01 42 72 10 16; temporary exhibits adult/14-25 yr/senior & student €7.50/3.50/5, permanent collections free, under 14 yr free; ☉ 10am-6pm Tue-Sun) is now a municipal museum devoted to the life and times of the celebrated novelist and poet, with a very impressive collection of his personal drawings and portraits. Admission includes a free audioguide.

PLETZL Map pp436-7
Ⓜ St-Paul

When renovation of the Marais (4e) began in the late 1960s, the area around rue des Rosiers and rue des Écouffes – traditionally known as the Pletzl and home to a poor but vibrant Jewish community – was pretty run-down. Now trendy and expensive boutiques sit side-by-side with Jewish bookshops and stores selling religious goods and cacher (kosher) grocery shops, butchers, restaurants and falafel takeaway joints. The area is very quiet on the Sabbath (sundown Friday to sundown Saturday).

The Art Nouveau Guimard synagogue (Map pp436–7; 10 rue Pavée, 4e) was designed in 1913 by Hector Guimard, who originated the city's famous metro entrances (p104). The interior is closed to the public.

THE ISLANDS
ÎLE DE LA CITÉ
Drinking p245; Eating p191; Shopping p290; Sleeping p314

The site of the first settlement in Paris (c 3rd century BC) and later the centre of the Roman town of Lutèce the Île de la Cité (Map pp436–7), remained the centre of royal and ecclesiastical power even after the city spread to both banks of the Seine during the Middle Ages. And as the institutions on the island grew, so grew the island – over a millennium the island more than doubled in size from eight to 17 hectares. The buildings on the middle part of the island were demolished and rebuilt during Baron Haussmann's great urban renewal scheme of the late 19th century (p76); the population – considered the poorest in the city – fell from 15,000 in 1860 to 5000 less than a decade later.

The Île de la Cité, most of which lies in the 4e arrondissement though its western tip is in the 1er arrondissement, is now home to two institutions devoted to maintaining public order: the judiciary (Palais de Justice) and the police (Préfecture de Police). Directly north is the Marais while the Latin Quarter and Saint Germain lie to the south.

CATHÉDRALE DE NOTRE DAME DE PARIS Map pp436-7

☎ 01 42 34 56 10; www.cathedraledeparis.com; place du Parvis Notre Dame, 4e; audioguide €5; ⏰ 8am-6.45pm Mon-Fri, 8am-7.45pm Sat & Sun, information desk 10am-5.30pm Mon-Sat; Ⓜ Cité
The Cathedral of Our Lady of Paris is the true heart of Paris; in fact, distances from Paris to every part of metropolitan France are measured from **place du Parvis Notre Dame**, the square in front of the basilica. A bronze star, set in the pavement across the street from the cathedral's main entrance, marks the exact location of *point zéro des routes de France* (point zero of French roads). Nearby, Charlemagne (768–814), emperor of the Francs, rides his steed under the trees in front of the cathedral.

Notre Dame, the most visited site in Paris with 10 million people crossing its threshold a year, is not just a masterpiece of French Gothic architecture but has also been the focus of Catholic Paris for seven centuries. In recent years its western façade has had a thorough cleaning, which makes it even more attractive and inspiring (though be aware that many of the saints carved in stone in the main portals are modern-day copies).

Built on a site occupied by earlier churches – and, a millennium before that, a Gallo-Roman temple perhaps dedicated to the god **Mithra** (p69) – it was begun in 1163 according to the design of Bishop Maurice de Sully and largely completed by the early 14th century. The cathedral was badly damaged during the Revolution; architect Eugène Emmanuel Viollet-le-Duc carried out extensive renovations between 1845 and 1864. The cathedral is on a very grand scale; the interior alone is 130m long, 48m wide and 35m high and can accommodate more than 6000 worshippers.

Notre Dame is known for its sublime balance, though if you look closely you'll see all sorts of minor asymmetrical elements introduced to avoid monotony, in accordance with standard Gothic practice. These include the slightly different shapes of each of the three main **portals**, whose statues were once brightly coloured to make them more effective as a *Biblia pauperum* – a 'Bible of the poor' to help the illiterate understand the Old Testament stories, the Passion of the Christ and the lives of the saints. One of the best views of Notre Dame is from square Jean XXIII, the lovely little park behind the cathedral, where you can view the forest of ornate **flying buttresses** that encircle the chancel and support its walls and roof.

Sights

THE ISLANDS

Ballon Eutelsat in Parc André Citroën (p94)

Inside, exceptional features include three spectacular **rose windows**, the most renowned of which is the 10m-wide one over the western façade above the 7800-pipe organ, and the window on the northern side of the transept, which has remained virtually unchanged since the 13th century. The central choir with its carved wooden stalls and statues representing the Passion of the Christ is also noteworthy. There are free **guided tours** (☉ noon Wed & Thu, 2.30pm Sat) of the cathedral, in English.

The **trésor** (treasury; adult/3-12 yr/student €3/1/2; ☉ 9.30am-6pm Mon-Sat, 1.30-5.30pm Sun) in the southeastern transept contains artwork, liturgical objects, church plate and first-class relics, some of them of dubious origin. Among these is the **Ste-Couronne**, the 'Holy Crown', which is purportedly the wreath of thorns placed on Jesus' head before he was crucified and was brought here in the mid-13th century. It is exhibited at 3pm on each first Friday of the month, every Friday during Lent and from 10am to 5pm on Good Friday.

The entrance to **Tours de Notre Dame** (Towers of Notre Dame; ☎ 01 53 10 07 02; www.monum.fr; rue du Cloître Notre Dame; adult/student & 18-25 yr €7.50/4.80, under 18 yr free, 1st Sun of the month Oct-Mar free; ☉ 9.30am-7.30pm Apr-Jun & Sep, 9am-7.30pm Mon-Fri, 9am-11pm Sat & Sun Jul & Aug, 10am-5.30pm Oct-Mar) is from the **North Tower**, which is to the right and around the corner as you walk out of the cathedral's main doorway. Climb the 387 spiralling steps to the top of the **western façade**, where you'll find yourself face-to-face with the cathedral's most frightening gargoyles, the 13-tonne bell **Emmanuel** (all the cathedral's bells are named) in the **South Tower**, and a spectacular view of Paris.

CONCIERGERIE Map pp436-7

☎ 01 53 40 60 97; www.monum.fr; 2 blvd du Palais, 1er; adult/18-25 yr €6.50/4.50, under 18 free, 1st Sun of the month Oct-Mar free; ☉ 9.30am-6pm Mar-Oct, 9am-5pm Nov-Feb; Ⓜ Cité

The Conciergerie was built as a luxurious royal palace in the 14th century for the concierge of the Palais de la Cité, but it later lost favour with the kings of France and was turned into a prison and torture chamber. During the Reign of Terror

(1793–94), the Conciergerie was used to incarcerate alleged enemies of the Revolution before they were brought before the Revolutionary Tribunal, which met next door in the Palais de Justice. Among the 2700 prisoners held in the *cachots* (dungeons) here before being sent in tumbrels to the guillotine were Queen Marie-Antoinette and, as the Revolution began to turn on its own, the radicals Danton, Robespierre and, finally, the judges of the Tribunal themselves.

The huge Gothic **Salle des Gens d'Armes** (Cavalrymen's Hall) dates from the 14th century and is a fine example of the Rayonnant Gothic style. It is the largest surviving medieval hall in Europe. The **Tour de l'Horloge** (Map pp436–7; cnr blvd du Palais & quai de l'Horloge), built in 1353, has held a public clock aloft since 1370.

A joint ticket with **Ste-Chapelle** (opposite) costs adult/18-25 yr €9.50/7.

CRYPTE ARCHÉOLOGIQUE Map pp436-7

☎ 01 55 42 50 10; 1 place du Parvis Notre Dame, 4e; adult/14-25 yr/senior & student €3.30/1.60/2.20, under 14 yr free; ☉ 10am-6pm Tue-Sun; Ⓜ Cité

The Archaeological Crypt is under the square in front of Notre Dame. The 117m long and 28m wide area displays *in situ* the remains of structures built on this site during the Gallo-Roman period (including actual rooms), a 4th-century enclosure wall, the foundations of the medieval foundlings hospice and a few of the sewers sunk by Haussman.

MARCHÉ AUX FLEURS Map pp436-7

place Louis Lépin, 4e; ☉ 8am-7.30pm Mon-Sat; Ⓜ Cité

The Île de la Cité's flower (and plant) market, surprisingly the oldest in Paris, has been at this square just north of the Préfecture de Police since 1808. On Sunday, it is transformed into the **Marché aux Oiseaux** (bird market; ☉ 9am-7pm).

MÉMORIAL DES MARTYRS DE LA DÉPORTATION Map pp436-7

square de l'Île de France, 4e; ☉ 10am-noon, 2-7pm Apr-Sep, 10am-noon, 2-5pm Oct-Mar; Ⓜ St-Michel Notre Dame

The Memorial to the Victims of the Deportation, erected in 1962 on the southeastern tip of the Île de la Cité, is a haunting monument to the 160,000 residents of France – including 76,000 Jews – who were killed in Nazi concentration camps during WWII. A single barred 'window' separates the bleak, rough concrete courtyard from the waters of the Seine.

The **Tomb of the Unknown Deportee** is flanked by hundreds of thousands of bits of back-lit glass, and the walls are etched with inscriptions from celebrated writers and poets.

MUSÉE DE NOTRE DAME DE PARIS

Map pp436-7

☎ 01 43 25 42 92; 10 rue du Cloître Notre Dame, 4e; adult/3-12 yr/student €3/1.50/2; ⊙ 2.30-6pm Wed, Sat & Sun; Ⓜ Cité

The small Museum of Notre Dame traces the cathedral's history and life on the Île de la Cité from Gallo-Roman times to today, via scale models, contemporary paintings, engravings and lithographs. An interesting document in the collection is a petition signed by Victor Hugo, the artist Ingres and others who sparked the campaign to restore the cathedral.

PONT NEUF Map pp436-7

Ⓜ Pont Neuf

The now sparkling white stone spans of Paris' oldest bridge, ironically called 'New Bridge', have linked the western end of the Île de la Cité with both banks of the Seine since 1607 when Henri IV inaugurated it by crossing the bridge on a white stallion. The occasion is commemorated by an equestrian **Henri IV statue**, who was known to his subjects as the Vert Galant ('jolly rogue' or 'dirty old man', depending on your perspective). The bridge's seven arches, decorated with humorous and grotesque figures of barbers, dentists, pickpockets, loiterers and the like, are best viewed from the river.

The Pont Neuf and the nearby place Dauphine were used for public exhibitions in the 18th century. In the last century the bridge itself became an *objet d'art* on at least three occasions: in 1963, when School of Paris artist Nonda built, exhibited and lived in a huge Trojan horse of steel and wood on the bridge; in 1984 when the Japanese designer Kenzo covered it in flowers; and in 1985 when the Bulgarian-born 'environmental sculptor' Christo famously wrapped the bridge in beige fabric.

STE-CHAPELLE Map pp436-7

☎ 01 53 40 60 97; www.monum.fr; 4 blvd du Palais, 1er; adult/18-25 yr €6.50/4.50, under 18 yr free, 1st Sun of the month Oct-Mar free; ⊙ 9.30am-6pm Mar-Oct, 9am-5pm Nov-Feb; Ⓜ Cité

The gemlike Holy Chapel, the most exquisite of Paris' Gothic monuments, is tucked away within the walls of the **Palais de Justice** (Law Courts). The 'walls' of the **upper chapel** are sheer curtains of richly coloured and finely detailed **stained glass** (the oldest and finest in Paris), which bathe the chapel in an extraordinary light on a sunny day. Built in just under three years (compared with nearly 200 for Notre Dame), Ste-Chapelle was consecrated in 1248. The chapel was conceived by Louis IX to house his personal collection of holy relics (including the Holy Crown now kept in the treasury at Notre Dame). The chapel's exterior can be viewed from across the street from the law courts' magnificently gilded 18th-century gate, which faces Rue de Lutèce.

A joint ticket with the **Conciergerie** (opposite) costs adult/18-25 yr €9.50/7.

ÎLE ST-LOUIS

Drinking p245; Eating p191; Shopping p290; Sleeping p314

The smaller of the Seine's two islands, Île St-Louis (Map pp436–7), is just downstream from the Île de la Cité and entirely in the **4e arrondissement**.

In the early 17th century, when Île St-Louis was actually two uninhabited islets – sometimes used for duels – called Île Notre Dame (Our Lady Isle) and Île aux Vaches (Cows Island), a building contractor called Christophe Marie and two financiers worked out a deal with Louis XIII to create one island out of the two and build two stone bridges to the mainland. In exchange they would receive the right to subdivide and sell the newly created real estate.

This they did with great success, and by 1664 the entire island was covered with fine, airy houses facing the quays and the river rather than the inner courtyards (as formerly). The **Pont Marie** linking the island with the Marais bears the contractor's name.

Today, the island's 17th-century, greystone houses and the small-town shops that line the streets and quays impart a village-like, provincial calm.

The central thoroughfare, the attractive rue St-Louis en l'Île built between 1614 and 1646, is home to a number of upmarket art galleries, boutiques and the French Baroque **Église St-Louis en l'Île** (Map pp436–7; ☎ 01 46 34 11 60; 19bis rue St-Louis en l'Île, 4e; ⓥ 9am-noon & 3-7pm Tue-Sun; Ⓜ Pont Marie) built between 1664 and 1726.

At the island's western end, the area around **Pont St-Louis** (Map pp436–7), the bridge linking Île de St-Louis with the Île de la Cité, and **Pont Louis-Philippe** (Map pp436–7), the bridge to the Marais, is one of the most romantic spots in all of Paris. On warm summer days, lovers mingle with cello-playing buskers and teenaged skateboarders. After nightfall, the Seine dances with the watery reflections of streetlights, headlamps, stop signals and the dim glow of curtained windows. Occasionally, tourist boats with super bright flood lamps cruise by. There's no doubt: you are really in Paris.

LATIN QUARTER & JARDIN DES PLANTES

Drinking p245; Eating p192; Shopping p290; Sleeping p315

Known as the **Quartier Latin** (Map pp436–7 & Map pp444–5) because all communication between students and professors here took place in Latin until the Revolution, what is now the **5e arrondissement** has been the centre of Parisian higher education since the Middle Ages. It has become increasingly touristy in the past several decades, however, and its near monopoly on the city's academic life has waned as students have moved to other campuses, especially since 1968. The Latin Quarter does have a large population of students and academics affiliated with the Sorbonne, which is now part of the University of Paris system, the Collège de France, the École Normale Supérieure and other institutions of higher learning. Bookshops and libraries, cafés and cheap restaurants are like annexes to these venerable institutions and are packed at all times.

Young people like to linger on the terraces spilling out over place St-Michel or place de la Sorbonne in the warmer months. In rue de la Harpe, rue Mouffetard, rue de la Huchette or place de la Contrescarpe, restaurant windows display set menus appealing to customers' cravings for Mediterranean or Asian food. Movie buffs flock to rue des Écoles to see classics while activists and sympathisers come together under the same banner at the Mutualité, chanting slogans and fighting the good fight.

The Institut du Monde Arabe offers a glimpse of the Arab world, and the lush Jardin des Plantes, with its tropical greenhouses and Musée National d'Histoire Naturelle, opens new horizons in a bucolic, romantic setting.

ARÈNES DE LUTÈCE Map pp444-5

49 rue Monge, 5e; admission free; ⓥ 9am-5.30 to 9.30pm Apr-Oct, 8am-5.30 to 9.30pm Nov-Mar; Ⓜ Place Monge

The Roman amphitheatre called Lutetia Arena, dating from the 2nd century, could once seat around 10,000 people for gladiatorial combats and other events. Discovered in 1869 by accident while Rue Monge was under construction and heavily rebuilt in 1917, it is now used by neighbourhood youths playing *boules* and football.

CENTRE DE LA MER Map pp444-5

☎ 01 44 32 10 70, 01 44 32 10 95; www.oceano .org in French; Institut Océanographique; 195 rue St-Jacques, 5e; adult/3-12 yr/senior & student €4.60/2/3; ⓥ 10am-12.30pm & 1.30-5.30pm Tue-Fri, 10am-5.30pm Sat & Sun; Ⓜ Luxembourg

France has a long history of success in the field of oceanography (think Jacques Cousteau and, well, Jules Verne) and the Sea Centre cruises through that science, as well as marine biology, through temporary exhibitions, aquariums, scale models and audiovisuals. It's educational, and also a great deal of fun. Kids will love the aquarium and the audiovisuals.

ÉGLISE ST-ÉTIENNE DU MONT

Map pp444-5

☎ 01 43 54 11 79; 1 place Ste-Geneviève, 5e; ⓥ 8am-noon & 2-7pm Tue-Sat, 9am-noon & 2.30-7pm Sun Ⓜ Cardinal Lemoine

The lovely Church of Mount St-Stephen, built between 1492 and 1655, contains Paris' only surviving **rood screen** (1535) separating the chancel from the nave; all the others were removed during the late Renaissance because they prevented the faithful assembled in the nave from seeing the priest celebrate Mass. In the southeastern corner of the nave, a chapel contains the **tomb of St Geneviève**, largely destroyed during the Revolution. A highly decorated **reliquary** nearby contains all that is left of her earthly remains – a finger bone. St Geneviève, patroness of Paris, was born at Nanterre in 422 and turned Attila the Hun away from Paris in AD 451. You can see a likeness of her – ghostly pale and turning her back on the city – high above the **Pont de la Tournelle** (Map pp436–7), just south of Île St Louis in the 5e.

Also of interest in the church is the carved **wooden pulpit** of 1650, held aloft by a figure of Samson, and the 16th- and 17th-century **stained glass**. Just inside the entrance, a plaque in the floor marks the spot where a defrocked priest stabbed an archbishop to death in 1857.

INSTITUT DU MONDE ARABE
Map pp444-5
☎ 01 40 51 38 38; www.imarabe.org in French; 1 place Mohammed V, 5e; Ⓜ Cardinal Lemoine or Jussieu

The Institute of the Arab World set up by France and 20 Arab countries to promote cultural contacts between the Arab world and the west, is housed in a highly praised building (1987) that successfully mixes modern and traditional Arab and western elements (p46). Thousands of mushrabiyah (or *mouche-arabies*, photo-electrically sensitive apertures built into the glass walls) that were inspired by the traditional latticed wooden windows that let you see out without being seen, are opened and closed by electric motors in order to regulate the amount of light and heat that reach the interior of the building.

The **museum** (adult/senior, student & 18-25 yr €5/4, under 18 free; Ⓗ 10am-6pm Tue-Fri, 10am-7pm Sat & Sun), spread over three floors and entered via the 7th floor, displays 9th- to 19th-century art and artisanship from all over the Arab world, as well as instruments from astronomy and other fields of scientific endeavour in which Arab technology once led the world. **Temporary exhibitions** (enter from Quai Saint Bernard; Map pp444–5) involve a separate fee (usually between €7 and €9 for adults and €5 and €7 for the reduced tariff). Audioguides are €5. A ticket valid for the permanent collection and exhibitions costs €13/11.

People relaxing outside Église St-Eustache (p99)

JARDIN DES PLANTES
Map pp444-5
☎ 01 40 79 56 01, 01 40 79 36 00; 57 rue Cuvier, 5e; Ⓗ 7.30am-5.30pm to 7.30pm (seasonal); Ⓜ Gare d'Austerlitz, Censier Daubenton or Jussieu

Paris' 24-hectare botanical garden was founded in 1626 as a medicinal herb garden for Louis XIII. Here you'll find the Eden-like **Jardin d'Hiver** (Winter Garden), also called the **Serres Tropicales** (Tropical Greenhouses) and under renovation, the **Jardin Alpin** (Alpine Garden; Sat & Sun admission €1.50; Ⓗ 8-5pm Mon-Fri, 1.30-6pm Sat, 1.30-6.30pm Sun Apr-Sep), with 2000 mountainous plants; and the gardens of the **École de Botanique** (admission free; Ⓗ 8-5pm Mon-Fri), which is where students of the School of Botany 'practice'.

The **Ménagerie du Jardin des Plantes** (☎ 01 40 79 37 94; 57 rue Cuvier & 3 quai St-Bernard, 5e; adult/senior, student & 4-15 yr €7/5; Ⓗ 9am-6pm Mon-Sat, 9am-6.30pm Sun Apr-Sep, 9am-5pm Mon-Sat, 9am-5.30pm Sun Oct-Mar), a medium-sized (5.5-hectare, 1000 animals) zoo in the northern section of the garden, was founded in 1794. During the Prussian siege of Paris in 1870, most of the animals were eaten by starving Parisians. While a recreational animal park, it also does much research into the reproduction of rare and endangered species.

MOSQUÉE DE PARIS Map pp444-5

☎ 01 45 35 97 33; www.mosquee-de-paris.org;
2bis place du Puits de l'Ermite, 5e; adult/senior
& 7-25 yr €3/2; ⊗ 9am-noon & 2-6pm Sat-Thu;
Ⓜ Censier Daubenton or Place Monge

Paris' central mosque with its striking
26m-high minaret was built in 1926 in
the ornate Moorish style popular at the
time. Visitors must be modestly dressed
and remove their shoes at the entrance
to the prayer hall. The complex includes
a North African-style salon de thé (tearoom)
and restaurant (p194) and a hammam (p280), a
traditional Turkish bath open to men and
women on different days.

MUSÉE DE L'ASSISTANCE PUBLIQUE-HÔPITAUX DE PARIS Map pp436-7

☎ 01 40 27 50 05; www.aphp.fr/musee; Hôtel de
Miramion, 47 quai de la Tournelle, 5e; adult/senior,
student & 13-18 yr €4/2, under 13 free, admission
1st Sun of the month free; ⊗ 10am-6pm Tue-Sun;
Ⓜ Maubert Mutualité

A museum devoted to the history of hospitals in Paris since the Middle Ages doesn't
sound like a crowd-pleaser but some of the
items on display – paintings, sculptures,
drawings, medical instruments etc – are
fascinating and very evocative of their times.
A must-see for nurses and nurse-wannabes.
The lovely Hôtel Miramion, dating from the
17th century and the city's central pharmacy
until the mid-1970s, is a positive delight.

MUSÉE NATIONAL D'HISTOIRE NATURELLE Map pp444-5 & Map pp446-7

☎ 01 40 79 30 00; www.mnhn.fr in French; 57
rue Cuvier, 5e; Ⓜ Censier Daubenton or Gare
d'Austerlitz

The National Museum of Natural History,
created by a decree of the Revolutionary
Convention in 1793, was the site of important scientific research in the 19th century.
It is housed in three different buildings
along the southern edge of the Jardin des
Plantes.

The Grande Galerie de l'Évolution (Map
pp444–5; Great Gallery of Evolution; 36 rue
Geoffroy St-Hilaire, 5e; adult/4-13 yr €8/6;
⊗ 10am-6pm Wed-Mon) has some imaginative exhibits on evolution and humanity's
effect on the global ecosystem, including
global warming, spread over four floors
and 6000 sq metres of space. The Salle des

Espèces Menacées et des Espèces Disparues (Hall of
Threatened and Extinct Species) on level 2
displays extremely rare specimens of endangered and extinct species while the Salle
de Découverte (Room of Discovery) on level 1
houses interactive exhibits for kids.

The Galerie de Minéralogie et de Géologie
(Map pp444–5; 36 rue Geoffroy St-Hilaire;
adult/4-13 yr €6/4; ⊗ 10am-5pm Mon-Fri,
10am-6pm Sat & Sun Apr-Oct, 10am-5pm
Wed-Mon Nov-Mar), which covers mineral-
ogy and geology, has an amazing exhibit
of giant natural crystals and a basement
display of jewellery and other objects made
from minerals.

The Galerie d'Anatomie Comparée et de Paléontologie (Map pp446–7; 2 rue Buffon; adult/4-13
yr €6/4; ⊗ 10am-5pm Mon-Fri, 10am-6pm
Sat & Sun Apr-Oct, 10am-5pm Wed-Mon
Nov-Mar) has displays on comparative
anatomy and palaeontology (the study of
fossils).

MUSÉE NATIONAL DU MOYEN AGE Map pp436-7

☎ 01 53 73 78 16, 01 53 73 78 00; www.musee
-moyenage.fr; Thermes & Hôtel de Cluny, 6 place
Paul Painlevé, 5e; adult/senior, student & 18-25 yr
€6.50/4.50, under 18 yr free, 1st Sun of the month
free; ⊗ 9.15am-5.45pm Wed-Mon; Ⓜ Cluny-La
Sorbonne or St-Michel

The National Museum of the Middle Ages,
sometimes called the Musée de Cluny, is
housed in two structures: the *frigidarium*
(cooling room), which holds remains of
Gallo-Roman baths dating from around AD
200, and the late-15th-century Hôtel de Cluny,
considered the finest example of medieval
civil architecture in Paris. The spectacular displays include statuary, illuminated
manuscripts, weapons, furnishings and
objets d'art made of gold, ivory and enamel.
But nothing compares with *La Dame à
la Licorne* (The Lady with the Unicorn), a
sublime series of late-15th-century tapestries from the southern Netherlands hung
in circular room 13 on the 1st floor. Five of
them are devoted to the senses while the
sixth is the enigmatic *À Mon Seul Désir* (To
My Sole Desire), a reflection on vanity.

Small gardens northeast of the museum,
including the Jardin Céleste (Heavenly Garden)
and the Jardin d'Amour (Garden of Love), are
planted with flowers, herbs and shrubs that
appear in masterpieces hanging through-

out the museum. To the west the **Forêt de la Licorne** (Unicorn Forest) is based on the illustrations in the tapestries.

PANTHÉON Map pp444-5

☎ 01 44 32 18 00; www.monum.fr; place du Panthéon, 5e; adult/18-25 yr €7.50/4.80, under 18 yr free, 1st Sun of the month Oct-Mar free; ⊙ 10am-6.30pm Apr-Sep, 10am-6.15pm Oct-Mar; Ⓜ Luxembourg

The domed landmark was commissioned by Louis XV around 1750 as an abbey church dedicated to Ste-Geneviève in thanksgiving for his recovery from an illness, but due to financial and structural problems it wasn't completed until 1789 – not a good year for church openings in Paris. The Constituent Assembly converted it into a secular mausoleum for the *grands hommes de l'époque de la liberté française* (great men of the era of French liberty) two years later and bricked up most of the windows.

The Panthéon is a superb example of 18th-century neoclassicism but its ornate marble interior is gloomy. It reverted to its religious duties two more times after the Revolution but has played a secular role ever since 1885, when God was evicted in favour of Victor Hugo. Among the other 80 or so permanent residents of the crypt are Voltaire, Jean-Jacques Rousseau, Louis Braille, Émile Zola and Jean Moulin. Personages removed for reburial elsewhere after a re-evaluation of their greatness include Mirabeau and Marat. The first woman to be interred in the Panthéon was the two-time Nobel Prize–winner Marie Curie (1867–1934), who was reburied here (along with her husband Pierre) in 1995.

SORBONNE Map pp444-5

12 rue de la Sorbonne, 5e; Ⓜ Luxembourg or Cluny-La Sorbonne

The imposing buildings of the Sorbonne, which dominate the heart of the Latin Quarter, testify to the long and distinguished career of one of the most famous universities in the world. Founded in 1253 by Robert de Sorbon, confessor to Louis IX, as a college for 16 impoverished theology students, it soon grew into a powerful body with its own government and laws. Today, the Sorbonne's main complex, bounded by rue de la Sorbonne, rue des Écoles, rue St-Jacques and rue Cujas, and other build-

TOP FIVE: LATIN QUARTER & JARDINS DES PLANTES

- Centre de la Mer (p114)
- Grande Galerie de l'Évolution (Musée Nationale d'Histoire Naturelle; opposite)
- Institut du Monde Arabe (p115)
- Musée National du Moyen Age (opposite)
- Panthéon (left)

ings in the vicinity house most of the 13 autonomous universities created when the University of Paris was reorganised after the student protests of 1968.

Place de la Sorbonne links blvd St-Michel and the **Chapelle de la Sorbonne** (Map pp444–5), the university's gold-domed church built between 1635 and 1642 and currently under renovation. The remains of Cardinal Richelieu (1585–1642) lie in a very camp tomb here with an effigy of a cardinal's hat suspended above it.

ST-GERMAIN, ODÉON & LUXEMBOURG

Drinking p247; Eating p206; Shopping p292; Sleeping p319

Centuries ago, the Église St-Germain des Prés and its affiliated abbey owned most of today's 6e and 7e. The neighbourhood around the church began to develop in the late 17th century, and these days the **6e arrondissement** is celebrated for its heterogeneity. Cafés such as **Les Deux Magots** (p248) and **Café de Flore** (p247) were once favourite hangouts of postwar Left Bank intellectuals, but bohemia and jazz have deserted its streets and basements and today *la vie germanopratin* (St-Germain life) is more touristy. Artists and writers, students and journalists, actors and musicians cross paths in the shadow of the École Nationale Supérieure des Beaux Arts, the Académie Française and the Odéon-Théâtre de l'Europe.

The arrival of the fashion industry many years ago changed the general tenor of the districts. Since then, clothing and footwear shops exist alongside bookshops, art galleries, publishing houses, antique dealers and interior design boutiques; but while *haute couture* and *prêt-à-porter* make flirtatious neighbours, each sector keeps for the most part to itself. Cinemas still advertise their multiple screenings, making no distinction between new films and old, small works and big blockbusters. The statue of Georges Danton, a leader of the Revolution and later one of its victims sent to the guillotine, stands near the site of his house at carrefour de l'Odéon and is a favourite meeting spot, with groups flocking to this landmark before invading the area's cafés, bars and restaurants. In the nearby rue de Seine, market stalls still groan under the weight of fresh fruit and vegetables, a reminder that village life here survives despite the passing fashions.

ÉGLISE ST-GERMAIN DES PRÉS
Map pp436-7

☎ 01 55 42 81 33; 3 place St-Germain des Prés, 6e; ☽ 8am-7pm Mon-Sat, 9am-8pm Sun; Ⓜ St-Germain des Prés

The Romanesque church of St Germanus of the Fields, the oldest church still standing in Paris, was built in the 11th century on the site of a 6th-century abbey and was the dominant church in Paris until the arrival of Notre Dame. It has been altered many times since, but the Chapelle de St-Symphorien, to the right as you enter, was part of the original abbey and is believed to be the resting place of St Germanus (AD 496–576), the first bishop of Paris. The Merovingian kings were buried here during the 6th and 7th centuries, but their tombs disappeared during the Revolution. Columns in the chancel were taken from the Merovingian abbey. The bell tower over the western entrance has changed little since AD 990, although the spire dates only from the 19th century. The vaulted ceiling is a starry sky that seems to float forever upward.

ÉGLISE ST-SULPICE Map pp436-7

☎ 01 46 33 21 78; place St-Sulpice, 6e; ☽ 8.30am-7.15pm Mon-Sat, 8.30am-7.45pm Sun; Ⓜ St-Sulpice

The Church of St Sulpicius, lined with small side chapels inside, was built between 1646 and 1780 on the site of earlier churches dedicated to the eponymous 6th-century archbishop of Bourges. The Italianate façade, designed by a Florentine architect, has two rows of superimposed columns and is topped by two towers. The neoclassical décor of the vast interior is influenced by the Counter-Reformation.

The frescoes in the Chapelle des Sts-Anges (Chapel of the Holy Angels), first to the right as you enter, depict Jacob wrestling with the angel (to the left) and Michael the Archangel doing battle with Satan (to the right) and were painted by Eugène Delacroix between 1855 and 1861. The monumental organ loft dates from 1781. The 10.30am Mass on Sunday is accompanied by organ music.

Place St-Sulpice is adorned by the very energetic Fontaine des Quatre Évêques (Fountain of the Four Bishops) dating from 1844. Nearby streets are known for their couture houses (p292).

Until recently, Église St-Sulpice was 'just another church' visited by handfuls of dedicated architecture buffs or fans of Delacroix. Than Dan Brown used it as the setting for a crucial discovery (and murder) in his *The Da Vinci Code* and the rest is, well, history. Use your elbows to enter.

INSTITUT DE FRANCE Map pp436-7

☎ 01 44 41 44 41; www.institut-de-france.fr; 23 quai de Conti, 6e; Ⓜ Mabillon or Pont Neuf

The French Institute, created in 1795, brought together five of France's academies of arts and sciences. The most famous of these is the Académie Française (French Academy), founded in 1635 by Cardinal Richelieu. Its 40 members, known as the Immortels (Immortals), have the Herculean (some say impossible) task of safeguarding the purity of the French language. The other academies are the Académie des Inscriptions et Belles-Lettres, the Académie des Sciences, the Académie des Beaux-Arts, and the Académie des Sciences Morales et Politiques.

The domed building housing the institute, across the Seine from the Louvre's eastern end, dates from the mid-17th century. It's a masterpiece of French neoclassical architecture. There are usually tours (adult/under 25 €8/6) at 10.30am or 11am on at least one Saturday (often the first) of the month. Contact the Centre des Monuments Nationaux (Monum; ☎ 01 44 54 19 30; www .monum.fr) for current schedules or check *Pariscope* or *L'Officiel des Spectacles* (p258) under 'Conférences'.

In the same building is the Bibliothèque Mazarine (Mazarine Library; ☎ 01 44 41 44 06; www.bibliotheque-mazarine.fr; ☽ 10am-6pm Mon-Fri), founded in 1643 and the oldest public library in France. You can visit the bust-lined, late-17th-century reading room or consult the library's collection of 500,000 volumes, using a free two-day admission pass obtained by leaving your ID at the office to the left of the entrance. Annual membership to borrow books costs €15; a carnet of 10 visits costs €7.50. You'll need two photos.

JARDIN DU LUXEMBOURG Map pp444-5
⏰ 7.30 to 8.15am-5 to 10pm (seasonal);
Ⓜ Luxembourg

When the weather is warm Parisians of all ages flock to the formal terraces and chestnut groves of the 23-hectare Luxembourg Garden to read, relax and romance. In the southern part of the garden you'll find urban **orchards** and the honey-producing **Rucher du Luxembourg** (Luxembourg Apiary).

Palais du Luxembourg (Luxembourg Palace; rue de Vaugirard, 6e), at the northern end of the garden, was built in the 1620s for Marie de Médici, Henri IV's consort, to assuage her longing for the Pitti Palace in Florence, where she had spent her childhood. The palace has housed the **Sénat** (Senate), the upper house of the French parliament, since 1958. There are **tours of the interior** (☎ reservations 01 44 5419 30; adult/under 25 €8/6) at 10.30am usually on the first Sunday of each month, but you

must book by the preceding Tuesday. The palace gardens, the main draw, are strewn with **sculptures**, including likenesses (real and imagined) of the queens of France. East of the palace is the Italianate **Fontaine des Médici**, a long, ornate fish pond built around 1630.

The **Musée du Luxembourg** (Luxembourg Museum; ☎ 01 42 34 25 95; www.museedu luxembourg.fr in French; 19 rue de Vaugirard, 6e; ⏰ 11am-10pm Mon, Fri & Sat, 11am-7pm Tue-Thu, 9am-7pm Sun) opened at the end of the 19th century in the orangery of the Palais du Luxembourg as an exhibition space for artists still living. It now hosts very prestigious temporary art exhibitions (eg Botticelli). Admission can cost up to €10 (students & 10-25 yr €8), but it depends on the exhibit. An audioguide is €4.50.

Luxembourg Garden offers all the delights of a Parisian childhood a century ago and is one of the best places in Paris to take kids. At the octagonal **Grand Bassin**, model sailboats can be rented (around €4) from 2pm until sometime between 4.30pm (in winter) and 7pm (in spring and summer) on Wednesday, Saturday and Sunday (daily during school holidays).

About 200m southwest of the pond, the pint-sized **Théâtre du Luxembourg** (☎ 01 43 26 46 47) puts on marionette shows, which can be enjoyed even if you don't understand French. There are performances

Église du Dôme, Hôtel des Invalides (p124)

(€4.20) at 3.15pm on Wednesday, Saturday and Sunday, with an additional one at 11am on Saturday and Sunday. They're staged daily during the school holidays.

Next to the Théâtre du Luxembourg is the modern **playground** (adult/child €1.50/2.50). One half of it is for kids aged up to seven (blue zone), the other half is for children aged seven to 12 (green zone). The nearby **carousel** (merry-go-round) costs €1.40.

At a spot about 100m north of the theatre, kids weighing up to 35kg can ride **Shetland ponies** (€2.30, or €6/11 for three/six rides) from about 11am.

MUSÉE DE LA MONNAIE DE PARIS
Map pp436-7

☎ 01 40 46 55 35; www.monnaiedeparis.fr; 11 quai de Conti, 6e; admission €8, under 16 yr free; ☽ 11am-5.30pm Tue-Fri, noon-5.30pm Sat & Sun; Ⓜ Pont Neuf

The Parisian Mint Museum traces the history of French coinage from antiquity to the present and displays presses and other minting equipment. There are some excellent audiovisual and other displays, which help to bring to life this otherwise niche subject. The entrance fee includes audioguide.

The **Hôtel de la Monnaie**, which houses the museum, became the royal mint during the 18th century and is still used by the Ministry of Finance to produce commemorative medals and coins, as well as official weights and measures. One-hour tours of the *ateliers* (workshops) leave at 2.15pm on Wednesday and Friday (€3).

MUSÉE NATIONAL EUGÈNE DELACROIX Map pp436-7

☎ 01 44 41 86 50; www.musee-delacroix.fr in French; 6 rue de Furstemberg, 6e; adult €5, under 18 yr free, 1st Sun of the month free; ☽ 9.30am-5pm Wed-Mon; Ⓜ Mabillon or St-Germain des Prés

The Eugène Delacroix Museum, in a courtyard just off a delightfully leafy 'square', was the Romantic artist's home and studio at the time of his death in 1863 and contains many of his oils, watercolours, pastels and drawings. If you want to see his major works, such as *Liberty Leading the People*, visit the **Louvre** (p100) or the **Musée d'Orsay** (p124); here you'll find many of his more intimate works (eg *An Unmade Bed*, 1828) and his paintings of Morocco. What is now

called rue de Furstemberg – the former place de Furstemberg takes on a special hue on summer evenings, when magnolias scent the air and buskers serenade lovers under the old-fashioned street lamp.

MUSÉE ATELIER ZADKINE Map pp444-5

☎ 01 55 42 77 20; www.v1.paris.fr/musees /zadkine; 100bis rue d'Assas, 6e; temporary exhibits adult/14-25 yr/senior & student €4/2/3, permanent collections free, under 14 yr free; ☽ 10am-6pm Tue-Sun

This museum is devoted to the life and work of Russian Cubist sculptor Ossip Zadkine (1890–1967), who arrived in Paris in 1908, and lived and worked in this cottage in a lovely courtyard opposite the Jardin du Luxembourg for almost 40 years. Though he is scarcely known outside France, Zadkine produced an enormous catalogue of work in wood, clay, stone and bronze.

MONTPARNASSE
Drinking p249; Eating p208; Sleeping p321

After WWI, writers, poets and artists of the avant-garde abandoned **Montmartre** (p148) on the Right Bank and crossed the Seine, shifting the centre of Paris' artistic ferment to the area around **blvd du Montparnasse** (Map pp434–5). Chagall, Modigliani, Léger, Soutine, Miró, Kandinsky, Picasso, Stravinsky, Hemingway, Ezra Pound and Cocteau, as well as such political exiles as Lenin and Trotsky, all hung out here at some point or another, talking endlessly in the cafés and restaurants for which the quarter became famous. Montparnasse remained a creative centre until the mid-1930s. Today, especially since the construction of the Gare Montparnasse complex, there is little to remind visitors of the area's bohemian past except those now very touristy restaurants and cafés.

Although the Latin Quarter crowd considers the area hopelessly nondescript, blvd du Montparnasse (on the southern border of the 6e) and its many fashionable restaurants, cafés and cinemas attract large numbers of people in the evening. In fact, the **14e arrondissement**, which is where the lion's share of the district falls, has a lot to offer: delightful Parc Montsouris (Map pp422–3); the Cimetière du Montparnasse, final resting place of such luminaries as Sartre and Serge Gainsbourg; posh place de Catalogne; and place Denfert Rochereau, gateway to the Catacombes (below). To the south the extraordinary Cité Universitaire (Map pp422–3), a lush oasis reserved for students, acts as a sort of buffer between Parc Montsouris and the blvd Périphérique, the ring road or beltway encircling Paris. The somewhat cold elegance of rue Froidevaux, which runs along the southern border of the Cimetière du Montparnasse, stands in sharp contrast to the neon signs and louche nightlife of the rue de la Gaîté. Pedestrians have the run of rue Daguerre, whose market, shops and bars attract friendly hordes on the weekends. Less flamboyant than the Latin Quarter, less hip than Bastille and less audacious than Bercy, the unpretentious 14e arrondissement has perhaps struck a better balance than many others.

CATACOMBES Map p448

☎ 01 43 22 47 63; www.catacombes.paris.fr in French; 1 av Colonel Henri Roi-Tanguy, 14e; adult/14-25 yr/senior & student €5/2.50/3.30, under 14 yr free; ☷ 10am-5pm Tue-Sun; Ⓜ Denfert Rochereau

In 1785 it was decided to solve the hygiene and aesthetic problems posed by Paris' overflowing cemeteries by exhuming the bones and storing them in the tunnels of three disused quarries. One quarried created in 1810 is now known as the Catacombes and is without a doubt the most macabre place in Paris. After descending 20m (130 steps) from street level, visitors follow 1.7km of underground corridors in which the bones and skulls of millions of Parisians are neatly stacked along the walls. During WWII, these tunnels were used as a headquarters by the Resistance; so-called *cataphiles* looking for cheap thrills are often caught roaming the tunnels at night (there's a fine of €60).

The route through the Catacombes begins at a small, dark green *belle époque*-style building in the centre of a grassy area of av Colonel Henri Roi-Tanguy, the new name of place Denfert Rochereau. The exit is at the end of 83 steps on rue Remy Dumoncel (metro Mouton Duvernet), 700m southwest of av Colonel Henri Roi-Tanguy, where a guard will check your bag for 'borrowed' bones.

CIMETIÈRE DU MONTPARNASSE
Map pp434-5

blvd Edgar Quinet & rue Froidevaux, 14e; ☷ 8am-6pm Mon-Fri, 8.30am-6pm Sat, 9am-6pm Sun mid-Mar–early Nov, 8am-5.30pm Mon-Fri, 8.30am-5.30pm Sat, 9am-5.30pm Sun early Nov–mid-Mar; Ⓜ Edgar Quinet or Raspail

Montparnasse Cemetery received its first 'lodger' in 1824. It contains the tombs of such illustrious personages as the poet Charles Baudelaire, writer Guy de Maupassant, playwright Samuel Beckett, sculptor Constantin Brancusi, painter Chaim Soutine, photographer Man Ray, industrialist André Citroën, Captain Alfred Dreyfus of the infamous affair, actress Jean Seberg, philosopher Jean-Paul Sartre and his lover, writer Simone de Beauvoir, and the crooner Serge Gainsbourg, whose grave in division No 1 just off av Transversale is a pilgrimage site for fans who place metro tickets atop his tombstone, a reference to *Le Poinçonneur des Lilas*, one of his more famous songs.

Maps showing the location of the tombs are available free from the conservation office (☎ 01 44 10 86 50; 3 blvd Edgar Quinet, 14e) at the main entrance. Guided tours (adult/child €6/3) depart at 2.30pm or 3pm on different days of the week. Ring ☎ 01 40 71 75 60 for information.

FONDATION CARTIER POUR L'ART CONTEMPORAIN Map pp434-5

☎ 01 42 18 56 50; www.fondation.cartier.fr; 261 blvd Raspail; adult/senior, student 11-26 €6.50/4.50, under 10 yr free; ☷ noon-8pm Tue-Sun; Ⓜ Raspail

This stunning contemporary building just east of the Cimetière du Montparnasse and designed by Jean Nouvel is a work of art in itself. It hosts temporary exhibits on contemporary art (from the 1980s till today) in a wide variety of media – from painting, photography and video to fashion.

FONDATION DUBUFFET Map pp434-5

☎ 01 47 34 12 63; www.dubuffetfondation.com in French; 137 rue de Sèvres, 6e; admission €4; ☷ 2-6pm Mon-Fri; Ⓜ Duroc

Situated in a lovely 19th-century *hôtel particulier* accessible at the end of a courtyard, the foundation houses and administers the collection of Jean Dubuffet (1901–85), chief of the Art Brut school, a term he himself coined to describe all works of artistic expression not officially recognised. Much of his work is incredibly modern and expressive.

GARE MONTPARNASSE Map pp434-5
place Raoul Dautry, 14e; Ⓜ Montparnasse Bienvenüe
This sprawling train station has several unusual attractions on – of all places – its rooftop. The unique Jardin de l'Atlantique (Atlantic Garden; place des Cinq Martyr du Lycée Buffon, 15e; Ⓜ Montparnasse Bienvenüe), whose 3.5 hectares of landscaped terraces veil the top of the station, offers a bit of greenery and tranquillity in the heart of a very busy district. Don't miss the futuristic Observatoire Météorologique 'sculpture', in the centre of the garden, which measures precipitation, temperature and wind speed.

Next to the garden the small Musée Jean Moulin (☎ 01 40 64 39 44; www.ml-leclerc-moulin.paris.fr; 23 allée de la 2e DB, 15e; temporary exhibits adult/14-25 yr/senior & student €4/2/3, permanent collections free, under 14 yr free; 🕙 10am-6pm Tue-Sun) is devoted to the WWII German occupation of Paris, with the focus on the Resistance and its leader, Jean Moulin (1899–1943). The attached Mémorial du Maréchal Leclerc de Hauteclocque et de la Libération de Paris shows a panoramic film on the eponymous general (1902-47) who led the Free French units during the war and helped to liberate the city in 1944.

To reach all these attractions, avoid going through the station. Instead board the bubble lift on the pavement opposite 25 blvd de Vaugirard (15e) and go up one floor. From there take the escalator and follow the signs to the garden and museums.

MUSÉE BOURDELLE Map pp434-5
☎ 01 49 54 73 73; www.bourdelle.paris.fr in French; 18 rue Antoine Bourdelle, 15e; temporary exhibits adult/14-25 yr/senior & student €4.50/2.20/3, permanent collections free, under 14 yr free; 🕙 10am-6pm Tue-Sun; Ⓜ Falguière
The Bourdelle Museum, due north of Gare Montparnasse, contains monumental bronzes in the very house and workshop where the sculptor Antoine Bourdelle (1861–1929), a pupil of Rodin, lived and worked. The three sculpture gardens, one of which faces rue Antoine Bourdelle, are particularly lovely and impart a flavour of

the Montparnasse of the *belle époque* and post-WWI periods.

MUSÉE DE LA POSTE Map pp434-5
☎ 01 42 79 24 24; www.museedelaposte.fr; 34 blvd de Vaugirard, 15e; adult/senior, student & 13-18 yr €5/3.50, under 13 free; 🕙 10am-6pm Mon-Sat; Ⓜ Montparnasse Bienvenüe or Pasteur
The Postal Museum, a few hundred metres southwest of Tour Montparnasse, has some pretty impressive exhibits illustrating the history of the French postal service – a matter of importance in a highly centralised state like France. The exhibition rooms, dispersed over several floors, showcase the original designs of French stamps, antique postal and telecommunications equipment and models of postal conveyances. The museum's exhibits (from €7/5.50 including access to the permanent collection) are particularly inspired; think travel and exploration, not stamps.

MUSÉE DU MONTPARNASSE
Map pp434-5
☎ 01 42 22 91 96; 21 av du Maine, 15e; adult /senior & student €5/4, under 12 yr free; 🕙 12.30-7pm Tue-Sun; Ⓜ Montparnasse Bienvenüe
Housed in the studio of Russian Cubist artist Marie Vassilieff (1884–1957) down a charming narrow alleyway off the av du Maine, the Museum of Montparnasse does not have a permanent collection but recalls the great role Montparnasse played during various artistic periods of the 20th century through temporary exhibitions. It's always well worth visiting when something is on.

MUSÉE ERNEST HÉBERT Map pp434-5
☎ 01 42 22 23 82; www.rmn.fr; 85 rue du Cherche Midi, 6e; adult/senior & student €3/2.30, 1st Sun of the month free; 🕙 12.30-6pm Mon & Wed-Fri, 2-6pm Sat & Sun; Ⓜ St-Placide
Portrait painter Ernest Hébert (1817–1908) did likenesses of society people of the

---

TOP FIVE: MONTPARNASSE

- Catacombes (p121)
- Cimetière de Montparnasse (p121)
- Fondation Cartier pour l'Art Contemporain (p121)
- Musée de la Poste (above)
- Tour Montparnasse (view from top only; opposite)

Place Vendôme (p103)

Second Empire and *belle époque* and was thus not short of a sou or two. The artist's wonderful 18th-century townhouse and its baubles – not his saccharine, almost cloying portraits – is the draw here though – alas – the museum was closed for renovations at research time.

MUSÉE PASTEUR Map pp434-5

☎ 01 45 68 82 83; www.pasteur.fr; Institut Pasteur, 25 rue du Docteur Roux, 15e; adult/senior & student €3/1.5; ☺ 2-5.30pm Mon-Fri Sep-Jul; Ⓜ Pasteur

Housed in the apartment where the famous chemist and bacteriologist spent the last seven years of his life (1888–95), a tour of this museum takes you through Pasteur's private rooms, a hall with such odds and ends as gifts presented to him by heads of state and drawings he did as a young man. After Pasteur's death, the French government wanted to entomb his remains in the Panthéon, but his family, acting in accordance with his wishes, obtained permission to have him buried at his institute. The great savant lies in the basement crypt.

TOUR MONTPARNASSE Map pp434-5

☎ 01 45 38 52 56; www.tourmontparnasse56.com; rue de l'Arrivée, 15e; adult/7-15 yr/student & 16-20 yr €8.50/4/6.50, under 7 yr free; ☺ 9.30am-11.30pm Apr-Sep, 9.30am-10.30pm Sun-Thu, 9.30am-11pm Fri & Sat Oct-Mar; Ⓜ Montparnasse Bienvenüe

The 210m-high Montparnasse Tower, built in 1973 with steel and smoked glass and housing offices for 5000 workers, affords spectacular views over the city and is just about the best place to be since it is one of the few spots in Paris where you can't see this startlingly ugly oversized lipstick tube. A lift carries you up in 38 seconds to the renovated indoor observatory on the 56th floor, with an exhibition centre, film about Paris, interactive terminals and bar. You can finish your visit with a hike up the stairs to the open-air terrace on the 59th floor.

FAUBOURG ST-GERMAIN & INVALIDES

Drinking p249; Eating p211; Shopping p293; Sleeping p322

The 7e arrondissement has the reputation of being rather staid. At first glance, its formal beauty and conventional manners give an impression of restraint and distance. But this world of elaborate ironwork, flashing gold leaf and hewn stone has an extravagance all of its own.

Faubourg St-Germain (Map pp434–5), the area between the Musée d'Orsay and, 1km south, rue de Babylone, was Paris' most fashionable neighbourhood in the 18th century. Some of the most interesting mansions, many of which now serve as embassies, cultural centres and government ministries, are along three streets running east to west: rue de Lille, rue de Grenelle and rue de Varenne. Hôtel Matignon at 57 rue de Varenne has been the official residence of the French prime minister since the start of the Fifth Republic (1958).

Watching over the district and the city, the Eiffel Tower dominates the Paris skyline. At its feet, the Seine flows in a gracious curve and the smooth lawns of the Champ de Mars stretch away. Somehow it always feels like Sunday in the alleys of this park, with its sweeping prospects and precise design. To the east, the well-to-do and sleepy rue de l'Université and rue St-Dominique make their calm way down to the blvd St-Germain, leaving behind the bright dome of Les Invalides. The National Assembly is over by the river as is the celebrated Musée d'Orsay, housed in the cavernous shell of an old railway station and displaying the patrimony's rich collection of impressionist art. The architecturally impressive **Musée du Quai Branly** (p44), opened in mid-2006 to great fanfare. For details see www.quai branly.fr/.

ASSEMBLÉE NATIONALE Map pp434-5

☎ 01 40 63 60 00; www.assemblee-nat.fr; 33 quai d'Orsay & 126 rue de l'Université, 7e; Ⓜ Assemblée Nationale or Invalides

The National Assembly, the lower house of the French parliament, meets in the 18th-century Palais Bourbon fronting the Seine. Tours are now available only through local deputies, thus only citizens or residents are eligible. Next door is the Second Empire-style **Ministère des Affaires Étrangères** (Ministry of Foreign Affairs; ☎ 01 43 17 53 53; 37 quai d'Orsay), built between 1845 and 1855 and often referred to as the 'Quai d'Orsay'.

HÔTEL DES INVALIDES Map pp434-5

Ⓜ Invalides, Varenne or La Tour Maubourg
A 500m-long expanse of lawn called the **Esplanade des Invalides** separates Faubourg St-Germain from the Eiffel Tower area. At the southern end of the esplanade, laid out between 1704 and 1720, is the final resting place of Napoleon, the man many French people consider to be the nation's greatest hero.

The **Hôtel des Invalides** was built in the 1670s by Louis XIV to provide housing for 4000 *invalides* (disabled war veterans). On 14 July 1789, a mob forced its way into the building and, after fierce fighting, seized 32,000 rifles before heading on to the prison at Bastille and the start of the French Revolution.

North of the Hôtel des Invalides' main courtyard, the so-called **Cour d'Honneur**, is the **Musée de l'Armée** (Army Museum; ☎ 01 44 42 38 77; www.invalides.org; 129 rue de Grenelle, 7e; adult/senior, student & 18-25 yr €7.50/5.50, under 18 yr free; ☺ 10am-6pm Apr-Sep, 10am-5pm Oct-Mar, closed 1st Mon of the month), which holds the nation's largest collection on the history of the French military.

To the south are the **Église St-Louis des Invalides**, once used by soldiers, and the **Église du Dôme**, with its sparkling dome (1677–1735), considered to be one of the finest religious edifices erected under Louis XIV. It received the remains of Napoleon in 1840. The very extravagant **Tombeau de Napoléon 1er** (Napoleon's Tomb; ☺ 10am-6pm Apr-Sep, 10am-5pm Oct-Mar, closed 1st Mon of the month), in the centre of the church, consists of six coffins that fit into one another like a Russian *matryoshka* doll.

Admission to the Army Museum allows entry to all the other sights in the Hôtel des Invalides, including the **Musée des Plans-Reliefs** (☎ 01 45 51 95 05), a rather esoteric museum full of scale models of towns, fortresses and chateaus across France that keeps the same hours as the Army Museum.

MUSÉE D'ORSAY Map pp434-5

☎ 01 40 49 48 14; www.musee-orsay.fr; 62 rue de Lille, 7e; adult/senior & 18-25 yr €7.50/5.50, under 18 yr free, 1st Sun of the month free; ☺ 9.30am-6pm Tue, Wed, Fri-Sun, 9.30am-9.45pm Thu; Ⓜ Musée d'Orsay or Solférino

The Musée d'Orsay, in a former train station (1900) facing the Seine from quai Anatole France, displays France's national collection of paintings, sculptures, *objets d'art* and other works produced between the 1840s and 1914, including the fruits of the impressionist, postimpressionist and Art Nouveau movements; the Musée National d'Art Moderne at the **Centre Pompidou** (p98) then picks up the torch.

Many visitors head straight to the upper level (lit by a skylight) to see the famous impressionist paintings by Monet, Renoir, Pissarro, Sisley, Degas and Manet and the postimpressionist works by Van Gogh, Cézanne, Seurat and Matisse, but there's also a great deal to see on the ground floor, including some early works by Manet, Monet, Renoir and Pissarro. The middle level has some magnificent Art Nouveau rooms.

PARIS ON THE CHEAP

The permanent collections at 11 of the 15 *musées municipaux* (city museums), run by the **Mairie de Paris** (www.paris .fr), are now open to one and all for free. Remember, however, this does not apply to temporary or special exhibitions, which always incur a separate admission fee.

City museums taking part in the scheme include the following:

Maison de Balzac (p128)

Maison de Victor Hugo (p110)

Musée Bourdelle (p122)

Musée Carnavalet (p107)

Musée Cernuschi (p133)

Musée Cognacq-Jay (p108)

Musée d'Art Moderne de la Ville de Paris (p128)

Musée de la Vie Romantique (p149)

Musée des Beaux-Arts de la Ville de Paris (Petit Palais; p131)

Musée Jean Moulin & Mémorial du Maréchal Leclerc de Hauteclocque et de la Libération de Paris (p122)

Musée Atelier Zadkine (p120)

At the same time, the *musées nationaux* (national museums) in Paris have a reduced rate for those aged over 60 and between 18 and 25 and sometimes for everyone else on one day or part of a day (eg Sunday morning) per week. They are always free for those under 18 years of age and for everyone on the first Sunday of each month. Again, this does not include temporary exhibitions, for which you will have to pay separately.

The museums and monuments in question are:

Arc de Triomphe (p130) October to March only.

Conciergerie (p112) October to March only.

Musée d'Art et d'Histoire (p158)

Musée de l'Assistance Publique-Hôpitaux de Paris (p116)

Musée de l'Histoire de France (Archives Nationales; p106)

Musée d'Orsay (opposite)

Musée du Louvre (p100)

Musée Guimet des Arts Asiatiques (p129)

Musée Ernest Hébert (p122)

Musée National d'Art Moderne (Centre Pompidou; p98)

Musée National du Moyen Age (Musée de Cluny; p116)

Musée National Eugène Delacroix (p120)

Musée National Gustave Moreau (p150)

Musée Picasso (p109)

Musée Rodin (p126)

Panthéon (p117) October to March only.

Ste-Chapelle (p113) October to March only.

Tours de Notre Dame (p111) October to March only.

English-language tours (information ☎ 01 40 49 48 48; tour €6.50/4.70 plus admission fee), lasting 1½ hours, include 'Masterpieces of the Musée d'Orsay', departing at 11.30am Tuesday to Saturday, and an in-depth tour focusing on the impressionists at 2.30pm on Tuesday and 4pm on Thursday at least once a month. The 1½-hour audioguide tour (€5.50), available in six languages, points out 80 major works. Be aware that tickets are valid all day so you can leave and re-enter the museum as you please. The reduced entrance fee of €5.50 applies to everyone after 4.15pm (8pm on Thursday) and all day on Sunday.

The excellent *Guide to the Musée d'Orsay* (€14.50) is in full colour and has detailed maps. The less comprehensive *Pocket Guide* to the *Musée d'Orsay* is €5.50. Both can be purchased at the ticket counter.

MUSÉE MAILLOL-FONDATION DIANA VIERNY Map pp434-5

☎ 01 42 22 59 58; www.museemaillol.com; 61 rue de Grenelle, 7e; adult/student & 16-25 yr €8/6, under 16 yr free; ☺ 11am-6pm Wed-Mon; Ⓜ Rue du Bac This splendid small museum focuses on the work of the sculptor Aristide Maillol (1861–1944) and also includes works by Matisse, Gauguin, Kandinsky, Cézanne and Picasso from the private collection of Dina Vierny (1915–), who was Maillol's principal model for 10 years from the age of 15. The museum is located in the stunning 18th-century Hôtel Bouchardon.

Avenue of trees in front of the Eiffel Tower

MUSÉE RODIN Map pp434–5

☎ 01 44 18 61 10; www.musee-rodin.fr; 79 rue de Varenne, 7e; adult/senior & 18-25 yr €7/5, under 18 yr free, 1st Sun of the month free, garden only €1; ⏰ 9.30am-5.45pm Tue-Sun Apr-Sep, 9.30am-4.45pm Tue-Sun Oct-Mar; Ⓜ Varenne

The Rodin Museum, the favourite cultural attraction in Paris for some visitors, is also one of the most relaxing spots in the city. It has a delightful garden full of sculptures and shade trees in which to rest and contemplate *The Thinker*. Rooms on two floors of the 18th-century Hôtel Biron display extraordinarily vital bronze and marble sculptures by Auguste Rodin, including casts of some of his most celebrated works: *The Hand of God, The Burghers of Calais, Cathedral,* that perennial crowd-pleaser *The Thinker* and the sublime, the incomparable, that romance-hewn-in-marble called *The Kiss*. There are also some 15 works by Camille Claudel (1864–1943), sister to the writer Paul and Rodin's mistress. An excellent audioguide (€4) is the perfect accompaniment to your visit. The garden closes its gates later than the museum: at 6.45pm in summer and at 5pm in winter.

EIFFEL TOWER AREA & 16E ARRONDISSEMENT

Eating p212

Paris' very symbol, the **Eiffel Tower** (Map pp434–5), is surrounded by open areas on both banks of the Seine, which take in both the **7e arrondissement** and the **16e arrondissement**.

Neuilly, Auteil and especially Passy – known as 'NAP' in local parlance – are among the city's most prestigious neighbourhoods. The wide avenues radiating out from the place du Trocadéro are lined with sober, elegant buildings from the Haussmann era. Luxury boutiques abound, frequented by posh customers who desert the area come nightfall. It's here, on the banks of the Seine, that the architectural curiosity known as the 'Maison Ronde' – the Maison de Radio France – was constructed. Just north, the Maison de Balzac keeps alive the memory of the illustrious author of *Le Père Goriot*. Further north, the ultra bourgeois av Foch thumbs its nose at the restless av de la Grande Armée, teeming with motorbike fanatics. The 16e arrondissement also hosts football meets at the Parc des Princes and, as summer approaches, the thud of tennis balls on clay can be heard at Stade Roland Garros. There are some fabulous cultural institutions here, including the Musée d'Art Moderne de la Ville de Paris, the Musée de la Marine, the Musée de l'Homme and the beautiful Musée Guimet as well as lots and lots of smaller and lesser known museums on such diverse subjects as wine, radio, crystal and the pen.

EIFFEL TOWER Map pp434-5

☎ 01 44 11 23 23; www.tour-eiffel.fr; ⏰ lifts 9am-midnight mid-Jun-Aug, 9.30am-11pm Sep–mid-Jun; stairs 9am-midnight mid-Jun-Aug, 9.30am-6.30pm Sep–mid-Jun; Ⓜ Champ de Mars-Tour Eiffel or Bir Hakeim

La Tour Eiffel faced massive opposition from Paris' artistic and literary elite when it was built for the 1889 Exposition Universelle (World Fair), marking the centenary of the Revolution.

The 'metal asparagus', as some Parisians snidely called it, was almost torn down in 1909 but was spared because it proved an ideal platform for the transmitting antennas needed for the newfangled science of radiotelegraphy. It welcomed two million visitors the first year it opened and just under three times that number – 5.8 million, in fact – make their way to the top each year today.

The Eiffel Tower, named after its designer, Gustave Eiffel, is 324m high, including the TV antenna at the tip. This figure can vary by as much as 15cm, however, as the tower's 10,000 tonnes of iron, held together by 2.5 million rivets, expand in warm weather and contract when it's cold.

Three levels are open to the public. The lifts (in the west and north pillars), which follow a curved trajectory, cost €4.20 to the 1st platform (57m above the ground), €7.70 to the 2nd (115m) and €11 to the 3rd (276m). Children aged three to 11 pay €2.30, €4.20 or €6, respectively; there are no senior, youth or student discounts though children under three years are free. If you're feeling fit and/or energetic you can avoid the lift queues by taking the stairs (€3.80/3 over/under 25 yr) in the south pillar to the 1st and 2nd platforms. The east pillar is normally reserved for groups.

FLAME OF LIBERTY MEMORIAL

Map pp426-7

Ⓜ Alma-Marceau

On 31 August 1997 in the Place d'Alma underpass, Diana, Princess of Wales, was killed in a devastating car accident, along with her companion, Dodi Fayed, and their chauffeur, Henri Paul. A little bit to the east of the underpass, the bronze Flame of Liberty became something of a memorial to Diana. The sculpture – a replica of the one topping the torch of the Statue of Liberty – was originally placed here in 1987 on the centenary of the launch of the *International Herald Tribune* newspaper and was intended as a symbol of friendship between France and the USA. After Diana's death, the Flame of Liberty was decorated with flowers, photographs, graffiti and personal notes for almost five years. It was renovated and cleaned in 2002 and, this being the age of short (or no) memories, there are no longer any reminders of the tragedy that happened so close by and had so much of the Western world in grief at the time.

An illuminated bronze replica of the entire Statue of Liberty in New York faces the Big Apple from a long and narrow artificial island in the Seine (Map pp434–5).

GALERIE-MUSÉE BACCARAT

Map pp426-7

☎ 01 40 22 11 00; www.baccarat.fr; 11 place des États-Unis, 16e; adult/student & 18-25 yr €7/3.50, under 18 yr free; ⏰ 10am-6.30pm Mon, Wed & Sat; Ⓜ Boissière or Kléber

That's gratitude for you... For decades the glittering Baccarat Gallery-Museum displayed its 1000 stunning pieces of crystal, many of them custom-made for princes and dictators of desperately poor excolonies, at the CIAT (Centre International des Arts de la Table) building, a fine example of Napoleon III-era industrial architecture in the gritty but gracious 10e arrondissement. And then the Noailles stately home became available in the uppity 16e, interior designer Philippe Starck was called in and the museum was at home precisely where you'd expect it to be. Shame... Rue de Paradis (Paradise St) will never be the same. There is an excellent restaurant called the Crystal Room attached now, though.

MUSÉE D'ART MODERNE DE LA VILLE DE PARIS Map pp426-7

☎ 01 53 67 40 00; www.mam.paris.fr in French; 11 av du Président Wilson, 16e; temporary exhibits from adult/12-17 yr/senior, student & 18-26 yr €4.50/2.20/3, permanent collections free, under 12 yr free; ☷ 10am-6pm Tue & Thu-Sun, 10am-10pm Wed; Ⓜ Iéna

The Modern Art Museum of the City of Paris was established in 1961. The museum is housed in what was the Electricity Pavilion at the time of the 1937 Exposition Universelle and displays works representative of just about every major artistic movement of the 20th and nascent 21st centuries: Fauvism, cubism, Dadaism, surrealism, the School of Paris, expressionism, abstractionism and so on. Artists who have works on display include Matisse, Picasso, Braque, Soutine, Modigliani and Chagall.

MUSÉE DAPPER Map pp426-7

☎ 01 44 00 91 75; www.dapper.com.fr in French; 35 rue Paul Valéry, 16e; adult/senior & student €6/3, under 16 yr free, last Wed of the month free; ☷ 11am-7pm Wed-Sun; Ⓜ Victor Hugo

This fantastic museum of Sub-Saharan African art collected and exhibited by the nonprofit Dapper Foundation in a 16th-century *hôtel particulier* (private mansion) with wonderful 21st-century add-ons stages two major exhibitions each year. The collection is mostly of carved wooden figurines and masks, which famously influenced the work of Picasso, Braque and Man Ray.

MAISON DE BALZAC Map pp434-5

☎ 01 55 74 41 80; www.balzac.paris.fr in French; 47 rue Raynouard, 16e; temporary exhibits adult/14-25 yr/senior & student €4/2/3, permanent collections free, under 14 yr free; ☷ 10am-6pm Tue-Sun; Ⓜ Passy or Kennedy Radio France

Balzac's House, about 800m southwest of the Jardins du Trocadéro, is the Passy spa house where the realist novelist Honoré de Balzac (1799–1850) lived and worked from 1840 to 1847, editing the entire *Comédie Humaine* and writing various books. There's lots of memorabilia, letters, prints and portraits, but this place is decidedly for dyed-in-the-wool Balzac fans only.

MUSÉE DES ÉGOUTS DE PARIS

Map pp434-5

☎ 01 53 68 27 81; place de la Résistance, 7e; adult/student & 5-16 yr €4/3.20, under 5 free; ☷ 11am-5pm Sat-Wed May-Sep, 11am-4pm Sat-Wed Oct-Dec & Feb-Apr; Ⓜ Pont de l'Alma

The Paris Sewers Museum is a working museum whose entrance, a rectangular maintenance hole topped with a kiosk, is across the street from 93 quai d'Orsay, 7e. Raw sewage flows beneath your feet as you walk through 480m of odoriferous tunnels, passing artefacts illustrating the development of Paris' waste-water disposal system. It'll take your breath away, it will. The sewers keep regular hours except – God forbid – when rain threatens to flood the tunnels.

MUSÉE DU STYLO ET DE L'ÉCRITURE

Map pp422-3

☎ 06 07 94 13 21; 3 rue Guy de Maupassant, 16e; adult/senior & student €2/1; ☷ 2-6pm Sun; Ⓜ Ave Henri Martin or Rue de la Pompe

The Museum of the Pen and of Penmanship has the most important collection of writing utensils in the world, with pens dating back to the early 18th century, as well as paper and calligraphy. It can be visited on other days if you phone and book in advance.

MUSÉE DU VIN Map pp434-5

☎ 01 45 25 63 26; www.museeduvinparis.com; rue des Eaux, 5 square Charles Dickens, 16e; admission €8; ☷ 10am-6pm Tue-Sun; Ⓜ Passy

The not-so-comprehensive Wine Museum, headquarters of the prestigious International Federation of Wine Brotherhoods, introduces visitors to the fine art of viticulture with mock-ups and displays of tools. Admission includes a glass of wine at the end of the visit. Entry is free if you have lunch at the attached restaurant of which we hear very good things from readers.

MUSÉE GALLIERA DE LA MODE DE LA VILLE DE PARIS Map pp426-7

☎ 01 56 52 86 00; www.galliera.paris.fr; 10 av Pierre 1er de Serbie, 16e; adult/14-25 yr/student & senior €7/3.50/5.50, under 13 yr free; ☷ 10am-6pm Tue-Sun; Ⓜ Iéna

The Fashion Museum of the city of Paris, housed in the 19th-century Palais Galliera, warehouses some 100,000 outfits and accessories from the 18th century to the present day and exhibits them – and items borrowed from collections abroad – in tremendously successful temporary exhibitions. The sumptuous Italianate building and gardens are worth a visit in themselves.

MUSÉE GUIMET DES ARTS ASIATIQUES Map pp426-7

☎ 01 56 52 53 00; www.museeguimet.fr; 6 place d'Iéna, 16e; permanent collections adult/18-25 yr & everyone on Sun €7/5, under 18 free, 1st Sun of the month free; ⏰ 10am-6pm Wed-Mon; Ⓜ Iéna

The Guimet Museum of Asiatic Arts is France's foremost repository for Asian art and has sculptures, paintings, *objets d'art* and religious articles from Afghanistan, India, Nepal, Pakistan, Tibet, Cambodia, China, Japan and Korea. The entrance fee includes an audioguide. Part of the collection – Buddhist paintings and sculptures brought to Paris in 1876 by collector Émile Guimet – is housed in the **Galeries du Panthéon Bouddhique du Japon et de la Chine** (Buddhist Pantheon Galleries of Japan & China; ☎ 01 47 23 61 65; 19 av d'Iéna; admission free; ⏰ 9.45am-5.45pm Wed-Mon; Ⓜ Iéna) in the scrumptious Hôtel Heidelbach a short distance to the north. Don't miss the wonderful **Japanese garden** (⏰ 1-5pm Wed-Mon) here.

MUSÉE HENRI BOUCHARD Map pp422-3

☎ 01 46 47 63 46; www.musee-bouchard.com; 25 rue de l'Yvette, 16e; adult/senior & student €4/2.50; ⏰ 2-7pm Wed & Sat; Ⓜ Jasmin

The workshop of the sculptor Henri Bouchard (1875–1960), who produced some 1300 works in his prolific career, is a jumble sale of sculptures, sketches and tools, and an interesting place to visit to get a feel of how the 16e once was – artsy and creative. The museum, with very limited opening hours, is run by the sculptor's son and daughter-in-law.

PALAIS DE CHAILLOT & JARDINS DU TROCADÉRO Map pp434-5

Ⓜ Trocadéro

The two curved, colonnaded wings of the Palais de Chaillot, built for the 1937 World Exhibition held in Paris, and the terrace in between them afford an exceptional panorama of the Jardins du Trocadéro, the Seine and the Eiffel Tower.

TOP FIVE: EIFFEL TOWER AREA & 16E

- Eiffel Tower (p127)
- Musée des Égouts de Paris (opposite)
- Musée Dapper (opposite)
- Musée Guimet des Arts Asiatiques (left)
- Palais de Tokyo (below)

The palace's western wing contains two interesting museums. The **Musée de l'Homme** (Museum of Mankind; ☎ 01 44 05 72 72; www.mnhn.fr in French; 17 place du Trocadéro, 16e; adult/4-16 yr/senior & student €7/3/5; ⏰ 9.45am-5.15pm Mon, Wed-Fri, 10am-6.30pm Sat & Sun) focuses on human development, ethnology, population and population growth; it's a branch of the **Musée National d'Histoire Naturelle** (p116). There are also excellent scientific and ethnographical temporary exhibits on everything from the personality and the brains to the Inuit people of Greenland.

The **Musée de la Marine** (Maritime Museum; ☎ 01 53 65 69 69; www.musee-marine.fr; 17 place du Trocadéro; adult/student & 18-25 yr €6.50/4.50, under 18 yr free; ⏰ 10am-6pm Wed-Mon) focuses on France's naval adventures from the 17th century until today and boasts one of the world's finest collections of model ships as well as ancient compasses, sextants, telescopes etc.

Unfolding below the Palais de Chaillot are the **Jardins du Trocadéro** (Map pp434–5; Ⓜ Trocadéro), whose fountains and statue garden are grandly illuminated at night. They are named after a Spanish stronghold near Cádiz captured by the French in 1823.

PALAIS DE TOKYO Map pp426-7

☎ 01 47 23 38 86; www.palaisdetokyo.com; 13 av du Président Wilson, 16e; adult/senior & 18-26 yr €6/4.50, under 18 yr free, 1st Sun of the month €1; ⏰ noon-midnight Tue-Sun; Ⓜ Iéna

The Tokyo Palace, like the Musée d'Art Modern de la Ville de Paris next door in yet another 1937 World Exhibition building, opened in 2002 as a Site de Création Contemporain (Site for Contemporary Arts). It has no permanent collection and plans no exhibitions of a single artist or theme but will showcase ephemeral artwork, installations and performances. It's event-driven rather than static, and worth a visit.

PARC DU CHAMP DE MARS Map pp434-5

Ⓜ Champ de Mars-Tour Eiffel or École Militaire
Running southeast from the Eiffel Tower,
the grassy 'Field of Mars' (named after
Mars, the Roman god of war) was originally used as a parade ground for the
cadets of the 18th-century École Militaire
(Military Academy), the vast, French-
classical building (1772) at the southeastern end of the park, which counts none
other than Napoleon Bonaparte among its
graduates.

On 14 July 1790 the Fête de la Fédération (Federation Festival) was held on the
Champ de Mars to celebrate the first anniversary of the storming of the Bastille. Four
years later it was the location of the Fête
de l'Être-Suprême (Festival of the Supreme
Being), at which Robespierre presided over
a ceremony that established a revolutionary 'state religion'.

The Marionettes du Champ de Mars (☎ 01 48
56 01 44; Ⓜ École Militaire) stage puppet
shows (€3) in a covered and heated *salle*
(hall) in the park at 3.15pm and 4.15pm on
Wednesday, Friday, Saturday and Sunday.

ÉTOILE & CHAMPS-ÉLYSÉES

Eating p213; Shopping p296; Sleeping p324

The **8e arrondissement** was born under a lucky
star, it would seem. Its avenues radiate from
place de l'Étoile – officially **place Charles de
Gaulle** (Map pp426–7) – bathing in the glow
of fame (and flame; see p132). First among
them is the av des Champs-Élysées. From
the Arc de Triomphe in the northwest to
the place de la Concorde in the southeast,
this broad boulevard rules supreme. On
New Year's Eve and after major sporting
victories there's always a party here. Like a
splendid, regal hostess, the avenue receives
its guests, makes them mingle and moves
them along. And the guests keep coming.
Just a short walk away, the av Montaigne
haughtily displays its designer wares. Mo-
torboats are moored by the pont de l'Alma.
And members of the jet set go shopping in
the av George V and the rue du Faubourg
St-Honoré. Here fashion, art and luxury hotels go hand in hand. Only the finest are on
display, as in the neighbourhood's theatres
and museums, such as the Grand Palais and
Petit Palais.

Sandwiched between the parks at the
eastern end of the av des Champs-Élysées
and the Jardin des Tuileries is the cobblestone expanse of place de la Concorde, a
huge 18th-century square with more than
a few Revolutionary ghosts haunting it.
Delightful place de la Madeleine, with its
lovely neoclassical church and fine-food
shops lies to the north.

ARC DE TRIOMPHE Map pp426-7

☎ 01 55 37 73 77; www.monum.fr; viewing
platform adult/18-25 yr €8/6, under 18 yr free, 1st
Sun of the month Oct-Mar free; ⌚ 10am-11pm
Apr-Sep, 10am-10.30pm Oct-Mar; Ⓜ Charles de
Gaulle-Étoile
The Triumphal Arch is 2km northwest of
place de la Concorde in the middle of place
Charles de Gaulle (or place de l'Étoile), the
world's largest traffic roundabout and the
meeting point of 12 avenues (and three
arrondissements). It was commissioned in
1806 by Napoleon to commemorate his
imperial victories but remained unfinished
when he started losing – first battles and
then whole wars. It was finally completed
in 1836. Among the armies to march trium-
phantly through the Arc de Triomphe were
the Germans in 1871, the Allies in 1919,
the Germans again in 1940 and the Allies
in 1944.

The most famous of the four high-relief
panels at the base is to the right, facing
the arch from the av des Champs-Élysées
side. Entitled *Départ des Volontaires de
1792* (Departure of the Volunteers of 1792)
and also known as *La Marseillaise* (France's
national anthem), it is the work of François
Rude. Higher up, a frieze running around
the whole monument depicts hundreds of
figures, each one 2m high.

From the viewing platform on top of
the arch (via 284 steps and well worth
the climb) you can see the dozen broad
avenues – many of them named after
Napoleonic victories and illustrious gener-
als – radiating toward every part of Paris.
Av de la Grande Armée heads northwest to
the skyscraper district of La Défense (p155),
where the Grande Arche, a hollow cube 110m
on each side, defines the western end
of the Grand Axe (the 'Great Axis' linking the Louvre and the Arc de Triomphe).
Tickets to the viewing platform of the Arc
de Triomphe are sold in the underground
passageway that surfaces on the even-

numbered side of av des Champs-Élysées. It is the only *sane* way to get to the base of the arch and is *not* linked to nearby metro tunnels. Driving around the roundabout is Paris' ultimate driving challenge, especially during rush hour.

AV DES CHAMPS-ÉLYSÉES Map pp426-7

Ⓜ Charles de Gaulle-Étoile, George V, Franklin D Roosevelt or Champs-Élysées Clemenceau

Av des Champs-Élysées (the name refers to the 'Elysian Fields' where happy souls dwelt after death according to Greek myth) links place de la Concorde with the Arc de Triomphe. The avenue has symbolised the style and *joie de vivre* of Paris since the mid-19th century and remains a popular tourist destination.

Some 400m north of av des Champs-Élysées is rue du Faubourg St-Honoré (8e), the western extension of rue St-Honoré. It has renowned couture houses, jewellers, antique shops and the 18th-century **Palais de l'Élysée** (cnr rue du Faubourg St-Honoré & av de Marigny, 8e; Ⓜ Champs-Élysées Clemenceau), which is the official residence of the French president.

At the bottom of av des Champs-Élysées is a 3.6m-tall bronze **statue** depicting Gen-

Fountain in place de la Concorde (132)

eral Charles de Gaulle in full military gear ready to march down the broad avenue to the Arc de Triomphe in a liberated Paris on 26 August 1944.

GRAND PALAIS Map pp426-7

☎ 01 44 13 17 17, reservation 0 892 684 694; www.rmn.fr/galeriesnationalesdugrandpalais; 3 av du Général Eisenhower, 8e; with/without booking adult €11/9.30, student & 13-25 €10/8, under 13 yr free; ◷ 10am-8pm Thu-Mon, 10am-10pm Wed; Ⓜ Champs-Élysées Clemenceau

The 'Great Palace', erected for the 1900 Exposition Universelle, houses the **Galeries Nationales du Grand Palais** beneath its huge Art Nouveau glass roof. Special exhibitions, among the biggest the city stages, last three or four months. You'll understand just how popular most of the exhibitions here are – and the importance of booking in advance – when you see the queues (especially at the weekend) looping halfway round the building.

PALAIS DE LA DÉCOUVERTE
Map pp426-7

☎ 01 56 43 20 21; www.palais-decouverte.fr in French; av Franklin D Roosevelt, 8e; adult/senior, student & 5-18 yr €6.50/4, under 5 yr free; ◷ 9.30am-6pm Tue-Sat, 10am-7pm Sun; Ⓜ Champs-Élysées Clemenceau

The Palace of Discovery, inaugurated during the 1937 Exposition Universelle and thus the world's first interactive museum, is a fascinating place to take kids thanks to its hands-on exhibits on astronomy, biology, medicine, chemistry, mathematics, computer science, physics and earth sciences. The **planetarium** (admission €3.50 extra) usually has four shows a day in French at 11.30am, and 2pm, 3.15pm and 4.30pm; ring or consult the website for current schedules.

PETIT PALAIS Map pp426-7

☎ 01 53 43 40 00; www.petitpalais.paris.fr in French; av Winston Churchill, 8e; permanent collections free, temporary exhibits entrance fee varies; ◷ 10am-6pm Wed-Sun, 10am-8pm Tue; Ⓜ Champs-Élysées Clemenceau

The 'Little Palace', like the Grand Palais opposite also built for the 1900 Exposition Universelle, is home to the **Musée des Beaux-Arts de la Ville de Paris**, the Paris municipality's

Museum of Fine Arts. It reopened in late 2005 after a protracted, four-year renovation and now looks fantastic.

It specialises in medieval and Renaissance *objets d'art* like porcelain and clocks, tapestries, drawings and 19th-century French painting and sculpture.

PLACE DE LA CONCORDE Map pp426-7
Ⓜ Concorde

Place de la Concorde was laid out between 1755 and 1775. The 3300-year-old pink granite **obelisk** with the gilded top standing in the centre of the square was presented to France in 1831 by Muhammad Ali, viceroy and pasha of Egypt. Weighing 230 tonnes and towering 23m over the cobblestones, it once stood in the Temple of Ramses at Thebes (modern-day Luxor). The eight **female statues** adorning the four corners of the square represent France's largest cities (at least in the late 18th century).

In 1793, Louis XVI's head was lopped off by a **guillotine** set up in the northwest corner of the square near the statue representing the city of Brest. During the next two years, another guillotine – this one near the entrance to the Jardin des Tuileries – was used to behead 1343 more people, including Marie-Antoinette and, six months later, the Revolutionary leader Danton. Shortly thereafter, Robespierre lost his head here, too. The square was given its present name after the Reign of Terror had come to an end in the hope that it would become a place of peace and harmony.

The two imposing buildings on the north side of Place de la Concorde are the **Hôtel de la Marine**, headquarters of the French Navy, and the **Hôtel de Crillon** (p323), one of the most luxurious and exclusive hotels in Paris. In 1778, the treaty in which France recognised the independence of the new USA was signed in the Hôtel de Crillon by Louis XVI and Benjamin Franklin.

PLACE DE LA MADELEINE Map pp426-7
Ⓜ Madeleine

Ringed by a plethora of fine-food and gourmet shops, the place de la Madeleine is 350m north of place de la Concorde along at the end of rue Royale. The *place* is named after the 19th-century neoclassical church in its centre, the **Église de la Madeleine** (Church of St Mary Magdalene; ☎ 01 44 51 69 00; www.eglise-lamadeleine. com in French; place de la Madeleine, 8e; ⏲ 10am-7pm). Constructed in the style of a Greek temple, La Madeleine was consecrated in 1845 after almost a century of design changes and construction delays. It is surrounded by 52 Corinthian columns standing 20m tall, and the marble and gilt interior is topped by three sky-lit cupolas. You can hear the massive organ being played at Mass at 9.30am and 11am on Sunday.

The **monumental staircase** on the south side affords one of the city's most quintessential Parisian panoramas: down rue Royale to place de la Concorde and its obelisk and across the Seine to the Assemblée Nationale. The gold dome of the Invalides appears in the background.

Paris' cheapest *belle époque* attraction is the **public toilet** on the east side of La Madeleine, which dates from 1905. There has been a **flower market** (⏲ 8am-7.30pm Tue-Sun) on the east side of the church since 1832.

LIGHT MY FIRE

Since 1920, the body of an unknown soldier from WWI removed from the battlefields of Verdun in the Lorraine has lain beneath the Arc de Triomphe, his fate and that of countless others like him commemorated by a memorial flame burning in perpetuity. The idea for the memorial first came from French journalist Gabriel Boissy (1879–1949), who suggested in an article in 1923 that an 'eternal flame' be used in connection with war memorials or shrines to represent remembrance and to symbolise the eternity of the soul. On 11 November – Armistice or Remembrance Day – of that year a flame that was supposed to stay lit forever was installed.

Well, at least it made it for almost three quarters of a century. In July 1998 a drunken 24-year-old Mexican football fan named Rodrigo Rafael Ortega who was attending the World Cup in which France beat Brazil (p18) – he was clearly supporting the losers – extinguished the flame by urinating on it. He was arrested and charged with public drunkenness and offending the dead. The incident will no doubt live on in British lads' 'zines as the event of the last century, but we know what we would have done with this *bandito*. And the gallows just wouldn't have been tall enough.

CLICHY & GARE ST-LAZARE

Drinking p251; Eating p214; Sleeping p324

This area stretches from the elegant residential districts of the *haute bourgeoisie* (upper middle class) that surround 8.25-hectare **Parc de Monceau** (Map pp426–7; Ⓜ Monceau) in the 8e eastward to the Gare St-Lazare, an impressive iron structure built in 1851 and the inspiration for the market *pavillons* at Les Halles built in the same year, and then north to Clichy and the **17e arrondissement.**

The 17e suffers from acute schizophrenia. Its southern neighbourhoods – with their beautiful, Haussmann-era buildings – seem like an extension of the 8e and 16e arrondissements, while its northern neighbourhoods assert their working-class, anarchistic identity. The wide av de Wagram, av des Ternes and av de Villiers have both a residential and commercial vocation and boast some of the capital's most famous shops and restaurants. A maze of small streets with a pronounced working-class character stretches out around the av de Clichy, a pocket of old Paris that has survived without becoming ossified.

The Clichy-Batignolles district to the west of the av de Clichy was chosen as the site of a 62-hectare 'Olympic Village' as part of Paris' bid for the 2012 Olympiad. After the games, the village was meant to form a new *quartier* boasting socially integrated housing around a 10-hectare park. Work had already begun on the site in 2004 before Paris lost in its bid to London and will continue, though perhaps not with the same amount of enthusiasm. You can have a look at the plans of this impressive project at the Pavillon de l'Arsenal.

CHAPELLE EXPIATOIRE Map pp426-7

☎ 01 44 32 18 00; www.monum.fr; square Louis XVI, 8e; admission €3, under 18 yr free; ⏰ 1-5pm Thu-Sat; Ⓜ St-Augustin

The austere, neoclassical Atonement Chapel, opposite 29 rue Pasquier, sits atop the section of a cemetery where Louis XVI, Marie-Antoinette and many other victims of the Reign of Terror were buried after their executions in 1793. It was erected by Louis' brother, the restored Bourbon king Louis XVIII, in 1815. Two years later the royal bones were removed to the **Basilique de St-Denis** (p157).

MUSÉE CERNUSCHI Map pp426-7

☎ 01 53 96 21 50; www.cernuschi.paris.fr; 7 av Vélasquez, 8e; temporary exhibits adult/14-25 yr/student & senior €7/3.50/5.50, permanent collections free, under 13 yr free; ⏰ 10am-6pm Tue-Sun; Ⓜ Villiers

The Cernuschi Museum, recently renovated and its exhibition space redefined and enlarged, houses a collection of ancient Chinese art (funerary statues, bronzes, ceramics) and some works from Japan assembled during an 1871–73 world tour by the banker and philanthropist Henri Cernuschi (1821–96), who settled here from Milan before the unification of Italy.

MUSÉE JACQUEMART-ANDRÉ

Map pp426-7

☎ 01 45 62 11 59; www.musee-jacquemart-andre .com; 158 blvd Haussmann, 8e; adult/student & 7-17 yr €9.50/7, under 7 yr free; ⏰ 10am-6pm; Ⓜ Miromesnil

The Jacquemart-André Museum, founded by collector Édouard André and his portraitist wife Nélie Jacquemart, is in an opulent mid-19th-century residence on one of Paris' posher avenues. It contains furniture, tapestries and enamels, but it is most noted for its paintings by Rembrandt and Van Dyck and Italian Renaissance works by Bernini, Botticelli, Carpaccio, Donatello, Mantegna, Tintoretto, Titian and Uccello. The museum is often compared to the Frick Collection in New York. The relatively high price of admission includes an audio-guide. Don't miss the Jardin d'Hiver (Winter Garden), with its marble statuary, tropical plants and double-helix marble staircase. Just off it is the delightful *fumoir* (smoking room) filled with exotic objects collected by Jacquemart in the course of her travels.

MUSÉE NISSIM DE CAMONDO

Map pp426-7

☎ 01 53 89 06 50; www.ucad.fr; 63 rue de Monceau, 8e; adult/18-25 yr €6/4.50, under 18 yr free; ⏰ 10am-5.30pm Wed-Sun; Ⓜ Monceau or Villiers

The Nissim de Camondo Museum, housed in a sumptuous mansion modelled on the **Petit Trianon at Versailles** (p336), displays 18th-century furniture, wood panelling, tapestries, porcelain and other *objets d'art* collected by Count Moïse de Camondo, a Jewish banker who settled in Paris from

Constantinople in the late 19th century. He bequeathed the mansion and his collection to the state on the proviso that it would be a museum named in memory of his son Nissim (1892–1917), a pilot killed in action during WWI. The museum is run by the Union Centrale des Arts Décoratifs, which is responsible for the Musée des Arts Décoratifs (p102) and two other museums in the Rohan Wing of the Louvre.

OPÉRA & GRANDS BOULEVARDS

Drinking p251; Eating p216; Shopping p299; Sleeping p325

Place de l'Opéra (Map pp426–7), site of Paris' world-famous opera house, abuts the eight contiguous 'Grands Boulevards' (Madeleine, Capucines, Italiens, Montmartre, Poissonnière, Bonne Nouvelle, St-Denis and St-Martin) that stretch from elegant place de la Madeleine in the 8e eastwards to the up-and-coming place de la République (Map pp428–9) in the 3e, a distance of just under 3km. The Grands Boulevards were laid out in the 17th century on the site of obsolete city walls and served as a centre of café and theatre life through much of the 18th and 19th centuries, reaching the height of fashion during the belle époque (p78). North of the western end of the Grands Boulevards is blvd Haussmann (8e and 9e), the heart of the commercial and banking district and known for some of Paris' most famous department stores, including Galeries Lafayette (p300) and Le Printemps (p300).

Place de l'Opéra and the lion's share of the Grands Boulevards are in the 9e arrondissement, a somewhat misleading district where the smart set and the riff-raff, the foodies and the gluttons all rub shoulders. It's not uncommon to find wildly different establishments just across the road or round the corner from one other. Leaving the Opéra or Drouot auction house in the southern part of the arrondissement, you can wander and window-shop on the boulevards. Department stores and little boutiques jostle for space on blvd Haussmann and blvd des Capucines. On rue de Provence, rue Richer and rue du Faubourg-Montmartre, fast-food outlets and restaurants are crammed into every bit of space, and it's a Babel Tower of foreign languages.

MUSÉE DE LA FRANC-MAÇONNERIE
Map pp428-9
☎ 01 45 23 74 68, 01 45 23 20 92; 16 rue Cadet, 9e; admission €2; 2-6pm Tue-Fri, 2-5pm Sat; Ⓜ Cadet or Peletier

This museum housed in the colossal and quite impressive Grande Orient de France building provides a brief introduction to the secretive world of Freemasonry, which grew out of medieval stone masons' guilds of the 16th century, and the museum is a much more popular sight since the publication of *The Da Vinci Code* (p160). A visit to the museum and guided tour of the building in French on Wednesday at 10.30am costs €6.

MUSÉE DU PARFUM Map pp426-7
☎ 01 47 42 04 56; www.fragonard.com; 9 rue Scribe, 2e; admission free; 9am-5.30pm Mon-Sat, 9.30am-3.30pm Sun mid-Mar-Oct, 9am-5.30pm Mon-Sat Nov–mid-Mar; Ⓜ Opéra

The Perfume Museum run by the *perfumerie* Fragonard is a fragrant collection opposite the Palais Garnier tracing the history of scent and perfume-making from ancient Egypt (those mummies wouldn't have smelled very nice undoused) to today's designer brands. A short distance to the south is the Théâtre-Musée des Capucines (Map pp426–7; ☎ 01 42 60 37 14; 39 blvd des Capucines, 2e; 9am-5.30pm Mon-Sat; Ⓜ Opéra), a kind of branch in an early 20th-century theatre that concentrates largely on bottling (for example, crystal flasks from Bohemia) and packaging the heady substance. There's a decent short film here and, of course, a shop selling Fragonard scent.

MUSÉE GRÉVIN Map pp428-9
☎ 01 47 70 85 05; www.grevin.com; 10 blvd Montmartre, 9e; adult/6-14 yr/senior/student €17/10/14.50/15.50; 10am-6.30pm Mon-Fri, 10am-7pm Sat & Sun; Ⓜ Grands Boulevards

This large waxworks museum inside the passage Jouffroy boasts an impressive 300 wax figures that largely look more like caricatures than characters, but where else do you get to see Marilyn Monroe, Charles de Gaulle and Spiderman face-to-face or the original death masks of some of the French Revolutionary leaders? The admission fee is positively outrageous and just keeps a-growin'.

PALAIS GARNIER Map pp426-7

☎ 0 892 899 090; place de l'Opéra, 9e; Ⓜ Opéra
This renowned opera house was designed in 1860 by Charles Garnier to showcase the splendour of Napoleon III's France. Unfortunately, by the time it was completed – 15 years later – the Second Empire was only a distant memory and Napoleon III was six feet under. Still, this is one of the most impressive monuments erected in Paris during the 19th century and today stages operas, ballets and **classical-music concerts** (p271). If you're not catching a performance here, it can be can be visited on English-language **guided tours** (☎ 01 41 10 08 10; http://visites.operadeparis.fr; adult/10-26 yr/senior €11/6/9; ⏱ 11.30am & 2.30pm Jul & Aug, 11.30am Sat & Sun Sep-Jun).

The Palais Garnier also houses the **Bibliothèque-Musée de l'Opéra** (☎ 01 47 42 07 02; www.bnf.fr; adult/senior, student & 10-26 yr €7/4, under 10 yr free; ⏱ 10am-5pm Sep-Jun, 10am-6pm Jul & Aug), which contains a lot of documentation (it also functions as an important research library) and some memorabilia. Of more of interest to the visitor though, is a self-paced visit to the opera house itself, included in the admission to the museum, as long as there's not a daytime rehearsal or performance scheduled.

GARE DU NORD, GARE DE L'EST & RÉPUBLIQUE

Drinking p252; Eating p219; Sleeping p326
Two sorts of foot traffic give the **10e arrondissement** its distinctive feel. The banks of the **Canal St-Martin** (Map pp428–9) draw leisurely strollers, while travellers part and are reunited on the platforms of the Gare du Nord and Gare de l'Est. Each arrival and departure announced over the loudspeakers produces a burst of frenetic activity. Outside, the cafés and brasseries do a brisk trade, catering to travellers and locals. Nearby, the blvd de Magenta rushes like a swollen river, the noisy, impatient crowd spreading through the adjoining streets and pouring out onto the place de la République.

The buzzy working-class area around blvd de Strasbourg and rue du Faubourg St-Denis, especially south of blvd de Magenta, is home to large communities of Indians, Bangladeshis, Pakistanis, West Indians, Africans, Turks and Kurds. Strolling through **passage Brady** (p219) is almost like stepping into a back alley in Mumbai or Dhaka.

Canal St-Martin, especially the quai de Jemmapes and the quai de Valmy with their rows of plane and chestnut trees, seems a

Oscar Wilde's tomb in Cimetière du Père Lachaise (p137)

world away. Barges appear, pass silently, then vanish behind a lock. Little iron bridges and walkways span the still water. Rundown not so long ago, the canal has a new lease of life, helped in a large part by the upmarket restaurants and bistros lining it.

CANAL ST-MARTIN Map pp428-9
Ⓜ République, Jaurès, Jacques Bonsergent
The tranquil, 4.5km-long St-Martin Canal, which has undergone a major renovation and clean-up recently, links the 10e with Parc de la Villette (Map pp422–3) in the 19e via the Bassin de la Villette and Canal de l'Ourcq and the canal makes its famous dogleg turn in this arrondissement. Its shaded towpaths are a wonderful place for a romantic stroll or a bike ride and take you past nine locks, metal bridges and ordinary Parisian neighbourhoods. Parts of the waterway – built between 1806 and 1825 to link the Seine with the 108km-long Canal de l'Ourcq – are higher than the surrounding land. The best way to see the canal is from a canal barge (p95).

MUSÉE DE L'ÉVANTAIL Map pp428-9
☎ 01 42 08 90 20; 2 blvd de Strasbourg, 10e; adult/student/senior €6/3/4; ⏱ 2-6pm Mon-Wed; Ⓜ Strasbourg St-Denis
Big fans of this museum, we always find it impossible to walk by without checking in on our favourite fans – screen, folding and brisé (the kind with overlapping struts). Around 900 breeze-makers are on display, dating as far back as the mid-18th century.

The small museum is housed in what was once a well-known fan manufactory, and its original showroom, dating from 1893, is sublime.

PORTE ST-DENIS & PORTE ST-MARTIN Map pp428-9
cnr rue du Faubourg St-Denis & blvd St-Denis, 10e; Ⓜ Strasbourg St-Denis
St Denis Gate, a 24m-high triumphal arch, was built in 1673 to commemorate Louis XIV's campaign along the Rhine. On the northern side, carvings represent the fall of Maastricht in the same year.

Two blocks east is a similar arch, the 17m-high Porte St-Martin (St Martin Gate) at the corner of rue du Faubourg St-Martin and blvd St-Denis. It was erected two years later to commemorate the capture of Besançon and the Franche-Comté region by Louis XIV's armies (note the gilded fleur-de-lis).

MÉNILMONTANT & BELLEVILLE
Drinking p253; Eating p222; Sleeping p328
A solidly working-class *quartier* with little to recommend it until the last decade, Ménilmontant, which shares the 11e arrondissement with Bastille (p105), now boasts almost as many restaurants, bars and clubs as the Marais, especially along rue Ménilmontant (Map pp428–9). On the other hand, the inner-city 'village' of Belleville (p170), centred on blvd de Belleville in the

GRAVE CONCERNS
Camp as a row of tents and as fresh as the air, Oscar Wilde (1854–1900) is apparently as flamboyant in death as he was on his hotel deathbed when he proclaimed 'My wallpaper and I are fighting a duel to the death – one of us has *got* to go.' It seems that the Père Lachaise grave of the Irish playwright and humorist, who was sentenced to two years in prison in 1895 for gross indecency stemming from his homosexual relationship with Lord Alfred 'Bosie' Douglas (1870–1945), is attracting admirers, who plaster the ornate tomb with indelible lipstick kisses. The problem has got so serious (and expensive) that authorities have asked a major cosmetic company to pay for a cleanup.

But Wilde's tomb is not the only grave concern at Père Lachaise these days. A security guard had to be posted near the grave of rock singer Jim Morrison (1943–71) after fans began taking drugs and having sex on his tomb. The cemetery's conservation office has even issued a leaflet outlining the rules of conduct when visiting the grave. Meanwhile, over in division 92, a protest by women has seen the removal of a metal fence placed around the grave of one Victor Noir, pseudonym of the journalist Yvan Salman (1848–70), who was shot and killed by Pierre Bonaparte, great-nephew of the Napoleon, at the age of just 22. The protest had not to do with freedom of the press or anything as highbrow as that. According to legend, a woman who strokes the amply filled crotch of Monsieur Noir's prostrate bronze effigy will quickly become pregnant. Apparently some would-be mothers were rubbing a bit too enthusiastically, and the larger-than-life-size package was being worn down – and so the (now dismantled) fence was built to protect the statue.

20e to the east, remains for the most part unpretentious and working-class – though that is changing too – and is home to large numbers of immigrants, especially Muslims and Jews from North Africa and Vietnamese and ethnic Chinese from Indochina. The **20e arrondissement** has retained its working-class character. The city centre is far away, the Eiffel Tower but a beacon on the horizon; this Paris is rough and rebellious, friendly and alive. The multicultural tone of rue de Belleville and rue de Ménilmontant is amplified by blvd de Belleville, blvd de Ménilmontant and blvd de Charonne. The air is filled with the aroma of coriander, saffron and cumin, and the exotic sounds of African and Asian languages. A colourful, abundant market spills out over the footpaths of blvd de Belleville.

CIMETIÈRE DU PÈRE LACHAISE

Map pp422-3 & Map pp440-1

☎ 01 55 25 82 10; ☾ 8am-6pm Mon-Fri, 8.30am-6pm Sat, 9am-6pm Sun mid-Mar–early Nov, 8am-5.30pm Mon-Fri, 8.30am-5.30pm Sat, 9am-5.30pm Sun early Nov–mid-Mar; Ⓜ Philippe Auguste, Gambetta or Père Lachaise

The world's most visited cemetery, Père Lachaise (named after a confessor of Louis XIV) opened its one-way doors in 1804. Its 69,000 ornate, even ostentatious, tombs of the rich and/or famous form a verdant 43-hectare sculpture garden. Among the 800,000 people buried here are: the composer Chopin; the playwright Molière; the poet Apollinaire; writers Balzac, Proust, Gertrude Stein and Colette; the actors Simone Signoret, Sarah Bernhardt and Yves Montand; the painters Pissarro, Seurat, Modigliani and Delacroix; the *chanteuse* (singer) Édith Piaf; the dancer Isadora Duncan; and even those immortal 12th-century lovers, Abélard and Héloïse (p26), whose remains were disinterred and reburied here together in 1817 beneath a neogothic tombstone.

Particularly frequented graves are those of Oscar Wilde, interred in Division 89 in 1900, and 1960s rock star Jim Morrison, who died in an apartment at 17–19 rue Beautreillis (4e; Map pp440–1) in the Marais in 1971 and is buried in Division 6 (see opposite).

On 27 May 1871, the last of the Communard insurgents, cornered by government forces, fought a hopeless, all-night battle among the tombstones. In the morning, the 147 survivors were lined up against the Mur des Fédérés (Wall of the Federalists), shot and buried where they fell in a mass grave. It is in the southeastern section of the cemetery.

Père Lachaise has five entrances, two of which are on blvd de Ménilmontant. Maps indicating the location of noteworthy graves are available free from the conservation office (Map pp440–1; 16 rue du Repos, 20e) in the southwestern corner of the cemetery. Two-hour guided tours (☎ 01 40 71 75 60; adult/under 25 €6/3) depart from the main entrance near the conservation office usually at 2.30pm on Saturday year-round.

MUSÉE DU FUMEUR Map pp440-1

☎ 01 46 59 05 51; www.museedufumeur.net; 7 rue Pache, 11e; admission €2; ☾ 1-7pm Tue-Sun; Ⓜ Voltaire

The Smoking Museum traces the history of one of mankind's greatest vices: the smoking of tobacco as well as lots and lots of other substances of various strengths and weaknesses. Hard-core butt-fiends will feel vindicated, though the museum takes an impartial stance, providing (as it states on its website) 'a vantage point for the observation of changing behaviours'.

MUSÉE ÉDITH PIAF Map pp428-9

☎ 01 43 55 52 72; 5 rue Crespin du Gast, 11e; admission free; ☾ by appointment 1-6pm Mon-Wed, 10am-noon Thu; Ⓜ Ménilmontant

Some 1.5km from the birthplace of the iconic chanteuse Édith Piaf (p264) and even closer to her final resting place in the Cimetière du Père Lachaise, this small museum follows the life and career of the 'urchin sparrow' through memorabilia, recordings and video.

PARC DE BELLEVILLE Map pp428-9

Ⓜ Couronnes

A few blocks east of blvd de Belleville, this lovely park occupies a hill almost 200m above sea level set amid 4.5 hectares of greenery. Little known by visitors, the park (which opened in 1992) offers some of the best views of the city. The Maison de l'Air (☎ 01 43 28 47 63; 27 rue Piat, 20e; admission €2; ☾ 1.30-5.30pm Mon-Fri, 1.30-6.30pm Sun Mar-Oct, 1.30-5pm Mon-Fri, 1.30-5.30pm Sun Nov-Feb; Ⓜ Pyrénées) stages temporary exhibitions related to ecology and the environment.

GARE DE LYON, NATION & BERCY

Drinking p255; Eating p226; Shopping p301;
Sleeping p329

The southern part of the 12e arrondissement, which borders the Bois de Vincennes
(Map pp422–3), is fairly well-to-do, and at
the weekend hordes of cyclists and soccer
players head for the woods. Walkers can clear
away the cobwebs with a stroll along the Promenade Plantée (Map pp446–7), a path along the
av Daumesnil viaduct. Within the arches,
upmarket shops, art galleries and cafés have
opened up. On the other side of the Gare de
Lyon, there's the pretty parc de Bercy, where
an orchard, a vegetable patch and a garden
have replaced the old wine market.

Long cut off from the rest of the city but
now joined to the Left Bank by the driverless
Météor metro line (number 14) and Pont
Charles de Gaulle, Bercy has some of Paris'
most important new buildings, including
Palais Omnisports de Paris-Bercy (Map pp446–7),
serving as both an indoor sports arena and
a venue for concerts, ballet and theatre, the
giant Ministère de l'Économie et des Finances (Map
pp446–7) and the stunning new Cinémathèque
Française (Map pp446–7; p268). The development of Bercy Village (Map pp422–3), a row of
former wine warehouses dating from 1877
that now house bars and restaurants, and the
arrival of river barges fitted out with more
glitzy eateries and music clubs has turned the
12e into a seriously active district after dark.

CINÉMATHÈQUE FRANÇAISE

Map pp446-7

☎ 01 71 19 33 33; www.cinemathequefrancaise
.com in French; 51 rue de Bercy, 12e; permanent
collection adult/under 12 yr/senior, student & 12-26
yr €4/2/3, temporary exhibitions €9/6/7; ☯ noon-
7pm Mon, Wed & Fri, noon-10pm Thu, noon-8pm
Sat & Sun; Ⓜ Bercy

After a protracted gestation this national
institution, better known for screening classic French and cutting-edge foreign films,
has moved to its stunning postmodern
premises and unveiled exhibition spaces
for its permanent collection and temporary
exhibitions. It also houses screening rooms
and the Bibliothèque du Film (Film Library)
for researchers. Enter from place Leonard
Bernstein.

MUSÉE DES ARTS FORAINS Map p449

☎ 01 43 40 16 22; www.pavillons-de-bercy.com;
Les Pavillons de Bercy, 53 av des Terroirs de France,
12e; adult/senior & student €5/4; ☯ by appointment; Ⓜ Cour St-Émilion

The Museum of the Fairground Art,
housed in an old *chai* (wine warehouse) in
trendy Bercy Village, is a wonderful collection of old amusements from 19th-century
funfairs – carousels, organs, stalls etc. Most
of the items still work and are pure works
of art. The place is usually only rented out
for corporate events with minimum numbers but give a call and try your luck.

PARC DE BERCY

Map p4490 & Map pp446-7

41 rue Paul Belmondo, 12e; ☯ 8am-5.30pm to
9.30pm Mon-Fri, 9am-5.30pm to 9.30pm Sat & Sun
(seasonal); Ⓜ Bercy or Cour St-Émilion

This park, which links the Palais Omnisports
with Bercy Village, is a particularly attractive 14-hectare public garden. On an island
in the centre of one of its large ponds is the
Maison du Lac du Parc de Bercy (Map p449; ☎ 01
53 46 19 34; ☯ 10am-6pm Apr-Sep, 11am-
5pm Oct-Mar), with temporary exhibitions.

The Maison du Jardinage (☎ 01 53 46 19
19; ☯ 1.30-5.30pm Tue-Fri, 1.30-6.30pm
Sat & Sun Apr-Sep, 1.30-5.30pm Tue-Sun
Mar & Oct, 1.30-5pm Tue-Sat Nov-Feb) in
the centre of the park takes a close look at
gardening and the environment.

VIADUC DES ARTS Map pp446-7

Ⓜ Gare de Lyon or Daumesnil

The arches beneath this disused railway viaduct running along av Daumesnil southeast
of place de la Bastille are now a showcase
for trendy designers and artisans; if you
need your Gobelins tapestry restored, porcelain repainted or the bottom of your antique
saucepan re-coppered, this is the place to
come. The top of the viaduct forms a leafy,
4km-long promenade called the Promenade
Plantée (Map pp446–7; ☯ 8am-5.30pm to
9.30pm Mon-Fri, 9am-5.30pm to 9.30pm
Sat & Sun seasonally), which offers excellent
views of the surrounding area. Don't miss
the spectacular Art Deco police station (Map
pp446–7; 85 av Daumesnil, 12e), opposite
rue de Rambouillet, which is topped with a
dozen huge marble torsos.

(Continued on page 147)

lais Royal-Musee du
re metro entrance (p100)
e very chic place du Tertre
0) in Montmartre **3** Shops
etzl, the historic Jewish
rter (p110)

139

1 *Institut du Monde Arabe* (p115)
2 *Man playing guitar on steps of Sacré Cœur* (p148) 3 *Exterior of Opéra Bastille* (p109) 4 *Statue at the Arc de Triomphe du Carrousel* (p98)

ple pass advertising
ard on av des Champs-
es (p131) **2** Viaduc des
p138) **3** Riding a motor-
hrough place de Tertre
), Montmartre

1 *Detail of column on place Vendôme (p103)* 2 *Moulin Rouge (p272)* 3 *Centre Pompidou (p98)*

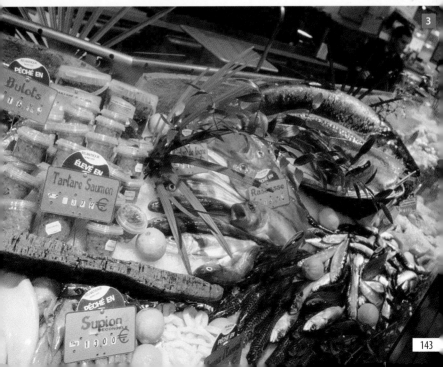

Vins de Loire **1**
Chinon (Domaine Gouron)
St Nicolas de Bourgueil
Saumur (domaine de l'enchantoir)

2

3

1 *North pillar of the Eiffel Tower (p127)* **2** *Fountain at place de la Concorde (p132)* **3** *Exterior of the Panthéon (p117)*

1

2

1 *Gargoyle's view of the city* **2** *Exterior of Musee du Louvre (p100) and the Grande Pyramide* **3** *Arc de Triomphe at night (p130)*

3

1 *Meat hanging in window of Tricotin Chinese restaura (p230)* **2** *Exterior of shop Antoine et Lili (p286)* **3** *Fru shop on rue Mouffetard (p*

(Continued from page 138)

13E ARRONDISSEMENT & CHINATOWN

Drinking p255; Eating p229; Sleeping p329

The **13e arrondissement** begins a few blocks south of the **Jardin des Plantes** (Map pp444–5) in the 5e and has been undergoing a true renaissance after the opening of the **Bibliothèque Nationale de France** (Map p449), the arrival of the high-speed Météor metro line and the start of the massive ZAC Paris Rive Gauche redevelopment project. The stylishness of the neighbouring 5e extends to the **av des Gobelins** (Map pp444–5 & Map p448), while further south, between av d'Italie and av de Choisy, the succession of Chinese and Vietnamese restaurants, stalls and shops in the capital's version of **Chinatown** (Map pp422–3) gives passers-by the illusion of having imperceptibly changed continents. This place is proud of its history. A working-class district if ever there was one, it's home to both a blvd Auguste Blanqui and place Nationale, a pairing propitious to the reconciliation between anarchism and patriotism. At the **butte aux Cailles** (Map p448), the jewel in this arrondissement's crown, people still sing revolutionary songs from the time of the Paris Commune – over chichi cuisine, of course.

BIBLIOTHÈQUE NATIONALE DE FRANCE Map p449

☎ 01 53 79 53 79, 01 53 79 40 41; www.bnf.fr; 11 quai François Mauriac, 13e; temporary exhibitions adult/student 18-26 yr from €5/3.50, under 18 yr free; ☯ 10am-7pm Tue-Sat, 1-7pm Sun; Ⓜ Bibliothèque

Across the Seine from Bercy are the four glass towers of the late President François Mitterrand's controversial €2 billion National Library of France, conceived as a 'wonder of the modern world' and opened in 1995. No expense was spared to carry out a plan that many said defied logic. While books and historical documents were shelved in the sunny, 23-storey and 79m-high towers (shaped like half-open books), patrons sat in artificially lit basement halls built around a 'forest courtyard' of 140 50-year-old pines, trucked in from the countryside. The towers have since been fitted with a complex (and expensive) shutter system and the basement is prone to flooding from the Seine. The national library contains around 12 million tomes stored on some 420km of shelves and can hold 2000 readers and 2000 researchers. Temporary exhibitions revolve around 'the word', focusing on everything from storytelling to bookbinding. Using the study library costs €3.30/35 per day/year while the research library costs €7/53 for three days/year.

MANUFACTURE DES GOBELINS
Map p448

☎ 01 44 08 52 00; 42 av des Gobelins, 13e; adult/7-25 yr €8/6, under 7 yr free; ☯ 2pm & 2.45pm Tue-Thu; Ⓜ Les Gobelins

The Gobelins Factory has been weaving *haute lisse* (high relief) tapestries on specialised looms since the 18th century along with Beauvais-style *basse lisse* (low relief) ones and Savonnerie rugs. The visit, by guided tour, takes you through the workshops and exhibits of the carpets and 5000 tapestries woven here.

15E ARRONDISSEMENT

Eating p231; Sleeping p330

After the war, entire battalions of steelworkers were drawn into the orbit of the **15e arrondissement** (Map pp434–5), clocking in every morning at the Citroën factory or one of the neighbourhood's numerous aeronautical companies. Over the years, the area has become more gentrified and residential. Av de la Motte-Picquet, blvd Pasteur and av Félix Faure are peaceful places – too peaceful for some tastes. For Unesco, the area seemed just right and, not far away, the republic's future officers converge on the majestic **École Militaire** (p130). But the 15e offers much more than bourgeois homes and institutions. Parisians flock to the shops and restaurants that line rue de la Convention, rue de Vaugirard (the longest street in Paris), rue St-Charles and rue du Commerce. On the quays, the towers of the Centre Beaugrenelle have long since abandoned their monopoly on futurism to the stylish, functional buildings occupied by TV stations Canal Plus and France Télévision, and Parisians with their heart in the country can enjoy the parc André-Citroën, one of the capital's most beautiful open spaces.

MONTMARTRE & PIGALLE

Drinking p255; Eating p232; Shopping p301; Sleeping p330

During the late 19th and early 20th centuries the bohemian lifestyle of **Montmartre** (Map p432) in the 18e attracted a number of important writers and artists, many of whom lived in a studio called **Bateau Lavoir** (p174) at 11bis place Émile Goudeau between 1892 and 1930. Picasso worked from here between 1904 and 1912 during his so-called Blue Period.

Although the activity shifted to Montparnasse after WWI, the **18e arrondissement** thrives on crowds and a strong sense of community. Its old-fashioned village atmosphere is lovingly preserved without being dolled up. When you've got Montmartre and Sacré Coeur, what more do you need? Cascading steps, cobblestone streets, small houses with wooden shutters in narrow, quiet lanes… The charm of the Butte de Montmartre (Montmartre Hill) is eternal. Rue Caulaincourt and rue Junot flaunt their bourgeois credentials, while the streets around the square Willette, place des Abbesses and rue Lepic become steeper and narrower, the inhabitants younger and hipper. The northern part of the **9e arrondissement** has a rough and ready charm. The lights of the Moulin Rouge dominate blvd de Clichy, and a few blocks southeast is lively, neon-lit place Pigalle, one

of Paris' two main sex districts. The other, which is *much* more low-rent, is along **rue St-Denis, 1er** (Map pp436–7). Pigalle is more than just a sleazy red-light district: the area around blvd de Clichy between Pigalle and Blanche metro stations is lined with erotica shops and striptease parlours, but there are also plenty of trendy nightspots, clubs and cabarets. On **place Gustave Toudouze** (Map pp428–9) the shops, cafés and restaurants are a colourful feast for the eye. Between Pigalle and the church of the Trinity, the Nouvelles Athènes (New Athens) district with its beautiful Greco-Roman architecture has a singular elegance. This little corner of Paris, full of grand houses and private gardens, has long been favoured by artists.

The easiest way to reach Butte de Montmartre is via the RATP's sleek **funicular** (p370). **Montmartrobus**, a bus run by the RATP, makes a circuitous route from place Pigalle through Montmartre to the 18e Mairie on place Jules Joffrin (detailed maps are posted at bus stops); it costs one RATP ticket. There's also the **Petit Train de Montmartre** (☎ 01 42 62 24 00; www.promotrain.fr; adult/3-12 yr €5.50/3.50), a touristy 'train' with commentary, runs through Montmartre every 30 minutes or so from 10am or 10.30am to between 6pm and midnight daily, depending on the season.

BASILIQUE DU SACRÉ CŒUR

Map p432

☎ 01 53 41 89 00; www.sacre-coeur-montmartre .com; place du Parvis du Sacré Cœur, 18e; ⊕ 6am-11pm; Ⓜ Anvers

Sacred Heart Basilica, perched at the very top of Butte de Montmartre, was built from contributions pledged by Parisian Catholics as an act of contrition after the humiliating Franco-Prussian War of 1870–1. Construction began in 1873, but the basilica was not consecrated until 1919. In a way, atonement here has never stopped; a perpetual prayer 'cycle' that began at the consecration of the basilica continues till this day.

Some 234 spiralling steps lead you to the basilica's **dome** (admission €5; ⊕ 9am-7pm Apr-Sep, 9am-6pm Oct-Mar), which affords one of Paris' most spectacular panoramas; they say you can see for 30km on a clear day. The chapel-lined **crypt**, which can be visited in conjunction with the dome and keeps the same hours, is huge but not very interesting.

Jardin du Luxembourg (p119)

TOP FIVE: MONTMARTRE

- Basilique du Sacré Cœur (opposite)
- Cimetière de Montmartre (below)
- Musée de l'Érotisme (right)
- Musée de Montmartre (below)
- Place du Tertre (p150)

CIMETIÈRE DE MONTMARTRE
Map p432

☎ 01 53 42 36 30; ☽ 8am-6pm Mon-Fri, 8.30am-6pm Sat, 9am-6pm Sun mid-Mar–early Nov, 8am-5.30pm Mon-Fri, 8.30am-5.30pm Sat, 9am-5.30pm Sun early Nov–mid-Mar; Ⓜ Place de Clichy
Established in 1798, Montmartre Cemetery is perhaps the most celebrated necropolis in Paris after Père Lachaise. It contains the graves of writers Émile Zola, Alexandre Dumas and Stendhal, composer Jacques Offenbach, artist Edgar Degas, film director François Truffaut and dancer Vaslav Nijinsky – among others. The entrance closest to the Butte de Montmartre is at the end of av Rachel, just off blvd de Clichy or down the stairs from 10 rue Caulaincourt.

Maps showing the location of the tombs are available free from the **conservation office** (☎ 01 53 42 36 30; 20 av Rachel, 18e) at the cemetery's entrance.

DALÍ ESPACE MONTMARTRE
Map p432

☎ 01 42 64 40 10; www.daliparis.com in French; 11 rue Poulbot, 18e; adult/student & 8-16 yr/senior €8/5/7, under 8 yr free; ☽ 10am-6pm; Ⓜ Abbesses
Some 330 works by Salvador Dalí (1904–89), the flamboyant Catalan surrealist printmaker, painter, sculptor and self-promoter, are on display at this surrealist-style basement museum just west of place du Tertre. The collection includes Dalí's strange sculptures (most in reproduction), lithographs, many of his illustrations and furniture (including the famous 'lips' sofa).

MUSÉE D'ART NAÏF MAX FOURNY
Map p432

☎ 01 42 58 72 89; www.hallesaintpierre.org in French; 2 rue Ronsard, 18e; adult/student, senior & 4-16 yr €7/5.50; ☽ 10am-6pm; Ⓜ Anvers
Founded in 1986, the Max Fourny Museum of Naive Art is housed in Halle St-Pierre,

across from square Willette and the base of the funicular. The dozen or so paintings in the permanent collection represent both the primitive and Art Brut schools and were gathered from around the world. The museum stages some three temporary exhibitions a year.

MUSÉE DE LA VIE ROMANTIQUE
Map pp426-7

☎ 01 55 31 95 67; www.vie-romantique.paris.fr; 16 rue Chaptal, 9e; temporary exhibitions adult/14-25 yr/student & senior €7/3.50/5.50; permanent collection free, ☽ 10am-6pm Tue-Sun; Ⓜ Blanche or St-Georges
In the centre of the district once known as 'New Athens' (due to all the writers and scholars who once lived here), the Museum of the Romantic Life in the lovely Hôtel Scheffer-Renan is devoted to the life and work of the Baronne Aurore Dupkin (1804–76), better known to the world as George Sand, and her intellectual circle of friends.

MUSÉE DE L'ÉROTISME Map p432
☎ 01 42 58 28 73; 72 blvd de Clichy, 18e; adult/student €8/6; ☽ 10am-2am; Ⓜ Blanche
The Museum of Erotic Art tries to put some 2000 titillating statuary, stimulating sexual aids and fetishist items from days gone by on a loftier plane, with antique and modern erotic art from four continents spread over seven floors and lots of descriptive information. But most of the punters know why they are here. Still, some of the exhibits are, well, breathtaking to say the least.

MUSÉE DE MONTMARTRE Map p432
☎ 01 49 25 89 39; www.museedemontmartre.com; 12-14 rue Cortot, 18e; adult/senior, student & 10-25 yr €5.50/3.50, under 10 yr free; ☽ 10am-6pm Tue-Sun; Ⓜ Lamarck Caulaincourt
The Montmartre Museum displays paintings, lithographs and documents mostly relating to the area's rebellious and bohemian/artistic past in a 17th-century manor house, the oldest structure in the *quartier*. It also stages exhibitions of artists still living in the *quartier*. There's an excellent bookshop here that also sells small bottles of the wine produced from grapes grown in the Close du Montmartre (p174).

MUSÉE NATIONAL GUSTAVE MOREAU Map pp428-9

☎ 01 48 74 38 50; www.musee-moreau.fr; 14 rue de La Rochefoucauld, 9e; adult/senior, student, 18-25 yr & everyone on Sun €4/2.60, under 18 yr free, 1st Sun of the month free; ☼ 10am-12.45pm & 2-5.15pm Wed-Mon; Ⓜ Trinité

The National Gustave Moreau Museum, about 500m southwest of place Pigalle, is dedicated to the eponymous symbolist painter's work. Housed in what was once Moreau's studio, the two-storey museum is crammed with 4800 of his paintings, drawings and sketches. Some of Moreau's paintings are fantastic – in both senses of the word. We particularly like *La Licorne* (The Unicorn), inspired by *La Dame à la Licorne* (The Lady with the Unicorn) cycle of tapestries in the Musée National du Moyen Age (p116).

PLACE DU TERTRE Map p432

Ⓜ Abbesses

Half a block west of Église St-Pierre de Montmartre, which once formed part of a 12th-century Benedictine abbey, is what was once the main square of the village of Montmartre. These days it's filled with cafés, restaurants, tourists and rather obstinate portrait artists and caricaturists who will gladly do your likeness. Whether it looks even remotely like you is another matter.

LA VILLETTE

The Buttes Chaumont, the Canal de l'Ourcq (Map pp428–9) and the Parc de la Villette (Map pp422–3), with its wonderful museums and other attractions, create the winning trifecta of the 19e arrondissement. Combining the traditional with the innovative, the old-fashioned with the contemporary, this district makes a virtue of its contradictions. It may not have the beauty of central Paris, but it is nonetheless full of delightful surprises. An aimless stroll finds narrow streets lined with small houses. The Parc des Buttes Chaumont, with its strange rocky promontory, attracts local inhabitants at dawn, who run, cycle or do t'ai chi exercises. The quays along the Canal de l'Ourcq have been transformed over the past several years and are now one of the area's main attractions. But the centrepiece is the Parc de la Villette, the former abattoirs of which have made way for a cultural centre

(Cité de la Musique), a concert hall (Zénith) and the impressive Cité des Sciences et de l'Industrie and its museums.

CITÉ DE LA MUSIQUE Map pp422-3

☎ 01 44 84 44 84; www.cite-musique.fr; 221 av Jean Jaurès, 19e; ☼ noon-6pm Tue-Sat, 10am-6pm Sun; Ⓜ Porte de Pantin

The City of Music, on the southern edge of Parc de la Villette, is a striking triangular-shaped concert hall whose brief is to bring nonelitist music from around the world to Paris' multiethnic listeners. (For information on concerts and other musical events, see p259). Next door is the prestigious Conservatoire National Supérieur de Musique et de Danse (National Higher Conservatory of Music & Dance; ☎ 01 40 40 45 45; 209 av Jean Jaurès, 19e; Ⓜ Porte de Pantin), with concerts and dance performances.

The Musée de la Musique (Music Museum; ☎ 01 44 84 44 84; adult/senior, student & 18-25 yr €7/3.40, under 18 yr free; ☼ noon-6pm Tue-Sat, 10am-6pm Sun) in the Cité de la Musique displays some 900 rare musical instruments (from a collection of 4500 warehoused); you can hear many of them being played through the earphones included in the admission cost. They also have some excellent temporary exhibitions, including a recent one on John Lennon called 'Unfinished Music'. The museum's Médiathèque (☎ 01 44 84 89 45; noon-6pm Tue-Sat, 1-8pm Sun) can answer your music questions via the Internet; it has terminals with about 500 music-related sites.

CITÉ DES SCIENCES ET DE L'INDUSTRIE Map pp422-3

☎ 01 40 05 80 00, reservations 0 892 697 072; www.cite-sciences.fr; 30 av Corentin Cariou, 19e; ☼ 10am-6pm Tue-Sat, 10am-7pm Sun; Ⓜ Porte de la Villette

The enormous City of Science and Industry, at the northern end of Parc de la Villette, has all sorts of high-tech exhibits.

Free attractions include Carrefour Numérique (level -1; ☼ noon-7.30pm Tue, noon-6.45pm Wed-Sun) Internet centre; Médiathèque (levels 0 & -1; ☼ noon-7.45pm Tue, noon-6.45pm Wed-Sun), with multimedia exhibits dealing with childhood, the history of science and health; Cité des Métiers (level -1; ☼ 10am-6pm Tue-Fri, noon-6pm Sat), with information about trades, professions and employment; and a small **Aquarium** (level -2; ⏰ 10am-6pm Tue-Sat, 10am-7pm Sun).

A free and very useful map/brochure in English called the *Keys to the Cité* is available from the circular information counter at the main entrance to the complex. If you really want more detail, buy a copy of the 80-page *Guide to the Permanent Exhibitions* (€3) at reception, though it's now pretty out of date. An audioguide costs €4.

The huge, rather confusingly laid-out **Explora** (levels 1 & 2; adult/7-25 yr €7.50/5.50, under 7 yr free), the heart of the exhibitions at the Cité des Sciences et de l'Industrie, look at everything from space exploration and automobile technology to biology and sound. Tickets are valid for a full day and allow you to enter and exit up to four times.

The **Planétarium** (level 1; admission €3, child 3-7 yr free; ⏰ 11am-5pm Tue-Sun) has six shows a day on the hour (except at 1pm) on a screen measuring 1000 sq metres. Children under three are not admitted.

The highlight of the Cité des Sciences et de l'Industrie is the brilliant **Cité des Enfants** (Children's Village; level 0), with imaginative hands-on demonstrations of basic scientific principles in two sections: for three- to five-year-olds, and for five- to 12-year-olds. In the first, kids can explore, among other things, the conduct of water (waterproof ponchos provided). The second allows children to build toy houses with industrial robots, and stage news broadcasts in a TV studio. A third section has special exhibitions on everything from electricity to light devoted largely to the five-to-12 age group.

Visits to Cité des Enfants lasting 1½ hours begin four times a day: at 9.45am, 11.30am, 1.30pm and 3.15pm on Tuesday, Thursday and Friday and at 10.30am, 12.30pm, 2.30pm and 4.30pm on Wednesday, Saturday and Sunday. Each child (€5) must be accompanied by an adult (maximum two per family). During school holidays, book two or three days in advance by phone or via the Internet.

The **Cinaxe** (☎ 01 42 09 85 83, reservations 0 892 684 540; admission €5.40, if holding another ticket to Cité des Sciences €4.80; ⏰ screenings 11am-1pm & 2-5pm Tue-Sun), a cinema with hydraulic seating for 60 people, moves in synchronisation with the action on the screen. It's across the walkway from the southwestern side of the Cité des Sciences. Shows begin every 15 minutes.

Pont Neuf (p113)

The **Géode** (☎ 01 40 05 79 99, reservations 0 892 684 540; www.lageode.fr; 26 av Corentin Cariou; 19e, adult/senior & 3-25 yr €9/7 except 1.30-5.30pm Sun, double feature €12; ☯ 10.30am-9.30pm Tue-Sat, 10.30am-8.30pm Sun) is a 36m-high sphere with a mirrorlike surface of thousands of polished, stainless-steel triangles, and is one of Paris' architectural calling-cards. Inside, high-resolution, 70mm 45-minute films on topics such as virtual reality, special effects and nature are projected onto a 180° screen to surround you by the action. There is a double feature at 6.30pm. Headsets for an English soundtrack are available for free. Reach the Géode level 0 of the Cité des Sciences et de l'Industrie.

The **Argonaute** (admission €3, under 7 yr free; ☯ 10am-6pm Tue-Sat, 10am-7pm Sun), a French Navy submarine commissioned in 1957 and dry-docked in the park in 1989, is just southeast of the Géode. The Argonaute is also accessible from level 0.

PARC DE LA VILLETTE Map pp422-3

☎ 01 04 03 75 75; www.villette.com; Ⓜ Porte de la Villette or Porte de Pantin

This 35-hectare park in the city's far north-eastern corner, which opened in 1993, stretches from the **Cité des Sciences et de l'Industrie** (p150) southwards to the **Cité de la Musique** (p150). Split into two sections by the Canal de l'Ourcq, the park is enlivened by shaded walkways, imaginative street furniture, a series of themed gardens and fanciful, bright-red pavilions known as *folies*. It is the largest open green space in central Paris and has been called 'the prototype of the urban park of the 21st century'.

There are 10 themed gardens/play-grounds, including the **Jardin des Îles** (Garden of Islands), **Jardin des Bambous** (Bamboo Gardens) and **Jardin des Miroirs** (Mirror Gardens). The best for kids are the **Jardin du Dragon** (Dragon Garden), with an enormous dragon slide between the Géode and the nearest bridge, and the **Jardin des Dunes** (Dunes Garden), which is across Galerie de la Villette (the covered walkway) from the **Grande Halle**, a wonderful old abattoir of wrought iron and glass now used for concerts, theatre performances, expos and conventions.

PARC DES BUTTES-CHAUMONT

Map pp428-9

rue Manin & rue Botzaris, 19e; ☯ 7am-10.15pm May-Sep, 7am-9.15pm Oct-Apr; Ⓜ Buttes-Chaumont or Botzaris

Encircled by tall apartment blocks, the 25-hectare Buttes-Chaumont Park is the closest thing in Paris to Manhattan's Central Park. The park's forested slopes hide grottoes and artificial waterfalls, and the lake is dominated by a temple-topped island linked to the mainland by two footbridges. Once a quarry and rubbish tip, the park was given its present form by Baron Haussmann in the 1860s.

BEYOND CENTRAL PARIS

Eating p236; Shopping p302

Worth a visit are several places just 'outside the walls' of central Paris. To the southeast and the southwest are the 'lungs' of Paris, the **Bois de Vincennes** and the **Bois de Boulogne** (Map pp422–3), both important recreational areas. The modern cityscape of La Défense (Map p155), a mere 20 minutes away at the end of metro line No 1 or RER line A, is so different from the rest of centuries-old Paris that it's worth a visit to put it all in perspective. To the north on metro line 13 is St-Denis (Map p157), France's royal resting place and site of an impressive medieval basilica.

TOP FIVE: BEYOND CENTRAL PARIS

- Basilique de St-Denis (p157)
- Château de Vincennes (opposite)
- Grande Arche de la Défense (p156)
- Musée Marmottan-Monet (p154)
- Stade de France (p158)

BOIS DE VINCENNES & SURROUNDS

The 'Vincennes Wood' encompasses some 995 hectares in the southeastern corner of Paris. Most of it, however, is just outside the blvd Périphérique. Nearby is the city's largest aquarium.

AQUARIUM TROPICAL Map pp422-3

☎ 01 44 74 84 80; www.musee-afriqueoceanie.fr in French; Palais de la Porte Dorée, 293 av Daumesnil, 12e; adult/senior & student €5.50/4; ⏰ 10am-5.15pm Wed-Mon; Ⓜ Porte Dorée

The Tropical Aquarium, at the western edge of the Bois de Vincennes, is Paris' most ambitious, with fish and other sea creatures from around the world in tanks spread throughout a dozen rooms. It was established in 1931 and housed in one of the few buildings left from the Exposition Coloniale of that year. Its role is as much a teaching venue as a tourist attraction.

BOIS DE VINCENNES Map pp422-3

blvd Poniatowski, 12e; Ⓜ Porte de Charenton or Porte Dorée

Located at the wood's northern edge, the Château de Vincennes (Palace of Vincennes; ☎ 01 48 08 31 20; www.monum.fr; av de Paris, 12e; ⏰ 10am-noon & 1.15-6pm May-Aug, 10am-noon & 1.15-5pm Sep-Apr; Ⓜ Château de Vincennes) is a *bona fide* royal chateau with massive fortifications and a moat. Louis XIV spent his honeymoon at the mid-17th-century Pavillon du Roi, the westernmost of the two royal pavilions flanking the Cour Royale (Royal Courtyard). The 52m-high dungeon, closed to visitors at present, was completed in 1369 and used as a prison during the 17th and 18th centuries. You can walk around the grounds for free, but the only way to see the Gothic Chapelle Royale (Royal Chapel), built between the 14th and 16th centuries, is to take a guided tour (in French; information booklet in English). Long-tour (1½ hours) tickets are €6.50 for seniors and students, €4.50 for ages 18 to 25, under 18 free; short tours (45 minutes) €5 and €3.50. There are an average of three short and five long tours daily from April to September but only one long tour a day at 4.30pm the rest of the year; ring ahead for exact times. There are guided tours in English at 11am and 3pm daily in July and August.

The wood's main attraction, the Parc Floral de Paris (Paris Floral Park; ☎ 3975, 0 820 007 575; www.parcfloraldeparis.com in French; esplanade du Château de Vincennes, 12e; adult/7-18 yr €1/.50 or when event is on €3/1.50; ⏰ 9.30am-5pm to 8pm seasonally; Ⓜ Château de Vincennes), is south of the Château de Vincennes, and amusements for kids aged six to 14 include the Bibliothèque-Ludothèque Nature (Nature Library & Puppetry;

☎ 01 43 28 47 63; ⏰ 1.30-5.30pm Tue-Sat, to 6.30pm Sun Apr-Sep, to 5.30pm Tue-Sun Oct-Mar) and a lovely Jardin des Papillons (Butterfly Garden), with 40 species of butterfly. The Jardin d'Agronomie Tropicale (Garden of Tropical Agronomy; ☎ 01 43 94 73 33; 45bis av de la Belle Gabrielle; ⏰ 11.30am-5.30pm Sat & Sun; Ⓜ Nogent-sur-Marne), a vestige of the 1907 Exposition Coloniale, is at the park's eastern edge.

Every year a huge amusement park known as the Foire du Trône (p10) installs itself on the Pélouse de Reuilly for eight weeks in April and May at the Bois de Vincennes. The 15-hectare Parc Zoologique de Paris (Paris Zoological Park; ☎ 01 44 75 20 10; www.mnhn.fr in French; 53 av de St-Maurice, 12e; admission €5, under 4 yr free; ⏰ 9am-6pm Mon-Sat, 9am-6.30pm Sun Apr-Sep, 9am-5pm Mon-Sat, 9am-5.30pm Sun Oct-Mar; Ⓜ Porte Dorée), just east of Lac Daumesnil and also known as the Zoo du Bois de Vincennes, was established in 1934. It has some 600 animals.

BOIS DE BOULOGNE & SURROUNDS

The 845-hectare Boulogne Wood (Map pp422-3) on the western edge of Paris owes its informal layout to Baron Haussmann, who was inspired by Hyde Park in London. Renovation of the Bois de Boulogne, which includes 125 hectares of forested land, was completed after it suffered severe storm damage in late 1999. Be warned that the Bois de Boulogne becomes a distinctly adult playground after dark, especially along the Allée de Longchamp, running from the northeast to the Étang des Réservoirs (Reservoirs Pond) where all kinds of prostitutes cruise for clients.

BOIS DE BOULOGNE Map pp422-3

blvd Maillot, 16e; Ⓜ Porte Maillot or Pont de Neuilly

The wood's enclosed Parc de Bagatelle (☎ 3975; 8am-8pm Mon-Fri, 9am-8pm Sat & Sun May-Aug, 8am-7pm Mon-Fri, 9am-7pm Sat & Sun Sep-Apr) in the northwestern corner, is renowned for its beautiful gardens surrounding the 1775-built Château de Bagatelle (☎ 01 40 67 97 00; route de Sèvres à Neuilly, 16e; adult/student & 7-18 yr €3/1.50, under 7 yr free; ⏰ 9am-6pm Apr-Sep, 9am-5pm Oct-Mar). There are areas dedicated to irises (which bloom in May), roses (June to October) and water lilies (August). The Pré Catalan

Grande Arche de la Défense (p156)

(Catalan Meadow) to the southeast includes the **Jardin Shakespeare** (8.30am-7pm) in which plants, flowers and trees mentioned in Shakespeare's plays are cultivated.

Located at the southeastern end of the Bois de Boulogne is the **Jardin des Serres d'Auteuil** (01 40 71 75 23; av de la Porte d'Auteuil, 16e; adult/6-18 yr €1.50/1, under 6 yr free; 10am-6pm Apr-Sep, 10am-5pm Oct-Mar; Porte d'Auteuil), a garden with impressive conservatories that opened in 1898.

The 20-hectare **Jardin d'Acclimatation** (01 40 67 90 82; av du Mahatma Gandhi; adult/4-18 yr €2.70/1.35, under 4 yr free; 10am-7pm Jun-Sep, 10am-6pm Oct-May; Les Sablons), a kids-oriented amusement park whose name is another word for 'zoo' in French, includes the hi-tech **Exploradôme** (01 53 64 90 40; www.exploradome.com in French; adult/4-18 yr €5/3.50, under 4 yr free), a tented structure devoted to science and the media.

The southern part of the wood takes in two horse-racing tracks, the **Hippodrome de Longchamp** for flat races and, for steeple-chases, the **Hippodrome d'Auteuil** (p276) as well as the **Stade Roland Garros**, home of the French Open tennis tournament (p275). Also here is the **Tenniseum-Musée de Roland Garros** (01 47 43 48 48; www.rolandgarros.com; 2 av Gordon Bennett, 16e; adult/under 18 yr €7.5/4, with stadium visit €15/10; 10am-6pm Wed & Fri-Sun; Porte d'Auteuil), the world's most extravagant tennis museum, tracing the sport's 500-year history through

paintings, sculptures and posters. Visitors to the museum can watch at least 200 hours of play from 1897 till today, including all the men's singles matches since 1990 and interviews with all the key players.

Rowing boats (01 42 88 04 69; per hr around €8.50; noon-6pm Mon-Fri, 10am-7pm Sat & Sun mid-Apr-mid-Oct) can be hired at **Lac Inférieur** (av Henri Martin), the largest of the wood's lakes and ponds. **Paris Cycles** (01 47 47 76 50; 30 min/1hr/day €3.50/5/10; 10am-sunset mid-Apr-mid-Oct, 10am-sunset Wed, Sat & Sun mid-Oct-mid-Apr) hires out bicycles at two locations in the Bois de Boulogne: on av du Mahatma Gandhi (Les Sablons), across from the Porte Sablons entrance to the Jardin d'Acclimatation amusement park, and near the Pavillon Royal (Avenue Foch) at the northern end of Lac Inférieur.

MUSÉE DE LA CONTREFAÇON
Map pp426-7

 01 56 26 14 00; www.museedelacontrefacon.com; 16 rue de la Faisanderie, 16e; adult/12-16 yr €4/3, under 12 yr free; 2-5.30pm Tue-Sun; Porte Dauphine

This fascinating museum east of Porte Dauphine is the real thing, dedicated to the not-so-fine art of counterfeiting. Apparently nothing is sacred to the manufacturers of the ersatz: banknotes, liqueurs, designer clothing, even Barbie and Ken. What makes this museum, established by the Union des Fabricants (Manufacturers' Union) so interesting is that it displays the real against the fake and lets you spot the difference. Most of the time it's as plain as the nose (the real one) on your face.

MUSÉE MARMOTTAN-MONET
Map pp422-3

 01 44 96 50 33; www.marmottan.com; 2 rue Louis Boilly, 16e; adult/8-25 yr €7/4.50, under 8 yr free; 10am-6pm Tue-Sun; La Muette

This museum, two blocks east of the Bois de Boulogne between Porte de la Muette and Porte de Passy, has the largest collection of works by impressionist painter Claude Monet (1840–1926) – about 100 – as well as paintings by Gauguin, Sisley, Pissarro, Renoir, Degas, Manet and Berthe Morisot. It also contains an important collection of French, English, Italian and Flemish miniatures from the 13th to the 16th centuries.

LA DÉFENSE

When development of 750-hectare La Défense (Map p155), Paris' skyscraper district on the Seine to the west of the 17e arrondissement, began in the late 1950s, it was one of the world's most ambitious civil-engineering projects. Its first major structure was the vaulted, largely triangular-shaped **Centre des Nouvelles Industries et Technologies** (CNIT; Centre for New Industries & Technologies), a giant 'pregnant oyster' inaugurated in 1958 and extensively rebuilt 30 years later. But after the economic crisis of the mid-1970s, office space in La Défense became hard to sell or lease. Buildings stood empty and further development of the area all but ceased.

Things picked up, and now La Défense counts over 100 buildings, the tallest of which is 187m-tall **Total Coupole** (1985). One of the most attractive is the 161m twin-towered, aptly named **Cœur Défense** (Défense Heart), more or less in the centre. The towers stand over a light-filled atrium bigger than the nave of Notre Dame. Diagonally opposite, the elongated oval-shaped **Tour EDF** (2001) appears to undulate in the breeze that forever whips across the place de la Défense. It's a triumphal solution to a relatively small space and as attractive a steel and glass skyscraper as you'll find anywhere. The new **Tour t1** (2005) near the Sofitel La Défense can only be described as a sail in glass and at 185m, it's almost in the record books.

The head offices of 14 of France's 20 largest corporations are housed here, and 1500 companies of all sizes employ some 150,000 people. About 20,000 people live here.

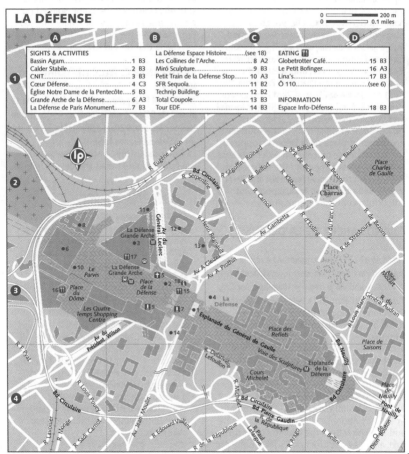

LA DÉFENSE

0 — 200 m
0 — 0.1 miles

SIGHTS & ACTIVITIES		
Bassin Agam	1	B3
Calder Stabile	2	B3
CNIT	3	B3
Cœur Défense	4	C3
Église Notre Dame de la Pentecôte	5	B3
Grande Arche de la Défense	6	A3
La Défense de Paris Monument	7	B3

La Défense Espace Histoire	(see 18)	
Les Collines de l'Arche	8	A2
Miró Sculpture	9	B3
Petit Train de la Défense Stop	10	A3
SFR Sequoïa	11	B2
Technip Building	12	B2
Total Coupole	13	B3
Tour EDF	14	B3

EATING 🍴		
Globetrotter Café	15	B3
Le Petit Bofinger	16	A3
Lina's	17	B3
Ô 110	(see 6)	

INFORMATION		
Espace Info-Défense	18	B3

La Défense is easy enough to explore on foot or you could hop aboard the **Petit Train de la Défense** (☎ 01 42 62 24 00; www.promotrain.fr; adult/3-12 yr €5.50/3.50; ⊙ 11am-5pm Mar-Jul & Sep-Nov, 11am-6pm Aug), which covers all the major sights in a 6km, 40-minute loop starting at the foot of the Grande Arche every 30 minutes or so.

Reach La Défense by taking metro line 1 to the terminus (La Défense Grande Arche). RER Line A also serves that station but know that La Défense is in zone three and you must pay a supplement (€1.40) if you are carrying a travel pass for zones 1 and 2.

GARDENS & MONUMENTS Map p155

Le Parvis, place de la Défense & Esplanade du Général de Gaulle; Ⓜ **La Défense Grande Arche or Esplanade de la Défense**

The Parvis, place de la Défense and Esplanade du Général de Gaulle, which form a pleasant 1km walkway, have been turned into a **garden of contemporary art**. The 60 sculptures and murals along the **Voie des Sculptures** (Sculptures Way) here, and west of the Grande Arche in the **Quartier du Parc** (Park District) and **Jardins de l'Arche**, a 2km-long extension of the Axe Historique, include colourful and imaginative works by Calder, Miró, Agam, César and Torricini. In the southeastern corner of place de la Défense (opposite the Info-Défense office) is an older **La Défense de Paris monument** honouring the defence of Paris during the **Franco-Prussian War of 1870–71** (right). Behind is **Bassin Agam**, a pool with colourful mosaics and fountains.

GRANDE ARCHE DE LA DÉFENSE

Map p155

☎ 01 49 07 27 27; www.grandearche.com in French; 1 parvis de la Défense; adult/student & 6-17 yr €7.50/6, under 6 yr free, ⊙ 10am-8pm Apr-Sep, 10am-7pm Oct-Mar; Ⓜ La Défense Grande Arche

La Défense's biggest draw card is the remarkable, cubelike **Grande Arche** (Great Arch). Designed by Danish architect Johan-Otto von Sprekelsen and housing government and business offices, it is made of white marble, grey granite and glass, and measures 110m along each side. Inaugurated on 14 July 1989, it marks the western end of the 8km-long **Axe Historique** (Historic Axis), begun in 1640 by André Le Nôtre of Versailles fame and stretching from the Louvre's glass pyramid, along av des Champs-Élysées to the Arc

de Triomphe, Porte Maillot and finally the Esplanade du Général de Gaulle. The arch symbolises a window open to the world and is slightly out of alignment with the Axe Historique – on purpose. Who wants perfection? Lifts whisk you up to the 35th floor, but some think neither the views from the rooftop nor the temporary art exhibits justify the ticket price.

ÉGLISE NOTRE DAME DE LA PENTECÔTE Map p155

☎ 01 47 75 83 25; http://catholiques.aladefense.cef.fr in French; 1 place de la Défense; ⊙ 8am-6.30pm Mon-Fri; Ⓜ La Défense Grande Arche

If the hub and the bub and the crowds of 'suits' get you down, head for the futuristic Our Lady of the Pentecost Catholic Church next to the CNIT building. The interior is sublime; check out the flame-shaped pulpit, the image of the Virgin Mary that looks uncannily like the Buddha and the individual chairs that unfold to create benches.

LA DÉFENSE ESPACE HISTOIRE

Map p155

☎ 01 47 74 84 24; www.ladefense.fr in French; 15 place de la Défense; admission free; ⊙ 10am-6pm Mon-Sat Apr-Sep, 9.30am-5.30pm Mon-Sat Oct-Mar; Ⓜ La Défense Grande Arche

La Défense History Space below the **Espace Info-Défense** (p386) traces the development

---

IN DEFENCE OF PARIS

La Défense is named after La Défense de Paris, a sculpture erected here in 1883 to commemorate the defence of Paris during the Franco-Prussian war of 1870–71. Removed in 1971 to facilitate construction work, it was placed on a round pedestal just west of the Bassin Agam in 1983.

Many people don't like the name La Défense because of its militaristic connotation, and it has caused some peculiar misunderstandings. A high-ranking official of EPAD, the authority that manages the business district, was once denied entry into Egypt because his passport indicated he was the 'managing director of La Défense', which Egyptian officials apparently assumed was part of France's military-industrial complex. And the story goes that a visiting Soviet general once expressed admiration at how well the area's military installations had been camouflaged underneath the stunning office blocks.

of La Défense via drawings, architectural plans and scale models. Especially interesting are the projects that were never built: the 750m-tall Tour Tourisme TV (1961) designed by the Polak brothers; Hungarian-born artist Nicholas Schöffer's unspeakable Tour Lumière Cybernetque (1965), a 'Cybernetic Light Tower' that, at 324m, would stand at the same height as the Eiffel Tower; and the horrendous Tour sans Fin, a 'Never-Ending Tower' that would be 425m high, but only 39m in diameter. Ouch.

ST-DENIS

For 1200 years St-Denis (Map p157) was the burial place of the kings of France; today it is a suburb just north of Paris' 18e arrondissement with a very mixed population. The ornate **royal tombs**, adorned with some truly remarkable statuary, and the **Basilique de St-Denis** (the world's first major Gothic structure) containing them are worth a visit and the town is easily accessible by metro in just 20 minutes or so. St-Denis can also boast the **Stade de France**, the futuristic stadium just south of the Canal de St-Denis where France beat Brazil to win the World Cup at home in 1998.

You can reach St-Denis most easily by metro line 13; take it to Basilique de St-Denis station for the basilica and tourist office and to St-Denis-Porte de Paris station for the Musée d'Art et d'Histoire and the Stade de France. Make sure to board a train heading for St-Denis Université, not for Gabriel Péri/Asnières-Gennevilliers, as the line splits at La Fourche station.

BASILIQUE DE ST-DENIS Map p157

☎ 01 48 09 83 54; www.monum.fr; 1 rue de la Légion d'Honneur; tombs adult/senior, student & 18-25 yr €6.50/4.50, basilica admission free, under 18 yr free; ✆ 10am-6.15pm Mon-Sat, noon-6.15pm Sun Apr-Sep, 10am-5.15pm Mon-Sat, noon-5.15pm Sun Oct-Mar; Ⓜ Basilique de St-Denis

St-Denis Basilica was the burial place for all but a handful of France's kings and queens from Dagobert I (ruled 629–39) to Louis XVIII (ruled 1814–24), constituting one of Europe's most important collections of funerary sculpture. The single-towered basilica, begun around 1136, was the first major structure to be built in the Gothic style, serving as a model for other 12th-century French cathedrals including the one at Char-

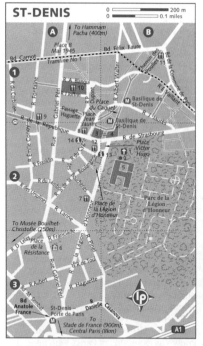

ST-DENIS

tres (p351). Features illustrating the transition from Romanesque to Gothic can be seen in the **choir** and **ambulatory**, which are adorned with a number of 12th-century **stained-glass windows**. The **narthex** (the portico running along the western end of the basilica) also dates from this period. The **nave** and **transept** were built in the 13th century.

During the Revolution and the Reign of Terror, the basilica was devastated; remains from the royal tombs were dumped into two

SIGHTS & ACTIVITIES

|---|---|
Basilique de St-Denis	1 B2
Crypt Entrance	2 B2
Hôtel de Ville	3 A2
Hôtel de Ville (Modern Annexe)	4 B2
Maison d'Éducation de la Légion d'Honneur	5 B2
Musée d'Art et d'Histoire	6 A3

EATING 🍴

Au Petit Breton	7 A2
Food Market	8 A2
Franprix	9 A1
Halle du Marché	10 A1
Le Café de l'Orient	11 B1
Les Arts	12 A2

INFORMATION

Le Kiosk	13 B2
Office de Tourisme de St-Denis-Plaine Commune	14 A2

157

big pits outside the church. The mausoleums were put into storage in Paris, however, and survived. They were brought back in 1816, and the royal bones were reburied in the crypt a year later. Restoration of the structure was begun under Napoleon, but most of the work was carried out by the Gothic Revivalist architect Eugène Viollet-le-Duc from 1858 until his death in 1879. The tombs in the crypt are decorated with life-sized figures of the deceased. Those built before the Renaissance are adorned with *gisants* (recumbent figures). Those made after 1285 were carved from death masks and are thus fairly, well, lifelike; the 14 figures commissioned under Louis IX (St Louis; ruled 1214–70) are depictions of how earlier rulers *might* have looked. The oldest tombs (from around 1230) are those of Clovis I (died 511) and his son Childebert I (died 558). Just south of the basilica is the former royal abbey and now the Maison d'Éducation de la Légion d'Honneur, a school for 500 pupils.

Self-paced 1¼-hour tours of the Basilique on CD-ROM headsets cost €4 (€6.50 for two sharing), available at the crypt ticket kiosk.

The basilica is named in honour of St Denis, the patron saint of France (also known as Dionysius of Paris), who introduced Christianity to Paris and was beheaded by the Romans in Montmartre for his pains. Legend has it that he then walked with his head under his arm to the very spot where the basilica was built. You can see a likeness of him carrying his unfortunate head under his arm on the carved western portal of Notre Dame Cathedral (p111).

MUSÉE BOUILHET-CHRISTOFLE
Map p157
☎ 01 49 22 40 40; 112 rue Ambroise Croizat; adult/senior & student €3, under 16 yr free; ⏰ 9.30am-1pm & 2-5.30pm Mon-Fri; Ⓜ St-Denis-Porte de Paris
About 250m to the southwest of the Musée d'Art et d'Histoire and just over the Seine is the ivy-covered Bouilhet-Christofle Mu-

seum, with some 2000 pieces of silverware created by the same family concern from its founding in 1830 to the present day. The silversmiths' skills seemed to have reached their apogee in the 1920s and '30s when they turned out some exquisite Art Deco pieces.

MUSÉE D'ART ET D'HISTOIRE Map p157
☎ 01 42 43 05 10; www.musee-saint-denis.fr; bis rue Gabriel Péri; adult/student, senior & everyone on Sun €4/2, under 16 yr free, 1st Sun of the month free; ⏰ 10am-5.30pm Mon, Wed & Fri, 10am-8pm Thu, 2-6.30pm Sat & Sun; Ⓜ St-Denis-Porte de Paris
To the southwest of the basilica is the Museum of Art and History, housed in a restored Carmelite convent founded in 1625 and later presided over by Louise de France, the youngest daughter of Louis XV. Displays include reconstructions of the Carmelites' cells, an 18th-century apothecary and, in the archaeology section, items found during excavations around St-Denis. There's a section on modern art, with a collection of work by local boy, the surrealist artist Paul Éluard (1895–1952), as well as politically charged posters, cartoons, lithographs and paintings from the 1871 Paris Commune.

STADE DE FRANCE Map p157
☎ 0 892 700 900; www.stadefrance.com; rue Francis de Pressensé, ZAC du Cornillon Nord, 93216 St-Denis la Plaine; adult/student & 6-11 yr €10/8, under 8 yr free; ⏰ tours on the hr in French 10am-5pm year-round, in English 10.30am & 2.30pm Jun-Aug; Ⓜ St-Denis-Porte de Paris
The 80,000-seat Stadium of France just south of central St-Denis and in full view from rue Gabriel Péri was built for the 1998 football World Cup, which France won by miraculously defeating Brazil 3-0. The futuristic and quite beautiful structure, with a roof the size of place de la Concorde, is used for football and rugby matches, major gymnastic events and big-ticket music concerts. It can be visited on guided tours only.

Walking Tours

Walking Tours

Paris is best seen on foot, and the five thematic walks outlined in this chapter are designed to help you appreciate Paris' rich cultural heritage (architectural, literary, artistic and ethnic) on both the Left and Right Banks by simply strolling. The first takes you to the Marais, where the finest Renaissance residences in Paris are located. The second explores the Left Bank and the hikes and haunts of important 20th-century literary figures, especially American expatriate writers. The third walk concentrates on the Right Bank's sumptuous covered shopping arcades dating from the 19th century. The fourth takes you though the heart of *Paris Mondial* (literally 'World Paris') on a walk that will have you visiting Africa, Asia and the Middle East within a few hours. The fifth and last is Montmartre as seen through its artistic denizens of the 19th and 20th centuries.

The times provided to complete each walk are not exact as they depend on your own pace and the number of stops you make along the way. Don't worry about doing every tour or even finishing each one; linger as long as you like in a museum or market that takes your fancy, do a little shopping or even stop at a café and watch *les flâneurs* (strollers) do their thing.

MARAIS MEDIEVAL MEANDERINGS

Monks and the Knights Templar settled in the Marais as early as the 13th century, which explains the religious nature of many of its street names (eg rue du Temple, rue des Blancs Manteaux). But it wasn't until Henri IV began construction of place Royale (today's place des Vosges) in the early 17th century that the aristocracy began building the *hôtels particuliers* (private mansions) and *pavillons* (somewhat less-grand houses) so characteristic of the district. These gold and cream-coloured brick buildings are among the most beautiful Renaissance structures in the city and, because so many were built at more or less the same time, the Marais enjoys an architectural harmony unknown elsewhere in Paris.

VENI, VIDI, DA VINCI

With apologies to J Caesar, we came, we saw, we Da Vinci'd – and not willingly. The shooting of the film of Dan Brown's runaway bestselling novel was wrapping up in Paris as we researched part of this book and *la code* – and we're not talking about the one to the *porte cochère* street door downstairs – was on everyone's *lèvres* (lips). But certainly not ours. We'll be honest – we didn't like *The Da Vinci Code* and what's more we don't like the idea that fiction should play the role of guidebook – especially when the author gets his compass points as mixed up as Mr Brown does. Versailles (p336) is 'northwest of Paris' while rue Haxo (where the Depository Bank of Zurich and the cryptex is located) is to the west near the Bois de Boulogne – where we get a little tour of the unusual sexual activity that takes place (we're told) there after dark (p153). Rue Haxo is actually on the opposite side of Paris near the Cimetière du Père Lachaise where, with the exception of Jim Morrison's grave (p136), there is probably little action in the wee hours. And those are just the author's directions… No, we say leave guidebooks to the experts – horses for courses and all that – so that's why you if you are really keen on seeing the sites named in the book, you should take a tour like the one offered by Paris Walks (p97). No one knows their way round like these guys do and why shouldn't they? One of the co-founders, Peter Caine, has written *The Definitive Guide to the Da Vinci Code* (Bartillat; €12). What we want to know is how come no one ever mentions the fact that Leonardo gave up the ghost in France (at Amboise in the Loire region on 2 May 1519 to be precise)? Is that in the sequel or have we just told Mr Brown something valuable? Can we, like the tourism industry in Paris, ca$h in? No one in Paris is complaining about the book. It's brought the free-spending Yanks back – 1.4 million dear souls a year, in fact – after that 'significant dip' in trans-Atlantic arrivals in the wake of 9/11 and the fracas between the USA and France over the war in Iraq. Like Mr Brown, Parisians in tourism are laughing – all the way to the bank (wherever it might be).

The golden age of the Marais' *hôtels particuliers* was the 17th century, though construction continued into the first half of the 18th. The removal of the royal court – lock, stock and satin slipper – to Versailles in 1692 sounded the death knell for the Marais, and the mansions passed into the hands of commoners, who used them as warehouses, markets and shops. The quarter was given a major face-lift in the late 1960s and early '70s, and today many of the *hôtels particuliers* house government offices, libraries and museums.

Begin the tour at St-Paul metro station on rue François Miron, 4e, facing rue de Rivoli. Walk south on narrow rue du Prévôt to rue Charlemagne, once called rue des Prestres (Street of the Priests). To the right (west) on the corner of rue des Nonnains d'Hyères at 7 rue de Jouy stands the majestic **Hôtel d'Aumont 1**, built around 1650 for a financier and one of the most beautiful *hôtels particuliers* in the Marais. It now contains offices of the Tribunal Administratif, the body that deals with – *sacré bleu!* – internal disputes in the bloated and litigious French civil service. Opposite Hôtel d'Aumont, at the corner of rue de Jouy and rue de Fourcy, is a wonderful **17th-century relief of a winemaker 2**.

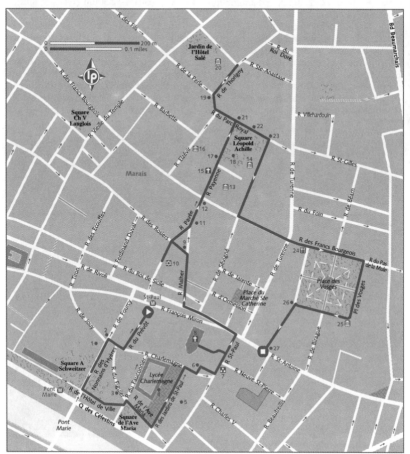

Continue south along rue des Nonnains d'Hyères past the Hôtel d'Aumont's geometrical gardens on the right and turn left (east) onto rue de l'Hôtel de Ville. On the left at 1 rue du Figuier is **Hôtel de Sens 3**, the oldest private mansion in the Marais. Begun around 1475, it was built as the Paris digs for the powerful archbishops of Sens, under whose authority Paris fell at the time. When Paris was made an archbishopric, the Hôtel de Sens was rented out to coach drivers, fruit sellers, a hatter and even a jam-maker. It was heavily restored in mock Gothic style (complete with turrets) in 1911; today it houses the **Bibliothèque Forney** (Forney Library; ☎ 01 42 78 14 60; adult/senior & student €4/2; ⊙ 1.30-7pm Tue-Sat) with temporary exhibitions.

Continue southeast along rue de l'Ave Maria and then go northeast along rue des Jardins de St-Paul. The two truncated and crumbling towers across the basketball courts on the left are all that remain of **Philippe-Auguste's enceinte 4**, a fortified medieval wall built around 1190 and once guarded by 39 towers. They are now part of the prestigious Lycée Charlemagne. To the right along rue des Jardins de St-Paul are the entrances to **Village St-Paul 5**, a courtyard of antique shops and boutiques.

Cross over rue Charlemagne and duck into **rue Eginhard 6**, a street with a tiny courtyard and a grated well built during the reign of Louis XIII. The street doglegs into rue St-Paul; at the corner above 23 rue Neuve St-Pierre housing a bed-linen shop are the remains of the medieval **Église St-Paul 7**. Tiny passage St-Paul leads to the side entrance of the **Église St-Paul St-Louis (8;** ☎ 01 42 72 30 32; ⊙ 8am-7.30pm Mon-Sat, 9.30am-12.30pm & 4-7pm Sun), a Jesuit church completed in 1641 during the Counter-Reformation.

Rue St-Paul debouches into rue St-Antoine. Turn left, passing the front entrance of Église St-Paul St-Louis at No 99, cross over rue de Rivoli and head north up rue Malher. A **former boulangerie-pâtisserie 9**, or bakery-cake shop, at No 13 (now a clothes shop) has fine old shop signs advertising *pains de seigle et gruau* (rye and wheaten breads), *gateaux secs* (biscuits) and *chaussons de pommes* (apple turnovers). Head west on rue des Rosiers and a short distance south on rue Pavée to No 10 and the Art Nouveau **Guimard synagogue 10** (p110). Continue north on rue Pavée (Paved Street), the first cobbled road in Paris. At No 24 stands **Hôtel Lamoignon 11**, built between 1585 and 1612 for Diane de France (1538–1619),

People relaxing around a fountain in Place des Vosges (p110)

duchess of Angoulême and legitimised daughter of Henri II. It is a fine example of late-Renaissance architecture; note the Corinthian capitals in the courtyard and, above the main gate, the cherubs holding a mirror (symbolising truth) and snake (for prudence). It now houses the **Bibliothèque Historique de la Ville de Paris** (☎ 01 44 59 29 40; ☯ 1-6pm Mon-Fri, 9.30am-6pm Sat).

The corner of rue Pavée and rue des Francs Bourgeois marks the site of the medieval **priory of Ste-Catherine 12**. Walk north along rue Payenne. The building immediately on the right at No 2 is the back of the mid-16th-century, Renaissance-style **Hôtel Carnavalet 13** built between 1548 and 1654 and home to the letter-writer Madame de Sévigné (1626–96). Further north is the **Hôtel Le Peletier de St-Fargeau 14**, which dates from the late 17th century. Both now form the Musée Carnavalet (p107).

From the grille just past the **Chapelle de l'Humanité 15**, a Revolutionary-era 'Temple of Reason' (p74) at 5 rue Payenne (the quote on the façade reads: 'Love as the principal, order as the base, progress as the goal'), you can see the rear of **Hôtel Donon 16** at 8 rue Elzévir, built in 1598 and now the Musée Cognacq-Jay (p108). At 11 rue Payenne is the lovely **Hôtel de Marle 17**, built in the late 16th century and now the Swedish Cultural Institute.

Opposite is a pretty green space called **square George Cain 18** with the remains of what was once the Hôtel de Ville on the south wall. Have a look at the relief of Judgement Day and the one-handed clock on the tympanum (the façade beneath the roof) on the southern side. From the square walk a short distance northwest to two spectacular 17th-century *hôtels particuliers*: **Hôtel de Libéral Bruant 19** (now the Galerie Libéral Bruant; ☎ 01 42 77 96 74; ☯ 2-7pm Tue-Sat) at 1 rue de la Perle and **Hôtel Aubert de Fontenay 20** at rue de Thorigny, whose three floors and vaulted cellars house the wonderful Musée Picasso (p109).

Retrace your steps to rue du Parc Royal. Heading east you'll pass three hôtels (**Hôtel de Croisille 21** at No 12, **Hôtel de Vigny 22** at No 10 and pink-brick **Hôtel Duret de Chevry 23** at No 8, the loveliest of the trio) before turning south down rue de Sévigné. All of these date from about 1620 and now do civic duty as archives and historical libraries.

You have already seen the two hotels on rue de Sévigné from the back – Hôtel Le Peletier de St-Fargeau at No 29 and Hôtel Carnavalet at No 23. Take a moment to check out the spaghetti-like monogram of the former's original owner, Michel Le Peletier de Souzy, on the front gate, and the exterior courtyard of the latter, with its wonderful reliefs. To the north are Roman gods and goddesses, to the south the elements, and to the west reliefs of the four seasons attributed to the Renaissance sculptor Jean Goujon (1510–68), who created the Fontaine des Innocents near the Forum des Halles (1549). In the centre of the courtyard is a statue of Louis XIII that was placed in front of the Hôtel de Ville on 14 July 1689 – a century to the day before an armed mob attacked the Bastille prison and sparked the revolution that would change the course of history. Little did they know...

Follow rue des Francs Bourgeois eastwards to the sublime place des Vosges (p110), with its four symmetrical fountains and an 1829 copy of a mounted statue of Louis XIII, originally placed here in 1639. In the northwestern corner at No 19 is **Ma Bourgogne 24** (p188), a delightfully situated place for a meal, snack or just a drink. In the southeastern corner at No 6 is **Hôtel de Rohan-Guéménée 25**, home to Victor Hugo for 16 years in the first half of the 19th century and now the Maison de Victor Hugo (p110).

In the southwestern corner of place des Vosges is the **back entrance 26** to **Hôtel de Sully 27** (p106), a restored aristocratic mansion at 62 rue St-Antoine built in 1624, now housing a branch of the Jeu de Paume (p100), an excellent bookshop (p289) and, appropriately enough, the Centre des Monuments Nationaux, the body responsible for France's national historical monuments.

Behind the Hôtel de Sully are two beautifully decorated late Renaissance–style court-yards, both of which are festooned with allegorical reliefs of the seasons and the elements. In the northern courtyard look to the southern side for spring (flowers and a bird in hand) and summer (wheat); in the southern courtyard turn to the northern side for autumn (grapes) and winter, with a symbol representing both the end of the year and the end of life. On the western side of the second courtyard are 'air' on the left and 'fire' on the right. On the eastern side look for 'earth' on the left and 'water' on the right. St-Paul metro station is about 250m west of the Hôtel de Sully's main entrance or catch bus 67 to the better-served metro stations of Hôtel de Ville or Châtelet.

LATIN QUARTER LITERARY LOOP

Writers have found their way to Paris ever since that 16th-century hedonist François Rabelais forsook his monastic vows and hightailed it to the capital. The 1920s saw the greatest influx of outsiders, particularly Americans. Many assume it was Paris' reputation for liberal thought and relaxed morals that attracted the likes of Ernest Hemingway, F Scott Fitzgerald, Ezra Pound and so on, but that's just part of the story. Paris was cheap, particularly the Left Bank, and in France, unlike in Prohibition-era America, you could drink alcohol to your heart's (or liver's) content.

> **Walk Facts**
>
> **Start** Metro Cardinal Lemoine
> **End** Dingo Bar (metro Vavin)
> **Distance** 7km
> **Time** Three hours
> **Fuel stop** Les Deux Magots or Café de Flore

Begin your tour at the Cardinal Lemoine metro station, where rue du Cardinal Lemoine meets rue Monge, 5e. Walk southwest along rue du Cardinal Lemoine, peering down the **passageway** 1 at No 71, which may or may not be closed off. The Irish writer James Joyce (1882–1941) lived in the courtyard flat at the back marked 'E' when he first arrived in Paris in 1921, and it was here that he finished

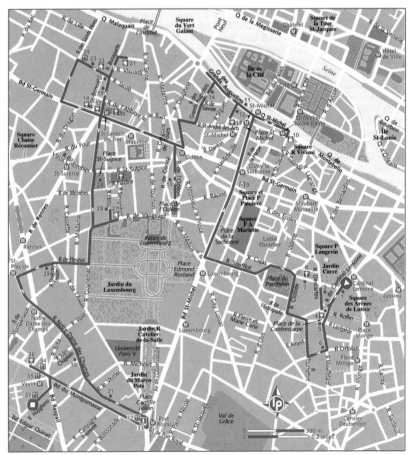

editing *Ulysses*. Further south at **74 Cardinal Lemoine** 2 is the 3rd-floor apartment where Ernest Hemingway (1899–1961) lived with his first wife Hadley from January 1922 until August 1923. The flat figures prominently in his book of memoirs, *A Moveable Feast*, from which the quotation on the wall plaque (in French) is taken: 'This is how Paris was in our youth when we were very poor and very happy'. Just below the flat was the Bal au Printemps, a popular *bal musette* (dancing club), which served as the model for the one where Jake Barnes met Brett Ashley in Hemingway's *The Sun Also Rises*. It is now a bookshop called **Les Alizées** (The Trade Winds; ☎ 01 43 25 20 03; ⏱ 10am-10pm Tue-Fri, 10am-7pm Sat & Sun), which stocks Hemingway's books in both English and French.

Hemingway lived on rue du Cardinal Lemoine, but he actually wrote in a top-floor garret of a hotel round the corner at **39 rue Descartes** 3, the very hotel where the poet Paul Verlaine (1844–96) had died less than three decades before. The plaque, on what is now a restaurant, incorrectly states that Hemingway lived here from 1921 to 1925. Japanese historical novelist Kunio Tsuji lived here from 1980 to 1999.

Rue Descartes runs south into place de la Contrescarpe, now a well-scrubbed square with Judas trees and a fountain, but once a 'cesspool' (or so Hemingway said), especially the **Café des Amateurs** 4 at No 2–4, which is now the popular Café Delmas (p245). The **Au Nègre Joyeux** 5 at No 12, which sports a large painting of a jolly black servant and his white master, was another popular music club in the early 20th century.

Rue Mouffetard (from *mofette*, meaning 'skunk') runs south of place de la Contrescarpe. Turn west (right) at the first street on the right (pedestrian rue du Pot de Fer); in 1928 one Eric Blair – better known to the world as George Orwell (1903–50) – stayed in a cheap and dirty boarding house above **6 rue du Pot de Fer** 6 called the Hôtel des Trois Moineaux (Hotel of the Three Sparrows) while working as a dishwasher. He wrote all about it and the street, which he called 'rue du Coq d'Or' (Street of the Golden Rooster), in *Down and Out in Paris and London* (1933).

Turn north (right) on rue Tournefort (the street where much of Balzac's novel *Père Goriot* takes place) and go left into rue de l'Estrapade. The large building on the right is the prestigious Lycée Henri IV; the tower in the northern part of the school is the 13th-century (but heavily restored) **Tour Clovis** 7, all that remains of an abbey founded by Clovis I.

From here follow Hemingway's own directions provided in *A Moveable Feast* as he made his way to a favourite café in the Place St-Michel. Walk along rue Clotilde, past the ancient **Église St-Étienne-du-Mont** (8; p114) on your right and through the large place du Panthéon, with the Panthéon on your left. Walk west along rue Soufflot and turn right onto the blvd St-Michel and follow it past **Hôtel de Cluny** 9, now the Musée National du Moyen Age (p116). The cafés on place St-Michel were taken over by tourists decades ago and **Shakespeare & Company** (10; p291) around the corner at 37 rue de la Bûcherie has nothing to do with the real bookshop of that name frequented by Hemingway, but that comes later in the tour. Follow the Seine west along quai des Grands Augustins. Hemingway used to buy books from the **bouquinistes** (11; second-hand booksellers), some of whom still line the embankment. At No 9 of tiny rue Gît le Cœur to the south is the **Relais Hôtel du Vieux Paris** 12, a favourite of the poet Allen Ginsberg (1926–97) and Beat writer Jack Kerouac (1922–69) in the 1950s. There's a not-wholly-substantiated story that when Truman Capote first read Kerouac's stream-of-consciousness *On the Road* he exclaimed: 'That's not writing – that's typewriting!' Ginsberg and Kerouac drank just down the road in a bar called **Le Gentilhomme** 13 at 28 rue St-André des Arts. It's now a large Irish pub called Corcoran's.

Pablo Picasso (1881–1973) had his studio at **7 rue des Grands Augustins** 14, the street that runs south from quai des Grands Augustins. Picasso lived here from 1936 to 1955 and completed his masterpiece *Guernica* here in 1937 – exactly a century after Balzac's *Le Chef d'Œuvre Inconnu* (The Unknown Masterpiece), set in this *hôtel particulier*, was published.

Walk south to rue St-André des Arts, follow it westwards and then turn south (right) through Cour du Commerce Saint André, a covered passage that empties into blvd St-Germain just opposite the statue of Georges Danton (p117). At No 12 rue de l'Odéon, the street running north, stood the original **Shakespeare & Company** 15 bookshop, where founder-owner Sylvia Beach (1887–1962) lent books to Hemingway, and edited, retyped and published *Ulysses* for Joyce in 1922. The bookshop was closed during the occupation when Beach refused to sell her last copy of Joyce's *Finnegan's Wake* to a Nazi officer.

Sign to Musée Picasso (p109)

Return to blvd St-Germain and walk westwards to the 11th-century **Église St-Germain des Prés** (16; p118). Just opposite is **Les Deux Magots** (17; p248) and beyond it **Café de Flore** (18; p247), favourite hang-outs of post-war Left Bank intellectuals such as Jean-Paul Sartre (1905–80) and Simone de Beauvoir (1908–86) and good (though pricey) places to stop for a snack or a drink.

From place St-Germain des Prés (half of which is now called place Sartre-Beauvoir) walk north along rue Bonaparte. In spring 1930 Henry Miller (1891–1980) stayed in a 5th-floor mansard room in the **Hôtel St-Germain des Prés 19** at No 36 and later wrote about the experience in *Letters to Emil* (1989). The philosopher Auguste Comté (1798–1857), the founder of positivism, lived in the same building from 1818 to 1822. A few doors down at No 30 is the **Bistrot Le Pré aux Clercs 20**, another Hemingway hang-out.

Continue north on rue Bonaparte and turn east (right) onto rue des Beaux-Arts. Walk to No 13 and you'll reach what is now **L'Hôtel 21**, the former Hôtel d'Alsace, where Oscar Wilde (born 1854) died of meningitis in 1900, but not before proclaiming, in his typical style, that he and the wallpaper of his room were 'fighting a duel to the death' (see p136). The Argentinian writer Jorge Luis Borges (1899–1986) also stayed in the same hotel many times in the late 1970s and early '80s.

Rue Jacob, which runs perpendicular to rue Bonaparte, has literary associations from the sublime to the ridiculous. At No 44, the **Hôtel d'Angleterre** (22; p319) is where Hemingway spent his first night in Paris (in room No 14 on 20 December 1921, to be precise). A few doors down at No 56, the former **Hôtel d'York 23** is of great historic, if not literary, significance – this is where David Hartley, George III's representative, met with Benjamin Franklin, John Adams and John Hay on 3 September 1783 to sign the treaty recognising American independence.

At 52 rue Jacob is a nondescript café called **Le Comptoir des Sts-Pères 24**, which under normal circumstances would not deserve a second glance. But this was the fashionable restaurant Michaud's, where Hemingway stood outside watching Joyce and his family dine and, later, when he was on the inside looking out, where a memorable event may – or may not – have taken place. According to Hemingway in his *A Moveable Feast*, the writer F Scott Fitzgerald (1896–1940), concerned about not being able to sexually satisfy his wife, Zelda, asked Hemingway to inspect him in the café's toilet. 'It is not basically a question of the size in repose…' Hemingway advised him, in what could be one of best examples of the 'big lie' in American literary history.

Go south (left) on rue des Saints Pères, then east (left) on blvd St-Germain and south (right) on rue Bonaparte. Follow it south past **Église St-Sulpice 25**, where a pivotal clue is left and a murder takes place in Dan Brown's *The Da Vinci Code* (p160). It eventually leads to the northwestern corner of the Jardin du Luxembourg, rue de Vaugirard and the **Fontaine des Quatre Évêques** (**26**; Fountain of the Four Bishops). Hemingway and many other members of the so-called 'lost generation' moved to this area after slumming it for a few years in the Latin Quarter. William Faulkner (1897–1962) spent a few months at 42 rue de Vaugirard in what is now the posh **Hôtel Luxembourg Parc** (**27**; p320) in 1925. Hemingway spent his last few years in Paris in a rather grand flat at **6 rue Férou 28**, within easy striking (the operative word, as they had fallen out – and big time – by then) distance of **27 rue de Fleurus 29**, where the American novelist Gertrude Stein (1874–1946) first lived with her brother Leo and then her lifelong companion, Alice B Toklas, for 35 years. Stein entertained such luminaries as Matisse, Picasso, Braque, Gauguin, Pound and of course the young Hemingway and Hadley, who were treated as though they were 'very good, well-mannered and promising children' according to the latter. It's odd to think that this splendid *belle époque* block (1894) was less than 10 years old when Stein first moved here in 1903. Pound (1885–1972) lived not far away at **70bis rue Notre Dame des Champs 30** in a flat filled with Japanese paintings and with packing crates posing as furniture, as did Katherine Anne Porter (1890–1980) in the same flat in 1934. Hemingway's first apartment in this part of town was above a sawmill at **113 rue Notre Dames des Champs 31**, now part of the École Alsacienne (Alsatian School) complex. Further to the east is **La Closerie des Lilas** (**32**; p209) on blvd du Montparnasse, where Hemingway often met John Dos Passos or just sat alone, contemplating the **Maréchal Ney statue 33** in front of it.

Port Royal metro station, where you might end the tour, is just opposite. But west of here and clustered around place Pablo Picasso and Vavin metro station is a triad of café-restaurants that have hosted more literary luminaries than any others in the world: **La Rotonde 34**, **Le Dôme** (**35**; p209) and, as Jake Barnes puts it in *The Sun Also Rises*, 'that new dive, the **Select**' (**36**; p249). Just off blvd Raspail at 10 rue Delambre is the former **Dingo Bar 37**, now an ordinary Italian restaurant called the Auberge de Venise. It was here that Hemingway, the ambitious, middle-class kid from the Midwest, and Fitzgerald, the well-heeled, dissolute Princeton graduate, met for the first time, became friends (of sorts) and went on to change the face of American literature. For at least one of us, the erstwhile Dingo is a church.

LES PASSAGES: PARIS UNDER COVER

Stepping into the *passages couverts* (covered shopping arcades) of the Right Bank is the simplest way to get a feel for what life was like in early-19th-century Paris. These arcades emerged during a period of relative peace and prosperity under the restored House of Bourbon after Napoleon's fall and the rapid growth of the new industrial classes. In a city without sewers, pavements or sheltered walkways, these arcades allowed shoppers to stroll from boutique to boutique protected from the elements and the filth and noise of the streets.

The *passages* quickly became some of Paris' top attractions – visitors from the provinces made the arcades their first port of call in order to kit themselves out for the capital – and by the mid-19th century Paris counted around 150 of these sumptuously decorated temples to Mammon. As well as shopping, visitors could dine and drink, play billiards, bathe (all the *passages* had public baths), attend the theatre and, at night (the *passages* were open 24 hours a day back then), engage in activities of a carnal nature; the arcades were notorious for attracting prostitutes after dark and there were rooms available on the 1st floor.

The demise of the *passages* came about for a number of reasons, but the most significant death knell was the opening of the first of the capital's department stores, Le Bon Marché, in 1852. Today there are only 18 arcades remaining – mostly in the 1er, 2e and 9e arrondissements – in various states of repair.

These are among the best places to get an idea of how Parisians and their tastes have changed over the years, with traditional millinery and cane shops mixing happily with postmodern designer fashion, and hand-worked printing presses sitting next to Internet cafés. And if you really wanted to you could spend your entire time in Paris under the glass roofs of the *passages;* they still contain everything you need – from restaurants, bars and theatres to hotels and, of course, shops. This might be the walking tour you save for a rainy day.

Begin the walk at the Louvre-Rivoli metro station (1er) on rue de Rivoli; go north along rue du Louvre, turn left (west) onto rue St-Honoré and then right (north) again on rue Jean-Jacques Rousseau. The entrance to the **Galerie Véro Dodat** 1, built in 1823 by two well-heeled *charcutiers* (butchers), is at No 19. The arcade retains its 19th-century skylights, ceiling murals, Corinthian columns, tiled floor, gas globe fittings (though now electric, of course) and shop fronts, among the most interesting of which include the Luthier music store with guitars, violins, banjos and ukuleles at No 17 and the Marini France stained-glass workshop at No 28.

The gallery's western exit leads to rue du Bouloi and rue Croix des Petits Champs. Head north on the latter to the corner of rue du Colonel Driant – the massive building ahead of you is the headquarters of the Banque de France – and turn left (west) and walk to rue de Valois. At No 5 is one of the entrances to the **Galeries du Palais Royal** 2. Strictly speaking, these galleries are not *passages* as they are arcaded rather than covered, but since they date from 1786 they are considered to be the prototypes of what was to come. The Café de Foy, from where the Revolution broke out on a warm mid-July day just three years after the galleries opened, once stood on the western side at what is today's **Galerie de Montpensier** 3. Charlotte Corday, Jean-Paul Marat's assassin, once worked in a shop in the **Galerie de Valois** 4. Galerie de Montpensier has more traditional shops, such as A Bacqueville at No 6–8 with medals and ribbons, Les Drapeaux de France at 13–15 with tin soldiers and Didier Ludot (p284) at No 19–20 and No 23–24 with exquisite antique clothes. The **Café du Théâtre** 5 at No 67 is a decent place to stop for something to eat or drink.

Galerie de Valois is more upmarket, with posh galleries and designer shops such as an outlet of Hong Kong–based boutique Joyce at shop No 168–173. Other shops worth a peek include Le Prince Jardinier gardening shop at No 114–121, the FC autograph shop at 149 and the *graveur héraldiste* (coat of arms engraver) Guillaumot – truly a niche concern – which prints family coats-of-arms at No 153.

The tiny arcade that doglegs from the north of the Galeries du Palais Royal into rue de Beaujolais is **passage du Perron** 6; the writer Colette (1873–1954) lived the last

Walk Facts

Start Metro Louvre-Rivoli
End Metro Le Peletier
Distance 3km
Time Two hours
Fuel stop Café du Théâtre

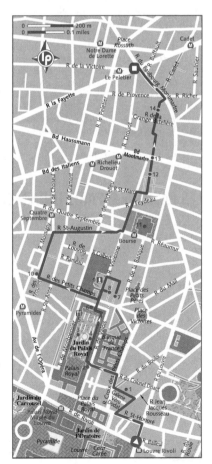

years of her life in a flat above here (9 rue de Beaujolais), from which she wrote her *Paris de Ma Fenêtre* (Paris from My Window), her description of the German occupation of Paris. Diagonally opposite from where you exit at 4 rue des Petits Champs are the entrances to two of the most stunningly restored *passages* in Paris. **Galerie Vivienne** 7, built in 1823 and decorated with bas-reliefs of snakes (signifying prudence), anchors (hope) and beehives (industry), and floor mosaics, was (and still is) one of the poshest of the *passages*. As you enter, look to the stairwell to the left at No 13 with its false marble walls; François Eugène Vidocq (1775–1857), master burglar *and* later the chief of detectives in Paris in the early 19th century, lived upstairs. Some shops to check out are Legrand Fille et Fils, which sells wine and wine-related paraphernalia, at No 7–11 as well as opposite at No 16; Wolff et Descourtis and its silk scarves at No 18; L'Atelir Emilio Robbo, one of the most beautiful flower shops in Paris, at No 29–33; the Librairie Ancienne & Moderne at No 45–46, which Colette frequented; and designer Jean-Paul Gaultier's first boutique (main entrance: 6 rue Vivienne, 2e).

The major draw of the **Galerie Colbert** 8, built in 1826 and now part of the University of Paris, is its huge glass dome and rotunda, which served as a car workshop and garage as recently as the early 1980s. Check out the bizarre fresco above the rue des Petits Champs exit; it's completely disproportionate. Enter and exit from rue Vivienne.

From here head south along rue Vivienne – passing the original home of the Bibliothèque Nationale (p147) before it moved to Bercy with its curiously leaning **statue of Sartre** 9 in the courtyard – to rue des Petits Champs and turn right (west). At No 40 is the entrance to **passage Choiseul** 10. Passage Choiseul (1828), some 45m long and containing scores of shops, is more ordinary than many of the other *passages* covered here but is rapidly raising its profile. Discount clothing and shoe shops (Nos 7–9 and 35), Asian fast-food shops (for example Nos 19, 32 and 46) and second-hand bookshops (No 74-76) are getting fewer and fewer. The *passage* has a long literary pedigree: Paul Verlaine (1844–96) drank absinthe here and Céline (1894–1961) grew up in his mother's shop at No 62, which now sells costume jewellery. Check out the Théâtre des Bouffes Parisiens, where comedies are performed, at No 61 (main theatre around the corner at 4 rue Monsigny, 2e).

Leave passage Choiseul at 23 rue St-Augustin and walk eastwards to where it meets rue du Quatre Septembre. The building across the square is the **Bourse du Commerce** 11, built in 1826. Head north and walk up rue Vivienne, and then east (right) along rue St-Marc. The entrance to the mazelike **passage des Panoramas** 12 is at No 10.

Built in 1800, passage des Panoramas is the oldest covered arcade in Paris and the first to be lit by gas (1817). It was expanded in 1834 with the addition of four other interconnecting *passages:* Feydeau, Montmartre, St-Marc and Variétés. It's a bit faded around the edges, but keep an eye open for Jean-Paul Belmondo's Théâtre des Variétés at No 17, the erstwhile vaudeville Théâtre d'Offenbach, from where spectators would come out to shop during the interval, and the old engraver Stern at No 47. Exit at 11 blvd Montmartre. Directly across the road, at No 10–12, is the entrance to **passage Jouffroy** 13.

Passage Jouffroy, the last major *passage* to open in Paris (1846) – and the first to use metal and glass in its skylights and to have central heating – remains a personal favourite; no other *passage* offers so much or feels so alive. There are two hotels here, including the Hôtel Chopin (p325) as well as the Musée Grévin (p134) of wax figures. There are also some wonderful boutiques, including the bookshops Librairie du Passage (Nos 37 and 62), with lots of old postcards, and Paul Vulin (No 46–50); M&G Segas (No 34), where Toulouse Lautrec bought his walking sticks; Brésilophile (No 40) filled with colourful rocks and minerals.

Leave passage Jouffroy at 9 rue de la Grange Batelière, cross the road to No 6, and enter **passage Verdeau** 14, the last and most modest of this stretch of covered arcades. Verdeau wasn't particularly successful because of its 'end-of-the-line' location. Still, there's lots to explore here: Le Cabinet des Curieux (No 12) with weird and curious objects; daguerreotypes at Photo Verdeau (No 14); vintage Tintin and comic books at Librairie Roland Buret (No 6); and needlepoint at Le Bonheur des Dames (No 8).

The northern exit from passage Verdeau is at 31bis rue du Faubourg Montmartre. Walk north and turn left (west) on rue La Fayette and you'll soon reach Le Peletier metro station.

PARISIAN ROUND-THE-WORLD TOUR

And you thought it was all berets, baguettes and bistros... To be sure, Paris is and will always be *français* – the *couturiers* (designers) will continue to spin their glad rags, the *boulangeries* (bakeries) will churn out those long, crispy loaves and the terrace cafés will remain the places to watch the world go by. But it's a much more international world nowadays, and *Paris Mondial,* a diverse, dynamic, multicultural city, vibrates to its rhythms.

France ruled a considerable part of the world until the middle of the 20th century, and today its population includes a large number of immigrants and their descendants from its former colonies and protectorates in Africa, Indochina, the Middle East, India, the Caribbean and the South Pacific (p12). At the same time, France has continued to accept significant numbers of exiles and refugees from around the world. Most of these immigrants have settled in specific areas of the capital, especially Belleville in the 19e and 20e, rue du Faubourg St-Denis in the 10e and La Goutte d'Or and Château Rouge in the 18e. A stroll through these quarters will have you touring the globe without even boarding an aeroplane.

Begin the walk at the Pyrénées metro stop in Belleville, a district where Jewish kosher and Muslim halal butchers share the same streets with cavernous Chinese noodle shops, their windows festooned with dripping *cha siu* (roast pork). Walk west on rue de Belleville past the **birthplace of Édith Piaf** (1; p264) at No 72 and turn left (south) onto rue Piat, which you will be forgiven for thinking says 'Piaf'. Rue Piat will bring you to the Parc de Belleville (p137) which, at 200m above sea level, affords some of the best views in what is a very flat city. Descend the steps at 27 rue Piat, which lead to the **Maison de l'Air** (2; p137) exhibition space, and follow the path downhill to the right to passage de Pékin and rue de Pali Kao to blvd de Belleville.

Blvd de Belleville is a microcosm of *Paris Mondial* and on market mornings (p52), you might think you've been transported to the Mediterranean, Africa or even Asia. Watch the elegant, turbaned African women in technicolour boubous brush past frenzied young Asians with mobile phones glued to their ears, and more relaxed Orthodox Jews wearing yarmulkes alongside North Africans in jellabas heading for the mosque. At No 39

Basilique du Sacré Cœur de Montmartre (p170)

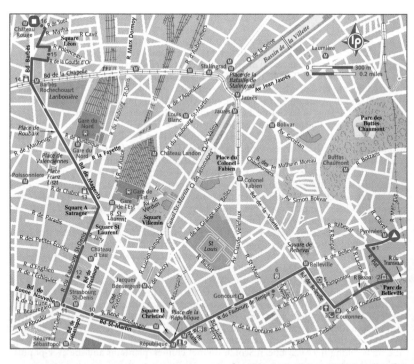

Walk Facts

Start Metro Pyrénées
End Metro Château Rouge
Distance 8km
Time 3½ hours
Fuel stop Passage Brady

is the **Mosquée Abu-Bakr as Siddio 3** just a few doors down from the modern **Église Notre Dame Réconciliatrice 4**, a 'Sri Lankan Christian' church at No 57. About 100m up on the right-hand – or Tunisian – side of blvd de Belleville is the **Synagogue Michkenot Yaachov 5** at No 118. In nearby rue Ramponeau you'll encounter a Jewish shop called La Maison du Taleth at No 10 with religious tomes and articles, a kosher butcher, Boucherie Zlassi, at No 7 and a kosher couscous restaurant called Bebert at No 8.

Walk north up blvd de Belleville and turn left (west) onto rue du Faubourg du Temple, 11e. The walk along rue du Faubourg du Temple to place de la République is a long one and you can take the metro for a couple of stops. But in doing so you'd miss the vibrancy and assorted sights: **La Java** (**6**; p263) at No 105, where Piaf once warbled, and the **Épicerie Asie, Antilles, Afrique 7** at No 88, which sells goods from three worlds.

Once you've crossed the placid Canal St-Martin and walked past the decrepit entrances to the popular clubs La Favela Chic (p265) and **Gibus** (**8**; p265), the enormous place de la République, where many political rallies and demonstrations in Paris start and/or end, and its **statue of the Republic 9** (erected in 1883), pop into view. Make your way to the square's northwest corner and follow blvd St-Martin past the **Porte St-Martin 10** and the **Porte St-Denis** (**11**; p136). Turn right (north) and follow rue du Faubourg St-Denis, the main artery linking Tamil Nadu with Turkey. **Passage Brady** (**12**; p221) at No 46, built in 1828 and once housing 100 tiny boutiques, is now a warren of Indian, Pakistani and Bangladeshi cafés and restaurants and the perfect spot for a break and some refuelling. Alternatively you might pop into a Turkish *çay salonu* (tea house) or *döner yemek ve çorba salon* (kebab and soup restaurant), which offer kebabs, soup, *pide* (Turkish pizza, for lack of a better term) and *lahmacun* (thin pitta bread topped with minced meat, tomatoes, onions and fresh parsley) for a cheap and tasty snack.

A few blocks up, the grocers betray their British colonial past: Horlicks, Bird's Custard, Glenrych pilchards, HP sauce and Tetley tea bags stand proud among naan and *dosas* (paper-thin lentil-flour pancakes) mixes in the well-stacked shop fronts of Wembley Bazaar, Asia Cash & Carry and Broadway Foods just off rue du Faubourg St-Denis in rue Jarry.

Turn left onto blvd de Magenta and carry on north past the 19th-century **Marché St-Quentin** (13; p52) and the Gare du Nord. The big pink sign announcing the **Tati department store** (14; p301) marks the start of La Goutte d'Or, the North African quarter called the 'Golden Drop' after a white wine that was produced here in the 19th century. The district is contiguous with African Château Rouge and outside the metro station you'll most likely be presented with the calling cards of various *médiums* (mediums) or *voyants* (fortune tellers) promising to effect the return of your estranged spouse, unrequited love or misspent fortune.

From the Barbès Rochechouart metro stop walk north up blvd Barbès past numerous goldsmiths with dazzling window displays. Turn east into rue de la Goutte d'Or, a great souk of a street selling everything from gaudy tea glasses and pointy-toed leather *babouches* (slippers) to belly dancers' costumes. From every direction the sounds of *raï* (a fusion of Algerian folk music and rock) fill the air.

A gate at 42 rue de la Goutte d'Or leads up **Villa Poissonnière** 15, a cobbled street that looks straight out of a 19th-century daguerreotype, and turn left and then right onto rue des Poissonniers – the 'Street of Fishermen' where you'll find halal butchers offering special deals on sheep heads and 5kg packets of chicken but no fish.

Rue Myrha on your left is the frontier between Central and West Africa and the Maghreb; *raï* music quickly gives way to Cameroonian *bikutsi* (a fusion of ancestral rhythms and fast electric guitars) and Senegalese *mbalax* (drum music). After crossing over rue Myrha, turn left (west) into **rue Dejean** 16 where an open-air market is held from 8am to 1pm on Sunday and 3.30pm to 7.30pm Tuesday to Saturday. Here you *will* find fish and lots of it, especially fresh *capitaine* (Nile perch) and *thiof* from Senegal, alongside stalls selling fiery Caribbean Scotch Bonnet chillies, plantains and the ever-popular *dasheen* (taro).

The Château Rouge metro station is a few steps to the southwest.

MONTMARTRE ART ATTACK

Montmartre (from the French words *mont* for hill and *martyr*) has been a place of legend ever since St Denis was executed here in c AD 250 and began his headless journey on foot to the village north of Paris that still bears his name (p152). In recent times the Montmartre of myth has been resurrected by music, books and especially films like *Le Fabuleux Destin d'Amélie Poulain* (just *Amelie* in English; 2002), which presented the district in various shades of rose, and *Moulin Rouge* (2001), which also made it pretty but gave it a bit more edge.

For centuries Montmartre was a simple country village filled with the *moulins* (mills) that supplied Paris with its flour. But then it was incorporated into the capital in 1860, and its picturesque charm and low rents attracted painters and writers – especially after the Communard uprising of 1871 (p78), which began here. The late 19th and early 20th centuries were Montmartre's heyday, when Toulouse-Lautrec drew his favourite cancan dancers and Picasso, Braque and others introduced the world to cubism.

After WWI such creative activity shifted to Montparnasse, but Montmartre retained an upbeat ambience that all the tourists in the world still can't spoil. The real attractions here, apart from the great views from the Butte de Montmartre (Montmartre Hill), are the area's little parks and steep, winding cobblestone streets, many of whose houses seem about to be engulfed by creeping vines and ivy.

In English-speaking countries, Montmartre's mystique of unconventionality has been magnified by the supposed notoriety of places like the Moulin Rouge, a nightclub on the edge of the Pigalle district that was founded in 1889 and is known for its scantily clad – ooooh lá lá! – chorus girls. The garish nightlife that Toulouse-Lautrec loved to portray has spread along blvd de Clichy, and Pigalle has become decidedly sleazy, though it's pretty tame stuff.

Begin the walk at the Blanche metro station. Diagonally opposite to the left is the legendary **Moulin Rouge** (1; p272) beneath its trademark red windmill while appropriately located to the right is the **Musée de l'Érotisme** (2; p149), an institution that portrays itself as educational rather than titillating. Walk up rue Lepic, which is lined with food shops, and halfway up on the left is the **Café des Deux Moulins** (3; ☎ 01 42 54 90 50; 15 rue Lepic, 18e; ☺ 7am-2am Mon-Fri, 7.30am-2am Sat, 9am-2am Sun), where our heroine Amélie worked in the eponymous film. Follow the curve to the west (left); Théo Van Gogh owned the **house at No 54** 4 and his brother, the artist Vincent, stayed with him on the 3rd floor for two years from 1886.

Further along rue Lepic are Montmartre's famous twinned windmills. The **Moulin de la Galette** 5, the better known, was turned into a popular open-air dance hall in the late 19th century and was immortalised by Pierre-Auguste Renoir in his 1876 tableau *Le Bal du Moulin de La Galette*. About 100m to the east, at the corner of rue Girardon is the **Moulin Radet** 6. Confusingly, it's now a restaurant called Le Moulin de la Galette.

Turn left (north) into rue Girardon, cross through leafy square St-Buisson (Holy Bush) and past the charmingly named Allée des Brouillards (Fog Path) and descend the stairs from place Dalida into rue St-Vincent; on the other side of the wall is **Cimetière St-Vincent** 7, final resting place of the great and the good, including Maurice Utrillo (1883–1955), the so-called Painter of Montmartre. Just over rue des Saules is the celebrated cabaret **Au Lapin Agile** (8; p263), whose name seems to suggest a nimble rabbit but actually comes from *Le Lapin à Gill,* a mural of a rabbit jumping out of a cooking pot by caricaturist André Gill, which can still be seen on the western exterior wall. Among the cabaret's regulars was the poet Guillaume Apollinaire, the great proponent of cubism and futurism, who was killed in combat in 1918.

Walk Facts

Start Metro Blanche
End Metro Abbesses
Distance 2.5km
Time Two hours
Fuel stop La Maison Rouge

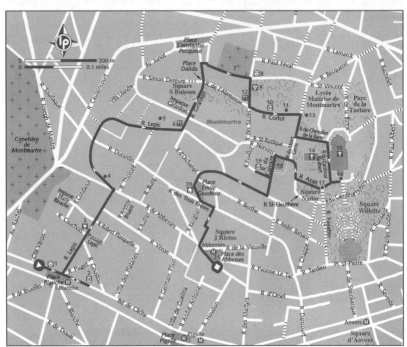

Turn right (south) onto rue des Saules. Just opposite is the **Close du Montmartre 9**, a small vineyard dating from 1933 whose 2000 vines produce an average of 850 bottles of wine each October (p12), which are auctioned off for charity in the 18e. You can buy sample bottles of the hooch at the **Musée de Montmartre** (10; p149), which is on rue Cortot at No 12–14, the first street on the left after the vineyard. The museum is housed in Montmartre's oldest building, a manor house built in the 17th century, and one-time home to painters Renoir, Utrillo and Raoul Dufy. **Eric Satie's house** 11, where the celebrated composer lived from 1892 to 1898, is at No 6. A great place for a bite to eat is **La Maison Rose** (12; p234), the quintessential Montmartre bistro and the subject of an eponymous lithograph by Utrillo.

Turn right (south) onto rue du Mont Cenis (the attractive **water tower 13** just opposite dates from the early 20th century), left onto (tiny) rue de Chevalier de la Barre and then right onto rue du Cardinal Guibert; this will lead you past the back of **Église St-Pierre de Montmartre 14**, which was built on the site of a Roman temple to Mercury and did time as a Temple of Reason under the Revolution and as a clothing factory during the Commune. The entrance to the **Basilique du Sacré Cœur 15** (p148) and the stunning vista over Paris from **place du Parvis du Sacré Cœur 16** are just a few steps to the south.

From the basilica follow rue Azaïs west past the upper station of the **funicular** (17; p370) and then rue St-Eleuthère north into **place du Tertre** (18; p150), arguably the most touristy place in all of Paris but buzzy and still fun. Just off the southwestern side of the square is rue Poulbot leading to the **Dalí Espace Montmartre** (19; p149), surprisingly the only 'art' museum on the Butte. From place du Calvaire take the steps – actually rue du Calvaire – into rue Gabrielle, turning right (west) to reach place Émile Goudeau. At No 11b is the so-called **Bateau Lavoir 20**, where Kees Van Dongen, Max Jacob, Amedeo Modigliani and Pablo Picasso, who painted his seminal *Les Demoiselles d'Avignon* (1907) here, once lived in great poverty in an old piano factory later used as a laundry that Jacob dubbed the 'Laundry Boat' because of the way it swayed in a strong breeze. Originally at No 13, the Bateau Lavoir burned down in 1970 and was rebuilt in 1978.

Take the steps down from place Émile Goudeau and follow rue des Abbesses south into place des Abbesses, where you can't the miss **metro station entrance 21** designed by Hector Guimard (p104).

Eating

Eating

As the culinary centre of the most aggressively gastronomic country in the world, Paris has more 'generic French', regional and ethnic restaurants, gourmet food shops and markets than any other place in France. Generally speaking, *la cuisine parisienne* (Parisian cuisine) is a poor relation of that extended family known as *la cuisine des provinces* (provincial cuisine), and today very few dishes are associated with the capital as such. Still, the surfeit of other cuisines available in Paris – from Lyonnais and Corsican to Vietnamese and Moroccan – will have you spoilt for choice and begging for more.

Opening Hours

Restaurants generally open from noon to 2.30pm or 3pm for lunch and from 7pm or 7.30pm to between 10pm and midnight for dinner. Only brasseries serve full meals continuously throughout the day (usually from 11am or noon to as late as 1am). National and local laws require that restaurants close for 1½ days a week and that employees work no more than 35 hours a week (though exceptions can be made). That means most eateries will be shut for a full day and (usually) an afternoon. Be advised that the vast majority of restaurants in Paris close on Sunday – there's a distressing tendency for many to shut down for the entire weekend. Supermarkets are generally open from 8.30am or 9am till 8pm Monday to Saturday with very few open Sunday (9am to 12.30pm or 1pm). Please note that opening hours are only listed in this chapter if they differ by more than one hour either way from these or if the business closes on certain other days.

How Much?

When it comes to eating out in Paris, the question 'How much?' is like asking 'How long is a piece of string?' It all depends… A three-course dinner *menu* (fixed-price meal with two or three courses) can be had for as little as €12 at budget places, and one-plate *plats du jour* (daily specials) at lunch are sometimes available for under €10. On the other hand,

L'Encrier restaurant (p190)

three courses for lunch at **Le Grand Véfour** (p180) overlooking the Jardin du Palais Royal will set you back €75 and dinner is well over three times that amount.

In general, however, you should be able to enjoy a substantial sit-down lunch for about €15 at a medium-priced restaurant and an excellent three-course dinner with wine for around €35. Cheap eats are under €12.

Generally, higher-priced *menus* are available at lunch and dinner. Lower-priced good-value *menus* that are available at lunch only (and usually just on weekdays) are noted as such throughout the chapter.

Booking Tables

It is always advisable to book in advance at midrange restaurants and absolutely manda-tory at top-end ones. If you do arrive at a restaurant without a reservation, you will be treated more seriously if you state the number of *couverts* (covers) required *(Avez-vous deux couverts?)* upon entry rather than referring to the number of places.

Paying & Tipping

With the exception of *cafétérias* (cafeterias), *restaurants libre-service* (self-service restaur-ants) and the like, most eateries in Paris take credit cards though there is usually a minimum charge of €15. A hand-held machine used to verify your credit card and payment is brought to the table, where the transaction takes place; if your card has a chip you will almost surely require a PIN number. Always check your bill before paying; small 'mistakes' do happen from time to time in Paris.

Many French people traditionally seemed to feel that 'going Dutch' (ie splitting the bill) at restaurants was an uncivilised custom, and in general the person who did the inviting would pay for the meal. That may still happen but nowadays close friends and colleagues will usually share the cost equally. They never calculate it down to the last euro and cent, however.

French law requires that restaurant and café bills include the service charge, which is usually between 12% and 15%. But a word of warning is in order. *Service compris* (service included, sometimes abbreviated as 'sc' at the bottom of the bill) means that the service charge is built into the price of each dish; *service non-compris* (service not included) or *service en sus* (service in addition) means that the service charge is calculated after the food and/or drink you've consumed has been added up. In either case you pay only the total of the bill so a *pourboire* (tip) on top of that is neither necessary nor expected in most cases. However, many Parisians will leave a few coins on the table in a restaurant, unless the service was particularly bad, although they rarely tip in cafés and bars when they've just had a coffee or a drink.

CON FUSION: FOOLISH FEELINGS ABOUT FOODING

In this ever-globalising world, it was, as they say, inevitable. In 1999 French journalists Alexandre Cammas and Emmanuel Rubin combined the English words 'food' and 'feeling' and came up not with self-evident 'fooling' but 'fooding'. Apparently they used it to describe the art of appreciating not only the contents on your plate but also what's going on around you – ambience, décor, scene. Before long it was *the* word in the mouths of *branché* (trendy) Parisians and within a year an annual Fooding Festival in late November/early December was established. Fooding guide books were written, a fooding dictionary published and the *Libération* newspaper started calling its restaurant pullout section 'Le Fooding Guide'.

The word pops up like a bad penny everywhere and you'll see it again and again and again. But what on God's green earth is 'fooding' all about, really? The funny (perhaps predictable) thing is that no-one seems to know. The *foodeur* (ie he/she who 'foods') frequents places as different as **Spoon** (p214), the chichi Georges at the **Pompidou Centre** (p98) and the **Atelier de Joël Robouchon** (p211). It would seem, then, that 'food' is not really a big part of 'fooding'; after all, the truly trendy Parisians are much more concerned with appearance than taste. So paying through the nose for mediocre food in a really trendy spot has got to be better than eating a superb meal somewhere that is uncool, right? Indeed it is. Just ask any Londoner.

CHEAP EATS

Along with the less-expensive places listed under specific quarters and arrondissements in this chapter, French chain and university restaurants offer excellent value for those counting their centimes.

Fast-Food & Chain Restaurants

American fast-food chains have busy branches all over Paris as does the local hamburger chain **Quick** (www.quick .fr in French). In addition, a number of local chain restaurants have outlets around Paris with standard menus. They are definitely a cut above fast-food outlets and can be good value in areas such as the av des Champs-Élysées, where restaurants tend to be overpriced.

Bistro Romain (www.bistroromain.fr in French; starters €4.90-9.70, pasta €12.80-15.90, mains €14.20-18.60, *menu* €13.90-22.70; ☽ 11.30am-1am) This ever-popular bistro-restaurant chain, which has some 15 branches in Paris proper and another nine in the *banlieues* (suburbs), is a surprisingly upmarket place for its price category, and service is always pleasant and efficient. The **Champs-Élysées Bistro Romain** (Map pp426–7; ☎ 01 43 59 93 31; 122 av des Champs-Élysées, 8e; Ⓜ George V), one of a pair along the city's most famous thoroughfare, is a stone's throw from place Charles de Gaulle and the Arc de Triomphe.

Buffalo Grill (www.buffalo-grill.fr; starters €3.90-9.50, mains €9.20-20.50, *menu* from €9; ☽ usually 11am-11pm Sun-Thu, 11am-midnight Fri & Sat) This successful chain has some eight branches in Paris, including the **Gare du Nord Buffalo Grill** (Map pp428–9; ☎ 01 40 16 47 81; 9 blvd de Denain, 10e; Ⓜ Gare du Nord). Not surprisingly, the emphasis here is on grills and steak – everything from Canadian buffalo burgers (€9.80) to 350g T-bone steaks (€17).

Hippopotamus (www.hippopotamus.fr in French; starters €4.50-9.90, mains €10.90-19.50, *menu* €9.90-24.50; ☽ usually 11.45am-12.30am Sun-Thu, 11.45am-1am Fri & Sat) This ever-expanding chain, which has 20 branches in Paris proper, specialises in solid, steak-based meals. Three of the outlets here stay open to 5am daily, including the **Opéra Hippopotamus** (Map pp428–9; ☎ 01 47 42 75 70; 1 blvd des Capucines, 2e; Ⓜ Opéra).

Léon de Bruxelles (www.leon-de-bruxelles.com in French; starters €4.30-6.80, mains €10.50-15, *menu* €10.50-16.90; ☽ 11.45am-11pm) At Léon the focus is on one thing and one thing only: *moules* (mussels). Meal-size bowls of the meaty bivalves, served with chips and bread, start at about €10 and are exceptionally good value, especially at lunch. There are 12 Léons in Paris, including the Les Halles branch of **Léon de Bruxelles** (Map pp436–7; ☎ 01 42 36 18 50; 120 rue Rambuteau, 1er; Ⓜ Châtelet-Les Halles).

University Canteens

Stodgy but filling *cafétéria* food is available in copious quantities at Paris' 17 *restaurants universitaires* (student restaurants). Another 20 cafés (usually in the same building) serve drinks, snacks and lighter meals from 8am to between 3pm and 6pm on weekdays. Tickets for three-course meals at Paris' university restaurants are €2.70 for students with a French university or college ID card, €4.80 with an ISIC or youth card and €6.30 for guests.

Centre Régional des Œuvres Universitaires et Scolaires (CROUS; ☎ 01 40 51 36 00; www.crous-paris.fr in French) restaurants (usually called *restos U*) have variable hours that change according to university holiday schedules and weekend rotational agreements; check the schedule posted outside any of the following or the CROUS website for current times. The only one open all year and on Sunday (for brunch) is Bullier.

Branches include **Assas** (Map pp444–5; ☎ 01 44 41 58 01; 92 rue d'Assas, 6e; ☽ lunch 11.15am-2.30pm Mon-Fri; Ⓜ Port Royal or Notre Dame des Champs); **Bullier** (Map pp444–5; ☎ 01 40 51 37 85; 39 av Georges Bernanos, 5e; ☽ lunch 11.30am-2pm Mon-Sat, brunch 10.30am-2pm Sun, dinner 6.15-8pm; Ⓜ Port Royal); **Censier** (Map pp444–5; ☎ 01 45 35 41 24; 31 rue Geoffroy St-Hilaire, 5e; ☽ lunch 11am-2.30pm Mon-Fri; Ⓜ Censier Daubenton or Jussieu); **Châtelet** (Map pp444–5; ☎ 01 43 31 51 66; 8-10 rue Jean Calvin, 5e; ☽ lunch 11.30am-2pm, dinner 6.30-8pm Mon-Fri; Ⓜ Censier Daubenton); **Mabillon** (Map pp436–7; ☎ 01 43 25 66 23; 3 rue Mabillon, 6e; ☽ lunch 11.30am-2.30pm, dinner 6-8pm; Ⓜ Mabillon); and **Mazet** (Map pp436–7; ☎ 01 46 34 23 83; 55bis rue André Mazet, 6e; ☽ lunch 11.30am-2pm Mon-Fri; Ⓜ Odéon).

Self-Catering

There is a wide variety of self-catering options available from small neighbourhood stores specialising in just one or two products to large supermarkets and Paris' great covered and open-air markets. Details are included at the end of neighbourhood sections in this chapter. Also see p52 for a list of markets.

LOUVRE & LES HALLES

The area between Forum des Halles (1er) and the Centre Pompidou (4e) is filled with a number of trendy restaurants, but few of them are particularly good and they mostly cater to tourists. Streets lined with places to eat include rue des Lombards, the narrow streets to the north and east of Forum des Halles and pedestrian-only rue Montorgueil, a market street and probably your best bet for something quick. In addition, there are several worthwhile places in the *passages couverts* (covered shopping arcades; p167).

Those in search of Asian food flock to rue Ste-Anne and other streets of Paris' so-called Japantown, which is just west of the Jardin du Palais Royal. There are also some good-value restaurants serving other Asian cuisine in the area.

AU DAUPHIN Map pp436-7   French, Basque

☎ 01 42 60 40 11; 167 rue St-Honoré, 1er; menus lunch €19 & €25, dinner €35; ☽ lunch & dinner to 10.30pm; Ⓜ Palais Royal-Musée du Louvre
The force behind this unassuming bistro facing place André Malraux and Palais Royal is two pedigreed chefs from Biarritz on the southwest coast who have brought the flavours of the Basque country and coastal Landes region to Paris. There are two hard-to-choose routes through the menu – the first being jars of wonderful rustic starters such as a tuna confit, *rillettes* (shredded potted meat) and foie gras, to be shared and with excellent bread, while the other offers combinations of classic Spanish *parrillada* (mixed grill).

AU PIED DE COCHON

Map pp436-7   French, Brasserie
☎ 01 40 13 77 00; 6 rue Coquillère, 1er; starters €6.50-19.50, mains €15.50-33, 2-/3-course menus €18.50/24; ☽ 24hr; Ⓜ Les Halles
This venerable establishment, which once satisfied the appetites of both market porters and theatre-goers with its onion soup and *pied de cochon* (pig's foot), has become more uniformly upmarket and touristy since Les Halles was moved to the suburbs, but it still opens round the clock seven days a week. If you've never eaten a trotter before, give it a go. Generous breakfasts are a snip at €11.

AUX CRUS DE BOURGOGNE

Map pp428-9   French, Bistro
☎ 01 42 33 48 24; 3 rue de Bachaumont, 2e; starters €6.50-18.50, mains €15-26.50, menu €27; ☽ lunch & dinner to 11pm Mon-Fri; Ⓜ Les Halles or Sentier
This excellent bistro on a pedestrian street just off busy rue Montorgueil has a penchant for fish and seafood – especially lobster (half a lobster with mayonnaise €16, lobster with foie gras and salad €18.50). As its name implies, Burgundy is the wine of choice. A real plus is the open terrace in the warmer months, which allows you to enjoy your crustaceans without a side order of exhaust fumes.

BAAN BORAN Map pp428-9   Thai

☎ 01 40 15 90 45; 43 rue de Montpensier, 1er; starters €6.10-13.70, mains €11-16; ☽ lunch Mon-Fri, dinner to 11pm Mon-Sat; Ⓜ Palais Royal-Musée du Louvre
The fare at this eatery, just opposite the Théâtre du Palais Royal and run by two Thai women, is provincial and about as authentic as you'll find in this part of Paris. It makes a convenient stop before or after touring the Louvre. There are several vegetarian dishes, priced between €8 and €14.

CAFÉ BEAUBOURG

Map pp436-7   French, International
☎ 01 48 87 63 96; 100 rue St-Martin, 4e; starters €6.50-12, mains €14.50-15; ☽ 8am-1am Sun-Wed, 8am-2am Thu-Sat; Ⓜ Châtelet-Les Halles
This upbeat minimalist café across from Centre Pompidou has been drawing a

Eating   **LOUVRE & LES HALLES**

TOP FIVE EAT STREETS IN PARIS

- Ave de Choisy, ave d'Ivry and rue Baudricourt (p229) have any number of Chinese and Southeast Asian eateries.
- Blvd de Belleville (p222) is the place for Middle Eastern food and kosher couscous.
- Rue Montorgueil (p52), a pedestrians-only market street, is one of the best places around for something quick.
- Rue Mouffetard (p52) is not just a food market but an excellent street to find ethnic and French restaurants in the budget category.
- Passage Brady (p221), a covered arcade, is the place to come for Indian, Pakistani and Bangladeshi food.

well-heeled crowd for breakfast and Sunday brunch (€13 to €24) on the terrace since 1986; there's always free entertainment on the *parvis* (large square) just opposite.

CAFÉ DE L'ÉPOQUE

Map pp436-7   French, Café

☎ 01 42 33 40 70; 12 rue Croix des Petits Champs, 1er; starters €6-10, mains €14.50-21; ⏰ lunch daily, dinner to midnight Mon-Sat; Ⓜ Louvre-Rivoli

A lovely old relic of the *belle époque* when the *passages couverts* were *the* places to shop. This café can be entered from the covered *passage* itself or the lovely terrace facing rue du Bouloi.

CAFÉ MARLY Map pp436-7   French, Café

☎ 01 46 26 06 60; 93 rue de Rivoli, 1er; starters €10-25, mains €12-28; ⏰ 8am-2am; Ⓜ Palais Royal-Musée du Louvre

This classic venue facing the cour Napoléon du Louvre serves contemporary French fare throughout the day under the colonnades of the Louvre. The views of the glass pyramid are priceless – if you don't know you're in Paris now, you never will – and depending on how *au courant* (familiar) you are with French starlets and people who appear in *Match*, you should get an eyeful. Decent pastas are €15 to €23 while sandwiches and snacks are €10 to €20.

CAFÉ MODERNE

Map pp428-9   French

☎ 01 53 40 84 10; 40 rue Notre Dames des Victoires, 2e; 2-/3-course menus €27/32; ⏰ lunch Mon-Fri, dinner to 11pm Mon-Sat; Ⓜ Bourse

A relative newcomer, just opposite the Bourse, it feels more New York than Paris but so much the better for that. The food on offer is more contemporary than classic bistro; the fish dishes are particularly recommended as is the wonderful *millefeuille* of pastry, cream and fresh fruit.

CHEZ LA VIEILLE

Map pp436-7   French

☎ 01 42 60 15 78; 1 rue Bailleul, 1er; starters €15-24, mains €18-25, menu €27; ⏰ lunch Mon-Fri, dinner to 9.30pm Thu; Ⓜ Louvre-Rivoli

This little restaurant on the corner of rue de l'Arbre à Sec and also known by its Corsican owner's *prénom*, Adrienne, is on two floors, but don't expect a slot on the more rustic

ground floor; that's reserved for regulars. The small menu reflects the size of the place but is universally sublime. Try the excellent terrine and splendid pot-au-feu (€23).

JOE ALLEN Map pp436-7   American

☎ 01 42 36 70 13; 30 rue Pierre Lescot, 1er; starters €7-9.80, mains €12.90-16.50, menus €12.90 (lunch only), €18 & €22.50; ⏰ noon-1am; Ⓜ Étienne Marcel

An institution in Paris for some 35 years, Joe Allen is a little bit of New York in Paris, with a great atmosphere and a good selection of Californian wines. There's an excellent brunch (€17 to €19.50) from noon to 4pm at the weekend, where many can be seen slumped over a Bloody Mary and trying to make sense of the night – or was that the morning? – before. The food is simple but finely prepared; the ribs (€16.50) are particularly recommended and some say Joe serves the best hamburgers in town.

LE GRAND COLBERT

Map pp428-9   French

☎ 01 42 86 87 88; 2-4 rue Vivienne, 2e; starters €9.50-15.50, mains €16.50-37, menus €26.50 (lunch only) & €30; ⏰ noon-3am; Ⓜ Pyramides

This former workers' *cafétéria* transformed into a *fin de siècle* showcase is more relaxed than many of its restored kind and a convenient spot for lunch if visiting Galerie Vivienne and Galerie Colbert or cruising the streets late at night (last orders: 1am). Don't expect gastronomic miracles, but portions are huge and service is friendly.

LE GRAND VÉFOUR Map pp428-9   French

☎ 01 42 96 56 27; 17 rue de Beaujolais, 1er; starters €68-86, mains €71-86, menus lunch/dinner €75/252; ⏰ lunch Mon-Fri, dinner to 9.30pm Mon-Thu; Ⓜ Pyramides

This 18th-century jewel on the northern edge of the Jardin du Palais Royal has been a dining favourite of the Paris elite since 1784; just look at who gets their names ascribed to each table – from Napoleon to Victor Hugo and Colette (who lived next door). And the food is tiptop; expect a voyage of discovery in one of the most beautiful restaurants in the world.

LE LOUP BLANC Map pp428-9 International
☎ 01 40 13 08 35; 42 rue Tiquetonne, 2e; veg dishes €10.50-13, mains €12.50-18.50; ☽ dinner to midnight Sun-Thu, to 12.30am Fri, to 1am Sat, brunch 11am-4.30pm Sun; Ⓜ Étienne Marcel
Some inventive and inexpensive dishes are on offer here: meat and fish marinated with herbs and spices (eg cardamom, star anise, marjoram) and then grilled. For accompaniments, you can choose from up to four vegetables and grains, according to your appetite and the season: red lentils, *quinoa* (a South American grain), creamed corn with peppers (a must) or carrots with cumin. We like the chicken with rosemary and savoury, prawns with tamarind and ginger and pork with tangerine.

LE PETIT MÂCHON
Map pp436-7 French, Lyons
☎ 01 42 60 08 06; 158 rue St-Honoré, 1er; starters €7-12.50, mains €14-22, menu lunch €16.50; ☽ lunch & dinner to 11pm Tue-Sun; Ⓜ Palais Royal-Musée du Louvre
Close to the Louvre, this is an upbeat bistro with Lyons-inspired specialities. It takes its

name from a Burgundian variety of *galette des rois* (kings' cake), a puff pastry filled with frangipane cream that is eaten at Epiphany (Twelfth night; p61). It serves some of the best Lyonnaise-inspired food in town.

LE TAMBOUR Map pp428-9 French, Bistro
☎ 01 42 33 06 90; 41 rue Montmartre, 2e; starters €6.50-14, mains €11-19, ☽ lunch Tue-Sat, dinner to 3.30am daily; Ⓜ Étienne Marcel or Sentier
The 'Drummer' is a Paris landmark with crazy hours and friendly but brisk service. It attracts a mixed, somewhat rowdy crowd; you'll enjoy the recycled street furniture, straightforward cuisine (served well into the night) and the cocky, moustached staff. The café-bar is open noon to 6am Tuesday to Saturday and 6pm to 6am Sunday and Monday.

LE VAUDEVILLE
Map pp428-9 French, Brasserie
☎ 01 40 20 04 62; 29 rue Vivienne, 2e; starters €6.50-14.50, mains €17-33, menus €19.90 & €29.90; ☽ lunch & dinner to 1am; Ⓜ Bourse
This stunning brasserie opposite the stock exchange is to Art Deco what the **Bouillon Racine** (p193) is to Art Nouveau. OK, the food might be something of an afterthought, but at least you can be guaranteed a certain standard. Come for the fabulous décor – engraved glass, extravagant lighting, domed ceiling and intricate ironwork – designed in the 1920s by the Solvet brothers, who also did **La Coupole** (p209).

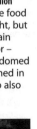

Patrons inside 404 (p183)

LE VÉRO DODAT

Map pp436-7　　　　　　　　　　　　French

☎ 01 45 08 92 06; 19 Galerie Véro Dodat, 2 rue du Bouloi, 1er; starters/mains/desserts €5/10.50/5, menus €14.50 & €16.50; ☽ lunch & dinner to 10.30pm Tue-Sat; Ⓜ Louvre-Rivoli

This friendly little place in the heart of the Véro Dodat (p168) *passage couvert* has seating both downstairs and upstairs. At lunchtime it's especially popular with workers from the nearby Bourse de la Commerce who come for the reasonably priced plats du jour (€10).

L'ÉPI D'OR Map pp436-7　　　French, Bistro

☎ 01 42 36 38 12; 25 rue Jean-Jacques Rousseau, 1er; starters €6-15, mains €16-22, 2-/3-course menus €18/22; ☽ lunch Mon-Fri, dinner to 10pm Mon-Sat; Ⓜ Louvre-Rivoli

The 'Golden Sword' has been an institution since the *belle époque*, when it would open at 10pm to serve the *'forts des halles'*, the brutes who stacked the *'devils'*, huge bags of potatoes and cabbage, all night at the old Marché des Halles. Today it's an oh-so-Parisian bistro serving well-prepared, classic dishes – such as *gigot d'agneau* (leg of lamb) cooked for seven hours – to a surprisingly well-heeled crowd. The *menus* are available at lunch and till 9pm only.

MACÉO Map pp428-9　　　　International

☎ 01 42 97 53 85; 15 rue des Petits Champs, 1er; starters €11-18, mains €24-30, menus €27 (lunch only) & €30-50; ☽ lunch Mon-Fri & dinner to 11pm Mon-Sat; Ⓜ Bourse or Opéra

From the people who brought us Willi's Wine Bar (right) comes this very upper crust restaurant with Second Empire décor and innovative cuisine, including a very sophisticated vegetarian menu.

RESTAURANT DU THÉÂTRE

Map pp428-9　　　　　　　　French, Bistro

☎ 01 42 97 59 46; 36 rue de Montpensier, 1er; starters €11.50-17.50, mains €14-18, menus €29 & €37; ☽ lunch & dinner to 10pm; Ⓜ Pyramides

This civilised bistro and wine bar facing the Jardin du Palais Royal is next door to the little-known Théâtre du Palais Royal (hence the name). It's a convenient spot if visiting the *passages couverts* around Palais Royal or even the Louvre and is best entered via 67 Galerie de Montpensier. The plat du jour is €16.

RESTAURANT VOYAGEURS
DU MONDE Map pp428-9　　　International

☎ 01 42 86 17 17; 51bis rue Ste-Anne, 2e; starters/mains/desserts €12/26/9, menus lunch/dinner €23/42; ☽ lunch & dinner to 10pm Mon-Fri; Ⓜ Pyramides or Quatre Septembre

Voyageurs du Monde, comprising an extensive travel agency (p370), shop and exhibition spaces, also boasts a restaurant that explores the cuisine of every continent in a single menu devoted to a different country each day – from Australia and the Pacific to Poland and Chile. It's an ambitious task and the results – it must be said – are not always 100% successful. But in a street where Japanese restaurants jostle for space, it's a delight to find this little culinary Babel.

TANA Map pp428-9　　　　　　　Thai

☎ 01 42 33 53 64; 36 rue Tiquetonne, 2e; starters €7-12.50, mains €9-20; ☽ dinner to 11.30pm; Ⓜ Étienne Marcel

In a street where each restaurant is more original than the next, Tana takes the tart. Customers are greeted by rather sexy Thai 'waitresses' and then plunged into a highly exotic world where the extravagant 'hostesses' are equal to the dishes on offer. The subtle flavours of the mixed hors d'oeuvre and the *homok pla* (steamed fish served in a banana leaf; €10) are both excellent choices.

WILLI'S WINE BAR

Map pp428-9　　　　　　　　French, Bistro

☎ 01 42 61 05 09; 13 rue des Petits Champs, 1er; starters €8-14, mains €13-18, menus lunch/dinner €22/33; ☽ lunch & dinner to 11pm Mon-Sat; Ⓜ Bourse

This civilised and very convivial wine bar-cum-bistro was opened in the mid-1980s by British expats who introduced the wine-bar concept to Paris. The food is still excellent, the wines (especially Côtes du Rhône) well chosen and Willi's legendary status lives on – and deservedly so.

CHEAP EATS

KUNITORAYA Map pp428-9　　　Japanese

☎ 01 47 03 33 65; 39 rue Ste-Anne, 1er; soup & noodle dishes €8.50-16, menu lunch €12.50; ☽ 11.30am-10pm; Ⓜ Pyramides

With seating on two floors, this simple and intimate place has a wide and excellent range of Japanese shop-made noodle dishes and set lunches and dinners. If headed here, aim to arrive before 1pm for lunch or before 8pm for dinner, or prepare to join a queue that functions as a noodle vacuum cleaner.

LA VICTOIRE SUPRÊME DU CŒUR

Map pp436-7   Vegetarian

☎ 01 40 41 93 95; 41 rue des Bourdonnais, 1er; starters & salads €4.70-10.70, mains €9.70-12.50, menus €12.50 (lunch only), €15.30 & €19.30; ⌚ lunch & dinner to 10pm Mon-Sat; Ⓜ Châtelet
This Indian-inspired vegan restaurant is a welcome addition to the hubbub of Les Halles. Food is actually quite good, but avoid the mock-meat dishes like the seitan (wheat gluten) 'steak'. For drinks try the mango lassi or spiced tea. No smoking, no alcohol, no guilt.

L'ARBRE À CANNELLE

Map pp428-9   French, Tea Room

☎ 01 45 08 55 87; 57 passage des Panoramas, 2e; dishes €6.50-12; ⌚ 11.30am-6.30pm Mon-Sat; Ⓜ Grands Boulevards
The 'Cinnamon Tree' is a lovely tea room with *tartes salées* (savoury pies; €6.50 to €7), excellent salads (€6.50 to €9.50), great plats du jour (€10) and red-fruit crumble for dessert. The original 19th-century décor is worth a visit in itself; seating is on the ground and 1st floors.

SELF-CATERING

Rue Montorgueil (p52), one of the busiest and best-stocked *rues commerçantes* (commercial streets not unlike open-air markets) in Paris, is north of Les Halles.

There are several supermarkets around Forum des Halles. Other options are: **Ed l'Épicier** (Map pp436-7; 80 rue de Rivoli, 4e; Ⓜ Hôtel de Ville), **Franprix Les Halles** (Map pp436-7; 35 rue Berger, 1er; Ⓜ Châtelet) and a **Franprix Châtelet branch** (Map pp436-7; 16 rue Bertin Poirée, 1er; Ⓜ Châtelet).

MARAIS & BASTILLE

The Marais, filled with small restaurants of every imaginable type, is one of Paris' premier neighbourhoods for eating out.

Towards République there's a decent selection of ethnic places. If you're after authentic

TOP FIVE MARAIS & BASTILLE RESTAURANTS

- Chez Nénesse (p185)
- L'Ambassade d'Auvergne (p186)
- Le Petit Marché (p187)
- L'Encrier (p190)
- Les Amis de Messina (p187)

Chinese food but can't be bothered going to the larger Chinatown in the 13e (see p229), check out the small noodle shops and restaurants along rue Au Maire, 3e. The kosher and kosher-style restaurants along **rue des Rosiers** (Map pp436–7; 4e), the so-called Pletzl, serve specialities from North Africa, Central Europe and Israel. Many are closed on Friday evening, Saturday and Jewish holidays. Takeaway falafel and *shwarma* (kebabs) are available at several places along the street.

Bastille is another area chock-a-block with restaurants, some of which have added a star or two to their epaulets in recent years. Narrow rue de Lappe and rue de la Roquette, 11e, just east of place de la Bastille, may not be as hip as they were a dozen years ago, but they remain popular streets for nightlife and attract a young, alternative crowd.

404 Map pp436-7   North African, Moroccan

☎ 01 42 74 57 81; 69 rue des Gravilliers, 3e; starters €7-9, couscous & tajines €14-24, menus lunch/brunch €17/21; ⌚ lunch Mon-Fri, dinner to midnight daily, brunch 10am-4pm Sat & Sun; Ⓜ Arts et Métiers
As comfortable a Maghreb (North African) caravanserai as you'll find in Paris, the 404 not only has excellent couscous and *tajines* but superb grills (€12 to €22) and pigeon pastillas. The weekend *brunch berbère* (Berber brunch) is available at the weekend. You'll just love the One Thousand and One Nights décor with real antiques and the waiters' free-flowing uniforms, but the tables are set too close to one another.

À LA RENAISSANCE

Map pp440-1   French, Café

☎ 01 43 79 83 09; 87 rue de la Roquette, 11e; starters €7.60-9.50, mains €11.50-16; ⌚ lunch & dinner to 11.30pm; Ⓜ Voltaire
This large, café-like *bistro de quartier* with its huge bar and plate-glass windows looking

onto the street is open daily. Food is reliable if unadventurous – herring fillets on a bed of warm potatoes, mackerel *rillettes*, steak tartare. The daily specials are particularly good value.

AU BASCOU Map pp428–9 French, Basque

☎ 01 42 72 69 25; 38 rue Réaumur, 3e; starters/mains/desserts €9/16/8; ⏱ lunch & dinner to 10.30pm Mon-Fri; Ⓜ Arts et Métiers;
This is a popular eatery serving such Basque classic dishes as *pipérade* (peppers, onions, tomatoes and ham cooked with scrambled eggs), *ttoro* (a kind of Basque bouillabaisse), *axoa* (veal shoulder with a sauce of pimento and peppers) and Bayonne ham in all its guises. Round off the meal with a piece of Ardi Gasna *brebis*, a ewe's milk cheese served with *confiture de cerise* (cherry jam) or a slice of *gâteau basque*, a relatively simple layer cake filled with cream and cherry jam.

AUX VINS DES PYRÉNÉES

Map pp440–1 French
☎ 01 42 72 64 94; 25 rue Beautreillis, 4e; starters €7.50-13, mains €13-18.50, menu lunch €12.50; ⏱ lunch Sun-Fri, dinner to 11.30pm; Ⓜ St-Paul or Bastille
Located in a former wine warehouse a couple of doors down from the house where rock singer Jim Morrison of the Doors died in 1971 (No 17–19), this is a good place to enjoy a no-nonsense French meal with a lot of wine. The place has been able to retain its old-world charm and it's not surprising that a crowd of locals have set up headquarters here. The fish, meat and game dishes are all equally good, but worth a special mention is the foie gras and the top-notch *pavé de rumsteak* (thick rump steak). The wine list offers a wide choice of celebrated and little-known estate wines.

BARACANE Map pp440–1 French

☎ 01 42 71 43 33; 38 rue des Tournelles, 4e; starters €10, mains €16-21, 2-/3-course menus €11/16 (lunch only) & €23/38; ⏱ lunch Mon-Fri, dinner to midnight Mon-Sat; Ⓜ Bastille or Chemin Vert
A poor cousin of the chic L'Oulette (p228), what Baracane lacks in looks during the day, it certainly makes up for at night when it's bustling with a mix of locals and tourists here for the capable southwestern provin-

cial cooking. Duck features heavily – try the *foie gras de canard* (€15) or the *magret de canard* (fillet of duck breast; €16). Wines include some 10 from the southwest.

BEL CANTO Map pp436–7 French

☎ 01 42 78 30 18; 72 quai de l'Hôtel de Ville, 4e; menu €68; ⏱ dinner to midnight Tue-Sat; Ⓜ Hôtel de Ville or Pont Marie
If London, New York and even Budapest can have one – a restaurant where the waiters sing (arias) for their supper, that is – why can't Paris have not one but two (there's now a branch in the 14e)? So if you fancy Bizet with your beef, Verdi with your veg and Puccini with your pud, this place and its *dîners lyriques* is the place for you.

BLUE ELEPHANT Map pp440–1 Thai

☎ 01 47 00 42 00; 43-45 rue de la Roquette, 11e; starters €10-14, mains €14.50-21, menus €44 & €48; ⏱ lunch Sun-Fri, dinner to midnight daily; Ⓜ Bastille
This is Paris' most famous upmarket Thai restaurant and part of an international chain, with a dozen branches in cities round the world from Brussels to Beirut (and more on the way). Although it has become a little too successful for its own good (it also sells knick-knacks and gift items), the indoor tropical rainforest and well-prepared spicy dishes (look for the one, two or three elephant symbols on the menu) are still worth the somewhat inflated prices.

BOFINGER

Map pp440–1 French, Brasserie
☎ 01 42 72 87 82; 5-7 rue de la Bastille, 4e; starters €6-18.50, mains €16.50-37.50, 2-/3-course menus €22.90/29.90; ⏱ lunch & dinner to 1am Mon-Fri, noon-1am Sat & Sun; Ⓜ Bastille
Founded in 1864, Bofinger is reputedly the oldest brasserie in Paris, though its polished Art Nouveau brass, glass and mirrors throughout suggest a redecoration a few decades later. As at most Parisian brasseries, specialities include Alsatian-inspired dishes such as *choucroute* (sauerkraut with assorted meats; €17.50 to €19), and seafood dishes (€18.90 to €37.50). There's a budget *menu* of €19.90 available after 11pm. Ask for a seat downstairs, under the *coupole* (stained-glass dome); it's the prettiest part of the restaurant.

CAFÉ DE L'INDUSTRIE

Map pp440-1   French, Café

☎ 01 47 00 13 53; 16 & 17 rue St-Sabin, 11e; starters €5.10-6.80, mains €8.70-14, menu lunch €10.50; ⏰ 10am-2am; Ⓜ Bastille

This popular café-restaurant with neocolonial décor has two locations directly opposite one another. It's a pleasant space and the perfect spot to meet a friend instead of at one of the crowded cafés or bars in Bastille. Food is competitively priced but not always up to scratch; to avoid disappointment stick with the simple entrees or just graze off the fabulous dessert table (€4 to €5.50). Brunch (€18) is served on Saturday and Sunday.

CHEZ NÉNESSE

Map pp440-1   French, Bistro

☎ 01 42 78 46 49; 17 rue de Saintonge, 3e; starters €4.50-14, mains €12-16; ⏰ lunch & dinner to 10.30pm Mon-Fri; Ⓜ Filles du Calvaire

Chez Nénesse is an oasis of simplicity and good taste in a district that can sometimes go over the top. The atmosphere is very 'old Parisian café' and unpretentious; the dishes made with fresh, high-quality ingredients such as *salade de mesclun au foie gras de canard* (mixed green salad with duck foie gras) and *fricassée de volaille aux morilles* (poultry fricassee with morel mushrooms). The lunchtime plats du jour are €10 to €12.

Le Petit Zinc (p207)

CHEZ OMAR

Map pp436-7   North African

☎ 01 42 72 36 26; 47 rue de Bretagne, 3e; couscous & tajines €12-24, grills €15-22; ⏰ lunch Mon-Sat, dinner to 11.30pm daily; Ⓜ Arts et Métiers

Once a favourite of celebrity types, Chez Omar doesn't seem to attract the very rich or particularly famous these days, which means more room for the likes of us. The quality of the couscous remains top notch, judging from the crowds. Apart from the food and the serving staff, don't expect anything else to be North African at Chez Omar: it looks almost exactly like the corner street café it was a quarter of a century ago.

GRAND APÉTIT

Map pp440-1   Vegetarian

☎ 01 40 27 04 95; 9 rue de la Cerisaie, 4e; soups €3-4, dishes €5.20-10.50; ⏰ lunch Mon-Fri, dinner to 9pm Mon-Wed; Ⓜ Bastille or Sully Morland

Set back from Bastille in a small, quiet street, this place offers light fare such as miso soup and cereals plus strength-building *bols garnis* (rice and vegetable bowls) and *assiettes* (platters) for big eaters only. The menu features delicious, filling dishes served with 100% organic cereals, raw and cooked vegetables and seaweed. Next door there's an excellent organic and macrobiotic shop (⏰ 9.30am-7.30pm Mon-Thu, 9.30am-4pm Fri).

ISAMI

Map pp436-7   Japanese

☎ 01 42 46 06 97; 4 quai d'Orléans, 4e; starters €5.50-17.50, mains €24-36; ⏰ lunch & dinner to 10pm Tue-Sat; Ⓜ Pont Marie

Japanese customers flock to this tiny, packed place for impeccably fresh sushi and sashimi (delicacies made with sea urchins and eels are especially popular) and 'sets' that include a small starter and a soup. The reception could be a bit warmer, though.

JO GOLDENBERG

Map pp436-7   Jewish, Kosher

☎ 01 48 87 20 16; 7 rue des Rosiers, 4e; starters €6-14, mains €13-18; ⏰ 8.30am-midnight; Ⓜ St-Paul

Since it's the oldest (established 1920) and most famous Jewish eatery in Paris, this kosher-style restaurant rates a mention, but the quality of what is served (and how) is uneven. The mixed starters (€8), stuffed carp and apple strudel (€7) are OK, but the plats du jour (€13) and pastrami don't measure up to even a generic New York deli. Dining is on two levels, one for nonsmokers.

LA MAIN D'OR

Map pp440-1   French, Corsican

☎ 01 44 68 04 68; 133 rue du Faubourg St-Antoine, 11e; starters €6.50-14.80, mains €13-19.50, menu €12; ⏱ lunch & dinner to 11pm Mon-Sat; Ⓜ Ledru Rollin

The unprepossessing cafélike 'Golden Hand' serves authentic Corsican dishes – a surprisingly elusive cuisine in Paris. *Sturza preti* (spinach and fine *brocciu* cheese) and traditional omelette with *brocciu* and *jambon sec* (dried ham, matured for two years) are some of the appetisers on the menu. For mains, favourites include the *tian de veau aux olives* (veal ragout). Plats du jour usually come in at about €8.50.

LA PERLA Map pp436-7   Mexican, Tex-Mex

☎ 01 42 77 59 40; 26 rue François Miron, 4e; starters €5.70-8.70, mains €7.50-12, menu lunch €9.90; ⏱ lunch & dinner to midnight; Ⓜ St-Paul or Hôtel de Ville

La Perla is a Californian-style Mexican bar-restaurant serving guacamole (€6.60), nachos (€5.70 to €8.70) and quesadillas (€5.70 to €7.10) to an appreciative audience. Margaritas (€8.80 to €12) at the **bar** (⏱ noon to 2am) are excellent. Happy hour is 6pm to 8pm Monday to Friday.

LA SOUMMAM

Map pp436-7   North African, Berber

☎ 01 43 54 12 43; 43 rue Mazarine, 6e; couscous & tajines €16.50-24, grills €13.20-16.50, menus lunch €11.50 & €14, dinner €32; ⏱ lunch & dinner to 11.30pm; Ⓜ Odéon or St-Michel

The Left Bank of the Seine is a long way from the North African home of the Berbers. But here, in this restaurant decorated with carpets, pottery and artworks, you can taste the unusual *tammekfoult (*a couscous of steamed vegetables accompanied by milk curds) as well as a superb veal *tajine* with olives, artichokes, prunes and other vegetables. The *hasban* are unique: semolina croquettes flavoured with mint and served with vegetables and chickpeas.

L'ALIVI Map pp436-7   French, Corsican

☎ 01 48 87 90 20; 27 rue du Roi de Sicile, 4e; starters €8.50-16, mains €15-21, menus €17 (lunch only) & €22; ⏱ lunch & dinner to 11.30pm; Ⓜ St-Paul

This is a rather fashionable Corsican restaurant within the Marais. The ingredients are fresh and refined, with *brocciu* cheese, charcuterie and basil featuring strongly on the menu. Try *starzapreti* (*brocciu* and spinach quenelles) and the unrivalled *cabri farci au brocciu et aux noix* (kid stuffed with *brocciu* cheese and nuts) with a Leccia wine to fully experience the pleasures of what the French call *l'île de beauté* (the beautiful island).

L'AMBASSADE D'AUVERGNE

Map pp436-7   French, Auvergne

☎ 01 42 72 31 22; 22 rue du Grenier St-Lazare, 3e; starters €7-16, mains €14-21, menu €27; ⏱ lunch & dinner to 10.30pm; Ⓜ Rambuteau

The 'Auvergne Embassy' is the place to head if you are a carnivore and well and truly hungry. This 100-year-old restaurant offers traditional dishes from the Auvergne such as *salade tiède de lentilles vertes du Puy* (warm salad of green Puy lentils; €9), a great lead-up to the house speciality: *saucisse d'Auvergne à l'aligot* (Auvergne sausage served with a potato and cheese purée; €14). A fitting conclusion to this magnificent feast is the sublime *clafoutis*, a custard and cherry tart baked upside down like a *tarte Tatin* (caramelised apple pie).

LE DÔME BASTILLE

Map pp440-1   French, Seafood

☎ 01 48 04 88 44; 2 rue de la Bastille, 4e; starters €8.70-12, mains €19.70-23; ⏱ lunch & dinner to 11pm; Ⓜ Bastille

This lovely restaurant, little sister to the more established **Dôme** (p209) in Montparnasse and awash in pale yellows, specialises in superbly prepared fish and seafood dishes. The blackboard menu changes daily. Wines are a uniform (and affordable) €21.70 per bottle.

LE DÔME DU MARAIS

Map pp436-7   French

☎ 01 42 74 54 17; 53bis rue des Francs Bourgeois, 4e; 2-/3-course menus lunch €17/23, dinner €32/45; ⏱ lunch & dinner to 11pm Tue-Sat; Ⓜ Rambuteau

This place serves both classic French dishes such as *tête de veau* (calf's head) and lighter fare – often shellfish and fish. The location is sublime: a pre-Revolution building and former auction room just down from the Archives Nationales so, though you can dress down, it is a place to mark a special occasion. The octagonal-shaped dining room is a knockout.

LE PETIT DAKAR

Map pp436-7   African, Senegalese

☎ 01 44 59 34 74; 6 rue Elzévir, 3e; starters €7, mains €13-15, menu lunch €15; 🕓 lunch & dinner to 11pm Mon-Sat; Ⓜ St-Paul

Some people think this is the most authentic Senegalese restaurant in Paris, and with both a popular African club and the CSAO Boutique (p287) opposite, it does feel like a little bit of Africa has fallen onto a quiet Marais street.

LE PETIT MARCHÉ

Map pp440-1   French, Café

☎ 01 42 72 06 67; 9 rue de Béarn, 3e; starters €7-16, mains €14-19, menu lunch €13.80; 🕓 lunch & dinner to midnight; Ⓜ Chemin Vert

This great little bistro just up from the place des Vosges fills up both at lunch and then again in the evening with a mixed crowd who come to enjoy the hearty cooking and friendly service. The salad starters are popular and the duck breast with ginger is great, but the open kitchen is in less safe territory with more adventurous fare.

LE PETIT PICARD

Map pp436-7   French

☎ 01 42 78 54 03; 42 rue Ste-Croix de la Bretonnerie, 4e; starters €5.50-14, mains €9.50-14.50, menus €13.50 (lunch only), €16 & €24.50; 🕓 lunch Tue-Fri, dinner to 11pm Tue-Sun; Ⓜ Hôtel de Ville

This popular little restaurant in the centre of gay Marais serves traditional French cuisine (try the generous menu traditionel at €24.50). Despite its name, the only dish from Picardy (unless you count herrings) that we could spot on the menu was flamiche aux poireaux, a Flemish-style leek pie. The place is always packed so book well in advance.

LE RÉCONFORT   Map pp436-7   French

☎ 01 49 96 09 60; 37 rue de Poitou, 3e; starters €7-11, mains €16-21, menus lunch €13 & €18; 🕓 lunch Mon-Fri, dinner to 11pm daily; Ⓜ St-Sébastien Froissart

Unusual for a restaurant in the Marais, the 'Comfort' has generous space between tables and is quiet enough to chat without yelling. The kitchen produces very tasty and inventive dishes, including homemade foie gras. For mains, consider morue caramélisée au vinaigre balsamique (caramelised cod) or crumble de confit de canard (duck confit with crumbs). The plat du jour at lunch is €10.

LE SQUARE TROUSSEAU

Map pp446-7   French

☎ 01 43 43 06 00; 1 rue Antoine Vollon, 12e; starters €6-17, mains €19-25, menus €20 & €25; 🕓 lunch & dinner to 11.30pm Tue-Sat; Ⓜ Ledru Rollin

This vintage (c 1900) bistro with etched glass, zinc bar and polished wood panelling is comfortable rather than trendy and attracts a jolly, mixed clientele. Most people come to enjoy the lovely terrace overlooking a small park. The set meals are available at lunchtime and to 9pm only. Attached to the main restaurant is the informal La Cave du Square (menus €12-20; 🕓 lunch & dinner to 11.30pm Tue-Sat), where you can have one, two or three courses or even pick up that bottle of Touraine you so much enjoyed over lunch next door.

L'ENOTECA   Map pp436-7   Italian

☎ 01 42 78 91 44; 25 rue Charles V, 4e; starters €8-14, mains €18-21, menu lunch €13; 🕓 lunch & dinner to 11.30pm; Ⓜ Sully Morland or Pont Marie

The 'Vinotheque', a trattoria in the historic Village St-Paul quarter of the Marais, serves haute cuisine à l'italienne, and there's an excellent list of Italian wines by the glass (€3 to €7). Some of the more difficult-to-find wines are on hand too. It's no secret that this is one of the few Italian wine bars in Paris to take its vino seriously so book ahead. Pasta dishes (€10 to €18) are good, as is the generous tavola antipasti (antipasto buffet table) at lunch. the plat du jour is €9.

LES AMIS DE MESSINA

Map pp446-7   Italian, Sicilian

☎ 01 43 67 96 01; 204 rue du Faubourg St-Antoine, 12e; starters €7.80-13.80, mains €17.50-24.90; 🕓 lunch Mon-Fri, dinner to 11.30pm Mon-Sat; Ⓜ Faidherbe Chaligny

The décor of this wonderful little neighbourhood trattoria is stylish, with clean lines, an open kitchen and the inevitable Italian football pennant. For starters, try the boulettes farcies (stuffed meatballs), a speciality of Palermo, or share a mixed antipasto (€17.80). For mains, the escalope farcie aux aubergines (veal escalope stuffed with aubergine) is a huge hit, or go for any of the exquisite Sicilian pastas (€11.80 to €17.20). Friday is fish day; watch out for the specials.

LES CAVES ST-GILLES

Map pp440-1 Spanish

☎ 01 48 87 22 62; 4 rue St-Gilles, 3e; tapas €5.30-17, mains €14.50-18; ⊙ lunch & dinner to 11.30pm; Ⓜ Chemin Vert

This Spanish wine bar a short distance northeast of place des Vosges is the most authentic place on the Right Bank for tapas, paella (at the weekend only; €19) and sangria (€28 for 1.4cL). If you don't believe us, just ask the Spanish expats who arrive here in droves. We like the bowls of complimentary olives provided on tables and at the bar.

LES GALOPINS Map pp440-1 French, Bistro

☎ 01 47 00 45 35; 24 rue des Taillandiers, 11e; starters €6.10-10.50, mains €12.50-19, menus lunch €11.50 & €14.50; ⊙ lunch Mon-Fri, dinner to 11pm Mon-Thu, to 11.30pm Fri & Sat; Ⓜ Bastille or Voltaire

The décor of this cute neighbourhood bistro is simple, the meals are straightforward and in the best tradition of French cuisine with offerings such as *poêlée de pétoncles* (pan-fried queen scallops), *magret de canard*, *cœur de rumsteck* (tenderloin rump steak) and *compotée d'agneau aux aubergines* (lamb and aubergine ragout). It's not a secret find, so it can feel like a bit of a factory at lunch or on a weekend night.

LES GRANDES MARCHES

Map pp440-1 French, Brasserie

☎ 01 43 43 90 32; 6 place de la Bastille, 12e; starters €7.60-17.50, mains €15.90-29, 2-/3-course menus €23/30; ⊙ noon-midnight; Ⓜ Bastille

This futuristic modern brasserie next to the 'Great Steps' of the Opéra Bastille was designed by Elisabeth and Christian Portzamparc for the Flo group. The result has been disappointing – both in décor and food served – but it has a convenient (and much coveted) location. If you do find yourself here, settle for the cheaper set *menu* or a couple of starters. After 10.30pm there's a €20 night *menu* available.

LES SANS CULOTTES

Map pp440-1 French, Bistro

☎ 01 48 05 42 92; 27 rue de Lappe, 11e; starters €9-15, mains €14-20, 2-/3-course menu €18/23; ⊙ lunch & dinner to 11pm Tue-Sun; Ⓜ Bastille

You wouldn't cross Paris to eat at Sans Culottes – the place takes its name from

the working-class 'men without fancy breeches' who fought in the French Revolution – but in a neighbourhood that has become über-trendy over the past decade it's a comforting reminder of the past. The interior, with frosted glass, huge zinc bar, ornate ceilings and wooden floors, positively glows in the evening. Food is uneven, though relatively low-priced; service is friendly and attentive. The set *menus* include wine.

MA BOURGOGNE

Map pp440-1 French, Bistro

☎ 01 42 78 44 64; 19 place des Vosges, 4e; starters €7-20, mains €17-26, menu €32; ⊙ noon-1am; Ⓜ St-Paul

With its terrace under the arcades of the place des Vosges and looking onto what is arguably the most beautiful square in Paris, this is a wonderful place to have lunch or just a drink. The plats du jour are good value at €11.50 to €17, when you consider the location. Specialities include the *saucisson du Beaujolais* (Beaujolais sausage) and the steak tartare.

ROBERT ET LOUISE

Map pp436-7 French

☎ 01 42 78 55 89; 64 rue Vieille du Temple, 3e; starters €5-12, mains €13-18, menu lunch €12; ⊙ lunch & dinner to 10pm Tue-Sat; Ⓜ St-Sébastien Froissart

This 'country inn', complete with its red gingham curtains, offers delightful, simple and inexpensive French food, including *côte de bœuf* (side of beef, €39), which is cooked on an open fire and prepared by a husband-and-wife team. If you arrive early, choose to sit at the farmhouse table, right next to the fireplace. It's a jolly, truly Rabelaisian evening.

SWANN ET VINCENT

Map pp446-7 Italian

☎ 01 43 43 49 40; 7 rue St-Nicolas, 12e; starters €6.40-10.50, mains €12-17, menu lunch €14.50; ⊙ lunch & dinner to 11.45pm; Ⓜ Ledru Rollin

If you're visiting this fine restaurant, ask for a table in the front room, which will hopefully be awash with sunlight. Unpretentious French staff can help you select from the huge blackboard, where at least two of the starters, pastas (€12 to €13) and main dishes change every day. Go slow on the complimentary basket of olive and sweet herb bread, though; you need to leave room for the tiramisu (€6.50). And, if you must know, Swann and Vincent, whose larger-than-life portraits face you through the front window, are the children of the owner.

THANKSGIVING Map pp436-7   American, Cajun
☎ 01 42 77 68 28; 20 rue St-Paul, 4e; starters €7-16, mains €15-22, menu lunch €15; ⊙ lunch & dinner to 11pm Wed-Sat, brunch 7am-4pm Sun; Ⓜ St-Paul

Thanksgiving serves all-American regional dishes. OK, you didn't come all the way to Paris for jambalaya and gumbo, but where else are you going to find Cajun in the City of Light? We especially like the rock oysters, the blackened redfish and, for afters, the pecan pie is to die for. There's a traditional brunch (as only Yanks know how to do them) on Sunday (€17 to €20).

WALY FAY Map pp440-1   African, Creole
☎ 01 40 24 17 79; 6 rue Godefroy Cavaignac, 11e; starters €6-8, mains €10-15; ⊙ dinner to midnight Mon-Sat; Ⓜ Charonne

This easygoing 'loungin' restaurant' attracts a rather hip crowd after the African food with a West Indian twist served to the sounds of soul and jazz. For starters, the *pepe* (fish soup) is deliciously smooth and highly spiced. For mains, the *tiéboudienne*

(rice, fish and vegetables) and fish *n'dole* are recommended by the staff, but try instead the copious *mafé* (beef simmered in peanut sauce) served with rice and *aloko* (fried plantain bananas).

CHEAP EATS

BAGEL STORE Map pp440-1   American
☎ 01 44 78 06 05; 31 rue de Turenne, 3e; dishes €3.50-9; ⊙ 8am-8pm Sun-Thu, to 7pm Fri; Ⓜ Chemin Vert

This small place just up from the Marais is a great spot if you want something *sur le pouce* (literally 'on the thumb', meaning on the run). There are soups, salads, plates of charcuterie and, of course, its signature bagels (€3.30 to €6.90) with a dozen different fillings.

BOLLYWOOD LINK CAFÉ
Map pp440-1   Indian
☎ 01 48 06 18 57; 33-35 rue de Lappe, 11e; starters €5.40-8.40, mains €12-22, menu lunch €9; ⊙ lunch & dinner to 2am; Ⓜ Bastille

Despite its ever-changing name (it was Coffee India until a year ago), this restaurant (and cocktail bar, lounge, tea room, café and film set wannabe) on busy rue de Lappe serves surprisingly authentic southern Indian fare. After 10pm on Friday and Saturday a DJ plays Indian music – from traditional to electro-acoustic. Happy hour is from 4pm to 8pm.

Inside Café de l'Industrie (p185)

CRÊPES SHOW Map pp440-1 — French, Brittany

☎ 01 47 00 36 46; 51 rue de Lappe, 11e; crepes & galettes €3-9.10, menu lunch €8.50; ⌚ lunch Mon-Fri, dinner to 1am Sun-Thu, to 2am Fri & Sat; Ⓜ Ledru Rollin

This unpretentious little restaurant specialises in sweet crepes (€3 to €7.90) and savoury buckwheat *galettes* (pancakes; €3 to €9.10). OK, they may not be the most authentic in town, but the location is convenient and the welcome warm. There are lots of vegetarian choices, including great salads from €4 to €7.90.

CHEZ HEANG Map pp440-1 — Korean

☎ 01 48 07 80 98; 5 rue de la Roquette, 11e; barbecue €8.50-17.50, menus lunch €9, dinner €11-23; ⌚ lunch & dinner to midnight; Ⓜ Bastille

Also known as 'Barbecue de Seoul', this is where you cook your food on a grill in the middle of your table. The *fondue maison*, a kind of spicy hotpot in which you dip and cook your food, costs €21 per person, with a minimum of two.

CHEZ MARIANNE

Map pp436-7 — Jewish, Kosher

☎ 01 42 72 18 86; 2 rue des Hospitalières St-Gervais, 4e; dishes €2.50-20, sandwiches €5.50-8.50; ⌚ noon-midnight; Ⓜ St-Paul

This is a Sephardic kosher alternative to the Ashkenazi Jo Goldenberg (p185). Platters containing four to 10 different meze (such as falafel, hummus, purées of aubergine and chickpeas) cost from €12 to €26. The window of the adjoining deli sells good takeaway falafel sandwiches for €4 and there's also an excellent bakery attached. The set *menus* include a number of vegetarian options.

CHEZ PAUL Map pp440-1 — French, Bistro

☎ 01 47 00 34 57; 13 rue de Charonne, 11e; starters €3.80-15, mains €13.50-21; ⌚ lunch & dinner to 12.30am; Ⓜ Ledru Rollin

When Central Staging orders up 'French restaurant' in Hollywood, this is what it must look like. An extremely popular bistro, it has traditional French main courses handwritten on a yellowing menu and brusque service – Paris in true form! Stick with the simplest of dishes – the steak or foie gras with lentils – and be prepared to wait even if you've booked.

CRÊPERIE BRETONNE

Map pp440-1 — French, Brittany

☎ 01 43 55 62 29; 67 rue de Charonne, 12e; starters €3.50-7, crepes & galettes €2.30-7.20; ⌚ lunch Mon-Fri, dinner to 11.30pm Mon-Sat; Ⓜ Charonne

Head here if you fancy savoury buckwheat *galettes* – try the ham, cheese and egg *complète* – or a sweet crepe and wash it down with dry *cidre de Rance* (Rance cider; €5.90 for 50cL). The Breton paraphernalia and B&W photos will keep you occupied if there's a lull in the chatter.

L'AS DE FELAFEL

Map pp436-7 — Jewish, Kosher

☎ 01 48 87 63 60; 34 rue des Rosiers, 4e; dishes €4-7.50; ⌚ noon-midnight Sun-Thu, noon-5pm Fri; Ⓜ St-Paul

This has always been our favourite place for those deep-fried balls of chickpeas and herbs (€3.50 to €4). It's always packed, particularly at weekday lunch, so avoid that time if possible.

LE TRUMILOU Map pp436-7 — French, Bistro

☎ 01 42 77 63 98; 84 quai de l'Hôtel de Ville, 4e; starters €4-12, mains €13-21, menu €17.50 & €19; ⌚ lunch & dinner to 11pm; Ⓜ Hôtel de Ville

This no-frills bistro just round the corner from the Hôtel de Ville and facing the posh Île de St-Louis square is a Parisian institution in situ for over a century. If you're looking for an authentic menu from the early 20th century and prices (well, almost) to match, you won't do better than this. The *confit de canard* (*confit* of duck) and the *tête de veau sauce au gribiche* (calf's head in a cold sauce of lemon, hard-boiled egg yolks, herbs, capers and mustard) are particularly good.

L'ENCRIER Map pp446-7 — French, Bistro

☎ 01 44 68 08 16; 55 rue Traversière, 12e; starters €5-10, mains €9-16.50, menus lunch €13, dinner €17-21; ⌚ lunch Mon-Fri, dinner to 11pm Mon-Sat; Ⓜ Ledru Rollin or Gare de Lyon

You can always expect a relaxed atmosphere at the popular 'Inkwell'. For starters, the classic salmon *tartare* alternates on the menu with less-common dishes like *cervelle des canuts* (a herbed cheese from Lyons). To follow, try the *bar entier grillé* (whole grilled bass) or delicate *joues de cochon aux épices* (pig's cheeks with spices). A variety of set *menus* for lunch and dinner, an open kitchen, exposed beams and a large picture window make this a winner.

PARIS HANOI Map pp440-1 · Vietnamese
☎ 01 47 00 47 59; 74 rue de Charonne, 11e; starters €3.10-7.50, mains €6.60-10; ⏱ lunch Mon-Sat, dinner to 10.30pm; Ⓜ Charonne
This upbeat restaurant is an excellent place to come for *pho* (soup noodles, usually with beef) and shrimp noodles. Judging from the clientele, the local Vietnamese community thinks so too.

PICCOLO TEATRO
Map pp436-7 · Vegetarian
☎ 01 42 72 17 79; 6 rue des Écouffes, 4e; starters €3.80-7.50, mains €8.90-11.70, menus lunch €8.90-14.70, dinner €15.10 & €21.50; ⏱ lunch & dinner to 11.30pm; Ⓜ St-Paul
This vegetarian restaurant is an intimate place with exposed stone walls, a beamed ceiling and cosy little tables lit by candles. The tasty *assiette végétarienne* (vegetarian plate; €12.10) is always popular but try any of the main gratin dishes, which are the speciality of the house. They combine vegetables, cream and cheese and are then baked.

SELF-CATERING
Markets in the Marais and Bastille area include the incomparable (and open-air) Marché Bastille (p52).

There are a number of food shops and Asian delicatessens on the odd-numbered side of rue St-Antoine, 4e (Map pp440–1; Ⓜ St-Paul) as well as several supermarkets. Closer to Bastille there are lots of food shops along rue de la Roquette (Map pp444–5; Ⓜ Voltaire or Bastille) towards place Léon Blum.

Supermarkets include: Franprix Marais (Map pp436–7; 135 rue St-Antoine, 4e; Ⓜ St-Paul), Franprix (Map pp436–7; 87 rue de la Verrerie, 4e; Ⓜ Hôtel de Ville), Monoprix (Map pp440–1; 71 rue St-Antoine, 4e; Ⓜ St-Paul), Monoprix Bastille branch (Map pp440–1; 97 rue du Faubourg St-Antoine, 11e; ⏱ 9am-10pm Mon-Sat; Ⓜ Ledru Rollin), Supermarché G20 (Map pp436–7; 81-83 rue de la Verrerie, 4e; Ⓜ Hôtel de Ville), Supermarché G20 Bastille (Map pp440–1; 115 rue St-Antoine, 4e; Ⓜ St-Paul), and the late-

opening Monop' (Map pp440-1; 62-64 rue de la Roquette, 11e; ⏱ 9am-midnight Mon-Sat; Ⓜ Voltaire).

LE NÔTRE Map pp440-1 · Delicatessen
☎ 01 53 01 91 91; www.lenotre.fr; 10 rue St-Antoine, 4e; ⏱ 9.30am-10pm Mon-Fri, 9am-10pm Sat & Sun; Ⓜ Bastille
This branch of the famous *traiteur* chain at the corner of rue des Tournelles has picnic supplies and some of the most delectable pastries and chocolate in Paris. There are 15 other outlets sprinkled across the capital.

THE ISLANDS
Famed for its ice cream as much as anything else, the Île St-Louis is generally an expensive place to eat and restaurants are few and far between. It's best suited to those looking for a light snack at one of the lovely tea rooms along rue St-Louis en l'Île, 4e (Map pp436–7; Ⓜ Pont Marie) or ingredients for a picnic along the Seine, though there are a couple of places worth checking out.

BRASSERIE DE L'ÎLE ST-LOUIS
Map pp436-7 · French, Brasserie
☎ 01 43 54 02 59; 55 quai de Bourbon, 4e; dishes €14-17; ⏱ 6pm-1am Thu, noon-midnight Fri-Tue; Ⓜ Pont Marie
Founded in 1870, this brasserie enjoys a spectacular location on the Seine just over the footbridge between Île de St-Louis and Île de la Cité. It serves favourites such as *choucroute garnie* (sauerkraut with meat), *jarret* (veal shank), cassoulet and *onglet de bœuf* (prime rib of beef; all €16.80). You can also enjoy the location by ordering a coffee/beer (€1.10/2.30 at the bar, €2.50/4.50 at a table or on the terrace).

LES FOUS DE L'ÎLE
Map pp436-7 · French, Café
☎ 01 43 25 76 67; 33 rue des Deux Ponts, 4e; starters 6.50-9, mains €12-15, menu €15 (lunch only) & €19; ⏱ lunch Tue-Sat, dinner to 10pm Thu-Sat; Ⓜ Pont Marie
This friendly, down-to-earth tea room and restaurant serves rather innovative café-style dishes and moonlights as an exhibition space, with some cutting-edge photography and art shows.

MON VIEIL AMI

Map pp436-7   French, Alsatian

☎ 01 40 46 01 35; 69 rue St-Louis en l'Île, 4e; menus €15 (lunch only) & €39; ⏱ lunch Wed-Sun, dinner to 10.15pm Tue-Sun; Ⓜ Pont Marie
You're treated like an old friend – thus the name – the minute you enter this sleek black bistro in one of Paris' most sought-after neighbourhoods, and the complimentary aperitif of Alsatian Pinot Blanc is ideal while you peruse the interesting menu. The pâté in pastry crust is a fabulous starter and any of the Alsatian mains are worth exploring. The chocolate tart is the pick of the desserts.

CHEAP EATS

BERTHILLON Map pp436-7   Ice Cream

☎ 01 43 54 31 61; 31 rue St-Louis en l'Île, 4e; ⏱ 10am-8pm Wed-Sun; Ⓜ Pont Marie
Berthillon is to ice cream what Château Lafite Rothschild is to wine and Valhrona is to chocolate. While the fruit flavours (eg cassis) produced by this celebrated *glacier* (ice-cream maker) are justifiably renowned, the chocolate, coffee, *marrons glacés* (candied chestnuts), Agenaise (Armagnac and prunes), *noisette* (hazelnut) and *nougat au miel* (honey nougat) are much richer. The takeaway counter of this café has one/two/three/four small scoops for €2/3.50/4.50/5.50. Choose from among 70 flavours.

SELF-CATERING

Along rue St-Louis en l'Île, on Île de St-Louis, there are a number of *fromageries* (cheese shops) and groceries (usually closed on Sunday afternoon and all day Monday). There are more food shops on rue des Deux Ponts.

LATIN QUARTER & JARDIN DES PLANTES

Rue Mouffetard (Map pp444–5; Ⓜ Place Monge or Censier Daubenton) and its side streets are filled with places to eat. It's especially popular with students, in part because of the number of stands and small shops selling baguettes, *panini* (Italian toasted bread with fillings) and crepes.

One of Paris's largest concentrations of ethnic restaurants is squeezed into a labyrinth of narrow streets in the 5e arrondissement across the Seine from Notre Dame. The Greek, North African and Middle Eastern restaurants between rue St-Jacques, blvd St-Germain and blvd St-Michel, including rue de la Huchette, attract mainly foreign tourists, often under the mistaken impression that this little maze is the whole of the famous Latin Quarter. But you'd be far better off looking elsewhere for ethnic food: blvd de Belleville in the 20e for Middle Eastern; nearby rue de Belleville in the 19e for Asian (especially Thai and Vietnamese); and Chinatown in the 13e for Chinese, especially ave de Choisy, ave d'Ivry and rue Baudricourt.

AL DAR Map pp436-7   Middle Eastern, Lebanese

☎ 01 43 25 17 15; 8-10 rue Frédéric Sauton, 5e; meze €6.50-9.80, mains €9-20, menus lunch €15.90 & €17, dinner €27; ⏱ lunch & dinner to midnight; Ⓜ Maubert Mutualité
This is a popular, award-winning Lebanese restaurant with a lovely terrace open in the warmer months. For those in a hurry, attached is an excellent **delicatessen** (⏱ 7am-midnight daily) with meze, little pizzas, sandwiches and the like for between €2.60 and €7.50.

ANAHUACALLI Map pp444-5   Mexican

☎ 01 43 26 10 20; 30 rue des Bernadins, 5e; starters €7.80-9.50, mains platters €14.50-19; ⏱ lunch Sun, dinner to 11pm Mon-Sat; Ⓜ Maubert Mutualité
The ample menu at the lovely 'House by the Water' (hey, the Seine is just due north) takes you off the usual beaten track of Mexican food, starting with the delicate *napolitos compuestos* (cactus salad; €8.80). The *poulet et sa sauce de cuitlacoche* (chicken in mushroom and corn sauce) and the *mole poblano* (chocolate-based meat dish; €17.50) are light years from the typical *cuchina mexicana* (Mexican cuisine).

AU COCO DE MER

Map pp444-5   Seychelles, Creole

☎ 01 47 07 06 64; 34 blvd St-Marcel, 5e; starters €6-12, mains €12-16, menus lunch/dinner €15/30; ⏱ lunch & dinner to 10.30pm Mon-Sat; Ⓜ St-Marcel
Partially done up like a blue clapboard beach hut, this is one of the few places in

Paris you'll be able to dine with your feet in the sand (literally). The *découverte* (discovery) menu at dinner is a great option, allowing you to compare the flavours of *requin au tamarin* (shark with tamarind) and *vindail de dorade coryphène* (dolphinfish).

AU P'TIT CAHOUA

Map pp444-5   North African, Moroccan
☎ 01 47 07 24 42; 39 blvd St-Marcel, 13e; starters €7-7.50, tajines & couscous €15-21.50, menu €24; ⏰ lunch & dinner to 11pm; Ⓜ St-Marcel
This is one of the better couscous and *tajine* restaurants on the Left Bank, with lovely modernist décor including fake mosaic tables under a Berber tent (no sand). We especially liked the black banquette by the window overlooking the terrace and the carefree service.

BOUILLON RACINE

Map pp444-5   French, Bistro
☎ 01 44 32 15 60; 3 rue Racine, 6e; starters €7.50-14.50, mains €14.50-28, menus €15.50 (lunch only) & €27; ⏰ lunch & dinner to 11pm; Ⓜ Cluny La Sorbonne
We've visited, inspected and eaten in lots and lots of historical restaurants in our day,

Deli on rue Mouffetard (p179)

but we've never – ever – seen anything quite like the Bouillon Racine, a 'soup kitchen' built in 1906 to feed city workers. It's an Art Nouveau palace and a positive delight. Oh, and the food? With a change in management, much better than it was but still with classic French dishes like *caille confite* (preserved quail) and *cochon de lait* (milk-fed pork).

CAFÉ LATIN

Map pp444-5   French, Café
☎ 01 46 33 02 06; 30 rue St-André des Arts, 6e; starters €7-12, mains €13-20; ⏰ 11am-2am; Ⓜ St-Michel
This café-restaurant in the heart of the Latin Quarter is a welcome and stylish addition to a part of town overwhelmed by deadbeat, cookie-cutter venues. Food runs the gamut from starters of quiche, onion soups and salads to mains of chicken and steaks. Lighter fare includes cheeseburgers (€13) and several plats du jour that change daily.

CHEZ ALLARD

Map pp436-7   French, Lyons
☎ 01 43 26 48 23; 41 rue St-André des Arts; starters €7.70-19.50, mains €19-35, 2-/3-course menus €24/32; ⏰ lunch & dinner to 11.30pm Mon-Sat; Ⓜ St-Michel
One of our favourite new (to us) places on the Left Bank is this positively charming bistro where the staff couldn't be kinder and more professional – even during its enormously busy lunchtime – and the food is superb. Try the excellent (and massive) *canard aux olives vertes* (duck with green olives). Enter from 1 rue de l'Éperon, 6e.

CHEZ LÉNA ET MIMILLE

Map pp444-5   French
☎ 01 47 07 72 47; 32 rue Tournefort, 5e; starters/mains/desserts €9/22/9, 2-/3-course menus lunch €21/28, dinner with wine €39; ⏰ lunch Tue-Fri, dinner to 11pm Tue-Sat; Ⓜ Censier Daubenton
This intimate but very elegant restaurant has one of the most fabulous terraces in Paris, overlooking a little park with a fountain and comical equestrian statue. And the food is excellent; seize the rare opportunity to taste *pieds de cochon farcis* (stuffed pig's trotters). Classic mains with a twist include *navarin d'agneau* (a kind of lamb stew) and *ravioles de romans au beurre basilique* (ravioli with basil butter). The plat du jour at lunch is €15.

FOGÓN ST-JULIEN

Map pp436-7   Spanish

☎ 01 43 54 31 33; 45 quai des Grands Augustins, 6e; mains €18, menu €35; ☻ lunch Sat & Sun, dinner to midnight Tue-Sun; Ⓜ St-Michel

Fogón St-Julien, which some say is the best Spanish restaurant in Paris, has moved to a new location in the slightly more chichi 6e. It continues to go well beyond 'tapas mania', serving up a half-dozen excellent paellas (vegetable, rabbit, chicken, seafood; €18). Try the *arroz negro* (€18), rice blackened with squid ink and hiding shrimps, cuttlefish and chunks of fish.

FOUNTI AGADIR

Map pp444-5   North African, Moroccan

☎ 01 43 37 85 10; 117 rue Monge, 5e; starters €6-7.50, mains €13.20-19; menus lunch/dinner €19/25; ☻ lunch & dinner to 10.30pm Tue-Sun; Ⓜ Censier Daubenton

This popular Moroccan restaurant serves some of the best couscous (€13.20 to €19), *tajines* (€14.60 to €15.50) and pastillas (€8 to €9) on the Left Bank.

LA MOSQUÉE DE PARIS

Map pp444-5   North African

Ⓜ 01 43 31 38 20; 39 rue Geoffroy St-Hilaire, 5e; starters & snacks €4-12, mains €11-25; ☻ lunch & dinner to 10.30pm; Ⓜ Censier Daubenton or Place Monge

The central Mosquée de Paris (p11600) has an authentic restaurant serving couscous (€11 to €25), *tajines* (€12 to €16) and grills (€11 to €13). There's also a North African–style tea room (☻ 9am-midnight) where you can get a cup of peppermint tea (€2) and a range of *pâtisseries orientales* (€2).

LA TOUR D'ARGENT

Map pp444-5   French

☎ 01 43 54 23 31; 15 quai de la Tournelle, 5e; meals from €180, menu lunch €70; ☻ lunch Wed-Sun, dinner to 9pm Tue-Sun; Ⓜ Cardinal Lemoine or Pont Marie

Famous for its *caneton* (duckling) prepared in a myriad of ways, La Tour d'Argent is equally celebrated for its rooftop garden and stunning views of the Seine and Notre Dame. You have to book well in advance (eight to 10 days before for lunch, three weeks ahead for dinner) and make sure

to try the signature *quenelles de brochet* (pike-perch dumplings) and pressed duck (which carries a €22 supplement at lunchtime). Though it lost one of its two coveted Michelin stars in 2006, the 'Silver Tower' has been around since 1582 so it must be doing something right.

LE BUISSON ARDENT

Map pp444-5   French, Bistro

☎ 01 43 54 93 02; 25 rue Jussieu, 5e; starters/mains €9/12, menus lunch €13 & €16, dinner €29; ☻ lunch & dinner to 10.30pm Mon-Fri; Ⓜ Jussieu

A modern bistro with the curious name of the 'Burning Bush', this place serves inventive starters (crayfish ravioli) and mains such as pork tenderloin with ceps and polenta in a subdued but upbeat atmosphere. With the university so close, expect a well-informed crowd at lunch. More elaborate tasting menus are available at €35 and €45.

LE COSI Map pp444-5   French, Corsica

☎ 01 43 29 20 20; 9 rue Cujas, 5e; starters €8.50-15, mains €15-24, 2-/3-course menu lunch €15/20; ☻ lunch & dinner to 11.15pm Mon-Sat; Ⓜ Luxembourg

Le Cosi is a Corsican restaurant that occasionally strays to other Mediterranean lands but is usually pretty faithful to its homeland. The *stufatu* (fragrant mutton stew with olives) is legendary and there is a good selection of Corsican wines. Lovely upbeat surrounds and large picture windows complete the picture.

LE PETIT PONTOISE

Map pp436-7   French

☎ 01 43 29 25 20; 9 rue de Pontoise, 5e; starters €8-13.50, mains €15-25; ☻ lunch & dinner to 10.30pm; Ⓜ Maubert Mutualité

This charming bistro, just down from the Institut du Monde Arabe (p115), offers up a blackboard menu of seasonal delights. Regular dishes to look out for are the homemade foie gras with figs (€12) and *poulet fermier avec pommes purée* (roasted farm chicken with mashed potato; €13), which transcends its simple ingredients. It's a great find in a quarter not overwhelmed with authentic eateries.

(Continued on page 203)

1 *Woman walking past temporary façade on av des Champs-Élysées (p131)* 2 *Books inside Shakespeare & Company bookshop (p291)* 3 *Eiffel Tower souvenirs in a shop window* 4 *Perfume bottles*

1 Customers inside Chez Omar (p185) **2** Culinary delights at the open air market on rue Mouffetard (p179) **3** Man working at doner kebab stand **4** Legumes at Agha Epicerie, rue Montorgueil (p52)

arisian stall vendor slicing
eese at Marché Maubert
2) **2** Interior of wine shop
rue Mouffetard (p179)
aiters in motion in Chartier
18)

1 *Man painting flowers, Giverny (p356)* **2** *Grandes Écuries (great stables) of Chateau de Chantilly (p349)* **3** *Statue at the Chateau de Versailles (p336)*

çade of the Vaux-le-
mte chateau (p347) **2** View
s the lake at the exquisite
eau de Fontainebleau
!) **3** Intricate gardens at
illes (p336)

1 *Géode, Parc de la Villette (p152)*
2 *Notre Dame viewed from the Seine (p111)* 3 *Behind the mixing desk at Le Nouveau Casino (p266)*
4 *Playing board games at place St-Sulpice (p118)*

1

Illuminated carousel spinning
next to the Eiffel Tower (p127)
Musicians performing at Le
Caveau de la Huchette (p261)
Commuters on the platform
at Opéra metro station (p271)

2

3

1 *Merchandise for sale inside Kili-watch store (p285)* 2 *An Hermès (p298) tie* 3 *Window display at Le Printemps department store (p300)* 4 *Window display in Fauchon (p297)*

(Continued from page 194)

LE TOURNEBRIDE

Map pp444-5   French, Auvergne

☎ 01 43 31 42 98; 104 rue Mouffetard, 5e; meals €13.20-16.20 ⌚ lunch Mon-Sat; Ⓜ Censier Daubenton

The Tournebride's restaurant is closed in the evening (though the bar stays open till 1am), so come here at lunchtime, when you can savour simple but well-prepared Auvergne cuisine in the company of journalists from the nearby offices of Le Monde. The real treasure here though is the bleu d'Auvergne (blue-veined cheese), straight from the countryside. At night you might get a plate of Auvergne charcuterie from the bar.

LE VIGNERON Map pp444-5 French, Southwest

☎ 01 47 07 29 99; 18-20 rue du Pot de Fer, 5e; starters €7-18, mains €14-23, menus €10.50 & €13.50 (lunch only), €18 & €30; ⌚ lunch & dinner to midnight; Ⓜ Place Monge

The 'Wine Grower', one of the best French restaurants in the Mouffetard quarter (not as big a superlative as you might think), specialises in the cuisine of southwest France. There are any number of menus available throughout the day and an annexe next door called L'Auberge de Vigneron handles overflow during the busiest months so you're always likely to get a table if you're prepared to wait. Lunch menus are available until 8pm.

LES VIGNES DU PANTHÉON

Map pp444-5   French, Southwest

☎ 01 43 54 80 81; 4 rue des Fossés St-Jacques, 5e; starters €8-15, mains €18-31, menus €30 & €35; ⌚ lunch Mon-Fri, dinner to 10pm Mon-Sat; Ⓜ Luxembourg

This charming eatery, owned and managed by a husband-and-wife team and just a few

TOP FIVE LATIN QUARTER & JARDIN DES PLANTES RESTAURANTS

- Allard (p193)
- Bouillon Racine (p193)
- Au Coco de Mer (p192)
- Le Petit Pontoise (p194)
- Mavrommatis (right)

paces down the hill from the Panthéon, stands out for its southwest-inspired food and fish dishes as well as its choice of wines. The back dining room, with exposed stone walls and candlelight, is a romantic choice.

MAVROMMATIS Map pp444-5   Greek

☎ 01 43 31 17 17; 42 rue Daubenton, 5e; starters €11.50-14, mains €20-26, menus €22 (lunch only) & €34; ⌚ lunch & dinner to 11pm Tue-Sat; Ⓜ Censier Daubenton

If your experience of Greek food in Paris is of takeaway outlets and restaurants in rue de la Huchette and streets like rue St-Séverin – and you have lived to tell the tale – visit Mavrommatis to sample the real thing. It's hard to choose between the assortment of tarama (fish roe dip), aubergines fumées (smoked aubergine) and tzatziki on one hand, and the salade grecque (tomatoes, lettuce, peppers and feta) on the other. Delicious moussaka or the crépines d'agneau sur lit de tomates, courgettes et pommes de terre (lamb tripe with tomatoes, courgette and potatoes) don't make it any easier. Enter from 5 rue du Marché des Patriarches.

MOISSONIER Map pp444-5   French

☎ 01 43 29 87 65; 28 rue des Fossés St-Bernard, 5e; starters €7-13, mains €14-23, menu lunch €23; ⌚ lunch & dinner to 9.30pm Tue-Sat; Ⓜ Cardinal Lemoine

Don't shout out about it while in Paris, but many French people believe that Lyons is the true food capital of France and this elegant eatery affords a great opportunity to sample that cuisine. The food is hearty, starting with the quenelles (fish dumplings; €16) through to boudin noir (black pudding; €14) and your best chance to try tripe as it should be. If you get through that, an extensive dessert list awaits.

PERRAUDIN Map pp444-5   French

☎ 01 46 33 15 75; 157 rue St-Jacques, 5e; starters €8-19, mains €15-29, menus lunch/dinner €18/28; ⌚ lunch & dinner to 11.30pm Mon-Fri; Ⓜ Luxembourg

Perraudin is a traditional French restaurant that hasn't changed much since it first opened. For classics such as bœuf bourguignon (beef marinated and cooked in red wine with mushrooms, onions, carrots and bacon; €15), gigot d'agneau (leg of lamb;

€16) or *confit de canard* (€16), try this reasonably priced and atmospheric (if somewhat shabby) place. If the *flamiche* (leek pie from northern France; €8) is on the menu, try that.

PIROSMANI Map pp436-7 — Georgian

☎ 01 43 26 17 65; 6 rue Boutebrie, 5e; starters €6-9, mains €8.90-12.50, menus €10 (lunch only) & €16; ☺ lunch & dinner to 1am; Ⓜ Cluny La Sorbonne
The cuisine of Georgia (as in Stalin's homeland not 'midnight train to') is an unusual but tasty one and relies heavily on walnuts. Try *adjapsandal,* Georgian ratatouille, for lack of a better definition (which will contain some of the nuts), as well as the *tchacapouli* (lamb with tarragon and white wine). No experts on things Caucasoid, we assume it's all authentic (though there's a lot more of the Cyrillic alphabet here than we'd anticipated).

SAVANNAH Map pp444-5 — International

☎ 01 43 29 45 77; 27 rue Descartes, 5e; starters €7-16, mains €13-14.50; ☺ dinner to 11pm Mon-Sat; Ⓜ Cardinal Lemoine
The food at this little bistro just north of the place de la Contrescarpe is as eclectic as its carnival-like decorations and choice of world music; tabouli mixes with tortellini here as does hummus with mozzarella and *fromage blanc* (cream cheese) with baklava. This place remains a welcome treat in an area overrun with tourist traps.

TEA CADDY Map pp436-7 — Tea Room

☎ 01 43 54 15 56; 14 rue St-Julien le Pauvre, 5e; set lunches & teas €26; ☺ noon-7pm Wed-Mon; Ⓜ St-Michel
Arguably the most English of the 'English' tea rooms in Paris, this institution, founded in 1928, is a fine place to break for lunch or tea (€5.90 to €7.80) and pastries (€5.30 to €8.10) after a tour of nearby Notre Dame, Ste-Chapelle or the Conciergerie.

CHEAP EATS
BREAKFAST IN AMERICA

Map pp444-5 — American, Deli

☎ 01 43 54 50 28; 17 rue des Écoles, 5e; meals €6.95-9.50; ☺ 8.30am-11pm; Ⓜ Cardinal Lemoine
The decision to open an almost authentic American-style diner, complete with red banquettes and Formica surfaces, was an inspired one. Breakfast, served all day and

with free coffee refills, starts at €6.95 and there are generous burgers, chicken wings and fish and chips (€7.50 to €8.95) as well.

INDIAN LOUNGE Map pp444-5 — Indian

☎ 01 47 07 77 18; 4 blvd de Port Royal, 5e; starters €4.50-15, mains €10-22, menus €9.50-12.50 (lunch only) & €18.10-21.10; ☺ lunch & dinner to 11.30pm; Ⓜ Les Gobelins
This is a relatively cheap, reasonably authentic place in south Paris should you require a fix of curry or tandoori grills. The décor is Mogul but not too over the top, and there are a half-dozen set *menus* to choose from.

KOOTCHI

Map pp444-5 — Middle Eastern, Afghani

☎ 01 44 07 20 56; 40 rue du Cardinal Lemoine, 5e; starters €4.50-6.50, mains €10.50-14.50, menus lunch €9.20 & €12.50, dinner €15.50; ☺ lunch & dinner to 10.30pm Mon-Sat; Ⓜ Cardinal Lemoine
Kootchi is an Afghan restaurant with décor – carpets, traditional instruments on the walls – reminiscent of a Central Asian caravanserai; it's a warm and welcoming place for a meal. Specialities include *qhaboli palawo* (veal 'stew' with nuts and spices) and *dogh*, a drink not unlike salted Indian lassi.

LA PETIT LÉGUME

Map pp444-5 — Vegetarian

☎ 01 40 46 06 85; 36 rue des Boulangers, 5e; dishes €6.50-13, menus €9-15; ☺ lunch & dinner to 10pm Mon-Sat; Ⓜ Cardinal Lemoine
The 'Little Vegetable', a tiny place on a narrow road, is a great choice for homemade vegetarian and organic fare. The ample salads (€11.50 to €13) are particularly good. It also has a good selection of organic wines.

LA VOIE LACTÉE

Map pp444-5 — Turkish

☎ 01 46 34 02 35; 34 rue du Cardinal Lemoine, 5e; starters €5.50-7, mains €9.50-12.50, menus lunch €11.50 & €14, dinner €16.50-19; ☺ lunch & dinner to 11pm Mon-Sat; Ⓜ Cardinal Lemoine
The 'Milky Way' is a Turkish place with both traditional and modern Anatolian cuisine, including a generous buffet of Turkish meze and salads. For mains, go for the grills, especially the various types of meatballs on offer. There's a good three-course vegetarian *menu* available for €16.50.

LE FOYER DU VIETNAM

Map pp444-5   Vietnamese

☎ 01 45 35 32 54; 80 rue Monge, 5e; starters €3.10-6, mains €6-8.50, menus €8.20 & €12.20; ⏲ lunch & dinner to 10pm Mon-Sat; Ⓜ Place Monge

The 'Vietnam Club', with its self-proclaimed *ambiance familiale* (family atmosphere), is a favourite meeting place among the capital's Vietnamese community. It's nothing but a long room with peeling walls and tables covered in oilcloths and plastic flowers. But if you're up for a one-dish meal choose one of the hearty house specialities – 'Saigon' or 'Hanoi' soup (noodles, soya beans and pork flavoured with lemon grass, coriander and chives). All dishes are available in either medium or large servings.

LE JARDIN DES PÂTES

Map pp444-5   Organic

☎ 01 43 31 50 71; 4 rue Lacépède, 5e; starters & snacks €4.50-6, mains €8-14; ⏲ lunch & dinner to 11pm; Ⓜ Place Monge

The 'Pasta Garden' may not be strictly vegetarian but it is 100% *bio* (organic) and offers as many types of noodle as you care to name – barley, buckwheat, rye, wheat, rice, chestnut and so on – all served with the freshest of ingredients. One especially delicious dish is barley pasta with salmon, crème fraîche, seaweed and leeks (€13.50). There's also a **13e arrondissement branch** (Map p448; ☎ 01 45 35 93 67; 33 blvd Arago, 13e; ⏲ lunch & dinner to 11pm Mon-Sat; Ⓜ Les Gobelins).

LES CINQ SAVEURS D'ANANDA

Map pp444-5   Organic

☎ 01 43 29 58 54; 72 rue du Cardinal Lemoine, 5e; soups & starters €5.20-9, mains €9.20-14.90; ⏲ lunch & dinner to 10.30 Tue-Sun; Ⓜ Cardinal Lemoine

Set back from the place de la Contrescarpe, this bright semi-vegetarian restaurant is extremely popular among health-food lovers. All ingredients are fresh and guaranteed 100%. Whet your appetite with miso soup (€5.20) then enjoy the hearty, delectable *assiette complète au seitan* (mixed plate with cooked wheat gluten; €13.90) served with artistically presented *crudités* (white radishes pickled in plum vinegar, seaweed, beans, rice and millet). Patrons should note that fish is served here.

MACHU PICCHU   Map pp444-5   South American

☎ 01 43 26 13 13; 9 rue Royer Collard, 5e; starters €5.80-8.80, mains €9.80-13.90, menu lunch €8.50; ⏲ lunch & dinner to 10.30pm Mon-Fri, dinner to 11pm Sat; Ⓜ Luxembourg

Peruvian food? Doesn't that mean guinea pig fricassee? Apparently not always; this small place serves up excellent meat and seafood dishes (eg *ceviche de pescado*, raw fish cured in lemon juice) from a tiny kitchen. It has a bargain-basement lunch *menu* and plats du jour (€6).

TASHI DELEK   Map pp444-5   Tibetan

☎ 01 43 26 55 55; 4 rue des Fossés St-Jacques, 5e; soups & bowls €3.80-6.50, mains €6.60-9.50, menus lunch €9.50 & €10, dinner €19; ⏲ lunch & dinner to 11pm Mon-Sat; Ⓜ Luxembourg

An intimate little place whose name means *bonjour* in Tibetan, Tashi Delek offers food that may not be gourmet but it is tasty and inexpensive. For starters, try the *tsampa* (vegetable and barley soup), followed by the delicious *daril seu* (meatballs with garlic, ginger and rice) or the *tselmok* (cheese and vegetable ravioli). Wash everything down with traditional or salted-butter tea, and don't forget the desserts, including the delicious *dressil* (yogurt with dried fruit). There are also vegetarian choices (€6.30 to €8.60).

SELF-CATERING

Place Maubert becomes a **lively food market** (p52) three mornings a week and has some great provisions shops here. Other good food markets are along **rue Mouffetard** (p52) and three days a week on **place Monge** (p52).

Supermarkets in the area include: **Champion** (Map pp444–5; 34 rue Monge, 5e; Ⓜ Cardinal Lemoine), **Ed l'Épicier** (Map pp444–5; 37 rue Lacépède, 5e; ⏲ 9am-1pm & 3-7.30pm Mon-Fri, 9am-7.30pm Sat; Ⓜ Place Monge) and **Franprix** (Map pp444–5; 82 rue Mouffetard, 5e; Ⓜ Censier Daubenton or Place Monge).

CRÉMERIE DES CARMES

Map pp444-5   Fromagerie

☎ 01 43 54 50 93; 47ter blvd St-Germain, 5e; ⏲ 7.30am-7.30 Mon-Sat, 7.30am-1pm Sun; Ⓜ Maubert Mutualité

This shop on lively place Maubert in the Latin Quarter sells cheese and high-quality dairy products.

Eating

LATIN QUARTER & JARDIN DES PLANTES

Interior of Bofinger (p184)

ST-GERMAIN, ODÉON & LUXEMBOURG

Rue St-André des Arts (Map pp436–7; M St-Michel or Odéon) is lined with restaurants, including a few down the *passage couvert* Cour du Commerce St-André, which empties into blvd St-Germain just opposite the statue of Georges Danton de Rohan. There are lots of eateries between Église St-Sulpice and Église St-Germain des Prés as well, especially along rue des Canettes, rue Princesse and rue Guisarde. Carrefour de l'Odéon has a cluster of lively bars, cafés and restaurants. Place St-Germain des Prés itself is home to celebrated cafés such as **Les Deux Magots** and **Café de Flore** (p247) as well as the equally celebrated Brasserie Lipp.

AZABU Map pp436-7   Japanese
☎ 01 46 33 72 05; 3 rue André Mazet, 6e; starters €8.50-13.50, mains €19-26, menus €18 (lunch only) & €33; ⏰ lunch Tue-Sat, dinner to 10.30pm Tue-Sun; M Odéon
For relatively cheap and somewhat cheerful Japanese food in the heart of St-Germain, head for Azabu. It was mostly filled with *gaijin* (non-Japanese) the last time we visited but the noodles and the teppanyaki looked authentic enough.

BRASSERIE LIPP Map pp434-5   French
☎ 01 45 48 53 91; 151 blvd St-Germain, 6e; starters €8.20-13.10, mains €15.60-20; ⏰ noon-2am; M St-Germain des Prés
The Lipp is a wood-panelled café-brasserie that was opened by one Léonard Lipp in 1880. Politicians rub shoulders with intellectuals, while waiters in black waistcoats, bow ties and long white aprons serve such brasserie favourites as *choucroute garnie* (€18.50) and *jarret de porc aux lentilles* (pork knuckle with lentils; €17.90). Everyone wants to sit downstairs, where smoking is permitted, rather than upstairs, which is the nonsmoking section and considered nowheresville; Lippistes call upstairs *L'Enfer* (Hell) and downstairs *Le Paradis* (Heaven). Look smart and like you know what you're doing; you might find yourself in the window seat in *Paradis*.

FISH LA BOISSONNERIE
Map pp436-7   Mediterranean, Seafood
☎ 01 43 54 34 69; 69 rue de Seine, 6e; starters/mains €7/14, menu lunch €21.50; ⏰ lunch & dinner to 10.45pm Tue-Sun; M Mabillon
A hybrid of a Mediterranean place run by a New Zealander and an American, with its rustic communal seating and bonhomie, Fish has surely taken its cue from London, where

such places have been a mainstay for several years. The wine selection is excellent – it's almost as much a wine bar as a restaurant – and the wonderful old mosaic on the front (which actually says *'la poissonnerie'* indicating it was a fishmonger) is a delight.

L'ARBUCI

Map pp436-7   French, Brasserie

☎ 01 44 32 16 00; 25 rue de Buci, 6e; starters €5.60-17, mains €14.50-28, menus lunch €15.50 & €20; ☽ noon-midnight; Ⓜ Mabillon

Though this marble and glass restaurant no longer looks like the retro-style brasserie it once was, the specialities remain: seafood (especially oysters) and spit-roasted beef, chicken, pork, salmon and – for dessert – pineapple. All-you-can-eat access to oysters of modest size costs €30, the lunch *menus* are available till 7pm and there's a *Faim de Nuit* (Night Hunger) *menu* for €19.50. There's live jazz downstairs on Friday and Saturday.

LE MÂCHON D'HENRI

Map pp436-7   French, Lyons & Mediterranean

☎ 01 43 29 08 70; 8 rue Guisarde, 6e; starters €6-8, mains €12-14; ☽ lunch & dinner until 11.30pm; Ⓜ St-Sulpice or Mabillon

A very Parisian bistro in an area awash with bars, this *mâchon* (in Lyons, a restaurant serving light meals) serves Lyons-inspired dishes lightened up with some Mediterranean accents. Dishes include *poivrons grillés à l'huile d'olive* (grilled capsicum with olive oil) and *terrine de courgettes et son coulis de tomates* (courgette terrine with tomato coulis). Regional dishes such as *saucisson de Lyon* (Lyons sausage) and sumptuous *boudin noir aux pommes* (black pudding with apple) come in generous serves. Rustic décor and excellent service makes this an easy choice.

LE PETIT ZINC

Map pp436-7   French, Brasserie

☎ 01 42 86 61 00; 11 rue St-Benoît, 6e; starters €7.50-19.50, mains €15-38, 2-/3-course menu €29.50/35; ☽ noon-2am; Ⓜ St-Germain des Prés

Not a 'little bar' but a wonderful, largish brasserie, serving traditional French cuisine and regional specialities from the south-west in true Art Nouveau splendour. The term brasserie is used loosely here; you'll feel more like you're in a starred restaurant so book ahead and dress accordingly.

LE ROUSSEAU Map pp434-5   French

☎ 01 42 22 51 07; 45 rue du Cherche Midi, 6e; starters €4.50-11.80, mains €13.80-17.80; ☽ 11am-11pm Mon-Sat; Ⓜ Rennes

This modern bar/brasserie comes highly recommended from a reader who seemed to eat every meal here during his stay in Paris. The *andouillette* (sausage made from the pig's small intestines that is grilled and eaten with onions and potatoes; €13.80) and the *onglet grillé* (grilled prime cut of beef; €13.80) look especially good but heavy; there's also lighter brasserie-style fare like omelettes and *croques-messieurs* (toasted ham and cheese sandwiches) for €6.40 to €9.80.

LES ÉDITEURS Map pp436-7   French, Café

☎ 01 43 26 67 76; 4 carrefour de l'Odéon, 6e; starters €9-16.50, mains €17.50-25; ☽ 8am-2am; Ⓜ Odéon

This place goes to great lengths to describe itself as a café, a restaurant, a library, a bar and a *salon de thé*, but for us it's just a good place to eat. It is intended for writers – there are more than 5000 books on hand and it's done up to feel like a slightly faded and dingy library – but it has big windows through which you can watch the Germanopratin – yes, there is an adjective for St-Germain des Prés – goings-on, and the generous Sunday brunch is a snip at €24.50.

YEN Map pp436-7   Japanese

☎ 01 45 44 11 18; 22 rue St-Benoît, 6e; mains around €22, menu dinner €55; ☽ lunch & dinner to 10.30pm Mon-Sat; Ⓜ St-Germain des Prés

This Japanese eatery – all blond wood and minimalist décor – is very popular with resident Japanese and knowledgeable Parisians. It has a real flair for *soba* (Japanese noodles) and tempura and you shouldn't leave without trying the aubergine in miso. Unusual for Paris, Yen serves and sells bento boxes at lunch.

CHEAP EATS

AMORINO Map pp436-7   Ice Cream

☎ 01 43 26 57 46; 4 rue de Buci, 6e; 1/2/3 scoops €3/4/5; ☽ noon-midnight; Ⓜ St-Germain des Prés

Though not such dedicated *lécheurs* (lickers) as some, we're told that **Berthillon** (p192) has serious competition and Amorino's homemade ice cream (yogurt, caramel, kiwi, strawberry etc) is, in fact, better. Expect long queues here and at the **Amorino Luxembourg branch** (Map pp434–5; ☎ 01 42 22 66 86; 4 rue Vavin, 6e; Ⓜ Vavin).

GUENMAÏ Map pp436-7 *Vegetarian*

☎ 01 43 26 03 24; 6 rue Cardinal & 2bis rue de l'Abbaye, 6e; soups €4.50, mains €7-11; ⓨ lunch Mon-Sat; Ⓜ St-Germain des Prés or Mabillon
On a corner and with two entrances, Guenmaï is essentially a **health food shop** (ⓨ 9am-8.30pm Mon-Sat) with a kitchen serving up macrobiotic and organic plats du jour and soups. It's a cosy, friendly place and, as the name suggests, the dishes are Asian-inspired. Try one of the wonderful juices (though they also serve beer and wine).

INDONESIA Map pp444-5 *Indonesian*

☎ 01 43 25 70 22; 12 rue de Vaugirard, 6e; menus lunch €9.90-13.50, dinner €17-23; ⓨ lunch Mon-Fri, dinner to 10.30pm daily; Ⓜ Luxembourg
One of a couple of Indonesian restaurants in Paris, this creatively named eatery has all the old favourites, from an elaborate, nine-dish *rijstafel* (rice with side dishes; €17 to €23) to *lumpia* (a type of spring roll; €5.50), *rendang* (spicy beef or chicken curry; €8.95) and *gado-gado* (vegetable salad with spicy peanut sauce; €6). Numerous *menus* are available at lunch and dinner. Traditional décor, incense and the gentle rhythm of the gamelan orchestra create a convincing atmosphere.

LE GOLFE DE NAPLES

Map pp436-7 *Italian, Pizzeria*
☎ 01 43 26 98 11; 8 rue Clément, 6e; starters €8-16, pizza & pasta dishes €10-16.50, mains €13-15; ⓨ lunch & dinner to 11pm Tue-Sun; Ⓜ Mabillon
Despite its location in the heart of tourist town, the 'Gulf of Naples' has some of the best pizza and fresh pasta in Paris – but more elaborate main courses can be disappointing. Make sure you try the *assiette napolitaine*, a dish of grilled fresh vegetables (€13.50). Enter from 5 rue de Montfaucon, 6e.

POLIDOR Map pp444-5 *French*

☎ 01 43 26 95 34; 41 rue Monsieur le Prince, 6e; starters €4-15, mains €10-19, menus €12 (lunch only), €20 & €30; ⓨ lunch & dinner to 12.30am Mon-Sat, to 11pm Sun; Ⓜ Odéon
A meal at Polidor, a quintessentially Parisian *crèmerie-restaurant*, is like a trip to Victor

Hugo's Paris – the restaurant and its décor date from 1845. Everyone knows about it and it's pretty touristy. Still, *menus* of tasty, family-style French cuisine are available. Specialities include *bœuf bourguignon* (€11), *blanquette de veau* (veal in white sauce; €13) and the most famous *tarte Tatin* (€6) in Paris. Don't bother booking in advance; you'll just have to wait anyway.

SELF-CATERING

With the Jardin du Luxembourg nearby, this is the perfect area for a picnic lunch. There is a cluster of food shops on rue de Seine and rue de Buci, 6e (Ⓜ Mabillon) as well as nearby rue St-Jacques, 5e (Ⓜ Luxembourg). The renovated and covered **Marché St-Germain** (Map pp436–7; 4-8 rue Lobineau, 6e; ⓨ 8.30am-1pm & 4-7.30pm Tue-Sat, 8.30am-1pm Sun; Ⓜ Mabillon), just north of the eastern end of Église St-Sulpice, has a huge array of produce and prepared food and opens Sunday morning. **Champion** (Map pp436–7; 79 rue de Seine, 6e; ⓨ 1-9pm Mon, 8.40am-9pm Tue-Sat, 9am-1pm Sun; Ⓜ Mabillon) supermarket is nearby.

TOP FIVE ST-GERMAIN & MONTPARNASSE RESTAURANTS

- La Cagouille (opposite)
- L'Assiette (opposite)
- Le Mâchon d'Henri (p207)
- Les Éditeurs (p207)
- Yen (p207)

MONTPARNASSE

Since the 1920s, the area around blvd du Montparnasse has been one of the city's premier avenues for enjoying that most Parisian of pastimes: sitting in a café and checking out the scenery on two (or maybe four) legs. Many younger Parisians now consider the area somewhat *démodé* and touristy and avoid it. Around metro Vavin, blvd du Montparnasse is home to a number of legendary brasseries and cafés, made famous between the wars by writers (p164) and artists such as Picasso, Dalí and Cocteau. Before the Russian Revolution, these cafés attracted exiles, including Lenin and Trotsky.

Montparnasse offers all types of eateries, especially traditional creperies, as Gare Montparnasse is where Bretons arriving in Paris to look for work would disembark (and apparently venture no further). At 18 & 20 rue d'Odessa there are three creperies and at least half a dozen more round the corner on rue du Montparnasse.

14 JUILLET Map pp422-3 French

☎ 01 40 44 91 19; 99 rue Didot, 14e; starters €7.80-9.30, mains €14.80-16.80, menu lunch €9.90; ⊗ lunch & dinner to 11pm; Ⓜ Porte de Vanves

It's always a fête (complete with lanterns) at this place with the ultra-budget weekday lunch *menu*. Here you'll eat favourites like *rillettes* and other charcuteries (€9.30), marrow bone (€7.80) and *blanquette de veau* (veal stew in white sauce enriched with cream, vegetables and often mushrooms; €14.80). Admittedly this place is very much off the beaten track, but the profiteroles alone are worth the trip.

LA CAGOUILLE Map pp434-5 French, Seafood

☎ 01 43 22 09 01; 10 place Constantin Brancusi, 14e; starters €11-15, mains €18-33, 2-/3-course menu €26/42; ⊗ lunch & dinner to 10.30pm; Ⓜ Gaîté

Chef Gérard Allemandou, one of the best seafood cooks (and cookery book writers) in Paris, gets rave reviews for his fish and shellfish dishes at this café-restaurant opposite 23 rue de l'Ouest. The *menus* here are exceptionally good value.

LA CLOSERIE DES LILAS

Map pp444-5 French, Brasserie

☎ 01 40 51 34 50; 171 blvd du Montparnasse, 6e; starters €6.50-17, mains €19-39, menu lunch €45; ⊗ noon-1.30am daily; Ⓜ Port Royal

As anyone who has read Hemingway will know, what is now the American Bar at the 'Lilac Enclosure' is where Papa did a lot of writing, drinking and eating of oysters (€11.40 to €20.60 a half-dozen); brass plaques tell you exactly where he and other luminaries such as Picasso, Apollinaire, Man Ray, Jean-Paul Sartre and Samuel Beckett stood or sat (or fell) and whiled away the hours. Along with the bar there is a chic restaurant and our favourite, the brasserie, where the décor is warm and romantic and the terrace a superb place for a drink in the warmer months.

LA COUPOLE Map pp434-5 French, Brasserie

☎ 01 43 20 14 20; 102 blvd du Montparnasse, 14e; starters €6.50-19, mains €12.50-32, menus €15 (lunch only), €24 & €32; ⊗ 8am-1am Sun-Thu, to 1.30am Fri & Sat; Ⓜ Vavin

The famous mural-covered columns (painted by such artists as Brancusi and Chagall), dark wood panelling and soft lighting have hardly changed an iota since the days of Sartre, Soutine, Man Ray, the dancer Josephine Baker and other regulars. The reason for visiting this enormous, 450-seat brasserie, designed by the Solvet brothers and opened in 1927, is thus history not gastronomy. You can book for lunch, but you'll have to queue for dinner; though there's always breakfast (€8). The more expensive *menus* are available until 6pm and after 10.30pm.

LA RÉGALADE

Map pp422-3 French

☎ 01 45 45 68 58; 49 av Jean Moulin, 14e; menu €30; ⊗ lunch Tue-Fri, dinner to midnight Tue-Sat; Ⓜ Porte d'Orléans

It's not exactly on the doorstep but this superb bistro, now under new management with chef Bruno Doucet in charge, offers some of the freshest and most carefully prepared seasonal food in Paris. Fish (especially mackerel and turbot) figures prominently and the desserts should be licensed. The staff are charming and service excellent.

L'ASSIETTE

Map pp422-3 French, Southwest

☎ 01 43 22 64 86; 181 rue du Château, 14e; menu with wine €50; ⊗ lunch Sat & Sun, dinner to 10.30pm Tue-Sun; Ⓜ Gaîté

This engaging bistro, with its ever-changing menu, is a bit off the beaten track southwest of the Cimitière du Montparnasse but has an unusual claim to fame: a woman chef. It's pricey for a bistro but the freshness and quality of the produce and the precision of the preparation and cooking justifies the cost. The wine list is well considered but you won't find a bottle for less than €50.

LE DÔME Map pp434-5 French, Seafood

☎ 01 43 35 25 81, 01 43 35 23 95; 108 blvd du Montparnasse, 14e; starters €12.50-25, mains €29-56; ⊗ lunch & dinner to 12.30am; Ⓜ Vavin

An Art Deco extravaganza dating from the 1930s, Le Dôme is a monumental place for a meal, with both a restaurant and a *poissonnerie*, where the emphasis, of course, is on the freshest of oysters, shellfish and fish dishes such as *sole meunière* (sole sautéed in butter and garnished with lemon and parsley). It's safest to stick with the basics at this historical venue and leave fussier dishes to the 'fooding' upstarts.

LES DIX VINS Map pp434-5   French
☎ 01 43 20 91 77; 57 rue Falguière, 15e; menus lunch/dinner €20/24; ⏱ lunch & dinner to 11pm Mon-Fri; Ⓜ Pasteur

This tiny restaurant, on the far side of Montparnasse, is so successful that you will probably have to wait at the bar even if you've booked. Not such a bad thing in this temple devoted to Bacchus, as you'll be able to sample one of the carefully chosen wines. The unique set *menu* may offer *pâté de sanglier aux cèpes* (boar pâté with ceps) or a tempting *Tatin boudin* (black pudding tart), followed by an excellent rabbit tournedos. Excellent value, good service and stylish décor combine to form a true winner.

CHEAP EATS

AQUARIUS Map pp422-3   Vegetarian
☎ 01 45 41 36 88; 40 rue de Gergovie, 14e; starters €4-7, mains €9-12, menus lunch/diner €11/15; ⏱ lunch & dinner to 10.30pm Mon-Sat; Ⓜ Pernéty or Plaisance

This vegetarian restaurant, the first to open in Paris, offers meals inspired by traditional French cuisine. From classic *chèvre chaud* (warm goat's cheese) to *ravioles de romans* (French-style ravioli), starters are substantial. For the main course, meat has been replaced with tofu or seitan. You can enjoy lasagne, cassoulet or *tartiflette* (a baked potato and cheese concoction). Organic wines are on offer as well. The outermost of three rooms opens onto a little garden that is pleasantly cool in summer.

DIETETIC SHOP Map pp434-5   Vegetarian
☎ 01 43 35 39 75; 11 rue Delambre, 14e; starters & snacks €5.50-11.20, mains €10.80; ⏱ lunch Mon-Sat, dinner to 10.30pm Mon-Fri; Ⓜ Vavin or Edgar Quinet

In this tiny no-nonsense eatery you can choose your meal from the kitchen in the middle of the room. Among the cold dishes there's a homemade vegetable pâté, *caviar*

d'algues marines (seaweed 'caviar') with pasta and an assortment of raw vegetables or lentils served with smoked tofu. Hot dishes include soups, couscous and more innovative specialities such as *tarte aux graines germées* (bean sprout tart). Fish is also served here. The Dietetic Shop is essentially just that – a place selling vegetarian and organic products with a few tables added.

MUSTANG CAFÉ
Map pp434-5   Mexican, Tex-Mex
☎ 01 43 35 36 12; 84 blvd du Montparnasse, 14e; starters €6-13.50, mains €8.20-15.45; ⏱ 9am-5am Mon-Sat, 11am-5pm Sun; Ⓜ Montparnasse Bienvenüe

A café that *almost* never sleeps, the Mustang has passable Tex-Mex combination platters and nachos (€8.20 to €15.45), fajitas (€15.45), burgers (€10.80 to €13.60) and salads (€6.60 to €8.90). Come here when the rest of Paris has gone to bed. Happy hour, when all drinks are half-price, is between 4pm and 8pm.

THUY LONG Map pp434-5   Vietnamese
☎ 01 45 49 26 01; 111 rue de Vaugirard, 6e; starters €5-9.90, mains €9.90-10.90, menus €10.90 & €12.90; ⏱ 11.30am-9pm Mon-Sat; Ⓜ St-Placide or Montparnasse Bienvenüe

Thuy Long, a tiny café just north of Gare Montparnasse, offers some of the best-value Vietnamese food in Paris. Try the generous bowl of *pho* or the *bo bun* (rice noodles with beef, small spring rolls and vegetables). It's hectic here at lunchtime; you might visit in the afternoon.

SELF-CATERING

Opposite the Tour Montparnasse is the open-air **Blvd Edgar Quinet food market** (Map pp434–5; blvd Edgar Quinet; ⏱ 7am-2pm Wed & Sat; Ⓜ Edgar Quinet or Montparnasse Bienvenüe). Two organic markets are also close by: **Marché Raspail** to the north and **Marché Brancusi** to the south (p52).

Supermarkets convenient to the area include: **Atac** (Map pp434–5; 55 av du Maine, 14e; ⏱ 9am-10pm Mon-Sat; Ⓜ Gaîté), **Franprix Delambre branch** (Map pp434–5; 11 rue Delambre; Ⓜ Vavin) and **Inno** (Map pp434–5; 29-31 rue du Départ, 14e; ⏱ 9am-9.50pm Mon-Fri, 9am-8.50pm Sat; Ⓜ Montparnasse Bienvenüe).

FAUBOURG ST-GERMAIN & INVALIDES

This district, effectively the entire 7e arrondissement, has the reputation of being rather staid and that's not too far from the truth; it seems there's a ministry or embassy on every other block. The National Assembly sits sentry by the river alongside the Musée d'Orsay, and visible from every angle is the Tour Eiffel's elaborate ironwork.

IL VIAGGIO Map pp434-5 Italian

☎ 01 45 55 80 75; 34 rue de Bourgogne, 7e; starters €13.50-16.50, mains €18-24, menus lunch/dinner €26/30; Ⓨ lunch Mon-Fri, dinner to 11pm Mon-Sat; Ⓜ Varenne

The intimate interior, irreproachable service, and stylish food and wine make this one of the most elegant Italian restaurants in Paris. Predictably, various sorts of pasta (€15 to €19) figure on the short, classic menu, but there are also delicious antipasti (notably the very tasty Parma ham and mozzarella) and some subtle variations on veal – the meat that rules in Italy. With the National Assembly just round the corner, the clientele is top-heavy with politicians.

L'ATELIER DE JOËL ROBOUCHON

Map pp434-5 International

☎ 01 42 22 56 56; 5 rue de Montalembert, 7e; starters €19-45, mains €25-59; Ⓨ lunch & dinner to midnight; Ⓜ Rue du Bac

More Soho than St-Germain, this palace of gastronomy overseen by His Royal Highness 'King' Joël Robouchon is an understated mix of red leather seats and black lacquer bars (there are no individual tables). The cuisine is 'modern mix' (ie everything goes) and you can run the gamut by ordering any of the small dishes (*tapas à la française*, for lack of a better term; €11 to €27) on offer. It's an extensive world tour, but with all of Paris along for the ride, it's well worth it.

LE 7E SUD Map pp434-5 Mediterranean

☎ 01 44 18 30 30; 159 rue de Grenelle, 7e; starters €8, mains €13-24.50, menu lunch €23; Ⓨ lunch & dinner to midnight; Ⓜ La Tour Maubourg

Specialising in bringing together the full gamut of Mediterranean flavours and the décor, this cosmopolitan place with its long tables and low lighting, has a warm, eastern feel, especially in the vaulted cellar. Organise your own culinary itinerary by starting with light-as-a-feather *fritellis calamares grecs* (Greek-style calamari; €10). For mains have a stopover in Italy with *rigatoni ricotti au jambon de Parme* (rigatoni with Parma ham; €13), a *tajine* in the purest Moroccan tradition, a mixed kebab on a bed of baby beans from the market or just a pasta dish (€13). There's a decent brunch (€21) on Sunday.

LE SALON D'HÉLÈNE

Map pp434-5 French

☎ 01 42 22 00 11; 4 rue d'Assas, 6e; average per person €60; Ⓨ lunch & dinner to 10.15pm Tue-Sat; Ⓜ Sèvres Babylone

While culinary star and darling of the media Hélène Darroze has a fine-dining restaurant upstairs with two Michelin stars, this more

Exterior of La Maison Rose (p234)

casual 'salon' is much more fun. The best way to experience her wonderful creations is to order the tapas-sized tasting menu (€79). Five courses come in matched pairs – each dish with descriptions longer than this review – but it's all fantastic stuff.

THOUMIEUX

Map pp434-5   French, Brasserie

☎ 01 47 05 49 75; 79 rue St-Dominique, 7e; starters €8-22, mains €18-33, menus €14 (lunch only) & €33; ☽ lunch & dinner to 11pm; Ⓜ La Tour Maubourg

Founded in 1923, Thoumioux is an institution just south of the Quai d'Orsay and popular with politicians and tourists alike. The cassoulet (€22) is justifiably renowned for its quality and size though you might also try such favourites as *saumon aux épinards rouges* (salmon with red spinach; €20) or *tête de veau* (€20).

SELF-CATERING

Arguably the finest grocery store in the district is Le Bon Marché's **La Grande Épicerie de Paris** (Map pp434–5; 26 rue de Sèvres; Ⓜ Sèvres Babylone). **Rue Cler** (p52), a wonderful market street open daily except Monday, is just west of Invalides.

TOP FIVE FAUBOURG ST-GERMAIN, INVALIDES & EIFFEL TOWER AREA RESTAURANTS

- L'Atelier de Joël Robouchon (p211)
- Le 7e Sud (p211)
- Le Petit Rétro (right)
- Le Salon d' Hélène (p211)
- Thoumieux (above)

EIFFEL TOWER AREA & 16E ARRONDISSEMENT

The 16e arrondissement is perhaps the most chichi and snobby part of Paris, the kind of area where a waiter will ask a fluent though non-native speaker of French whether they would like *la carte en anglais* (English menu). It's not everyone's *tasse de thé* (cup of tea), but a couple of its ethnic restaurants are worth a visit.

LA CANTINE RUSSE

Map pp426-7   Russian

☎ 01 47 20 56 12; 26 av de New York, 16e; starters €7-23, mains €12-20, menus €15 & €25; ☽ lunch & dinner to 10pm Tue-Sat; Ⓜ Alma Marceau

Established for the bulk of the students at the prestigious Conservatoire Rachmaninov in 1923, the 'Russian Canteen' is still strong more than eight decades on. At communal tables you can savour herrings served with blinis, aubergine 'caviar', *pojarski* (chicken meatballs with dill), beef Stroganov, *chachliks* (marinated lamb kebabs) and, to complete the tableau, *vatrouchka* (cream cheese cake).

LA CHAUMIÈRE EN CHINE

Map pp426-7   Chinese

☎ 01 47 20 85 56; 26 av Pierre 1er de Serbie, 16e; starters €7.5-9, mains €8-18, menus lunch €12, dinner €17 & €22; ☽ lunch & dinner to 10.30pm Mon-Sat; Ⓜ Alma Marceau

Parisians in the know would warn you against eating in ethnic restaurants outside ethnic *quartiers*, but the Chinese embassy just next door to this place makes it a notable exception to that rule. The largely Chinese clientele favour the *crabes mous en friture* (soft-shell crab fritters), made with a crustacean fished in the waters of Vietnam and Madagascar, the *canard farci* (stuffed duck) and pungent fermented bean curd.

LE PETIT RÉTRO Map pp426-7   French

☎ 01 44 05 06 05; 5 rue Mesnil, 16e; starters €6.50-14, mains €15.50-22, menus lunch €19.50, dinner €24 & €33; lunch Mon-Fri, dinner to 11.30pm Mon-Sat; Ⓜ Victor Hugo

From the gorgeous 'Petit Rétro' emblazoned on the zinc bar to the Art Nouveau folk tiles, this is a handsome space and one that serves up hearty dishes year-round. With dishes such as *blanquette de veau* and *choucroute maison* as house specials, it's hearty, heart-warming stuff. Service could be warmer and less rushed, though.

SELF-CATERING

Marché Président Wilson (p52) is not our favourite open-air market in Paris but it's convenient to the neighbourhood.

ÉTOILE & CHAMPS-ÉLYSÉES

The 8e arrondissement seems to have been born under a lucky star. Its broad avenues radiate from place Charles de Gaulle – also known as place de l'Étoile or simply Étoile – and among them is the celebrated av des Champs-Élysées; from the Arc de Triomphe to the place de la Concorde, the 'Elysian Fields' rules unchallenged. With very few exceptions, eateries lining this touristy thoroughfare offer little value for money, but those in surrounding areas can be excellent.

BUGSY'S Map pp426-7   American
☎ 01 42 68 18 44; 15 rue Montlivet, 8e; salads €10.20-11.70, mains €10.30-16.50; ☽ lunch & dinner to 11pm; Ⓜ Madeleine
This immensely popular place – it's positively heaving at lunchtime, especially with expats – is done up to resemble a Prohibition-era Chicago speakeasy. Food is the please-everyone easy option: Tex-Mex, salads, ploughman's lunches, and, of course, burgers (€11 to €12.50). The huge bar keeps going till 1am daily.

GRAINDORGE Map pp426-7   Belgian
☎ 01 47 64 33 47; 15 rue de l'Arc de Triomphe, 17e; starters €11-16, mains €22-25, menus lunch/ dinner €28/32; ☽ lunch Mon-Fri, dinner to 11pm Mon-Sat; Ⓜ Charles de Gaulle-Étoile
The name of this stylish restaurant, with its soft lighting, burgundy chairs and banquettes, and Art Deco touches, means 'barleycorn' and alludes to the great breweries of Flanders (check out the drinks list). The signature dish is *potjevleesch* (€11), four kinds of meat cooked slowly together and served in aspic, though you'll find plenty of other dishes that hint at the Low Countries.

L'ARDOISE Map pp426-7   French, Bistro
☎ 01 42 96 28 18; 28 rue du Mont Thabor, 1er; menu €31; ☽ lunch & dinner to 11pm Tue-Sun; Ⓜ Concorde or Tuileries
This is a little bistro with no menu as such (*ardoise* means 'blackboard', which is all there is) but who cares? The food – rabbit stuffed with plums and beef fillet with morels, prepared dextrously by chef Pierre Jay (ex-Tour d'Argent) – is superb and the *prix fixe* (set menu) offers good

value. L'Ardoise is bound to attract a fair number of tourists due to its location, but generally they too are on a culinary quest.

LE MANDALA RAY
Map pp426-7   Fusion
☎ 01 56 4 88 36 36; 34 rue Marbœuf, 8e; starters €6-16, mains €23-28, menus €27 & €35; ☽ dinner to midnight; Ⓜ Franklin D Roosevelt
What was until recently the Man Ray, named after the seminal surrealist photographer, is now the Mandala Ray (the current owner is Buddhist). It is still as cavernous as ever, with fusion food, great scenery (of all kinds) and a bar open till 2am daily and a club until 6am on Friday.

L'ÉTOILE VERTE Map pp426-7   French
☎ 01 43 80 69 34; 13 rue Brey, 17e; starters €8-15, mains €12-22, menu lunch €14, dinner with wine €18 & €25; ☽ lunch & dinner to 11pm; Ⓜ Charles de Gaulle-Étoile
Founded in 1951, the 'Green Star' is where all the old French classics remain: the onion soup, the snails, the rabbit. When one of us was a student in Paris (back when the glaziers were installing the stained glass at Ste-Chapelle) this was the place for both Esperanto speakers (a green star is their symbol) and students on a splurge. That may have changed, but the lunch *menu* is still a great deal for this neighbourhood.

MAISON PRUNIER
Map pp426-7   French
☎ 01 44 17 35 85; 16 av Victor Hugo, 16e; starters €15-59, mains €28-70, menu lunch €60; ☽ lunch & dinner to midnight Mon-Sat; Ⓜ Charles de Gaulle-Étoile
A venerable restaurant founded in 1925, Prunier is as famed for its Art Deco interior as for its own brand of caviar, fish and seafood dishes and dozens of vodkas. Definitely a place for celebrations; hang the expense and order the caviar (€60 to €140 for 30g).

MARKET Map pp426-7   French
☎ 01 56 43 40 90; 15 av Matignon, 8e; starters €11-22, mains €25-40, 2-/3-course menu lunch €34/51; ☽ lunch Mon-Fri, brunch noon-6pm Sat & Sun, dinner to 11.30; Ⓜ Franklin D Roosevelt
Jean-Georges Vongerichten's very swish restaurant focuses on fresh market produce

delivered with signature eclectic combinations and Asian leanings. While it's less formal than his accolade-adorned restaurants in the US and China, it's still a refined experience with lunch attracting a business crowd and dinner a somewhat sexier proposition. It's a place for everyone; breakfast is served from 8am to 11am during the week.

PIERRE GAGNAIRE

Map pp426-7   French

☎ 01 58 36 12 50; 6 rue Balzac, 8e; menu lunch/dinner €90/195; ☯ lunch Mon-Fri, dinner to 10pm Mon-Fri & Sun; Ⓜ George V

The controversial owner/chef (Pierre Gagnaire, see p50) of this very haute cuisine establishment changes his menus to reflect seasonal produce in a way that few chefs match. His artistic presentation (think painter's palette) and flavour combinations are now legendary. No matter which *menu* you choose (the tasting *menu* is a cool €230) make sure to try his signature *le grand dessert Pierre Gagnaire* – simply the seven wonders of desserts.

SPOON Map pp426-7   Fusion

☎ 01 40 76 34 44; 14 rue de Marignan, 8e; starters €14-20, mains €24.50-38, menu lunch €38 & €45, dinner €85; ☯ lunch & dinner to 11pm Mon-Fri; Ⓜ Franklin D Roosevelt

Diners at this Ducasse/Starck-inspired, recently renovated venue reserved for nonsmokers are invited to mix and match their own main courses and sauces – grilled calamari, say, with a choice of satay, curry and Béarnaise sauces or hummus and aubergine salad with samosas. It has an unheard of (for Paris) selection of New World and other European wines, with only a portion being French. The evening *menu* is a multicourse tasting one, which frees you from making all those choices.

CHEAP EATS

LINA'S Map pp426-7   Sandwiches

☎ 01 40 15 94 95; 4 rue Cambon, 1er; soups & salads €4.50-6.10, sandwiches €3.50-6.90; ☯ 9.30am-4.30pm Mon-Fri, 10am-5.30pm Sat; Ⓜ Concorde

This branch of a popular chain of lunch spots across Paris (some 20 outlets so far) has upmarket sandwiches, salads and soups. Other outlets include Bercy (Map pp446-7; ☎ 01 43 40 42 42; 104 rue de Bercy, 12e;

Bercy), La Défense (Map p155 ; ☯ 01 46 92 28 47; parvis de la Défense; Ⓜ La Défense) and Opéra (Map pp428-9; ☎ 01 47 03 30 29; 7 av de l'Opéra, 1er; Ⓜ Pyramides).

SELF-CATERING

Rue Poncelet and rue Bayen have some excellent food shops, including the incomparable Fromagerie Alléosse (p296). The huge Monoprix (Map pp426-7; 62 av des Champs-Élysées, 8e; ☯ 9am-midnight Mon-Sat; Ⓜ Franklin D Roosevelt) at the corner of rue La Boétie has a big supermarket section in the basement, and there's a Franprix (Map pp426-7; 12 rue de Surène, 8e; Ⓜ Madeleine) near place de la Madeleine.

TOP FIVE ÉTOILE, CHAMPS-ÉLYSÉES & CLICHY RESTAURANTS

- Charlot, Roi des Coquillages (opposite)
- L'Ardoise (p213)
- Market (p213)
- Pierre Gagnaire (left)
- Velly (p216)

CLICHY & GARE ST-LAZARE

Unlike their neighbour to the west, these areas are not gentrified in the least. Indeed, heading east in the 8e arrondissement, by the time you reach Gare St-Lazare, the shops and architecture have changed and another journey has begun. Around place de Clichy and the eponymous avenue leading north and south from it, a maze of small streets with a pronounced working-class character stretches out, a pocket of old Paris that has survived. These are happy hunting grounds for ethnic eateries and restaurants with character.

À LA GRANDE BLEUE

Map pp422-3   North African, Berber

☎ 01 42 28 04 26; 4 rue Lantiez, 17e; starters €4.50-7, mains €10-18.50, menu lunch €9.90; ☯ lunch Mon-Fri, dinner to 10.30pm Mon-Sat; Ⓜ Brochant or Guy Moquet

The rare *crêpes berbères* (Berber crepes; €8.50 to €11.50) must be ordered in advance. You'll also find unusual barley couscous (€11.80 to €18.50) prepared in the style of the Berbers (Kabyles) of eastern Algeria as well as the semolina variety (€10 to €17), and the savoury-sweet *pastilla au poulet* (chicken pastilla; €18.50). Add to that the cool blue and yellow décor, art on the walls and warm welcome and you've got a winner.

AU BON COIN Map pp426-7   French, Café
☎ 01 58 60 28 72; 52 rue Lemercier, 17e; starters €4-6, mains €10-15; 🕑 lunch Mon-Fri, dinner to 10.30pm Tue & Wed, to 11pm Thu & Fri; Ⓜ La Fourche

There's nothing particularly spectacular about this café up from place de Clichy that moonlights as a restaurant three nights a week. In fact, it's crowded and rather noisy. But if you are looking for solid café food and a quintessential Parisian eating experience, look no further.

BISTRO DES DAMES
Map pp426-7   French
☎ 01 45 22 13 42; 18 rue des Dames, 17e; starters €6-14, mains €12-18; 🕑 lunch & dinner to 11.30pm; Ⓜ Place de Clichy

The Bistro des Dames, the restaurant of Hôtel Eldorado (p325), will appeal to lovers of simple, authentic cuisine, such as hearty salads, tortillas and glorious charcuterie platters of *pâté de campagne*, authentic Guéméné *andouille* sausage (a smoked sausage made of pork tripe usually eaten cold) and paper-thin Serrano ham. The dining room, which looks out onto the street, is lovely, but during those humid Parisian summers it's the cool and tranquillity of the small back garden that pulls in the punters.

CHARLOT, ROI DES COQUILLAGES
Map pp426-7   French, Seafood
☎ 01 53 20 48 00; 12 place de Clichy, 9e; starters €10.50-25, mains €19-39, menus lunch €19 & €25; 🕑 lunch & dinner to midnight Sun-Wed, to 1am Thu-Sat; Ⓜ Place de Clichy

'Charlot, the King of Shellfish' is an Art Deco palace that some Parisians think is the best place in town for no-nonsense seafood. The seafood platters and oysters are why everyone is here, but don't ignore the wonderful fish soup and mains such as grilled sardines, *sole meunière* and bouillabaisse (€38).

Chez Omar (p185)

CHEZ JEAN Map pp428-9   French
☎ 01 48 78 62 73; 8 rue St Lazare, 9e; starters €16-19, mains €27-37, menu €35; 🕑 lunch Mon-Fri, dinner to 10.30pm Mon-Sat; Ⓜ Notre Dame de Lorette

This stylish gourmet restaurant manages to balance just the right amounts of sophistication and genuine warmth. Dark-red banquette seats liven up the large, quiet dining room. A sample meal might include *fricassée de langoustines* (scampi) served with a julienne of vegetables, *magret de canard rôti au miel et ses navets et échalotes confites* (honey-roasted fillet of duck breast served with preserved turnips and shallots) and a modern version of profiteroles – a scoop of vanilla ice cream between two crunchy, chocolate-coated meringues. There's a multi-course tasting menu available at €75.

LA GAIETÉ COSAQUE
Map pp426-7   Russian
☎ 01 44 70 06 07; 6 rue Truffaut, 17e; starters €1.70-18, mains €14.50-19, menu lunch €9.50 & €11, dinner €19 & €23; 🕑 lunch & dinner to 11.45pm Mon-Sat; Ⓜ Place de Clichy or Rome

This bistrolike restaurant with the oxymoronic name (Cossack Cheerfulness?)

is the place for *zakuski* (Russian starters), typically drunk with ice-cold vodka. Among the stand-outs are *salades de choux blancs aux baies roses* (a coleslaw-like salad with bay), the various herring dishes and aubergine 'caviar'. If you're stumped, try one of the mixed platters (€8 to €35). Hearty main dishes include *chachlyik* (lamb kebab; €17) and *koulibiaka* (pie filled with fish, rice, veg and boiled eggs; €19).

LA TÊTE DE GOINFRE

Map pp426-7   French, Café

☎ 01 42 29 89 80; 16 rue Jacquemont, 18e; average per person €30; ⏱ lunch & dinner to 10.30pm Mon-Sat; Ⓜ La Fourche

This funny place, whose name translates as 'Glutton Head' has a piggy theme and cute little figurines pepper the joint. As for the joints and other comestibles on the plate, it's (mostly) pork – from the charcuterie to munch on while you wait for a table to *jarret de porc*. It's a lively place, always packed and an evening to experience rather than taste.

MACIS ET MUSCADE

Map pp426-7   French

☎ 01 42 26 62 26; 110 rue Legendre, 17e; starters €10-11, mains €11-18, menus lunch €13 & €16, dinner €25; ⏱ lunch Sun-Fri, dinner to 10.30pm Sun-Thu, to 11pm Fri & Sat; Ⓜ La Fourche

The owners of this restaurant like to talk about 'tastes and scents' and you'll find both in excess on the plate: a *feuilleté de maroilles et sa salade à l'essence de ciste* (Maroilles cheese and a rose-essence salad), perhaps, or *carré d'agneau à l'infusion de thym* (loin of lamb with thyme). People rave about the Sunday brunch (€20).

VELLY Map pp428-9   French

☎ 01 48 78 60 05; 52 rue Lamartine, 9e; starters €10, mains €20, 2-/3-course menus €23/31; ⏱ lunch & dinner to 10.30pm Mon-Fri; Ⓜ Notre Dame de Lorette

The eclectic mix of locals that comes to this bistro with two dining rooms know they're onto a good thing. With a regularly changing menu, just order what sounds appealing – mushroom risotto, maybe, or *ravioles d'escargots* – it's all well prepared and attractively presented. There's a short but interesting wine list.

CHEAP EATS

LA MAFFIOSA DI TERMOLI

Map pp426-7   Italian, Pizzeria

☎ 01 55 30 01 83; 19 rue des Dames, 17e; pizzas & pasta €7.50-9; ⏱ lunch Mon-Sat, dinner to 11pm; Ⓜ Place de Clichy

This place has some 40 pizzas that are too good to ignore, as well as decent garlic bread with or without Parma ham. It does a thriving takeaway business, too.

SELF-CATERING

Marché Batignolles-Clichy (p52) is excellent for *produits biologiques* (organic goods).

OPÉRA & GRANDS BOULEVARDS

The neon-lit blvd Montmartre and nearby sections of rue du Faubourg Montmartre (neither of which are anywhere near the neighbourhood of Montmartre in the 18e) form one of the Right Bank's most animated café and dining districts. This area also has a couple of French restaurants that could almost be declared national monuments. A short distance to the north there's a large selection of Jewish and North African kosher restaurants on rue Richer, rue Cadet and rue Geoffroy Marie, 9e, south of metro Cadet.

AUX DEUX CANARDS

Map pp428-9   French

☎ 01 47 70 03 23; 8 rue du Faubourg Poissonnière, 10e; starters €5-14.50, mains €16-25, menu lunch €17; ⏱ lunch Tue-Fri, dinner to 10.15pm Mon-Sat; Ⓜ Bonne Nouvelle

The tradition at this long-established innlike place is that you ring first (is this a speakeasy?) before you are allowed entry. The name of the restaurant – 'At the Two Ducks' – reflects much of the menu (there's everything from foie gras to *magret*) but you'll find starters as diverse as mussels with leek and marrow on toast and many of the desserts are orange-based. This restaurant is reserved for nonsmokers.

AUX LYONNAIS Map pp428-9   French, Lyons

☎ 01 42 96 65 04; 32 rue St-Marc, 2e; starters €10-13, mains €20-22, 3-course menu €28; ⏱ lunch & dinner to 11pm Tue-Fri; Ⓜ Richelieu Drouot

This is where Alain Ducasse (who's got three Michelin stars at his restaurant over at the Plaza Athénée) and his followers 'slum' it. The venue is an Art Nouveau masterpiece that feels more real than movie set and the food is restructured Lyonnais classics on the short, seasonal menu; any item based on *cochon* (pig) comes with an ironclad guarantee to satisfy and everything goes well with Beaujolais. Two complaints: there are too many covers in the small space and service is rushed and impersonal.

BISTROT DU SOMMELIER

Map pp426-7   French

☎ 01 42 65 24 85; 97 blvd Haussman, 8e; starters €14-19, mains €22-27, 2-/3-course menu lunch €32/39, with wine €42/54; ☽ lunch & dinner to 10.30pm Mon-Fri; Ⓜ St-Augustin

This is the place to choose if you are as serious about wine as you are about food. The whole point of this attractive eatery is to match wine with food, and owner Philippe Faure-Brac, one of the world's foremost sommeliers, is at hand to help. The best way to sample his wine-food pairings is to order one of the tasting menus (€60 to €100, including the wine). The food, prepared by chef Jean-André Lallican, is hearty bistro fare and surprisingly not all the wines are French.

JULIEN Map pp428-9   French, Brasserie

☎ 01 47 70 12 06; 16 rue du Faubourg St-Denis, 10e; starters €5.90-15.50, mains €14-33, menu with wine €24.50 & €34.50; ☽ lunch & dinner to 1am; Ⓜ Strasbourg St-Denis

Located in the less-than-salubrious neighbourhood of St-Denis, Julien offers food that you wouldn't cross town for. But – *mon Dieu!* – the décor and the atmosphere: it's an Art Nouveau extravaganza perpetually in motion and a real step back in time. Service is always excellent here; you'll feel welcome at any time of day.

LE GÉNÉRAL LA FAYETTE

Map pp428-9   French, Café

☎ 01 47 70 59 08; 52 rue La Fayette, 9e; starters €4.90-6.80, mains €15-18; ☽ 10am-3am; Ⓜ Poissonnière

With its all-day menu, archetypal *belle époque* décor and Belgian beers, this is an excellent stop if you're hungry outside normal restaurant hours. Stick to the classics,

like the hearty onion soup and crisp *confit de card* (preserved duck leg cooked very slowly in its own fat; €14) with tasty potatoes, and you can't go wrong. For something lighter go for one of the generous *salades composées* (mixed salad; €6.80 to €11.80).

LE ROI DU POT AU FEU

Map pp426-7   French

☎ 01 47 42 37 10; 34 rue Vignon, 9e; starters €5-7, mains €16-17, 2-/3-course menus €23/28; ☽ noon-10.30pm Mon-Sat; Ⓜ Havre Caumartin

The typical Parisian bistro atmosphere, '30s décor and checked tablecloths all add to the charm of the 'King of Hotpots', and we always go back when we're in Paris. What you really want to come here for is a genuine pot-au-feu, a stockpot of beef, aromatic root vegetables and herbs stewed together, with the stock served as an entree and the meat and vegetables as the main course. Other offerings – the chef's terrine, leeks *à la vinaigrette*, *hachis Parmentier* (chopped beef with potatoes), crème caramel, *tarte Tatin* or chocolate mousse, and the complimentary *cornichons* at the start – are equally traditional fare but less noteworthy. You drink from an open bottle of wine and pay for what you've consumed. No reservations.

LE Y Map pp426-7   Greek

☎ 01 42 68 08 51; 24 rue Godot de Mauroy, 9e; menu €12.50 (lunch only) & €18; ☽ lunch Mon-Sat, dinner to midnight Tue-Sat; Ⓜ Havre Caumartin

Don't expect very much from Le Y (pronounced 'i grec' in French) except traditional, family-style Greek cooking and a warm welcome. The lunch *menu* is available until 8pm. The mezzanine area is a pleasant place to sit and there are occasional photographic exhibits here.

LES AILES Map pp428-9   Jewish, Kosher

☎ 01 47 70 62 53; 34 rue Richer, 9e; starters €7.50-17, mains €18-25; ☽ lunch & dinner to 11.30pm; Ⓜ Cadet

Next door to the Folies-Bergère and with a delicatessen and bakery attached, 'Wings' is a kosher North African (Sephardic) place that has superb couscous with meat or fish (€19 to €24) and grills. Don't even consider a starter; you'll be inundated with little plates of salad, olives etc before you can say *shalom*. Sabbath meals (pre-ordered and prepaid) are also available.

Meal in Market restaurant (p213)

MOTHER EARTH'S

Map pp428-9   Vegetarian

☎ 01 47 70 06 88; 40 rue du Faubourg Montmartre, 9e; dishes €9, menu €10 (lunch only) & €16.50; ⏰ lunch & dinner to 10pm Mon-Sat; Ⓜ Le Peletier

Situated at the back of a minuscule courtyard off rue du Faubourg Montmartre, this place is more of a '60s-style eatery with a homey dining room and Formica décor. At lunchtime, regulars make themselves at home and, without a moment's hesitation, order the *assiette céréalière* (cereal platter; €9), a hearty dish comprising an assortment of grains (bulgur wheat, brown rice, semolina and buckwheat). They also serve fish here.

WALLY LE SAHARIEN

Map pp428-9   North African

☎ 01 42 85 51 90; 36 rue Rodier, 9e; menu lunch/dinner €25/40; ⏰ lunch & dinner to 10.30pm Tue-Sat; Ⓜ St-Georges or Cadet

This is several cuts above most Maghreb restaurants in Paris, offering couscous in its pure Saharan form – without stock or vegetables, just a finely cooked grain served with a delicious sauce – and excellent *tajines*. It's fixed price here at both lunch and dinner and rather pricey for what it is. But one guarantee: you won't walk away hungry.

CHEAP EATS

CHARTIER

Map pp428-9   French, Bistro

☎ 01 47 70 86 29; 7 rue du Faubourg Montmartre, 9e; starters €2-11.50, mains €6.30-11.60, menu with wine €20; ⏰ lunch & dinner to 10pm; Ⓜ Grands Boulevards

Chartier is a real gem that is justifiably famous for its 330-seat *belle époque* dining room, virtually unaltered since 1896. With a 25/50cL *pitchet* (pitcher) of wine for €1.60/2.60, you should spend no more than €15/20 for two/three courses per person. The menu changes (well, alters) daily, but don't expect gourmet. Reservations are not accepted so expect a queue at busy times. Lone diners will have to share a table.

CHEZ HAYNES

Map pp428-9   American, Southern

☎ 01 48 78 40 63; 3 rue Clauzel, 9e; starters €7, mains €8-16; ⏰ dinner to midnight Tue-Sat; Ⓜ St-Georges

A legendary, funky hang-out set up by an African American ex-GI in 1947, Haynes dishes up such genuine soul food as shrimp gumbo, fried chicken, barbecued ribs and cornbread. There's usually a lively crowd for the blues, dance and performance art sessions on Friday and Saturday from 8.30pm or 9pm (€5) and jamming from 11pm to midnight.

SELF-CATERING

Both av de l'Opéra and rue de Richelieu have several supermarkets, including a large one in the basement of **Monoprix** (Map pp426–7; 21 av de l'Opéra, 2e; ✆ 9am-10pm Mon-Fri, 9am-9pm Sat; **M** Pyramides).

TOP FIVE OPÉRA, GRANDS BOULEVARDS, GARE DU NORD, GARE DE L'EST & RÉPUBLIQUE RESTAURANTS

- Bistrot du Sommelier (p217)
- Julien (p217)
- Le Chansonnier (p220)
- Le Roi du Pot au Fer (p217)
- Terminus Nord (p221)

GARE DU NORD, GARE DE L'EST & RÉPUBLIQUE

These areas offer all types of food but most notably Indian and Pakistani, which can be elusive in Paris. There's a cluster of brasseries and bistros around the Gare du Nord. They're decent options for a first (or final) meal in the City of Light.

CHEZ JENNY Map pp428-9   French, Alsace
✆ 01 44 54 39 00; 39 blvd du Temple, 3e; starters €5.80-17.50, mains €16-33, 2-/3-course menus €19/23.50; ✆ noon-midnight Sun-Thu, noon-1am Fri & Sat; **M** République
This cavernous brasserie dating from 1932 serves a huge *choucroute garnie* (€20.50 to €25.50), but we suspect that most people visit to admire the stunning marquetry of Al-satian scenes by Charles Spindler on the 1st floor. A quick and tasty lunch at Chez Jenny is *flammekuche* (€9), an Alsatian-style tart made with cream, onion, bacon and cheese.

CHEZ PAPA (ESPACE SUD-OUEST)
Map pp428-9   French, Southwest
✆ 01 42 09 53 87; 206 rue La Fayette, 10e; starters & salads €7.05-13.40, mains €14.55-26.10, menus €15.95 & €23.90; ✆ 11am-1am; **M** Louis Blanc
Chez Papa serves all sorts of specialities of the southwest, including cassoulet (€17.35) and *pipérade* (€14.55), but most diners are

here for the famous *salade Boyarde*, an enormous bowl filled with lettuce, tomato, sautéed potatoes, two types of cheese and ham – all for the princely sum of €7.45 (or €8.35 if you want two fried eggs thrown in). There's a branch called **La Ferme de Chez Papa** (Map pp426–7; ✆ 01 42 65 43 68; rue de l'Arcade, 8e; **M** Havre Caumartin), which keeps the same hours.

DA MIMMO Map pp428-9   Italian
✆ 01 42 06 44 47; 39 blvd de Magenta, 10e; starters €7-15, mains €17-22, menu lunch €26; ✆ lunch & dinner to 11.30pm Tue-Sat; **M** Jacques Bonsergent
Neither the less-than-salubrious neigh-bourhood nor the relatively high prices are enough to keep fans away from this eatery with its authentic Neapolitan cuisine. Naples is, of course, the birthplace of pizza (€12 to €14); try one with rocket and forget about pizzas of the past.

EL PALADAR
Map pp428-9   Cuban
✆ 01 43 57 42 70; 26bis rue de la Fontaine au Roi, 11e; starters €4-7, mains €10-14; ✆ dinner to 2am; **M** Goncourt
While the name of this place suggests the restaurants run from private homes in today's cash-strapped Havana, the food and sheer exuberance recalls the Cuba of the 1950s when everything was plentiful. It's a convivial, graffiti-covered place with super *cäpirinhas* (€6): cocktails made from a sugarcane-based alcohol, lime juice and sugarcane syrup. Dishes – *pescado guisado* (fried fish), *pollo piopio* (chicken cooked with citrus) and *yuca con mojo* (manioc with onions and garlic) – are only so-so.

GUILLAUME Map pp440-1   Modern French
✆ 01 44 54 20 60; 32 rue de Picardie, 3e; starters €6.50-12, salads €12-14, mains €13-17.50; ✆ lunch Mon-Fri, dinner to 11.30pm Mon-Sat; **M** Temple or République
What was the Web Bar for several years has morphed in this sophisticated venue, a hop, skip and a jump from place de la République. A couple of the *petites assiettes* ('little dishes' but let's call them French tapas; €4.50 to €6) make an ideal light lunch – try the tomato Tatin and the tape-nade – and there's a three-dish *formule* (set

menu) for €12.50; eat either in the front bar or in the spacious dinning room behind. There's a lovely art gallery on the 1st floor and, if you're a group (something unusual in Paris), there's a huge round table seating at least a dozen people.

LA 25E IMAGE Map pp428-9 — French

☎ 01 40 35 80 88; 9 rue des Récollets, 10e; mains €11-14; ☽ lunch & dinner to 12.30am Mon-Fri; Ⓜ Gare de l'Est

The original painted-tile ceiling of this former bakery is still intact, and brightly coloured ceramic tables give this 'bar-galerie-resto' a lively, upbeat feel. The '25th Image' (it's a reference to the number of frames per second on moving film) has simple, very authentic cuisine, for example tarte aux légumes et au chèvre (vegetable and goat's cheese tart) and other savoury pies (€9.50 to €12). The welcome is warm and the service excellent.

LA MARINE Map pp428-9 — French

☎ 01 42 39 69 81; 55bis quai de Valmy, 10e; starters €7.50-12, mains €14.10-18.80, menu lunch €12; ☽ lunch & dinner to 11.30pm Mon-Sat; Ⓜ République

This large, airy bistro overlooking Canal St-Martin is a favourite, especially in the warmer months, among les branchés du quartier (neighbourhood trendies), who nibble on dishes like millefeuille de rouget à la vinaigrette (mullet in layered pastry with vinaigrette) and brick de poisson à la crème océane (fish fritter with seafood sauce).

LA PAELLA Map pp428-9 — Spanish

☎ 01 46 07 28 89; 50 rue des Vinaigriers, 11e; starters €6.10-16, mains €20.20-25, 3-course menu €27; ☽ lunch & dinner to 11pm; Ⓜ Jacques Bonsergent

This homely place, which almost feels like a buzzy café (especially on weekend nights), specialises in Spain's most famous culinary export – though it does a mean zarzuela de pescado (Spanish 'bouillabaisse'; €25) as well. The paella is cooked to order so count on at least a 30-minute wait and don't overdo the tapas.

LE CHALAND Map pp428-9 — French, Café

☎ 01 40 05 18 68; 163 quai de Valmy, 10e; starters & salads €6.50-11, mains €12.50-15, menu lunch

€11; ☽ lunch & dinner to midnight Tue-Fri, to 10pm Sat & Sun; Ⓜ Louis Blanc

The 'Barge' is a pleasant café du quartier serving rock-solid favourites like bœuf bourguignon and tartes salées (savoury pies) with the occasional leap into the 21st century with gigantic salads. It's one of the more approachable (and affordable) eateries on the canal.

LE CHANSONNIER

Map pp428-9 — French

☎ 01 42 09 40 58; 14 rue Eugène Varlin, 10e; starters €5.50-12, mains €15-18, menus €10.50 (lunch only), €22 & €23.50; ☽ lunch Mon-Fri, dinner to 11pm Mon-Sat; Ⓜ Château Landon or Louis Blanc

If ever there was ever a perfect example of a restaurant du quartier, the 'Singer', named after Lyonnais socialist singer-songwriter Pierre Dupont (1821–70), is it. With its curved zinc bar and Art Nouveau mouldings, it could be a film set. The food is authentic, excellent and very substantial; the €23.50 formule bistro includes terrine maison à valonté (all you can eat of four types of terrine). The noix St-Jacques provençal (scallops in herbed tomato sauce) is an excellent starter while the bouillabaisse is the main course of choice.

LE RÉVEIL DU XE

Map pp428-9 — French, Auvergne

☎ 01 42 41 77 59; 35 rue du Château d'Eau, 10e; starters €4-9, mains €9-13; ☽ lunch Mon-Sat, dinner to 9.30pm Thu; Ⓜ Chateau d'Eau

The 'Awakening of the 10th Arrondissement', taking its name from a left-wing newspaper of the late 19th century, is an authentic and historic institution, where hearty and flavoursome family cooking is served in a friendly atmosphere. Produce from the Auvergne dominates the menu: tripoux (small parcels of highly seasoned sheep's or calf's tripe), pounti (a hash of bacon, Swiss chard and onions bound with milk and eggs) and, of course, cheese.

LE SPORTING Map pp428-9 — International

☎ 01 46 07 02 00; 3 rue des Récollets, 10e; starters €7-14, mains €13-18.50; ☽ lunch & dinner to 11.30pm; Ⓜ Gare de l'Est

This is one of the more sophisticated café-restaurants along the Canal St-Martin and the minimalist décor – all browns and ash greys and bare wooden floors – suggests an up-to-the-moment bar or club in London. Brunch on Sunday (noon to 3.30pm) is when Le Sporting is at its busiest.

NOUVEAU PARIS-DAKAR

Map pp428-9   African, Senegalese

☎ 01 42 46 12 40; 11 rue de Montyon, 9e; starters €6.90, mains €12.50-16, menus lunch €9.90, dinner €24 & €32; ☽ lunch Mon-Thu & Sat, dinner to 1am Mon-Sat; Ⓜ Grands Boulevards

This is a little bit of Senegal in Paris, with Mamadou still reigning as the 'King of Dakar' despite the new location. Specialities here include *yassa* (chicken or fish marinated in lime juice and onion sauce; €12) and *mafé Cap Vert* (lamb in peanut sauce; €13). There's live African music most nights.

TERMINUS NORD

Map pp428-9   French, Brasserie

☎ 01 42 85 05 15; 23 rue de Dunkerque, 10e; starters €7.50-18, mains €15-33, menus with wine €24.90 & €34.50; ☽ 8am-1am; Ⓜ Gare du Nord

The 'North Terminus' has a copper bar, waiters in white uniforms, brass fixtures and mirrored walls that look as they did when it opened in 1925. Breakfast (from €8) is available from 8am to 11am, and full meals are served continuously from 11am to 12.30am. It's a museum-quality time piece!

CHEAP EATS

CHEZ SÉBASTIEN

Map pp428-9   Turkish

☎ 01 42 78 58 62; 22 passage Vendôme, 3e; dishes €4-7; ☽ 11.30am-8pm Mon-Sat; Ⓜ République

This simple little Turkish café on two levels in a scruffy *passage* south of place de la République is just the ticket if you're looking for something cheap, filling and tasty to eat 'on the thumb' as the French say. Try any of the meze or the Iskender kebab, lamb slices served with pide bread and yogurt.

LE CAMBOGE Map pp428-9   Cambodian

☎ 01 44 84 37 70; 10 av Richerand, 10e; dishes €3-10; ☽ lunch & dinner to 11.30pm Mon-Sat; Ⓜ Goncourt

Hidden in a quiet street between the gargantuan Hôpital St-Louis and Canal St-Martin, this favourite spot among students serves enormous *rouleaux de printemps*

(spring rolls) and the ever-popular *pique-nique cambodgien* ('Cambodian picnic' of rice vermicelli and sautéed beef, which you wrap up in lettuce leaves). The food tastes homemade – the vegetarian platters are especially good – and the staff are always run off their feet. Try to arrive before 9pm so you don't have to wait for a table.

LE MAURICIEN FILAO

Map pp428-9   Mauritian, Creole

☎ 01 48 24 17 17; 9 passage du Prado, 10e; dishes around €5; ☽ lunch & dinner to 10pm; Ⓜ Strasbourg St-Denis

This hole-in-the-wall canteen in passage du Prado, a derelict covered arcade accessible from 12 rue du Faubourg St-Denis and 18-20 blvd St-Denis, serves cheap but tasty Mauritian dishes such as spicy *rougaille de poisson* (a Creole dish of fish cooked with onions, garlic, ginger, chilli and coriander). It's won the approval of several readers. Only certain dishes from the main menu are available daily, though.

MADRAS CAFÉ Map pp428-9   Indian

☎ 01 05 29 56; 180 rue du Faubourg St-Denis, 10e; starters €4.50-10, mains €6-11; ☽ lunch & dinner to 11.30pm; Ⓜ Gare du Nord

You wouldn't cross town to eat at this simple restaurant with specialities from both northern and southern India – the one-dish thalis (€7) are good – but if you've just arrived at or are just about to leave from the Gare du Nord and need a curry fix, this café is right around the corner.

PASSAGE BRADY

Map pp428-9   Indian, Pakistani

46 rue du Faubourg St-Denis & 33 blvd de Strasbourg, 10e; ☽ lunch & dinner to 11pm; Ⓜ Château d'Eau

Joining rue du Faubourg St-Denis and blvd de Strasbourg in the 10e, this derelict covered arcade could easily be in Calcutta. Its incredibly cheap Indian, Pakistani and Bangladeshi cafés offer some of the best-value lunches in Paris (meat curry, rice and a tiny salad €5 to €7, chicken or lamb biryani €8 to €12, thalis €12); dinner *menus* are from €9 to €22. There are lots of places to choose from, but the pick of the crop are **Roi du Kashmir** (☎ 01 48 00 08 85; 76 passage Brady), **Passage de Pondicherry** (☎ 01 53 32 63 10; 84 passage Brady) and **Pooja** (☎ 01 48 24 00 83; 91 passage Brady).

SELF-CATERING

Two covered markets in this area are the Marché aux Enfants Rouges and the more extravagant Marché St-Quentin. For details, see p52.

Rue du Faubourg St-Denis, 10e, which links blvd St-Denis and blvd de Magenta, is one of the cheapest places to buy food, especially fruit and vegetables; the shops at Nos 23, 27-29 and 41-43 are laden with produce. The street has a distinctively Middle Eastern air, and quite a few of the groceries offer Turkish, North African and subcontinental specialities. Many of the food shops, including the *fromagerie* at No 54, are open Tuesday to Saturday and until noon on Sunday.

Supermarkets convenient to this area include **Franprix Petites Écuries branch** (Map pp428–9; 7-9 rue des Petites Écuries, 10e; M Château d'Eau), **Franprix Magenta branch** (Map pp428–9; 57 blvd de Magenta, 10e; M Gare de l'Est) and **Franprix Bretagne branch** (Map pp436–7; 49 rue de Bretagne, 3e; ⏰ 9am-8.30pm Tue-Sat, 9am-1.20pm Sun; M Arts et Métiers).

MÉNILMONTANT & BELLEVILLE

In the northern part of the 11e and into the 19e and 20e arrondissements, rue Oberkampf and its extension, rue de Ménilmontant are popular with diners and denizens of the night, though rue Jean-Pierre Timbaud, running parallel, is stealing some of their glory these days. Rue de Belleville and the streets running off it are dotted with Chinese, Southeast Asian and a few Middle Eastern places; blvd de Belleville has some kosher couscous restaurants, most of which are closed on Saturday.

AU VILLAGE

Map pp440-1   African, Senegalese

☎ 01 43 57 18 95; 86 av Parmentier, 11e; starters €5.50-8, mains €11-16; ⏰ dinner to midnight Mon-Thu, to 2am Fri-Sun; M Parmentier

Newcomers to African cuisine can choose from a range of classic Senegalese dishes such as *aloko* (fried plantain bananas with red sauce; €5.50), followed by the delicious, lightly spiced fish/chicken *yassa* (€12/11) or the hearty beef *mafé* (€11) For dessert, check out the amazing *thiakry* (semolina

and cream cheese salad; €5.50). The plat du jour is usually €13. The atmosphere is warm, friendly and a bit hip and the décor is delightful; you'll think you're in a Senegalese village.

BISTRO FLORENTIN

Map pp428-9   Italian

☎ 01 43 55 57 00; 40 rue Jean-Pierre Timbaud, 11e; starters €8-14, mains €15-17, menu lunch €11.50; ⏰ lunch Mon-Fri, dinner to 11pm Mon-Sat; M Parmentier

Excellent Italian fare in cosy surroundings: grilled, finely seasoned aubergine for starters, tiramisú as light as a feather for dessert and, between those two courses, a wide choice of mains and pastas (€11.50 to €16). The *penne à la crème d'artichauts et de truffes blancs* (penne with cream, artichokes and white truffles; €15) is superb as is the *ravioli à la ricotta et aux épinards, sauce aux champignons* (spinach and cheese ravioli with a mushroom sauce).

BISTROT GUILLAUME

Map pp440-1   French, Bistro

☎ 01 47 00 43 50; 5 rue Guillaume Bertrand, 11e; starters €5-13, mains €12.50-16, menus lunch €10.50, dinner €17 & €25; ⏰ lunch Mon-Fri, dinner to 11pm Mon-Sat; M St-Maur

This smart bistro, close to the flashy rue Oberkampf, has a dozen tables with gingham tablecloths arranged around a polished wooden bar. Add a few Venetian dolls, a touch of greenery and background music from Vivaldi to Abba *et voilà*: 'Bill's Place'. The *ravioles de saumon crème ciboulette* (ravioli with salmon, cream and chives) will tickle your taste buds; for mains, the menu offers a range of traditional provincial dishes such as *jarret de porc sur choucroute* (pork knuckle with sauerkraut), but also more enlightened *chou farci au saumon* (stuffed cabbage with salmon). Expect friendly, attentive service.

JUAN ET JUANITA

Map pp428-9   French

☎ 01 43 57 60 15; 82 rue Jean-Pierre Timbaud, 11e; starters €8.50, mains €15-16, menus €14 (lunch only) & €17; ⏰ lunch & dinner to 2am Tue-Sat, brunch to 5pm Sun; M Parmentier or Couronnes

This delightful little restaurant and lounge stands out for its over-the-top, slightly camp décor – there are four *coins* (corners) with as many atmospheres: country, chic bistro, salon and bar – and the exceedingly high standards of its kitchen. The menu features such dishes as *tajine d'agneau aux abricots secs* (lamb *tajine* with dried apricots), *mignon de porc au raifort* (tenderloin of pork with horseradish) and *clafoutis aux fruits* (upside-down cake with fresh fruit).

LA TOCCATA Map pp440-1   Italian
☎ 01 40 21 04 59; 52 av de la République, 11e; starters €7.50-9.50, mains €14.50-16, menus €17 (lunch only), €25 & €38; ⏱ lunch & dinner to midnight Tue-Sat; Ⓜ Parmentier

It's said (by the French, of course) that Neapolitan cuisine still bears traces of the French occupation in the 18th century and makes abundant use of seafood: *il piatto del guarracino* (local bouillabaisse) and sardines in *escabèche* (seasoned marinade). Also to die for is the *fusili al ragú* (ham, bacon, onion and meat cooked in wine for six hours).

TOP FIVE MÉNILMONTANT & BELLEVILLE RESTAURANTS

- Bistro Florentin (opposite)
- Juan et Juanita (opposite)
- L'Ave Maria (p225)
- Le Villaret (p224)
- Ossek Garden (p225)

LE BARATIN Map pp428-9   French, Bistro
☎ 01 43 49 39 70; 3 rue Jouye-Rouve, 20e; meals from €35, menu lunch €14; ⏱ lunch Tue-Fri, dinner to midnight Tue-Sat; Ⓜ Pyrénées or Belleville

This animated wine bar just a step away from the lively Belleville quarter offers some of the best French food in the 20e on its ever-changing blackboard. The wine selection (by the glass or carafe) is excellent; most are between €18 and €30 a bottle.

LE C'AMELOT Map pp440-1   French, Bistro
☎ 01 43 55 54 04; 50 rue Amelot, 11e; menus lunch €17 & €24, dinner €34; ⏱ lunch Tue-Fri, dinner to 10.30pm Mon-Sat; Ⓜ St-Sébastien Froissart

The 'Street Pedlar', making an awkward pun with the street name, is the perfect little neighbourhood bistro, but it's on everyone's list so book well in advance. For starters, the *tarte feuilletée de sardines marinées et confit d'oignons* (tart with marinated sardines and onion confit) is a discovery. The *agneau de Lozère rôti, de l'ail en chemise et des haricots coco mitonnés au jus* (roast lamb cooked with whole cloves of garlic and borlotti beans simmered in the juice) offers a perfect combination of flavours. Staid atmosphere but great food.

LE CLOWN BAR Map pp440-1   French, Bistro
☎ 01 43 55 87 35; 114 rue Amelot, 11e; starters/mains €7.50/15, menus lunch/dinner €13.50/25; ⏱ lunch & dinner to midnight Mon-Sat; Ⓜ Filles du Calvaire

A wonderful wine bar-cum-bistro next to the Cirque d'Hiver (Map pp440-1), the Clown Bar is like a museum with its painted ceilings, mosaics on the wall, lovely zinc bar and circus memorabilia that touches on one of our favourite themes: the evil clown. The food is simple and unpretentious traditional French; the charcuterie platter is substantial and goes well with a half-bottle of Brouilly, while the *Parmentier de boudin aux pommes* (black pudding Parmentier with apple) is deservedly one of the restaurant's most popular dishes.

LE GRAND MÉRICOURT
Map pp440-1   French
☎ 01 43 38 94 04; 22 rue de la Folie Méricourt, 11e; starters €11-17, mains €16-19, menus €14 (lunch only), €17 & €27; ⏱ lunch Mon-Fri, dinner to 10.30pm Tue-Sat; Ⓜ St-Ambroise

Young chef Gregory Merten offers his version of *'la cuisine créative'* (basically traditional French that is light on oils and fat and heavy on seasonal produce) in a very English, almost fussy (floral wallpaper, wooden floors, starched white tablecloths and napkins) place just a stone's throw from trendy rue Oberkampf.

LE KRUNG THEP Map pp428-9   Thai
☎ 01 43 66 83 74; 93 rue Julien Lacroix, 20e; starters €7-8.50, mains €8.50-18; ⏱ dinner to 11pm; Ⓜ Pyrénées

Krung Thep means 'Bangkok' in Thai. It's a small – some might say cramped – and kitsch place with all our favourites (and then some: there are dozens and dozens of dishes on the menu): green curries, *tom yum goong* (spicy soup with prawns) and fish or chicken steamed in banana leaves. The steamed shrimp ravioli and curried crab will hit the spot. There is also a generous number of vegetarian dishes (€5.50 to €7).

LE POROKHANE

Map pp428-9 African, Senegalese

☎ 01 40 21 86 74; 3 rue Moret, 11e; starters €5.80, mains €11.50-14.80, menu €15; ⏰ dinner to 2am; Ⓜ Ménilmontant or Parmentier

A large dining room in hues of ochre and terracotta, Le Porokhane is a popular meeting place for Senegalese artists – the clientele have *un peu tendance show-biz*, we're told –and live *kora* (a traditional string instrument) music is not unusual at the weekend. Try the *tiéboudienne*, *yassa* or *mafé*.

LE REPAIRE DE CARTOUCHE

Map pp440-1 French

☎ 01 47 00 25 86; 8 blvd des Filles du Calvaire & 99 rue Amelot, 11e; starters €8-14, mains €18-30, menus lunch €13 & €24; ⏰ lunch & dinner to 11pm Tue-Sat; Ⓜ St-Sébastien Froissart;

With entrances at both front and back, Cartouche's Den – a reference to the 18th-century Parisian 'Robin Hood' Louis-

Dominique Cartouche – looks to the past and the future. It's an old-fashioned place that takes a very modern, innovative approach to French food under the direction of Norman chef Rodolphe Paquin. As its name implies and the rifle on the wall underscores, it focuses on meat and (poached?) game, though there are some excellent fish and shellfish dishes on the menu.

LE TROISIÈME BUREAU

Map pp428-9 French, Café

☎ 01 43 55 87 65; 74 rue de la Folie Méricourt, 11e; starters €540-10.70, mains €12.80-18, menus lunch €11 & €13.30; ⏰ lunch & dinner to midnight Mon-Fri, noon-2am Sat & Sun; Ⓜ Oberkampf

An interesting clientele frequents this pub-cum-bistro, where you can read, listen to music and enjoy Sunday brunch (€15) from noon to 4pm.

LE VILLARET Map pp440-1 French

☎ 01 43 57 89 76; 13 rue Ternaux, 11e; starters €8.50-20, mains €17-35, 2-/3-course menu lunch €21/26; ⏰ lunch Mon-Fri, dinner to 11.30pm Mon-Thu, to 1am Fri & Sat; Ⓜ Parmentier

An excellent neighbourhood bistro serving very rich food, Le Villaret has diners coming from across Paris to sample the house specialities. The *velouté de cèpes à la mousse de foie gras* (cep mushroom soup with foie gras mousse), the *solette au beurre citronné* (baby sole with lemon-flavoured butter) and the *gigot d'agneau de Lozère rôti et son gratin de topinambours* (roast lamb with Jerusalem artichoke gratin) are all recommended but only the chef knows what will be available as he changes the menu daily. Tasting menus can range from around €45, to €80 when truffles are in season.

LE VIN DU ZINC

Map pp440-1 French, Wine

☎ 01 48 06 28 23; 25 rue Oberkampf, 11e; starters €7-10, mains €13-22; ⏰ lunch & dinner to 1pm Tue-Sat; Ⓜ Filles du Calvaire

This distressed-look bistro is the kind of spot every neighbourhood wishes it had – with a blackboard menu that actually changes regularly, plenty of interesting wines and flavoursome food that makes a great excuse to try another *vin*. It's a very relaxed spot and there is usually no need to book.

Produce for sale at La Maison de la Truffe (p298)

LES JUMEAUX Map pp440-1   French

☎ 01 43 14 27 00; 73 rue Amelot, 12e; menus lunch/dinner €27/33; ☻ lunch & dinner to 10.30pm Tue-Sat; Ⓜ St-Sébastien Froissart or Chemin Vert

The 'Twins' is owned and run by a pair of men – Erich and Karl – much changed from their picture, at the entrance, as babies. There's not much to say about the décor except that crockery is different for each person and each course; it's the food that demands attention. Start with *galette de foie gras chaud aux oignons et citrons confits* (buckwheat crepe with warm foie gras and preserved onions and lemons) and move on to the extraordinary flavours offered by the *coquilles Saint-Jacques à la purée de pois cassés, sauce pamplemousse rose* (scallops with split-pea puree and pink-grapefruit sauce). The grand finish has to be the *pastilla de poires aux amandes, sorbet poire* (almond and pear turnover with pear sorbet).

OSSEK GARDEN Map pp428-9   Korean

☎ 01 48 07 16 35; 14 rue Rampon, 11e; starters €6-14.80, barbecue €15.90-17.90, menus €9.50-29.90; ☻ lunch & dinner to 11pm; Ⓜ Oberkampf

Things Korean – especially films – seem to be taking the world by storm these days and Paris is no exception. This place not far from place de la République has excellent barbecues on offer but we particularly like the *bibimbab* (€12 to €17.90), rice served in a sizzling pot topped with thinly sliced beef (or other meat) and cooked with preserved vegetables, then bound by a raw egg and flavoured with chilli-laced soy paste. Staff, in traditional Korean dress, are welcoming.

CHEAP EATS

AU TROU NORMAND Map pp428-9   French

☎ 01 48 05 80 23; 9 rue Jean-Pierre Timbaud, 11e; starters €5.50-12, mains €8.50-16, ☻ lunch & dinner to 11.30pm Sun-Thu, to midnight Fri & Sat; Ⓜ Oberkampf

Ever since a young dynamic team got hold of the 'Norman Hole', it's no longer been the bargain-basement *cafétéria* of the 11e arrondissement that it once was. Still, the food, in keeping with the surrounds, is simple and portions are fairly generous. There are dozens of starters to choose from; main courses include various cuts of beef (tournedos, steak tartare etc) and other meat dishes, served with homemade chips.

DONG HUONG Map pp428-9   Vietnamese

☎ 01 43 57 42 81; 14 rue Louis Bonnet; dishes €5-7.60; ☻ lunch & dinner to 11.30pm Wed-Mon; Ⓜ Belleville

Despite a name that sounds like a Spanish Lothario, this Vietnamese noodle shop-cum-restaurant serves up great bowls of *pho* to rooms full of appreciative regulars. The fact that the regulars are all Asian (and mainly Vietnamese) and the food is coming out so fast is a testament to its authenticity and freshness. A real nonsmoking section is an added and unexpected bonus.

LA PIRAGUA

Map pp440-1   South American, Colombian

☎ 01 40 21 35 98; 6 rue Rochebrune, 11e; starters €5.50-7.50, mains €12-19, menus €18 & €20; ☻ lunch Sun, dinner to 1am daily; Ⓜ St-Ambroise

This small, brightly coloured eatery, which pays homage to a type of canoe, has been here since 1990. It serves such Colombian favourites as various types of *ceviche* (fish marinated in lemon juice) dishes as well as *badeja paisa* (a concoction of chopped meat, kidney beans, rice and the kitchen sink). The list of Chilean wines is excellent, and there's decent canned Latin American music here too.

LAO SIAM Map pp428-9   Thai

☎ 01 40 40 09 68; 49 rue de Belleville, 19e; starters €5.80-9.20, mains €6-21.50; ☻ lunch & dinner to 11.30pm; Ⓜ Belleville

This Thai-Chinese place, with neon lights and spartan décor, looks like any other Asian restaurant in Belleville. But it must be doing something right because it's always packed. There are more than 120 dishes on the menu – from the classic beef and duck with coconut milk and bamboo to the more unusual *méduse à la citronnelle* (jellyfish with lemon grass).

L'AVE MARIA Map pp440-1   Fusion

☎ 01 47 00 61 73; 1 rue Jacquard, 11e; dishes €12-15; ☻ dinner to midnight; Ⓜ Parmentier

This great place is a chic and colourful canteen combining flavours of the southern hemisphere and creating hearty, hybrid and harmonious dishes. You might be treated to *bœuf mijoté aux noyaux de palmes rouges* (beef stew with red palm seeds), served with cassava and baby white aubergine. Tropical fruit, unknown wild grasses, and heavenly vegetation provide a lush garnish and an extra touch of exoticism. The music livens up towards midnight and dancing carries on to 2am.

NEW NIOULLAVILLE

Map pp428-9   Chinese
☎ 01 40 21 96 18; 32 rue de l'Orillon, 11e; starters €4.90-7.50, mains €7.50-16, menus €7-14; ☺ lunch & dinner to 1am; Ⓜ Belleville or Goncourt
This cavernous, 400-seat place resembles the Hong Kong stock exchange on a busy day. The food is a bit of a mishmash – dim sum sits next to beef satay, as do scallops with black bean alongside Singapore noodles, though whether they do so comfortably is another matter. Order carefully and you should be able to approach authenticity. Rice and noodle dishes are between €6.90 and €9.

REUAN THAI Map pp428-9   Thai
☎ 01 43 55 15 82; 36 rue de l'Orillon, 11e; starters €4.50-13, mains €7.50-15, lunch buffet €8; ☺ lunch & dinner to 11.30pm; Ⓜ Belleville
This fragrant place offers some of the most authentic Thai food in Paris and has all your favourite Thai dishes, including soups. About a half-dozen of the choices are vegetarian. Décor is on the kitsch side but we weren't here for the figurines and the bolsters piled a mile high.

SELF-CATERING

Supermarkets in these two areas include **Franprix Jean-Pierre Timbaud branch** (Map pp428–9; 23 rue Jean-Pierre Timbaud, 11e; Ⓜ Oberkampf) and **Franprix Jules Ferry branch** (Map pp428–9; 28 blvd Jules Ferry, 11e; Ⓜ République or Goncourt); **Marché Belleville** (p52) is one of the most exotic in Paris.

GARE DE LYON, NATION & BERCY

The waterfront southwest of Gare de Lyon has had a new lease of life in recent years. The development of the old wine warehouses in **Bercy Village** (p138) attract winers and diners till the wee hours. There are loads of decent restaurants on the roads fanning out from huge place de la Nation.

À LA BANANE IVOIRIENNE

Map pp440-1   African, Côte d'Ivoire
☎ 01 43 70 49 90; 10 rue de la Forge Royale, 11e; starters €4.50-7, mains €10-15.50, menu €16.50; ☺ dinner to midnight Tue-Sat; Ⓜ Ledru Rollin
West African specialities are served in a relaxed and friendly setting, with lots of West African gewgaws on display. There's live African music in the cellar restaurant starting at 10pm on Friday.

ATHANOR Map pp446-7   Romanian
☎ 01 43 43 49 15; 4 rue Crozatier, 12e; starters €8-12, mains €15-21, menus lunch/dinner €12/23; ☺ lunch & dinner to 11.30pm Tue-Sat; Ⓜ Reuilly Diderot
It's not easy to get a fix of Romanian cuisine in Paris, but Athanor can provide. The décor (puppets, red curtains and candle light) is theatrical in the extreme; grab a vodka (or two) and tune in to the baroque music. Try the grilled blinis with *tarama* (fish roe dip) and herrings in cream. Seasoned freshwater river fish (pike, sturgeon, carp and eel) is the speciality of the house though you mustn't miss the *sarmale* (stuffed cabbage), the national dish.

AU VIEUX CHÊNE

Map pp440-1   French
☎ 01 43 71 67 69; 7 rue du Dahomey, 11e; starters €8-16, mains €17.50-25, menus €13 (lunch only) & €29; ☺ lunch & dinner to 10.30pm Mon-Fri, dinner to 11pm Sat; Ⓜ Faidherbe Chaligny
Along a quiet side street in a neighbourhood full of traditional woodworking studios, 'At the Old Oak' offers an excellent seasonal menu and some well-chosen wines. The surrounds are fabulous – and important. Three of the cast-iron columns holding the place up are classified monuments.

CAFÉ CANNELLE

Map pp440-1   North African, Moroccan
☎ 01 43 70 48 25; 1bis rue de la Forge Royale, 11e; starters €5.50-10.50, mains €11.50-15; ☺ dinner to midnight; Ⓜ Ledru Rollin
This is a festive Moroccan restaurant run by an Algerian maths professor who decided to branch out. The restaurant and its open kitchen do couscous and especially *tajines* with a twist – with olives and preserved lemon, fresh dates etc. For dessert try the orange salad flavoured with cinnamon.

CAFFÈ COSY

Map pp422-3   French, Café

☎ 01 43 43 08 21; 50 av de St-Mandé, 12e; starters €7-16, mains €15-22; Ⓥ 7.30am-10.30pm; Ⓜ Picpus

We love this, well, cosy café-restaurant with the great terrace south of place de la Nation. There are nice little touches throughout, including lovely art work on the walls and unusually designed coffee cups on the table. The menu includes simple but well-prepared dishes like grilled spiced salmon (€19) as well as simple things like wraps (€13 to €14) and tortillas rolled with salad, guacamole and chicken or salmon. A brunch *formule* (€26) is available between 10am and 4pm.

CHEZ RAMULAUD

Map pp440-1   French

☎ 01 43 72 23 29; 269 rue du Faubourg St-Antoine, 11e; starters €9-13, mains €18-23, menu €29; Ⓥ lunch Mon-Fri, dinner to 11pm Mon-Sat; Ⓜ Faidherbe Chaligny

With its peaceful, retro atmosphere, this enormous establishment is reminiscent of one of those famous provincial restaurants. The blackboard offerings are not overly adventurous but they are comforting and substantial – daily soups, terrine, *œufs cocotte aux champignons de saison* (coddled eggs with seasonal mushrooms). For mains, the fish dishes are usually winners.

COMME COCHONS

Map pp446-7   French

☎ 01 43 42 43 36; 135 rue de Charenton, 12e; starters €6.50-10, mains €15-19, 2-/3-course menu lunch €12/15; Ⓥ lunch & dinner to 11pm Mon-Sat; Ⓜ Gare de Lyon

You may not be attracted by the name ('Like Pigs'), but the excellent traditional dishes and the sunny terrace at Comme Cochons will undoubtedly change your mind. This bistro is like a page out of the past – only the contemporary paintings on the wall by local artists will keep you in the present. Among the specialities are *paleron aux endives meunières* (beef served with endives) and *ganache de chocolat noir aux grillotines* (a rich dark-chocolate concoction). There's also live jazz on Thursday evening.

KHUN AKORN Map pp422-3   Thai

☎ 01 43 56 20 03; 8 av de Taillebourg, 11e; starters €11-16, mains €13-17; Ⓥ lunch & dinner to 11pm Tue-Sun; Ⓜ Nation

This Thai eatery near place de la Nation is an oasis of sophistication and good taste – in every sense. Among the traditional dishes, the *tom yum*, and the beef and chicken satays with scrumptious peanut sauce are outstanding. More innovative offerings include *fruits de mer grillés sauce barbecue maison* (grilled seafood with barbecue sauce) or the *larmes du tigre* (tears of the tiger; grilled fillet of beef marinated in honey and herbs). In fine weather, try the terrace upstairs.

LA MUSE VIN Map pp440-1   French, Wine

☎ 01 40 09 93 05; 101 rue de Charonne; starters €8, mains €18, menus lunch €9.50-15.50; Ⓥ lunch & dinner to 11pm Mon-Sat; Ⓜ Charonne

Primarily a wine bar and bottle shop, the 'Wine Muse' does food too and its offerings go well beyond plates of cold meats and cheese; the evening menu changes every three weeks. It takes its wines very seriously, though, so keep that foremost in your mind.

LE MANSOURIA

Map pp440-1   North African, Moroccan

☎ 01 43 71 00 16; 11 rue Faidherbe, 11e; starters €7-16, mains €15-25, menu €30, with wine €46; Ⓥ lunch Wed-Sat, dinner to 11pm Mon-Sat; Ⓜ Faidherbe Chaligny

This is an especially attractive Moroccan restaurant that serves excellent milk-fed steamed lamb, if not the best *kascsou* (couscous) and *touagin* (tajine) in town. Someone in your group should at least order the *mourouzia*, lamb simmered in a complex combination of more than two dozen spices and served with a honey sauce. Be sure to book ahead.

LE TEMPS AU TEMPS

Map pp440-1   French

☎ 01 43 79 63 40; 3 rue Paul Bert, 11e; 3-course menu €26; Ⓥ lunch & dinner to 10.30pm Tue-Sat; Ⓜ Faidherbe Chaligny

This tiny little place with about 10 tables has a very exciting menu that changes daily; some of the dishes have been inspired by the cuisine of the great Catalan chef Ferran Adria. Come here for lunch; you're much more likely to get a seat.

LE VIADUC CAFÉ

Map pp446-7   International, Café

☎ 01 44 74 70 70; 43 av Daumesnil, 12e; starters €7-14, mains €13-15, menu lunch €17; ☽ 9am-2am; Ⓜ Gare de Lyon

This New York-style café-bar with a terrace in one of the glassed-in arches of the **Viaduc des Arts** (p138) is an excellent spot to while away the early hours and enjoy brunch (€25) with live jazz from noon to 4pm on Sunday.

L'ÉBAUCHOIR Map pp446-7   French

☎ 01 43 42 49 31; 45 rue de Cîteaux, 12e; starters €6.40-8.30, mains €14-21; ☽ lunch & dinner to 11pm Mon-Sat; Ⓜ Faidherbe Chaligny

This convivial neighbourhood workers' eatery attracts a loyal clientele who mix with an 'outside' crowd who have recently discovered it. The usual menu of bistro food is well prepared and dishes such as marinated herrings and *foie de veau au miel* (veal liver with honey sauce) keep customers coming back.

L'ÉCAILLER DU BISTROT

Map pp440-1   French, Seafood

☎ 01 43 72 76 77; 22 rue Paul Bert, 11e; starters €10-12, mains €20-30; ☽ lunch Tue-Sat, dinner to 11.30pm Mon-Sat; Ⓜ Faidherbe Chaligny

Oyster lovers should make a beeline for the 'Bistro Shucker', a neighbourhood resto done up in nautical kitsch that serves up to a dozen varieties of fresh bivalves, freshly shucked and accompanied by a little lemon juice. Other seafood delights are treated with equal respect – such as minute-cooked tuna steak with sesame oil and the extravagant lobster *menu* (€45).

LES AMOGNES Map pp446-7   French

☎ 01 43 72 73 05; 243 rue du Faubourg St-Antoine, 11e; starters €8-18, mains €12-16, menus lunch/dinner €29/33; ☽ lunch Tue-Fri, dinner to 11pm Tue-Sat; Ⓜ Faidherbe Chaligny

This quiet place with its faux cottage frontage offers discreet service and an atmosphere that is *correcte* (proper), even provincial. A meal here is a quintessentially French – rather than Parisian – experience: *côte de veau cuite sur le sel* (veal chop cooked in salt), *ragoût de fèves et pois gourmands* (vegetable stew of pulses). Chef Thierry Coué is especially adept at desserts, especially traditional ones like *gâteau Breton* (butter cake from Brittany). The lunch plat du jour is €19.

TOP FIVE GARE DE LYON, NATION & BERCY RESTAURANTS

- Comme Cochons (p227)
- Le Temps au Temps (p227)
- Le Viaduc Café (left)
- L'Écailler du Bistro (left)
- L'Oulette (below)

L'OULETTE

Map pp446-7   French, Southwest

☎ 01 40 02 02 12; 15 place Lachambeaudie, 12e; starters €14-21, mains €22-34, 2-/3-course menu lunch €25/32, with wine €47; ☽ lunch & dinner to 10.15pm Mon-Fri; Ⓜ Cour St-Émilion

A distance relative of **Baracane** (p184) near Bastille, this is a lovely restaurant with a terrace overlooking a pretty church in a rather dreary neighbourhood. Chef Marcel Baudis' *menu du marché* (market menu) might include *soupe de poisson à la crème de coquillages au safran* (fish soup with saffron cream) and *la chartreuse de queue de bœuf braisée aux poivrons* (ox tail braised with leeks).

CHEAP EATS
LA PARTIE DE CAMPAGNE

Map p449   French

☎ 01 43 40 44 00; 36 cour St-Émilion, 12e; dishes €9.50-13; ☽ 8am-10.30pm Sun-Tue, to 11pm Wed-Sat; Ⓜ Cour St-Émilion

Located in one of the old *chais* (wine warehouses) of Bercy, the 'Country Outing' serves some of the best food in the area. Business people and strollers from the Jardin de Bercy sit cheek by jowl at a large communal table set up at the back of the room, and order from a menu that includes soups, tartines and pies. It's also a great place for breakfast (€5.50 to €6.90). The inviting terrace is open in the warmer months.

LE PURE CAFÉ

Map pp440-1   French, International

☎ 01 43 71 47 22; 14 rue Jean Macé, 11e; starters €8.40-15, mains €15-20, menus €10 & €14 (lunch only), €25.50; ☽ lunch & dinner to midnight; Ⓜ Charonne

This restaurant that moonlights as a café (open 7am to 2am Monday to Friday, 8am to 2am Saturday and noon to midnight

Diners at Tricotin (p230)

Sunday) has a modern kitchen (some dishes veer toward 'world') and an old café that just must be a national monument. Best of all it's open on Sunday.

SELF-CATERING

West of Parc de Bercy there's a **Franprix** (Map p449; 3 rue Baron le Roy, 12e; ⊗ 8.30am-8.30pm Tue-Sun; Ⓜ Cour St-Émilion) that's open on Sunday .

13E ARRONDISSEMENT & CHINATOWN

Until the opening of the high-tech Météor metro line (No 14) linking Gare St-Lazare with the Bibliothèque Nationale de France François Mitterrand, few travellers ventured as far south as this unless they were in search of authentic Chinese food. But all that has changed. Dozens of Asian restaurants – not just Chinese ones – line the main streets of Paris' Chinatown, including av de Choisy, av d'Ivry and rue Baudricourt.

Another wonderful district for an evening out is the Butte aux Cailles southwest of place d'Italie. It's chock-a-block with interesting addresses.

CHEZ JACKY Map p449   French
☎ 01 45 83 71 55; 109 rue du Dessous des Berges, 13e; starters €18-20, mains €18-29, menu €30, with wine €43; ⊗ lunch & dinner to 10.30pm Mon-Fri; Ⓜ Bibliothèque
In the shadow of the national library, Chez Jacky is a serious, traditional restaurant with thoughtful service and a nice old-fashioned provincial atmosphere. The three brothers in charge know how to find good regional produce and present it with great panache, even if originality isn't their cardinal virtue.

LA CHINE MASSÉNA
Map pp422-3   Chinese
☎ 01 45 83 98 88; 18 av de Choisy, 13e; soups & starters €4.10-11, mains €6.10-13.50; ⊗ lunch & dinner to 11pm; Ⓜ Porte de Choisy
This enormous restaurant, which specialises in Cantonese and Chiu Chow cuisine, is our current favourite place in Chinatown and to ensure it would have good joss for the coming year we fed the dragon lettuce at the last Lunar New Year celebrations. The dim sum here is especially good and women still go around the dining area with trolleys calling out their wares.

TOP FIVE 13E & 15E ARRONDISSEMENTS RESTAURANTS

- Chez Gladines (right)
- Kim Anh (opposite)
- La Chine Masséna (p229)
- Le Temps des Cérises (below)
- Le Troquet (opposite)

L'AUDIERNES

Map p449   French, Brasserie

☎ 01 44 24 86 23; 22 rue Louise Weiss, 13e; starters €4-13, mains €10.20-14, menu €12.50; ⓧ lunch Mon-Sat; Ⓜ Chevaleret

In an annexe of the Department of the Economy & Finance, this brasserie-bar serves well-prepared and traditional French dishes to demanding civil servants. The contemporary décor gives the place a lively feel; the menu is good (although hardly original), featuring such dishes as *bœuf à l'échalote* (beef with shallots), *pavé de rumsteck* (thick-cut rump steak), *faux-filet* (beef sirloin) and a range of main-course salads with cutesy names. There's also a lovely terrace where you can sit on sunny days.

L'AVANT-GOÛT Map p448   French, Bistro

☎ 01 53 80 24 00; 26 rue Bobillot, 13e; starters/ mains €9.5/16, menus €14 (lunch only) & €31; ⓧ lunch & dinner to 11pm Tue-Fri; Ⓜ Place d'Italie

A prototype of the Parisian 'neo-bistro' (classical yet modern), the 'Foretaste' has chef Christophe Beaufront serving some of the most inventive modern cuisine around. It can get noisy, however, and there are occasional lapses in service but the food is well worth it. For starters, we recommend the *ravioles de thon et de morue avec velouté de crustacés* (tuna and cod ravioli with a seafood velouté sauce) followed, in season, by the excellent pot-au-feu.

LE TEMPS DES CÉRISES Map p448   French

☎ 01 45 89 69 48; 18-20 rue de la Butte aux Cailles, 13e; starters €4.50-16, mains €10-23, menus lunch/dinner €14.50/22.50; ⓧ lunch Mon-Fri, dinner to 11.30pm Mon-Fri, to midnight Sat; Ⓜ Corvisart or Place d'Italie

The 'Time of Cherries' (ie 'days of wine and roses' to English speakers), an easygoing restaurant run by a workers' cooperative for three decades now, keeps regulars coming back for more with its good, solid fare (rabbit with mustard, steak and chips) and low prices. It's in the centre of the Butte aux Cailles quarter and provides the quintessential Parisian night out.

CHEAP EATS

CHEZ GLADINES Map p448   French, Basque

☎ 01 45 80 70 10; 30 rue des Cinq Diamants, 13e; starters €4.50-9, mains €7.30-11, menu lunch €10; ⓧ lunch & dinner to midnight Sun-Tue, to 1am Wed-Sat; Ⓜ Corvisart

This lively Basque bistro in the heart of the Buttes aux Cailles quarter is always a hoot and you're bound to meet someone at one of the communal tables. Most people come for the enormous 'meal-in-a-bowl' salads (€5 to €9), but the traditional Basque specialities, such as *pipérade* and *poulet basque* (chicken cooked with tomatoes, onions, peppers and white wine), are also worth consideration.

LA FLEUVE DE CHINE

Map pp422-3   Chinese

☎ 01 45 82 06 88; 15 av de Choisy, 13e; starters €3.50-9, mains €7-15; ⓧ lunch & dinner to 11pm Fri-Wed; Ⓜ Porte de Choisy

Here you'll find the most authentic Cantonese and Hakka food in Paris and, as is typical, both the surroundings and the service are forgettable. Go for the superb dishes cooked in clay pots. La Fleuve de Chine can also be reached through the Tour Bergame housing estate at 130 blvd Masséna.

TRICOTIN Map pp422-3   Chinese, Thai

☎ 01 45 84 74 44 (Chinese), ☎ 01 45 85 51 52 (Southeast Asia); 15 av de Choisy, 13e; meals €8-15; ⓧ 9am-11.30pm; Ⓜ Porte de Choisy

If you're going into Chinatown and want something cheap and cheerful, Tricotin, in a dreary 13e housing estate, offers two dining areas to satisfy your craving for Asian fare. On the left is the Southeast Asian room, offering decent green curries and Vietnamese spring rolls, while the one on the right does a roaring trade with its dim sum, duck dishes and soups. The Chinese section is open daily, but the Southeast Asian one closes on Tuesday.

15E ARRONDISSEMENT

Solidly working class until well after WWII, the 15e arrondissement has become more gentrified and residential over the years. Av de la Motte-Picquet, blvd Pasteur and av Félix Faure are peaceful residential places, but the 15e arrondissement offers much more than bourgeois homes and institutions. Parisians flock to the shops and restaurants that line rue de la Convention, rue de Vaugirard, rue St-Charles, rue du Commerce and those south of blvd de Grenelle.

FEYROUZ

Map pp434-5   Middle Eastern, Lebanese

☎ 01 45 78 07 02; 8 rue de Lourmel, 15e; starters €7-12.50, mains €17.90-19.50, menus lunch €11 & €15.50, dinner €23; ⓨ 7am-2am; Ⓜ Dupleix
This bright, busy *traiteur* (delicatessen) has excellent Lebanese meze and other dishes to take away and a small restaurant in the back where you can enjoy them *sur place* (on the spot). The food and the surrounds are a cut above the usual Lebanese restaurant.

KIM ANH Map pp434-5   Vietnamese

☎ 01 45 79 40 96; 49 av Émile Zola, 15e; starters €12-15, mains €20-40, menu €34; ⓨ dinner to 11.15pm Tue-Sun; Ⓜ Charles Michels
The antithesis of the typically Parisian canteen-style Vietnamese restaurant, Kim Anh greets its customers with tapestries, white tablecloths and fresh flowers. What's more, the freshness of the food, elaborate presentation and quality service make eating here a pleasure. The *émincé de bœuf à la citronnelle* (beef with lemon grass) is a skilful combination of flavours and the *éventail de brochettes au bœuf, poulet et porc* (assortment of beef, chicken and pork satays) offers a variety of tastes. For something really sensational try caramelised langoustine.

LA GITANE Map pp434-5   French

☎ 01 47 34 62 92; 53bis av de la Motte-Picquet, 15e; starters €4.90-14.70, mains €14.40-18.70, menu lunch from €19; ⓨ lunch & dinner to 11pm Mon-Sat; Ⓜ La Motte-Picquet Grenelle
Over the past two decades the 'Gypsy' has established itself as an ideal spot to have lunch. While not exceptional, everything here bears the mark of good taste and

high quality and the place is always packed with regular locals and expats over from the Unesco building. The *terrine de Saint-Jacques à la sauce aigrelette* (scallop terrine with a vinegary sauce) is a nice starter and, in winter, a favourite main dish is *cassoulet avec ses haricots tarbais* (cassoulet with Tarbes beans; €18.90).

LAL QILA Map pp434-5   Indian

☎ 01 45 75 68 40; 88 av Émile Zola, 15e; starters €4.50-9.60, mains €8.70-12.80, menus €12.50 (lunch only), €21.50 & €25.50; ⓨ lunch & dinner to 11.30pm; Ⓜ Charles Michels
Outside it's Disneyland meets the Red Fort of Delhi; inside the stucco colonnade and multicoloured mirrors make this restaurant feel like a true Bollywood set. Kitsch it may be, but the food is hardly B grade. Main roles are played by such classics as fish curry or chicken biryani as well as less known ones like chicken *shami kebab*. Special award goes to *shahi korma*, lamb served with cream of cashew flavoured with cardamom and cinnamon.

LE TIPAZA

Map pp434-5   North African, Moroccan

☎ 01 45 79 22 25; 150 av Émile Zola, 15e; starters €4.50-12, mains €12.60-18; ⓨ lunch & dinner to midnight; Ⓜ Av Émile Zola
This relatively classy Moroccan place has good couscous (€12.60 to €18.80), *tajines* (€14.60 to €16.50) and grills (€13.80 to €18) done on a wood stove. Service is warm and very efficient.

LE TROQUET Map pp434-5   French, Bistro

☎ 01 45 66 89 00; 21 rue François Bonvin, 15e; 2-/3-course menu lunch €24/28, dinner €30 & €38; ⓨ lunch & dinner to 11.30pm Tue-Sat; Ⓜ Sèvres Lecourbe
Basque chef Christian Etchebest takes 'ordinary' things and puts a spin on them: veal bouillon flavoured with aniseed and served with vegetable quenelles, caramelised pork on puréed vegetables, and seared whiting on a bed of fresh green beans. Breathtaking presentation, startling tastes and a restaurant that changes its menu every day according to what's on offer at the market will get our vote any time. The décor is nothing special, but top-flight service brightens things up.

L'OS À MOËLLE Map pp434-5   French, Bistro

☎ 01 45 57 27 27; 3 rue Vasco de Gama, 15e; menus lunch/dinner €32/38; 🕙 lunch Tue-Sat, dinner to 11.30pm Tue-Thu, to midnight Fri & Sat; Ⓜ Lourmel

The 'Marrowbone' is well worth a trip to this far-flung corner of the 15e and chef Thierry Faucher (ex-Hotel Crillon) offers one of the best and most affordable *menus dégustation* (sampling menus) in town. The six-course menu (portions are modest) could include such delicacies as scallops with coriander, sea bass in cumin butter, half a quail with endives and chestnuts and the chef's award-winning chocolate quenelle with saffron cream.

SAWADEE Map pp434-5   Thai

☎ 01 45 77 68 90; 53 av Émile Zola, 15e; starters €7-14, mains €12-15, menu lunch €13.50; 🕙 lunch & dinner to 10.30pm Mon-Sat; Ⓜ Charles Michels

For 20 years this well-known restaurant has been bidding *sawadee* (welcome) to lovers of Thai food. The sophisticated cuisine more than makes up for the rather impersonal décor. You'll be able to enjoy the classic dishes of Siam, such as prawn or chicken soup flavoured with lemon grass, spicy beef salad (a real treat), or satay sticks (chicken, beef, lamb and pork) with peanut sauce.

CHEAP EATS
EL FARÈS

Map pp434-5   Middle Eastern, Lebanese

☎ 01 47 83 54 38, 01 42 79 88 55; 166 blvd de Grenelle, 15e; starters €5-6.50, mains €11-15.50, menus €9 & €11 (lunch only), €20; 🕙 lunch & dinner to 11pm Tue-Sun; Ⓜ Cambronne

The décor's banal but who comes for the surrounds? The tabouli, *mtabal* (aubergine purée with sesame and lemon) and *labni* (cow's milk cheese) make delicious starters or order the mixed meze for €12. There are also delicious falafels, chicken wings and layered cheese dishes served warm. Big eaters will go for the *chiche taouk* (kebab of marinated chicken fillets) or the traditional *kefta* (mincemeat kebab with onions and parsley).

SELF-CATERING

Two excellent open-air markets in the 15e are Marché Grenelle and Marché St-Charles (p52). Supermarkets include Monoprix (Map pp434-5; 2 rue du Commerce, 15e; 🕙 9am-10pm

Mon-Sat; Ⓜ La Motte Picquet-Grenelle) and Franprix (Map pp434-5; 34 rue de Lourmel, 15e; Ⓜ Dupleix).

MONTMARTRE & PIGALLE

The 18e arrondissement, where you'll find Montmartre and the northern half of place Pigalle, thrives on crowds and little else. When you've got Sacré Coeur, place du Tertre and its portrait artists and Paris literally at your feet, who needs decent restaurants? But that's not to say everything is a write-off in this well-trodden tourist area. You just have to pick and choose a bit more carefully than elsewhere in Paris. The restaurants along rue des Trois Frères, for example, are generally a much better bet than their touristy counterparts in and around place du Tertre.

À LA CLOCHE D'OR Map p432   French

☎ 01 48 74 48 88; 3 rue Mansart, 9e; 2-/3-course menus €25/29; 🕙 lunch & dinner to 4am Mon-Sat; Ⓜ Blanche or Pigalle

This place, at the foot of the Butte Montmartre since 1928 and once the property of actress Jeanne Moreau's parents, is the antithesis of where the 'fooding' crowd (see p177) hangs out. Decorated in 'old bistro' style with photos of stars of stage (mostly) and screen (some) plastering the walls, the 'Gold Bell' serves up favourites like steak tartare (its signature dish), massive steaks and fish of the day. Order the baked Camembert and, in winter, sit by the fire.

AU PETIT BUDAPEST

Map p432   Hungarian

☎ 01 46 06 10 34; 96 rue des Martyrs, 18e; starters €9.50-17.50, mains €10.50-18.50, menu €17.50; 🕙 lunch Sat & Sun, dinner to midnight Tue-Sun; Ⓜ Abbesses

With old etchings and the requisite Gypsy music, the owner (a former artist) has recreated the atmosphere of a late-19th-century Hungarian *csárda* (traditional inn). From the *paprikash au bœuf épicé* (beef paprika) to the *gâteau au fromage blanc* (cream cheese cake), there are refined versions of popular Hungarian dishes. The *crepe à la Hortobagy* (crepe with meat and crème fraîche) is delicious.

AUX NÉGOCIANTS Map p432 French

☎ 01 46 06 15 11; 27 rue Lambert, 18e; starters €6-10, mains €12-15; ⏱ lunch Mon-Fri, dinner to 10.30pm daily; Ⓜ Château Rouge

This old-style wine bar is far enough from the madding crowds of Montmartre to attract a faithful local clientele. Patés, terrines, traditional mains like *bœuf bourguinon*, and wine paid for according to consumption – it feels like the Paris of the 1950s.

CHEZ PLUMEAU Map p432 French

☎ 01 46 06 26 29; 4 place du Calvaire, 18e; starters €8-16, mains €15-18, menu lunch €16; ⏱ lunch & dinner to midnight daily Apr-Oct, lunch & dinner to 11pm Thu-Mon Nov-Mar; Ⓜ Abbesses

Once the popular Auberge du Coucou restaurant and cabaret, today's 'Feather Duster' caters mainly to tourists fresh from having their portraits done on place du Tertre. But for a tourist haunt it's not too bad and the back terrace is great on a warm spring afternoon. Plats du jour are a snip at about €14.

CHEZ TOINETTE Map p432 French

☎ 01 42 54 44 36; 20 rue Germain Pilon, 18e; starters €5-8, mains €14-20; ⏱ dinner to 11pm Tue-Sat; Ⓜ Abbesses

The atmosphere of this convivial restaurant is rivalled only by its fine cuisine. In the heart of one of the capital's most touristy neighbourhoods, Chez Toinette has kept alive the tradition of old Montmartre with its simplicity and culinary expertise. Game lovers won't be disappointed; *perdreau* (partridge), *biche* (doe), *chevreuil* (roebuck) and the famous *filet de canard à la sauge et au miel* (fillet of duck with sage and honey) are the house specialities and go well with a glass of Bordeaux.

IL DUCA Map p432 Italian

☎ 01 46 06 71 98; 26 rue Yvonne le Tac, 18e; starters €11-14, mains €15-18, menu lunch €13; ⏱ lunch & dinner to 11.30pm daily; Ⓜ Abbesses

This intimate little Italian restaurant has good, straightforward food, including homemade pastas (€11 to €15). The selection of Italian wine and cheese is phenomenal and themed weeks, with various regions and types of produce, are scheduled throughout the year.

LA MASCOTTE Map p432 French, Seafood

☎ 01 46 06 28 15; 52 rue des Abbesses, 18e; starters €6.50-12, mains €17-23, menu €17.50 (lunch only) & €29; ⏱ lunch & dinner to 11.30pm Tue-Sat; Ⓜ Abbesses

La Mascotte is a small, unassuming spot much frequented by regulars who can't get enough of its seafood and regional cuisine. In winter, don't hesitate to sample the wide variety of seafood, especially the shellfish. In summer sit on the terrace and savour the delicious *fricassée de pétoncles* (fricassee of queen scallops). Meat lovers won't be disappointed with various regional delicacies such as Auvergne sausage and Troyes *andouillette* (sausage made of pork/veal tripe). Plats du jour are between €14 and €16.

Café Marly (p180)

TOP FIVE MONTMARTRE & PIGALLE RESTAURANTS

- À La Cloche d'Or (p232)
- Chez Toinette (p233)
- La Table d'Anvers (below)
- La Maison Rose (right)
- Relais Gascon (opposite)

LA TABLE D'ANVERS

Map p432   French

☎ 01 48 78 35 21; 2 place d'Anvers, 9e; starters €12, mains €18, 2-/3-course menus lunch €15/23, dinner €26/33; ☽ lunch Tue-Fri, dinner to 11pm Mon-Sat; Ⓜ Anvers
Just far enough off the Montmartre tourist track to keep the hordes away, this local favourite overlooking a stylish (and grassy) square offers some great dishes and some very decent fixed-price *menus*. The dishes are contemporary French, with Mediterranean (and especially Provençale) influences.

LE MAQUIS

Map p432   French

☎ 01 42 59 76 07; 69 rue Caulaincourt, 18e; starters €10, mains €16, menus €19 & €29; ☽ lunch & dinner to 10pm Mon-Sat; Ⓜ Lamarck Caulaincourt
If you're in Montmartre and despairing over the choice of eateries (overpriced with poor service) there, give the Butte the boot and head the short distance north to rue Caulaincourt and this typical bistro with *cuisine traditionelle* (traditional cooking). The name suggests both the French Resistance (unlikely connection) and the herbal underbrush of Corsica, which might explain some of the Mediterranean-inspired dishes.

LE REFUGE DES FONDUS

Map p432   French, Savoie

☎ 01 42 55 22 65; 17 rue des Trois Frères, 18e; menu €16; ☽ dinner to 2am daily; Ⓜ Abbesses or Anvers
This odd place has been a Montmartre favourite for more than four decades. The single *menu* provides an aperitif, hors d'oeuvre, red wine (or beer or soft drink) in a *biberon* (baby bottle) and a good quantity of either *fondue savoyarde* (melted cheese) or *fondue bourguignonne* (meat fondue; minimum two people). Dessert is €2. The last sitting is at midnight.

CHEAP EATS
AU GRAIN DE FOLIE

Map p432   Vegetarian

☎ 01 42 58 15 57; 24 rue de la Vieuville, 18e; dishes €10-12, menus €12 & €16; ☽ lunch & dinner to 10.30pm Mon-Sat, 12.30-10.30am Sun; Ⓜ Abbesses
This hole-in-the-wall macrobiotic and organic eatery has excellent vegetarian pâté and vegan quiche. There are also lots of good dippy things like hummus and guacamole.

KASTOORI

Map pp428-9   Indian, Pakistani

☎ 01 44 53 06 10; 4 place Gustave Toudouze, 9e; starters €3-6, mains €8-11; menus lunch/dinner €8/15; ☽ lunch Tue-Sun, dinner to 11.30pm daily; Ⓜ St-Georges
This eatery just a stone's throw from place Pigalle is a delight in summer, with its large terrace looking onto a quiet, leafy square. The excellent value set *menus* include three generous courses; if you want one dish go for the excellent vegetable biryani.

LA MAISON ROSE   Map p432   French

☎ 01 42 57 66 75; 2 rue de l'Abreuvoir, 18e; starters €7.80-13, mains €14.50-16.50, menu €16.50; ☽ lunch & dinner to 11pm daily Mar-Oct, lunch Thu-Mon, dinner to 9pm Mon, Thu-Sat Nov-Feb; Ⓜ Lamarck Caulaincourt
Looking for the quintessential Montmartre bistro in a house that was the subject of a lithograph by Utrillo (p172)? Head for the tiny 'Pink House' just north of the Place du Tertre.

LE MONO   Map p432   African, Togolese

☎ 01 46 06 99 20; 40 rue Véron, 18e; dishes €5-10.50; ☽ dinner to 1am Thu-Tue; Ⓜ Abbesses or Blanche
Le Mono offers Togolese and other West African specialities, including *lélé* (flat, steamed cakes of white beans and shrimp; €5), *azidessi* (beef or chicken with peanut sauce; €9.50), *gbekui* (goulash with spinach, onions, beef, fish and shrimp; €10.50) and *djenkoumé* (grilled chicken with semolina noodles; €10.50). Roast milk-fed pork is a house speciality served on Saturday and Sunday evening only. The rum-based punches are excellent.

LE SOLEIL GOURMAND

Map p432   French, Mediterranean

☎ 01 42 51 00 50; 10 rue Ravignan, 18e; dishes €8-12.50; ⏱ lunch Tue-Sat, dinner to 11pm Mon-Sat; Ⓜ Abbesses

This cheery boutique and restaurant exudes the south of France with its warm décor and simple dishes like salads, savoury tarts and baked *bricks* (stuffed fritters). Treat yourself to the *tarte aux oignons, poivrons, raisins et pignons grillés* (tart with onion, green peppers, grapes and grilled pine nuts) and any of the homemade ice creams: gingerbread, almond milk, tiramisu or wild peach.

RELAIS GASCON

Map p432   French, Southwest

☎ 01 42 58 58 22; 6 rue des Abbesses, 18e; starters €5.50-11, mains €9-12, menus €8 (lunch only), €13.50 & €19.50; ⏱ lunch & dinner to midnight; Ⓜ Abbesses

Just a short stroll from the place des Abbesses, the Relais Gascon has a re-laxed atmosphere and authentic regional cuisine at rock-bottom prices. The *salade géante* (giant salad, a house speciality) and the *confit sud-ouest* (southwest confit) will satisfy big eaters, while the traditional Basque *pipérade* and *tartiflette* are equally tasty and filling. After, try the traditional *gâteau basque* (a simple layer cake filled with cream and cherry jam) or a *crème brûlée*.

SELF-CATERING

Towards place Pigalle there are lots of groceries, many of them open until late at night; try the side streets leading off blvd de Clichy (eg rue Lepic). Heading south from blvd de Clichy, rue des Martyrs, 9e, is lined with food shops almost all the way to the Notre Dame de Lorette metro station. Supermarkets in the area include **8 à Huit** (Map p432; 24 rue Lepic, 18e; Ⓜ Abbesses) and **Ed l'Épicier** (Map p432; 6 blvd de Clichy, 18e; Ⓜ Pigalle).

Eating

MONTMARTRE & PIGALLE

FRESH TARTS & SWEET MEMORIES

Parisians love *sucreries* (sweet or sugary things) and fruit and, judging from the eye-catching and saliva-inducing window displays at pastry shops throughout the city, they can't get enough of either in combination. But trying to compile a list of the best *pâtisseries* in Paris is like setting out to determine the length of a piece of string – it can just go on and on. We asked half a dozen of our sweet-toothed friends to choose their favourites, based on the *spécialités de la maison* (house specialities). The proof, as they say, is in the pudding.

Au Levain du Marais (Map pp440–1; ☎ 01 42 78 07 31; 32 rue de Turenne, 3e; ⏱ 7am-8.30pm Mon-Sat; Ⓜ St-Paul) Specialities include *tartes aux fruits* (fruit tarts), *macarons au citron* (lemon macaroons) and two-dozen speciality breads.

Dalloyau (Map pp426–7; ☎ 01 42 99 90 00; 101 rue du Faubourg St-Honoré, 8e; ⏱ 8.30am-9pm; Ⓜ St-Philippe du Roule) Specialities include *pain aux raisins* (raisin bread), *millefeuille* (pastry layered with cream) and *tarte au citron* (lemon tart).

Florence Finkelsztajn (Map pp436–7; ☎ 01 48 87 92 85; 24 rue des Écouffes, 4e; ⏱ 10am-7pm Thu-Tue; Ⓜ St-Paul) This pâtisserie has scrumptious Jewish and Central European–style breads and pastries, including apple strudel and poppy-seed cakes.

Gérard Mulot (Map pp436–7; ☎ 01 43 26 85 77; 76 rue de Seine, 6e; ⏱ 7am-8pm Thu-Tue; Ⓜ Odéon) Specialities include various fruit tarts (peach, lemon, apple), *tarte normande* (apple cake) and *mabillon* (caramel mousse with apricot conserves).

Jean Millet (Map pp434–5; ☎ 01 45 51 49 80; 103 rue St-Dominique, 7e; ⏱ 9am-7pm Mon-Sat, 8am-1pm Sun; Ⓜ École Militaire) Specialities include *délice au chocolat praliné* (a heavenly almond and chocolate concoction) and *bavarois d'abricots* (a cold moulded mousse dessert of cream and apricot fruit purée).

Ladurée (Map pp426–7; ☎ 01 40 75 08 75; 75 av des Champs-Élysées, 8e; ⏱ 7.30am-11pm; Ⓜ George V) Specialities include *macarons au chocolat* (chocolate macaroons) and *macarons à la pistache* (pistachio macaroons).

Stohrer (Map pp428–9; ☎ 01 42 33 38 20; 51 rue Montorgueil, 2e; ⏱ 7.30am-8.30pm; Ⓜ Les Halles or Sentier) Specialities include *galette des rois* (kings' cake; puff pastry with frangipane cream) and *marrons glacées* (candied chestnuts).

BEYOND CENTRAL PARIS

LA DÉFENSE

For the most part La Défense is fast-food territory, including a branch of the sandwich shop **Lina's** (see p214), but there are some independent outlets from which to choose.

GLOBETROTTER CAFÉ

Map p155   Island

☏ 01 55 91 96 96; 16 place de la Défense; starters €4.90-13.80, mains €14-26; ☺ lunch Mon-Fri; Ⓜ La Défense Grande Arche

This attractive restaurant, which is located next to the La Défense tourist office, has a tropical theme and it attempts to take diners on a culinary tour of the world through various islands. It does this with dishes like *carpaccio d'espadon et ananas des Caraïbes* (carpaccio of swordfish with Caribbean pineapple) and *millefeuille de canard aux fruits secs* (layered duck breast with dried fruit). The glassed-in bar is open until 8pm on weekdays.

LE PETIT BOFINGER

Map p155   French, Brasserie

☏ 01 46 92 46 46, 1 place du Dôme; menu €20.50 & €25; ☺ lunch & dinner until 11pm; Ⓜ La Défense Grande Arche

Formerly Le Petit Dôme (it sits under what was once the IMAX dome), this glassed-in dining room is a perennial favourite of La Défense *gens d'affaires* (businesspeople). The atmosphere is a bit industrial but the food is fine.

Ô 110 Map p155   French

☏ 01 49 07 27 32; Grande Arche; starters (for 2) €13.50, mains €13-20; ☺ lunch 11.30am-2.30pm, bar (with snacks) 10am-7pm daily; Ⓜ La Défense Grande Arche

Sitting atop the Grande Arche on the 35th floor, this brasserie offers acceptable food at lunch and some of the best views in Paris from – guess how high – 110m up.

ST-DENIS

There are a number of restaurants in the modern shopping area around the Basilique de St-Denis metro station.

AU PETIT BRETON

Map p157   French, Bretagne

☏ 01 48 20 11 58; 18 rue de la Légion d'Honneur; menus €11 & €13; ☺ 8.30am-4pm Mon-Sat; Ⓜ St-Denis Porte de Paris

'At the Little Breton' is a decent spot for a lunch of traditional French fare (don't expect *galettes* or crepes despite the name). The plat du jour is a bargain-basement €8.

LE CAFÉ DE L'ORIENT

Map p157   Tea Room

☏ 01 48 20 30 83; 8 blvd de la Commune de Paris; teas €3-8, cocktails €5-6; ☺ noon-midnight; Ⓜ Basilique de St-Denis

If you fancy some North African mint tea and pastries, a toke on the hookah or a cocktail, this is a comfortable café with overstuffed cushions and Moroccan décor northeast of the basilica.

LES ARTS Map p157   North African, French

☏ 01 42 43 22 40; 6 rue de la Boulangerie; starters €4.50-7.90, mains €10.50-19.50, menus lunch/dinner €12.90/21.50; ☺ lunch Tue-Sun, dinner to 10.30pm Tue-Sat; Ⓜ Basilique de St-Denis

This central restaurant has mostly Maghreb cuisine (couscous, *tajines* etc), with a few traditional French dishes as well, and comes recommended by local people. It's just opposite the basilica.

Self-Catering

The large, multiethnic **food market** (Map p157; place Jean Jaurès; ☺ 8am-2pm Tue, Fri & Sun; Ⓜ Basilique de St-Denis) is opposite the tourist office. **Halle du Marché**, the large covered market a short stroll to the northwest, is known for its selection of spices.

Franprix (Map p157; 34 rue de la République; ☺ 9am-1pm & 3-7.15pm Tue-Sat, 8.30am-1pm Sun; Ⓜ Basilique de St-Denis) is in the centre of town by the post office.

Drinking

Drinking

At first glance the Parisian bar scene can seem either daunting or soporific, with ultrapretentious VIP spots at one end and dime-a-dozen bar-*tabacs* (bar-tobacconists) at the other. You'd be forgiven for yearning for a few more chilled venues where you need neither a gold-plated credit card nor membership to the local anarchists' association to feel at ease. Instead the middle ground seems filled with a vast array of nondescript or wannabe-trendy cafés that tend to all blur into one. But fear not, intrepid tipplers – a gold mine of excellent and atmospheric drinking spots can be unearthed with a little insider information.

The best thing is to let yourself be absorbed by the local way of doing things. In Paris this could mean any of the following: eating thin slices of sausage with a glass of Sauvignon on a terrace at sundown; dancing on tables to bossa nova beats; hovering at a counter with local winos; or enjoying a martini on a dark leather couch in a place where jazz and Ernest Hemingway haunt the air. In France, eating and drinking go together like wine and cheese, so the line between bars, restaurants and cafés is usually very fuzzy. Most of the places listed serve food, but are more noteworthy as happening drinking venues. Also listed are some cafés and tea salons that are more suited to daytime dwindling or a gentle apéritif (early-evening drinks). Many cafés in Paris have important literary and/or historical associations (see p164).

Unless otherwise stated, a glass of wine starts at €3 or €4 and increases with quality; a cocktail is usually €7 to €10 and a *demi* (half-pint) of beer is €3 to €5. In clubs and the fanciest bars, however, those prices can double. Essentially, drinking in Paris means paying the rent for the space you take up. So it costs more sitting at tables than standing at the counter, more on a fancy square than a back street, more in the 8e than in the 18e. Think of it as a short-term investment that varies ac-

TOP FIVE PUBS, BARS & CAFÉS

- China Club (p242)
- De la Ville Café (p251)
- Harry's New York Bar (p252)
- La Caravane (p254)
- Le 10 (p248)

Le Clown Bar (p223)

cording to the décor and the property price per square metre in that neighbourhood! If you're looking for the place with the cheapest drinks, just follow the trail of students. Most venues have a happy hour from around 5pm to 9pm with reduced-price drinks – we've mentioned it specifically whenever there's a significant discount. Closing times tend to be 2am, though some bars have later licences. See p265 for clubbing spots and p259 for live music venues, many of which are great places to head for a drink.

LOUVRE & LES HALLES

Some great bars skirt the no-man's-land of Les Halles (but avoid crossing the garden above the Forum des Halles at night). Rue des Lombards is the place for jazz (p261), while sophisticated bars are clustered towards the Louvre and Palais Royal. The Étienne Marcel area, especially along rue Tiquetonne and rue Montorgueil, has a fine selection of hip cafés. This area is right next to the happening bars of rue Montmartre, which are listed on p251.

CAFÉ OZ
Map pp436-7

☎ 01 40 39 00 18; 18 rue St-Denis, 1er; ✆ 5pm-3am Sun-Thu, 5pm-5am Fri, 1pm-5am Sat; Ⓜ Châtelet

A militantly proud Aussie pub at the bottom of sleazy rue St Denis, Oz is authentic – from its wood-and-ochre décor to its strong commitment to maximising your drink intake. Convivial bordering on raucous, it's popular with Anglos but the French love it too. The place is packed on Friday and Saturday nights, when it heats up with DJs and dancing. There's also a smaller and more chilled-out branch in **Pigalle** (Map p432; ☎ 01 40 16 11 16; 1 rue de Bruxelles, 9e; Ⓜ Blanche), which closes at 2am.

KONG
Map pp436-7

☎ 01 40 39 09 00; 1 rue du Pont Neuf, 1er; ✆ noon-2am; Ⓜ Pont Neuf

This Philippe Starck–designed bar is carefully perched upon the Kenzo building. The concept is kind of postmodern Japanese, a cradle for new generation wannabes who trail their Vuitton handbags along the bar and click their fingers for more bottles of

champagne. The cocktails are around €11, not bad for a place this pretentious, and DJs playing hip-hop somehow get everyone dancing on the tables. Dress up; no running shoes.

LE CAFÉ DES INITIÉS
Map pp436-7

☎ 01 42 33 78 29; 3 place des Deux-Ecus, 1er; ✆ 8am-1am; Ⓜ Louvre-Rivoli

This modern-design café almost on rue du Louvre is popular with journalists and communications types. While not a late night destination, it has a pleasant terrace and is great for evening drinks, coffees and light meals. Slick service, nondeafening music and good food attract a trendy 30-something mix of suits and hooded tops.

LE FUMOIR
Map pp436-7

☎ 01 42 92 00 24; 6 rue de l'Amiral de Coligny, 1er; ✆ 11am-2am; Ⓜ Louvre-Rivoli

A stylish establishment from the owners of **China Club** (p242), this elegant colonial-style bar-restaurant is opposite the eastern flank of the Louvre. It's a fine place to sip top-notch gin from quality glassware while nibbling on olives; during happy hour (6pm to 8pm) cocktails are around half-price at €6. There's a buoyant, corporate crowd on weekday evenings. The restaurant is popular for Sunday brunch; try to get a seat in the 'library'.

LE TROISIÈME LIEU
Map pp436-7

☎ 01 48 04 85 64; 62 rue Quincampoix, 4e; ✆ 6pm-2am; Ⓜ Rambuteau

This friendly bar has rapidly become the new happening place for chic young lesbians, and for everyone else, for that matter. Boys are welcome. There's a large, colourful bar and big wooden tables at street level, with good-value canteen meals. Downstairs leaves space for dancing to DJs, rock/alternative music concerts and live singers.

L'IMPRÉVU
Map pp436-7

☎ 01 42 78 23 50; rue Quincampoix, 4e; ✆ 5pm-2am; Ⓜ Rambuteau

A bit of an oasis if you're looking for a cosy place in Les Halles, this bar is relatively

GAY & LESBIAN VENUES

The Marais (4e), especially those areas around the intersection of rue Ste-Croix de la Bretonnerie and rue des Archives, and eastwards to rue Vieille du Temple, has been Paris' main centre of gay and – to a lesser extent – lesbian nightlife for over two decades. There are also a few bars and clubs within walking distance of blvd de Sébastopol. Other venues are scattered throughout the city.

For a predominantly boys-only night out there's the **Open Café** (p244), **Le Quetzal** (p243), **Amnésia** (below) and, of course, **Le Dépôt** (p266). Gay men's nights happen at various clubs including **Le Queen** (p267), **Red Light** (p267) and **Les Bains** (p267).

Women have found a space in **Bliss Kfé** (opposite), **3W Kafé** (below) and the club **Le Pulp** (p267), while younger girls love **Le Troisième Lieu** (p239), which, like the boys' **Mixer Bar** (p244), makes people of all inclinations welcome.

Indeed, the need for exclusiveness appears to be relaxing – as is, perhaps, the general public's mentality towards homosexuality. Bars and clubs are generally all gay friendly, while specifically gay venues are increasingly mixing things up – becoming some of the coolest spots in Paris. If you're looking for a chilled, open-to-all atmosphere there's the **AOC Café** (opposite), **Politburo** (p244) and **Interface Bar** (p242), to name only a few.

inexpensive, with mismatched furniture and a relaxed charm. It's quite large but the different rooms and corners mean you'll soon find your niche. Popular with students.

MARAIS & BASTILLE

The Marais is a great place to go out for drinks. It's a fascinating mix of gay-friendly (and gay-only) café society and bourgeois arty spots, with an interesting sprinkling of eclectic bars and pubs. Bastille has become increasingly crass over the years but it invariably draws a crowd, particularly as seething rue de Lappe. Things get quieter – and better – as you go further up rue de la Roquette and rue de Charonne; rue Keller has some good cafés.

3W KAFÉ
Map pp436-7
☎ 01 48 87 39 26; 8 rue des Écouffes, 4e; ☷ 6pm-2am; Ⓜ Hôtel de Ville
This glossy lesbian cocktail bar has replaced the former 'Les Scandaleuses'. It aims to be more relaxed and elegant than its previous incarnation. There's no ban on men but the clientele is almost exclusively women.

À LA RENAISSANCE
Map pp440-1
☎ 01 43 79 83 09; 87 rue de la Roquette, 11e; ☷ 8.30am-8pm Mon, 8.30am-midnight Tue-Sat, 9.30am-8pm Sun; Ⓜ Voltaire
If you're looking for the typical Parisian café du quartier (neighbourhood café)

not too far from the Bastille area, head up to the Renaissance. Regulars drop in for a late breakfast, a drink or a quality meal either at the pavement tables or the indoor booths. Intrepid souls can enjoy the house speciality – steak tartare (raw minced steak).

AMNÉSIA
Map pp436-7
☎ 01 42 72 16 94; 42 rue Vieille du Temple, 4e; ☷ 10am-2am; Ⓜ Hôtel de Ville
In the heart of the Marais, the cosy, warmly lit Amnésia is far from forgettable. Friendly and stylish, it remains resolutely popular with gay guys but is more mixed than many of its counterparts. There's an attractive lounge area upstairs and a tiny dance floor in the cave (wine cellar) downstairs.

ANDY WAHLOO
Map pp436-7
☎ 01 42 71 20 38; 69 rue des Gravilliers, 3e; ☷ noon-2am; Ⓜ Arts et Métiers
Casablanca meets pop art meets candy store in this cool, multicoloured cocktail lounge hidden away just north of the Centre Georges Pompidou. Its clever name means 'I have nothing' in Arabic. The acid colours, sweet cocktails, pushy staff and loud house music may be a bit too much for some palates, but it's a lively, spirited little bar that most will enjoy. There are great olives as well as promising mezze plates. During happy hour (5pm to 8pm) a cocktail/beer is €5/3 – after that prices double.

AOC CAFÉ

Map pp436-7

☎ 01 48 87 43 36; 62 rue du Roi de Sicile, 4e; ⏰ 8am-2am; Ⓜ St-Paul

Run by some of the eminent ladies from lesbian club Le Pulp (p267), this modern wine bar–café is a new local favourite, with great coffee and meals. The clientele is relaxed, mixed and street smart with a penchant for electronic music and good wine.

AU PETIT FER À CHEVAL

Map pp436-7

☎ 01 42 72 47 47; 30 rue Vieille du Temple, 4e; ⏰ 9am-2am; Ⓜ Hôtel de Ville or St-Paul

The original horseshoe-shaped bar leaves little room for much else, but nobody seems to mind at this genial bar. It overflows with friendly regulars enjoying a drink or a sandwich (simple meals are served from noon), and it's nestled in with adjacent sister cafés: L'Étoile Manquante (p244), Les Philosophes and La Chaise au Plafond – all worthwhile. The latter two have terraces leading onto tranquil passage du Trésor; worth knowing about in summer.

BARRIO LATINO

Map pp440-1

☎ 01 55 78 84 75; 46-48 rue du Faubourg St-Antoine, 11e; ⏰ 11am-2am Sun-Thu, 11am-3am Fri & Sat; Ⓜ Bastille

Still squeezing the salsa theme for all that it's worth, this enormous bar-restaurant with serious dancing is spread over three highly decorated floors. It attracts Latinos, Latino wannabes and Latino wannahaves. The delicious *mojitos* (Cuban cocktails created with rum, mint and limes) go down a treat.

BLISS KFÉ

Map pp436-7

☎ 01 42 78 49 36; 30 rue du Roi de Sicile, 4e; ⏰ 5.30pm-2am; Ⓜ St-Paul

This lesbian café and lounge bar at the corner of rue des Écouffes (in what was once a *boulangerie*-patisserie) has a stylish vibe and a somewhat mixed crowd. Guys are welcome, and there's a smoky club downstairs that operates on Friday and Saturday nights.

BOCA CHICA

Map pp440-1

☎ 01 43 57 93 13; 58 rue de Charonne, 11e; ⏰ 10am-1.30am Sun-Thu, 10am-4am Fri & Sat; Ⓜ Ledru Rollin

This enormous, colourfully decorated place attracts a trendy, tanned, salsa-lovin' crowd that isn't shy about getting up to dance. When the multilevel bar areas and terrace are not hosting salsa soirees you'll find DJs, flamenco artists and '80s theme nights. The extensive tapas selection is unsatisfying; stick to the sangria.

BOTTLE SHOP

Map pp440-1

☎ 01 43 14 28 04; 5 rue Trousseau, 11e; ⏰ noon-2am; Ⓜ Ledru Rollin

A popular lunch café by day, this great little local has a lively pub feeling in the evenings. There's a welcoming mix of regulars and travellers – at least half the friendly banter going on is in English.

CAFÉ DES PHARES

Map pp440-1

☎ 01 42 72 04 70; 7 place de la Bastille, 4e; ⏰ 7am-3am Sun-Thu, 7am-4am Fri & Sat; Ⓜ Bastille

If you wake in the night wondering 'What does speaking mean?' or 'How to go from ethics to morality?', and then wake in the morning with a craving for *croque monsieur* (grilled ham and cheese sandwich; €8), this place is your dream come true. It was the original philosopher's café

Drinking

MARAIS & BASTILLE

(many more have spawned across town), established by the late philosopher and Sorbonne professor Marc Sautet (1947–98). Debates on diverse topics take place at 11am Sunday.

CENTRE CULTUREL SUÉDOIS
Map pp440-1

☎ 01 44 78 80 20; 11 rue Payenne, 3e; ☺ noon-6pm Tue, Wed & Fri-Sun, noon-9pm Thu; M Chemin Vert

There's a lot of mutual admiration between the Swedes and the French, and this gorgeous café in the Swedish Cultural Centre is doing a lot for bilateral relations. Housed in the beautiful Hôtel de Marle, a 16th-century mansion, the Centre hosts a variety of exhibitions, concerts and debates, with rich resources on Swedish history and culture. But what we're interested in is the lovely café, with modern indoor seating and tables outside in the tranquil paved courtyard. Delicious soups, salads and teas.

CHINA CLUB
Map pp446-7

☎ 01 43 43 82 02; 50 rue de Charenton, 12e; ☺ 7pm-2am; M Ledru Rollin or Bastille

Evocative of a colonial gentleman's club, this is an exquisite destination for cocktails, which start at €6 during happy hour (7pm to 9pm). Cigar aficionados can travel upstairs to the *fumoir* (smoking room), with glowing fire. Jazz buffs prefer the Sing Song club in the cellar, which is styled like 1930s Shanghai. The restaurant is well-reputed (*menus* from €28).

HAVANITA CAFÉ
Map pp440-1

☎ 01 43 55 96 42; 11 rue de Lappe, 11e; ☺ 4pm-2am; M Bastille

Flashy Cuban style every inch of the way, from the *mojitos* to the main courses to the murals on the walls. This attractive but commercial bar-restaurant has stood the test of time on the increasingly lurid rue de Lappe, thanks to its always reliably festive atmosphere.

IGUANA CAFÉ
Map pp440-1

☎ 01 40 21 39 99; 15 rue de la Roquette, 11e; ☺ 8am-2am Sun-Thu, 9am-5am Fri & Sat; M Bastille

A contemporary, two-level café-pub whose clientele is slipping progressively from 30-somethings to early-20s punters. Its best of a mediocre bunch if you're after accessible cocktails in the immediate Bastille vicinity, and has the merit of closing late on Friday and Saturday nights.

INTERFACE BAR
Map pp440-1

☎ 01 47 00 67 15; 34 rue Keller, 11e; ☺ 4pm-2am; M Ledru Rollin

This is a very laid-back neighbourhood gay bar that attracts locals and habitués of the nearby Centre Gai et Lesbien de Paris Île de France (Gay & Lesbian Centre; p377).

JOKKO BAR
Map pp436-7

☎ 01 42 74 35 96; 5 rue Elzévir, 3e; ☺ 5pm-12.30am Wed-Sun; M St-Paul or Chemin Vert

A fantastic little bar, part of a small African colony incongruously established on this quiet Marais backstreet. Set up by the founder of the Compagnie du Sénégal et de l'Afrique de l'Ouest (CSAO; Senegal and West Africa Company; p287) and Senegalese musician Youssou N'Dour, Jokko hits the spot with colourful décor, world music and cocktails with rum and fresh ginger. There are concerts most nights at 7.30pm (jazz, African beats, soul…), and rotating exhibitions.

L'APPAREMMENT CAFÉ
Map pp440-1

☎ 01 48 87 12 22; 18 rue des Coutures St-Gervais, 3e; ☽ noon-2am Mon-Fri, 4pm-2am Sat, 12.30pm-midnight Sun; Ⓜ St-Sébastien Froissart

A tasteful haven tucked behind the Musée Picasso and at a merciful distance from the Marais shopping hordes. It's a bit like a private living room with wood panelling, leather sofas, scattered parlour games, dog-eared books – and Parisians languidly studying their Sunday brunches (served to 4pm).

LE BISTROT DU PEINTRE
Map pp440-1

☎ 01 47 00 34 39; 116 av Ledru-Rollin, 11e; ☽ 8am-2am; Ⓜ Bastille

This quintessential *belle époque* bistro should really count more as a restaurant than a drinking place; after all, the food is great. But the 1902 Art Deco bar, elegant terrace and spot-on service put this café on our apéritif A-list – and that of local artists, *bobos* (bohemian bourgeois) and celebs.

LE CAFÉ DU PASSAGE
Map pp440-1

☎ 01 49 29 97 64; 12 rue de Charonne, 11e; ☽ 6pm-2am; Ⓜ Ledru Rollin

This is the destination of choice for willing wine buffs, who relax in armchairs while sampling Loire vintages from the excellent range on offer. Le Café du Passage has hundreds of wines available, including many by the glass (from €5). Whisky aficionados are also catered for and won't be disappointed by the selection of pure malts. It's a touch exclusive but the conversation flows as smoothly as the Pinot. Light meals and gourmet snacks are available.

LE DIVAN
Map pp440-1

☎ 01 48 05 72 36; 60 rue de la Roquette, 11e; ☽ 8am-2am; Ⓜ Bastille

Although nondescript and a touch sombre, the Divan bar-restaurant scores a mention for three reasons. First, a quality long copper bar with stools: highly suitable for that moody apéritif or *Le Monde*–scrutinising coffee break. Second, a local clientele that's older and considerably less hysterical than the rue de Lappe lot. And, finally, it opens onto a little passage – great on warm nights.

LE LÈCHE-VIN
Map pp440-1

☎ 01 43 55 98 91; 13 rue Daval, 11e; ☽ 6.30pm-1.30am Mon-Thu, 6.30pm-2am Fri & Sat, 5pm-midnight Sun; Ⓜ Bastille

A divine surprise in a tawdry neighbourhood, this irreverent shambles is devoted to good wines and religious bric-a-brac. Note the electric pietà, Pope John XXIII plate and the Last Supper bathmat amid the multiple icons of the Virgin Mary. Be aware, however, that eternal damnation is just a visit to the toilet away.

LE PICK CLOPS
Map pp436-7

☎ 01 40 29 02 18; 16 rue Vieille du Temple, 4e; ☽ 7.30am-2am; Ⓜ Hôtel de Ville or St-Paul

This retro café-bar – all shades of yellow and lit by neon – has Formica tables, ancient bar stools and plenty of mirrors. Attracting a friendly flow of locals and passers-by, it's a great place for morning or afternoon coffee, or that last drink.

LE QUETZAL
Map pp436-7

☎ 01 48 87 99 07; 10 rue de la Verrerie, 4e; ☽ 5pm-3am Mon-Thu, 5pm-5am Fri-Sun; Ⓜ Hôtel de Ville

This dimly lit bar that's popular with 30-something gay men is opposite rue des Mauvais Garçons (Bad Boys' Street), a street named after the brigands who congregated here in 1540. It seems to have lost its relaxed vibe but it's always busy, with house and dance music playing at night. During their almost never-ending happy hour – from 5pm to midnight – a pint costs €3.60.

LES ÉTAGES

Map pp436-7

☎ 01 42 78 72 00; 35 rue Vieille du Temple, 4e;
🕑 3.30pm-2am; Ⓜ Hôtel de Ville or St-Paul

This bar lost its distressed 'squat' charm when it brought in all those stupid purple chairs and ditched the couches. However, students and expats find it a viable alternative to the standard Marais fare, and happily appropriate the lounge rooms upstairs. Before 9.30pm certain cocktails are €4 (instead of €7.50). Its Left Bank clone **Les Étages Odéon** (Map pp436-7; ☎ 01 46 34 26 26; 5 rue Buci, 6e; 🕑 11am-2am; Ⓜ Odéon) has a popular terrace but eschews happy hour.

L'ÉTOILE MANQUANTE

Map pp436-7

☎ 01 42 72 48 34; 34 rue Vieille du Temple, 4e;
🕑 5pm-2am; Ⓜ Hôtel de Ville or St-Paul

A long elegant room with a long elegant wine and cocktail list, 'the missing star' takes standard décor up a slight notch with modern art, metal frames and fittings, clustered mirrors and dim lighting. There are light meals but it's not a proper restaurant. It's part of the Caffeine group that runs four cafés on this corner, including **Au Petit Fer à Cheval** (p241).

LIZARD LOUNGE

Map pp436-7

☎ 01 42 72 81 34; 18 rue Bourg Tibourg, 4e;
🕑 noon-2pm; Ⓜ Hôtel de Ville or St-Paul

A quality outpost of Anglo-Saxon attitude in the heart of the Marais, this relaxed pub has beer on tap, cocktails and food (club sandwiches and burgers). Young expats with clutch purses file straight downstairs to the cellar, complete with stone walls, a DJ, and magnanimous little corners in which to schmooze. Just around the corner and run by the same team is the smaller **Stolly's** (Map pp436-7; ☎ 01 42 76 06 76; 16 rue de la Cloche Percée, 4e; 🕑 4.30pm-2am; Ⓜ St-Paul).

MIXER BAR

Map pp436-7

☎ 01 48 87 55 44; 23 rue Ste-Croix de la Bretonnerie, 4e; 🕑 5pm-2am; Ⓜ Hôtel de Ville

This bright and colourful club has regular party nights and chill-out sessions. Blended up in this hedonistic mix are an animated gay crowd, a happy sprinkling of heteros, and DJs spinning techno, electro and house.

OPEN CAFÉ Map pp436-7

☎ 01 42 72 26 18; 17 rue des Archives, 4e;
🕑 11am-2am Sun-Thu, 11am-4am Fri & Sat;
Ⓜ Hôtel de Ville

The huge, overflowing terrace here is the place for gay men to see and be seen, especially in the warmer months (though even in winter there's a lot of posing outdoors). This is a Marais institution, where most boyz of most ages head after work and before moving on to bigger and better things. It's packed, but it's more social than cruisy.

PAUSE CAFÉ Map pp440-1

☎ 01 48 06 80 33; 41 rue de Charonne, 11e;
🕑 7.30am-2am Mon-Sat, 9am-8.30pm Sun;
Ⓜ Ledru Rollin

Principally a restaurant, this attractive café with lots of windows remains a firmly popular destination for drinks, meals, coffee or brunch. Well situated a little away from the fray of Bastille, its generous terrace fills up with fashionable locals and the almost famous.

POLITBURO

Map pp436-7

☎ 01 42 77 01 78; 25 rue du Roi de Sicile, 4e;
🕑 6pm-2am; Ⓜ St-Paul

With red-washed walls and neo-Soviet style, this hip little mid-Marais drinking spot often has concerts, debates and DJs going on. It hasn't overdone the KGB décor and there's a friendly, mixed crowd, not to mention €3 vodkas during happy hour (6pm to 9pm).

PURE MALT BAR

Map pp440-1

☎ 01 42 76 03 77; 4 rue Caron, 4e; 🕑 5pm-2am;
Ⓜ St-Paul

A little Scottish pub just south of the lovely place du Marché Ste-Catherine, the Pure Malt is for the whisky connoisseur. More than 150 types of whisky are on hand to try at €7 to €17 a glass. It concentrates mainly on single malt whisky (though beer is available at €6 a pint).

SANZ SANS

Map pp440-1

☎ 01 44 75 78 78; 49 rue du Faubourg St-Antoine, 11e; ⏰ 9am-2am Sun-Thu, 9am-5am Fri & Sat; Ⓜ Bastille

A little cheesy, a lot sleazy, this lively bar clad in red velvet and zebra stripes continues to hold out as a busy drinking venue on the Bastille beat. DJs play a very mixed bag of music, mostly electronic or funk/soul, and the crowd is similarly unpredictable.

WAX

Map pp440-1

☎ 01 40 21 16 16; 15 rue Daval, 11e; ⏰ 6pm-2am Tue-Thu, 6pm-5am Fri & Sat; Ⓜ Bastille

Wax is a 'retro-futuristic' (think *A Clockwork Orange*) bar and club with yellow and red plastic furniture and walls, portholes on the walls and DJs playing mostly groove and House tunes. Slick and thoroughly overdone, it's kind of like Tupperware on acid. Happy hour is from 6pm to 9pm.

THE ISLANDS

LA CHARLOTTE EN ÎLE

Map pp436-7

☎ 01 43 54 25 83; rue St-Louis en l'Île 24, Île St-Louis, 4e; ⏰ noon-8pm Thu-Sun; Ⓜ Pont Marie

This tiny place is one of the loveliest *salons de thé* (tearooms) in all of Paris and is definitely worth crossing the bridge. The fairy-tale theme adds flavour (as if any is needed) to the chocolate and pastries, and the three dozen or so teas on offer are superbly chosen. Small concerts and events take place; pass by to get the latest flyer.

TAVERNE HENRI IV

Map pp436-7

☎ 01 43 54 27 90; 13 place du Pont Neuf, Île de la Cité, 1er; ⏰ 1.30am-9.30pm; Ⓜ Pont Neuf

One of the very few places to drink on the Île de la Cité, the 'Henry IV Tavern' is a serious wine bar and decent place for a nibble, with a choice of inexpensive *tartines* (slices of bread with toppings), *charcuterie* (cured, smoked or processed meats), cheese and quiche. It attracts lots of legal types from the nearby Palais de Justice and has become something of an institution. It sometimes closes in the evenings for private functions, so you may wish to call ahead.

LATIN QUARTER & JARDIN DES PLANTES

The Latin Quarter and the rue Mouffetard area are popular with downtrodden students, *Rive Gauche* (Left Bank) romantics and well-heeled café society types. Tending to stick with old-but-good recipes and nostalgic formulas, the 5e pleases those in search of a typically Parisian soiree. Expect good fun but nothing too ground-breaking.

CAFÉ DELMAS

Map pp444-5

☎ 01 43 26 51 26; 2 place de la Contrescarpe, 5e; ⏰ 8am-2am Sun-Thu, 8am-4am Fri & Sat; Ⓜ Cardinal Lemoine

The Delmas occupies one of the most enviable positions in Paris: its generous terrace overlooks the idyllic place de la Contrescarpe at the top of rue Mouffetard.

LES EXPATRIÉS

These predominantly Anglo pubs and cafés attract homesick travellers and expats from all over the world. They also tend to draw in lots of Parisians, often nostalgic for past travels or looking to find love from faraway shores…

- Americans love **Harry's New York Bar** (p252).
- For the English, **Frog & Princess** (p247) and **Cricketer Pub** (p250) are among many English-style pubs.
- Scottish pubs include crazy **Highlander** (p248) and more discerning **Pure Malt Bar** (opposite).
- Australians have their headquarters at busy **Café Oz** (p239).
- Swedes can take refuge at relatively sedate **Centre Culturel Suédois** (p242).
- Irish pubs, often of dubious authenticity, are practically on every corner, but popular ones include **Coolín** (p247), **O'Sullivan's** (p252).
- Canadians get their home away from home at **Moosehead Bar** (p249).
- Good all-rounders include **Lizard Lounge** (opposite), **Stolly's** (opposite), **Bottle Shop** (p241) and **SoMo** (p252) – incidentally all owned by the same people – as well as **Lush Bar** (p251).

FOR SOMETHING CHIC

Smoky *caves* (wine cellars) and café terraces have their place, but Paris also offers some wonderfully chic, atmospheric places for a fancy cocktail.

- Buddha Bar (p250)
- China Club (p242)
- Hemingway Bar (p250)
- Kong (p239)
- Le Fumoir (p239)
- Mezzanine de l'Alcazar (p248)

Although located in a solidly student neighbourhood, the café is surprisingly cosmopolitan, and you'll hear (and meet) all types here.

LE CROCODILE

Map pp444–5

☎ 01 43 54 32 37; 6 rue Royer Collard, 5e; ⏰ 10pm-6am Mon-Sat; Ⓜ Luxembourg

This bar has been dispensing cocktails (more than 200 on the list) since 1966. Apparently the '70s were 'epic' in this bar, and the dream kicks on well into the wee hours of the new century. Come knocking late at night for a truly eclectic crowd including lots of students, and an atmosphere that can go from quiet tippling to raucous revelry.

LE PIANO VACHE

Map pp444–5

☎ 01 46 33 75 03; 8 rue Laplace, 5e; ⏰ noon-2am Mon-Fri, 9pm-2am Sat & Sun; Ⓜ Maubert Mutualité

Just down the hill from the Panthéon, this bar is covered in old posters and couches and is drenched in 1970s and '80s rock ambience. Effortlessly underground and a huge favourite with students, it has bands and DJs playing mainly rock, plus some Gothic, reggae and pop.

LE RALLYE

Map pp444–5

☎ 01 43 54 29 65; 11 quai de la Tournelle, 5e; ⏰ 7.30am-2am Mon-Fri, 9.30am-2am Sat & Sun; Ⓜ Maubert Mutualité

A 1950s-style Provençal café where the speciality is, as you'd expect, *pastis* (aniseed liqueur). Its devotion to Tintin-themed décor is not so explicable. There's

not much else going on except typical bar-*tabac* living: locals engaged in the gentle pursuit of cigarettes, cheap lunch *menus*, early apéritifs and the odd game of *pétanque* (played with heavy metal balls on a sandy pitch).

LE VIEUX CHÊNE

Map pp444–5

☎ 01 43 37 71 51; 69 rue Mouffetard, 5e; ⏰ 4pm-2am Sun-Thu, 4pm-5am Fri & Sat; Ⓜ Place Monge

This rue Mouffetard institution is believed to be the oldest bar in Paris. A revolutionary circle met here in 1848, when most of Europe was in turmoil, and it was a popular *bal musette* (dancing club) in the late-19th and early-20th centuries. Today it is popular with students and often has jazz on weekends. Happy hour is from opening time to 9pm, with half-pints for €2.50 (usually €3.50).

LE VIOLON DINGUE

Map pp444–5

☎ 01 43 25 79 93; 46 rue de la Montagne Ste-Geneviève, 5e; ⏰ 8pm-4.30am Tue-Sat; Ⓜ Maubert Mutualité

A loud, lively bar adopted by revolving generations of students. The 'Crazy Violin' attracts lots of young English-speakers with big-screen sports shown upstairs and the flirty 'Dingue Lounge' downstairs. Pints/cocktails cost €3.50/5 during happy hour (8pm to 10pm), or €5.50/6.50 at other times. The name 'Crazy Violin' is a pun on the expression *le violon d'Ingres,* meaning 'hobby' in French, because the celebrated painter Jean-Auguste-Dominique Ingres (see p33) used to fiddle in his spare time.

L'URGENCE BAR

Map pp444–5

☎ 01 43 26 45 69; 45 rue Monsieur le Prince, 6e; ⏰ 9pm-2am Mon-Sat; Ⓜ Luxembourg

Just south of the École de Médecine is the medical-themed 'emergency room'. Here are the future doctors of France, busy imbibing luridly coloured liquor from babies' bottles and test tubes, loosening their stethoscopes and pointing to the 'X-ray art' – making comments like '*mais non!* Clarisse, that's so not the tibia'.

Swannie Vincendon • 50 rue de charenton 75012 Paris

CHINA CLU
live

HADJA KOUYATE

TAKE 3
vendredi 4 mars
22h00 • 5€00

LUCY DE

China Club (p242) sign

ST-GERMAIN, ODÉON & LUXEMBOURG

While much of the 6e is rather sleepy and snobby, the area around Odéon has quite a lot of action going on. Rue de Buci, rue St-André des Arts and rue de l'Odéon in particular have some picturesque, arty cafés as well as busy pubs. Meanwhile, the local and international student hordes, rugby players/watchers and Anglophiles have found their niche on atmospheric '*rue de la soif*' (street of thirst) down rue Princesse and rue des Canettes.

CAFÉ DE FLORE

Map pp436-7

☎ 01 45 48 55 26; 172 blvd St-Germain, 6e; ⏰ 7.30am-1.30am; Ⓜ St-Germain des Prés
The red upholstered benches, mirrors and marble walls haven't changed since the days when Jean-Paul Sartre, Simone de Beauvoir, Albert Camus and Pablo Picasso bent their elbows and wagged their chins here. This Art Deco landmark is slightly less touristy than **Les Deux Magots** (p248). Its lovely terrace draws in lunching ladies, posh business-folk and foreigners in search of the past. Try the house Pouilly Fumé (€7.50 a glass or €29 a bottle). A coffee will set you back €4.40.

CAFÉ DE LA MAIRIE

Map pp436-7

☎ 01 43 26 67 82; 8 place St-Sulpice, 6e; ⏰ 7am-2am Mon-Sat; Ⓜ St-Sulpice
Plain but with an excellent terrace opening onto place St-Sulpice, this bustling yet laid-back café attracts students, writers and film people with its tattered Left Bank ambience.

COOLÍN

Map pp436-7

☎ 01 44 07 00 92; 15 rue Clément, 6e; ⏰ 10.30am-2am Mon-Sat, 1pm-2am Sun; Ⓜ Mabillon
This rather upscale Irish pub in a renovated covered market is a friendly oasis in this part of St-Germain. Decked out in wood panels with lots of tables, it's an attractive, welcoming place that packs out with a mix of students and local post-office drinkers. It also serves food and bar snacks. Happy hour is from 6pm to 8pm, with pints of beer or cider for €5 (usually €6.80).

FROG & PRINCESS

Map pp436-7

☎ 01 40 51 77 38; 9 rue Princesse, 6e; ⏰ 5.30pm-2am Mon-Fri, 1pm-2am Sat & Sun; Ⓜ Mabillon
You could be anywhere on earth at this international pub. Crappy beer is €6 a

247

bottle, which does nothing to stop the jubilant young exchange-student crowd from crushing around the bar and, invariably, dancing on the tables to MTV hits before midnight has even struck. For an older, more relaxed version try the sister 'franglais' bars **Frog & Rosbif** (Map pp436–7; ☎ 01 42 36 34 73; 116 rue St-Denis, 1er; ✆ noon-2am; Ⓜ Etienne Marcel) and **Frog at Bercy Village** (Map p449; ☎ 01 43 40 70 71; 25 cour St-Émilion, 12e; ✆ noon-2am; Ⓜ Cour St-Émilion).

HIGHLANDER
Map pp436-7

☎ 01 43 26 54 20; 8 rue de Nevers, 6e; ✆ 5pm-5am Mon-Fri, noon-5am Sat; Ⓜ Odéon
Establishing a kind of love-hate relationship with its regulars, the jubilant Highlander scrapes up the after-hours remains of the Left Bank pub crowd. This mainly means French students, Anglophone lassies, rugby players, hobos and combinations thereof, all intent on drinking until dawn. Downstairs from the Scottish pub is a quasi dance floor, moved more by Long Island iced teas (€9, served in pint glasses) than any kind of rhythm. Pints of beer from €5.50.

LA PALETTE
Map pp436-7

☎ 01 43 26 68 15; 43 rue de Seine, 6e; ✆ 8am-2am Mon-Sat; Ⓜ Mabillon
This *fin-de-siècle* café and erstwhile stomping ground of Paul Cézanne and Georges Braque attracts a grown-up clientele of fashion people and local art dealers. The classic counter gives way to a mirrored, atmospheric room where you can drink at tables. It's in a quiet street and the terrace is beautiful in summer.

LA PLAZA DEL TORO
Map pp436-7

☎ 01 43 26 79 93; 2 rue Guisarde, 6e; ✆ 5pm-2am; Ⓜ Mabillon
Half the room faces the game on the TV screen while the other half canoodles over drinks and slices of baguette with Spanish ham (tapas €4). It's a warm and welcoming little bar on this animated strip of bars, indicative of the neighbourhood's southwest influence – hence the tapas-meets-rugby phenomenon.

LE 10
Map pp436-7

☎ 01 43 26 66 83; 10 rue de l'Odéon, 6e; ✆ 5.30pm-2am; Ⓜ Odéon
A local institution, this cellar pub groans with students, smoky ambience and cheap sangria (served in jugs for €3.30 per person). Posters adorn the walls and an eclectic selection emerges from the jukebox – everything from jazz and the Doors to *chanson française* ('French song'; traditional musical genre where lyrics are paramount). It's the ideal spot for plotting the next revolution or conquering a lonely heart.

LE COMPTOIR DES CANNETTES (CHEZ GEORGES)
Map pp436-7

☎ 01 43 26 79 15; 11 rue des Canettes, 6e; ✆ noon-2am Tue-Sat, closed Aug; Ⓜ Mabillon
The friendly street-level wine bar has a faithful local following. From 10pm students pour into the cellar: a stuffy, atmospheric tribute to downtrodden romanticism – complete with red tablecloths, melting candles and nostalgic photos of musicians. The wine is cheap, the regulars are incorrigible and the whole thing spills back up the stairs and out onto the street on a good night.

LES DEUX MAGOTS
Map pp436-7

☎ 01 45 48 55 25; 170 blvd St-Germain, 6e; ✆ 7am-1am; Ⓜ St-Germain des Prés
This erstwhile literary haunt dates from 1914 and is best known as the favoured hang-out of Sartre, Hemingway and André Breton. Its name refers to the two *magots* (grotesque figurines) of Chinese dignitaries at the entrance. It's touristy, but just once you can give in to the nostalgia and sit on this inimitable terrace, which still attracts passing celebrities, retiring philosophers and remnants of noblesse. The famous shop-made hot chocolate is served in porcelain jugs (€6).

MEZZANINE DE L'ALCAZAR
Map pp436-7

☎ 01 53 10 19 99; 62 rue Mazarine, 6e; ✆ noon-3pm & 7pm-1am; Ⓜ Mabillon
Narcissistic but alluring – a modern white-and-glass mezzanine with fancy cocktails, *nouvelle cuisine* dinners and a fashionable

but restrained supper-club clientele. There are usually DJs 'passing records' in the corner – this place is famous for its excellent trip-hop/House lounge music compilations. It's attached to Le Wagg (p267) club next door, both designed by Sir Terence Conran.

MOOSEHEAD BAR

Map pp436-7

☎ 01 46 33 77 00; 16 rue des Quatre Vents, 6e; ⏰ 4pm-2am Mon-Fri, 11am-2am Sat & Sun; Ⓜ Odéon

It's forever Canada at this friendly pub, which has become a mecca for homesick Canucks. It is also popular with French students and the general expat crowd. A long bar serves big drinks, big screens serve long sports matches, and seating areas down the back provide for international mingling.

MONTPARNASSE
CUBANA CAFÉ

Map pp434-5

☎ 01 40 46 80 81; 47 rue Vavin, 6e; ⏰ 11am-3am Sun-Wed, 11am-5am Thu-Sat; Ⓜ Vavin

This the perfect place for cocktails and tapas plates (€2 to €8) before carrying on to the nearby La Coupole (p263). The *salon fumoir* (smoking lounge) indulges cigar lovers with comfy old leather armchairs and oil paintings of daily life in Cuba.

LE ROSEBUD

Map pp434-5

☎ 01 43 35 38 54; 11bis rue Delambre, 14e; ⏰ 7pm-2am; Ⓜ Edgar Quinet or Vavin

Like the sleigh of that name in *Citizen Kane*, Rosebud harkens back to the past. In this case it's to the time of the Montparnos (painters and writers who frequented Montparnasse during the neighbourhood's golden years of the early 20th century). Enjoy an expertly mixed champagne cocktail or whisky sour amid the quiet elegance of the polished wood and aged leather setting.

LE SELECT

Map pp434-5

☎ 01 42 22 65 27; 99 blvd du Montparnasse, 6e; ⏰ 7.30am-2.30am; Ⓜ Vavin

Along with La Coupole (p209) and Le Dôme (p209) this café is a great Montparnasse

institution. It has changed very little since it opened in 1923. Students congregate in the early evening; regulars tend to take over as the night wears on. *Tartines* made with Poilâne bread (Poilâne is a famous bakery; see boxed text, p65) are a speciality here (€5 to €15), but you can also have full meals.

FAUBOURG ST-GERMAIN & INVALIDES
CAFÉ DU MUSÉE RODIN

Map pp434-5

☎ 01 44 18 61 10; 77 rue de Varenne, 7e; ⏰ 9.30am-6.45pm Tue-Sun Apr-Sep, 9.30am-4.45pm Tue-Sun Oct-Mar; Ⓜ Varenne

A serene beauty pervades the garden of the Musée Rodin (p126), with the great master's sculptures popping up among the roses and lime trees that line the pathways. If the weather is fine you can have a drink and a snack at one of the tables hidden behind the trees (entry to garden €1).

CAFÉ THOUMIEUX

Map pp434-5

☎ 01 45 51 50 40; 4 rue de la Comète, 7e; ⏰ noon-2am Mon-Fri, 5pm-2am Sat; Ⓜ La Tour Maubourg

The trendy café and tapas annexe of the brasserie Thoumieux (p212) is just a hop, skip and a jump from Les Invalides and the bustle of shops on rue St-Dominique. As a consequence its single, long room is

LATE NIGHTS & EARLY MORNINGS

Most bars shut at 2am, but we've put together a selection of bars for serious night owls. We've also included places that stand out as one of the few late options in their area. Some only open late on weekends.

- Café Charbon (p253) in the 11e
- Café Oz (p239) in the 1er
- Chez Wolf Motown Bar (p253) in the 10e
- Cubana Café (left) at Montparnasse (6e)
- Harry's New York Bar (p252) in the 9e
- Highlander (opposite) in the 6e
- Iguana Café (p242) at Bastille (4e and 11e)
- Le Crocodile (p246) in the 5e
- Le Quetzal (p243) in the Marais (4e)
- Le Tambour (p181) in the 2e
- Le Violon Dinge (p246) in the 5e

always full of well-heeled young people who seem to enjoy the Iberian ambience. Tapas and San Miguel beer set the scene, but vodka is the house speciality, with no fewer than 40 different types (including chocolate and watermelon) on offer for around €9.

ÉTOILE & CHAMPS-ÉLYSÉES

The Champs-Élysées itself is still a popular place for drinking but the vast majority of venues are terribly expensive and tend to be either tacky traps or exceedingly pretentious lounge affairs. A few nondescript but less flashy pubs can be found in the side streets.

The chic quarters around Concorde are not great for finding a classic Parisian café or happening drinking hole, but there are some very memorable, glamorous venues with fantastic décor and, often, a rich history. While not on most Parisians' regular outing list, they definitely merit at least one visit. Most of the fancy hotels along rue de Rivoli have very classy bars and lounges.

ANGÉLINA

Map pp426-7

☎ 01 42 60 82 00; 226 rue de Rivoli, 1er;
⊗ 9am-7pm; Ⓜ Tuileries

Take a break from the long trek along the Tuileries gardens and line up for a table at Angélina, along with the lunching dames and their posturing poodles. This beautiful, high-ceilinged tearoom has exquisite furnishings, mirrored walls and fabulous fluffy cakes. More importantly, it serves the best and most wonderfully sickening 'African' liquid hot chocolate in the history of time (€6.20), served with a pot of whipped cream. It's positive meal replacement and is said to be the best hot chocolate in Paris.

BUDDHA BAR

Map pp426-7

☎ 01 53 05 90 00; 8 rue Boissy d'Anglas, 8e;
⊗ noon-2am Mon-Fri, 6pm-midnight Sat & Sun;
Ⓜ Concorde

Although vacillating in and out of A-list status as the supermodel/gold-card crowd

comes and goes, Buddha Bar has made a name for itself with its zen lounge CDs and remains a hit with suits and tourists. The décor is simply spectacular, with a two-storey golden Buddha, millions of candles, and intimate corners. It's definitely worth it for a cocktail (€12 to €15) or Asian-inspired bar snacks. The admittedly stunning Asian/fusion restaurant is a rip-off – better to peer over it from the bar area.

CRICKETER PUB

Map pp426-7

☎ 01 40 07 01 45; 41 rue des Mathurins, 8e;
⊗ noon-2am; Ⓜ St-Augustin or Madeleine

This English pub can stake a claim to authenticity – it was supposedly transported lock, stock and barrel from Ipswich. It's not a happening venue at night, but with Newcastle Brown on tap, salt 'n' vinegar chips, Brit tabloids and darts it is as close to England as you can get this side of the Channel.

HEMINGWAY BAR

Map pp426-7

☎ 01 43 16 30 30; Hôtel Ritz Paris, 15 place Vendôme, 1er; ⊗ 6.30pm-2am Tue-Sat;
Ⓜ Madeleine or Opéra

This epic bar, nestled in the finery and grandeur of the Ritz, is a paean to Papa and it's where he imbibed after making a name for himself. Legend has it that during the liberation of Paris, Hemingway himself was put in charge of the bar – complete with Jeep and machine gun. Fabulous décor, outstanding cocktails (from €20), and expert bar staff.

LA SUITE

MAP pp426-7

☎ 01 53 57 49 49; 40 av Georges V, 8e;
⊗ restaurant 9am-midnight Mon-Sat, bar 8pm-2am Tue & Wed, 8pm-5am Thu-Sun; Ⓜ Georges V

A *très chic* nesting ground for the creatures of the Champs-Élyseés night. The lurid main bar heats up at night, while 'suites', like kinky dolls' houses with bay windows and pink-and-white furnishings, allow for secluded dining and drinking. Breaching their selective entry system may require booking a table, which will be a very expensive neo-Mediterranean affair. They often host young designers' fashion shows.

Slick interior of Murano (p252)

CLICHY

LUSH BAR

Map pp426-7

☎ 01 43 87 49 46; 16 rue des Dames, 17e; ⏰ 10am-2am Mon-Fri, noon-2am Sat & Sun; Ⓜ Place de Clichy
Next to stylish **Hôtel Eldorado** (p325), this Clichy post has made a name for itself with a relaxed-but-hip local following and Anglo expats. It has excellent cocktails including killer white Russians, as well as wines and, in true English style, affordable beers. DJs often play on weekends.

OPÉRA & GRANDS BOULEVARDS

Mr Haussman's windswept boulevards are unwelcoming and traffic-clogged, but some excellent bars stand out along the main axes and in the side streets. There are some interesting bars near the Bourse (stock exchange) and Opéra, catering mainly to the trader/corporate crowds. Another nocturnal niche is rue Montmartre in the Sentier district, with trendy bars and clubs.

CAFÉ NOIR

Map pp428-9

☎ 01 40 39 07 36; 65 rue Montmartre, 2e; ⏰ 8am-2am Mon-Fri, 3pm-2am Sat; Ⓜ Sentier
An excellent, dependable bar on the edge of the Sentier garment district, the 'Black Café' is one of those bars you decide to make into a regular haunt. It's always packed, with a mix of French and Anglo imbibers attracted by the friendly and very hip ambience.

DE LA VILLE CAFÉ

Map pp428-9

☎ 01 48 24 48 09; 24 blvd de Bonne Nouvelle, 10e; ⏰ 5pm-2am; Ⓜ Bonne Nouvelle
Another success story from the founders of **Café Charbon** (p253) and **Le Nouveau Casino** (p266. This grand former brothel has an alluring, slightly confused mix of restored history and modern design; the mosaic tiles were uncovered by accident during renovations. Between the high-ceilinged restaurant, the extensive terrace and the bar/lounge areas, you're sure to find your niche. DJs play most nights, making it a quality 'before' venue for nearby **Rex Club** (p267) and **Le Pulp** (p267).

FOOTSIE

Map pp426-7

☎ 01 42 60 07 20; 10-12 rue Daunou, 2e; ⏰ noon-2am Mon-Thu, noon-4am Fri & Sat; Ⓜ Opéra
An almost nauseatingly successful gimmick: drink prices floated like stocks, with prices changing according to demand. You stand in this gorgeous wood-panelled bar, with the same pub tracks stuck on repeat and watch way-too-young girls batting eyelashes at be-suited brokers while you

stare at the screen that says if the price of a Heineken has risen or fallen in the last two minutes.

HARRY'S NEW YORK BAR
Map pp426-7

☎ 01 42 61 71 14; 5 rue Daunou, 2e; ⏰ 10.30am-4am; Ⓜ Opéra

Thick with American class of a bygone era, Harry's evokes a golden prewar past without feeling like a museum piece. Lean on the bar where F Scott Fitzgerald and Hemingway once hovered, and have the expert, white-smocked gentlemen prepare you a killer martini or the house creation: the Bloody Mary. The Cuban mahogany interior dates from the mid-19th century and was brought over from a Manhattan bar in 1911. There's a basement piano bar and, for the peckish, old school hot dogs and tasty club sandwiches.

LE CŒUR FOU
Map pp428-9

☎ 01 42 33 91 33; 55 rue Montmartre, 2e; ⏰ 5pm-2am; Ⓜ Étienne Marcel

The 'Crazy Heart' is hip without attaining the too-cool-for-school pretentiousness that reigns in the Étienne Marcel environs. It's a tiny, gallery-like bar with little candles nestled in whitewashed walls and a dapper late-20s crowd that doesn't keep to itself.

O'SULLIVAN'S
Map pp428-9

☎ 01 40 26 73 41; 1 blvd Montmartre, 2e; ⏰ noon-2am Sun-Tue, noon-5am Wed-Fri, 1pm-5am Sat; Ⓜ Grands Boulevards

From the outside it looks like another supermarket-chain Irish pub, but O'Sullivan's is much more. It's hugely popular thanks to its prominent location and friendly vibe. The spacious surrounds are always packed for big sporting events, plus there are live concerts, including jazz, rock, pop and Irish music on weekends, when entry can cost around €10. Different areas like an outdoor terrace mean you can always find a tranquil place to chat.

SOMO
Map pp428-9

☎ 01 40 13 08 80; 168 rue Montmartre, 2e; ⏰ noon-2am Mon-Fri, 6pm-2am Sat, noon-4am Sun; Ⓜ Grands Boulevards

A hip, modern-design bar that caters to an Anglo-oriented crowd has grown out of the student pub scene and moved on to bigger and better things. Loft style with a mezzanine area, SoMo has DJs on weekends – mainly House and lounge music – as well as music concerts on occasions (which can involve an entry fee). There's a fashionable but friendly atmosphere and you can also have lunch or dinner here. SoMo likes to bemuse Parisians with its odd cuisine combinations.

GARE DU NORD, GARE DE L'EST & RÉPUBLIQUE

Canal St-Martin offers a trendy bohemian atmosphere and wonderful summer nights (and days) in casual canalside cafés. The proliferation of bars and cafés in the 10e is gradually joining up this area with Belleville and Ménilmontant. There are also some bars around Gare du Nord and Gare de l'Est.

CHEZ PRUNE
Map pp428-9

☎ 01 42 41 30 47; 71 quai de Valmy, 10e; ⏰ 8am-2am Mon-Sat, 10am-2am Sun; Ⓜ République

This Soho-boho café put Canal St-Martin on the map. It has such a reputation that you

BEST BAR-HOPPING STREETS

These streets have a concentration of bars that makes them great for a leisurely bar crawl.
- Rue Princesse and rue des Canettes in the 6e (p247) are full of student bars, sports bars, tapas bars, pubs.
- Rue Oberkampf and rue Jean-Pierre Timbaud in the 11e (opposite) offer an endless array of hip bars, bohemian hang-outs and atmospheric cafés.
- Rue de la Roquette, rue Keller and rue de Lappe at Bastille (p240) have a huge, diverse range of bars; take your pick.
- Rue Montmartre in the 2e (p251) has some modern, slick bars and pubs.
- Canal St-Martin in the 10e (above) offers a strip of canal-side cafés that are great in warm weather.
- Rue Vieille du Temple and the surrounding streets in the Marais (p240) have a mix of gay bars and chic cafés.

could be forgiven for wondering what the fuss is about. But it's a classic Parisian café-bar, nicely rough around the edges with good vibes – a canalside terrace in summer and a cosy atmosphere in winter.

CHEZ WOLF MOTOWN BAR

Map pp428-9

☎ 01 46 07 09 79; 81-83 blvd de Strasbourg, 10e; ☻ closed 6am-7pm Sat; Ⓜ Gare de l'Est

This little 24-hour find is the place to come in the wee hours when you have a thirst and a few bob but, alas, no friends. You can drink at any time of day and eat (mains €8.50 to €13.50) until 5am, and live singers croon on some nights. There's a warm and festive feel, and the staff and the patrons are friendly.

LE RELAIS DU NORD

Map pp428-9

☎ 01 48 78 03 51; 22 rue de Dunkerque, 10e; ☻ 6am-9pm; Ⓜ Gare du Nord

This gem of an Art Nouveau café is a short distance to the west of the Gare du Nord and an excellent, down-to-earth choice if you're in the mood to celebrate your departure or arrival with a drink or light meal.

LE PANIER

Map pp428-9

☎ 01 42 01 38 18; rue Ste-Marthe, 10e; ☻ 11am-2am Sun-Tue; Ⓜ Belleville

Out in the western flanks of Belleville, it's easy to miss the little street of rue St-Marthe, filled with colourful restaurants and bars, exerting a dilapidated, funky charm. At the top, literally and figuratively, is this splendid and convivial café with an enormous terrace on sheltered place Ste-Marthe. It's brilliant for warm afternoons, casual meals and an extended apéritif; it often hosts live music.

LE VERRE VOLÉ

Map pp428-9

☎ 01 48 03 17 34; 67 rue de Lancry, 10e; ☻ 10.30am-11pm Tue-Sat, 11am-8pm Sun; Ⓜ Jacques Bonsergent

The tiny 'Stolen Glass' – a wine shop with a few tables – is just about the most perfect wine bar in Paris, with excellent wines from southeastern France (€18 to €54 a bottle) and expert advice. Unpretentious and hearty *plats du jour* (daily specials) from €11.

MÉNILMONTANT & BELLEVILLE

Rue Oberkampf is the essential hub of the Ménilmontant bar crawl, springing from a few cafés to being the epicentre of a vibrant, rapidly expanding bar scene. As Oberkampf commercialises, the arty/edgy crowd is moving steadily outwards, through cosmopolitan Belleville and towards La Villette.

CAFÉ CHARBON

Map pp428-9

☎ 01 43 57 55 13; 109 rue Oberkampf, 11e; ☻ 9am-2am Sun-Thu, 9am-4am Fri & Sat; Ⓜ Parmentier

With its postindustrial *belle époque* ambience, this was the first of the hip cafés and bars to catch on in Ménilmontant. Now it's somewhat of a victim of its own success, but it's always crowded and worth heading to for the distressed décor with high ceilings, chandeliers and perched DJ booth. It gives way to Le Nouveau Casino (p266) next door. The food is good; it's popular for Sunday brunch.

CAFÉ CHÉRI(E)

Map pp428-9

☎ 01 42 02 02 05; 44 blvd de la Villette, 19e; ☻ 8am-2am; Ⓜ Belleville

The quintessential of Belleville 'before', this formidably successful bar-café has a lively, gritty, art-chic crowd and nightly electro DJs. An imaginative, colourful bar with its signature red lighting, infamous rum punches and commitment to quality tunes, it's become everyone's *chéri(e)* (darling) and the preclubbing icon of this area. There's a great terrace for warm days.

CANNIBALE CAFÉ

Map pp428-9

☎ 01 49 29 95 59; 93 rue Jean-Pierre Timbaud, 11e; ☻ 8.30am-2am; Ⓜ Couronnes

Warm and welcoming, with an awesome rococo-style bar, wood panelling, high ceilings, Formica tables and red leatherette bench seats. It's a laid-back, almost frayed alternative to the rue Oberkampf hype, great for daytime lingering or night-time mingling. There's an extensive menu with popular breakfasts (€7), and brunch (served between noon and 4pm on the weekend) is €17.90.

LA CARAVANE
Map pp428-9

☎ 01 49 23 01 86; 35 rue de la Fontaine au Roi, 11e; ☺ 11am-2am Sun-Fri, 5pm-2am Fri & Sat; Ⓜ Goncourt

This funky, animated bar is a little jewel tucked away between République and Oberkampf. The bar is surrounded by colourful kitsch furnishings, the people around it and behind it are amiable and relaxed, and the drinks served over it are reasonably priced. The kitchen was into Thai dishes when last we looked, somewhat of a rarity in Paris. It packs out on weekends, but the chilled weeknight atmosphere is worth savouring.

L'ARAM
Map pp440-1

☎ 01 48 05 57 79; 7 rue de la Folie Méricourt, 11e; ☺ noon-2am Mon-Sat, 4pm-midnight Sun; Ⓜ St-Ambroise

Despite its proximity to the heady bustle of Oberkampf, this café-bar théâtre has far more going on than just drinking. Exhibitions, theatre performances, community TV broadcasts and clairvoyant readings are just some of the happenings here. There is usually an 'events night' on Thursday at around 9pm. Even without all the entertainment, l'Aram is worth discovering for its friendly service and somewhat eclectic décor.

L'AUTRE CAFÉ
Map pp428-9

☎ 01 40 21 03 07; 62 rue Jean-Pierre Timbaud, 11e; ☺ 8am-1.30am Mon-Fri, 11.30am-1.30am Sat & Sun; Ⓜ Parmentier

A young mixed crowd of locals, artists and party-goers remains faithful to this quality café with its long bar, spacious seating areas, relaxed environment and reasonable prices. And the food is very good. A springboard for young artists, the Autre Café organises exhibition openings and film screenings. There are also philosophical afternoon teas for children. It's a great place to do a little work, and there is a small lounge upstairs.

LE CHAT NOIR
Map pp428-9

☎ 01 48 06 98 22; 76 rue Jean-Pierre Timbaud, 10e; ☺ 9am-2am; Ⓜ Parmentier

Slightly removed from the overexcitement of Oberkampf and with a slightly older crowd, this attractive corner café with high ceilings and a long wooden bar is a happening but relaxed drinking space at night. It's also a great café in which to hang out or read during the day. Downstairs is more animated with live concerts – usually jazz or world music.

L'ÎLE ENCHANTÉE
Map pp428-9

☎ 01 42 01 67 99; 65 blvd de la Villette, 19e; ☺ 8am-2am Mon-Fri, 5pm-2am Sat & Sun; Ⓜ Belleville

In a similar vein to Café Chéri(e) (p253), this enchanted island in Belleville has become a popular stop-off for the before-clubbing crowd. With its colourful façade, huge windows and large, modern interior, it's a relaxed restaurant and terrace by day that turns electric at nightfall, with quality House/electro DJs mixing most evenings.

MURANO
Map pp440-1

☎ 01 42 71 20 00; 13 blvd du Temple, 3e; ☺ 7am-2am; Ⓜ Filles du Calvaire

This chic bar is located within the Murano hotel, or 'urban resort' as they would have it. Ultramodern and very classy, this establishment is evidence of the new trend of setting up swish boutique hotels in more cosmopolitan areas of Paris. The bar, with its colourful sleek design and lounge ambience, makes a very chichi spot for a cocktail (€16 to €20).

ON CHERCHE ENCORE
Map pp428-9

☎ 01 49 20 79 56; www.onchercheencore.com; 2 rue des Goncourt, 11e; ☺ 9am-2am; Ⓜ Goncourt

A work in progress at the time of writing, this is a space to watch. A relaxed, modern loft-style café-bar is set to materialise, intent on providing quality tunes (electro and funk), quality wines and quality mingling. Whatever eventuates, the corner terrace is positioned for all-afternoon sun and will certainly be worth pouncing on.

POP IN
Map pp440-1

☎ 01 48 05 56 11; 105 rue Amelot, 11e;
🕙 6.30pm-1.30am Tue-Sun; Ⓜ St-Sébastien
Froissart

All skinny jeans and cultivated pop-rock nonchalance, the Pop In somehow got itself on the in-crowd map but maintains a relaxed regulars' vibe. It's popular with expats and Parisian students, the drinks are reasonable and the air is heavy with cigarette smoke and East London influences.

GARE DE LYON, NATION & BERCY

The erstwhile desert of Bercy is an increasingly happening place that draws in crowds for its cinemas and wine bars, though it's a somewhat artificially created scene. Gare de Lyon and Nation are close to drinking spots in Bastille (p240), and to the eastern side of the 11e (p253).

CHAI 33
Map p449

☎ 01 53 44 01 01; 33 cour St-Émilion, 12e;
🕙 noon-2am; Ⓜ Cour St-Émilion

The converted wine warehouses in Bercy Village house a variety of restaurants and bars, including this enormous new wine-oriented concept space with a restaurant, lounge, tasting room and shop. Wine (French and foreign) is divided into six categories, and colour-coded: red is 'fruity and intense', green is 'light and spirited' etc. We never thought we'd see this happen in Paris but, all in all, it seems to work well. There are cocktails and decent food here too, as well as two terraces.

LA FLÈCHE D'OR CAFÉ
Map pp422-3

☎ 01 43 72 04 23; www.flechedor.com; 102bis rue de Bagnolet, 20e; 🕙 8am-2am Tue-Thu, 11am-6am Fri & Sat, noon-5pm Sun; Ⓜ Alexandre Dumas

Just over 1km northeast of place de la Nation, this smoky music bar has a striking setup in a former railway station on the outer edge of central Paris. It attracts a young, arty and alternative crowd; this could very well be Berlin. The big café serves food until 1.30am and does a decent Sunday brunch, but the place is known for its DJ nights and concerts. Reggae, House/electro and rock feature; the Flèche d'Or has a solid reputation for promoting young talent.

LA LIBERTÉ
Map pp446-7

☎ 01 43 72 11 18; 168 rue de Faubourg St-Antoine, 12e; 🕙 11am-2am; Ⓜ Faidherbe-Chaligny

A beautifully messy little bar infused the spirit of the '68 revolution. Simple meals and wine by day, by night it's a heaving mix of regulars and randoms, eclectic songs, red Marlboros, raspy-voiced arguments and glasses going clink. The kind of place where *bobos*, artists, old rockers and the semihomeless find their common point: a passionate love of drink and talk.

13E ARRONDISSEMENT & CHINATOWN

While Chinatown isn't exactly a hopping spot for bars, the area around the Butte aux Cailles, a kind of molehill southwest of Place d'Italie, has some good options. It is a pretty area that is popular with students and local residents: places tend to have die-hard regulars.

LE MERLE MOQUEUR
Map p448

☎ 01 45 65 12 43; 11 rue de la Butte aux Cailles, 13e; 🕙 5pm-2am; Ⓜ Corvisart

Friendly, convivial, and boasting the largest selection of rum punches (€5) we've ever seen, this is the perfect place for an apéritif or late-night drink before or after crossing the street for a meal at Le Temps des Cérises (p230) or up the road at the L'Avant-Goût (p230). Happy hour is from 5pm to 8pm.

MONTMARTRE & PIGALLE

Crowded around the hill side of Montmartre you'll find an utterly eclectic selection of places to drink. This area offers a strange medley of tourist-trap *chanson* bars at Sacré Cœur, sleazy sex-shop venues at Pigalle, African outposts at Château Rouge and picturesque Parisian spots around Abbesses.

JUNGLE MONTMARTRE

Map p432

☎ 01 46 06 75 69; 32 rue Gabrielle, 18e; ☾ 7pm-2am; Ⓜ Abbesses

A corner of West Africa on an outcrop of the Butte Montmartre. We'd walk a million miles for the ginger punch (€5), which soon gets you chatting and boogieing. The atmosphere is hyperfestive thanks to nonstop DJ mixes and a *kora* (West African stringed instrument) player nearly every night. West African dishes (around €12) such as chicken *yassa* (onion and lemon–based sauce) and beef *mafé* (peanut-based stew) are available to 1am.

LA FOURMI

Map p432

☎ 01 42 64 70 35; 74 rue des Martyrs, 18e; ☾ 8am-2am Mon-Thu, 10am-4am Fri-Sun; Ⓜ Pigalle

This Pigalle stayer hits the mark with its lively yet unpretentious atmosphere. The décor is hip but not overwhelming, the zinc bar is long and inviting and the people are laid-back. The music is mostly rock – quality, well-known tunes that get you going while leaving space in the airways for the rise and fall of unbridled conversation. If you're hungry, its *plat du jour* costs €9.

LE CHÀO BÀ

Map p432

☎ 01 46 06 72 90; 22 blvd de Clichy, 18e; ☾ 8.30am-2am Sun-Thu, 9am-4am Fri & Sat; Ⓜ Pigalle

This loungy café-restaurant, transformed from the old-style Café Pigalle, is straight out of the film *Indochine,* decorated in colonial-oriental style with huge plants and bamboo chairs. It serves great cocktails (from €8.50) in goldfish-bowl-sized glasses, and somewhat bland Franco-Vietnamese food. And don't hesitate to ask what *chào bà* means.

LE PROGRÈS

Map p432

☎ 01 42 51 33 33; 7 rue des Trois Frères, 18e; ☾ 5pm-2am; Ⓜ Abbesses

A real live *café du quartier* perched in the heart of Abbesses. Occupying a corner with huge windows and simple seating, it attracts a relaxed mix, of local artists, shop staff, writers and hangers-about, that's very telling of the local population. It's great for convivial evenings, with DJs and bands some nights, but also for inexpensive meals and daytime coffees.

LE SANCERRE

Map p432

☎ 01 42 58 08 20; 35 rue des Abbesses, 18e; ☾ 7am-2am Sun-Thu, 7am-4am Fri & Sat; Ⓜ Abbesses

Le Sancerre is a popular, rather brash bistro-cum-bar that's often crowded to capacity in the evening, especially on Saturday. Scruffy yet attractive with its classic bistro décor and hip local mood, it has a prized terrace that gets the late morning sun. It serves bistro food and breakfasts from 11.30am to 11.30pm.

OLYMPIC CAFÉ

Map p432

☎ 01 42 52 29 93; 20 rue Léon, 18e; ☾ 7pm-2am Mon-Sat; Ⓜ Château Rouge

This community bar in the Goutte d'Or neighbourhood is full of surprises. From plays and film screenings to concerts of Afro punk, Balkan folk, hip-hop, klezmer and so on in the basement, this is a breeding ground for creative young people bursting with original ideas. Events are €5 to €7 and drinks are in the €3 range. The monthly program available at the bar also includes events at the Lavoir Moderne Parisien (Map pp428–9; ☎ 01 42 52 09 14; 35 rue Léon, 18e), another springboard for young talent just down the road.

Entertainment

Entertainment

Parisians are fanatical about culture and theirs is the capital of savoir-vivre, so there are endless ways and means to find entertainment in this city. It's a spectacular place to absorb the abundance of performing arts, fantastic for a night out dancing and probably the film-lover's ultimate city. From jazz bars to comic theatre, from Gipsy beats to go-go dancers, whatever your taste, this chapter will help you plan your personalised delve into the cultural depths and nocturnal heights of the City of Light. Cultural festivals of all genres flourish so be sure to check what's on when you're in town (see p9).

Paris holds a firm place on the touring circuit of the world's finest artists and boasts historic, often legendary concert venues, so seeing a performance here is an absolute treat, and something worth organising before you leave home. Here you can catch world-class French and international opera and ballet companies in such magnificent venues as the **Palais Garnier** (p271); or enjoy classic theatre at the world-famous **Comédie Française** (p269). There are eternal crowd pleasers like traditional French *chansons* and the incorrigible cancan dancers in cabarets of the likes of the Moulin Rouge.

In addition to the classics and the big names of dance and theatre, Paris is a hotbed for creativity and fringe art, and at any moment there are innumerable local performances and productions, often very avant-garde.

When it comes to live concerts, in addition to excellent locally cultivated acts, Paris is a great place to catch the many impressive overseas artists and musicians that are always passing through. All kinds of music from around the world flourish here, while the club scene is peculiar but exerts its own special appeal.

Last but not least the cinema: Parisians are film fetishists *par excellence* and wonderful movie theatres abound. As well as new flicks and avant-garde cinema, Paris is a fantastic place to catch priceless classics.

Information & Listings

In order to sample the richness of Paris' entertainment scene, first take a close look at either *Pariscope* (€0.40) or *L'Officiel des Spectacles* (€0.35), both of which come out on Wednesday and are available at any newsstand. *Pariscope* includes a six-page English-language insert at the back courtesy of London's *Time Out* magazine, though many people think *L'Officiel des Spectacles* is easier to use. The weekly magazine *Zurban* (www.zurban.com in French; €1) also appears on Wednesday and has fresh, informed listings on soirees and cultural events. A number of free, French-language weeklies such as *A nous Paris,* available at metro stations and in the street, also list hot new venues and events. *Les Inrockuptibles* (www.lesinrocks .com in French; €2.90) is a national culture and entertainment weekly mostly devoted to Paris. Its website lists events and concerts.

For up-to-date information on clubs and the music scene, check the above magazines or pick up a copy of *LYLO* (short for *les yeux, les oreilles,* meaning 'eyes and ears'), a free booklet of 50 pages or so with excellent listings of rock concerts and other live music. It is available at many cafés, bars and clubs across town. Check out any of the Fnac outlets (opposite), especially the ones in the Forum des Halles shopping centre, Bastille and the Champs-Élysées, for free flyers, schedules and programmes.

Musicians playing at Le Limonaire (p264)

Other excellent sources for what's on include Radio FG on 98.2 mHz FM (www.radiofg .com in French) and Radio Nova on 101.5 mHz FM.

In addition to the above, for information on the club scene you can also check out www .france-techno.fr (in French) or www.parissi.com (in French).

Tickets & Reservations

You can buy tickets for cultural events at many ticket outlets, including Fnac (rhymes with 'snack') and Virgin Megastore branches, for a small commission. Both accept reservations, ticketing by phone and the Internet, and most credit cards. Tickets generally cannot be returned or exchanged unless a performance is cancelled.

Agence Marivaux (Map pp428–9; ☎ 01 42 97 46 70; 7 rue de Marivaux, 2e; ⏰ 11.30am-7.30pm Mon-Fri, noon-4pm Sat; Ⓜ Richelieu Drouot) is just opposite the Opéra Comique.

Agence Perrossier & SOS Théâtres (Map pp426–7; ☎ 01 42 60 58 31, 01 44 77 88 55; www.agence detheatresdeparis.fr; 6 place de la Madeleine, 8e; ⏰ 10am-7pm Mon-Fri, 10am-5.30pm Sat; Ⓜ Madeleine), one agency with two names, faces the Église de la Madeleine.

Fnac (☎ 08 92 68 36 22; www.fnac.com in French; ⏰ 10am-7.30pm Mon-Sat) has 10 outlets in Paris with *billeteries* (ticket offices) including **Fnac Champs-Élysées** (Map pp426–7; ☎ 01 53 53 64 64; 74 av des Champs-Élysées, 8e; ⏰ 10am-midnight Mon-Sat, 11am-midnight Sun; Ⓜ Franklin D Roosevelt); **Fnac Forum** (Map pp436–7; ☎ 01 40 41 40 00; Forum des Halles shopping centre, Level 3, 1-7 rue Pierre Lescot, 1er; Ⓜ Châtelet Les Halles); **Fnac Montparnasse** (Map pp434–5; ☎ 01 49 54 30 00; 136 rue de Rennes, 6e; Ⓜ St-Placide); **Fnac Musique Bastille** (Map pp440–1; ☎ 01 43 42 04 04; 4 place de la Bastille, 12e; ⏰ 10am-8pm Mon-Sat; Ⓜ Bastille); **Fnac Étoile** (Map pp426–7; ☎ 01 44 09 18 00; 26-30 av des Ternes, 17e; Ⓜ Ternes) and **Fnac St-Lazare** (Map pp426–7; ☎ 01 55 31 20 00; 109 rue St-Lazare, 9e; ⏰ 10am-7.30pm Mon-Wed, Fri & Sat, 10am-9.30pm Thu; Ⓜ St-Lazare).

There are a half-dozen **Virgin Megastores** (www.virginmega.fr in French) in Paris, including **Barbès** (Map p432; ☎ 01 56 55 53 70; 15 blvd Barbès, 18e; ⏰ 10am-9pm Mon-Sat; Ⓜ Barbès Rochechouart); **Champs-Élysées** (Map pp426–7; ☎ 01 49 53 50 00; 52-60 av des Champs-Élysées, 8e; ⏰ 10am-midnight Mon-Sat, noon-midnight Sun; Ⓜ Franklin D Roosevelt), with a large *billeterie* in the basement, and **Galerie du Carrousel du Louvre** (Map pp436–7; ☎ 01 44 50 03 10; 99 rue de Rivoli, 1er; ⏰ 10am-8pm Mon & Tue, 10am-9pm Wed-Sun; Ⓜ Palais Royal Musée du Louvre) with a ticket office in the shopping centre behind the inverted glass pyramid.

Discount Tickets

Two main outlets for discount tickets are **Kiosque Théâtre Madeleine** (Map pp426–7; opp 15 place de la Madeleine, 8e; ⏰ 12.30-7.45pm Tue-Sat, 12.30-3.45pm Sun; Ⓜ Madeleine) and **Kiosque Théâtre Montparnasse** (Map pp434–5; parvis Montparnasse, 15e; Ⓜ Montparnasse Bienvenüe) which keeps the same hours. On the same day of the performance, they sell tickets to plays and other events (concerts, operas, ballets etc) at half price plus commission of about €2.50. However, the seats are often the most expensive ones in the stalls or 1st balcony. The French websites www.billetreduc.com and www.ticketac.com have online discounts.

MUSIC

Music of all kinds thrives in Paris, allowing visitors to indulge in some of the best music that France – and the world – has to offer. Of course, the city is excellent for classical music and big-name rock, pop and independent acts, not to mention some world-renowned jazz. But it is also a cosmopolitan society, whose musical culture is deeply influenced by its rich immigration. Vibrant subcultures and an open-minded public make it a real breeding ground for experimental music of all kinds, and world music in particular – especially from Africa and South America.

Music festivals take place for just about every genre imaginable, so check listings to see what's on when you're in town. Summer is particularly good for outdoor music concerts which often take place along the Seine and in parks. And then of course there are the buskers – from the accordion players of the metro to the amateur opera singers in front of the Centre Pompidou, there's music in the streets (often whether you like it or not). In June the **Fête de la Musique** (p10) sees the whole city taken over by official and improvised concerts and street performances.

Here we have listed the most significant and most interesting venues according to music type; but many *salles* (halls) have eclectic programmes covering different musical types. See also the Drinking chapter (p238), which lists numerous bars that have live bands, singers or DJs.

ROCK, POP & INDIE

There's rock, pop, alternative and indie music around Paris, and a number of venues regularly host international performers. It's often easier to see big-name Anglophone acts in Paris than in their home countries, and it has become a testing ground for up-and-coming British acts. The most popular stadiums and other big venues for international acts are the **Palais Omnisports de Paris-Bercy** (Map pp446–7; ☎ 08 25 03 00 31, 01 46 91 57 57; www.bercy.fr in French; 8 blvd de Bercy, 12e; Ⓜ Bercy); the **Stade de France** (Map p157; ☎ 08 92 70 09 00, 01 55 93 00 00; www.stadedefrance.fr; rue Francis de Pressensé, ZAC du Cornillon Nord, 93216 St-Denis La Plaine; Ⓜ St-Denis-Porte de Paris); and **Le Zénith** (Map pp422–3; ☎ 01 55 80 09 38; www.le-zenith.com in French; 211 av Jean Jaurès, 19e; Ⓜ Porte de Pantin) at the Cité de la Musique in Parc de la Villette, 19e. These are huge impersonal venues, whereas some of the smaller concert halls in Paris have real history and charm and are favoured by fans. *Les Inrockuptibles* (p258) is particularly good for information on concerts.

LA CIGALE Map p432

☎ 01 49 25 89 99; www.lacigale.fr; 120 blvd de Rochechouart, 18e; admission €22-45; Ⓧ box office noon-7pm Mon-Fri; Ⓜ Anvers or Pigalle

Now classed as a historical monument, this music hall dates from 1887 but was redecorated 100 years later by Philippe Starck. Having welcomed artists from Jean Cocteau to Les Rita Mitsouko, today it prides itself on its avant-garde programme, with rock and jazz concerts by international and French acts.

LE BATACLAN Map pp440-1

☎ 01 43 14 00 30; www.bataclan.fr in French; 50 blvd Voltaire, 11e; admission €15-50; Ⓧ box office 3pm-7pm Mon-Sat; Ⓜ Oberkampf or St-Ambroise

Built in 1864 and Maurice Chevalier's debut venue in 1910, this excellent little concert hall draws French and international acts. It also masquerades as a theatre and dance hall. The Bataclan holds concerts, shows, live DJ acts and theatre. Attached is the wonderful **Batadan Café** (☎ 01 49 23 96 33; Ⓧ 7am-2am).

L'ÉLYSÉE-MONTMARTRE Map p432

☎ 01 44 92 45 36, 01 55 07 16 00; www.elyseemontmartre.com; 72 blvd de Rochechouart, 18e; admission €10-34; Ⓜ Anvers

A huge old music hall with a great sound system, L'Élysée-Montmartre is one of the better venues in Paris for one-off rock and indie concerts. It opens at 7.30pm for concerts. It also hosts club events and big-name DJs.

L'OLYMPIA Map pp426-7

☎ 08 92 68 33 68; www.olympiahall.com; 28 blvd des Capucines, 9e; admission €20-50; Ⓧ box office noon-7pm Mon-Fri; Ⓜ Opéra

The Olympia was opened by the Moulin Rouge founder in 1888 and is said to be the oldest concert hall in Paris. It's an atmospheric venue of manageable size with a sloping floor. It has hosted all the big names over the years, from Johnny Hallyday to Jimi Hendrix. This is the hallowed venue of one of Édith Piaf's last performances, and what Jeff Buckley considered his best ever concert, the seminal *Live at l'Olympia* in 1995.

CLASSICAL

Paris plays host to dozens of orchestral, organ and chamber-music concerts each week. In addition to the theatres and concert halls listed below, Paris' beautiful churches have much-celebrated organs and can be wonderful places to hear music. The concerts don't keep to any fixed schedule, but are advertised on posters around town. Admission fees can vary, but they usually range from €10 for children and students to €20 for adults.

CHÂTELET-THÉÂTRE MUSICAL DE PARIS Map pp436-7

☎ 01 40 28 28 40; www.chatelet-theatre.com in French; 2 rue Édouard Colonne, 1er; concert tickets €9-60, opera €11-106, ballet €9-62; Ⓧ box office 11am-7pm, no performances Jul & Aug; Ⓜ Châtelet

The central Théâtre du Châtelet hosts concerts (including ones by the Orchestre de

Paris) as well as operas, ballets and theatre performances. Tickets go on sale at the box office 14 days before the performance date. Subject to availability, anyone under 26 or over 65 can get reduced-price tickets from 15 minutes before curtain time. The entrance is on Place du Châtelet.

SALLE PLEYEL Map pp426-7
☎ 01 42 56 13 13; www.sallepleyel.fr; 252 rue du Faubourg St-Honoré, 8e; Ⓜ Ternes
This highly regarded hall dating from the 1920s hosts many of Paris' finest classical music concerts and recitals. It closed in July 2002 for renovations and plans to re-open in September 2006 with prestigious French and foreign orchestras on the programme.

THÉÂTRE DES CHAMPS-ÉLYSÉES
Map pp426-7
☎ 01 49 52 50 50; www.theatrechampselysees .fr in French; 15 av Montaigne, 8e; tickets €5-120; ⏰ box office 1-7pm Mon-Sat; Ⓜ Alma Marceau
This prestigious Right Bank orchestral and recital hall holds concerts throughout the year. It also serves as a theatre called the Comédie des Champs-Élysées (☎ 01 53 23 99 19; www.comediedeschampselysees.com).

JAZZ & BLUES
After WWII, Paris was Europe's most important jazz centre and, though the style has only a niche following today, the city's better clubs and cellars attract international stars. Top acts play at the wonderful **Paris Jazz Festival** (Parc Floral de Paris; ☎ 01 43 41 16 26; www.parc floraldeparis.com), which takes place in the Parc Floral in June and July each year, with interactive events and jazz concerts. The **Banlieues Bleues** (Suburban Blues; ☎ 01 49 22 10 10; www.banlieuesbleues.org), a jazz festival held in St-Denis and other Paris suburbs in March and early April, also attracts big-name talent. Paris' soothing jazz radio station **TFS** (89.9 mHz; www.tsfjazz.com) has concert information in French both on the airwaves and on its website.

CAFÉ UNIVERSEL Map pp444-5
☎ 01 43 25 74 20; 267 rue St-Jacques, 5e; admission free; ⏰ 9.30pm-2am Mon-Sat; Ⓜ Port Royal
The Café Universel has been much talked about of late. It hosts a brilliant array of live concerts with everything from bebop and

Latin sounds to vocal jazz sessions. Entry is free and there's a lot of freedom given to young producers and artists. Its convivial relaxed atmosphere attracts a mix of students and jazz lovers.

LE BAISER SALÉ Map pp436-7
☎ 01 42 33 37 71; 58 rue des Lombards, 1er; admission free-€22; ⏰ 7pm-late; Ⓜ Châtelet
One of several jazz clubs on this street, the *salle de jazz* (jazz room) on its 1st floor has concerts of jazz, Afro-jazz and jazz fusion. Sometimes there's also room for pop rock or *chansons*. Combining big names and unknown artists, it is known for its relaxed vibe and a gift for discovering new talents. The cover charge depends on the act; the bar on the ground floor is open from 6pm to 6am.

LE CAVEAU DE LA HUCHETTE
Map pp436-7
☎ 01 43 26 65 05; www.caveaudelahuchette.fr; 5 rue de la Huchette, 5e; adult Sun-Thu €11, Fri & Sat €13, student €10; ⏰ 9.30pm-2.30am Sun-Thu, 9pm-4am Fri & Sat; Ⓜ St-Michel
Housed in a medieval *caveau* (cellar) that was used as a courtroom and torture chamber during the Revolution, this club is where virtually all the jazz greats have played since the end of WWII. It's touristy, but the atmosphere can be more electric than at the more serious jazz clubs. Sessions start at 9.30pm.

LE DUC DES LOMBARDS Map pp436-7
☎ 01 42 33 22 88; www.ducdeslombards.com; 42 rue des Lombards, 1er; admission €16-20; ⏰ 9pm-4am; Ⓜ Châtelet
A cool venue decorated with posters of jazz greats (including the eponymous Duke), this place attracts a far more relaxed (and less reverent) crowd than the other jazz clubs in the same street. The ground-floor bar is packed out from 9pm, when sets start, to 4am nightly and the Duc continues to bring in some of the greatest names in jazz.

LE PETIT JOURNAL ST-MICHEL
Map pp444-5
☎ 01 43 26 28 59; www.petitjournalsaintmichel .com in French; 71 blvd St-Michel, 5e; admission €15-17.50; ⏰ 8pm-2am Mon-Sat; Ⓜ Luxembourg
This is a sophisticated jazz venue with everything from Dixieland and vocals to big

band and swing. Classic jazz concerts take place in the atmospheric downstairs cellar from 9pm until 1am. Monday night jam sessions are free.

L'OPUS Map pp428-9

☎ 01 40 34 70 00; 167 quai de Valmy, 10e; admission free-€15; ✆ 8pm-2am Sun & Tue-Thu, 8pm-4am Fri & Sat; Ⓜ Louis Blanc

Housed in a former officers' mess by the Canal St-Martin, the Opus has moved on from hip-hop to the cool sounds of jazz, soul, blues, gospel and *zouk* (a blend of African and Latin American dance rhythms). It's a welcoming venue with wood-panelled walls. It also serves food; sometimes concerts obligatorily include dinner for €22 to €31.

NEW MORNING Map pp428-9

☎ 01 45 23 51 41; www.newmorning.com in French; 7-9 rue des Petites Écuries, 10e; admission €15-21; ✆ 8pm-2am, box office 4.30-7.30pm Mon-Fri; Ⓜ Château d'Eau

New Morning is a highly regarded auditorium that hosts big-name jazz concerts as well as blues, rock, funk, salsa, Afro-Cuban and Brazilian music. Concerts take place three to seven nights a week at 9pm, with the second set ending at about 1am. Tickets are available at the box office, but can usually be purchased at the door.

SUNSET & SUNSIDE Map pp436-7

☎ 01 40 26 46 60, Sunside 01 40 26 21 25; www.sunset-sunside.com; 60 rue des Lombards, 1er; admission €10-22; ✆ 9.30pm-4am Mon-Sat; Ⓜ Châtelet

Two venues in one at this trendy, well-respected club. The Sunset downstairs has electric jazz and fusion concerts beginning at 10pm. It leans towards world music and sometimes runs salsa sessions during the week. The Sunside picks things up upstairs with jazz acoustics and concerts at 9pm, attracting musicians and actors (both film and theatre).

WORLD & LATINO

Sono mondiale (world music) is a very big deal in Paris and you'll hear everything from Algerian *raï* and other North African music to Senegalese *mbalax* and West Indian *zouk* at clubs. But nothing has caught

Moulin Rouge (p272)

on in the past decade like Latino music, especially Cuban salsa. Many of the concert and clubbing venues listed have salsa classes – look also for dancing along the Seine in summer. See also the Clubbing section (p265), as these and other clubs often have world beats and live acts.

BISTROT LATIN Map pp436-7

☎ 01 42 77 21 11; 20 rue du Temple, 4e; admission €6-10; ✆ 7pm-1am Mon, Wed & Thu, 7pm-2am Fri-Sun; Ⓜ Hôtel de Ville

This friendly club and restaurant upstairs from the cinema Le Latina (p269) is well plugged into the Latino music scene, with salsa and tango nights. Dance classes are usually held from 7pm to 8.30pm.

CITÉ DE LA MUSIQUE Map pp422-3

☎ 01 44 84 44 84; www.cite-musique.fr; 221 av Jean Jaurès, 19e; tickets €6-34; ✆ box office noon-6pm Tue-Sat, 10am-6pm Sun, to 8pm on day of performance; Ⓜ Porte de Pantin

At the Parc de la Villette, every imaginable type of music and dance, from Western classical to North African and Japanese, is hosted in its oval-shaped, 1200-seat main auditorium. Concerts are in the little Amphithéâtre du Musée de la Musique. Get tickets from the box office opposite the main auditorium next to the Fontaine aux Lions.

CONSERVATOIRE NATIONAL SUPÉRIEUR DE MUSIQUE ET DE DANSE Map pp422-3

National Higher Conservatory of Music & Dance; ☎ 01 40 40 45 45; www.cnsmdp.fr; 209 av Jean Jaurès, 19e; ⊗ box office noon-6pm Tue-Sat, 10am-6pm Sun, to 8pm on day of performance; Ⓜ Porte de Pantin

On the other side of the fountain from the Cité de la Musique (but sharing the same box office) students put on free orchestra concerts and recitals several times a week, in the afternoon or evening.

LA CHAPELLE DES LOMBARDS

Map pp440-1

☎ 01 43 57 24 24; 19 rue de Lappe, 11e; admission €15-19; ⊗ 11pm-dawn Tue-Sun; Ⓜ Bastille

This perennially popular Bastille dance club has happening Latino DJs and reggae, funk and zouk concerts – in a word, a bit of everything. Concerts take place at 8.30pm on Thursday and Friday.

LA COUPOLE Map pp434-5

☎ 01 43 27 56 00; 102 blvd du Montparnasse, 14e; admission €12-16; ⊗ 9.30pm-3am Thu, 11.30pm-5.30am Fri, 10am-5pm Sat; Ⓜ Vavin

Above La Coupole (p209) restaurant, this established club is famed for its salsa nights, which were credited with single-handedly passing Latin fever to most of Paris. Salsa and Latino nights still take place, but the venue hosts also hosts other kinds of music like zouk, reggae/funk and garage.

LA JAVA Map pp428-9

☎ 01 42 02 20 52; 105 rue du Faubourg du Temple, 10e; admission €8-16; ⊗ 11pm-5am Thu-Sat, 2-7pm Sun; Ⓜ Goncourt

Built in 1922 this is the dance hall where Édith Piaf (see the boxed text, p264) got her first break, and it now reverberates to the sound of live salsa and other Latino music. Live concerts of the world music variety usually take place at 9pm. After this a festive crowd gets dancing to Latino DJs.

L'ATTIRAIL Map pp428-9

☎ 01 42 72 44 42; 9 rue au Maire, 3e; admission free; ⊗ 10.30am-1.30am; Ⓜ Arts et Métiers

Free concerts of chansons françaises and world music (Gypsy music rap, Irish sets,

southern Italian folk and pop) almost daily at 8.30pm. With its cheap pots (460mL bottle) of wine and friendly staff, this cosmopolitan enclave in the heart the original Chinatown attracts a large crowd of students. Manic but friendly customers crowd the amazing Formica bar, which snakes its way down one side of a smoky room covered with posters.

LES ÉTOILES Map pp428-9

☎ 01 47 70 60 56; 61 rue du Château d'Eau, 10e; admission €9-20; ⊗ 9pm-4am Thu-Sat; Ⓜ Château d'Eau

Paris' first music hall in a former theatre opened in 1856 and is still going strong. It features live Latin bands and an ambiente popular (easygoing atmosphere) three nights a week. Salsa is the go – and they usually have a live orchestra. Part of the night is usually reserved for dinner (€20), and part for salsa classes.

SATELLIT CAFÉ Map pp440-1

☎ 01 47 00 48 87; www.satellit-café.com; 44 rue de la Folie Méricourt, 11e; admission €10-12; ⊗ 8pm-3am Tue-Thu, 10pm-6am Fri & Sat; Ⓜ Oberkampf

A great venue for world music and not as painfully trendy as some others in Paris. Come here to hear everything from blues and flamenco to tango and Peruvian folk music. Concerts usually take place at 9pm.

FRENCH CHANSONS

When French music comes to mind, most people hear accordions and chansonniers (cabaret singers) such as Édith Piaf, Jacques Brel, Georges Brassens and Léo Ferré. But though you may stumble upon buskers performing chansons françaises (French songs) or playing musette (accordion music) in the market, it can sometimes be difficult to catch traditional French music in a more formal setting. Following are a handful of venues where you're sure to hear it – both the traditional and the modern forms.

AU LAPIN AGILE Map p432

☎ 01 46 06 85 87; www.au-lapin-agile.com; 22 rue des Saules, 18e; adult €24, students except Sat €17; ⊗ 9pm-2am Tue-Sun; Ⓜ Lamarck Caulaincourt

This rustic cabaret venue was favoured by artists and intellectuals in the early 20th century and chansons are still performed here.

The four-hour show starts at 9.30pm and includes singing and poetry. Some love it, others feel it's a bit of a trap. Admission includes one drink. Named after *Le Lapin à Gill*, a mural of a rabbit jumping out of a cooking pot by caricaturist André Gill, which can still be seen on the western exterior wall.

CHEZ ADEL Map pp428-9

☎ 01 42 08 24 61; 10 rue de la Grange aux Belles, 10e; admission free; ☾ noon-2am; Ⓜ Jacques Bonsergent

Chez Adel is a truly Parisian concept: Syrian hosts with guest *chansonniers* (as well as Gypsy, folk and world music) performing most nights to a mixed and enthusiastic crowd. Mains cost €10. The part-Parisian part-Eastern décor of this simple bistro looks better as the owners' punch goes down.

CHEZ LOUISETTE Map pp422-3

☎ 01 40 12 10 14; Marché aux Puces de St-Ouen; ☾ noon-6pm Sat-Mon; Ⓜ Porte de Clignancourt

Here since 1967, this little bistro is one of the highlights of a visit to Paris' largest **flea market** (p302). Market-goers crowd around little tables to eat lunch (mains €12 to €20) and hear old-time *chanteuses* and *chanteurs* (they change regularly) belt out numbers by Piaf and other classic French singers, accompanied by accordion music; you might even get to see an inspired diner jump up to dance *la guinguette* (jig) in the aisles.

LE LIMONAIRE Map pp428-9

☎ 01 45 23 33 33; 18 cité Bergère, 9e; admission free; ☾ 6pm-midnight Tue-Sun; Ⓜ Grands Boulevards

This little wine bar, tucked far away from the big commercial cabarets off rue Bergère, is one of the best places to listen to traditional French *chansons*. The crowd can be convivial or almost reverential, depending on the night. The singers (who change regularly) perform on the small stage at 10pm every night. It's free entry, and simple meals are served for around €10; be generous when the hat comes your way.

ÉDITH PIAF: URCHIN SPARROW

Like her US contemporary Judy Garland, Édith Piaf was not just a singer but a tragic and stoic figure who the nation took to its heart and has never let go.

She was born Édith Giovanna Gassion to a street acrobat and a singer in the working-class district of Belleville in 1915. Spending her childhood with an alcoholic grandmother who neglected her and a stint with her father's family, who ran a local brothel in Normandy, Piaf's beginnings were far from fortunate. On tour with her father by the age of nine, by 15 she had left home to sing alone in the streets of Paris. It was her first employer, Louis Leplée, who dubbed her *la môme piaf* (urchin sparrow) and introduced her to the cabarets of the capital.

When Leplée was murdered in 1935 Piaf faced the streets again, but along came Raymond Asso, an ex-French Legionnaire who became her Pygmalion. He forced her to break with her pimp and hustler friends, put her in her signature black dress and was the inspiration for her first big hit, *Mon légionnaire* (My Legionnaire) in 1937. From a contract at what is now **La Java** (p263), one of the most famous Parisian music halls of the time, her career skyrocketed.

This frail woman, who sang about street life, drugs, unrequited love, violence, death and whores, seemed to embody all the miseries of the world yet sang in a husky, powerful voice with no self-pity. Her tumultuous love life earned her the reputation as *une dévoreuse d'hommes* (a man-eater); in fact she launched the careers of several of her lovers, including Yves Montand and Charles Aznavour. When one of her lovers, world middleweight boxing champion Marcel Cerdan, died suddenly in a plane crash, Piaf insisted that the show go on — and fainted on stage in the middle of *L'Hymne à l'amour* (Hymn to Love), a song inspired by Cerdan.

After suffering injuries in a car accident in 1951, Piaf began drinking heavily and became addicted to morphine. Despite her rapidly declining health she continued to take the world stage, including New York's Carnegie Hall in 1956, and recorded some of her biggest hits such as *Je ne regrette rien* (No, I regret nothing) and *Milord* (My Lord). In 1962, frail and once again penniless, Piaf married a 20-year-old hairdresser called Théophanis Lamboukas (aka Théo Sarapo), recorded the duet *À quoi ça sert l'amour?* (What Use Is Love?) with him and left Paris for the South of France, where she died the following year. Some two million people attended her funeral in Paris, and the grave of the beloved and much missed Urchin Sparrow at Père Lachaise Cemetery is still visited and decorated by thousands of loyal fans each year. Interest in her life and work continues unabated, as was seen in early 2004 when the City of Paris sponsored a highly successful and interactive exhibition called *Piaf, la Môme de Paris* (Piaf, the Urchin Sparrow of Paris).

CLUBBING

Paris does not have a mainstream club scene resembling that found in other major capitals. A night out in Paris can be anything from sauntering about with the champagne-guzzling Champs-Elysées crowd to opening an unmarked doorway in the city's industrial outskirts in search of a dance party. The music, theme and crowd to be found at most clubs changes regularly according to the whims of the moment. The Latin scene is huge with salsa dancing and Latino music nights taking place in many clubs; those with live music are listed on p262. There's a decent R & B and hip-hop following, although these styles are far less represented here than in, say, London. Electronic music is high quality in Paris' clubs, with some excellent local House and techno. Recently the predominance of dark minimal sounds seems to be giving way to more funk and groove. This scene remains somewhat underground and very mobile – the best DJs and their followings tend to have short stints in a certain venue before moving on. To keep in the loop, see Information & Listings, p258, and pick up flyers in shops; the website www.audiofamilies .com has information and downloads on top Parisian DJs. Some of the bars listed in the Drinking chapter (p238) have DJ nights and dancing.

Admission to clubs generally costs around €10 to €15 and includes a drink; often men cannot get in unaccompanied (by women, that is). Drink prices vary greatly but you're usually looking at upwards of €6 for a beer and €8 for mixed drinks and cocktails.

AU TANGO Map pp436-7

☎ 01 42 72 17 78; www.boite-a-frissons.fr; 13 rue au Maire, 3e; admission €7; ☾ 10.30pm-5am Fri & Sat, 5-11pm Sun; Ⓜ Arts et Métiers

Billing itself as a *boîte à frissons* (quivering club), Au Tango brings in a mixed and cosmopolitan gay and lesbian crowd. Housed in a historic 1930s dance-hall, its atmosphere and style are retro and festive. Dancing gets going when it opens at 10.30pm with waltzing, salsa and tango. From about 12.30am onwards DJs play disco and other sounds, but there's no techno allowed. It also has debates, concerts and meetings.

GIBUS Map pp428-9

☎ 01 47 00 78 88; www.gibus.fr in French; 18 rue du Faubourg du Temple, 11e; admission free-€18; ☾ 11pm-dawn Tue-Sat; Ⓜ République

A dark and dingy cave-like venue, the Gibus is huddled against the very different Favela Chic, halfway between Canal St-Martin and place de la République. Once a temple for rock music, today it's a kind of no-man's land, yielded over to other sounds, mainly techno and trance. Disco gets a word in also, and it has popular R & B and hip-hop nights, drawing a would-be gangsta crowd. Women usually get in free – not always a good sign.

LA FAVELA CHIC Map pp428-9

☎ 01 40 21 38 14; www.favelachic.com in French; 18 rue du Faubourg du Temple, 10e; admission €10; ☾ 7.30pm-2am Tue-Fri, 9.30pm-4am Sat; Ⓜ République

It starts as a chic, convivial restaurant and gives way to *cäpirinha*-fuelled bumping, grinding, flirting and dancing – mostly on the tables. The music is traditionally samba, *baile* (dance) funk and Brazilian pop but increasingly and disappointingly errs towards Western pop. This place is hot, packed and sultry, proudly bearing its motto of 'Disorder and Progress' (an iconoclastic jab at Brazil's national motto '*Ordem e Progresso*').

LA GUINGUETTE PIRATE Map p449

☎ 01 53 61 08 49; opp 11 quai François Mauriac, 13e; admission €6-12; ☾ 7pm-2am Tue-Sat, 5pm-midnight Sun; Ⓜ Quai de la Gare or Bibliothèque

A floating *boîte* (club), in a three-masted Chinese junk referred to as '*la dame de Canton*' (the lady from Canton), it usually hosts some sort of concert at 8pm – anything from pop and indie to electro and hip-hop – and the crowd is young and energetic.

LE BALAJO Map pp440-1

☎ 01 47 00 07 87; 9 rue de Lappe, 11e; admission €10-17; ☾ 9pm-2am Tue-Thu, 11pm-5am Fri & Sat, 3-7.30pm Sun; Ⓜ Bastille

A mainstay of Parisian nightlife since 1936, this ancient ballroom is devoted to salsa classes and Latino music during the week. Weekends see DJs spinning a very mixed bag of rock, disco, R & B and House. While a bit lower-shelf these days, it scores a mention for its historical value and its old-fashioned *musette* (accordion music) gigs

CLUBBING IN PARIS: BEFORE AND AFTER

Seasoned Parisian clubbers, who tend to have a finely tuned sense of the absurd, divide their night out into three main parts. First, *la before*, usually drinks in a bar that has a DJ playing (many are listed in the Drinking chapter, p238). Next they head to a club for *la soirée*, which rarely kicks off before 1am or 2am. When the party continues (or begins) at around 5am and goes until midday, it's called *l'after*. Often, however, the before and the after blend into one without any real 'during'. Meanwhile *'after d'afters'* are increasingly held in bars and clubs on Sunday afternoons and evenings, with a mix of strung-out clubbers kicking on and people out for a relaxed party that doesn't take place in the middle of the night. Go figure.

on Sundays: waltz, tango and cha-cha for aficionados of retro tea-dancing.

LE BARON Map pp426-7

☎ 01 47 20 04 01; 6 av Marceau, 8e; ⌚ 10pm-5am; Ⓜ Alma-Marceau

When it reopened in 2004, the Baron shot to fame as the place where everyone wanted to be but no-one could get into. Intimately located in a former brothel with a smouldering, luxury-cabaret ambience, it's graced by a continuous trail of St-Germain artists, hip writers and A-list celebrities (Björk, Sophia Coppola). This is what Parisians mean when they say a place is *hype*. You usually need to know a member or be a famous actor (or a brilliant liar) to get in.

LE BATOFAR Map p449

☎ 01 56 29 10 33; www.batofar.net in French; opp 11 quai François Mauriac, 13e; admission free-€15; ⌚ 9pm-midnight Mon & Tue, to 4am or later Wed-Sun; Ⓜ Quai de la Gare or Bibliothèque

This incongruous and much-loved red-metal tugboat moored next to the imposing Bibliothèque Nationale de France has a rooftop bar that's great in summer, while the club underneath provides memorable underwater acoustics between its metal walls and portholes. The *bateau* is known for its edgy, experimental music policy and live performances, mostly electro-oriented but also incorporating other sounds like hip-hop, new wave, rock, punk or jazz. Sometimes it doesn't open 'til 10pm.

LE CAB' Map pp436-7

☎ 01 58 62 56 25; www.cabaret.fr; 2 place du Palais Royal, 1er; admission €20; ⌚ 7.30pm-5am Tue-Sat; Ⓜ Palais Royal-Musée du Louvre

Another chic bar-club-restaurant reserved for the bold and the beautiful, it has a modern-design interior with circular lounge areas set around a House-and-disco dance floor. You need to be dressed up to get past the door staff, and cashed up to afford the drinks.

LE CITHÉA Map pp428-9

☎ 01 40 21 70 95; 114 rue Oberkampf, 11e; admission free-€4; ⌚ 5pm-5.30am Tue-Thu, 10pm-6.30am Fri & Sat; Ⓜ Parmentier or Ménilmontant

This popular and ever-hopping venue picks up the post-drinking crowd from rue Oberkampf. There's a pub-meets-concert-hall feel to it, with quality bands playing rock, soul, jazz and funk. Concerts usually run from 10.30pm, with DJs from 1am.

LE DÉPÔT Map pp436-7

☎ 01 44 54 96 96; 10 rue aux Ours, 3e; admission €6-12; ⌚ 2pm-8am; Ⓜ Rambuteau or Étienne Marcel

With a cop shop just next door you'd think this strictly men-only bar would be a titch more subdued. Fat chance. It proudly waves its gay flag just metres from the red, white and blue ones of the *commissariat* and is perhaps just as much of an institution. It's a major men's pick-up joint with theme nights, DJs and notorious backrooms.

LE DIVAN DU MONDE Map p432

☎ 01 40 05 06 99; 75 rue des Martyrs, 18e; admission free to €10-12; ⌚ 7pm-3am; Ⓜ Pigalle

Take some cinematographic events, bossa nova concerts and Gypsy gatherings. Then add in soul/funk fiestas, air-guitar face-offs and rock parties of the White Stripes/Smiths persuasion. You may now be starting to get some idea of the inventive, open-minded approach at this excellent cross-cultural venue in Pigalle. Check the programme and look out for their themed apéritifs that begin at 7pm.

LE NOUVEAU CASINO Map pp428-9

☎ 01 43 57 57 40; www.nouveaucasino.net in French; 109 rue Oberkampf, 11e; admission free-€18; ⌚ 9pm or 11pm-2am or 6am; Ⓜ Parmentier

This club/concert annexe of the Café Charbon (p253) rapidly made a name for itself with its intimate live music concerts and top DJs. Electro, pop, deep House, rock – the programme is eclectic, underground and always up to the minute. Small but well designed, it mixes sharp modern lines and chandeliers, with a tiny mezzanine lounge upstairs. Try to get there before everyone pours out of the surrounding bars at 2am.

LE PULP Map pp428-9
☎ 01 40 26 01 93; www.pulp-paris.com; 25 blvd Poissonnière, 2e; admission free-€10; ⌚ midnight-6am Thu-Sun; Ⓜ Grands Boulevards
A hip yet down-to-earth place with a hot little dance floor and a lounge area with couches, the Pulp was Paris' pre-eminent women's-only club. Men are allowed in (when accompanied by more women) on the mixed Thursday nights, which have been known for attracting the electronic in-crowd and some of Paris' best House/electro DJs.

LE QUEEN Map pp426-7
☎ 01 53 89 08 90; www.queen.fr; 102 av des Champs-Élysées, 8e; admission €9-20; ⌚ midnight-6am; Ⓜ George V
Once the king (as it were) of gay discos in Paris, Le Queen now reigns supreme with a very mixed crowd though it still has gay nights. While right on the Champs-Élysées, it's not as difficult to get into as it used to be – and not nearly as inaccessible as most of the nearby clubs. There's a festive atmosphere and mix of music with lots of House and funk. Currently famed for its hugely popular Disco Inferno Monday nights.

LE RÉSERVOIR Map pp440-1
☎ 01 43 56 39 60; 16 rue de la Forge Royale, 11e; admission free-€15; ⌚ 8pm-2am Mon-Thu, 8pm-4am Fri & Sat, noon-2am Sun; Ⓜ Ledru Rollin
This east Paris warehouse-turned-restaurant-club is a place to party, not to share a romantic dinner for two. It's an impressive, cave-like space lit with candles. There's an

TOP FIVE CLUBS
- La Favela Chic (p265)
- Le Baron (opposite)
- Le Batofar (opposite)
- Le Nouveau Casino (opposite)
- Rex Club (right)

imposing stage in the centre of the room where concerts take place most nights at 11pm. The music is eclectic – pop, tango, Latino, jazz etc – and the clientele fairly hip.

LE WAGG Map pp436-7
☎ 01 55 42 22 00; 62 rue Mazarine, 6e; admission €10-12; ⌚ 11pm-5am Wed-Sun; Ⓜ Odéon
The former Whisky a Go-Go is now a UK-style Conran club (associated with the popular Fabric in London). Compared with the usual scruffy style of Paris clubs, the Wagg is beautifully done in terms of slick fixtures and contemporary design, but the vibe is somewhat stifled and the in-crowd came and went. Last time we looked it had been taken over by the salsa craze.

LES BAINS Map pp436-7
☎ 01 48 87 01 80; www.lesbains-club.com in French; 7 rue du Bourg l'Abbé, 3e; admission €16-20; ⌚ 11pm-5am Mon-Sat; Ⓜ Étienne Marcel
Housed in a refitted old Turkish *hammam*, Les Bains recently reopened after a modern makeover: shiny but predictable with lots of couches, disco balls and giant screens with sharks swimming across them. Once famous for its glamorous clientele and impassable door, it has sought to shake off its inaccessible image with a new mix of themes including funk nights by Respect is Burning, Sunday morning 'afters' and gay soirees.

RED LIGHT Map pp434-5
☎ 01 42 79 94 94; 34 rue du Départ, 14e; admission €20; ⌚ 11pm-6am Thu-Sun; Ⓜ Montparnasse Bienvenüe
Previously and perhaps more fittingly named *l'enfer* (hell), this seedy underground (literally) venue beneath Tour Montparnasse refuses to perish. Huge and laser-lit, it's a popular choice for student drink-fest evenings during the week, while weekends see a young, exuberant gay crowd pack out its podiums.

REX CLUB Map pp428-9
☎ 01 42 36 10 96; 5 blvd Poissonnière, 2e; admission €8-13; ⌚ 11.30pm-6am Wed-Sat; Ⓜ Bonne Nouvelle
The Rex reigns majestic in the House and techno scene, always has and probably always will. The sound system is impeccable but the place sadly lacks a decent chill out. It

Entertainment

CLUBBING

welcomes big-name local and international DJs and getting in is more a question of lining up than looking right. Friday nights are a techno institution in Paris; after all this is the old stomping ground of Laurent Garnier.

TRIPTYQUE Map pp428-9

☎ 01 40 28 05 55; www.letryptique.com; 142 rue Montmartre, 2e; admission €3-10, more for concerts; ⏱ 9pm-2am Sun-Wed, 9pm-5am Thu-Sat; Ⓜ Grands Boulevards

A vast club set up in three stonewalled underground rooms decorated with video projections. Triptyque opened in 2003, filling somewhat of a gap in inner-city clubbing. Crowd-wise it's fairly unpretentious without being overly trashy. Musically they're on to it, with a serious sound system spanning electro, hip-hop and funk, as well as jazz and live acts.

CINEMA

Pariscope and *L'Officiel des Spectacles* (p258) list Paris' cinematic offerings alphabetically by their French title followed by the English (or German, Italian, Spanish etc). Going to the cinema in Paris does not come cheaply: expect to pay up to €9 for a first-run film. Students and those aged under 18 or over 60 usually get discounts of about 25% except on Friday nights, all day Saturday and until the evening on Sunday. On Wednesday (and sometimes Monday) most cinemas give discounts of 20% to 30% to everyone. At some cinemas the first film of the day (usually before noon) is half-price.

If a movie is labelled 'vo' or 'VO' (for *version originale*) it means it will be sub-titled rather than dubbed (labelled 'vf', *version française*). Thus English-language films marked 'vo' will still be in English.

Cinémathèque Française

Beyond the cinemas showing Hollywood blockbusters, the following are noteworthy.

CINÉMA DES CINÉASTES Map pp426-7

☎ 01 53 42 40 20, 0 836 68 97 17; 7 av de Clichy, 17e; adult €6.50-7.20, student & child €5.50-5.70, morning screenings €4.80; Ⓜ Place de Clichy

Founded by the three Claudes (Miller, Berri and Lelouch) and *Betty Blue* director Jean-Jacques Beneix, this is a three-screen theatre dedicated to quality cinema, be it French or foreign, but always avant-garde. Thematic seasons, documentaries and meet-the-director sessions round out the repertoire.

CINÉMATHÈQUE FRANÇAISE
Map pp446-7

☎ 01 71 19 33 33; www.cinemathequefrancaise .com in French; 51 rue Bercy, 12e; adult/student & child €8/6.50; Ⓜ Bercy

This national institution almost always leaves its foreign offerings – often rarely screened classics – in their original versions. Having had to close the *salles* on Palais de Chaillot and Grands Boulevards, it is now only at Bercy. The association is a nonprofit collective largely funded by the state. The new *cinémathèque* is a veritable temple to the 'seventh art' and also holds debates, cultural events, workshops and exhibitions.

FORUM DES IMAGES Map pp436-7

☎ 01 44 76 62 00; www.forumdesimages.net in French; 1 Grande Galerie, Porte St-Eustache, Forum des Halles, 1er; adult €6.50, senior, student & under 26 €5.50; ⏱ 1-10pm Tue, 1-9pm Wed-Sun; Ⓜ Les Halles

This archive cinema beneath the sprawling Forum des Halles is a superb place to see rarely screened and little-known films, especially ones that deal with Paris as a theme or have the City of Light as the setting. There are usually between four and five screenings a day.

LA PAGODE Map pp434-5

☎ 01 45 55 48 48; 57bis rue de Babylone, 7e; adult/student €7/4; Ⓜ Vaneau

Now classed as yet another historical monument, the pagoda was supposedly shipped to France for the wife of the proprietor of the Bon Marché during the 19th century. Set in the gardens of a private mansion, today its a fantastic, atmospheric cinema.

LE CHAMPO Map pp444-5

☎ 01 43 54 51 60; www.lechampo.com in French; 51 rue des Écoles, 5e; adult/student & child €7/5.50, 2pm matinée €4.50; Ⓜ St-Michel or Cluny la Sorbonne

This is one of the most popular of the many Latin Quarter cinemas, featuring classics and retrospectives looking at the films of actors and directors such as Alfred Hitchcock, Jacques Tati, Alain Resnais, Frank Capra and Woody Allen. There are two *salles*, one of which has wheelchair access.

LE LATINA Map pp436-7

☎ 01 42 78 47 86; www.lelatina.com in French; 20 rue du Temple, 4e; adult/student & child €7.50/6; Ⓜ Hôtel de Ville

This cinema, which dates back more than 90 years, is the premier spot in Paris for catching films in Spanish and Portuguese. It has two *salles,* one with 180 seats and one with 60 seats, and themed festivals and retrospectives are scheduled. Three films are usually screened each day.

MK2 BIBLIOTHÈQUE Map p449

☎ 0 892 69 84 84; www.mk2.com; 128-162 av de France, 13e; adult/student/child €9/6.50/5.70, everyone before noon €4.50; Ⓜ Quai de la Gare

This branch of the ever-growing chain (10 outlets at last count) is the most ambitious yet, with 14 screens, a café, brasserie, restaurant and late-night bar. MK2 cinemas show both blockbusters and studio films so there's always something for everyone. Prices may vary depending on the time and place.

THEATRE

Almost all of Paris' theatre productions, including those originally written in other languages, are performed in French. There are a few itinerant English-speaking troupes around, though; look for ads on metro poster boards and in English-language periodicals such as *Fusac* (see p382), *Paris Voice* and the *Irish Eyes*, which are free at English-language bookshops, pubs and so on, as well as the website www.parisfranceguide.com. Apart from the celebrated Théâtre des Bouffes du Nord, theatres that occasionally stage productions in English include **Théâtre de Nesle** (Map pp436–7; ☎ 01 46 34 61 04; 8 rue de Nesle, 6e; Ⓜ Odéon or Mabillon),

Théâtre des Déchargeurs (Map pp436–7; ☎ 01 42 36 00 02; 3 rue des Déchargeurs, 1er; Ⓜ Châtelet) and **Théâtre de Ménilmontant** (Map pp422–3; ☎ 01 46 36 03 43; 15 rue du Retrait, 20e; Ⓜ Gambetta).

For booking agencies for theatre tickets see p259.

COMÉDIE FRANÇAISE Map pp436-7

☎ 0 825 10 16 80; www.comedie-francaise.fr; place Colette, 1er; tickets €5-32; ⏰ box office 11am-6pm Tue-Sat, 1-6pm Sun & Mon; Ⓜ Palais Royal-Musée du Louvre

Founded in 1680 during the reign of Louis XIV, the 'French Comedy' theatre bases its repertoire around the works of classic French playwrights like Molière, Racine, Corneille, Beaumarchais, Marivaux and Musset, though in recent years contemporary and even non-French works have been staged.

There are three venues: the main Salle Richelieu on place Colette just west of the Palais Royal; the **Comédie Française Studio Théâtre** (Map pp436–7; ☎ 01 44 58 98 58; Galerie du Carrousel du Louvre, 99 rue de Rivoli, 1er; ⏰ box office 1-5pm Wed-Mon; Ⓜ Palais Royal-Musée du Louvre) and the **Théâtre du Vieux Colombier** (Map pp434–5; ☎ 01 44 39 87 00; 21 rue du Vieux Colombier, 6e; ⏰ box office 11am-6pm Tue-Sat, 1-6pm Sun & Mon; Ⓜ St-Sulpice).

Tickets for regular seats cost €10 to €35; tickets for the 95 places near the ceiling (€7) go on sale one hour before curtain time (usually 8.30pm), which is when those aged under 27 can purchase any of the better seats remaining for €7.50 to €10. The **discount ticket window** (Map pp436–7) is around the corner from the main entrance and facing place André Malraux.

ODÉON-THÉÂTRE DE L'EUROPE
Map pp436-7

☎ 01 44 85 40 40; www.theatre-odeon.fr in French; place de l'Odéon, 6e; tickets €12-30; ⏰ box office 11am-6.30pm Mon-Sat; Ⓜ Odéon

This huge, ornate theatre built in the early 1780s has recently undergone extensive renovations. It often puts on foreign plays in their original languages (subtitled in French), and hosts theatre troupes from abroad. Some plays are staged at the **Ateliers Berthier** (Map pp422–3; ☎ 01 44 85 40 40; 8 blvd Berthier, 17e; tickets €13-26; ⏰ box office 11am-6.30pm Mon-Sat; Ⓜ Porte de Clichy).

People aged over 60 get a discount on the pricier tickets, while students and under-30s can get good seats for as little as €7.50.

THÉÂTRE DE LA BASTILLE Map pp440-1
☎ 01 43 57 42 14; www.theatre-bastille.com in French; 76 rue de la Roquette, 11e; adult/concession €19/12.50; ⊗ box office 10am-6pm Mon-Fri, 2-6pm Sat; Ⓜ Bastille or Voltaire

One of the best fringe theatre venues in Paris, with two spaces and a variety of experimental works: spoken word, movement and music. Some excellent modern dance performances take place here.

THÉÂTRE DE LA VILLE-SALLE DES ABBESSES Map p432
☎ 01 42 74 22 77; www.theatredelaville-paris.com in French; 31 rue des Abbesses, 18e; adult €16-23, student €11.50; ⊗ box office 5-8pm Tue-Sat, 1hr before matinée; Ⓜ Abbesses

This red-and-cream neoclassical building in Montmartre mainly stages the contemporary dramatic productions of the Théâtre de la Ville (p272), but also some music and dance.

THÉÂTRE DES BOUFFES DU NORD
Map pp428-9
☎ 01 46 07 34 50; www.bouffesdunord.com in French; 37bis blvd de la Chapelle, 10e; adult €14-24.50, concession €8-17; ⊗ box office 11am-6pm Mon-Sat; Ⓜ La Chapelle

Perhaps best known as the Paris base of Peter Brooks' and Stéphane Lissner's experimental troupes, this theatre in the northern reaches of the 10e and just north

of the Gare du Nord also hosts works by other directors (eg Stéphane Braunschweig, Krzysztof Warlikowski), as well as classical and jazz concerts. It was renovating in 2006, but planning to reopen in October. It also stages music concerts.

COMEDY

Though it may come as a surprise to some, Parisians do like to laugh, and the capital is not short of comedy clubs where comedians such as Bourvil, Fernandel, Bernard Blier, Louis de Funès, Francis Blanche, Jean Poiret and Michel Serrault have enjoyed enormous popularity over the years. The 'one man show' (say it with a French accent) is increasingly popular. There is also a growing scene of English-language comedy.

CAFÉ DE LA GARE Map pp436-7
☎ 01 42 78 52 51; 41 rue du Temple, 4e; adult €17-20, under 26 yrs €10; ⊗ Sun-Thu; Ⓜ Hôtel de Ville or Rambuteau

In the erstwhile mews of a Marais hôtel particulier (private mansion), this is one of the best and most innovative café-theatres in Paris, with acts ranging from comic theatre and stand-up to reinterpreted classics.

LAUGHING MATTERS IN PARIS
Map pp428-9
☎ 01 53 19 98 88; www.anythingmatters.com; 116 quai de Jemmapes, 10e; tickets €20-22; Ⓜ République

At Espace Jemmapes next to the Hôtel du Nord, Laughing Matters presents the best

Musicians performing at Le Caveau de la Huchette (p261)

shows in town for English-language laughs. Its regular stream of stand-ups includes the likes of Rich Hall and Ross Noble. It also presents comedy in other venues in Paris.

POINT VIRGULE Map pp436-7

☎ 01 42 78 67 03; 7 rue Ste-Croix de la Bretonnerie, 4e; adult €15, student €10; Ⓜ Hôtel de Ville
This tiny, convivial and popular comedy spot in the Marais celebrated its silver anniversary in 2003. It offers café-theatre at its best – stand-up comics, performance artists, musical acts. The quality is variable, but it's great fun nevertheless and the place has a reputation for discovering new talent. There are three shows daily at 8pm, 9.15pm and 10.30pm.

OPERA

The Opéra National de Paris (ONP) splits its performance schedule between the Palais Garnier, its original home built in 1875, and the modern Opéra Bastille, which opened in 1989. Both opera houses also stage ballets and classical-music concerts performed by the ONP's affiliated orchestra and ballet companies. The season runs from September to July.

OPÉRA BASTILLE Map pp440-1

☎ 08 92 89 90 90; www.opera-de-paris.fr; 2-6 place de la Bastille, 12e; opera €6-114, ballet €13-70, chamber music €6-16; Ⓜ Bastille
Despite some initial resistance to this 2700-seat venue, the main opera house in the capital, it's now performing superbly. While far less alluring than the Palais Garnier, at least all seats have a view of the stage. Ticket sales begin at a precise date prior to each performance, with different opening dates for bookings by telephone, online or from the box office (Map pp440–1; 130 rue de Lyon, 11e; ☎ 10.30am-6.30pm Mon-Sat). In general, box office sales start 14 days before the performance date. According to local opera buffs, the only way to ensure a seat is to book by post (120 rue de Lyon, 75576 Paris CEDEX 12) two months in advance. The cheapest seats start at €6 and are only sold from the box office. Note, on the first day they are released box office tickets can only be bought from the opera house at which the performance is to be held. At Bastille, standing-only tickets for €10 are available 1½

hours before performances begin. Just 15 minutes before the curtain goes up, last-minute seats at reduced rates (usually €20) are released to people aged under 28 or over 65; these can sometimes be excellent seats.

OPÉRA COMIQUE Map pp428-9

☎ 0 825 00 00 58; www.opera-comique.com in French; 5 rue Favart, 2e; tickets €7-100; Ⓜ Richelieu Drouot
This century-old hall premiered many important French operas. It continues to host classic and less-known operas. Get tickets from Fnac (p259) or Virgin (p259) and directly from the box office (☎ 9am-9pm Mon-Sat, 11am-7pm Sun, 1hr before performances) on the southwest side of the theatre. Subject to availability, students and those under 26 can buy unsold tickets for less than €10.

PALAIS GARNIER Map pp426-7

☎ 0 892 89 90 90; www.opera-de-paris.fr; place de l'Opéra, 9e; Ⓜ Opéra
The city's original opera house is smaller and more glamorous than its Bastille counterpart, and boasts perfect acoustics. Due to its odd shape, however, some seats have limited or no visibility. Ticket prices and conditions (including last-minute discounts) at the box office (☎ 11am-6.30pm Mon-Sat) are almost the same as those at the Opéra Bastille (left).

DANCE

The Ballet de l'Opéra National de Paris (www.opera-de-paris.fr in French) performs at both the Palais Garnier and the Opéra Bastille. Other important venues for both classical and modern dance are the Châtelet-Théâtre Musical de Paris and Théâtre des Champs-Élysées as well as the Théâtre de la Bastille.

CAFÉ DE LA DANSE Map pp440-1

☎ 01 47 00 57 59; www.cafédeladanse.com in French; 5 passage Louis-Philippe, 11e; admission €8-30; ☎ box office noon-6pm Mon-Fri; Ⓜ Bastille
Located just a few metres down a small passage from 23 rue de Lappe, this large auditorium has 300 to 500 seats. An excellent venue for modern dance, it also plays host to rock and world music concerts, musical theatre and poetry readings.

LE REGARD DU CYGNE Map pp422-3

☎ 01 43 58 55 93; 210 rue de Belleville, 20e; adult/
concession €16/13; ✆ box office 1-3pm Mon-Fri;
Ⓜ Place des Fêtes

Le Regard du Cygne prides itself on being
an independent, alternative performance
space. Situated in the creative 20e, this is
where many of Paris' young and daring
talents in movement, music and theatre
congregate to perform. If you're in the
mood for some innovative and experimental modern dance, performance or partici-
pation, this is the place. There are discounts
for students and seniors half an hour before
curtain time; for performances at 3pm on
Friday all tickets are €10.

THÉÂTRE DE LA VILLE Map pp436-7

☎ 01 42 74 22 77; www.theatredelaville-paris.com
in French; 2 place du Châtelet, 4e; adult €16-23,
student €11.50; ✆ box office 11am-7pm Mon,
11am-8pm Tue-Sat; Ⓜ Châtelet

While the Théâtre de la Ville also hosts
theatre and music, it's most celebrated for
its avant-garde dance productions by such
noted choreographers as Merce Cunning-
ham, Angelin Preljocaj and Pina Bausch.
Depending on availability, students and
under-27-year-olds can buy up to two tickets for €11 or €12.50 each on the day of the
performance. There are no performances in
July and August.

CABARET

Paris' risqué cabaret revues – those dazzling, pseudo-bohemian productions where
the women wear two beads and a feather
(or was that two feathers and a bead?) –
are today another one of those things that
everyone sees in Paris except the Parisians.
However they still draw in the crowds and
can be a lot of fun. Times and prices vary
with the seasons, but shows usually begin at
7.30pm or 9pm, and tickets cost from €40
to €100 per person for the performance,
or from €100 to €400 when you include a
fancy dinner, usually with champagne.

CRAZY HORSE Map pp426-7

☎ 01 47 23 32 32; www.lecrazyhorseparis.com;
12 av George V, 8e; Ⓜ Alma Marceau

This popular cabaret, whose dressing (or,
rather, undressing) rooms were featured in
Woody Allen's film *What's New Pussycat?*
(1965), has been promoting what it calls
l'art du nu (nudity) for over half a century.

FOLIES-BERGÈRE Map pp428-9

☎ 01 44 79 98 98; www.foliesbergere.com in
French; 32 rue Richer, 9e; Ⓜ Cadet

The cabaret where the African-American
exotic dancer Josephine Baker made her
debut and where none other than Charlie
Chaplin, WC Fields and Stan Laurel appeared on stage together on a night in
1911 is celebrated for its high-kicking, pink
feather-clad cancan dancers but has been
staging more mainstream musicals lately
such as *Fame* and *Snow White*.

LE LIDO DE PARIS Map pp426-7

☎ 01 40 76 56 10; www.lido.fr; 116bis av des
Champs-Élysées, 8e; Ⓜ George V

Founded at the close of WWII, the Lido gets
top marks for its ambitious sets and the lavish costumes of its 70 artistes.

MOULIN ROUGE Map p432

☎ 01 53 09 82 82; www.moulinrouge.fr; 82 blvd
de Clichy, 18e; Ⓜ Blanche

Ooh la la… This legendary cabaret founded
in 1889, whose dancers appeared in the
celebrated posters by Toulouse-Lautrec, sits
under its trademark red windmill (actually a
1925 replica of the 19th-century original).

Activities

Activities

Parisians love to watch sport, and you can catch some big games at its world-class stadiums. As for playing sport, Paris may not seem, on the surface, like a very fit city, what with the pollution, the narrow streets and the population's general preference for eating, drinking and smoking over puffing and sweating. However, a huge number of Parisians are closet *sportifs* (sportspeople), and there are numerous ways to get active in the city. Cycling, swimming, in-line skating and tennis are among the most popular urban sports, and there are many gyms as well as authentic Turkish baths.

WATCHING SPORT

For details of upcoming sporting events, consult the sports daily **L'Équipe** (www .lequipe.fr in French; €0.80) or **Figaroscope** (www.figaroscope.fr in French), an entertainment and activities supplement published with **Le Figaro** daily newspaper each Wednesday.

Most big international sporting events are held at the magnificent Stade de France (p158) in St-Denis, north of central Paris.

FOOTBALL

France's home matches (friendlies and qualifiers for major championships) are held at the **Stade de France** (p158; tickets €12 to €70), which was built especially for the 1998 World Cup.

The city's only top-division football team, **Paris-St-Germain** (☎ 01 47 43 71 71; www.psg .fr in French), wears red and blue and plays its home games at the 45,500-seat **Parc des Princes** (Map pp422–3; ☎ 0 825 07 50 78; 24 rue du Commandant Guilbaud, 16e; tickets €12-80; ☉ box office 9am-9pm Mon-Sat; Ⓜ Porte de St-Cloud), built in 1972. Tickets are also available at the more centrally located **Boutique PSG** (Map pp426–7; ☎ 01 56 69 22 22; www.psg.fr in French; 27 av des Champs-Élysées, 8e; ☉ 10am-7.45pm Mon-Thu, 10am-9.45pm Fri & Sat, noon-7.45pm Sun; Ⓜ Franklin D Roosevelt), or from **Fnac** (p259) and **Virgin Megastore outlets** (p259) in central Paris.

RUGBY

There's a strong rugby following in the southwest of France, with the favourite teams being Toulouse, Biarritz, Castres and Perpignan. Paris-based team **Stade Français CASG** (☎ 01 40 71 71 00; www.stade.fr) catapulted the capital to rugby fame and fortune with its defeat of the favourites, Toulouse, in the national championship in 2003. The team has had good form in recent years but missed out on playing in the 2006 National Championship after losing the semifinal to Toulouse. Stade Français CASG plays its home games north of the Parc des Princes at the **Stade Jean Bouin** (Map pp422–3; ☎ 01 46 51 00 75; 26 av du Général Sarrail, 16; Ⓜ Exelmans), with room for 10,000 spectators, and sometimes at the Stade de France. Tickets are available at Stade Jean Bouin's **box office** (☎ 01 46 51 00 75; tickets €5-35; ☉ 11am-2pm & 3-7pm Tue-Fri, 2-7pm Mon & Sat) and at **Fnac outlets** (p259) throughout Paris. The finals of the Championnat de France de Rugby take place in late May and early June.

France has been particularly strong in recent Six Nations rugby with a 44–5 victory over Ireland in 2002. In 2004 they defeated England 24–21, while in 2006 they narrowly triumphed on points difference over Ireland. After an honourable loss to Australia in the 1999 World Cup, France

---

INFORMATION

The best single source of information on sports – both spectator and participatory – in Paris is the 500-page **Parisports: Le Guide du Sport à Paris** (www.sport .paris.fr in French). It's in French only and is available free from the **Mairie de Paris** (Paris Town Hall; map pp436–7; ☎ 39 75; www.paris.fr; Hôtel de Ville, 29 rue de Rivoli, 4e; Ⓜ Hôtel de Ville). The **tourism office website** (www.parisinfo.com) has information on sports stadiums, venues, public spaces and associations under 'Practical Paris – Long Stays'. Each local *mairie* also has information on sports for particular arrondissements.

failed to make the final in 2003, losing a third place playoff to New Zealand 40–13.

The Rugby World Cup will be held in France in 2007 with matches all over the country and major matches in Paris: it's set to be a huge year of rugby fever. See the pubs in the Drinking chapter (p238), especially those around St-Germain (p247), for good spots to watch the games. Having won the Six Nations Tournament in 2006, France is a hot (and very determined) favourite to win.

TENNIS

In late May and early June the tennis world focuses on the clay surface of 16,500-seat **Stade Roland Garros** (Map pp422–3; ☎ 01 47 43 48 00, 01 47 43 52 52; www.rolandgarros .com in French; 2 av Gordon Bennett, 16e; Ⓜ Porte d'Auteuil) in the Bois de Boulogne for Les Internationaux de France de Tennis (French Open), the second of the four Grand Slam tournaments. Tickets are quite expensive and very hard to come by; they go on sale mid-November and bookings must usually be made by March. One week prior to the competition (on the first day of the qualifiers), remaining tickets are sold from the **box office** (☎ 0 825 16 75 16; ⏱ 9.30am-5.30pm Mon-Fri) at the entrance to the stadium.

The top indoor tournament is the Open de Tennis de la Ville de Paris (Paris Tennis Open), which usually takes place in late October or early November at the **Palais Omnisports de Paris-Bercy** (Map pp446–7; ☎ 01 40 02 60 60, 08 92 39 04 90; www.bercy.fr in French; 8 blvd de Bercy, 12e; Ⓜ Bercy). Tickets are available from the **box office** (☎ 0 892 39 04 90, from abroad 33-1 46 91 57 57; ⏱ 11am-6pm Mon-Sat) or from **Fnac** (p259) and **Virgin Megastore outlets** (p259) in central Paris.

TOP FIVE SPORT VENUES

- AMF Bowling de Paris (p278)
- Espace Vit'Halles (p279)
- Hammam de la Mosquée de Paris (p280)
- Patinoire de l'Hôtel de Ville (p278)
- Piscine de la Butte aux Cailles (p279)

CYCLING

The **Tour de France** (www.letour.fr) is the world's most prestigious bicycle race. For three weeks in July, 189 of the world's top cyclists (in 21 teams of nine) take on a 3000km-plus route. In recent years the Tour has been starting in foreign capitals, and in 2007 London will host the take-off for the first time.

The route changes each year, but three things remain constant – the inclusion of the Alps, the Pyrenees and, since 1974, the race's finish on the av des Champs-Élysées. The final day varies from year to year but is usually the 3rd or 4th Sunday in July, with the race finishing sometime in the afternoon. If you want to see this exciting event, find a spot at the barricades before noon.

The race itself is divided into 22 stages: the prologue – a short time trial used essentially to put a rider (the prologue's winner) in the leader's jersey for the first stage; two more time trials; five or six stages in the mountains; and some long flat stages.

There's usually one rest day. Each stage is timed and the race's overall winner is the rider with the lowest aggregate time. The smallest winning margin was in 1989, when American Greg LeMond beat enigmatic Parisian Laurent Fignon by eight seconds after 23 days and 3285km of racing.

Activities

WATCHING SPORT

Ice-skating (p278) at place de l'Hôtel de Ville

Track cycling, a sport at which France excels, is held in the velodrome of the **Palais Omnisports de Paris-Bercy** (Map pp446–7; ☎ 01 40 02 60 60, 08 92 39 04 90; www.bercy.fr in French; 8 blvd de Bercy, 12e; Ⓜ Bercy).

HORSE RACING & SHOWJUMPING

One of the cheapest ways to spend a relaxing afternoon in the company of Parisians of all ages, backgrounds and walks of life is to go to the races. The most accessible of the Paris areas' seven racecourses is **Hippodrome d'Auteuil** (Map pp422–3; ☎ 01 40 71 47 47; www.france-galop.com; Champ de Courses d'Auteuil, Bois de Boulogne, 16e; Ⓜ Porte d'Auteuil) in the southeastern corner of the Bois de Boulogne, which hosts steeplechases from February to late June or early July, and from early September to early December.

Races are held about six times a month (check the Hippodrome d'Auteuil website for exact days), with half a dozen or so heats scheduled between 2pm and 5.30pm. There's no charge to stand on the lawn in the middle of the track, but a seat in the stands costs about €3 for adults and €1.50 for students and seniors on weekdays (on Sundays it costs €4 and €2, respectively). Those under 18 get in free. Race schedules are published in almost all of the national newspapers. If you can read French, pick up a copy of *Paris Turf* (€1.15), the horse-racing daily.

In recent years the International Show Jumping Competition has taken place as part of the annual Salon du Cheval (www.salon-cheval.com), usually held in December at the Porte de Versailles expo centre.

Showjumping also takes place at Bercy in the **Palais Omnisports de Paris-Bercy** (Map pp446–7; ☎ 01 40 02 60 60; www.bercy.fr in French; 8 blvd de Bercy, 12e; Ⓜ Bercy), with major jumping events usually held in March.

OUTDOOR ACTIVITIES

The entertainment weeklies *Pariscope* and *L'Officiel des Spectacles,* which come out on Wednesday, have up-to-date information in French on every imaginable sort of activity. For more information on Paris' sporting activities and facilities, consult the free *Parisports: Le Guide du Sport à Paris* (see boxed text, p274) or ring **Mairie de Paris** (☎ 39 75).

CYCLING

Including tracks in the Bois de Boulogne (16e) and Bois de Vincennes (12e), Paris now has some 220km of bicycle lanes running throughout the city, as well as a dedicated lane running parallel to about two-thirds of the blvd Périphérique. Also, on Sundays and holidays throughout most of the year, large sections of road are reserved for pedestrians, cyclists and skaters under a scheme called *Paris Respire* (Paris Breathes; see below).

The **Mairie de Paris** (Map pp436–7; ☎ 39 75; www.paris.fr; Hôtel de Ville, 29 rue de Rivoli, 4e; Ⓜ Hôtel de Ville) produces a free booklet called *Paris à Vélo* (Paris by Bicycle) with itineraries, rules and regulations listed as well as a map called *À Paris Sortez Vos Vélos* (In Paris Get Out Your Bikes). More detailed is *Paris de Poche: Cycliste et Piéton* (Pocket Paris: Cyclist and Pedestrian; €3.50), which is available in most bookshops.

PARIS BREATHES

The Paris Respire (Paris Breathes) operation has been going for some years. It began as an effort to stop traffic in parts of the city by reserving certain streets for pedestrians, cyclists, in-line skaters – basically, anything but cars! In fact, it seems to have done little to stop pollution and traffic jams, which were simply diverted to other parts of the city – much to the disgruntlement of die-hard motorists. But if Paris doesn't necessarily breathe any better, the initiative has been hugely successful with anyone on fewer than four wheels. The following tracks are now off limits to cars on Sunday and public holidays. For updates on the exact routes contact the Mairie de Paris (see the boxed text, p274).

All year round, the *quais* (river-bank lanes) from quai des Tuileries, 1e, to the Pont Charles de Gaulle in the 12e are freed up from 9am to 5pm. Same goes for the rue Mouffetard area in the 5e, including rue Mouffetard, rue de Cluny, rue des Descartes and rue de Lanneau, from 10am to 6pm; and rue des Martyrs in the 9e from 10am to 1pm. A particularly nice area is the Canal St-Martin, 10e, blocked off from quai de Valmy. The streets surrounding Bois de Vincennes and Bois de Boulogne are also closed off.

From March to November, the streets around the Jardin du Luxembourg, including parts of rue Auguste Compte, rue d'Assas, blvd St-Michel and rue des Chartreux, are free from vehicles from 10am to 6pm.

For information on guided bicycle tours in Paris, see p95.

Bicycle Hire

BIKE 'N' ROLLER Map pp434-5
☎ 01 45 50 38 27; 38 rue Fabert, 7e; 3hr/1 day €12/17; ⊙ 10am-8pm Mon-Sat, 10am-6.30pm Sun; Ⓜ Invalides or La Tour Maubourg

Just north of Hôtel des Invalides, this place hires out bikes and in-line skates (right). €250 deposit is required; credit cards accepted.

FAT TIRE BIKE TOURS Map pp434-5
☎ 01 56 58 10 54; www.fattirebiketoursparis .com; 24 rue Edgar Faure, 15e; 1hr/day/weekend/ week/month €2/15/25/50/65; ⊙ 9am-7pm; Ⓜ La Motte-Picquet Grenelle

Formerly known as Mike's Bike Tours, Fat Tire is a friendly Anglophone outfit that rents out three-speeds. You need to show identification (driver's licence or passport), as well as a Visa card or MasterCard for the €250 deposit.

GEPETTO & VÉLOS Map pp444-5
☎ 01 43 54 19 95; www.gepetto-et-velos.com in French; 59 rue du Cardinal Lemoine, 5e; half-/full day/weekend/week €7.50/14/23/50; ⊙ 9am-1pm & 2-7.30pm Tue-Sat, 9am-1pm & 2-7pm Sun; Ⓜ Cardinal Lemoine

This store rents out bikes and sells new and second-hand bicycles; it also does repairs. There is a 5e arrondissement branch (Map pp444–5; ⊙ 01 43 37 16 17; 46 rue Daubenton, 5e; ⊙ 9am-1pm & 2-7.30pm Mon-Sat; Ⓜ Censier Daubenton), but the bike rental is available from its rue Cardinal Lemoine office.

MAISON ROUE LIBRE Map pp436-7
☎ 01 44 76 86 43, 0 810 44 15 34; www.rouelibre .fr; Forum des Halles, 1 passage Mondétour, 1er; 1hr/4hr/10hr/weekend €4/10/15/27; ⊙ 9am-7pm mid-Jan–mid-Dec; Ⓜ Les Halles

Sponsored by the city's public transport system, this is *the* place to rent a bike. There are hourly, daily, weekly, monthly and yearly rates. Seniors, students and under-26s get a 10% discount. Insurance, helmet and baby seat are included. The deposit is €150, and you need some form of identification. There's an outlet at Bastille (Map pp440–1; ☎ 01 44 54 19 29; 37 blvd Bourdon, 4e; Ⓜ Bastille) with the same hours. From 9am to 7pm Sunday and public holidays from

April to October, bikes can also be rented from 'cyclobuses' (bikes stored on big buses) in locations around the city, such as Denfert-Rochereau (Map pp422–3; cnr rue Daguerre & av Général Leclerc, 14e; Ⓜ Denfert-Rochereau) and La Villette (Map pp428–9; 23 quai de la Loire, 19e; Ⓜ Laumière).

PARIS À VÉLO, C'EST SYMPA!
Map pp440-1
☎ 01 48 87 60 01; www.parisvelosympa.com in French; 22 rue Alphonse Baudin, 11e; half-day/10hr/ weekend/week €9.50/12.50/24/59; ⊙ 9.30am-1pm & 2-6.30pm Mon-Fri, 9am-7pm Sat & Sun Apr-Oct, 9.30am-1pm & 2-6pm Mon-Fri, 9am-6pm Sat & Sun Nov-Mar; Ⓜ St-Sébastien Froissart

This association with the cringey name (Paris by Bike, it's Nice!) also rents out tandems, which are the price of two bikes. There's a deposit of €200 (€610 for a tandem), which can be made with a credit card.

SKATING

Be it on Tarmac or ice, skating has taken Paris by storm in recent years. See the boxed text, opposite for information on traffic-free streets in which to skate down on Sundays.

In-line Skating

In-line skaters may want to join one of the two Randonnées en Roller (Skating Rambles) organised weekly throughout the year. Up to 15,000 people take part in each ramble.

The 30km Pari Roller Ramble (Friday Night Fever; ☎ 01 43 36 89 81; www.pari-roller.com in French) leaves place Raoul Dautry, 14e (Map pp434–5; Ⓜ Montparnasse Bienvenüe), the plaza between Gare Montparnasse and Tour Montparnasse, at 10pm Friday (meet there at 9.30pm), returning at 1am.

The Rollers & Coquillages Ramble (☎ 01 44 54 07 44; www.rollers-coquillages.org) Sunday Afternoon Skate departs from the rear of the Nomades bike store every Sunday at 2.30pm, returning between 5.30pm and 6pm.

BIKE 'N' ROLLER Map pp434-5
☎ 01 45 50 38 27; 38 rue Fabert, 7e; half-/full-day €9/12; ⊙ 10am-8pm Mon-Sat, 10am-6.30pm Sun; Ⓜ Invalides or La Tour Maubourg

This place has bicycles, *rollers* (in-line skates), *quads* (roller skates) and *trottinettes* (scooters) for rent. Elbow/knee guards cost €1/1.50.

Activities

OUTDOOR ACTIVITIES

NOMADES Map pp440-1

☎ 01 44 54 07 44; www.nomadeshop.com in French; 37 blvd Bourdon, 4e; half-/full-day weekdays €5/8, weekends €6/9, weekend €16, week Mon-Fri €23, full week €30; ⏰ 11am-1pm & 2-7pm Mon-Fri, 10am-7pm Sat, 10am-6pm Sun; Ⓜ Bastille
This enormous shop is the Harrods for roller-heads and, as well as renting out skates, it sells equipment and accessories and gives courses at five different levels. Elbow and knee guards cost €1, and helmets cost €2. You must leave a deposit of €150, or an identity card or passport.

Ice-Skating

From early December to early March, the city of Paris and the adjoining *département* (administrative division) of Hauts-de-Seine maintain several outdoor ice-skating rinks. Access to the rinks is free, but *patins* (skates) cost €5 to rent. Sites include the **Patinoire de l'Hôtel de Ville** (Map pp436–7; ☎ 39 75; Place de l'Hôtel de Ville; ⏰ noon-10pm Mon-Thu, noon-midnight Fri, 9am-midnight Sat, 9am-10pm Sun; Ⓜ Hôtel de Ville) and the **Patinoire de Montparnasse** (Map pp434–5; ☎ 39 75; place Raoul Dautry, 14e; ⏰ noon-8pm Mon-Fri, 9am-8pm Sat & Sun; Ⓜ Montparnasse Bienvenüe).

The **Patinoire Tour Eiffel** (Map pp434–5; ☎ 39 75; ⏰ 9.30am-11pm; Ⓜ Champ de Mars-Tour Eiffel), on the 1st floor of the Eiffel Tower was a huge success in 2004 and 2005. Initially a bit of a publicity stunt as Paris' unsuccessful bid for the 2012 Olympics, the vanilla-scented rink was such a hit that they decided to keep it going. Beware, however, that you may have to queue for hours.

Open year-round except in summer is **Patinoire Sonja Henie** (Map pp446–7; ☎ 01 40 02 60 60; www.bercy.fr in French; 8 blvd de Bercy, 12e; adult/student & under 26 yrs €4/3, Fri & Sat night €6/4; ⏰ 3-6pm Wed, 9.30pm-12.30am Fri, 3-6pm & 9.30pm-12.30am Sat, 10am-2pm & 3-6pm Sun Sep-May; Ⓜ Bercy), an ice-skating rink inside the Palais Omnisports de Paris-Bercy (use the garden-facing north entrance).

BOULES & BOWLING

France's most popular traditional games are *boules* and the similar but less formal *pétanque*. They are like lawn bowls but are played on a gravel or sandy pitch known as

a *boulodrome*, scratched out wherever a bit of flat, shady ground can be found. The object is to get your *boules* (biased metal balls) as close as possible to the *cochonnet* (little piggy), or jack – the small wooden target ball thrown at the start. *Boules* is especially popular in southern France, but you may come across a group (usually men) playing in the Jardin du Luxembourg.

Bowling is surprisingly popular in Paris and there are more than 24 tenpin alleys in the city. The ones listed here are among the best and/or the most central. Prices for games depend on the time and day of the week.

AMF BOWLING DE MONTPARNASSE
Map pp434-5

☎ 01 43 21 61 32; 25 rue du Commandant René Mouchotte, 14e; games €4.50-6, shoes €2; ⏰ 10am-2am Sun-Thu, 10-4am Fri, 10-5am Sat; Ⓜ Montparnasse Bienvenüe
This centre, just opposite the Gare Montparnasse, has 16 lanes. A *forfait* (set price) allows multiple games.

AMF BOWLING DE PARIS Map pp422-3

☎ 01 53 64 93 00; Jardin d'Acclimitation, rte du Mahatma Gandhi, 16e; games €4.50-6, shoes €2; ⏰ 10am-3am Sun-Thu, 10-5am Fri & Sat; Ⓜ Porte de Neuilly
Supermodern centre with 24 lanes on the northern edge of the Bois de Boulogne.

BOWLING MOUFFETARD Map pp444-5

☎ 01 43 31 09 35; 13 rue Gracieuse & 73 rue Mouffetard, 5e; games €2.90-6, shoes €1.90; ⏰ 3pm-2am Mon-Fri, 10am-2am Sat & Sun; Ⓜ Place Monge
This intimate and friendly eight-lane alley has two entrances.

TENNIS
MAIRIE DE PARIS

☎ 39 75, reservations ☎ 01 71 71 70 70 in French only; www.tennis.paris.fr; open court per hr adult/under 26yr €6.50/4, covered court €12.50/7
The city runs some 170 covered and open municipal tennis courts in dozens of locations (hours vary considerably). You can reserve by calling its reservations number or by logging on to its website. You need to sign in to the website first to get an identification number and password, which you then use for reservations. The following are

three very central tennis centres: **Luxembourg** (Map pp444–5; ☎ 01 43 25 79 18; Jardin du Luxembourg, 6e; Ⓜ Luxembourg) has six courts for hire, **Candie** (Map pp440–1; ☎ 01 43 55 84 95; rue Candie, 11e; Ⓜ Ledru Rollin) has two courts and **Neuve Saint Pierre** (Map pp440–1; ☎ 01 42 78 21 04; 5-7 rue Neuve St Pierre, 4e; Ⓜ St-Paul) has one court.

HEALTH & FITNESS

Consult the free *Parisports: Le Guide du Sport à Paris* (p274) or ring **Mairie de Paris** (☎ 39 75) to find out about activities available. The *mairie* (town hall) of each arrondissement will have details on local sports clubs and gyms, which are often the cheapest way of practising an activity or taking classes, though you may need a year-long subscription.

GYMS & FITNESS CLUBS

Like everywhere else in the world these days, in Paris gyms and fitness clubs are a penny a barrel, and several allow short-term memberships.

CLUB MED GYM

☎ 0 820 20 20 20; www.clubmedgym.com in French
In addition to twelve gym outlets (and more to come), there are also 'Club Med Waou' (basically, 'Club Med Wow') centres, which offer luxurious settings and spa facilities. Check the website to find the most convenient locations. Main Club Med Gym branches include **Palais Royal** (Map pp436–7; ☎ 01 40 20 03 03; 147bis rue St-Honoré, 1er; ☯ 7.30am-10pm Mon-Fri, 9am-7pm Sat, 9am-5pm Sun; Ⓜ Palais Royal-Musée

Volleyball in Jardin du Luxembourg (p119)

du Louvre), **République** (Map pp428–9; ☯ 01 47 00 69 98; 10 place de la République, 11e; ☯ 7.30am-10pm Mon-Fri, 8am-7pm Sat, 9am-5pm Sun; Ⓜ République), entry on rue du Faubourg du Temple, and **Montparnasse** (Map pp434–5; ☎ 01 45 44 24 35; 149 rue de Rennes, 6e; ☯ 8am-10pm Mon-Fri, 8am-8pm Sat, 9am-2pm Sun; Ⓜ St-Placide).

CLUB QUARTIER LATIN Map pp444-5

☎ 01 55 42 77 88; www.clubquartierlatin.com in French; 19 rue de Pontoise, 5e; pool/gym entry €3.70/18, 10-entry pool/gym carnet €30.20/147; ☯ 9am-midnight Mon-Fri, 9.30am-7pm Sat & Sun; Ⓜ Maubert Mutualité
This no-frills gym above **Piscine Pontoise-Quartier Latin** (p280) also has squash courts. Check with the gym for class details and times.

ESPACE VIT'HALLES Map pp436-7

☎ 01 42 77 21 71; www.vithalles.com in French; 48 rue de Rambuteau, 3e; admission €25, 10-entry carnet €199; ☯ 8am-10.30pm Mon-Fri, 10am-7pm Sat, 10am-6pm Sun; Ⓜ Rambuteau
This squeaky-clean health club just north of place Georges Pompidou gets fabulous reviews, especially for its exercise classes, from local residents and blow-ins.

SWIMMING

Paris has some 35 swimming pools open to the public; check with the **Mairie de Paris** (☎ 39 75; www.paris.fr) for the nearest pool. Most are short-length pools, and finding a free lane for laps can be nigh on impossible. Opening times vary widely, but avoid Wednesday afternoon and Saturday, when kids off from school take the plunge. Unless noted otherwise the entry cost for municipal pools in Paris is €2.60. Under-21s residing in Paris pay €1.35. A *carnet* of 10 tickets is €21.50.

PISCINE DE LA BUTTE AUX CAILLES
Map p448

☎ 01 45 89 60 05; 5 place Paul Verlaine, 13e; ☯ 7am-8am, 11.30am-1pm & 4.30-6.30pm Tue, 7am-6.30pm Wed, 7am-8am & 11.30am-6pm Thu & Fri, 7am-8am & 10am-6pm Sat, 8am-5.30pm Sun; Ⓜ Place d'Italie
This positively stunning pool, built in 1924 and now a listed building, takes advantage of the lovely warm water issuing from a nearby artesian well.

PISCINE PONTOISE-QUARTIER LATIN
Map pp444–5

☎ 01 55 42 77 88; 19 rue de Pontoise, 5e; adult/concession €3.70/2.20, 10-entry carnet €30.20/19.40; ⏰ 7-8.30am, 12.15-1.30pm, 4.30-8.45pm & 9-11.45pm Mon & Tue, 7-8.30am, 12.15-8.45pm & 9-11.45pm Wed, 7-8.30am, 12.15-1.30pm, 4.30-7.15pm & 9-11.45pm Thu, 7-8.45am, noon-1.30pm, 4.30-8pm & 9-11.45pm Fri, 10am-7pm Sat, 8am-7pm Sun; Ⓜ Maubert Mutualité
This beautiful Art Deco–style pool in the heart of the Latin Quarter measures 33m by 15m. In the evenings pool entry is €9 for everyone, but includes gym and sauna entry.

PISCINE ROGER LE GALL Map pp422–3
☎ 01 44 73 81 12; 34 blvd Carnot, 12e; ⏰ noon-2pm & 5-8pm Mon, noon-2pm & 5-9pm Tue, Thu & Fri, 8am-9pm Wed, 10am-7pm Sat, 8am-7pm Sun; Ⓜ Porte de Vincennes
Readers tell us that this is one of the best public pools in Paris, but the blvd Périphérique is a little too close for our comfort.

PISCINE SUZANNE BERLIOUX
Map pp436–7

☎ 01 42 36 98 44; Level 3, Forum des Halles, 10 place de la Rotonde, 1er; adult/child 4-15 yr €3.80/3, 10-entry carnet €35/28.95; ⏰ 11.30am-10pm Mon, Tue, Thu & Fri, 10am-10pm Wed, 9am-7pm Sat & Sun; Ⓜ Les Halles
This 50m by 20m pool, surrounded by a tropical garden, is in the bowels of Paris' largest shopping centre; it's always busy, but fun. The pool was closed for renovations for a while but should have reopened by mid-2006.

Water Parks
AQUABOULEVARD Map pp422–3
☎ 01 40 60 10 00; www.aquaboulevard.com in French; 4 rue Louis Armand, 15e; adult/child 3-11 yr €20/10; ⏰ 9am-11pm Mon-Thu, 9am-midnight Fri, 8am-midnight Sat, 8am-11pm Sun; Ⓜ Balard
A huge recreational centre in southwest Paris with a wide range of activities for adults and kids, including a swimming pool, a 'beach' and aquatic park, tennis, squash, golf practice, a gym, restaurants and so on. Children under the age of three cannot be brought into the park.

TURKISH BATHS
One of the best places to relax after a day of slogging through the streets and museums of Paris is in a hammam (Turkish bath).

HAMMAM DE LA MOSQUÉE DE PARIS
Map pp444–5

☎ 01 43 31 18 14, 01 43 31 38 20; 39 rue Geoffroy St-Hilaire, 5e; admission €15; ⏰ men 2-9pm Tue & 10am-9pm Sun, women 10am-9pm Mon, Wed, Thu & Sat, 2-9pm Fri; Ⓜ Censier Daubenton or Place Monge
Massages at this atmospheric hammam cost €10 for 10 minutes. There are several 'combination' tickets available, including the formule orientale (Oriental set menu), which includes admission to the hammam, a 10-minute massage, an exfoliating treatment, a mint tea and a couscous meal with drink for €58. The same deal without the meal costs €38. You must be over 12 years old and you must wear a swimsuit and sarong/towel.

HAMMAM DES GRANDS BOULEVARDS Map pp428–9
☎ 01 48 01 03 05; 28 blvd de Bonne Nouvelle, 10e; admission €21-23; ⏰ men 1-10pm Tue, 1-8pm Fri, women 1-5pm Sat, mixed with bathing suit required 2-10pm Mon, 1-5pm Wed, 5-9pm Sat & 1-9pm Sun, mixed with naturist association card required 5-10pm Wed, 1-10pm Thu; Ⓜ Bonne Nouvelle
This bath has two eucalyptus hammams (where the hammams use natural eucalyptus), sauna, cold pool etc. It was closed for part of 2006 but will be open by the time you read this.

HAMMAM PACHA Map p157
☎ 01 48 29 19 66; 147 rue Gabriel Péri, St-Denis; admission €29; ⏰ noon-midnight Mon-Wed & Fri, 10am-midnight Thu, 10am-8pm Sat & Sun; Ⓜ Basilique de St-Denis
This women-only hammam is one of the better ones around, though it is in far-flung St-Denis. Massage costs €22 for 15 minutes.

YOGA
One of the most active yoga centres in Paris, the Fédération Inter-Enseignements de Hatha Yoga (Hatha Yoga Teachings Federation; Map pp426–7; ☎ 01 42 60 31 10; www.fidhy .asso.fr in French; 322 rue St-Honoré, 1er; Ⓜ Tuileries), organises courses at various Paris venues. Check its website for details.

Shopping

Shopping

Shopping in Paris is not about finding that one main street and trucking up and down it, because there isn't one. Of course you have the large boulevards lined with international chains, the luxury avenues with high fashion, and the famous *grands magasins* (department stores). There are also some fabulous flea markets. But the real charm of Parisian shopping resides in a peripatetic stroll through the side streets, where tiny specialty stores and quirky boutiques alternate with cafés, galleries and churches – allowing for cultivated, scenic browsing. For where to shop, see the boxed text, below, and the introductions to each geographical area.

When in Paris, seek out those things that the French do best. First and foremost we're talking fashion – for our mini-guide to French *mode* see the boxed text, p294. They're also experts in jewellery, fine food and wine, perfumes and cosmetics, antique furniture and fine stationery.

Opening hours

Opening hours are generally from 10am to 7pm Monday to Saturday. Smaller stores are often shut all day Monday; on other days their proprietors may simply close up at midday and head off for a hot lunch. Larger stores often hold *nocturnes* on Thursdays, staying open until around 10pm. For Sunday shopping, the Champs-Élysées stays open and both Montmartre and the Marais and Bastille areas remain lively. During sales and around Christmas larger stores stay open later at night and all weekend.

Winter sales normally start in mid-January and the summer ones in the second week of June.

WHERE TO SHOP FOR WHAT

Shopping is very spread out in Paris; each area has a selection of different stores. However, some areas do have certain shopping strong points. The introduction to each neighbourhood explains what it has to offer. See also the boxed texts Odd Spots & Speciality Streets (p285), Top Five Bookshops (p290) and Top Gift Ideas (opposite). For a window into high fashion, see the boxed text, p294.

Antiques and art Fine antiques are centred in the area around the 1e (see opposite) and the 7e (p293). Rue de Seine and rue Jacob in the 6e are lined with galleries (p292), as is the place des Vosges in the Marais (p286).

Boutique shopping For a mixed selection of cute and quirky specialty stores, gifts, home decorations and design, the best spots are around the Marais in the 3e and 4e (p286) and around St-Germain in the 6e (p292). Parts of the 18e (p301) are also good.

Chain stores For major chain stores like Gap, H&M and Zara, head straight to rue de Rivoli and **Les Halles** (Map pp436–7, Ⓜ Châtelet or Les Halles) in the 1er and 2e, **rue de Rennes** (Map pp434–5; Ⓜ St-Sulpice and Montparnasse Bienvenüe) in the 6e and the area around the big **department stores** (Map pp428–9, Ⓜ Opéra and Grands Boulevards) in the 9e.

Deluxe purchases Couture, luxury jewellery and designer perfumes are concentrated around the Étoile & Champs-Élysées (p296) and Concorde & Madeleine (p297) areas.

Department stores The major ones are concentrated around blvd Haussman in the 9e (p299); in the 7e, there's also Le Bon Marché (p293) and in the Marais, BHV (Bazar de l'Hôtel de Ville; p287).

Fine food Little gourmet shops are dotted all over Paris, but place de la Madeleine in the 8e (p297) and the Bon Marché in the 7e (p293) are centres for designer foodstuffs.

Markets Most of the fabulous fleamarkets are just outside Paris (p302); closer in there's the Marché d'Aligre in the 12e (p301).

Original Fashion The areas mentioned under 'boutique shopping', above, are also the main zone for fashion; see the Fashion boxed text (p294) for more.

TOP GIFT IDEAS

- French perfume and scented candles from **Guerlain** (p296), **L'Artisan Parfumeur** (p288) or **Fragonard** (p288)
- Fine food and lovely wine from places such as **Fauchon** (p297), **À l'Olivier** (p286) or **La Maison du Miel** (p298)
- Beautiful stationery and paper from **Mélodies Graphiques** (p290)
- Tea from **Le Palais des Thés** (p289) or **Mariage Frères** (p289)
- Exotic and eclectic items from **Anna Joliet** (right), **CSAO Boutique** (p287) or **E Dehillerin** (p284)

Bargaining & Consumer Taxes

Many stores (eg large department stores and some 'duty-free' shops) will give discounts of 10% to foreign passport holders if asked. Otherwise bargaining is reserved for flea markets.

If you're not a resident of the EU, you can get a TVA (VAT; sales tax) refund of up to 17%, provided you have spent more than €182 in any one store; see Tax & Refunds (p384).

LOUVRE & LES HALLES

The upper realms of this area (in the 1e and 2e) around the Sentier garment district have become a centre for fashion. Rue Étienne Marcel, place des Victoires and rue du Jour (beside the Église St-Eustache; Map pp436–7) offer prominent labels, brilliant shoe shops and remarkable kitchenware. Nearby rue Montmartre and rue Tiquetonne are known for their streetwear and avant-garde designs. Les Halles itself, once the city's food market, now consists of a vast and commercial underground shopping complex. It is flanked to the east by the sleaze and sports stores of rue St-Denis, and to the south by the chain stores of rue de Rivoli. The eastern part of the 1e around the Palais Royal is far more conservative, with fancy antiques and label fashion.

AGNÈS B Map pp436-7 *Clothing & Accessories*
☎ 01 45 08 56 56; www.agnesb.fr; 6 rue du Jour, 1er; ⊙ 10.30am-8pm Mon-Sat; Ⓜ Les Halles
Style and photography guru agnès b excels in extremely wearable, durable and com-

fortable (yet sometimes quirky) clothes. The basics are excellent; the rest has somewhat lost its cachet of late. On the same street you'll find her **men's** (Map pp436–7; ☎ 01 42 33 04 13; 3 rue du Jour, 1er; Ⓜ Les Halles) and **children's** (Map pp436–7; ☎ 01 40 39 96 88; 2 rue du Jour, 1er) stores.

ANNA JOLIET Map pp428-9 *Gifts & Souvenirs*
☎ 01 42 96 55 13; passage du Perron, 9 rue de Beaujolais, 1er; ⊙ 10am-7pm Mon-Sat; Ⓜ Pyramides
This wonderful (and tiny) shop at the northern end of the Jardin du Palais Royal specialises in music boxes, both new and old. Just open the door and see if you aren't tempted in.

BARBARA BUI
Map pp436-7 *Clothing & Accessories*
☎ 01 40 26 43 65; www.barbarabui.fr; 23 rue Étienne Marcel, 2e; Ⓜ Étienne Marcel; ⊙ 10am-7.30pm Mon-Sat
Franco-Vietnamese Barbara Bui's **Kabuki store** (p286) in rue Étienne Marcel (1er) was an instant success. Bui went on to open her own shop, known for its elegant modernism and beautifully cut pants. She also has a fairly pretentious, minimalist café two doors up.

BONPOINT
Map pp428-9 *Clothing & Accessories*
☎ 01 40 26 20 90; 50 rue Étienne Marcel; ⊙ 10am-7pm Mon-Sat; Ⓜ Étienne Marcel
This is a timeless collection of immaculate, classic children's clothes (from newborn

Window display at Kenzo (p285)

CLOTHING SIZES

Measurements approximate only, try before you buy

Women's Clothing

Aus/UK	8	10	12	14	16	18
Europe	36	38	40	42	44	46
Japan	5	7	9	11	13	15
USA	6	8	10	12	14	16

Women's Shoes

Aus/USA	5	6	7	8	9	10
Europe	35	36	37	38	39	40
France only	35	36	38	39	40	42
Japan	22	23	24	25	26	27
UK	3½	4½	5½	6½	7½	8½

Men's Clothing

Aus	92	96	100	104	108	112
Europe	46	48	50	52	54	56
Japan	S		M	M		L
UK/USA	35	36	37	38	39	40

Men's Shirts (Collar Sizes)

Aus/Japan	38	39	40	41	42	43
Europe	38	39	40	41	42	43
UK/USA	15	15½	16	16½	17	17½

Men's Shoes

Aus/UK	7	8	9	10	11	12
Europe	41	42	43	44½	46	47
Japan	26	27	27½	28	29	30
USA	7½	8½	9½	10½	11½	12½

to 14 years). The chic babes of Paris have always been be-suited in Bonpoint – usually by their grandmothers. It's a longstanding tradition, but if you're looking to buy into it expect to pay €35 for a pair of perfectly crafted size-one booties.

CARROUSEL DU LOUVRE

Map pp436-7   Shopping Centre

☎ 01 43 16 47 10; www.carrouseldulouvre.com; 99 rue de Rivoli, 1er; ⏰ 11am-8pm; Ⓜ Palais Royal-Musée du Louvre
Built around IM Pei's inverted glass pyramid beneath the place du Carrousel, this shopping centre contains some three dozen upmarket shops, restaurants and even the Comédie Française Studio Théâtre (p269).

CLAUDIE PIERLOT

Map pp434-5   Clothing & Accessories

☎ 01 42 21 38 38; 1 rue Montmartre, 1e; ⏰ 10.30am-7pm Mon-Sat; Ⓜ Étienne Marcel
Much sought-after by visitors, this is that typically Parisian look worn by those girls

who drift by looking exactly like they walked out of a postcard. It's feminine and understated, with some unique and unusual prints, smart suits and a good accessories collection.

DIDIER LUDOT

Map pp428-9   Clothing & Accessories

☎ 01 42 96 06 56; 19-20 & 23-24 Galerie de Montpensier, 1er; ⏰ 10.30am-7pm Mon-Sat; Ⓜ Palais Royal-Musée du Louvre
Formed from old galleries that have been joined together, this fabulous shop in the equally fabulous Galerie de Montpensier (p103) just up from the Palais Royal is crammed with preloved couture creations from yesteryear, including original Chanel suits from the 1950s and Hermès bags and accessories.

DU PAREIL AU MÊME

Map pp436-7   Clothing & Accessories

☎ 01 42 36 07 57; 1 rue St-Denis, 1e; Ⓜ Châtelet
This chain has cute babies' and children's clothing and accessories that are more affordable than those in the designer baby stores.

E DEHILLERIN

Map pp436-7   Household Goods

☎ 01 42 36 53 13; 18-20 rue Coquillière, 1er; ⏰ 9am-12.30pm & 2-6pm Mon, 9am-6pm Tue-Sat; Ⓜ Les Halles
Spread out over two floors and dating back to 1820, this shop carries an incredible selection of professional-quality *matériel de cuisine* (kitchenware). You're sure to find something you desperately need, like a *coupe volaille* (poultry scissors) or perhaps a *turbotiére* (turbot poacher).

KABUKI Map pp436-7   Clothing & Accessories

☎ 01 42 33 13 44; www.barbarabui.fr; 25 rue Étienne Marcel, 2e; ⏰ 10am-7.30pm Mon-Sat; Ⓜ Étienne Marcel
Opened over 10 years ago, this is the shop that brought Barbara Bui to fame. Her own store is next door (p286). In addition to Bui's own designs you'll find a judicious selection from other brands. Miu Miu, Prada, Helmut Lang and Costume National are well represented and competitively priced, and there's a memorable range of shoes.

KENZO Map pp436-7 *Clothing & Accessories*

☎ 01 73 04 20 00; www.kenzo.com; 1 rue du Pont Neuf, 1er; ⏱ 11am-7.30pm Mon-Sat; Ⓜ Pont Neuf
While Kenzo himself may have retired from designing in 1999, Sardinian Antonio Marras has brought a new *joie de vivre* to the label. The Pont Neuf flagship store is a tantalising temple to fashion and beauty. The building also houses the Philippe Starck–designed **Kong bar** (p239).

KILIWATCH Map pp428-9 *Clothing & Accessories*

☎ 01 42 21 17 37; 64 rue Tiquetonne, 2e; ⏱ 11am-7pm Tue-Sat; Ⓜ Étienne Marcel
Kiliwatch is always packed with hip guys and dolls sorting through rack after rack of new and used street wear and designs. There's a startling vintage range including hats and boots, plus art/photography books and the latest sneakers. They also carry flyers for very on-to-it clubbing and cultural events.

LA SAMARITAINE

Map pp436-7 *Department Store*

☎ 01 40 41 20 20; www.lasamaritaine.com; 19 rue de la Monnaie, 1er; ⏱ closed at time of writing; Ⓜ Pont Neuf
The wonderful 'Samaritan' department store has closed due to its apparently insalubrious safety standards. It remains a Parisian landmark, and should it reopen while you're in Paris, check out the outstanding view from the rooftop.

LE SHOP Map pp428-9 *Clothing & Accessories*

☎ 01 40 28 95 94; 3 rue Argout, 2e; ⏱ 11am-8pm Tue-Sun; Ⓜ Sentier
With its many levels, colourful clothes and crowds and suspended dj-booth, Le Shop is almost like a daytime club. Covering a remarkable 1200 sq metres, it's packed with different streetwear labels and hip-hop gear. Pick up flyers and info on nightclubs and get your party outfit while you're at it.

LOUVRE DES ANTIQUAIRES

Map pp436-7 *Antiques*

☎ 01 42 97 27 27; 2 place du Palais Royal; www .louvre-antiquaires.com; ⏱ 11am-7pm Tue-Sun Sep-Jun, 11am-7pm Tue-Sat Jul & Aug; Ⓜ Palais Royal-Musée du Louvre
This extremely elegant 'mall' houses some 250 antique shops spread over three floors and is filled with *objets d'art*, furniture, clocks

and classical antiquities – affordable for anyone with a king's ransom. The basement is an Aladdin's cave of jewellery shops.

MARITHÉ ET FRANÇOIS GIRBAUD

Map pp428-9 *Clothing & Accessories*

☎ 01 53 40 74 20; www.girbaud.com; 38 rue Étienne Marcel, 2e; ⏱ 11.30am-7.30pm Mon, 10.30am-7.30pm Tue-Sat; Ⓜ Étienne Marcel
This globetrotting designer couple from the 1960s consider themselves 'jeanologists' having devoted themselves to over 30 years of denim; they have been highly influential in Tokyo as well as in Paris.

MARTIN MARGIELA

Map pp428-9 *Clothing & Accessories*

☎ 01 40 15 07 55; 23-25 rue de Montpensier, 1e; ⏱ 11am-7pm Mon-Sat; Ⓜ Palais Royale
The most Parisian of Belgian designers, the expressedly enigmatic Martin Margiela (b 1957) set up his own *maison* (house) in 1988 and has an immaculate gallerylike boutique. His clothes bear a blank label but can be recognised by their white stitching and other visible sewing techniques.

PRINCESSE TAM TAM

Map pp436-7 *Clothing & Accessories*

☎ 01 40 41 99 51; 5 rue Montmartre, 1e; Ⓜ Étienne Marcel
Beautiful, fun Frenchy lingerie at less outrageous prices than luxury brands. This brand can be found in department stores, and also puts out a great swimwear line.

SURFACE 2 AIR

Map pp436-7   Clothing & Accessories
☎ 01 49 27 04 54; www.surface2air.com; 144 rue de Rivoli, 1er; ⏱ 12.30pm-7.30am Mon-Sat; Ⓜ Les Halles

Relaxed in its conceptual niche, this shop has a lounge-meets-gallery thing going on, with arty books, accessories, graphic design and very edgy clothing. With an exceedingly up-to-date collection of daring local and international designs, the space also welcomes regular installations and collaborative events with artists.

MARAIS & BASTILLE

The Marais is a wonderful place for a stroll, with quaint speciality stores and an ever-expanding fashion presence. Note that the hip young designers are colonising the upper reaches of the 3e towards rue Charlot (Map pp436–7). Meanwhile rue des Francs Bourgeois and, towards the other side of rue de Rivoli, rue François Mirron in the 4e have well-established boutique shopping for clothing, hats, home furnishings and stationery. The place des Vosges is lined with art and antique galleries with some amazing sculpture for sale. Over towards the 11e, Bastille has some interesting shops on rue Keller (Map pp440–1; young designers, records and manga/comic stores) and rue de Charonne (clothes). See also the boxed text on fashion (p294).

À L'OLIVIER Map pp436-7   Food & Drink
☎ 01 48 04 86 59; 23 rue de Rivoli, 4e; ⏱ 9.30am-1pm & 2-7pm Mon-Sat; Ⓜ St-Paul

'At the Olive Tree' has been *the* place for oil, from olive and walnut to soy and sesame, since 1822. The stores (with branches throughout Paris) and their products are very nicely packaged. They also offer olive oil tastings and olive oil beauty products, as well as good vinegars, jams and honeys.

AB 33 Map pp436-7   Clothing & Accessories
☎ 01 42 71 02 82; 33 rue Charlot, 3e; ⏱ 11am-8pm Tue-Sun; Ⓜ Filles du Calvaire

Leading the new rue Charlot brat pack, AB has a small but extremely educated selection of the latest names in local fashion, such as Isabel Marant and See by Chloé. In the same street, their **l'Atélier d'Andréa** (Map pp440–1, ☎ 01 44 78 91 90; 60 rue

Charlot, 3e) has more adventurous creations from Sharon Wauchob (Collection K), Hussein Chalayan and Martin Margiela.

ABOU D'ABI BAZAR

Map pp440-1   Clothing & Accessories
☎ 01 42 77 96 98; 10 rue des Francs Bourgeois, 3e; ⏱ 2-7pm Sun & Mon, 10.30am-7.15pm Tue-Sat; Ⓜ St-Paul

This fashionable boutique is a treasure trove of smart and affordable ready-to-wear pieces from young designers such as Paul & Joe, Isabel Marant and Vanessa Bruno.

ALTERNATIVES

Map pp436-7   Clothing & Accessories
☎ 01 42 78 31 50; 18 rue du Roi de Sicile, 4e; ⏱ 1-7pm Tue-Sat; Ⓜ St-Paul

This men's and women's resale shop has great bargains in superb condition. This is an excellent place to pick up Japanese designer wear at a third of the original price. You can also come across Miu Miu, Prada, Martin Margiela and Isabel Marant here on a good day.

ANTOINE ET LILI

Map pp436-7   Clothing & Accessories
☎ 01 42 72 26 60; 51 rue des Francs Bourgeois, 3e; ⏱ 2-7pm Sun & Mon, 10.30am-7.15pm Tue-Sat; Ⓜ St-Paul

All the colours of the rainbow and all the patterns in the world congregate in this wonderful Parisian institution with designer clothing and hip home decorations. Antoine et Lili have a knack for choosing those things you wished you'd thought to bring back from India or Thailand. They also have a **Canal St Martin store** (Map pp428–9; ☎ 01 40 37 41 55; 95 quai Valmy, 10e; Ⓜ République).

APC Map pp440-1   Clothing & Accessories
Atélier de Production et Création; ☎ 01 42 71 78 18 02; www.apc.fr; 112 rue Vieille du Temple, 3e; ⏱ 11am-8pm Tue-Sun; Ⓜ Chemin Vert

The hip streetwear of APC is very popular with those young Parisian guys with accidental pop-rock haircuts, white sneakers and falling-off jeans. It also has women's clothes. The focus is on simple lines and straight cuts, though some pieces are more adventurous.

Fnac Musique (p288)

AZZEDINE ALAÏA

Map pp436-7   Clothing & Accessories

☎ 01 42 72 19 19; 7 rue Moussy, 4e; 🕙 10am-7pm Mon-Sat; Ⓜ St Paul

Tunisian-born Azzedine Alaïa studied sculpture at the École des Beaux-Arts de Tunis before moving to Paris in 1975. He worked with Dior and Guy Laroche before setting up his own label in 1981. Highly influential, Alaïa is best known for his slim silhouettes and beautiful shoes.

BAINS PLUS

Map pp436-7   Household Goods

☎ 01 48 87 83 07; 51 rue des Francs Bourgeois, 3e; 🕙 11am-7.30pm Tue-Sat, 2-7pm Sun; Ⓜ Hôtel de Ville

A bathroom supplier for the 21st century. True to its name, 'Baths Plus' stocks luxurious robes and gowns, soaps and oils, shaving brushes and mirrors.

BAZAR DE L'HÔTEL DE VILLE

Map pp436-7   Department Store

BHV; ☎ 01 42 74 90 00; www.bhv.fr in French; 14 rue du Temple, 4e; 🕙 9.30am-7.30pm Mon, Tue, Thu & Fri, 9.30am-9pm Wed, 9.30am-8pm Sat; Ⓜ Hôtel de Ville

BHV is a straightforward department store – apart from its huge but hopelessly chaotic hardware/DIY department in the basement, with every possible type of hammer, power tool, nail, plug or hinge you could ask for. Service is decidedly in the DIY vein too.

BOUTIQUE PARIS-MUSÉES

Map pp436-7   Gifts & Souvenirs

☎ 01 42 74 13 92; 29bis rue des Francs Bourgeois, 4e; 🕙 2-7pm Mon, 11am-1pm & 2-7pm Tue-Sun; Ⓜ Chemin Vert or St-Paul

This lovely boutique stocks museum reproductions, especially of art and sculpture on exhibit at museums run by the City of Paris, such as the Musée Carnavalet (p107) and the Musée d'Art Moderne de la Ville de Paris (p128).

CSAO BOUTIQUE

Map pp436-7   Gifts & Souvenirs

☎ 01 44 54 55 88; 1-3 rue Elzévir, 3e; 🕙 11am-7pm Tue-Fri, 11am-7.30pm Sat, 2-7pm Sun; Ⓜ St-Paul or Chemin Vert

This wonderful gallery and shop, owned and operated by the charitable Compagnie du Sénégal et de l'Afrique de l'Ouest (CSAO; Senegal and West Africa Company), distributes the work of African artists and craftspeople. Many of the colourful fabrics and weavings are exquisite. There are items handmade from recycled handbags, aluminium cans and tomato paste tins.

EROTOKRITOS

Map pp436-7   Clothing & Accessories

☎ 01 42 78 14 04; www.erotokritos.com; 99 rue Vieille du Temple; 🕙 11am-7pm Tue-Sat; Ⓜ Filles du Calvaire

Born of Greek parents in Cyprus, Erotokritos worked with Thierry Mugler before launching his own label in 1994 and rapidly gained a name for himself. The clothes are

Shopping · MARAIS & BASTILLE

287

chic and colourful, combining and contrasting fabrics with amazing prints. They're also quite affordable, considering the designer's hot reputation.

FNAC MUSIQUE Map pp440-1   Music
☎ 01 43 42 04 04; 4 place de la Bastille, 12e;
🕙 10am-8pm Mon-Sat; Ⓜ Bastille
Fnac's flagship music store at Bastille has a huge variety of local and international music. The **Fnac Forum des Halles** (Map pp428–9; ☎ 01 40 41 40 00; 1 rue Pierre Lescot, 1e; Ⓜ Les Halles) also has books and electronic equipment.

FRAGONARD
Map pp436-7   Cosmetics & Perfume
☎ 01 44 78 01 32; 51 rue des Francs Bourgeois, 4e; 🕙 10.30am-7.30pm Mon-Sat, 12-7pm Sun; Ⓜ St-Paul
This Parisian perfume maker has alluring natural scents in elegant bottles as well as candles, essential oils and soaps. In addition to the splendid smells, it has a small, expensive and very tasteful selection of clothing, hand-stitched linen napkins and jewellery. Fragonard also runs the **Musée du Parfum** (see p134).

GASPARD YURKIEVICH
Map pp440-1   Clothing & Accessories
☎ 01 42 77 55 69; www.gaspardyurkievich .com; 38 rue Charlot, 3e; 🕙 11am-7pm Tue-Sun; Ⓜ Filles du Calvaire
Everyone is talking about this designer, whose style, according to Yurkievich himself, is 'urban glamour'. The clothes are beautifully put together with original juxtapositions of fabrics and a resistance to anything that might be mass-produced. There are glorious fantasy stockings, and a sensational women's shoe collection.

ISABEL MARANT
Map pp440-1   Clothing & Accessories
☎ 01 49 29 71 55; 16 rue de Charonne, 11e; 🕙 11am-7pm Mon-Sat; Ⓜ Bastille
Great cardigans and pants, interesting accessories, ethnic influences and beautiful fabrics: just a few reasons why Isabel Marant has become the *chouchou* (darling) of Paris fashion. Bohemian and stylish (think Right Bank career girl moved by a trip to India) they're clothes people actually look good in.

JACENKO Map pp436-7   Clothing & Accessories
☎ 01 42 71 80 38; 38 rue de Poitou, 3e;
🕙 12-8pm Tue-Sat; Ⓜ Filles du Calvaire
Men get their turn to shine in this tiny but well-constructed boutique. There are eye-catching suits with exposed stitching and patterned lining, and great streetwear including excellent cargos and sweatshirts. Not to mention those pink-on-blue designer socks you've probably been looking for all your life.

JULIEN, CAVISTE
Map pp440-1   Food & Drink
☎ 01 42 72 00 94; 50 rue Charlot, 3e; 🕙 9.30am-1.30pm & 3.30-8.30pm Tue-Fri, 9.30am-8.30pm Sat, 10am-1pm Sun; Ⓜ Filles du Calvaire
This independent wine store on hip rue Charlot focuses on small, independent producers and organic wines. There's a unique selection of Rhône, Languedoc and Loire vintages and exceptional champagnes. The eminent Julien speaks very good English and will locate, explain (and wax lyrical about) the wine for you, whatever your budget.

LA BOUTIQUE DES INVENTIONS
Map pp436-7   Gifts & Souvenirs
☎ 01 42 71 44 19; Village St-Paul, 13 rue St-Paul, 4e; 🕙 11am-7pm Wed-Sun; Ⓜ St-Paul
This unique shop in the heart of Village St-Paul, a delightful little square with antique shops, galleries and boutiques, is a forum for inventors and their inventions. Make friends and influence people with your brand new self-twisting pepper grinder or your miraculous filter that turns water into wine.

L'ARTISAN PARFUMEUR
Map pp436-7   Cosmetics & Perfume
☎ 01 42 66 32 66; 32 rue Bourg Tibourg, 4e; 🕙 10am-7pm Mon-Sat; Ⓜ St-Paul
This artisan has been making exquisite original scents and candles for decades. The products are expensive but high quality and attractively packaged. There are several other outlets across town and stands in most department stores.

LE BOUDOIR ET SA PHILOSOPHIE
Map pp436-7   Gifts & Souvenirs
☎ 01 48 04 89 79; 18 rue Charlot, 3e; 🕙 2-7pm Tue-Sat; Ⓜ Filles du Calvaire
Like a 19th-century powder room bursting at the seams, this tiny boudoir's philosophy

is one of parlour games, floral prints and silky nightgowns. Overflowing with all sorts of things from soaps to carnival masks, it's not bad for finding that esoteric, non-functional gift.

LE PALAIS DES THÉS

Map pp436-7   Food & Drink

☎ 01 48 87 80 60; 64 rue Vieille du Temple, 3e; ⏰ 10am-8pm; Ⓜ Hôtel de Ville or St-Paul
The 'Palace of Teas' is not as well established as **Mariage Frères** (p286), but the selection is as large and the surroundings more 21st century. There are three other outlets in Paris including a **6e branch** (Map pp434–5; ☎ 01 42 22 03 98; 61 rue du Cherche Midi, 6e; Ⓜ Rennes).

L'ÉCLAIREUR

Map pp436-7   Clothing & Accessories

☎ 01 48 87 10 22; 9 89; www.leclaireur.com; 3ter rue des Rosiers, 4e; ⏰ 11am-7pm Mon-Sat; Ⓜ St-Paul
You'll find John Galliano and Dries Van Noten rubbing shoulders with objects by Garouste & Bonetti and Ron Arad. Part art space, part lounge and part deconstructionist fashion statement, this collection is known for having the next big thing first. There is also a **Marais branch** (Map pp436–7; ☎ 01 44 54 22 11; 12 rue Malher, 4e; Ⓜ St-Paul).

LES BELLES IMAGES

Map pp440-1   Clothing & Accessories

☎ 01 42 76 93 61; www.lesbellesimages.com; 74 rue Charlot, 3e; ⏰ 11am-8pm Tue-Sat; Ⓜ Filles du Calvaire
The clothes, shoes and accessories are all brand new – and straight off the shelves of designers like Gaspard Yurkievich and Vivienne Westwood – but the look is ultra-cultivated retro. Everything has been conceptualised, from the one-piece 70s-style Lacoste swimsuit down to the Art Deco coffee jugs.

LES MOTS À LA BOUCHE

Map pp436-7   Books

☎ 01 42 78 88 30; www.motsbouche.com in French; 6 rue Ste-Croix de la Bretonnerie, 4e; ⏰ 11am-11pm Mon-Sat, 2-8pm Sun; Ⓜ Hôtel de Ville
Paris' premier gay bookshop. Most of the left-hand side of the ground floor is de-voted to English-language books, including some guides and novels; 'naughty' books are downstairs.

LESAMIE

Map pp436-7   Clothing & Accessories

☎ 01 42 78 65 35; 60 rue Vieille du Temple, 3e; ⏰ 11am-2pm & 2.30-7.30pm Mon-Sat; Ⓜ St-Paul
Exquisite hand-stitched gloves and hand-knitted sweaters, bonnets and scarves are among the treasures here. There are also ethnic-influenced wraps, fine shawls and dresses in silks and linens. As its owner explains 'we dress all kinds of women'.

L'HABILLEUR

Map pp436-7   Clothing & Accessories

☎ 01 48 87 77 12; 44 rue de Poitou, 3e; ⏰ 11am-8pm Mon-Sat; Ⓜ St-Sébastien Froissart
For 10 years this shop has been known for its discount designerwear – offering 50% to 70% off original prices. It generally stocks last season's collections – including Plein Sud and Prada. The selection of men's clothes, including Helmut Lang designs, is quite extensive.

LIBRAIRIE DE L'HÔTEL DE SULLY

Map pp440-1   Books

☎ 01 44 61 21 75; 62 rue St-Antoine, 4e; ⏰ 10am-6pm Tue-Sun; Ⓜ St-Paul
This early-17th-century aristocratic mansion housing the body responsible for many of France's historical monuments, the Centre des Monuments Nationaux, has one of the best bookshops in town for titles related to Paris. From historical texts and biographies to picture books and atlases, it's all here.

MARIAGE FRÈRES

Map pp436-7   Food & Drink

☎ 01 42 72 28 11; www.mariagefreres.com in French; 30 rue du Bourg Tibourg, 4e; ⏰ shop 10.30am-7.30pm, tearooms noon-7pm; Ⓜ Hôtel de Ville
Founded in 1854, this is Paris' first and arguably its finest tea shop. Choose from 500 varieties of tea sourced from more than 30 countries. In addition, Mariage Frères has two other outlets – the **6e branch** (Map pp436–7; ☎ 01 40 51 82 50; 13 rue des Grands Augustins; Ⓜ Odéon) and the **8e branch** (Map pp426–7; ☎ 01 46 22 18 54; 260 rue du Faubourg St-Honoré;

Ⓜ Tuileries) as well as concessions in three major department stores, which are **Le Bon Marché** (p293), **Galeries Lafayette** (p300) and **Le Printemps** (p300).

MÉLODIES GRAPHIQUES

Map pp436-7   Gifts & Souvenirs

☎ 01 42 74 57 68; 10 rue du Pont Louis-Philippe, 4e; ☒ 2-7pm Mon, 11am-7pm Tue-Sat; Ⓜ Pont Marie

Here you'll find all sorts of items made from exquisite Florentine *papier à cuve* (paper hand-decorated with marbled designs). This is just one of several fine stationery shops along the same street.

RED WHEELBARROW BOOKSTORE

Map pp436-7   Books

☎ 01 48 04 75 08; 22 rue St-Paul, 4e; ☒ 10am-7pm Mon-Sat, 2-6pm Sun; Ⓜ St-Paul

This somewhat earnest English-language bookshop has arguably the best selection of literature and 'serious reading' in Paris and a helpful, well-read staff.

SHINE Map pp440-1   Clothing & Accessories

☎ 01 48 05 80 10; 15 rue de Poitou, 3e; ☒ 11am-7pm Tue-Sat; Ⓜ Filles du Calvaire

Another limited but discerning collection of designer stuff in the trendsetting 3e. Young women's clothing and some excellent shoes and handbags have been astutely selected, with plenty of Marc Jacobs, See by Chloé and the current jewellery fetish, Bijoux de Sophie.

SIC AMOR Map pp436-7   Jewellery

☎ 01 42 76 02 37; 20 rue du Pont Louis-Philippe, 4e; ☒ 10.30am-2pm & 3-7pm Tue-Sat, 2-7pm Sun & Mon; Ⓜ Pont Marie

This shop sells contemporary jewellery by local designers from a shop opposite the headquarters of the all-but-moribund Partie Communiste Française.

TUMBLEWEED Map pp440-1   Toys

☎ 01 42 78 06 10; 19 rue de Turenne, 4e; ☒ 11am-7pm Mon-Sat, 2-7pm Sun; Ⓜ St-Paul or Chemin Vert

This gorgeous little shop, which specialises in *l'arsinart d'art ludique* (crafts of the playing art), stocks wonderful wooden toys, some of which look too nice to play with. The jack-in-the-box collection is especially fine.

THE ISLANDS

GALERIE ALAIN CARION

Map pp436-7   Gifts & Souvenirs

☎ 01 43 26 01 16; 92 rue St-Louis en l'Île, 4e; ☒ 10.30am-1pm & 2-7.30pm Tue-Sat; Ⓜ Pont Marie

This small boutique has a stunning collection of museum-quality minerals, crystals, fossils and meteorites from 40 countries, some of them in the form of earrings, brooches and pendants. They also open some Sundays.

LA PETITE SCIERIE

Map pp436-7   Food & Drink

☎ 01 55 42 14 88; 60 rue St-Louis en l'Île, 4e; ☒ 11am-8pm; Ⓜ Pont Marie

This little hole-in-the-wall sells every permutation of duck edibles with the emphasis – *naturellement* – on foie gras (€30 for 180g). The products come direct from the farm with no intermediary involved so you can be assured of the highest quality.

LIBRAIRIE ULYSSE Map pp436-7   Books

☎ 01 43 25 17 35; 26 rue St-Louis en l'Île, 4e; ☒ 2-8pm Tue-Sat; Ⓜ Pont Marie

A delightful store full of travel guides, maps and sage advice from staff. The 20,000 back issues of *National Geographic* are not to be sniffed at.

TOP FIVE BOOKSHOPS

- Abbey Bookshop (below)
- Librairie Ulysse (above)
- Red Wheelbarrow Bookstore (left)
- Tea and Tattered Pages (p294)
- Village Voice (p293)

LATIN QUARTER & JARDIN DES PLANTES

The Latin Quarter is a particularly good hunting ground for bookshops, comics and sporting goods.

ABBEY BOOKSHOP Map pp436-7   Books

☎ 01 46 33 16 24; www.abbeybookshop.com; 29 rue de la Parcheminerie, 5e; ☒ 10am-7pm Mon-Sat; Ⓜ Cluny-La Sorbonne

The Abbey is a mellow Canadian-owned bookshop, not far from place St-Michel, known for its free tea and coffee and a good selection of new and used fiction and nonfiction. Ask about the weekend hikes around Paris.

ALBUM Map pp436-7
Books
☎ 01 43 25 85 19; 8 rue Dante, 5e; ☺ 10am-8pm Mon-Sat; Ⓜ Maubert Mutualité
Album specialises in *bandes dessinées* (comic books), which have an enormous following in France, with everything from Tintin and Babar to erotic comics and the latest Japanese manga. There's a **branch** (Map pp436–7; ☎ 01 53 10 00 60; 67 blvd St-Germain, 5e) just around the corner.

AU VIEUX CAMPEUR
Map pp444-5
Outdoor Gear
☎ 01 53 10 48 48; www.auvieuxcampeur.fr in French; 48 rue des Écoles, 5e; ☺ 11am-7.30pm Mon-Wed & Fri, 11am-9pm Thu, 10am-7.30pm Sat; Ⓜ Maubert Mutualité or Cluny La Sorbonne
This popular sporting gear chain in the Latin Quarter has more than 20 outlets, each specialising in equipment for a specific kind of outdoor activity: hiking, cycling, skiing, scuba diving, canyoning etc. Camping equipment is sold at several shops, including those at 18 rue du Som-

merard, 3 rue de Latran and 6 rue Thénard (Map pp444–5); check the website for the appropriate outlet.

EOL' MODELISME
Map pp444-5
Hobby Items
☎ 01 43 54 01 43; www.eol-model.fr; 62 blvd St-Germain, 5e; ☺ 10am-7pm Tue-Sat; Ⓜ Maubert Mutualité
This shop sells expensive toys for big boys and girls, including every sort of model imaginable – from radio-controlled aircraft to large wooden yachts. The main shop has an amazing collection of tiny cars. There are two nearby **branches** (Map pp444–5; 55 & 70 blvd St-Germain, 5e) that keep the same hours.

SHAKESPEARE & COMPANY
Map pp436-7
Books
☎ 01 43 26 96 50; 37 rue de la Bûcherie, 5e; ☺ noon-midnight; Ⓜ St-Michel
Paris' most famous English-language bookshop has a varied collection of new and used books, but the place has been resting on its laurels and is now an expensive tourist trap. Poetry readings are held at 8pm on most Mondays, and there's a library on the 1st floor. This isn't the original Shakespeare

Art stalls, place du Tertre, Montmartre (p301)

& Company owned by Sylvia Beach, who published James Joyce's *Ulysses*; that was closed by the Nazis.

ST-GERMAIN, ODÉON & LUXEMBOURG

The part of the 6e between the Église St-Germain des Prés and the Seine, including the charming rue de Seine and rue Jacob (Map pp436–7), is lined with lots of small art galleries, florists, antique stores and designer furnishings. Left Bank fashion and style snakes down rue Bonaparte and then congregates around place St-Sulpice in the 6e and rue de Grenelle in the 7e. For the bigger chain stores, head down rue de Rennes (Map pp434–5) towards Montparnasse. You'll find souvenirs and schoolbooks in Odéon.

CACAO ET CHOCOLAT

Map pp436-7   Food & Drink

☎ 01 46 33 77 63; 29 rue du Buci, 6e;
⌚ 10.30am-7.30pm Mon-Sat, 11am-1.30pm & 2.30-7pm Sun; Ⓜ Mabillon

You haven't tasted chocolate till you've tasted it here: citrus, spices and chilli flavours. This a contemporary and exotic take on chocolate, showcasing the cocoa bean in all its guises. You can drink a marvellous liquid hot choc in the shop. There are two other outlets including the **Marais branch** (Map pp436–7; ☎ 01 42 71 50 06; 36 rue Vieille du Temple, 4e; ⌚ 11am-7.30pm; Ⓜ St-Paul).

CACHAREL Map pp436-7   Clothing & Accessories

☎ 01 40 46 00 45; 64 rue Bonaparte, 6e;
⌚ 10am-7pm Mon-Sat; Ⓜ St-Sulpice

Original designer Corrine Sarut brought Cacharel back into vogue. Floaty garments, gentle floral prints, perfumes – everything you might need should you be planning to drift through Paris in the springtime.

COMPTOIR DES COTONNIERS

Map pp436-7   Clothing & Accessories

☎ 01 43 26 07 56; 59ter rue Bonaparte, 6e;
Ⓜ St-Germain des Prés

Beautifully cut and very typically Parisian women's wear can be found at this store

(there are several around Paris). Particularly popular are their fine coats, stylish knits and relaxed work outfits. They also have a girls' line.

FORMES Map pp434-5   Clothing & Accessories

☎ 01 45 49 09 80; 5 rue du Vieux Colombier, 6e;
Ⓜ St-Germain des Prés

This shop has a number of branches around Paris selling elegant, relaxed pregnancy wear for the chic-while-expecting.

LE MOUTON À CINQ PATTES

Map pp436-7   Clothing & Accessories

☎ 01 43 29 73 56; 19 rue Grégoire de Tours, 6e;
⌚ 10.30am-7.30pm Mon-Fri, 10.30am-8pm Sat;
Ⓜ Odéon

Specialises in heavily discounted designer clothing from last year's range. If you can spot a Jean-Paul Gaultier or Vivienne Westwood without a label, you'll walk away with a discount of up to 70%.

ODIMEX PARIS

Map pp436-7   Household Goods

☎ 01 46 33 98 96; 17 Rue de l'Odéon, 6e;
⌚ 10.30am-6.30pm Mon-Sat; Ⓜ Odéon

This shop sells teapots in all their guises: there are little ones, big ones, sophisticated, comic and very expensive ones. Some of the Japanese teapots are particularly beautiful.

ONWARD

Map pp436-7   Clothing & Accessories

☎ 01 55 42 77 56; 147 blvd St-Germain, 6e;
⌚ 11am-7pm Mon-Sat; Ⓜ St-Germain des Prés

Formerly called Kashiyama, Onward is a clean, modern-looking boutique that stocks fashion-forward clothes from numerous up-and-coming designers such as Dries Van Noten, Martin Margiela and Hussein Chalayan.

SONIA RYKIEL

Map pp434-5   Clothing & Accessories

☎ 01 49 54 60 60; www.soniarykiel.com; 175 blvd St-Germain, 6e; ⌚ 11am-7pm Mon-Sat;
Ⓜ St-Germain des Prés

Sonia Rykiel opened her first boutique in May 1968, with a guiding (if not exactly revolutionary) style philosophy that women should be able to adapt fashion to suit themselves rather than blindly follow the dictates of the latest trends. Not called the Queen of Knitwear for nothing, Rykiel is particularly famous for reinventing the sweater. The stripy Rykiel kingdom (which includes diffusion labels as well as children's clothes) can be found dotted along rue de Grenelle, rue des St Pères and blvd St-Germain. For the gentlemen, there's also **Sonia Rykiel men** (Map pp434–5; ☎ 01 45 44 83 19; 194 blvd St-Germain, 6e).

VANESSA BRUNO

Map pp436-7   Clothing & Accessories

☎ 01 43 54 41 04; 25 rue St-Sulpice, 6e; 🕑 10.30am-7.30pm Mon-Sat; Ⓜ St-Sulpice

Vanessa Bruno is another designer who has become quite the class favourite lately. Her feminine women's clothing is very popular with Parisians and her signature sequined carry bags can be seen – and have been mercilessly copied – all over town.

VENTILO Map pp436-7   Clothing & Accessories

☎ 01 43 26 64 40; 59 rue Bonaparte, 6e; Ⓜ St-Germain des Près

Parisian women's fashion with a slight ethnic twist, Ventilo has clothing and accessories for a variety of ages. The beading and detail on the clothes is often very well done.

VILLAGE VOICE

Map pp436-7   Books

☎ 01 46 33 36 47; www.villagevoicebookshop.com; 6 rue Princesse, 6e; 🕑 2-8pm Mon, 10am-8pm Tue-Sat, 2-6pm Sun; Ⓜ Mabillon

With an excellent selection of contemporary North American fiction and European literature, lots of readings and other events and helpful staff, the Village Voice is many people's favourite English-language bookshop in Paris.

VOYAGEURS & CURIEUX

Map pp436-7   Antiques

☎ 01 43 26 14 58; 2 rue Visconti, 6e; 🕑 2-7pm Wed-Sat; Ⓜ St-Germain des Prés

This wonderful shop looks and feels like an 18th-century cabinet of curiosities collected from around the world: chalices made from coconut shells, unusual feathers and beads, and odd masks.

ZADIG & VOLTAIRE

Map pp434-5   Clothing & Accessories

☎ 01 45 48 39 37; 3 rue du Vieux Colombier, 6e; Ⓜ St-Sulpice

Nudging its way into the higher echelons of fashion, this store now has a 'deluxe' range. Its main line is overpriced for what is essentially just casual wear, yet it is unshakably popular for its seductively simple tops, sexy knit sweaters and fantastic jeans.

FAUBOURG ST-GERMAIN & INVALIDES

Somewhat stuck in time – and also somewhat stuck behind the walls of private mansions and government buildings – most of this area is a little more austere to wander around than St-Germain or the Marais. There are still some lovely little shopping strips, however, and it's around here that you'll find the lion's share of Paris' wonderful top-end antique shops and art galleries, in particular around rue du Bac (Map pp434–5).

CARRÉ RIVE GAUCHE

Map pp434-5   Art & Antiques

☎ 01 42 60 70 10; www.carrerivegauche.com; quai Voltaire, rue de l'Université, rue des St-Pères & rue du Bac; 🕑 10am-6pm Mon-Sat; Ⓜ Rue du Bac or Solférino

Not really a shop but rather a group of 120 fine art and antique galleries, the 'Left Bank Square' is just east of the Musée d'Orsay. It represents one of the finest groupings of shops and merchants not just in Paris but in the world and should not be missed.

LE BON MARCHÉ

Map pp434-5   Department Store

☎ 01 44 39 80 00; www.bonmarche.fr; 24 rue de Sèvres, 7e; 🕑 9.30am-7pm Mon-Wed & Fri, 10am-9pm Thu, 9.30am-8pm Sat; Ⓜ Sèvres Babylone

Built by Gustave Eiffel as Paris' first department store in 1852, Le Bon Marché (which translates as Good Market but which also means 'bargain') is less frenetic than its rivals across the river, but no less chic. It has excellent collections of men's and women's fashion. Its glorious grocery store, **La**

FASHION

Fashion is not something that exists in dresses only. Fashion is in the sky, in the street; fashion has to do with ideas, the way we live, what is happening.

Coco Chanel

Parisians take fashion in much the same way they do food: very seriously. They savour it, dissect it and discuss it endlessly; they take their time. While fickle in their followings and avant-garde in their creations, they're firmly fastidious in their commitment to tradition and taste. They're ruthless critics, voracious consumers…and frightful snobs. After all, when it comes to fashion (or cuisine for that matter), as far as the French are concerned, they invented it. In fact an Englishman is credited with creating Parisian *haute couture* (literally 'high sewing'). Known as 'the Napoleon of costumers', **Charles Frederick Worth** (1825–95; www.charlesfrederickworth.org) arrived in Paris at the tender age of 20 and revolutionised fashion by banishing the crinoline (stiffened petticoat), lifting hemlines up to the oh-so-shocking ankle length and presenting his creations on live models.

These days a single *haute couture* made-to-measure creation can cost more than €60,000 and take 400 hours to assemble, under very specific guidelines. While talk of the 'death of couture' is perhaps far-fetched, it's true that the market for such garments is tiny while the cost is inordinate. The high fashion world is today fighting to keep the *haute couture* catwalk collections alive. These shows are scheduled in late January for the spring/summer collections and early July for autumn/winter ones. However, most established couturiers present a more affordable *prêt-à-porter* (ready-to-wear) line, and many have abandoned *haute couture* altogether. *Prêt-à-porter* shows are usually in late February and October. All major shows are ultra-exclusive affairs – even eminent fashion journalists must fight tooth and nail to get a spot on the sidelines.

Paris' self-proclaimed position at the summit of fashion is today contested by New York, Milan and London but fashion is fashion: Paris will always have that special something and its shows are still the *chouchou* (darling) of the designer pack, who are always relieved to arrive in the beautiful city for the final fashion week, which is known to be the most innovative and striking of the bunch. As actress Cathérine Deneuve rightly pointed out to the press during the 2006 *prêt-à-porter* shows (from her catwalk vantage point next to hip-hop star Pharrell Williams), 'I don't say that there are no other cities in America or Italy…but everybody wants to show in Paris.'

Fashion Shopping

Just as everyone wants to show here, everyone also wants to shop in Paris. Despite the globalisation of trends, the city retains a certain cachet when it comes to shopping, in part because the great couture houses were founded here. This is where you come for a classic, timeless recipe – the Hermès scarf, the Cartier watch, the little back Chanel dress – or recycled versions thereof. This is where you'll find that effortless Parisian street style women covet, the slick suits and casual wear sought after by men, and those intricate, inimitable children's clothes. And, of course, this is where you can dig around for the next big thing in fashion and peer over the cutting edge of design.

This is a society that coined the expression *lèche-vitrine* (literally 'window-licker'): tasting without buying is an art like any other so don't be shy about just having a good look. The fancy couture houses on av Montaigne may seem daunting, as many of their gleaming façades sit behind little fences, giving the impression of luxurious private homes. In most, however,

Grande Épicerie de Paris (Map pp434–5; 26 rue de Sèvres; Ⓜ Sèvres Babylone), is in store No 2.

SENNELIER   Map pp434-5   Hobby Items
☎ 01 42 60 72 15; 3 quai Voltaire, 7e; ☿ 9.30am-12.30pm & 2-6pm Tue-Sat; Ⓜ St- Germain des Prés
This artists' colour merchant has been in business for well over a century and still makes paints using rare pigments, as well as supplying other artists' materials.

TEA & TATTERED PAGES
Map pp434-5   Books
☎ 01 40 65 94 35; 24 rue Mayet, 6e; ☿ 11am-7pm Mon-Sat, noon-6pm Sun; Ⓜ Duroc
This is the best and most comprehensive shop selling used English-language books in Paris. There are more than 15,000 volumes squeezed onto two floors. There's also a lovely tea room in the back of the shop where you can sip, munch and browse.

no appointment is necessary and you can simply walk on in (except at Louis Vuitton where there is always a huge queue out the front). Don't expect overly friendly service but do expect courtesy; after all, how are they to know that behind your jeans-and-sneakers façade you're not hiding a significant trust fund and a penchant for Lagerfeld? Although, as one high-fashion salesperson confided, 'I can immediately smell whether a customer intends to buy something or not, but either way I am always polite, of course.' Which means that you will always be extended a courteous *bonjour*, which you must return, followed by a prefrozen smile and one of those looks that appraises you from head to foot in a flash before resuming its glazed indifference. Try ignoring them just as gracefully and go to try on sunglasses.

For a more accessible tour of Parisian fashion, check out the **Bon Marché department store** (see p293) which has an excellent collection of all the big labels and couture designs. For some catwalk action, there are weekly *defilés* (parades) in the **Galérie Lafayette and Printemps department stores** (see p300), while up-and-coming designers have recently been showing at the exclusive bar **La Suite** (p250). In some stores you can join mailing lists to receive fashion show invitations, but you need to be in Paris at the right time to attend.

Parisienne Style

Indicative of the somewhat intellectual approach Parisians have to fashion is their choice of icons. While reality TV stars and glamorous heiresses get their 15 minutes of fame, when it comes to fashion the personalities who become 'leaders' are more likely to be 'thinking actresses' than supermodels or popstars. Hence we see singer/actress (and Johnny Depp's girlfriend) Vanessa Paradis in megabudget ads for Chanel, actress Marie Gillain as the face of Lancôme and Charlotte Gainsbourg (actress and daughter of Serge Gainsbourg and Jane Birkin) for Gérard Darel. Other rising stars of cinema being noticed are Anna Mouglalis, muse of Karl Lagerfeld for Chanel (she's in the Allure perfume ads), and Nicolas Duvauchelle for Hugo Boss.

As for the fashion on the street, there's no need to feel overwhelmed as most people are relatively casual. There are, however, some characteristic Parisian looks which can often be related to certain geographical and social genres. The funky, streetwear style, heavily inspired by London, can be associated with the trendy shops around Etienne Marcel (near the Louvre/Les Halles area) and the Marais. Meanwhile your more upper-crust 'BCBG' *(bon chic bon genre)* girl tends to keep her pearls, twinsets and Hermes scarves safely in the 7e, 8e and 16e districts. The chic Left Bank mademoiselle struts her designer jeans, expensive knits and Balençiaga purse around St-Sulpice and St-Germain in the 6e; while the 11e (such as Oberkampf, Bastille) and 18e (Abbesses) tend to be the stomping ground of the 'Bobo' (bourgeois bohemian), whose take on style is doused in nostalgia for her voyage to India and her avowed commitment to free trade and beads.

But if anything defines the Parisian brand of chic it would have to be that quintessential combination of elegance, femininity and originality. The fashionable Parisian follows trends very closely while never sacrificing herself to them. She puts a great deal of thought into her outfits. 'Being broke is no excuse', declares one fashionista, whose perception of broke may require some nuancing. 'You must mix and match, choose carefully from cheap places like H&M or Zara and combine with one very expensive piece, and think properly about your shoes: the rest comes down to accessories.' The Parisian seeks out that little detail that makes simple clothes special: adding a brooch to a cardigan, mixing prints and fabrics, a judicious use of hats, tying your scarf just so. Jewellery and heels are almost always *de rigueur*, and sexiness remains the underlying – but understated – value. Nothing is worse than 'vulgarity', and the classy Parisienne avoids anything that is *trop* (too much). Too much make-up, too much flesh showing, too many colours, too much matching, too shiny, too fat: all things to be avoided like the plague. After all, looking effortless takes an awful lot of work.

EIFFEL TOWER AREA & 16E ARRONDISSEMENT

ESPACE CATHERINE MAX

Map pp426-7   Clothing & Accessories

☎ 01 53 70 67 47; www.espacecatherinemax.com; 17 av Raymond Poincaré, 16e; Ⓜ Trocadéro
The infinitely well-connected Catherine Max holds massive private sales in her huge showrooms, with hugely discounted designer stocks – both fashion and home decorations. With over 80 sales held per year you're bound to come across something you need or want. To participate you will need to pay an €18 subscription and join the queuing masses. You can also sign up for updates online. See their sale schedule for opening times. There's also a second Neuilly showroom (Map pp422–3; ☎ 01 53 70 67 48; 113 av Charles de Gaulle, Neuilly-sur-Seine, 92200; Ⓜ Les Sablons).

RÉCIPROQUE

Map pp426-7   Clothing & Accessories

☎ 01 47 04 30 28, 01 47 04 82 24; 88 & 95 rue de la Pompe, 16e; ⏰ 11am-7pm Tue-Fri, 10.30am-7pm Sat; Ⓜ Rue de la Pompe

The biggest *dépôt-vente* in Paris with half a dozen shops on the same street. You'll find rack after rack of Chanel suits as well as bits and pieces from the likes of Christian Lacroix, Hermès and John Galliano. It's an excellent place to pick up bags and shoes.

ÉTOILE & CHAMPS-ÉLYSÉES

The av des Champs-Élysées is somewhat of a giant wind tunnel, lined with super-sized chain stores. But if you came to the *Champs* to shop you're probably coming for the French dream: luxury fashion. The luxury fashion houses that make wonderful window-shopping, situated along av Montaigne (with the mammoth Louis Vuitton store on the corner) and the equally prestigious av Georges V. For more, see the Fashion boxed text, p294.

CHLOÉ Map pp426-7   Clothing & Accessories

☎ 01 47 23 74 12; www.chloe.com; 44 av Montaigne, 8e; ⏰ 9am-7pm; Ⓜ George V

Having presented its first collection in the Café de Flore (p247) in 1956, Chloé was led by Lagerfeld in the '60s and '90s. Thanks to a revamping by Stella McCartney and Phoebe Philo, it now prides itself on its 'street cred' and sexy image.

ESPACE IGN Map pp426-7   Books

☎ 01 43 98 80 00; www.ign.fr; 107 rue La Boétie, 8e; ⏰ 9.30am-7pm Mon-Fri, 11am-12.30pm & 2-6.30pm Sat; Ⓜ Franklin D Roosevelt

This is the place to find a full selection of Institut Géographique National (IGN) maps, as well as atlases, globes, walking maps, city plans, compasses, satellite images, historic maps and guidebooks.

FROMAGERIE ALLÉOSSE

Map pp426-7   Food & Drink

☎ 01 46 22 50 45; 13 rue Poncelet, 17e; ⏰ 9am-1pm & 4-7pm Tue-Sat, 9am-1pm Sun; Ⓜ Ternes

This is the best cheese shop in Paris and worth a trip across town. Cheeses are as they should be – grouped in five main categories: *fromage de chèvre* (goat's milk cheese), *fromage à pâte persillée* (veined or blue cheese), *fromage à pâte molle* (soft cheese), *fromage à pâte demi-dure* (semi-hard cheese) and *fromage à pâte dure* (hard cheese).

GUERLAIN Map pp426-7   Cosmetics & Perfume

☎ 01 45 62 52 57; 68 av des Champs-Élysées, 8e; ⏰ 10.30am-8pm Mon-Sat, 3-7pm Sun; Ⓜ Franklin D Roosevelt

Guerlain is Paris' most famous *perfumerie*, and its shop, dating from 1912, is one of the

Galeries Lafayette (p300)

most beautiful in the city. With its shimmering mirror and marble décor, it's a reminder of the former glory of the Champs-Élysées.

LANVIN Map pp426-7 — Cosmetics & Perfume

☎ 01 44 71 33 33; www.lanvin.com; 15 rue du Faubourg St-Honoré, 8e; ⊙ 10am-7pm; Ⓜ Concorde
Alber Elbaz has now nudged the elegant luxury of the house of Lanvin back into the style spotlight after it drifted into obscurity during the '90s. The suits and handbags are particularly prized.

SÉPHORA Map pp426-7 — Cosmetics & Perfume

☎ 01 53 93 22 50; www.sephora.com; 70 av des Champs-Élysées, 8e; ⊙ 10am-1am Mon-Sat, noon-1am Sun; Ⓜ Franklin D Roosevelt
Séphora's flagship store features over 12,000 fragrances and cosmetics for your sampling pleasure. You can spend hours in here (until 1am in fact) and will invariably come out with bags of stuff and a headache from all the perfume in the air.

VIRGIN MEGASTORE Map pp426-7 — Music

☎ 01 49 53 50 00; 52-60 av des Champs-Élysées, 8e; ⊙ 10am-midnight Mon-Sat, noon-midnight Sun; Ⓜ Franklin D Roosevelt
This French-owned version of the huge British music and bookshop chain has the largest music collection in Paris, as well as English-language books.

CONCORDE & MADELEINE

If the big fashion houses reign mainly on the other side the Champs Élysées, the class and couture continues along in the 8e rue du Faubourg St-Honoré and its eastern extension, rue St-Honoré in the 1e, where designer shops – and designer shoppers – abound. This area is also home to the grand gourmet food stores of place de la Madeleine and the luxury jewellery of place Vendôme. See also the Fashion boxed text, p294.

BOUTIQUE MAILLE

Map pp426-7 — Food & Drink
☎ 01 40 15 06 00; 6 place de la Madeleine, 8e; ⊙ 10am-7pm Mon-Sat; Ⓜ Madeleine
The mustard specialist has premade items, but can also prepare some two dozen

different varieties for you, designed to accompany your cuisine, like the Dijon cassis (to be served with game or fowl). There is a range of exclusive vinegars too.

COLETTE Map pp426-7 — Clothing & Accessories

☎ 01 55 35 33 90; www.colette.fr; 213 rue St-Honoré, 1er; ⊙ 10.30am-7.30pm Mon-Sat; Ⓜ Tuileries
This Japanese-inspired concept store is the ultimate place to see what's hot in Paris. Not just an exquisite selection of clothes and accessories, Colette has books, art, music and beauty products. Limited-edition sneakers, candles that smell like happiness, cutting-edge clocks – it's worth a look even if you're not buying. Colette's famous sales see huge reductions on the designer stock, including Prada, Marc Jacobs and far more. The Water Bar in the basement features still and sparkling waters from around the world.

ERES Map pp426-7 — Clothing & Accessories

☎ 01 47 42 28 82; www.eres.fr; 2 rue Tronchet, 8e; ⊙ 10am-7pm Mon-Sat; Ⓜ Madeleine
You will pay an arm and a leg for an Eres swimsuit, but anyone who has despaired at buying bathers in the past will understand why these have become a must-have item for those in the know. The stunning swimmers are cut to suit all shapes and sizes with bikini tops and bottoms sold separately. They also have magnificent lingerie.

FAUCHON Map pp426-7 — Food & Drink

☎ 01 47 42 60 11; 26-30 place de la Madeleine, 8e; ⊙ 8.30am-7pm Mon-Sat; Ⓜ Madeleine
Paris' most famous caterer has six departments in two buildings selling the most incredibly mouth-watering delicacies from pâté de foie gras to confitures (jams). There are a dozen smaller outlets throughout the city, including a Bastille branch (Map pp440–1).

HÉDIARD Map pp426-7 — Food & Drink

☎ 01 43 12 88 88; www.hediard.fr; 21 place de la Madeleine, 8e; ⊙ 8.30am-8.30pm Mon-Sat; Ⓜ Madeleine
This famous luxury food shop established in 1854 consists of two adjacent sections selling prepared dishes, teas, coffees, jams, wines, pastries, fruits, vegetables and so on, as well as a popular tea room (⊙ 8.30am-7pm Mon-Sat).

IL POUR L'HOMME

Map pp426-7   Gifts & Souvenirs

☎ 01 42 60 43 56; 209 rue St-Honoré, 1er;
⏱ 10.30am-7pm Mon-Sat; Ⓜ Tuileries

This men's gift store is housed in what was once a paint shop with 19th-century display counters and chests of drawers. Here you'll find everything a man could want and not really need – from hip flasks and cigar cutters to shaving brushes and designer tweezers.

LA MAISON DE LA TRUFFE

Map pp426-7   Food & Drink

☎ 01 42 65 53 22; www.maison-de-la-truffe.com
in French; 19 place de la Madeleine, 8e; ⏱ shop
9am-9pm Mon-Sat, eating area 11am-9pm Mon-
Sat; Ⓜ Madeleine

The 'House of Truffles' is the place for tasting these fine fungi – French black from late October to March, Italian white (over €450 per 100g) from mid-October to December. There's a small sit-down area where you can sample dishes.

LA MAISON DU MIEL

Map pp426-7   Food & Drink

☎ 01 47 42 26 70; 24 rue Vignon, 9e; ⏱ 9.15am-
7pm Mon-Sat; Ⓜ Madeleine

In business since 1898, it stocks over 40 kinds of honey, with perfumes such as Corsican wildflower.

MADELIOS

Map pp426-7   Clothing & Accessories

☎ 01 53 45 00 00; 23 blvd de la Madeleine, 8e;
⏱ 10am-7pm Mon-Sat; Ⓜ Madeleine

A head-to-toe men's store, with a fine selection of classic and modern suits, shoes

---

HISTORIC HAUTE COUTURE

A stroll down av Montaigne and av Georges V (in the infamous Golden Triangle), as well as rue du Faubourg St-Honoré (Map pp426–7), all in the 8e, essentially constitutes the walk of fame of top French fashion. The following is a far-from-complete description of some of the most influential French *maisons de couture* (fashion houses).

Chanel (Map pp426–7; ☎ 01 47 23 74 12; www.chanel.com; 40-42 av Montaigne, 8e; Ⓜ Georges V) Visionary and perfectionist, Gabrielle 'Coco' Chanel (1883–1971) revolutionised 20th-century fashion by shunning corsetry and dressing women in comfortable, often mannish clothes. By 1925 Chanel had presented her signature cardigan jacket and the following year saw the arrival of the celebrated little black dress. Today Karl Lagerfeld is Chanel's successor.

Christian Dior (Map pp426–7; ☎ 01 40 73 54 44; www.dior.com; 30-32 av Montaigne, 8e; Ⓜ Georges V) Christian Dior (1905–57) caused a sensation in 1947 when he unveiled his small-waisted, full-skirted 'new-look'. After a period of wartime austerity, Dior's creations became the dictate of style, re-establishing Paris as the world fashion capital. Yves Saint Laurent was appointed chief designer after Dior's death. Today flamboyant British designer John Galliano (b 1960; www.johngalliano.com) holds this position, with Hedi Slimane for Dior Homme (menswear).

Christian Lacroix (Map pp426–7; ☎ 01 42 68 79 00; www.christian-lacroix.fr; 73 rue Faubourg St-Honoré, 8e; Ⓜ Georges V) Christian Lacroix (b 1951) is known for his use of colour and often theatrical combinations: taffeta and lace flirt with denim and knits in contemporary combinations. Lacroix opened his own *maison de couture* in 1987. In 1994 he created his Bazar collection, zapping between folklore and different eras, a celebration of the melting pot that Paris had become. He went on to launch his Jeans collection two years later, the first collection combining past, present and future with denim as the common denominator.

Givenchy (Map pp426–7; ☎ 01 44 31 51 25, 01 44 31 51 09; www.givenchy.com; 3 & 8 av Georges V, 8e; Ⓜ Georges V) A classic couturier from the golden age of Paris fashion, Hubert de Givenchy (b 1927) opened his own *maison de couture* in 1952. A pioneer, Givenchy was the first to present a luxury collection of women's ready-to-wear. Audrey Hepburn and, to a lesser extent, Jacqueline Kennedy, became the label's unofficial style ambassadors in the '50s and '60s.

Hermès (Map pp426–7; ☎ 01 40 17 47 83; www.hermes.com; 24 rue du Faubourg St-Honoré, 8e; Ⓜ Concorde) This fashion house was founded in 1837 by saddle-maker Thierry Hermès, and the company is currently in the hands of his family's seventh generation; its logo – a horse-drawn carriage – reflects the company's original business. The famous scarves were first launched in 1930 and are considered by many to be *the* fashion accessory. Jean-Paul Gaultier presented his first collection for Hermès in 2004.

Jean-Paul Gaultier (Map pp426–7; www.jeanpaul-gaultier.com; ☎ 01 44 43 00 44; 44 av George V, 8e; Ⓜ Georges V) Jean-Paul Gaultier (b 1952), the shy kid from the Paris suburbs, worked for Pierre Cardin in the 1970s

and casual wear. It also has a hairdress-
ing and beauty salon, café and exhibition
space.

MARIA LUISA

Map pp426-7   Clothing & Accessories
☎ 01 47 03 96 15; 2 rue Cambon, 1er;
🕐 10.30am-7pm Mon-Sat; Ⓜ Concorde
Every fashionista knows and trusts this
eminent selection of classic and avant-
garde designers (including Alexander
McQueen, Stella McCartney and Helmut
Lang). This shop also stocks a range of
swimwear. Around the corner you'll find
an **accessories branch** (Map pp426–7; ☎ 01
47 03 48 08; 40 rue Mont Thabor, 1er)
and there's also a **menswear branch** (Map
pp428–9; ☎ 01 42 60 89 83; 19bis rue
Mont Thabor, 1er).

OPÉRA & GRANDS BOULEVARDS

The area around Opéra and the Grands
Boulevards is where you'll find Paris'
most popular *grands magasins* (department stores), around which are clustered
all the major French and international
chain stores. If here in December, check
out the fabulous Christmas shows in the
department store windows – but beware
the unbearable crowds.

BRENTANO'S Map pp426-7   Books
☎ 01 42 61 52 50; www.brentanos.fr; 37 av de
l'Opéra, 2e; 🕐 10am-7.30pm Mon-Sat; Ⓜ Opéra
Situated midway between the Louvre and
Palais Garnier, this US-based chain is a
good shop for tracking down books from

and launched his own line in 1975. Influenced by the punk movement in London, JPG quickly became known as the
enfant terrible of the fashion world, with his granny's corsets, men dressed in skirts and bracelets cut from tin cans.
The man responsible for Madonna's conical bra, Gaultier continues to surprise, seduce and innovate today.

Louis Vuitton (Map pp426–7; ☎ 01 53 57 24 00; www.vuitton.com; 101 av des Champs-Élysées, 8e; Ⓜ Georges
V) Louis Vuitton (1821–92) opened his first luggage and trunk shop in 1854 after working as the Empress Eugenie's
personal packer. The ever-popular canvas bag with the 'LV' monogram was created as far back as 1896. In 1987 Louis
Vuitton merged with the champagne maison Moët Hennessy to form the powerful LVMH group. American-born Marc
Jacobs (b 1963; www.marcjacobs.com) is now the creative director.

Yves Saint Laurent (Map pp436–7; ☎ 01 43 26 84 43; www.ysl.com; 6 & 12 place St-Sulpice, 6e; Ⓜ St-Sulpice)
The darling of the fashion world for almost half a century, Saint Laurent (b 1936) started with Dior at the tender age
of 17 and opened his own fashion house in 1962. Inspired by the arts and celebrated as the man who re-imagined
women's fashion, he shocked with designs that would go on to become classics: trouser suits with tuxedo tops, safari
jackets and see-through blouses. Today Stephano Pilatti has replaced Tom Ford as YSL chief, heralding a return to its
classic elegant origins that has caused much sighing in relief.

International couture in Paris

Comme des Garçons (Map pp426–7; ☎ 01 53 30 27 27; 54 rue du Faubourg St Honoré, 8e; Ⓜ Georges V)

Emilio Pucci (Map pp426–7; ☎ 01 47 20 04 45; 36 av Montaigne, 8e; Ⓜ Georges V)

Gianfranco Ferré (Map pp426–7; ☎ 01 42 89 90 91; 51 av Montaigne, 8e; Ⓜ Georges V)

Gucci (Map pp426–7; ☎ 01 56 69 80 80; 60 av Montaigne, 8e; Ⓜ Georges V)

Helmut Lang (Map pp426–7; ☎ 01 53 30 27 27; 219 rue du Faubourg St-Honoré, 8e; Ⓜ Tulieries)

Issey Miyake (Map pp440–1; ☎ 01 48 87 01 86; 5 place des Vosges, 4e; Ⓜ St-Paul)

Miu Miu (Map pp434–5; ☎ 01 53 63 20 30; 16 rue de Grenelle, 7e; Ⓜ St-Germain des Prés)

Nina Ricci (Map pp426–7; ☎ 01 40 88 64 51; 39 av Montaigne, 8e; Ⓜ Georges V)

Prada (Map pp426–7; ☎ 01 53 23 99 40; 10 av Montaigne, 8e; Ⓜ Georges V)

Ungaro (Map pp426–7; ☎ 01 53 57 00 00; 2 av Montaigne, 8e; Ⓜ Georges V)

Valentino (Map pp426–7; ☎ 01 47 23 64 61; 17-19 av Montaigne, 8e; Ⓜ Georges V)

Yohji Yamamoto (Map pp428–9; ☎ 01 45 08 82 45; 47 rue Étienne Marcel, 2e; Ⓜ Étienne Marcel)

Window shopping at E Dehillerin (p284)

the US, including fiction, business and children's titles, and magazines.

DROUOT Map pp428-9 — Antiques
☎ 01 48 00 20 20; www.gazette-drouot.com; 7-9 rue Drouot, 9e; ◔ sales 2-6pm; Ⓜ Richelieu Drouot
Paris' most established auction house has been selling fine lots for more than a century. Bidding is in rapid-fire French (also now available on the Internet) and a 10% to 15% commission is charged on top of the purchase price. Viewings (always a vicarious pleasure) are from 11am to 6pm the day before and 10.30am to 11.30am the morning of the auction. Details can be found in the weekly *Gazette de l'Hôtel Drouot*, available at the auction house and selected newsstands on Friday, and on the house's website.

GALERIES LAFAYETTE
Map pp426-7 — Department Store
☎ 01 42 82 34 56; www.galerieslafayette.com; 40 blvd Haussmann, 9e; ◔ 9.30am-7.30pm Mon-Wed, Fri & Sat, 9.30am-9pm Thu; Ⓜ Auber or Chaussée d'Antin
A vast *grand magasin* in two adjacent buildings linked by a pedestrian bridge over rue de Mogador, Galeries Lafayette features over 75,000 brand-name items, a wide range of fashion labels and the world's largest lingerie department. There's a fine view from the rooftop restaurant. A fashion show (☎ 01 42 82 30 25 to book a seat) takes place at 3pm Friday. The 10,000 sq metre Lafayette Maison (Map pp428-9; 35 blvd Haussmann, 9e; Ⓜ Auber or Chaussée

d'Antin) has each floor dedicated to a particular room in the house.

LE PRINTEMPS
Map pp426-7 — Department Store
☎ 01 42 82 50 00; www.printemps.com; 64 blvd Haussmann, 9e; ◔ 9.35am-7pm Mon-Wed, Fri & Sat, 9.35am-10pm Thu; Ⓜ Havre Caumartin
This is actually three separate stores – Le Printemps de la Mode (women's fashion), Le Printemps de l'Homme (for men) and Le Printemps de la Beauté et Maison (for beauty and household goods) – offering a staggering display of perfume, cosmetics and accessories, as well as established and up-and-coming designer wear. There's a fashion show under the 7th floor cupola at 10am on Tuesday; reservations are not required.

LEGRAND FILLES & FILS
Map pp428-9 — Food & Drink
☎ 01 42 60 07 12; 7-11 Galerie Vivienne, 1 rue de la Banque, 2e; ◔ 11am-7pm Mon-Sat; Ⓜ Pyramides
This shop beside a lovely covered arcade sells not just fine wines but all the accoutrements: corkscrews, tasting glasses, decanters etc. They also have a fancy wine bar and tasting room.

LES CAVES AUGÉ Map pp426-7 — Food & Drink
☎ 01 45 22 16 97; 116 blvd Haussmann, 8e; ◔ 1-7.30pm Mon, 9am-7.30pm Tue-Sat; Ⓜ St-Augustin
This should be the wine shop for you if you're following the advice of Marcel Proust. It's now under the stewardship of knowledgeable sommelier Marc Sibard.

GARE DE LYON, NATION & BERCY

The upmarket boutiques of Bercy have transformed the 12e and are always packed with shoppers. Elsewhere in the 12e, the area near the Viaduc des Arts has discerning furniture, antiques and art. The Marché d'Aligre flea-market is a must.

BERCY VILLAGE Map p449   Shopping Centre
☎ 01 40 02 90 80; www.bercyvillage.com; Cour St-Émilion, 12e; ⏱ 11am-9pm; Ⓜ Cour St-Émilion
This redevelopment of a row of 19th-century *chais* (wine warehouses) in southeast Paris contains dozens of shops, bars and restaurants, including the Chai 33 (p255) wine bar.

MARCHÉ AUX PUCES D'ALIGRE
Map pp446-7   Flea Market
place d'Aligre, 12e; ⏱ 7am-1.30pm Tue-Sun; Ⓜ Ledru Rollin
Smaller but more central than Paris' other flea markets, this is one of the best places to rummage through boxes of clothes and accessories worn decades ago by those fashionable (and not-so-fashionable) Parisians.

MUSÉE & COMPAGNIE
Map p449   Gifts & Souvenirs
☎ 01 40 02 98 72; 40-42 Cour St-Émilion, 12e; ⏱ 11am-9pm; Ⓜ Cour St-Émilion
This shop sells top-end copies of all those knick-knacks you admired in the museum but couldn't have: *Mona Lisa, Venus de Milo*, Celtic jewellery and so on. All fakes, of course – but good ones.

MONTMARTRE & PIGALLE

The area of the 9e and 18e along rue des Martyrs and climbing up rue des Abbesses from metro Pigalle constitutes a good stroll for the patient shopper who wants to enjoy the scenery. You'll find little designer-clothing shops and a mixed bag of second-hand fashion depots, vintage clothing and records, not to mention some excellent, typically Parisian bakeries and food stores. The rest of the 18e, especially around the less-than-salubrious Goutte d'Or area (rue Myrha and rue de la Goutte d'Or) has cheap fabrics, cut-price fashion, young designers and assorted frippery. Around metro Barbès Rochechouart and blvd Magenta it's working-class, bargain-basement shopping: take a detour from the glamorous avenues and see how the other half lives.

GASPARD DE LA BUTTE
Map p432   Department Store
☎ 01 42 55 99 40; 10bis rue Yvonne le Tac, 18e; ⏱ 11am-7pm Tue-Sun; Ⓜ Pigalle
Women's and children's wear, all locally made with beautiful cottons as well as colourful felts for the infants' clothing. Its very 'Montmartre' in style – you could imagine Amélie Poulain shopping here.

LA CITADELLE
Map p432   Clothing & Accessories
☎ 01 42 52 21 56; 1 rue des Trois Frères, 18e; ⏱ 11am-8pm Mon-Sat, 2-7pm Sun; Ⓜ Abbesses
This designer discount shop hidden away in Montmartre has some real finds from new French and Italian designers. Look out for labels like Noir Ebène, Les Chemins Blancs and Petit Bateau T-shirts.

TATI Map p432   Department Store
☎ 01 55 29 50 00; 4 blvd Rochechouart, 18e; ⏱ 10am-7pm Mon-Fri, 9.15am-7pm Sat; Ⓜ Barbès Rochechouart
With its war cry of *les plus bas prix* (the lowest prices) Tati has been Paris' great working-class department store for 50 years. Don't be surprised to see trendy Parisians fighting for bargains hidden in the crammed bins and piled onto tables. There's a smaller 3e branch (Map pp428–9; ☎ 01 48 87 72 81; 174 rue du Temple, 3e; Ⓜ République) as well.

WOCHDOM
Map pp428-9   Clothing and Accessories
☎ 01 53 21 09 72; 72 rue Condorcet, 18e; ⏱ 12-8pm Mon-Sat; Ⓜ Pigalle
Cool in a slightly creepy way, this self-consciously chic retro seconds store has painstakingly selected 'design vintage', mostly from the '70s. Shoes are on display directly across the street.

BEYOND CENTRAL PARIS

Venture beyond central Paris for shopping malls, designer outlets and wonderful flea markets.

LA VALLÉE VILLAGE
Shopping Centre

☎ 01 60 42 35 00; www.valueretail.com; 3 cours de la Garonne, 77700 Serris; ⏰ 10am-8pm Mon-Sat May-Sep, 10am-7pm Mon-Sat Oct-Apr, 11am-7pm Sun

This shopping centre within the Disneyland Resort (p359), 30km east of Paris, contains some 60 big-name outlets – from Christian Lacroix to Kenzo and Versace – offering discounts on last season's clothing, accessories and tableware. To get there from central Paris, take RER line A4 (€5.90, 30 to 35 minutes) and get off at Val d'Europe station. Alternatively Cityrama (p335) runs a coach (adult/child 3-11 yrs €15/10) from 4 place des Pyramides, 1er (Ⓜ Tuileries) at 10.15am on Tuesday, Thursday and Sunday, returning at 5pm. Be sure to book in advance.

MARCHÉ AUX PUCES DE LA PORTE DE VANVES Map pp422-3
Flea Market

av Georges Lafenestre & av Marc Sangnier, 14e; ⏰ 7am-6pm or later Sat & Sun; Ⓜ Porte de Vanves
The Porte de Vanves flea market is the smallest and, some say, friendliest of the lot. Av Georges Lafenestre has lots of 'curios' that don't quite qualify as antiques. Av Marc Sangnier is lined with stalls of new clothes, shoes, handbags and household items for sale.

MARCHÉ AUX PUCES DE MONTREUIL
Map pp422-3 ⏰ Flea Market

av du Professeur André Lemière, 20e; ⏰ 8am-6pm or later Sat-Mon; Ⓜ Porte de Montreuil
Established in the 19th century, the Montreuil flea market is known for its quality second-hand clothes and designer seconds. The 500 stalls also sell engravings, jewellery, linen, crockery, old furniture and appliances.

MARCHÉ AUX PUCES DE ST-OUEN
Map pp422-3
Flea Market

www.les-puces.com; rue des Rosiers, av Michelet, rue Voltaire, rue Paul Bert & rue Jean-Henri Fabre, 18e; ⏰ 10am-7pm Sat-Mon; Ⓜ Porte de Clignancourt
This vast flea market founded in the late 19th century and said to be Europe's largest, has 2500-odd stalls grouped into 10 marchés (market areas), each with its own speciality (eg Marché Serpette and Marché Biron for antiques, Marché Malik for second-hand clothing). There are miles of modern clothing and 'freelance' stalls selling anything from batteries to stolen phones. For more information about the market and its stalls check out www.libertys.com or www.vernaison.com.

MI-PRIX Map pp422-3
Clothing & Accessories

☎ 0148 28 42 48; 27 blvd Victor, 15e; ⏰ 10am-7pm Mon-Sat; Ⓜ Porte de Versailles
On the edge of Paris, another spot for reduced designer names. Word goes out of sudden arrivals of freshly discounted Miu Miu and Gaspard Yurkievich, and informed Parisians hot-foot it to this store to grab the bargains.

Sleeping ■

Sleeping

Paris has a very wide choice of accommodation options – 75,000 beds in 1450 establishments – that caters for all budgets throughout much of the city. There are four basic types: deluxe and top-end hotels, some of which count among the finest in the world; midrange hotels, many of which have personalities all of their own and by and large offer very good value when compared with similarly priced places to stay in other European capitals; adequate but generally uninspiring budget hotels; and hostels, which run the gamut from cramped, airless cupboards to party places with bars worth a visit in their own right. In this chapter, accommodation options are listed according to the sections of the city as outlined in the Sights chapter. The last two types of accommodation (budget hotels and hostels) can be found under the heading Cheap Sleeps in each neighbourhood.

The city of Paris levies a *taxe de séjour* (tourist tax) of between €0.20 (camp sites, unclassified hotels) and €1.20 (four-star hotels) per person per night on all forms of accommodation.

A note on the icons used in this chapter: those hotels that bear a nonsmoking icon (🚭) really do have at least a handful of rooms – in the case of several, entire floors – reserved for those who do not smoke and are not just places that make claims to 'airing out our rooms thoroughly after guests' use'. Also most hotels and hostels in Paris have some form of Internet access available nowadays. We have included an Internet icon (💻) only if the hotel has wi-fi (pronounced we-fee in French) or allows guests to use a terminal free of charge in the lobby or reception area. Some establishments (usually hostels) charge their guests an access fee, which we have noted in the review text. For information about rooms for travellers with disabilities and our use of that icon (♿), see p308.

Accommodation Styles

APARTMENTS
If you are interested in renting a furnished flat for anything from a night to a month, consult one of the many agencies listed under the heading 'Location Appartements Meublés' (Furnished Rentals) on sheets distributed by the **Office de Tourisme et de Congrès de Paris** (Paris Convention & Visitors Bureau; p386) and on its website. Accommodation for students and organisations that can arrange it are listed under 'Pour les Jeunes' (Young Paris).

Serviced flats – like staying in a hotel without all the extras – are an excellent option for those staying longer than a week, particularly if you're part of a small group. There are quite a few of them around Paris. Some options are listed in the boxed text, opposite.

For information about longer-term rentals in Paris, see p307.

HOTELS
Hotels in Paris are inspected by authorities at *département* (administrative division of France) level and classified into six categories – from no star to four-star 'L' (for

Card table in Hôtel Caron de Beaumarchais (p310)

SERVICED APARTMENTS

Apart'hotels Citadines (☎ 0 825 333 332, 01 41 05 79 05 from abroad; www.citadines.com; ⊠ 🖳 ⑤) This fabulously successful (now international) chain has 16 properties in Paris, including those listed below. Prices vary depending on the season and the property but, in general, a small studio for two with fully equipped kitchen (fridge, microwave, dishwasher, crockery and cutlery) for just under a week costs €108 to €255 per night and a one-bedroom flat sleeping four costs €175 to €396. For stays longer than six days there's a discount of 10% to 15%, and for 30 days or more about 20% to 25%. Central branches include: **Bastille Nation** (Map pp446–7; ☎ 01 40 04 43 50; bastillenation@citadines.com; 14-18 rue de Chaligny, 12e; Ⓜ Reuilly Diderot), **Les Halles** (Map pp436–7; ☎ 01 40 39 26 50; leshalles@citadines.com; 4 rue des Innocents, 1er; Ⓜ Châtelet-Les Halles), **Maine Montparnasse** (Map pp434–5; ☎ 01 53 91 27 00; montparnasse@citadines.com; 67 av du Maine, 14e; Ⓜ Gaîté), **Montmartre** (Map p432; ☎ 01 44 70 45 50; montmartre@citadines.com; 16 av Rachel, 18e; Ⓜ Blanche), **Opéra Grands Boulevards** (Map pp428–9; ☎ 01 40 15 14 00; operaboulevard@citadines.com; 18 rue Favart, 2e; Ⓜ Richelieu Drouot), **St-Germain des Prés** (Map pp436–7; ☎ 01 44 07 70 00; stgermain@citadines.com; 53ter quai des Grands Augustins, 6e; Ⓜ St-Michel) and **Tour Eiffel** (Map pp434–5; ☎ 01 53 95 60 00; eiffel@citadines.com; 132 blvd de Grenelle, 15e; Ⓜ La Motte Picquet Grenelle).

France Location (☎ 04 92 28 38 48; www.france-location.fr; 🖳)This chain has serviced apartments around France, including two in Paris. Daily prices quoted here are for up to seven nights' stay; there is a discount of 10% from eight to 27 nights and 20% after that. **Résidence Le St-Germain** (Map pp436–7; ☎ 01 46 34 22 33; reservation@france-location.fr; 16 rue Boutebrie, 5e; 2-person studio €93-113, 4-person apt €136-163; Ⓜ St-Michel) has 11 fully equipped studios and apartments for between two and six people measuring from 17 to 55 sq metres.

Résidence Passage Dubail (Map pp428–9; ☎ 01 44 89 66 70; reservation@france-location.fr; 5-7 Passage Dubail, 10e; 2-person studio €77-87, 4-person apt from €135; Ⓜ Gare de l'Est) has studios and apartments measuring 16 to 30 sq metres accommodating up to four people.

Park & Suites Grande Bibliothèque (Map p449; ☎ 01 53 61 62 00; www.parkandsuites.com; 15 rue de Tolbiac, 13e; ste with kitchenette for 1-2 people €138, for 3-4 people €154, €567/472.50 per week; Ⓜ Bibliothèque; 🖳) Close to the **Bibliothèque Nationale de France** (p147) these 70 fully equipped studios for up to four people are a good choice if you want to stay in the Bercy area. Rates drop to as low as €90 and €97 per night for longer stays.

Résidence des Arts (Map pp436–7; ☎ 01 55 42 71 11; www.residencedesarts.org; 14 rue Gît le Cœur, 6e; studio €130-190, ste for 2 people €195-280, apt for 4 people €210-300, 2-bed apt €370-490; Ⓜ St-Michel; ⊠ 🔲 🖳) This lovely *résidence* in a 15th-century private mansion just west of place St-Michel feels more like a luxury hotel than a flat. Studios have showers, suites have baths and all have fully equipped kitchenettes. The lift does not reach the top (6th) floor.

Résidence Pierre & Vacances City Montmartre (Map p432; ☎ 01 42 57 14 55; www.pierreetvacances-city.com; 10 place Charles Dullin, 18e; 2/3/4 person studios €114/126/144, 1/2 bed apt €177/224; Ⓜ Abbesses; ⊠ 🔲 🖳) An attractive *résidence* at the end of a leafy street in the heart of Montmartre, this place has 76 studios and apartments for between two and six people. There's a 10% discount on stays of eight nights or more and 20% on stays of 28 days or more. There are a half-dozen other Pierre & Vacances properties scattered throughout Paris, including two in La Défense.

luxe), the French equivalent of five stars. All hotels must display their rates, including TVA (VAT; valued-added tax) both outside the hotel and in guests' rooms.

Paris may not be able to boast the number of budget hotels it did a decade ago, but the choice is still more than ample, especially in the Marais, around the Bastille, near the major train stations and off the Grands Boulevards. Places with one star and those with the designations 'HT' (Hôtel de Tourisme) or 'NN' (Nouvelle Norme), which signifies that a hotel is awaiting its rating but assures you of a certain standard of comfort, are much of a muchness. Remember: the overall consideration at these places is cost, never quality. We've said it before and we'll say it again: you get what you pay for. Be advised also that relatively few budget hotels in Paris accept credit cards.

Breakfast – usually a simple continental affair of bread, croissants, butter, jam and coffee or tea, though American-style breakfast buffets are becoming more popular – is served at most hotels with two or more stars and costs from about €6 or €8.

Some hotels in Paris have different rates according to the season and are noted as such throughout the chapter. The high season is (roughly) from April to September while the low season is from October to March.

HOSTELS

Paris is awash with hostels, but such budget accommodation isn't as cheap as it used to be here. Beds under €20 are increasingly rare – especially in summer – so two people who don't mind sleeping in the same bed may find basic rooms in budget hotels a less-expensive proposition. Groups of three or four will save even more if they share two or three beds in a budget hotel.

Showers are always free at hostels in Paris, and rates include a simple breakfast. Internet access (about €2 for 15 minutes) is available at almost all the hostels listed here. If you don't have your own sheet bag, sheets can be rented at most hostels for a one-off charge of around €3 (plus deposit).

Some hostels only allow guests to stay a maximum of three nights, particularly in summer. Places that have upper age limits (for example, 30 years old) tend not to enforce them except at the busiest times. Only the official *auberges de jeunesse* (youth hostels), of which there are just two in Paris, require guests to present Hostelling International (HI) cards or their equivalent. Curfew – if enforced – is generally at 1am or 2am.

HOMESTAYS & B&BS

Under an arrangement known as *hôtes payants* (literally 'paying guests') or *hébergement chez l'habitant* (lodging with the occupants of private homes), students, young people and tourists can stay with French families. In general you rent a room and, for an additional fee, have access to the family's kitchen in the evening. Half and full board is also usually available.

One well-established agency that organises homestays is **Accueil Familial des Jeunes Étrangers** (Map pp434–5; ☎ 01 42 22 32 64; www.afje-paris.org; 1st fl, 23 rue du Cherche Midi, 6e; ⊙ 10am-4pm Mon-Fri, 10am-noon Sat; Ⓜ Sèvres Babylone). It can find you a room with a family in the suburbs/central Paris for €465/540 per month including breakfast, or €535/610 with evening access to the kitchen. For stays of less than a month, expect to pay from €23 (or €25 with access to the kitchen) per day. There's a registration fee of €35 and a subscription fee of €46/77 for one month/up to three months then €16 per month after that.

Some language schools (p374) can arrange home-stays for their students.

Price Ranges

When calculating accommodation costs, assume you'll spend from about €35 for a washbasin-equipped double in a budget hotel (count on anything up to €65 if you want your own shower). Bear in mind that you may be charged up to €5 to use communal

IT'S A FAMILY AFFAIR

Popular with students learning French are *pensions de famille*, which are similar to B&Bs but more intimate. Family guesthouses that have been recommended by the Paris tourist office in the past include the following four places.

Pension Au Palais Gourmand (Map pp434–5; ☎ 01 45 48 24 15; www.au-palais-gourmand.fr; 3rd fl, 120 blvd Raspail, 6e; s incl breakfast & dinner €67-72.50, d €78.50-87.50; Ⓜ Vavin or Notre Dame des Champs) The promisingly named 'At the Gourmet Palace' is on a busy street between the Jardin du Luxembourg and Montparnasse and is convenient to everything.

Pension Les Marronniers (Map pp434–5; ☎ 01 43 26 37 71; www.pension-marronniers.com; 78 rue d'Assas, 6e; s incl breakfast & dinner €37-62, d €68-83; Ⓜ Vavin or Notre Dame des Champs; 🖳) In a pretty building facing the Jardin du Luxembourg, it has monthly rates at 20% less. Vegetarian meals are also available. Use of microwave, fridge and Internet access.

Résidence des Palais (Map pp434–5; ☎ 01 43 26 79 32; pensionladagnous@wanadoo.fr; 2nd fl, 78 rue d'Assas, 6e; s/d incl breakfast €55/70; Ⓜ Vavin or Notre Dame des Champs) This is in the same building as the Pension Les Marronniers.

Résidence Cardinal (Map pp426–7; ☎ 01 48 74 16 16; http://pensioncardinal.free.fr; 2nd fl, 4 rue Cardinal Mercier, 9e; s incl breakfast €35, d €55-65; Ⓜ Liège or Place de Clichy) This place is on a quiet street with an old fountain at the end of it.

showers in budget hotels. If you can't go without your daily ablutions, it is often a false economy staying at such places.

Midrange hotels in Paris offer some of the best value for money of any European capital. Hotels at this level always have bathroom facilities. All rooms have showers or baths unless noted otherwise. These hotels charge between €65 and €150 for a double and generally offer excellent value, especially at the higher end.

Top-range places run the gamut from tasteful and discreet boutique hotels to palaces with 100+ rooms and will cost two people €150 or more a night. For details of some of the best deluxe hotels, see the boxed text, p323.

Reservations

During periods of heavy domestic or foreign tourism – Christmas and New Year, the winter (February to March) school holidays, Easter, July and August – a hotel reservation can mean the difference between a bed in a room and a bench in the park. For really popular places – think location and/or price – book several months ahead.

Many hotels, especially budget ones, accept reservations only if they are accompanied by *des arrhes* (a deposit). Some places, especially those with two or more stars, don't ask for a deposit if you give them your credit card number or if you send them confirmation of your plans by letter, fax or email in French or clear, simple English.

Most independent hotels will hold a room only until a set hour, rarely later than 6pm or 7pm without prior arrangement. If you're arriving later than expected and you haven't prepaid or given the hotel your credit-card details, let the staff know or they might rent your room to someone else.

BOOK ACCOMMODATION ONLINE

For more accommodation reviews and recommendations by Lonely Planet authors, check out the online booking service at www.lonelyplanet.com. You'll find the true, insider lowdown on the best places to stay. Reviews are thorough and independent. Best of all, you can book online.

Long-Term Rentals

Small (15 to 30 sq metres) studios with attached toilet start from about €18 per sq metre per month; expect to pay from about €800 for a one-bedroom flat and €550 for a studio. The per-metre cost theoretically decreases the larger the place, the further away it is from the city centre and if it is a walk-up (ie does not have access to a lift).

About €450 a month will get you a tiny garret room with a washbasin but no fixed-line telephone, no proper cooking facilities and no private toilet. There may not even be a communal shower. These rooms, often occupied by students, are usually converted *chambres de bonne* (maid's quarters) on the 6th or 7th floors of old apartment buildings without lifts, but in decent neighbourhoods.

The hardest time to find an apartment – especially a cheap one – in Paris is in September and October, when everyone is back from their summer holidays and students are searching for digs for the academic year. Moderately priced places are easiest to find towards the end of university semesters – ie between Christmas and early February and July to September.

If you've exhausted your word-of-mouth sources (expats, students, compatriots living temporarily in Paris), it's a good idea to check out the bulletin boards at the American Church (p382). People who advertise there are more likely to rent to foreigners, will usually speak at least some English and might be willing to sign a relatively short-term contract. FUSAC (p382), a free periodical issued every two weeks, is another good source. Also see p304 for other sources of information.

If you know some French (or someone who does), you'll be able to consult several periodicals available from newsagents: the weekly *De Particulier à Particulier* (€2.95) appears on Thursday while the biweeklies *À Vendre, à Louer* (€1.50) and *Se Loger* (€2.30) come out on Monday and Thursday respectively. You'll have to do your calling in French, though.

GET A GRIP: HOTELS FOR DISABLED TRAVELLERS

Most hotels with two or more stars in Paris are equipped with a lift but not much more for those in wheelchairs. Both Michelin's *Guide Rouge* and the Paris tourist office's free *Guide des Hôtels, Résidences de Tourisme et Chambres d'Hôtes Adhérents* indicate hotels with lifts and facilities for disabled people.

Hotels in this chapter that have one or two rooms fully equipped for disabled guests (bathrooms big enough for a wheelchair user to turn around in, access door on bath tubs, grip bars alongside toilets etc) include the 14 below. All hotels in Paris will be required to have at least one guest bathroom with these facilities by 2013.

Arioso Hôtel (p324)

Grand Hôtel St-Michel (p315)

Hôtel Costes (p323)

Hôtel de Nevers (p328)

Hôtel des Grandes Écoles (p316)

Hôtel du Panthéon (p316)

Hôtel Favart (p325)

Hôtel Henri IV (p317)

Hôtel Le Clos Médicis (p320)

Hôtel St-Christophe (p317)

Hôtel Sèvres Azur (p320)

Hôtel Sezz (p323)

La Villa St-Germain des Prés (p321)

Port Royal Hôtel (p318)

At the same time, another 10 hotels in this chapter have one or two bedrooms on the *rez-de-chaussée* (ground floor) that can be accessed by anyone in a wheelchair. Though the rooms are not equipped with anything else for travellers with disabilities, they may serve at a pinch.

Grand Hôtel Malher (p310)

Hôtel Aquarelle (p328)

Hôtel de l'Espérance (p316)

Hôtel des Arts (p326)

Hôtel des Grands Hommes (p316)

Hôtel Jeanne d'Arc (p311)

Hôtel Résidence des 3 Poussins (p331)

Hôtel St-Jacques (p317)

Hôtel Saintonge Marais (p312)

Hôtel Utrillo (p331)

If you have access to a phone, you could place a wanted ad in *De Particulier à Particulier* and have people call you.

Websites of commercial agencies that rent studios and apartments to visitors and have been recommended by readers include www.an-apartment-in-paris.com, www.parismarais.com, www.paris-apts.com and www.parislodging.fr.

Allô Logement Temporaire (Map pp436–7; ☎ 01 42 72 00 06; alt@claranet.fr; 1st fl, 64 rue du Temple, 3e; ⏱ noon-8pm Mon-Fri; Ⓜ Rambuteau) is a nonprofit organisation that links property-owners and foreigners looking for furnished apartments for periods of one week to one year. Small furnished studios of 15 sq metres cost €550 per month while double that size is about €800, depending on the location. October, when university classes resume, is the hardest month to find a place, but over summer and into September it's usually possible to rent something within a matter of days. Before any deals are signed, the company will arrange for you to talk to the owner by phone, assisted by an interpreter if necessary. There is a €50 annual membership fee and, in addition to the rent and one month's deposit (paid directly to the owner), you'll pay a charge of €35 for each month you rent.

LOUVRE & LES HALLES

The area encompassing the Musée du Louvre and the Forum des Halles, effectively the 1er and a small slice of the 2e, is more disposed to welcoming top-end travellers, but there are some decent midrange places to choose from and the main branch of a popular hostel is here as well.

HÔTEL LE RELAIS DU LOUVRE

Map pp436-7   Hotel

☎ 01 40 41 96 42; www.relaisdulouvre.com; 19 rue des Prêtres St-Germain l'Auxerrois, 1er; s €99-130, d & tw €150-190, tr €190, ste €210-410; Ⓜ Châtelet; ⊠ ▣

If you are someone who likes style but in a traditional sense, choose this lovely 21-room hotel just west of the Louvre and south of the Église St-Germain l'Auxerrois. It was given a face-lift for the millennium. The eight rooms facing the street and the church are on the petite side; if you are looking for something more spacious, ask for one of five rooms ending in a '2' and looking onto the garden/patio.

CHEAP SLEEPS

This part of the 1er and 2e is very central, but don't expect to find tranquillity or many bargains here. Both airports are linked to nearby metro station Châtelet-Les Halles by the RER (Réseau Express Régional – regional train service).

CENTRE INTERNATIONAL DE SÉJOUR

BVJ PARIS-LOUVRE Map pp436-7   Hostel

☎ 01 53 00 90 90; www.bvjhotel.com; 20 rue Jean-Jacques Rousseau, 1er; per person dm €25, d €28; Ⓜ Louvre-Rivoli; ⊠ ▣

This modern, 200-bed hostel run by the Bureau des Voyages de la Jeunesse (Youth Travel Bureau) has bunks in a single-sex room for two to eight people with showers down the corridor. Guests should be aged under 35. Rooms are accessible from 2.30pm on the day you arrive and all day after that. There are no kitchen facilities.

There is usually space in the morning, even in summer, so stop by as early as you can. All rooms are nonsmoking and Internet access is available for €1 for 10 minutes. The **Centre International de Séjour BVJ Paris-Quartier Latin** (Map pp444–5; ☎ 01 43 29 34 80; 44 rue des Bernardins, 5e; per person dm €26, s/d €35/28; Ⓜ Maubert Mutualité), its sister-hostel on the Left Bank, has 100 beds in single-sex dorm rooms for four to 10 people as well as singles and doubles. All rooms have showers and telephones.

HÔTEL DE LILLE LOUVRE

Map pp436-7   Hotel

☎ 01 42 33 33 42; 8 rue du Pélican, 1er; s €35, d €43-50, tr €65; Ⓜ Palais Royal-Musée du Louvre; ⊠

This old-fashioned but clean 13-room hotel is down a quiet side street just west of the bizarre Ministère de la Culture et de l'Information. A half-dozen of the rooms have just washbasin and bidet (communal showers cost €4.50) while the rest have *en suite* showers. The friendly and helpful manager speaks good English.

HÔTEL TIQUETONNE

Map pp436-7   Hotel

☎ 01 42 36 94 58; fax 01 42 36 02 94; 6 rue Tiquetonne, 2e; s €30-40, d €50; Ⓜ Étienne Marcel

If you're looking for good-value digs smack in the middle of party town, this vintage 47-room cheapie on a cobbled pedestrian street may not be inspirational but it's clean and comfortable. Some of the rooms are quite large. Forum des Halles is a short distance to the south.

MARAIS & BASTILLE

There are quite a few top-end hotels in the heart of the Marais as well as in the vicinity of the elegant place des Vosges, and the choice of lower-priced one- and two-star hotels is excellent. Two-star comfort is less expensive closer to the Bastille in the neighbouring 11e, however.

GRAND HÔTEL MALHER

Map pp436-7   Hotel

☎ 01 42 72 60 92; www.grandhotelmalher.com;
5 rue Malher, 4e; s €95-120, d €115-140, ste €170-185; Ⓜ St-Paul; ⓐ

This welcoming establishment run by the same family for three generations has nicely appointed rooms and a small, pretty courtyard at the back. Some of the public areas have been recently renovated, including the lobby. The hotel's 31 bedrooms are of a decent size and the bathrooms are modern and relatively large; two dozen are equipped with a bath and seven with shower.

HÔTEL BASTILLE DE LAUNAY

Map pp440-1   Hotel

☎ 01 47 00 88 11; www.albotel.com; 42 rue Amelot, 11e; s €73, d €102-129; Ⓜ Chemin Vert; ⓐ

This 36-room hotel offers good value for money due to its central location just up from place de la Bastille. Rooms are smallish and much of a muchness, with classic two-star furnishings and carpets. Double room No 41 and twin No 43 face rue Amelot and the steps up to blvd Beaumarchais.

HÔTEL BASTILLE SPERIA

Map pp440-1   Hotel

☎ 01 42 72 04 01; www.hotel-bastille-speria.com; 1 rue de la Bastille, 4e; s €98-131, d €125-160, tw €145-170; Ⓜ Bastille; ⓐ ⓐ

This 42-room hotel within spitting distance of place de la Bastille offers good value for its location. The rooms are nothing to write home about but some of them (No 103, for example) sit on the corner and boast two windows. Bathrooms are modern and relatively large. And the name? Well, they say the 'speria' part comes from the Greek for 'good evening' but it doesn't sound like *kali spera* to us. Rates depend on the season and type of room.

HÔTEL CARON DE BEAUMARCHAIS

Map pp436-7   Boutique Hotel

☎ 01 42 72 34 12; www.carondebeaumarchais .com; 12 rue Vieille du Temple, 4e; r €125-162; Ⓜ St-Paul; ⓐ ⓐ ⓐ

Decorated like an 18th-century private house contemporary with Beaumarchais, who wrote *Le Mariage de Figaro* (The Marriage of Figaro) at No 47 on this street, this award-winning themed hotel has to

be seen to be believed. The museumlike lobby, with its prized 18th-century pianoforte and candelabras, sets the tone of the place. The 19 rooms aren't huge but positively dripping in brocade, furniture decorated with tracery and ormolu-framed mirrors. The welcome could be a bit warmer here.

HÔTEL CASTEX Map pp440-1   Hotel

☎ 01 42 72 31 52; www.castexhotel.com; 5 rue Castex, 4e; s €85-115, d & tw €95-140, ste €160-220; Ⓜ Bastille; ⓐ ⓐ

Equidistant from the Bastille and the Marais, the 30-room Castex got a major face-lift a couple of years ago but has retained some of its 17th-century elements, including a vaulted stone cellar used as a breakfast room, terracotta tiles on the floor and Toile de Jouy wallpaper. Try to get one of the independent rooms (Nos 1 and 2) off the lovely patio; No 3 is a two-room suite or family room.

HÔTEL CENTRAL MARAIS

Map pp436-7   Hotel

☎ 01 48 87 56 08; www.hotelcentralmarais.com; 2 rue Ste-Croix la Bretonnerie, 4e; s & d €87, tr €107; Ⓜ Hôtel de Ville; ⓐ ⓐ

This small hotel in the centre of gay Paris caters essentially for gay men, though lesbians are also welcome. It's in a lovely 17th-century building and its seven rooms are spread over as many floors; there is no lift. Also there is only one bathroom for every two rooms, though the room on the 5th floor has an *en suite* bathroom and toilet. Reception, which is on the 1st floor, is open from 8am to 5pm; after that check in round the corner in the bar called Le Central (☎ 01 48 87 99 33; 33 rue Vieille du Temple, 4e; ☷ 4pm-2am Mon-Fri, 2pm-2am Sat & Sun; Ⓜ Hôtel de Ville), which is the oldest (in every sense) gay bar still open in Paris.

HÔTEL DAVAL Map pp440-1   Hotel

☎ 01 47 00 51 23; www.hoteldaval.com; 21 rue Daval, 11e; s/d/tr/q €67/71/84/98; Ⓜ Bastille; ⓐ ⓐ

This 21-room property is a clean and central option if you're looking for budget accommodation just off place de la Bastille. Rooms and baths are a bit on the small side and if you're looking for some peace and quiet choose a back room (eg No 13).

HÔTEL DE LA BRETONNERIE

Map pp436-7   Hotel

☎ 01 48 87 77 63; www.bretonnerie.com; 22 rue Ste-Croix la Bretonnerie, 4e; s & d €116-149, tr & q €174, ste €180-205; Ⓜ Hôtel de Ville; 🖳
This is a very charming three-star in the heart of the Marais nightlife area dating from the 17th century. The décor of each of the 22 rooms and seven suites is unique, and some rooms have four-poster and canopy beds. Three 'duplex' suites on two levels are huge and can easily accommodate three or four people.

HÔTEL DE LA PLACE DES VOSGES

Map pp440-1   Hotel

☎ 01 42 72 60 46; www.hotelplacedesvosges.com; 12 rue de Biragne, 4e; s & d €107-140, ste €207; Ⓜ Bastille; 🖳
This superbly situated 17-room hotel is an oasis of tranquillity due south of sublime place des Vosges. The public areas are quite impressive and the rooms have recently had a face-lift. A tiny lift serves the 1st to 4th floors but it's stairs only from the ground floor and to the 5th floor.

Interior of room of Hôtel Le Clos Médicis (p320)

HÔTEL DE NICE

Map pp436-7   Hotel

☎ 01 42 78 55 29; wwwhoteldenice.com; 42bis rue de Rivoli, 4e; s €65-75, d €95-105, tr €130; Ⓜ Hôtel de Ville
This is an especially warm, family-run place with 23 comfortable rooms. Some have balconies high above busy rue de Rivoli. Reception is on the 1st floor. Every square inch of wall space is used to display old prints, and public areas and bedrooms are full of Second Empire–style furniture, kilims and Indian carpets.

HÔTEL DU 7E ART

Map pp436-7   Hotel

☎ 01 44 54 85 00; hotel7art@wanadoo.fr; 20 rue St-Paul, 4e; s & d €85-135, tw €90-135; Ⓜ St-Paul; 🖳
This themed hotel on the south side of rue St-Antoine is a fun place for film buffs – *le septième art* (the seventh art) is what the French call cinema – and boasts a B&W-movie theme throughout, right down to the tiled floors and the bathrooms. The 23 rooms over five floors – there is no lift – are sizeable and quite different from one another. A single with just washbasin is €59.

HÔTEL DU BOURG TIBOURG

Map pp436-7   Boutique Hotel

☎ 01 42 78 47 39; www.hoteldubourgtibourg.com; 19 du Bourg Tibourg, 4e; s €150, d €200-250, ste €350; Ⓜ Hôtel de Ville or St-Paul; ❄ 🖳
This stunning 30-room boutique hotel is in the Hôtel Costes stable and was also done up by designer Jacques Garcia, one of the most fashionable interior decorators in Paris. The result: romantic 'French' neogothic combined with Orientalia. Be aware that this place is built more for romance than business; rooms are not particularly big.

HÔTEL JEANNE D'ARC

Map pp440-1   Hotel

☎ 01 48 87 62 11; www.hoteljeannedarc.com; 3 rue de Jarente, 4e; s €58-96, d €82-96, tr €115, q €145; Ⓜ St-Paul; ♿
This cosy 36-room hotel near lovely place du Marché Ste-Catherine is a great little base for your peregrinations among the museums, bars and restaurants of the Marais and almost has a country feel to it. About the only thing wrong with this place is that everyone knows about it, so you'll have to book well in advance.

HÔTEL LES JARDINS DU MARAIS

Map pp440-1   Hotel

☎ 01 40 21 22 23; www.homeplazza.com; 74 rue Amelot, 11e; r €350-455, ste from €600; Ⓜ Chemin Vert; ⊠ ⚉ ⌨ ♿

You'd never know you were in Paris after walking through the door of this 268-room hotel housed in nine separate buildings designed by Gustave Eiffel and surrounding an enormous courtyard of cobblestones and gardens. Rooms are Art Deco, with furnishings in maple and mahogany and the outlets always bursting at the seams. Check the Internet carefully for generous promotional offers.

HÔTEL LYON MULHOUSE

Map pp440-1   Hotel

☎ 01 47 00 91 50; www.1-hotel-paris.com; 8 blvd Beaumarchais, 11e; s €65-90, d €78-110, tr €110-130; Ⓜ Bastille; ⚉ ⌨

This former post house, from where carriages would set out for Lyon and Mulhouse, has been a hotel since the 1920s. The 40 rooms, though not particularly special, are comfortable, quiet and of a good size; some have recently been renovated. Place de la Bastille is just around the corner.

HÔTEL PRATIC Map pp440-1   Hotel

☎ 01 48 87 80 47; www.hotelpratic.com; 9 rue d'Ormesson, 4e; s €87-102, d €98-117, tr €135; Ⓜ St-Paul; ⊠

This 23-room hotel, which is opposite the delightful place du Marché Ste-Catherine, has been thoroughly renovated and the décor – exposed beams, gilt frames, half-timbered or stone walls – is almost too much. Rooms, dispersed over six floors, are rather pricey for what you get; there's no lift and not all rooms have their own toilet.

HÔTEL ST-LOUIS MARAIS

Map pp440-1   Hotel

☎ 01 48 87 87 04; www.saintlouismarais.com; 1 rue Charles V, 4e; s €99, d & tw €115-140, tr €150, ste €160; Ⓜ Sully Morland; ⌨

This especially charming hotel built within a converted 17th-century convent is more Bastille than Marais but still within easy walking distance of the latter. Wooden beams on ceilings, terracotta tiles on the floors and heavy brocade drapes tend to

darken the 19 renovated rooms but certainly add to the atmosphere. Be aware that there are four floors here but no lift.

HÔTEL ST-MERRY Map pp436-7   Hotel

☎ 01 42 78 14 15; www.hotelmarais.com; 78 rue de la Verrerie, 4e; d & tw €160-230, tr €205-275, ste €335-407; Ⓜ Châtelet

The interior of this 11-room hostelry, with beamed ceilings, church pews and confessionals, and wrought-iron candelabra, is a Gothic historian's wet dream; you have to see the architectural elements of room No 9 and the furnishings of Nos 12 and 20 to believe them. On the downside there is no lift connecting the postage-stamp lobby with the four upper floors, and it has no mod cons to speak of (including TVs).

HÔTEL SAINTONGE MARAIS

Map pp440-1   Hotel

☎ 01 42 77 91 13; www.hotelmarais.com; 16 rue Saintonge, 3e; s/d/tr €105/115/140, ste €170; Ⓜ Filles du Calvaire; ♿

This charming 23-room hotel, with exposed beams, vaulted cellar and period furniture, is really more Oberkampf/République than the Marais. But with the Musée Picasso practically next door, let's not quibble. You'll get much better value for money here than in the more central parts of the Marais, including at the Saintonge's sister property, the Hôtel St-Merry (above).

HÔTEL SÉVIGNÉ Map pp436-7   Hotel

☎ 01 42 72 76 17; www.le-sevigne.com; 2 rue Malher, 4e; s €64, d & tw €74-85, tr €100; Ⓜ St-Paul; ⚉ ⌨

This hotel in the heart of the Marais and named after the celebrated 17th-century writer the Marquise de Sévigné, whose letters give us such a wonderful insight into the Paris of her day, is excellent value for its

---

TOP FIVE HOTELS WITH A GARDEN

- Hôtel des Grandes Écoles (p316)
- Hôtel des Marronniers (p319)
- Hôtel de Nesle (p319)
- Hôtel Les Jardins du Marais (left)
- Hôtel Relais Christine (p323)

location. The hotel's 29 rooms, spread over six floors and accessible by lift, are basically but comfortably furnished.

NEW HOTEL CANDIDE

Map pp440-1   Hotel

☎ 01 43 79 02 33; www.new-hotel.com; 3 rue Pétion, 11e; s/d €95/120; Ⓜ Voltaire; ✗ ▣
This 48-room hotel within easy striking distance of the Bastille and the Marais offers relatively good value and is very convenient to the Marché Bastille (p52) on blvd Richard Lenoir. It's on a very quiet street and we've always been impressed by the friendly, helpful service.

CHEAP SLEEPS

The Marais is one of the liveliest parts of the Right Bank and its hostels are among the city's finest. Despite massive gentrification, there are also some less expensive hotels left. East of the Bastille, the relatively untouristy 11e is generally made up of unpretentious working-class areas and is a good way to see 'real' Paris up close.

AUBERGE INTERNATIONALE
DES JEUNES Map pp440-1   Hostel

☎ 01 47 00 62 00; www.aijparis.com; 10 rue Trousseau, 11e; per person dm Jul & Aug €17, Mar-Jun & Sep-Oct €15, Nov-Feb €13; Ⓜ Ledru Rollin
This clean, friendly hostel just 700m east of place de la Bastille attracts a young, international crowd and gets full in the summer. Beds are in dorms for two to four people; the larger ones have shower and toilet en suite. Rooms are closed for cleaning between 10am and 3pm daily but there 's no curfew. Internet access costs €2 for 15 minutes.

GRAND HÔTEL DU LOIRET

Map pp436-7   Hotel

☎ 01 48 87 77 00; hotelduloiret@hotmail.com; 8 rue des Mauvais Garçons, 4e; s €45-70, d €45-80, tr/q €90/100; Ⓜ Hôtel de Ville or St-Paul; ▣
This 27-room budget hotel in the heart of gay Marais is very popular with young male travellers, not just because it is within easy walking distance of just about everything after dark but because it sits – or does it lie? – on 'Street of the Bad Boys'. Nine of the rooms have neither private shower nor bath or toilet but share facilities off the corridors. They're a steal at €45. Internet access costs a whopping €9 an hour.

HÔTEL BAUDELAIRE BASTILLE

Map pp440-1   Hotel

☎ 01 47 00 40 98; www.paris-hotel-bastille.com; 12 rue de Charonne, 11e; s €62-65, d €67-74, tr €72-86, q €90-104; Ⓜ Bastille or Ledru Rollin; ▣
Formerly the Pax, this independent one-star hotel is in an ancient building that is coy about showing its age except for the odd worm-chewed beam. The 46 rooms are of a decent size and spotless, though there is no lift. Rooms look out onto a quiet courtyard or the street but double-glazing successfully keeps the din where it belongs. Internet costs €2 for 15 minutes.

HÔTEL BAUDIN Map pp440-1   Hotel

☎ 01 47 00 18 91; hotelbaudin@wanadoo.fr; 113 av Ledru Rollin, 11e; s €29-52, d €35-62, tr €40-76; Ⓜ Ledru Rollin
This once-grand, old-fashioned hostelry has 17 brightly coloured rooms and fairly weathered public areas, with reception on the 1st floor. The rooms at the lower end of the price scale have washbasins only (shared showers are free) while more expensive ones have shower or bath and toilet. The welcome here is always warm.

HÔTEL DE LA HERSE D'OR

Map pp440-1   Hotel

☎ 01 48 87 84 09; www.hotel-herse-dor.com; 20 rue St-Antoine, 4e; r €40-68; Ⓜ Bastille; ▣
This friendly place just east of place de la Bastille has 35 serviceable rooms off a long stone corridor lined with mirrors. It's very basic and very cheap; the lower-priced rooms have washbasins only. You can check your emails at an Internet station in the lobby for €1 for 15 minutes. And, just in case you wondered, *herse* in French is not 'hearse' but 'portcullis'. So let's just call it the 'Golden Gate Hotel'.

HÔTEL LES SANS CULOTTES

Map pp440-1   Hotel

☎ 01 49 23 85 80; www.lessansculottesfr.com; 27 rue de Lappe, 11e; s/d €53.50/61; Ⓜ Bastille
The nine rooms of this hotel above a nice little bistro of the same name (p188) are on the small side but are clean, tidy and decorated in bright colours and floral patterns.

Best of all, the place is very central to restaurants and nightlife of the Bastille and Marais. Be warned that there is no lift here, though.

HÔTEL RIVOLI Map pp436–7   Hotel
☎ 01 42 72 08 41; 44 rue de Rivoli or 2 rue des Mauvais Garçons, 4e; s €30-50, d €40-50, tr €66; Ⓜ Hôtel de Ville

Long a Lonely Planet favourite (there's no pretending who we are – or are not – with these guys), the Rivoli is forever cheery but not as dirt cheap as it once was, with 20 basic, somewhat noisy rooms. The cheaper singles and doubles have washbasins only but use of the shower room is free. Annoyingly – given that it is in the heart of the Marais nightlife area – the front door is locked from 2am to 7am. Reception is on the 1st floor. Its central location is a big attraction.

MAISON INTERNATIONALE DE LA JEUNESSE ET DES ÉTUDIANTS
Map pp436–7   Hostel
MIJE; ☎ 01 42 74 23 45; www.mije.com; per person dm €27, s/tw/tr €42/32/28; Ⓧ ▣

The MIJE runs three hostels in attractively renovated 17th- and 18th-century *hôtels particuliers* (private mansions) in the heart of the Marais, and it's difficult to think of a better budget deal in Paris. Costs are the same for all three; there are single-sex, shower-equipped dorms with four to eight beds per room as well as singles, twins and triples. Rooms are closed from noon to 3pm, and curfew is from 1am to 7am. The maximum stay is seven nights. Individuals can make reservations at any of the three MIJE hostels listed below by emailing (info@mije.com) or calling the central switchboard; reception will hold you a bed till noon. During summer and other busy periods, there may not be space after midmorning. There's an annual membership fee of €2.50.

MIJE Le Fourcy (Map pp436–7; 6 rue de Fourcy, 4e; Ⓜ St-Paul) with 185 beds is the largest of the three. There's a cheap eatery here called Le Restaurant, which offers a three-course fixed-price *menu* including a drink for €10.50, and a two-course *formule* (choice of two out of three courses) plus drink for €8.50.

MIJE Le Fauconnier (Map pp436–7; 11 rue du Fauconnier, 4e; Ⓜ St-Paul or Pont

Marie) has 122 beds, two blocks south of MIJE Le Fourcy.

MIJE Maubuisson (Map pp436–7; 12 rue des Barres, 4e; Ⓜ Hôtel de Ville or Pont Marie) – the pick of the three, in our opinion – is half a block south of the *mairie* (town hall) of the 4e. It has 103 beds.

THE ISLANDS

The smaller of the two islands in the middle of the Seine, the Île St-Louis is by far the more romantic and has a string of excellent top-end hotels. It's an easy walk from central Paris.

HÔTEL DE LUTÈCE Map pp436–7   Hotel
☎ 01 43 26 23 52; www.hotel-ile-saintlouis.com; 65 rue St-Louis en l'Île, 4e; s/d/tr €130/164/186; Ⓜ Pont Marie; Ⓧ ▣

An exquisite 23-room hotel and more country than city, the Lutèce has an enviable spot on delightful Île St-Louis and has friendly and helpful management. The comfortable rooms are tastefully decorated and the location is one of the most desirable in the city. The lobby/salon, with its ancient fireplace aglow in the cooler months, wood panelling, antique furnishings and terracotta tiles, sets the inviting tone of the whole place.

HÔTEL ST-LOUIS Map pp436–7   Hotel
☎ 01 46 34 04 80; www.hotel-saint-louis.com; 75 rue St-Louis en l'Île, 4e; d/tw €140/155, ste €220; Ⓜ Pont Marie; Ⓧ ▣ Ⓖ

One of several hotels lining posh rue St-Louis en l'Île, this one has 19 appealing but unspectacular rooms, though the public areas are lovely. The breakfast room in the basement dates from the early 17th century.

CHEAP SLEEPS

Believe it or not, the only hotel on the Île de la Cité is a budget one.

HÔTEL HENRI IV Map pp436–7   Hotel
☎ 01 43 54 44 53; 25 place Dauphine, 1er; s €27-34, d €35-72, tr €47; Ⓜ Pont Neuf or Cité; Ⓖ

This decrepit place, with 20 tattered and worn rooms, is popular for its location, location and – above all else – location on the tip of the Île de la Cité. It would be impossible to find a hotel more romantically located at such a price in all of Paris – much less then Île de la Cité. But it's not the most salubrious of establishments. Singles and triples have washbasin only; doubles are equipped with shower or bath.

LATIN QUARTER & JARDIN DES PLANTES

There are dozens of attractive two- and three-star hotels in the Latin Quarter, including a cluster near the Sorbonne and another group along the lively rue des Écoles. Midrange hotels in the Latin Quarter are very popular with visiting academics, so rooms are hardest to find when conferences and seminars are scheduled (usually from March to June and in October). In general this area offers better value among top-end hotels than the neighbouring 6e does. The Luxembourg and Port Royal RER stations are linked to both airports by RER and Orlyval.

FAMILIA HÔTEL Map pp444-5   Hotel
☎ 01 43 54 55 27; www.hotel-paris-familia.com; 11 rue des Écoles, 5e; s €72-93, d €83-125, tr €129-149, q €147-171; Ⓜ Cardinal Lemoine; 🖳
This very welcoming and well-situated family-run hotel has sepia murals of Parisian landmarks in its 30 rooms and is one of the most attractive 'almost budget' options on this side of the Seine. Eight rooms have little balconies, from which you can catch a glimpse of Notre Dame; the choicest rooms

Exterior of Hôtel Ritz Paris (p323)

which carry a premium – are Nos 61, 62 and 65 (the last has a four-poster bed). We love the flower-bedecked window and the complimentary breakfast.

GRAND HÔTEL DES GOBELINS
Map pp444-5   Hotel
☎ 01 43 31 79 89; www.hotel-des-gobelins.com; 57 blvd St-Marcel, 13e; s €83-105, d €95-160, tr €140-190; Ⓜ Gobelins; ☒ 🎲 🖳
This three-star Logis de France hotel may be a bit out of the way but rue Mouffetard and its **market** (p52) is just minutes away. Both the 45 rooms and the public areas are particularly stylish; framed fragments of 18th-century Gobelins tapestry and the painter Maladir's *Atelier à St-Petersbourg* add warmth to the already cosy lobby. You'll pay more for air-conditioned 'superior' rooms facing the back than for the noisy ones on the boulevard. Rates vary widely according to the season.

GRAND HÔTEL ST-MICHEL
Map pp444-5   Hotel
☎ 01 46 33 33 02; www.grand-hotel-st-michel .com; 19 rue Cujas, 5e; s/d €130/170, ste €220; Ⓜ Luxembourg; 🎲 🖳 ♿
This very well situated 46-room hotel is far away from the din of blvd St-Michel, making it feel almost remote. Some of the rooms have a balcony and the attached *salon de thé* (tea room) is quite pleasant. The 46 rooms are well proportioned and decorated; we especially like the folklike floral motifs painted on cupboard doors, bedheads and so on, and the well-chosen fabrics.

HÔTEL CLUNY SORBONNE
Map pp444-5   Hotel
☎ 01 43 54 66 66; www.hotel-cluny.fr; 8 rue Victor Cousin, 5e; s & d €83-85, tr & q €100-140; Ⓜ Luxembourg
This hotel, surrounded by the prestigious buildings of the Sorbonne and where the poet Arthur Rimbaud dallied in 1872, has 23 rooms that could use a refit. One of the choicest is No 63 for three to four people, which has memorable views of the college and the Panthéon. The lift may be the size of a telephone box but it will accommodate most travellers and their hatboxes. We love the cheery yellow lobby and equally cheery staff.

HÔTEL DE L'ESPÉRANCE

Map pp444-5   Hotel

☎ 01 47 07 10 99; www.hoteldelesperance.fr; 15 rue Pascal, 5e; s €71-79, d €79-87, tw/tr €87/102; Ⓜ Censier Daubenton; 🖥 ♿

Just a couple of minutes' walk south of lively rue Mouffetard is this quiet and immaculately kept 38-room hotel with *faux* antique furnishings and a warm welcome. Some of the larger rooms have two double beds.

HÔTEL DES GRANDES ÉCOLES

Map pp444-5   Hotel

☎ 01 43 26 79 23; www.hotel-grandes-ecoles .com; 75 rue du Cardinal Lemoine, 5e; s & d €105-130, tr €125-150; Ⓜ Cardinal Lemoine or Place Monge; ⊠ ♿

This wonderful, very welcoming 51-room hotel just north of place de la Contrescarpe has one of the loveliest situations in the Latin Quarter, tucked away in a courtyard off a medieval street with its own garden. Choose a room in one of three buildings but our favourites are those in the garden annexe, especially the five that are on the ground floor and have direct access to the garden (Nos 29 to 33).

HÔTEL DES GRANDS HOMMES

Map pp444-5   Hotel

☎ 01 46 34 19 60; www.hoteldesgrandshommes .com; 17 place de Panthéon, 5e; s €183-233, d €203-243, tw €244-266; Ⓜ Luxembourg; ⊠ 🖥 ♿

This 31-room hotel in a lovely 18th-century building was given a complete overhaul in 2002 and is now more opulent than ever. The style is Empire, and the rooms with balconies on the 2nd, 5th and 6th floors all have full views of the Panthéon. But if you want to see things further afield go for a room on either of the last two; on a clear day you'll see all the way to Montmartre and Sacré Coeur.

HÔTEL DU COLLÈGE DE FRANCE

Map pp444-5   Hotel

☎ 01 43 26 78 36; www.hotel-collegedefrance .com; 7 rue Thénard, 5e; s €70-85, d €78-115, tr €80-97; Ⓜ Maubert Mutualité; 🖥

Close by its prestigious educational namesake, this 29-room property is under new management. The rooms remain basic and

very similar; avoid the dark ones facing the courtyard and go for those overlooking the quiet street, especially the rooms with two windows. The lobby, with its roaring fire, stained glass and statue of Joan of Arc (go figure – unless it's to remind visiting Brits of their dastardly deed) is welcoming.

HÔTEL DU LEVANT Map pp436-7   Hotel

☎ 01 46 34 11 00; www.hoteldulevant.com; 18 rue de la Harpe, 5e; s €95-115, d €111-135, tw €150, tr €165-206, ste €285-303; Ⓜ Cluny-La Sorbonne or St-Michel

It's hard to imagine anything more central than this recently renovated 47-room hotel in the heart of the Latin Quarter; you'll never lack for a kebab at any time of day. The lobby, done up in yellows and reds, is warm and welcoming; the breakfast room is nicely decorated with a large *faux naïf* mural and lots of 19th-century fashion engravings. Rooms are of a decent size, furnishings two steps beyond pure functional and the bathrooms completely new.

HÔTEL DU PANTHÉON

Map pp444-5   Hotel

☎ 01 43 54 32 95; www.hoteldupantheon.com; 19 place du Panthéon, 5e; s €183-233, d €203-243, tr €244-266; Ⓜ Luxembourg; ⊠ 🖥 ♿

In the shadow of the capital's largest secular mausoleum and just uphill from the Jardin du Luxembourg, the Panthéon is an attractive 36-room hotel that is positively deluxe for the price. The rooms are, in a word, elegant and some rooms on the upper floors have balconies that look straight on to the Panthéon; the alternative is a leafy courtyard, which can actually boast a tree.

HÔTEL ESMERALDA

Map pp436-7   Hotel

☎ 01 43 54 19 20; fax 01 40 51 00 68; 4 rue St-Julien le Pauvre, 5e; s €35-85, d €80-95, tr/q €110/120; Ⓜ St-Michel

Tucked away in a quiet street with million-dollar views of Notre Dame, this renovated inn is about as central to the Latin Quarter as you're ever likely to get. Its charm is no secret, though, so book well ahead. At these prices and location the 19 rooms – the cheapest singles have washbasin only – are no great shakes, so expect little beyond the picture postcard through the window.

HÔTEL HENRI IV Map pp436-7   Hotel

☎ 01 46 33 20 20; www.hotel-henri4.com; 9-11 rue St-Jacques, 5e; s/d/tr €149/167/188; Ⓜ St-Michel Notre Dame or Cluny La Sorbonne; ⊠ 🖳 ⚬

This three-star place with 23 rooms awash with antiques, old prints and fresh flowers is an oasis in the Latin Quarter just steps from Notre Dame and the Seine. It's part of the same group as the Hôtel de Lutèce (p314) on the Île de St-Louis and exudes 'country chic'; the lobby with its 18th-century (working) fireplace, terracotta tiles and portraits could almost be in a manor house in Normandy.

HÔTEL LA DEMEURE Map pp444-5   Hotel

☎ 01 43 37 81 25; www.hotel-paris-lademeure .com; 51 blvd St-Marcel, 13e; s/d €155/190, ste €245; Ⓜ Les Gobelins; ⊠ ⋈ 🖳

This self-proclaimed hotel de caractère, owned and operated by a charming father-son team who always seem to be at hand, is a bit away from the action at the bottom of the 5e. But the refined elegance of its 43 rooms, the almost 'clubby' public areas and the wrap-around balconies of the corner rooms make it worth going the extra distance. Unusual for Paris, the entire hotel is nonsmoking.

HÔTEL MINERVE Map pp444-5   Hotel

☎ 01 43 26 26 04; www.hotel-paris-minerve.com; 13 rue des Écoles, 5e; s €84-132, d €98-132, tr €150-152; Ⓜ Cardinal Lemoine; ⋈ 🖳

This 54-room hotel in two buildings is owned by the same family who run the Familia Hôtel (p315). It has a reception area kitted out in Oriental carpets and antique books, which the affable owner/manager Erich Gaucheron collects, and some of the rooms have been enlarged. We like the frescoes of French monuments and reproduction 18th-century wallpaper. Some 10 rooms have small balconies, eight with views of Notre Dame and two have tiny courtyards that are swooningly romantic. There's covered parking (€20 per day) just 50m away.

HÔTEL RÉSIDENCE HENRI IV

Map pp444-5   Hotel

☎ 01 44 41 31 81; www.residencehenri4.com; 50 rue des Bernadins, 5e; s & d €175-185, 1-/2-person apt €220-230, 3-person apt €250-260, 4-person apt €300-310; Ⓜ Maubert Mutualité; 🖳

This exquisite late-19th-century hotel at the end of a quiet cul-de-sac near the Sorbonne has eight rooms and five two-room apartments – all with kitchenette (microwave, fridge, stove, crockery and cutlery). They are of a generous size – a minimum 17 sq metres for the rooms and 25 sq metres for the apartments – and all look out onto the street and leafy square, while the bathrooms all face a courtyard.

HÔTEL ST-CHRISTOPHE

Map pp444-5   Hotel

☎ 01 43 31 81 54; www.charm-hotel-paris.com; 17 rue Lacépède, 5e; s €106-116, d €118-128; Ⓜ Place Monge; ⊠ 🖳 ⚬

This classy small hotel with 31 well-equipped rooms is located on a quiet street between rue Monge in the Latin Quarter and the Jardin des Plantes. Rooms are hardly what you would call spectacular, but there are five sizes and shapes to choose from, and the welcome is always particularly warm at this Logis de France hotel.

HÔTEL ST-JACQUES Map pp444-5   Hotel

☎ 01 44 07 45 45; www.hotel-saintjacques.com; 35 rue des Écoles, 5e; s €52-80, d €90-118, tr €145; Ⓜ Maubert Mutualité; ⊠ 🖳 ⚬

This very stylish 38-room hotel has rooms at the corner with balconies overlooking the Panthéon. The singles are relatively spacious, but not all the rooms have toilets. Audrey Hepburn and Cary Grant, who filmed some scenes of Charade here in the 1960s, would commend the mod cons that now complement the original 19th-century details (trompe l'œil ceilings that look like cloud-filled skies, an iron staircase and so on). The comments book in the lobby is a welcome touch.

SELECT HÔTEL Map pp444-5   Boutique Hotel

☎ 01 46 34 14 80; www.selecthotel.fr; 1 place de la Sorbonne, 5e; d €139-175, tw €155-175, tr €179-189, ste €212; Ⓜ Cluny La Sorbonne; ⋈ 🖳

What was once a popular student hotel in the thick of the Sorbonne area, the Select has metamorphosed into an Art Deco mini-palace, with an atrium and cactus-strewn winter garden, an 18th-century vaulted breakfast room and 67 stylish bedrooms. The rooms are not always as large as you'd hope for, but the design solutions are ingenious, making great use of minimal space. The 1920s-style cocktail bar with an attached 'library' is a delight.

Bar at Hôtel Meurice (p323)

VILLA D'ESTRÉES Map pp436-7   Hotel
☎ 01 55 42 71 11; www.villadestrees.com; 17 rue Gît le Cœur, 6e; r €205-255, ste €235-295; Ⓜ St-Michel; ✕ 🕸 🖵

This luxurious property owned and run by a father and son on one of the Latin Quarter's quietest and quaintest streets is a stunner. The 10 rooms and five suites are positively huge and impeccably outfitted in various styles, including a lavish Second Empire room. Legend tells us that the odd street name came about when Henri IV, having dallied with his mistress Gabrielle d'Estrée in a nearby hotel – perhaps this very one – mused as he departed 'Ici gît mon cœur' (Here lies my heart). For a weekend à deux, it's hard to imagine anything more romantic.

CHEAP SLEEPS

The northern section of the 5e close to the Seine has been popular with students and young people since the Middle Ages. While truly budget places to stay are at a premium, there's at least a popular and well-maintained hostel to choose from.

HÔTEL GAY-LUSSAC Map pp444-5   Hotel
☎ 01 43 54 23 96; hotel.gay-lussac@club-Internet.fr; 29 rue Gay Lussac, 5e; s, d or tr with washbasin €49, s €55-59, d €64-68.50, tr/q €90/95; Ⓜ Luxembourg

The Gay-Lussac is a 35-room threadbare hotel with a certain amount of character in the southern part of the Latin Quarter. Though the single rooms are small, the others are large and have high ceilings. Furnishings are very basic and the whole place

could use a refit but the staff are friendly and helpful. Rates include breakfast.

PORT ROYAL HÔTEL Map pp444-5   Hotel
☎ 01 43 31 70 06; www.portroyal.fr; 8 blvd de Port Royal, 5e; s €41-89, d €52.50-89; Ⓜ Les Gobelins; 🕭

It's hard to imagine that this 46-room hotel, owned and managed by the same family for three generations, still only bears one star. The spotless and very quiet rooms overlook a small glassed-in courtyard (eg No 15) or the street (No 14) but we especially like room No 11 with its colourful bed frame and pretty bathroom. Of course, this value-for-money place is no secret; the last time we were here a former minister of the Interior was a paying guest. Rooms at the lower end of the scale have washbasins only.

YOUNG & HAPPY HOSTEL
Map pp444-5   Hostel
☎ 01 47 07 47 07; www.youngandhappy.fr; 80 rue Mouffetard, 5e; dm €21-23, d per person €24-26; Ⓜ Place Monge; ✕ 🖵

This is a friendly though slightly tatty place in the centre of the Latin Quarter. It's popular with a slightly older crowd than when it opened as Paris' first independent hostel some 15 years ago. The hostel rooms are shut tight between 11am and 4pm but reception stays open; the 2am curfew is enforced. Beds are in cramped rooms with washbasins, and accommodate two to eight people. In summer, the best way to get a bed is to stop by at about 8am. Internet access costs €2 for 30 minutes.

ST-GERMAIN, ODÉON & LUXEMBOURG

St-Germain des Prés is a delightful area to stay and offers some excellent midrange hotels. The three-star hotels in this area are around St-Germain des Prés.

HÔTEL D'ANGLETERRE

Map pp436-7   Hotel

☎ 01 42 60 34 72; www.hotel-dangleterre.com; 44 rue Jacob, 6e; s €135-250, d €195-260, ste €280-290; Ⓜ St-Germain des Prés; 🖳
A beautiful 27-room property in a quiet street close to busy blvd St-Germain and Musée d'Orsay. The loyal guests breakfast in the courtyard of this former British Embassy, where the Treaty of Paris ending the American Revolution was signed and where Hemingway once lodged (see p166). Duplex suite No 51 at the top has beamed ceilings and a four-poster bed: it's the finest in the house.

HÔTEL DANEMARK

Map pp434-5   Boutique Hotel

☎ 01 43 26 93 78; www.hoteldanemark.com; 21 rue Vavin, 6e; s €115-132, d €132-152; Ⓜ Vavin; ⊠ 🍴 🖳
This positively scrumptious boutique hotel southwest of the Jardin du Luxembourg has 15 very tastefully furnished rooms and eclectic contemporary décor contrasting with ancient stone walls. Public areas such as the reception and its corner rooms are full of vibrantly coloured furniture and objects that match and contrast; the bedrooms, well soundproofed and of a generous size (minimum 20 sq metres) for a boutique hotel in central Paris, contain original artwork – though not all of it is museum-quality.

HÔTEL DE NESLE Map pp436-7   Hotel

☎ 01 43 54 62 41; www.hoteldenesleparis.com; 7 rue de Nesle, 6e; s €55-75, d €75-100; Ⓜ Odéon or Mabillon
The Nesle is a relaxed, colourfully decorated hotel with 20 rooms, half of which are painted with murals taken from (mostly French) literature, in a quiet street west of place St-Michel. What is by far its greatest asset, though, is the huge (by Parisian standards) garden – a back yard really – accessible from the 1st floor, with pathways, trellis and

even a small pond. Reservations are only accepted by telephone and usually only up to a few days in advance.

HÔTEL DES 2 CONTINENTS

Map pp436-7   Hotel

☎ 01 43 26 72 46; www.continents-paris-hotel.com; 25 rue Jacob, 6e; s €123-138, d €132-160, tw €145-160, tr €175-190; Ⓜ St-Germain des Prés; 🍴 🖳
The 'Two Continents Hotel' – the name pays homage to the Treaty of Paris having been signed at the nearby Hôtel d'Angleterre (left) – is a very pleasant establishment with 41 spacious rooms in a quiet street. The mural in the breakfast room, viewed through parted drapes, is an early morning eye-opener. About a third of the rooms are air-conditioned.

HÔTEL DES MARRONNIERS

Map pp436-7   Hotel

☎ 01 43 25 30 60; www.hotel-marronniers.com; 21 rue Jacob, 6e; s €110-168, d & tw €153-173, tr €208, q €248; Ⓜ St-Germain des Prés; 🍴 🖳
At the end of a small courtyard 50m from the main street, this hotel has 37 cosy rooms and a delightful conservatory giving on to a magical garden at the back. It's a real oasis in the heart of St-Germain. From the 3rd floor up, rooms ending in 1 or 2 look onto the garden; the rooms on the two uppermost floors – the 5th and the 6th – have pretty views over the courtyard and the roofs of central Paris.

HÔTEL DU GLOBE

Map pp436-7   Boutique Hotel

☎ 01 43 26 35 50; www.hotel-du-globe.fr; 15 rue des Quatre Vents, 6e; s €95-120, d €105-130, ste €160; Ⓜ Odéon; 🖳
This eclectic caravanserai has 14 small but completely renovated rooms just south of the blvd St-Germain. Some of the rooms are verging on the miniscule, and there is no lift (but four floors to ascend via a very narrow staircase). Still, we're suckers for armour and there are at least two full sets here.

HÔTEL DU LYS Map pp436-7   Hotel

☎ 01 43 26 97 57; www.hoteldulys.com; 23 rue Serpente, 6e; s/d/tr €95/115/130; Ⓜ Odéon
This 22-room midrange hotel is a real find and you read about it here first. It's in a 17th-century erstwhile hôtel particulier and

owned and operated by the same family for six decades. We love the beamed ceiling and the chinoiserie wallpaper in the lobby; rooms to go for include the blue-toned No 13 with its striped ceiling and two windows or the darker (but more atmospheric) No 13 in terracotta but with rustic old furniture.

HÔTEL LE CLOS MÉDICIS
Map pp444-5   Hotel

☎ 01 43 29 10 80; www.closmedicis.com; 56 rue Monsieur le Prince, 6e; s €150, d & tw €185-225, tr €270, ste €270-470; Ⓜ Luxembourg; ✕ 🎧 🖳 ♿

Someone has taken an 18th-century building and spun it into the 21st century, with tasteful greys, blacks and burgundies in the 38 bedrooms. History stays for the most part in the lobby, with its antique furnishings, convivial bar and, in winter, open fire. The inner courtyard is a delight for drinks and/or breakfast in fine weather.

HÔTEL LUXEMBOURG PARC
Map pp444-5   Hotel

☎ 01 53 10 36 50; www.hotelluxparc.com; 42 rue de Vaugirard, 6e; r €200-300, ste €475; Ⓜ Luxembourg; 🎧 🖳 ♿

This stunner of a 23-room hotel overlooks the Jardin du Luxembourg and is not to be confused with the Hôtel Luxembourg at No 4 of the same street. Rooms are done up in 'royal French' style (think the late Louis and the last Napoleon), there's a very pleasant (and rather clubby-looking) bar off the lobby and a wonderful courtyard for catching the sun in the warmer months. It's very convenient to the Sénat and the Palais du Luxembourg. The American novelist William Faulkner holed up here in 1925 (p167).

HÔTEL MICHELET ODÉON
Map pp444-5   Hotel

☎ 01 53 10 05 60; www.hotelmicheletodeon.com; 6 place de l'Odéon, 6e; s €80, d €95-105, tw €105-115, tr/q €135/150, ste €170; Ⓜ Odéon; 🖳

Opposite the landmark Odéon-Théâtre de l'Europe (p269) and just a minute's walk from the Jardin du Luxembourg, this 42-room, two-star hotel has tasteful, generously proportioned rooms. It's a very short walk down to Odéon and the cafés and shops of blvd St-Germain.

HÔTEL ST-ANDRÉ DES ARTS
Map pp436-7   Hotel

☎ 01 43 26 96 16; hsaintand@wanadoo.fr; 66 rue St-André des Arts, 6e; s/d/tw/tr/q €66/85/90/108/119; Ⓜ Odéon

This hotel on a lively, restaurant-lined thoroughfare is an excellent choice if you're looking for reasonably priced but stylish accommodation in the centre of the action. The 31 rooms are not particularly spectacular, but the public areas are very evocative of vieux Paris (old Paris), with their beamed ceilings, ancient stone walls and mock-Gothic chairs. Room rates include breakfast.

HÔTEL ST-GERMAIN DES PRÉS
Map pp436-7   Hotel

☎ 01 40 46 83 63; www.hotel-paris-saint-germain.com; 36 rue Bonaparte, 6e; s & d €180-255, ste €310; Ⓜ St-Germain des Prés; 🎧 🖳

Situated just up from the cafés and hubbub of place St-Germain des Prés, this is a tastefully appointed 30-room hotel. We especially love the suite with the baronial four-poster bed. Rooms are often somewhat small; if you need more space, splurge on a 'superior' room (numbers ending in 4 and 5) or a 'deluxe' one (ending in 6). Many guests come to lay their head where Henry Miller did (p166).

HÔTEL SÈVRES AZUR
Map pp434-5   Hotel

☎ 01 45 48 84 07; www.hotelsevresazur.com; 22 rue de l'Abbé Grégoire, 6e; s €85-95, d €90-115, tr €135; Ⓜ St-Placide; 🖳 ♿

Well situated on a quiet street between Montparnasse and St-Germain, this 31-room hotel offers some of the best value for money on the Left Bank. Rooms are of a decent size; yellows and oranges predominate and the ones facing the courtyard are as bright as those on the street. The reception area, with its tiled floor and abundance of mirrors, is less impressive.

HÔTEL VERNEUIL
Map pp434-5   Hotel

☎ 01 42 60 82 14; www.hotelverneuil.com; 8 rue de Verneuil, 7e; s €130, d €155-200; Ⓜ St-Germain des Prés; 🎧 🖳

Chic and cosy, this lovely hotel is in a 17th-century building in a quiet street just off blvd St-Germain des Prés. It has 26 individually decorated rooms and the décor tries hard to reflect this *quartier* full of galleries and antique shops; there are engravings and original artwork on the walls throughout the hotel. The salon off the lobby feels like a library in a private home and there is some lovely stained glass in the hallways.

L'HÔTEL Map pp436-7
Boutique Hotel

☎ 01 44 41 99 00; www.l-hotel.com; 13 rue des Beaux Arts, 6e; s & d €255-640, ste €540-740; Ⓜ St-Germain des Prés; ✗ ⚒ 💻 🅿

With 20 rooms and tucked away in a quiet quayside street, this place with the most minimal of names is the stuff of romance, Parisian myths and urban legends. Rock-and film-star patrons alike fight to sleep in room 16 where Oscar Wilde died a century ago now decorated with a peacock motif, or in the Art Deco room (No 36) of legendary dancer Mistinguett with its huge mirrored bed. Rooms give off a large circular atrium; the public areas include a fantastic bar and restaurant under a glass canopy and, in the ancient cellar, a very modern swimming pool. Rates vary widely according to the seasons.

LA VILLA ST-GERMAIN DES PRÉS

Map pp436-7
Hotel

☎ 01 43 26 60 00; www.villa-saintgermain.com; 29 rue Jacob, 6e; s & d €260-335, ste €440; Ⓜ St-Germain des Prés; ⚒ 💻 ♿

This 31-room hotel helped set what has become almost a standard of the Parisian accommodation scene: small, minimalist, discreet. Fabrics, lighting and soft furnishings all are of the utmost quality and taste. Rooms are refreshingly modern but subtly designed, bathrooms are small but shimmering, and the lobby, with its popular bar, is large and bright.

MONTPARNASSE

Just east of Gare Montparnasse (the train station that is also home to Montparnasse Bienvenüe metro station), there are some two- and three-star places on rue Vandamme and rue de la Gaîté – though the latter is rife with sex shops and peep shows. Gare Montparnasse is served by Air France buses from both airports. Place Denfert Rochereau is also linked to both airports by Orlybus, Orlyval and RER.

HÔTEL AVIATIC

Map pp434-5
Hotel

☎ 01 53 63 25 50; www.aviatic.fr; 105 rue de Vaugirard, 6e; r €139-210; Ⓜ Montparnasse Bienvenüe; ⚒ 💻

This 43-room hotel with charming, almost Laura Ashley–style décor and a delightful Art Deco entrance has been around since 1856, so it must be doing something right. The tiny 'winter garden' is a breath of fresh air (literally). Some rooms face the street and a quieter courtyard. For more space choose a 'superior' or 'millennium' room. Book on the Internet and you'll save up to 25%.

HOTEL BLEU MARINE

Map pp434-5
Hotel

☎ 01 56 54 84 00; www.bleumarine.fr; 40 rue du Commandant René Mouchotte, 15e; r €140-250; Ⓜ Montparnasse Bienvenüe; ✗ ⚒ 💻 ♿

We don't usually give large international hotels a second (or a first) look but this one behind the Gare Montparnasse is an exception. With 354 rooms (more than half of which are twins) spread over seven floors, it's one of the largest hotels in town but service remains efficient and friendly. Unusual for a Paris hotel, it's almost entirely nonsmoking. The fitness room with sauna, Annick Goutal bath products in each room and the bar with live music three times a week are pluses.

HÔTEL DELAMBRE Map pp434-5
Hotel

☎ 01 43 20 66 31; www.hoteldelambre.com; 35 rue Delambre, 14e; s €75-115, d €85-115, ste €150-160; Ⓜ Montparnasse Bienvenüe; ⚒ 💻

This very attractive 30-room hotel just east of the Gare Montparnasse takes wrought iron as a theme and uses it both in functional pieces (bedheads, lamps) and decorative items throughout. Room 7 has its own little terrace while Nos 1 and 2 look onto a small private courtyard.

HÔTEL ODESSA MONTPARNASSE

Map pp434-5
Hotel

☎ 01 43 20 64 78; www.paris-hotel-odessa.com; 28 rue d'Odessa, 14e; s €68-71, d €80-85, tw €94, tr/q €105/113; Ⓜ Montparnasse Bienvenüe; ✗

This hotel on the street of creperies (p209) is just around the corner from the brasseries and bistros of Montparnasse. The rooms are unspectacular but bright and airy.

CHEAP SLEEPS

The budget places in the 14e don't usually see many foreign tourists because of the dearth of sights in the area but that means the accommodation is usually better value for money.

CELTIC HÔTEL Map pp434-5 Hotel

☎ 01 43 20 93 53; hotelceltic@wanadoo.fr; 15 rue d'Odessa, 14e; s €43-56, d €57-63, tr €75; Ⓜ Edgar Quinet

This 29-room hotel is an old-fashioned place that has undergone a few changes in recent years – there's now a lift (a small one but a lift nonetheless) and a new reception area. The cheaper singles are pretty bare and even the *en suite* doubles and triples are not exactly *tout confort* (with all the mod cons), but the Gare Montparnasse is only 200m away.

HÔTEL DE BLOIS Map pp422-3 Hotel

☎ 01 45 40 99 48; www.hoteldeblois.com; 5 rue des Plantes, 14e; s €45-56, d €49-62, tw €58-66, tr €55-72; Ⓜ Mouton Duvernet; ⊗ 🖳

This 25-room establishment just off the av du Maine underwent major renovations in 2006 and is now a very pleasant, very affordable one-star just south of Gare Montparnasse. Rooms, smallish but fully equipped, now have shower or bath but some share use of the toilet down the hall. Staff are very friendly.

HÔTEL DE L'ESPÉRANCE

Map pp434-5 Hotel

☎ 01 43 21 63 84; info@esperancehotelparis.com; 45 rue de la Gaîté, 14e; s €55-60, d €65-70, tw €75; Ⓜ Gaîté; 🟦

This 15-room place, along a street lined with sex shops and other less-than-salubrious establishments one usually finds around train stations, has had a somewhat cheesy refit but remains good value for what and where it is.

PETIT PALACE HÔTEL Map pp422-3 Hotel

☎ 01 43 22 05 25; http://paris-hotel-petit -palace.com; 131 av du Maine, 14e; s €57-65, d 75; Ⓜ Gaîté; 🖳

This friendly (and rather ambitiously named) two-star hotel right on a main boulevard south of Montparnasse has been run by the same family for half a

century. It has 41 smallish but spotless rooms, all of which have showers and toilets.

FAUBOURG ST-GERMAIN & INVALIDES

The 7e is a lovely arrondissement in which to stay, but apart from the northeast section – the area east of Invalides and opposite the Louvre – it's fairly quiet here.

HÔTEL LENOX ST-GERMAIN

Map pp434-5 Hotel

☎ 01 42 96 10 95; www.lenoxsaintgermain.com; 9 rue de l'Université, 7e; s €120-152, d €125-165, tw €152-165, ste €260-275; Ⓜ Rue du Bac; 🟦 🖳

This hotel has 34 simple, comfortable rooms and a late-opening 1930s-style bar called the Lenox Club that attracts a chic clientele. The Art Deco décor is a treat and the fine leather armchairs in the lobby are more than comfortable.

HÔTEL LINDBERGH Map pp434-5 Hotel

☎ 01 45 48 35 53; www.hotellindbergh.com; 5 rue Chomel, 7e; s & d €98-160, tr €156-180, q €166-190; Ⓜ Sèvres Babylone; 🖳

We still haven't figured out why this 26-room *hotel de charme* is totally kitted out in Charles Lindbergh photos and memorabilia, but somehow it works. The newly renovated bedrooms are done up in shades of chocolate and red with silk fabric on the walls and rush matting on the floors. We like the room-number plates on the doors with little Paris landmarks, the ample-sized bathrooms and the very friendly staff.

HÔTEL ST-DOMINIQUE

Map pp434-5 Hotel

☎ 01 47 05 51 44; www.hotelstdominique.com; 62 rue St-Dominique, 7e; s €82-101, d €95-123; Ⓜ Invalides; 🖳

This hotel, with its beamed ceilings, ancient stone walls and huge back patio, is located between Invalides and the Eiffel Tower. Only some of the 37 rooms have had a refit so insist on one of those (eg No 2). A very quiet choice is No 10, which looks out onto the patio, where breakfast is served in the warmer months.

EIFFEL TOWER AREA & 16E ARRONDISSEMENT

Surprisingly these very chic neighbour-hoods offer some decent choices in the way of midrange hotels.

GRAND HÔTEL LÉVÊQUE

Map pp434-5   Hotel

☎ 01 47 05 49 15; www.hotel-leveque.com; 29 rue Cler, 7e; s €57, d €87-110, tr €125; Ⓜ École Militaire; ⊠

This 50-room hotel is recommended less for its charms than for value for money and an excellent location overlooking rue Cler and its **market** (p52). Choose any room ending in 1, 2 or 3 (eg room 11 with its little balcony), all of which have two windows overlooking the market. For those travellers seeking silence, your best bet is one of the rooms facing the courtyard but they're darker and smaller (eg No 10). Singles here are miniscule.

HÔTEL DU CHAMP-DE-MARS

Map pp434-5   Hotel

☎ 01 45 51 52 30; www.hotelduchampdemars.com; 7 rue de Champ de Mars, 7e; s/d/tw/tr €78/84/88/105; Ⓜ École Militaire; ⊠ 🖵

This charming 25-room hotel in the shadow of the Eiffel Tower is on everyone's wish list so book a good month or two in advance if you want to wake up and smell the coffee here. The attractive shop-front entrance leads into a colourful lobby done up in yellows and greens. Rooms on the lower floors can be downright cupboardlike, though; go up higher (in floors and price) and you might earn a glimpse of Mademoiselle Eiffel herself.

HÔTEL SEZZ

Map pp434-5   Boutique Hotel

☎ 01 56 75 26 26; www.hotelsezz.com; 6 av Frémiet, 16e; s €250-275, d €300-350, ste €400-600; Ⓜ Passy; ⊠ 🔅 🖵 ♿

We've visited, inspected and stayed in lots of hotels in our day, but we seldom come

---

TOP OF THE CLASS: PARIS' FINEST DELUXE HOTELS

The following are our favourite four- and four-star 'L' (*luxe*, the local equivalent of five stars) hotels.

Hôtel Costes (Map pp426-7; ☎ 01 42 44 50 00; www.hotelcostes.com; 239 rue St-Honoré, 1er; s & d €350-800, ste from €1200; Ⓜ Concorde; 🔅 🖵 🐾 ♿) Jean-Louis Costes' eponymous caravanserai offers a 'luxurious and immoderate home away from home' to visiting *über-mensch* and A-listers. Outfitted in camp Second Empire cast-offs with a Byzantine twist, this 82-room hotel remains a darling of the rich and famous. A delightful restaurant takes pride of place in the central Italian-style courtyard in the warmer months; the basement pool, with underwater music and Art Deco-ish lounge chairs, is gorgeous; and the bar and its groovy music compilations are legendary.

Hôtel de Crillon (Map pp426-7; ☎ 01 44 71 15 00; www.crillon.com; 10 place de la Concorde, 8e; s €510-605, d €630-890, ste from €995; Ⓜ Concorde; ⊠ 🔅 🖵) This colonnaded 200-year-old 'jewel in the heart of Paris', whose sparkling public areas (including the recently renovated **Les Ambassadeurs** restaurant, with two Michelin stars) are sumptuously decorated with chandeliers, original sculptures, gilt mouldings and inlaid furniture, is the epitome of French luxury. The 157 rooms are spacious with king-sized beds and have floor-to-ceiling marble bathrooms with separate shower and bath.

Hôtel Meurice (Map pp426-7; ☎ 01 44 58 10 10; www.meuricehotel.com; 228 rue de Rivoli, 1er; s €510-600, d €610-800, ste from €810; Ⓜ Tuileries; ⊠ 🔅 🖵 ♿) With 60 rooms and facing the Jardin des Tuileries, the Meurice's gold leaf and Art Nouveau glass positively gleam and its restaurant, **Le Meurice**, is a bastion of good taste (in more ways than one). Don't miss the classical music under the glass dome of the Jardin d'Hiver (Winter Garden). The hotel is part of the Dorchester Group.

Hôtel Relais Christine (Map pp426-7; ☎ 01 40 51 60 80; www.relais-christine.com; 3 rue Christine, 6e; s & d €355-450, ste from €530; Ⓜ Mabillon or St-Michel; 🔅 🖵) Part of the Small Luxury Hotels of the World, the Relais Christine is a beautiful 51-room property with an unforgettable courtyard entrance off a quiet street, with a garden behind it, and a spa and fitness centre built in and around an original 13th-century cellar. Rooms are spacious and (unusual for a hotel of this category) the décor is more modern than classic.

Hôtel Ritz Paris (Map pp426-7; ☎ 01 43 16 35 29; www.ritzparis.com; 15 place Vendôme, 1er; s & d €680-770, ste from €900; Ⓜ Opéra; ⊠ 🔅 🖵) So famous it's lent its name to the English lexicon, the incomparable, unmistakable Ritz has 162 sparkling rooms and suites. Its **L'Espadon** restaurant has two Michelin stars and the **Hemingway Bar** (p250) is where the American author imbibed once he'd made a name for himself – and could afford it.

Statue outside Hôtel Relais Christine (p323)

across anything quite like this. Punning on the number of the posh arrondissement – 16 (*seize* in French) – in which it finds itself, this boutique bonanza is heavy on design (think Christophe Pillet), technology and *l'esprit zen* (zen spirit). The 27 rooms are spacious and done up in reds and blacks and lots of glass, there's a hammam, Jacuzzi and massage room, and the bar specialises in champagne. There is no reception; a personal butler is at your command during your stay.

ÉTOILE & CHAMPS-ÉLYSÉES

Like the 1er, the 8e is for the most part home to deluxe hotels (see the boxed text, Top of the Class, p323), though there are a few top-end favourites in the vicinity of place Charles de Gaulle.

ARIOSO HÔTEL Map pp426-7   Hotel
☎ 01 53 05 95 00; www.arioso-hotel.com; 7 rue d'Argenson, 8e; s €205-245, d €225-265, q €440; Ⓜ Miromesnil; ✗ ⊠ ▯ ♿
This late-18th-century building, a short hop from the blvd des Champs-Élysées, has been transformed into an elegant new four-star hotel. The 28 rooms, some of which have balconies, are furnished in a tasteful traditional style; each of the five floors has a different colour scheme. We love the back courtyard/patio with a fountain, the complimentary L'Occitane products in the bathroom and room 104 with the big balcony.

HÔTEL BEDFORD Map pp426-7   Hotel
☎ 01 44 94 77 77; www.hotel-bedford.com; 17 rue de l'Arcade, 8e; s/d €158/178, tw €198-230, ste €310; Ⓜ Madeleine; ✗ ⊠ ▯
This 145-room property in the posh 8e exudes class – in the way that only English-style hotels can. The décor is understated, the colour scheme (every imaginable version of white) muted. Rooms are of a good size except for the mansard ones on the top (8th) floor. Everything faces the street; for both tranquillity and fabulous views of Paris, choose anything on the 7th floor. The breakfast room, with its *belle époque* glass dome and wedding-cake ceiling, moonlights as a concert hall for students of the Conservatoire International de Musique de Paris (in the same arrondissement).

HÔTEL LE A Map pp426-7   Boutique Hotel
☎ 01 42 56 99 99; www.paris-hotel-a.com; 4 rue d'Artois, 8e; r €329-399, ste €450-590; ✗ ⊠ ▯ Ⓜ St-Philippe du Roule
One of our favourite new discoveries, the 'A' (think 'list') is an über-stylish minimalist hotel that doesn't have any of the attitude that generally goes with the concept. White, black and grey predominate and help 'frame' the fabulous contemporary art by painter Fabrice Hybert. The airy spaces (the breakfast area and bar are in a glassed-in courtyard), fireplace, and real books (as opposed to decorative items) in the lobby for guests' use are as welcome as the nonsmoking floor but rooms are somewhat petite. Rates are up to 30% less on the Internet.

CLICHY & GARE ST-LAZARE

These areas offer some excellent medium-range and reasonably priced top-end hotels. The better deals are away from Gare St-Lazare but there are several places along rue d'Amsterdam beside the station worth checking out.

HÔTEL BRITANNIA Map pp426-7   Hotel
☎ 01 42 85 36 36; www.hotelbritannia.com;
24 rue d'Amsterdam, 9e; s/d/tr €78/85/99;
Ⓜ St-Lazare; 🖳

This 46-room place with narrow hallways
but pleasant, clean rooms is just opposite
Gare St-Lazare and a quick walk to the
grands magasins (department stores) on
blvd Haussmann. We still haven't figured
out why there are plaster reliefs of Roman
citizens lining the entrance hall but it does
give the place something of a classical feel.
Ask about the three-night packages.

HÔTEL CONCORDE-ST-LAZARE
Map pp426-7   Hotel
☎ 01 40 08 44 44; www.concordestlazare-paris
.com; 108 rue St-Lazare, 8e; s & d €360-450, ste
from €685; Ⓜ St-Lazare; ⊠ 😾 🖳

Built in 1889 as the Grand Hôtel Terminus,
this fabulous 266-room railway hotel has
now been totally restored, declared a historical monument and must be seen to be
believed; the marble and the mirrors alone
must have broken the bank. Make sure you
bring a compass – the corridors are enormous. The staff are not as well-informed as
you would imagine at a four-star hotel.

HÔTEL FAVART Map pp428-9   Hotel
☎ 01 42 97 59 83; www.hotel-paris-favart.com;
5 rue Marivaux, 2e; s €89-110, d €110-135, tr €130-
160, q €155-176; Ⓜ Richelieu Drouot; ⊠ 😾 🚫

This stylish Art Nouveau hotel with 37
rooms facing the Opéra Comique feels like
it never let go of the *belle époque*. It's an excellent choice if you're interested in shopping, being within easy walking distance of
the *grands magasins* on blvd Haussmann.

NEW ORIENT HÔTEL Map pp426-7   Hotel
☎ 01 45 22 21 64; www.hotel-paris-orient.com;
16 rue de Constantinople, 8e; s €82-105, d €99-105,
tw €105-130, tr & q €140; Ⓜ Europe; ⊠ 😾 🖳

This 30-room hotel is situated in a neighbourhood of the 8e north of Gare St-Lazare
that seems to have only shops that sell
musical instruments and/or sheet music.
It has a lot of personality, especially in the
common areas. The bedrooms (all nonsmoking) are not as nice, though several
have Second Empire furnishings and busts.
Some (eg twin room No 7 and double No 8)
have little balconies.

CHEAP SLEEPS
Clichy offers a couple of very unusual places
to stay in the budget category.

HÔTEL ELDORADO Map pp426-7   Hotel
☎ 01 45 22 35 21; www.eldoradohotel.fr; 18 rue
des Dames, 17e; s €25-50, d & tw €45-70, tr €50-80;
Ⓜ Place de Clichy

This bohemian place is one of Paris' greatest finds: a welcoming, reasonably well-run
place with 40 colourfully decorated and
(often) ethnically themed rooms in a main
building on a quiet street and in an annexe
with a private garden at the back. We love
rooms 1 and 2 in the garden annexe; the
choicest rooms in the main building are
Nos 16 and 127 with their own terraces
giving onto the garden. Cheaper-category
rooms have washbasin only. The excellent Bistro des Dames (p215) next door, which
belongs to the hotel, is a bonus.

STYLE HOTEL Map pp426-7   Hotel
☎ 01 45 22 37 59; fax 01 45 22 81 03;
8 rue Ganneron, 18e; s & d €35-50, tr/q €57/67;
Ⓜ La Fourche

This 36-room hotel just north of place de
Clichy and west of Cimetière de Montmartre is a titch rough around the edges
(rough wooden floors, old runner carpets
in the hallways) but is loaded with character and the welcome is always charming.
There's a lovely double courtyard, but no
lift. The cheapest singles and doubles are
equipped with washbasin only.

OPÉRA & GRANDS BOULEVARDS
The avenues around blvd Montmartre are
popular for their nightlife area and it's a
lively area in which to stay. It's very convenient for shopping as this is where you'll find
Paris' premium department stores.

HÔTEL CHOPIN Map pp428-9   Hotel
☎ 01 47 70 58 10; fax 01 42 47 00 70; 46 passage
Jouffroy, 9e; s €58-73, d €75-86, tr €100; Ⓜ Grands
Boulevards

Dating back to 1846, the Chopin is down
one of Paris' most delightful 19th-century
passages couverts (covered shopping arcades) and a great deal for its location right

off the Grands Boulevards (entrance at 10 blvd Montmartre). The sprawling 36-room hotel may be a little faded, but it's still enormously evocative of the *belle époque* and the welcome is always warm. The cheapest singles have washbasin only. After the arcade closes at 10pm, ring the *sonnette de nuit* (night doorbell).

HÔTEL DES ARTS Map pp428-9 Hotel
☎ 01 42 46 73 30; hdag@free.fr; 7 Cité Bergère, 9e; s/d/tr €74/82/98; Ⓜ Grands Boulevards; ♿
This quirky place with pink geraniums bedecking each exterior window is in a quiet little alley off rue du Faubourg Montmartre. It has 25 rooms recently redone in shades of plum and burgundy and there seems to be a bird theme (ancient prints, caged parrot in the lobby) throughout. There are seven other hotels on this tranquil street.

HÔTEL LANGLOIS Map pp426-7 Hotel
☎ 01 48 74 78 24; www.hotel-langlois.com; 63 rue St-Lazare, 9e; s €89-104, d & tw €104-120, ste €160; Ⓜ Trinité; ⊠ ▣
Built in 1870, this 27-room hotel has retained its charming *belle époque* look and feel despite a massive makeover in 1997. The rooms and suites are unusually large for a smallish hotel in Paris; most have sandstone fireplaces that, sadly, have been decommissioned, and many retain original bathroom fixtures and tiles. The location is very convenient for the department stores on the blvd Haussmann.

HÔTEL PELETIER HAUSSMANN OPÉRA Map pp428-9 Hotel
☎ 01 42 46 79 53; www.peletieropera.com; 15 rue Le Peletier, 9e; s €72-80, d €82-90, tr €86-95; Ⓜ Richelieu Drouot; ▣
This is a pleasant 26-room hotel just off blvd Haussmann and close to the big department stores. Attractive packages are available at the weekend, depending on the season. Internet access here costs €2 for 15 minutes.

HÔTEL VIVIENNE Map pp428-9 Hotel
☎ 01 42 33 13 26; paris@hotel-vivienne.com; 40 rue Vivienne, 2e; s €54-104, d €69-104, tw €90-104; Ⓜ Grands Boulevards; ⊠ ▣ ▣
This stylish hotel is amazingly good value for Paris. While the 45 rooms are not huge, they have all the mod-cons, some even with little balconies and the public areas

are bright and cheery. The Vivienne is a very wise choice if you want to be close to the Palais Royal or the Vivienne and Colbert covered passages (p169).

GARE DU NORD, GARE DE L'EST & RÉPUBLIQUE

There are a few two- and three-star places around the train stations in the 10e that are convenient if you're catching an early train to London or want to crash immediately upon arrival.

AUSTIN'S ARTS ET MÉTIERS HÔTEL
Map pp428-9 Hotel
☎ 01 42 77 17 61; www.austinshotel.com; 6 rue Montgolfier, 3e; s/d €99/135; Ⓜ Arts et Métiers; ⊠ ▣
This three-star hotel southwest of place de la République and hard by the Musée des Arts et Métiers (p109) stands out primarily for its warm welcome and excellent service. The 29 rooms are minimally furnished but attractively done up in reds, yellows and blues. The brightest rooms face the street, while the largest ones overlook the courtyard. Choose No 12 if, like us, you like a bathroom with a window.

GRAND HÔTEL DE PARIS
Map pp428-9 Hotel
☎ 01 46 07 40 56; grand.hotel.de.paris@gofornet .com; 72 blvd de Strasbourg, 10e; s/d/tr/q €77/83/102/119; Ⓜ Gare de l'Est
The Grand Hôtel de Paris is a well-run establishment just south of the Gare de l'Est on blvd de Strasbourg. It has 49 soundproofed rooms and a tiny lift and is a pleasant place to stay if you're in the area. The quads are especially spacious and suitable for a small family.

HÔTEL FRANÇAIS Map pp428-9 Hotel
☎ 01 40 35 94 14; www.hotelfrancais.com; 13 rue du 8 Mai 1945, 10e; s €85-92, d €89-96, tr €124-131; Ⓜ Gare de l'Est; ⊠ ▣ ▣ Ⓟ
This two-star hotel facing the Gare de l'Est has 71 attractive, almost luxurious and very quiet rooms, some of which have balconies. Parking – always difficult around train stations in Paris – in the hotel garage costs €9.50 a day.

TOP FIVE BOUTIQUE HOTELS

- Hôtel La Manufacture (p330)
- Hôtel Le A (p324)
- Hôtel Sezz (p323)
- Le Général Hôtel (below)
- Murano Urban Resort (below)

HÔTEL LIBERTEL CROIX DE MALTE

Map pp440-1   Hotel

☎ 01 48 05 09 36; H2752@accor-hotels.com; 5 rue de Malte, 11e; s/d €97/107; Ⓜ Oberkampf; ✗ 🖳 This cheery hotel will have you thinking you're in the tropics, not Paris. The breakfast room just off the lobby is bathed in light and looks out onto a tiny glassed-in courtyard with a giant jungle mural; Walasse Ting prints (of parrots mostly) complete the picture. The 28 rooms are in two little buildings, only one of which has a lift.

LE GÉNÉRAL HÔTEL

Map pp428-9   Boutique Hotel

☎ 01 47 00 41 57; www.legeneralhotel.com; 5-7 rue Rampon, 11e; s €135-155, d €165-195, tr €195-225, ste €235-265; Ⓜ République; ✗ 🕱 🖳 ♿ This 48-room hotel near the place de la République, which opened in 2003, is a symphony in white on the outside and bonbon box of coloured goodies inside. The hotel's décor is fresh and fun and the rooms are beautifully furnished. The light 'sculpture' in the bar off the lobby is memorable and amenities include a fitness centre and sauna.

MURANO URBAN RESORT

Map pp440-1   Boutique Hotel

☎ 01 42 71 20 00; www.muranoresort.com; 13 blvd du Temple, 3e; s €350, d €400-650, ste €750-950; Ⓜ Filles du Calvaire; ✗ 🕱 🖳 This 52-room 'urban resort' south of place de la République wears a classical 19th-century exterior but has the 21st century inside. Its name suggests that you should come in, kick off your shoes and sink your toes in the hotel's figurative sand. And with public areas like a spa with heated pool and hammam, a courtyard restaurant under glass, a cool jazz and DJ bar and bedrooms that that allow you to change their colour scheme, that's easily accomplished.

NORD-EST HÔTEL

Map pp428-9   Hotel

☎ 01 47 70 07 18; hotel.nord.est@wanadoo.fr; 12 rue des Petits Hôtels, 10e; s/d/tr/q €63/73/97/123; Ⓜ Poissonnière; 🖳 This unusual 30-room hotel is set away from the street and fronted by a small terrace. What the enormous carved elephant is doing in the lobby is anyone's guess. It is convenient to both the Gare du Nord and the Gare de l'Est. Internet access costs an outrageous €8/12 for 30/60 minutes.

CHEAP SLEEPS

The areas east and northeast of the Gare du Nord and Gare de l'Est have always had a more than ample selection of hotels and now you'll also find a hostel within striking distance. Place de la République (Map pp428–9) is relatively convenient for the nightlife areas of Ménilmontant.

Gare du Nord is linked to Charles de Gaulle airport by RER and RATP (Régie Autonome des Transports Parisians) bus 350, and to Orly airport by Orlyval. Bus 350 to/from Charles de Gaulle airport also stops right in front of the Gare de l'Est.

AUBERGE DE JEUNESSE JULES FERRY

Map pp428-9   Hostel

☎ 01 43 57 55 60; www.fuaj.fr; 8 blvd Jules Ferry, 11e; per person dm €20, d €20; Ⓜ République or Goncourt; ✗ 🕱 🖳 This official hostel, three blocks east of place de la République, is somewhat institutional and the rooms could use a refit, but the atmosphere is fairly relaxed. The 99 beds are in two- to six-person rooms, which are locked between 10.30am and 2pm for housekeeping; there is no curfew. You'll have to pay an extra €2.90 per night if you don't have an HI card or equivalent. The only other official hostel in central Paris is the Auberge de Jeunesse Le D'Artagnan (Map pp422–3; ☎ 01 40 32 34 57; www.fuaj.fr; 80 rue Vitruve, 20e; dm €21.50; Ⓜ Porte de Bagnolet), which is far from the centre of the action but just one metro stop from the Gare Routière Internationale de Paris-Galliéni (International Bus Terminal). It has rooms with two to eight beds, big lockers, laundry facilities, a bar, cinema, and the same rules and regulations as the Jules Ferry hostel. It is the largest hostel in France, with 435 beds on seven floors.

HÔTEL AQUARELLE Map pp428-9   Hotel

☎ 01 48 05 79 76; www.hotel-aquarelle.com; 38 blvd du Temple, 11e; d & tw €65-72, tr €80, ste €110; Ⓜ République or Filles du Calvaire; ♿

This 32-room hotel due south of the place de la République would be that much more attractive if it wasn't on such a busy street. Still, the location just couldn't be better if you're planning to graze and/or cruise rue Oberkampf and its surrounds. The rooms are pretty small and fairly ordinary, though it's clear that some attempts have been made to give the bathrooms a fresher, more contemporary look. The free English newspapers are certainly a nice touch.

HÔTEL DE NEVERS Map pp428-9   Hotel

☎ 01 47 00 56 18; www.hoteldenevers.com; 53 rue de Malte, 11e; s & d €35-53, tr €66-78; Ⓜ Oberkampf; 💻 ♿

This excellent-value family-run budget hotel is around the corner from place de la République, and within easy walking distance of the nightlife of Ménilmontant. Hyper-allergenics may think twice about staying here, though; there are at least two cats on hand to greet you. The 32 rooms are sparingly furnished but nothing is threadbare and everything is proper and *propre* (clean).

HÔTEL LA VIEILLE FRANCE

Map pp428-9   Hotel

☎ 01 45 26 42 37; la.vieille.france@wanadoo.fr; 151 rue La Fayette, 10e; s €42, d €60-65, tr €90; Ⓜ Gare du Nord; 💻

This is an upbeat, 34-room place with relatively spacious and pleasant rooms though with the Gare du Nord so close it's bound to be somewhat noisy. Singles are basic, with washbasins only, but communal showers are free.

HÔTEL LIBERTY Map pp428-9   Hotel

☎ 01 42 08 60 58; www.libertyhotel.net; 16 rue de Nancy, 10e; s €31-40, d €35-47, tw €50, tr €60; Ⓜ Château d'Eau

The Liberty is a 42-room hotel just south of the Gare de l'Est with clean, partially renovated but very plain, very functional rooms. The cheapest singles and doubles have washbasins only. Communal showers cost €2.50.

PEACE AND LOVE HOSTEL

Map pp428-9   Hostel

☎ 01 46 07 65 11; www.paris-hostels.com; 245 rue La Fayette, 10e; per person dm €17-21, d €21-26; Ⓜ Jaurès or Louis Blanc; 💻

This modern-day hippy hang-out is a groovy though chronically crowded hostel with beds in 20 smallish, shower-equipped rooms for two to four people. There's a great kitchen and eating area, but most of the action seems to revolve around the ground floor bar (open till 2am), which boasts more than 30 types of beer, including the cheapest *blondes* (that's lagers) in Paris. Internet access costs from €2 for 15 minutes.

SIBOUR HÔTEL Map pp428-9   Hotel

☎ 01 46 07 20 74; sibour.hotel@wanadoo.fr; 4 rue Sibour, 10e; s €40-55, d €40-65, tr/q €75/85; Ⓜ Gare de l'Est

This friendly place has 45 well-kept rooms, including some old-fashioned ones – the cheapest singles and doubles – with washbasins only. Communal showers cost €3. Some of the rooms look down on pretty Église de St-Laurent.

MÉNILMONTANT & BELLEVILLE

The Ménilmontant nightlife area is an excellent area in which to spend the night, but the selection of accommodation in all price categories is unfortunately relatively limited.

HÔTEL BEAUMARCHAIS

Map pp440-1   Boutique Hotel

☎ 01 53 36 86 86; www.hotelbeaumarchais.com; 3 rue Oberkampf, 11e; s/d/ste/tr €75/90-110/150/170; Ⓜ Filles du Calvaire; 💥 💻

This brighter-than-bright 31-room boutique hotel, with its emphasis on sunbursts and bold primary colours, is just this side of kitsch. But it certainly makes for a different Paris experience, and it fits in with its surroundings very well indeed. The rooms are of a decent size and *la crème de la crème* is room No 1, which leads into the hotel's charming leafy terraced courtyard, where you can be served breakfast in fine weather.

Interior room of Murano Urban Resort (p327)

HÔTEL DU VIEUX SAULE

Map pp440-1   Hotel

☎ 01 42 72 01 14; www.hotelvieuxsaule.com; 6 rue de Picardie, 3e; s €91, d €106-136, tr €151; Ⓜ Filles du Calvaire; ✗ ♿ 💻
This flower-bedecked 31-room hostelry in the northern Marais is something of a 'find' because of its slightly unusual location. The hotel has a small sauna, there is a tranquil little garden on full display behind glass off the lobby and the 'superior' rooms on the 3rd and 4th floors have recently been renovated.

GARE DE LYON, NATION & BERCY

The development of Bercy Village, with its selection of restaurants and bars, has done much to resuscitate the 12e.

CHEAP SLEEPS

The neighbourhood around Gare de Lyon has a few budget hotels and a popular independent hostel.

HÔTEL LE COSY Map pp422-3   Hotel

☎ 01 43 43 10 02; www.hotel-cosy.com; 50 av de St-Mandé, 12e; s €35-85, d €48-85; Ⓜ Picpus; ♿ 💻
This family-run budget hotel immediately southeast of place de la Nation positively

oozes charm. The 28 rooms, though basic (the cheapest singles and doubles have washbasins only), are all different, decorated in warm pastels with original artwork by a young painter from Marseilles and hardwood floors. If feeling flush, choose one of four 'VIP' rooms in the courtyard annexe, especially No 3 or 4 on the 1st floor. The attached **Caffè Cosy** (p227) is an added bonus.

HOSTEL BLUE PLANET

Map pp446-7   Hostel

☎ 01 43 42 06 18; www.hostelblueplanet.com; 5 rue Hector Malot, 12e; dm €21; Ⓜ Gare de Lyon; ✗ 💻
This 43-room hostel is very close to Gare de Lyon – convenient if you're heading south or west at the crack of dawn or arriving in the wee hours. Dorm beds are in rooms for two to four people and the hostel closes between 11am and 3pm. There's no curfew. Internet access costs €3 for 30 minutes.

13E ARRONDISSEMENT & CHINATOWN

The 13e is where you'll find the Bibliothèque Nationale de France, as well as the *péniches* (barges) on the Seine fitted out with music clubs and restaurants, such as **Le Batofar** (p266) and **La Guinguette Pirate** (p265).

HÔTEL LA MANUFACTURE

Map p448   Boutique Hotel

☎ 01 45 35 45 25; www.hotel-la-manufacture
.com; 8 rue Philippe de Champagne, 13e; s
€125-145, d €133-145, tr €199-225, q €266-278;
Ⓜ Place d'Italie; ☒ ☒ 🖳

The graceful, minimalist La Manufacture
is located on the fringe of the Latin Quarter. The 57 individually decorated rooms
adhere to clean lines and sport very bold
plumage; the lobby bar is a delight. Rooms
on the top (7th) floor are the most spacious
and coveted; room No 71 boasts a view
of the Panthéon while No 74 glimpses the
Eiffel Tower. The Chinese and other Asian
eateries of the 13e (see p229) are within
easy sniffing distance.

CHEAP SLEEPS

The southern 13e is a happy hunting ground
for budget hotels.

HÔTEL DES BEAUX-ARTS

Map p448   Hotel

☎ 01 44 24 22 60; www.hotel-beaux-arts.fr; 2 rue
Toussaint Féron, 13e; s €34-46, d €34-58, tr €59-65;
Ⓜ Tolbiac; 🖳

This 25-room one-star hotel just north
of the Tolbiac metro station has a pretty
garden/courtyard and is run by a friendly
couple. It's a great budget choice if you
don't mind going the distance. The cheapest singles and doubles have just washbasins.

15E ARRONDISSEMENT

The 15e, some people's least favourite arrondissement in Paris, offers some decent
accommodation options, especially when
it comes to chain hotels.

HÔTEL FONDARY Map pp434-5   Hotel

☎ 01 45 75 14 75; lefondary@wandoo.fr; 30 rue
Fondary, 15e; s €70-74, d €76-80, tw €83; Ⓜ Av
Émile Zola; 🖳

This almost budget hotel in the far-flung
(but well-served by metro) 15e is an excellent choice for the price. The 22 rooms are
modest but well maintained; choose one
looking on to the pretty (and very leafy) little
courtyard that is such a delight in the warm
weather.

CHEAP SLEEPS

The 15e is home to two hostels under the
same management and very well known
among backpackers and budget travellers:
the Aloha Hostel and the Three Ducks
Hostel. Based on feedback from readers,
Lonely Planet no longer recommends the
Three Ducks, but the Aloha still gets the
thumbs up.

ALOHA HOSTEL Map pp434-5   Hostel

☎ 01 42 73 03 03; www.aloha.fr; 1 rue Borromée,
15e; per person dm/d Nov-Mar €18/22, Apr-Oct
€22/25; Ⓜ Volontaires; ☒ ☒ 🖳

The Aloha is a laid-back and safe hostel
north of rue de Vaugirard. The rooms,
which have two to six beds and sometimes
en suite shower, are locked from 11am to
5pm (though reception remains open)
and curfew is at 2am. Kitchen facilities are
available. Internet access costs €2 for 20
minutes.

MONTMARTRE & PIGALLE

Montmartre, encompassing the 18e and
the northern part of the 9e, is one of the
most charming neighbourhoods in Paris.
There is a bunch of top-end hotels in the
area, and the attractive two-star places on
rue Aristide Bruant are generally less full
in July and August than in the spring and
autumn.

HÔTEL DES ARTS Map p432   Hotel

☎ 01 46 06 30 52; www.arts-hotel-paris.com;
5 rue Tholozé, 18e; s €68, d & tw €82, tr €97;
Ⓜ Abbesses or Blanche; 🖳

This friendly and attractive 50-room hotel is
convenient to both place Pigalle and Montmartre. Towering over it is the old-style
windmill Moulin de la Galette. The resident
canine is very friendly.

HÔTEL REGYN'S MONTMARTRE

Map p432   Hotel

☎ 01 42 54 45 21; www.regynsmontmartre.com;
18 place des Abbesses, 18e; s €72-92, d & tw €84-
104, tr €104-124; Ⓜ Abbesses; ☒ 🖳

This 22-room hotel should be one of your
first choices if you want to stay in old Montmartre and not break the bank. It's just

TOP FIVE BUDGET HOTELS

- Hôtel Bonséjour Montmartre (right)
- Hôtel de Nevers (p328)
- Hôtel Eldorado (p325)
- Hôtel Le Cosy (p329)
- Port Royal Hôtel (p318)

(1883–1955) is smartly done up and can boast a few extras such as a little leafy courtyard and a small sauna.

VILLA ROYALE Map p432   Boutique Hotel
☎ 01 55 31 78 78; www.leshotelsdeparis.com;
2 rue Duperré, 9e; s & d €210-310, ste €350;
Ⓜ Pigalle; ⊠ ☒ 🖳
Part of the swish Les Hôtels de Paris chain, each of the 31 rooms in this 'luxury villa' just might be a Pigalle madam's boudoir, what with every shade of red on the spectrum represented, the sash curtains and the gilded taps. With all the theatres and dance halls in the district, there's also something of a theatrical/artistic theme amidst the baroque and rococo drippings. Ooh la la! Villa Royale might be just the ticket for a romantic and/or very dirty weekend *à Paris*.

opposite the Abbesses metro station, which happens to have one of the best preserved Art Nouveau entrance canopies designed by Hector Guimard (see p104), and outside the hotel is a lovely old plane tree. Some of the rooms have views out over Paris.

HÔTEL RÉSIDENCE DES 3 POUSSINS

Map pp428-9   Hotel

☎ 01 53 32 81 81; www.les3poussins.com;
15 rue Clauzel, 9e; s/d & tw €130/150, 1- or
2-person studio €185, 3- or 4-person studio €220;
Ⓜ St-Georges; ☒ 🖳 ♿
A lovely hotel due south of place Pigalle, it has 40 rooms, half of which are small studios with their own cooking facilities. This place reeks of style – from the classical music in the lobby to the artistically designed lift up to the bedrooms – and the back patio is a delightful place in the warmer months for breakfast or a drink.

TERRASS HOTEL Map p432   Hotel

01 46 06 72 85; www.terrass-hotel.com; 12 rue
Joseph de Maistre, 18e; s €208-280, d €248-320, ste
€36-360; Ⓜ Blanche; ⊠ ☒ 🖳
This very sedate, very stylish hotel at the southeastern corner of Montparnasse Cemetery and due east of the Butte de Montmartre (Montmartre Hill) has 100 spacious and well-designed rooms and suites, an excellent restaurant and bar, and quite simply the best views in town. For the ultimate Parisian experience, choose junior suite No 703 for stunning views of the Eiffel Tower and Panthéon from the Jacuzzi, or No 802, which boasts its own private terrace. Internet access costs from €4 for 15 minutes.

HÔTEL UTRILLO Map p432   Hotel

☎ 01 42 58 13 44; www.hotel-paris-utrillo.com;
7 rue Aristide Bruant, 18e; s €64, d & tw €76-82, tr
€96; Ⓜ Abbesses or Blanche; ☒ 🖳 ♿
This friendly 30-room hotel, named after the 'painter of Montmartre' Maurice Utrillo

CHEAP SLEEPS

The flat area around the base of the Butte de Montmartre has some surprisingly good deals. The lively, ethnically mixed area east of Sacré Cœur can be a bit rough; some people say it's prudent to avoid Château Rouge metro station at night. Both the 9e and the 18e have fine and recommended hostels.

HÔTEL BONSÉJOUR MONTMARTRE

Map p432   Hotel

☎ 01 42 54 22 53; www.hotel-bonsejour
-montmartre.fr; 11 rue Burq, 18e; s €25, d €32-48,
tr €59; Ⓜ Abbesses
At the end of a quiet street in Montmartre, this is a perennial budget favourite. It's a simple place to stay – no lift, linoleum or parquet floors – but welcoming, comfortable, very clean and getting a much needed facelift. Some rooms (eg Nos 14, 23, 33, 43 and 53) have little balconies attached and at least one room (No 55) offers a fleeting glimpse of Sacré Cœur. Communal showers cost €2.

HÔTEL DU MOULIN Map p432   Hotel

☎ 01 42 64 33 33; www.hotelmoulin.com; 3 rue
Aristide Bruant, 18e; s €55-63, d €59-67, tw €67-70;
Ⓜ Abbesses or Blanche; 🖳
This quiet little hotel has 27 good-sized rooms with toilet and bath or shower in both a main building and a garden annexe. The Korean family who own the place are very kind. Check out their fun website. Internet access costs €1.60 for 30 minutes.

LE VILLAGE HOSTEL

Map p432   Hostel

☎ 01 42 64 22 02; www.villagehostel.fr;
20 rue d'Orsel, 18e; per person Nov–mid-Mar
dm/d/tr €20/23/21.50, mid-Mar–Oct €23/27/25;
Ⓜ Anvers; ✗ 💻

A fine 25-room hostel with beamed ceilings, a lovely outside terrace and views of Sacré Cœur. Dormitory beds are in rooms for four to six people and all have shower and toilet. Kitchen facilities are available, and there's a popular bar too. Rooms are closed between 11am and 4pm for cleaning, and the 2am curfew is enforced. Internet access is available for €2.50 for 30 minutes.

WOODSTOCK HOSTEL

Map pp428-9   Hostel

☎ 01 48 78 87 76; www.woodstock.fr; 48 rue
Rodier, 9e; per person dm/d Oct-Mar €18/21, Apr-
Sep €21/24; Ⓜ Anvers; ✗ 💻

This friendly hostel is just down the hill from raucous place Pigalle in a quiet residential quarter. Dorm beds are in rooms sleeping four to six people in bunk beds, and each room has washbasin only; showers and toilets are off the corridor. Rooms are shut from 11am to 3pm, and the (enforced) curfew is at 2am. The spanking new eat-in kitchen down the steps from the patio has everything. Internet access is available for €2 for 30 minutes.

Excursions

To Reims (60km)

To Lille (175km)

TGV Nord

To Amiens (75km)

To Rouen (35km)

To Rouen (50km)

20 km
12 miles

Provins

Coulommiers

N34

N19

N4

SEINE ET MARNE

La Ferté sous Jouarre

Meaux

A4

N36

A5

E

TGV

Disneyland Resort Paris

Vaux-le-Vicomte

Sud Est

N2

Forêt d'Ermenonville

Ermenonville

Parc Astérix

Aéroport Roissy Charles de Gaulle

A104

N19

N104

TGV

C

Melun

N7

Barbizon

A1

Paris

SEINE ST-DENIS

N3

Héliport

Créteil

N

Senlis

Forêt de Chantilly

N17

A3

VAL DE MARNE

N6

A

St-Leu

Chantilly

Luzarches

N16

Ecouen

St-Denis

PARIS

A6

N7

Evry

A6

Seine

R

Persan

Beaumont

N1

Bois de Boulogne

Bois de Vincennes

A86

A20

Auvers-sur-Oise

A15

La Défense

HAUTS DE SEINE

Aéroport d'Orly

F

VAL D'OISE

Pontoise

Cergy

St-Germain en-Laye

Versailles

A10

ESSONNES

A10

N13

N10

E

A13

Rambouillet

A11

D

Forêt de Rambouillet

N14

Mantes la Jolie

Seine

E

TGV Atlantique

A10

EURE ET

L

Giverny

N12

YVELINES

N10

Vernon

Eure

Chartres

Marne

Marne

Oise

Seine

Excursions

Paris is encircled by the Île de France (Island of France), a 12,000-sq-km area shaped by five rivers: the Epte, the Aisne, the Eure, the Yonne and the Marne. The region was the seed from which the kingdom of France grew, beginning about AD 1100.

Today, the excellent rail and road links between the French capital and the exceptional sights of the Île de France and neighbouring *départements* (administrative divisions) make the region especially popular with day-trippers from Paris. At the same time, the many woodland areas around the city, including the forests of Fontainebleau and Chantilly, offer unlimited outdoor activities.

In Paris visit **Espace du Tourisme d'Île de France** (Tourism Office for Île de France; Map pp436–7; ☎ 08 26 16 66 66, from abroad ☎ 33-1 44 50 19 98; www.pidf.com; Galerie du Carrousel du Louvre; 99 rue de Rivoli, 1er; ☻ 10am-6pm; Ⓜ Palais Royal-Musée du Louvre) in the lower level of the Carrousel du Louvre shopping centre next to IM Pei's inverted glass pyramid. Staff can provide you with information and a free map of destinations in Île de France.

If you're visiting the area under your own steam, pick up a copy of IGN's 1:250,000 scale map *Île de France* (€4.80) or the more compact 1:100,000 scale *Paris et Ses Environs* (€4.90), both available from the **Espace IGN outlet** (p296) just off the av des Champs-Élysées.

ORGANISED TOURS

If you're pressed for time or don't want to do it yourself, several companies organise excursions to destinations outside Paris. Children aged four to 11 generally pay half-price.

Cityrama (Map pp426–7; ☎ 01 44 55 61 00; www.cityrama.fr; 4 place des Pyramides, 1er; Ⓜ Tuileries) This well-established outfit has half-day trips to **Versailles** (€36 to €61), **Chartres** (€55), **Vaux-le-Vicomte** (€57), and **Fontainebleau** and **Barbizon** (€61), as well as many combination trips such as Versailles apartments and Chartres (€97) and Versailles apartments and Fontainebleau (€97).

Paris Vision (Map pp428–9; ☎ 01 47 42 27 40; www.parisvision.com; 20 av de l'Opéra, 9e; Ⓜ place de l'Opéra) This company has eight-hour trips to Versailles and nine-hour ones to **Giverny** and Versailles, and **Auvers-sur-Oise** and Giverny, as well as combination tours that include Paris. Day trips to the destinations in this chapter cost €63 to €116. They also serve destinations further afield such as the **Loire Valley** and **Champagne** (day tours from €145). Departure takes place from its **Rivoli Branch** (Map pp426–7; 01 42 60 30 01; 214 rue de Rivoli, 1e, Ⓜ Tuileries)

Unless otherwise stated, all of the accommodation options listed in this section have showering facilities. Most hotels have nonsmoking rooms. While hotel Internet facilities are uncommon, wi-fi is increasingly available, so those with portable computers should be able to connect in most places.

CHATEAUX

Not all of France's most celebrated chateaux are in the Loire Valley. Versailles (below), one of the most extravagant palaces in the country, is only 21km southwest of Paris. Chantilly (p347), north of Paris, is well known for its artwork and gardens while Fontainebleau (p342), to the south of Paris, is one of the most important Renaissance chateaux in France. Vaux-le-Vicomte (p347), 20km north of Fontainebleau, is a much smaller version of Versailles (the same architects and landscape artist worked on both) and, for many, it's more accessible as a result.

CATHEDRALS

If you haven't had your fill of grand churches in Paris, travel the extra distance southwest to Chartres (p351), where the cathedral is one of the greatest achievements of Western architecture and contains some of the finest examples of medieval stained glass in Europe. The cathedral at Senlis (p350) to the north of Paris, parts of which influenced the construction of the cathedral at Chartres, is just a hop, skip and jump from Chantilly and its wonderful chateau.

ART TOWNS

Giverny (p356), where Claude Monet lived and painted from 1883 to 1926, is in the northwest just over the border from the Île de France in Normandy, but it's still easily accessible from the capital. Less visited but only 35km north of Paris is Auvers-sur-Oise (p357), where van Gogh arrived in May 1890, painted prolifically for just over two months, and then died in the upstairs bedroom of a cheap inn from a self-inflicted bullet wound.

THEME PARKS

It may not be everyone's *tasse de thé* (cup of tea) but kids have decided it's theirs – Disneyland Resort Paris (p359) is now the most popular fee-charging destination in Europe. If globalisation and cultural imperialism have you concerned, however, a home-grown alternative to the American theme park is Parc Astérix (p360). What's more, it's closer to Paris.

VERSAILLES

The prosperous, leafy and very bourgeois suburb of Versailles (population 85,300) is the site of the grandest and most famous palace in France. It served as the kingdom's political capital and the seat of the royal court for more than a century from 1682 to 1789, the year Revolutionary mobs massacred the palace guard and dragged Louis XVI and Marie-Antoinette back to Paris, where they eventually had their heads lopped off.

The enormous Château de Versailles was built in the mid-17th century during the reign of Louis XIV (1643–1715) – the Roi Soleil (Sun King) – to house the entire court of 6000 people, and to project at home and abroad the absolute power of the French monarchy. Its scale and décor also reflect Louis XIV's taste for profligate luxury and his appetite for self-glorification. To accomplish this he hired four very talented men: architect Louis Le Vau; Jules Hardouin-Mansart, who took over from Le Vau in the mid-1670s; painter and interior designer Charles Le Brun; and landscape designer André Le Nôtre, whose workers flattened hills, drained marshes and relocated forests to lay out seemingly endless gardens, ponds and fountains.

Le Brun and his hundreds of artisans decorated every moulding, cornice, ceiling and door of the interior with luxurious and ostentatious appointments: frescoes, marble, gilt

VERSAILLES

0 — 500 m
0 — 0.3 miles

SIGHTS & ACTIVITIES
Académie du Spectacle Équestre..(see 10)
Bassin d'Apollon..............................1 A4
Bassin de Neptune..........................2 C4
Cathédrale St-Louis.........................3 C6
Château Bike Hire............................4 A4
Château Bike Hire............................5 B4
Château de Versailles......................6 C5
Entrée A (Ticket Office)....................7 C5
Entrée B2 (Pass Holders)................8 C5
Entrée C (King's Chamber
  Audioguide Tour)..........................9 C5
Entrée H (Disabled Visitors)........(see 7)
Grand Écurie..................................10 C5
Grand Trianon................................11 A3
Hameau de la Reine.......................12 A2
Jeu de Paume.................................13 C5
Les Grandes Heures du Parlement.14 C5

Musée des Carrosses.................(see 10)
Musée Lambinet............................15 D4
Orangerie......................................16 B5
Parterre du Midi.......................(see 16)
Petit Trianon.................................17 A3
Petite Écurie.................................18 C5
Phébus Bike Hire..........................19 D6
Potager du Roi..............................20 C6
Versailles Tour........................(see 19)

EATING 🍴
À la Ferme....................................21 C6
Au Mandarin Royal.......................22 C4
Crêperie St-Louis..........................23 C5
Le Falher......................................24 C5
Le Potager du Roy........................25 C6
Marché Notre Dame......................26 D4
Monoprix......................................27 D5

Pizzeria Via Veneto.......................28 C5

SLEEPING 🏠
Hôtel d'Angleterre..........................29 C5
Hôtel du Palais..............................30 C5
Royal Hôtel....................................31 C6

TRANSPORT
Bus 171 (To/From Paris)...............32 C5
Local Bus Station...........................33 C5

INFORMATION
CCF Bank.......................................34 D5
Police...35 D5
Post Office.....................................36 C5
Tourist Office.................................37 C5

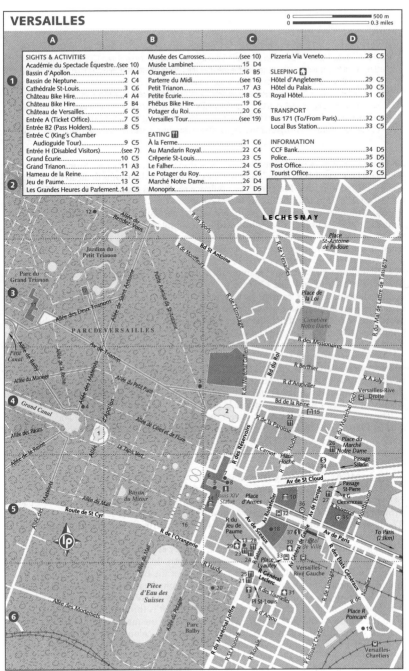

TENNIS COURT OATH

At Versailles in May 1789, in an effort to deal with huge national debt and to moderate dissent by reforming the tax system, Louis XVI convened the États-Généraux (States General). It was a body made up of over 1000 deputies representing the three 'estates': the nobility, the clergy and the so-called third estate (the latter representing the middle classes).

When the third estate's representatives, who formed the majority of the delegates, were denied entry to the usual meeting place of the États-Généraux, they met separately in a room of the **Jeu de Paume** (Royal Tennis Court), where, on 17 June, they constituted themselves as the National Assembly. Three days later they took the famous Serment du Jeu de Paume (Tennis Court Oath), swearing not to dissolve the assembly until Louis XVI had accepted a new constitution. This act of defiance sparked demonstrations of support and, less than a month later, a mob in Paris stormed the prison at Bastille.

and woodcarvings, with themes and symbols drawn from Greek and Roman mythology. The **Grand Appartement du Roi** (King's Suite), for example, includes rooms dedicated to Hercules, Venus, Diana, Mars and Mercury. The opulence reaches its peak in the **Galerie des Glaces** (Hall of Mirrors), a 75m-long ballroom with 17 huge mirrors on one side and, on the other, an equal number of windows looking out on the gardens. The Hall of Mirrors has been undergoing restoration, half of which had been completed by 2006.

The chateau has undergone relatively few alterations since its construction, though almost all the interior furnishings disappeared during the Revolution, and many of the rooms were rebuilt by Louis-Philippe (r 1830–48), who opened part of the chateau to the public. A €370 million renovation and maintenance program that began in late 2003 will affect 25 areas of the chateau and take 17 years.

The chateau complex consists of four main sections: the palace building, a 580m-long structure with innumerable wings, grand halls and sumptuous bedchambers (only parts of which are open to the public); the vast gardens, canals and pools to the west of the palace; the two smaller palaces – the Grand Trianon and, a few hundred metres to the east, the Petit Trianon; and the Hameau de la Reine (Queen's Hamlet).

The **Grands Appartements** (State Apartments) – the main section of the palace building – includes the Galerie des Glaces, the **Appartement de la Reine** (Queen's Suite), the **Musée de l'Histoire de France** (Museum of French History) and other halls and apartments. **Les Grandes Heures du Parlement** (Landmarks in the History of French Parliament), a rather esoteric exhibit on the history of France's Assemblée Nationale, is in the southwestern wing of the chateau.

The section of the vast gardens nearest the palace, laid out between 1661 and 1700 in the formal French style, is famed for its geometrically aligned terraces, flowerbeds, tree-lined paths, ponds and fountains. The many statues of marble, bronze and lead were by the most talented sculptors of the period. The more pastoral English-style **Jardins du Petit Trianon** have meandering, sheltered paths.

The **Grand Canal**, 1.6km long and 62m wide, is oriented to reflect the setting sun. It's traversed by the 1km-long **Petit Canal**, creating a cross-shaped body of water with a perimeter of over 5.5km. Louis XIV used to hold boating parties here. In summer you can paddle around the Grand Canal in four-person rowing boats; the dock is at the canal's eastern end. The **Orangerie**, built below the Parterre du Midi (a flowerbed) on the southwestern side of the palace by Le Vau in 1663, houses exotic plants in winter.

The gardens' largest fountains are the 17th-century **Bassin de Neptune** (Neptune's Fountain), 300m north of the palace, and the **Bassin d'Apollon** (Apollo's Fountain), built in 1668 at the eastern end of the Grand Canal. The straight side of the Bassin de Neptune abuts a small, round pond graced by a winged dragon. Emerging from the water in the centre of the Bassin d'Apollon is Apollo's chariot, pulled by rearing horses. There are **Grande Perspective** and **Grandes Eaux Musicales** fountain displays during the warmer months throughout the grounds.

In the middle of the park, about 1.5km northwest of the main building, are two smaller palaces, each surrounded by neat flowerbeds. The pink-colonnaded **Grand Trianon** was built in 1687 for Louis XIV and his family as a place of escape from the rigid etiquette of the court. Napoleon I had it renovated in the Empire style.

The much smaller, ochre-coloured **Petit Trianon**, built in the 1760s, was redecorated in 1867 by Empress Eugénie (the consort of Napoleon III) who added Louis XVI–style furnishings similar to the uninspiring pieces that now fill its 1st-floor rooms.

A bit further north is the **Hameau de la Reine**, a mock village of thatched cottages constructed from 1775 to 1784 for the amusement of Marie-Antoinette, who liked to play milkmaid here.

Because so many people consider it a must-see destination, Versailles attracts more than three million visitors a year. The best way to avoid the queues is to arrive first thing in the morning; if you're interested in just the Grands Appartements, another good time to get here is about 3.30pm or 4pm. The queues are longest on Tuesday, when many of Paris' museums are closed, and on Sunday.

The entrance for disabled visitors is Entrée H, northwest of Entrée A. You can ring ☎ 01 30 83 76 20 for general information or ☎ 01 30 83 75 05 for information about facilities for visitors with a disability.

Like its chateau, the attractive town of **Versailles**, crisscrossed by wide boulevards, is a creation of Louis XIV. Most of today's buildings, however, date from the 18th and 19th centuries. Av de St-Cloud, av de Paris and av de Sceaux, the three wide thoroughfares that fan out eastwards from place d'Armes in front of the chateau, are separated by two stables dating from the late 17th century. The recently restored **Grande Écurie** (Big Stables) contains the **Musée des Carrosses** (Coach Museum) as well as the **Académie du Spectacle Équestre** (Academy of Equestrian Arts), where riding and dressage displays are held. The **Petite Écurie** (Little Stables) is occupied by Versailles' celebrated school of architecture.

Some 100m southwest of the Petite Écurie is the **Jeu de Paume** (Royal Tennis Court), which was built in 1686 and played a pivotal role in the Revolution about a century later (see the boxed text, opposite). South of this is **Le Potager du Roi** (King's Kitchen Garden), which was built on 9 hectares of land in the late 17th century to meet the enormous catering requirements of the court. It retains its original patch divisions as well as some very old apple and pear orchards, and produces 70 tonnes of vegetables and fruit a year.

In the same *quartier* (neighbourhood), one of the prettiest in Versailles, is the neoclassical (and slightly baroque) **Cathédrale St-Louis**, a harmonious if austere work by Hardouin-Mansart. It was built between 1743 (when Louis XV himself laid the first stone) and 1754, and made a cathedral in 1802. It is known for its 3636-pipe Cliquot organ and is decorated with a

DID YOU KNOW?

The chateau at Versailles counts 700 rooms, 2153 windows, 352 chimneys and 11 hectares of roofing set on 900 hectares of garden, park and wood. The walls and rooms are adorned with 6300 paintings, 2000 sculptures and statues, 15,000 engravings and 5000 decorative art objects and furnishings.

TRANSPORT

Distance from Paris 21km

Direction Southwest

Travel time 35 minutes by RER/train

Car Route A13 from Porte de St-Cloud, exit 'Versailles Château'.

Bus 171 (€1.40 or one metro/bus ticket) from Pont de Sèvres (15e) to place d'Armes every eight to 15 minutes daily, with the last bus leaving Versailles just before 1am. It's faster to go by RER and you'll have to get to/from Pont de Sèvres metro station on line 9.

RER The RER line C5 (€2.55) from Paris' Left Bank RER stations to Versailles-Rive Gauche station is only 700m southeast of the chateau and is close to the tourist office. There are up to 70 trains a day (half that number on Sunday), with one every 15 minutes. The last train back to Paris leaves shortly before midnight. RER line C8 (€2.55) links Paris' Left Bank with Versailles-Chantiers station, a 1.3km walk from the chateau.

SNCF From Paris' Gare St-Lazare (€3.40) SNCF operates about 70 trains a day to Versailles-Rive Droite, which is 1.2km from the chateau. The last train to Paris leaves just after midnight. Versailles-Chantiers is also served by some 30 SNCF trains a day (20 on Sunday) from Gare Montparnasse; all trains on this line continue to Chartres (€9.90, 45 to 60 minutes).

number of interesting paintings and stained-glass panels. To the northeast of the chateau just around the corner from the Versailles-Rive Droite train station, and housed in a lovely 18th-century residence, the **Musée Lambinet** (Lambinet Museum) displays 18th-century furnishings (ceramics, sculpture, paintings and furniture) and objects connected with the history of Versailles, including the all-important Revolutionary period.

Information

CCF bank (17-19 rue du Maréchal Foch, Versailles; ⊙ 9am-5pm Mon-Fri)

Office de Tourisme de Versailles (Tourist Office; ☎ 01 39 24 88 88; www.versailles-tourisme.com; 2bis av de Paris, Versailles; ⊙ 9am-7pm Apr-Oct, 9am-6pm Tue-Sat, 9am-5pm Sun & Mon Nov-Mar) The tourist office has themed guided tours (adult/child €8/4) of the city throughout the week, year-round.

Post office (av de Paris, Versailles; ⊙ 8am-7pm Mon-Fri, 8am-noon Sat) On the opposite side of av de Paris from the tourist office.

Sights

Académie du Spectacle Équestre (Academy of Equestrian Arts; www.acadequestre.fr; ☎ 01 39 02 07 14; Grande Écurie, 1 av Rockefeller, Versailles; morning dressage adult/student & child 5-16 yr €8/4; ⊙ 9am-1pm Tue-Fri & 11am-3pm Sat & Sun Feb-Dec) In addition to the regular dressage displays held at 10.30am, the Academy also presents the 'Reprise musicale', a show with music, lighting and equestrian choreography – the show is held each year during July and August, on Saturday nights at 8.30pm (adult/student & child €20/10) and Sunday afternoons at 3.30pm (adult/student & child €16/8); call in advance for information and reservations. All dressage sessions and shows include a visit to the stables.

Appartement de Louis XIV & **Appartements du Dauphin et de la Dauphine** (King's Chamber; Château de Versailles; 1hr audioguide adult before/after 3.30pm €8/6, child under 10 free; ⊙ 9am-5.30pm Apr-Oct, 9am-4.30pm Nov-Mar) This ticket includes entrance to Musée des Carrosses. The audioguide included in the ticket is available at Entrée C; buying tickets here is also a good way to avoid the queues at Entrée A.

Cathédrale St-Louis (☎ 01 39 50 40 65; 4 place St-Louis, Versailles; ⊙ 8.30am-noon & 2-7.45pm)

Château bike hire (☎ 01 39 66 97 66; Château de Versailles; half-/1hr €3/6, half-/full day €13.50/15; ⊙ 10am-sunset Mon-Fri & 1pm-sunset Sat & Sun Jun-mid-Sep, 10am-sunset Sat & Sun Feb-May & mid-Sep-Nov) Rent these bicycles from kiosks at Petite Venise at the eastern end of the Grand Canal and next to Grille de la Reine. The bike hire closes when the gardens close, which varies according to season.

Château de Versailles (☎ 01 30 83 78 00, 01 30 83 77 77; www.chateauversailles.fr; Château de Versailles, Grande Ecurie; 1-day pass Apr-Oct adult/child €20/6, Nov-Mar €15.50/4; ⊙ 9am-6.30pm Tue-Sun Apr-Oct, 9am-5.30pm Tue-Sun Nov-Mar) The Passport (one-day pass) allows entry via Entrée B2 to the Grands Appartements, Appartement de Louis XIV, the Trianons, the gardens, Musée des Carrosses and fountain displays.

Château English-language guided tours (☎ 01 30 83 77 88; Château de Versailles; 1-/1½-/2hr tours adult €5/7/9.50, child 10-17 yr €4/5.50/7; ⊙ 9am-3.45pm Tue-Sun Nov-Mar, 9am-4pm Tue-Sun Apr-Oct) Tickets for the tours only are sold at Entrée D; they begin across the courtyard at Entrée F and must be booked ahead. All tours require you to purchase a ticket to the Grands Appartements. If you buy it at Entrée C or Entrée D you can later avoid the Grands Appartements queue at Entrée A by going straight to Entrée B.

Château gardens (Château de Versailles; Apr-Oct fountain displays adult/under 18 €3/free, Apr-Oct admission free except during fountain displays, Nov-Mar admission free; ⊙ 9am-sunset Apr-Oct, 8am-sunset Nov-Mar) The gardens are free for everyone except during weekends in summer when the Grandes Eaux Musicales fountain displays are held.

Grand Canal rowing boats (☎ 01 39 66 97 66; Château de Versailles; per half-/1hr €8/11; ⊙ Mar-Nov)

Grande Perspective & Grandes Eaux Musicales fountain displays (Château de Versailles; adult/student & child 11-18yr €7/5.50, admission free for all after 4.50pm; ⊙ 11am-noon & 3.30-5pm Sat early-May-late-Sep, 11am-noon & 3.30-5pm Sun early-Apr-early-Oct) On the same days the Bassin de Neptune flows for 10 minutes from 5.20pm.

Grand Trianon & Petit Trianon (Château de Versailles; adult before/after 3.30pm €5/3, under 18 free; ⊙ noon-6.30pm Apr-Oct, noon-5.30pm Nov-Mar)

Grands Appartements (State Apartments; Château de Versailles; adult before/after 3.30pm €8/6, under 18 free, 1hr audioguide €4.50; ⊙ 9am-6.30pm Tue-Sun Apr-Oct, 9am-5.30pm Tue-Sun Nov-Mar) This is the main section of the palace that can be visited without a guided tour. Tickets are on sale at Entrée A, to the right of the equestrian statue of Louis XIV as you approach the palace.

Jeu de Paume (Royal Tennis Court; ☎ 01 30 83 77 88; 1 rue du Jeu de Paume, Versailles; admission free; ⊙ 12.30-6.30pm Sat & Sun Apr-Oct)

Le Potager du Roi (King's Kitchen Garden; ☎ 01 39 24 62 62; 10 rue du Maréchal Joffre, Versailles; adult weekday/weekend €4.50/6.50, student & child 6-18 yr €3; ⊙ 10am-6pm Apr-Oct)

Musée des Carrosses (Coach Museum; ☎ 01 30 83 77 88; Grande Écurie, 1 av Rockefeller, Versailles; adult/under 18 €2/free; ⊙ 9am-6.30pm Sat & Sun Apr-Oct)

Musée Lambinet (Lambinet Museum; ☎ 01 39 50 30 32; 54 blvd de la Reine, Versailles; adult/student & child €5.30/2.50, 1st Sun of the month free; ⏰ 2-6pm Tue, Thu, Sat & Sun, 1-6pm Wed, 2-5pm Fri)

Phébus bike hire (☎ 01 39 20 16 60; www.phebus.tm.fr in French; place Raymond Poincaré, Versailles; 1hr/half-day €2/10; ⏰ 7-10am & 4-8pm Mon-Fri Sep-Jun, 7-10am & 4-8pm daily Jul & Aug) This place in front of the Versailles-Chantiers train station rents out bicycles; a deposit of €300 is required.

Versailles Tour (☎ 0810 001 722; day pass adult/child €10/5; ⏰ 9.30am-6.30pm Tue-Sun late-Apr-Jun, Sep & Oct,

CITY ESCAPES: FRANCE FURTHER AFIELD

There is life beyond Paris! If you have the time for more than just a day trip, some major metropolitan destinations in France – while many miles away – are actually easily and quickly reached on France's train system. Thanks to very fast TGV *(train à grande vitesse)* trains, of which the French are inordinately proud, many of the most exciting and scenic cities in provincial France are all within a few hours of the capital.

The only negative is the cost, which can vary greatly. The trick to getting cut-price tickets is to book as early as possible. Early-bird tickets, called *'prems'* (firsts), are usually much, much cheaper than full-price tickets and you should snap them up about two months before your journey. From one month prior to the date of travel, prices will rise considerably, but last-minute tickets are made available on Tuesdays, for the coming weekend. Prices also tend to increase around public holidays. Tickets can be purchased online from the Sociéte' Nationale des Chemins de Fer (SNCF) at www.sncf.com or from its offices.

Five ideas for ambitious train escapes from Paris that can be done in a weekend:

Lille (www.lille-tourism.com; €60 to €100 return, one hour from Paris Gare du Nord) Right on the border with Belgium, Lille is known for its rich cultural life, good restaurants and Flemish influences. Many Lillois pop over to Brussels to go partying on weekends.

Lyon (www.lyon-france.com; €50 to €150 return, two hours from Paris Gare de Lyon) In just two hours you can find yourself in this eminent city, famed for its wealth of historical sites and fine gastronomy. It also makes a good base for outdoor activities in the surrounding countryside.

Marseille (www.marseille-tourisme.com; €50 to €180 return, three hours from Paris Gare de Montparnasse) The Mediterranean may seem a bit far-fetched when talking about getaways from Paris, but sunny, cosmopolitan Marseille is easily accessible and makes a refreshing change. In just three hours you can be by the old port, sipping *pastis* (aniseed-flavoured alcoholic drink) and eating bouillabaisse…

Rennes (www.ville-rennes.fr; €50 to €140 return, two hours from Paris Gare de Montparnasse) This charming university town is the capital of Brittany. There is a lovely old city with creperies, churches and picturesque half-timbered houses.

Tours (www.ligeris.com; €40 to €100 return, 1¼ hours from Paris Gare de Montparnasse & Gare d'Austerlitz) The town is pretty, though nothing spectacular, with great cafés and a friendly university atmosphere. More importantly, however, Tours can function as the gateway to the magnificent castles of the Loire valley, including the Châteaux de Chenonceau and Chambord, which can be visited on day trips.

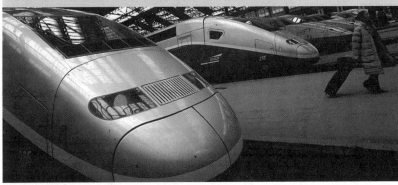

TGV trains at Gare de Lyon

to 5pm Jul & Aug) A tour bus run by Cityrama. The yellow buses do a circuit of the town that takes in both train stations (Versailles-Rive Droite and Versailles-Rive Gauche) as well as destinations inside the chateau grounds and the place St-Louis. Short-ride tickets are not available. If you have a Paris Open Tour Pass your day ticket at Versailles will only cost €8. You get information on headphones in six languages. There is no address per se in Versailles but the tourist office can give you information. You can also call the local transport company **Phebus** (01 39 20 16 20) for information.

Eating

À la Ferme (☎ 01 39 53 10 81; 3 rue du Maréchal Joffre, Versailles; starters €6-10, mains €10.50-15, menu lunch/dinner €14.50/21.80; ☾ lunch & dinner to 11pm Wed-Sun) 'At the Farm' specialises in grilled meats and the cuisine of southwest France. It's next door to le Potager du Roy and is much cheaper and more relaxed.

Au Mandarin Royal (☎ 01 39 50 48 03; 5 rue de Ste-Geneviève, Versailles; menu lunch/dinner €10/13.60 & 18; ☾ lunch Tue-Sun & dinner to 11pm Mon-Sat) This decent restaurant, not far from Musée Lambinet, also serves Vietnamese dishes.

Crêperie St-Louis (☎ 01 39 53 40 12; 33 rue du Vieux Versailles, Versailles; menus lunch & dinner €10-15; ☾ lunch & dinner to 11pm) A warm little Breton place that's very popular for lunch, with sweet and savoury crepes and *galettes* (savoury buckwheat pancakes; €3 to €8.50).

Le Falher (☎ 01 39 50 57 43; 22 rue Satory, Versailles; starters €14-20, mains €23-28, menu lunch/dinner €24/29 & 44; ☾ lunch Mon-Fri & dinner to 10.30pm Tue-Sat) This quiet and elegant place not far from the palace has French gastronomic *menus* (set menus).

Le Potager du Roy (☎ 01 39 50 35 34; 1 rue du Maréchal Joffre, Versailles; menus €33 & €48; ☾ lunch & dinner to 10.30pm Tue-Sat) This is a refined place with traditional *cuisine bourgeoise* (high-quality home cooking).

Pizzeria Via Veneto (☎ 01 39 51 03 89; 20 rue Satory, Versailles; mains €7-12; ☾ lunch & dinner to 11pm) A

modern restaurant with cosy tables, the Veneto serves pizzas and pasta dishes.

CHEAP EATS

Marché Notre Dame (place du Marché Notre Dame, Versailles; ☾ 7.30am-1.30pm Tue, Fri & Sun) If headed for this outdoor food market from the tourist office, enter via passage Saladin (33 av de St-Cloud). There are also food halls (open 7am to 1pm and 3.30pm to 7.30pm Tuesday to Saturday, and 7am to 2pm Sunday) surrounding the marketplace.

Monoprix (9 rue Georges Clemenceau, Versailles; ☾ 8.30am-8.55pm Mon-Sat) This department store north of av de Paris has a large supermarket section.

Sleeping

Hôtel d'Angleterre (☎ 01 39 51 43 50; www.hotel -angleterre-versailles.com; 2bis rue de Fontenay, Versailles; s €55-66, d & tw €72-87). Less than 300m from the chateau entrance, and around the corner from the Jeu de Paume, is this charming 18-room hotel. The clean, attractive rooms are very modern – aside from the red velvet curtains and squishy mattresses. Some rooms are considerably smaller and pokier than others.

Hôtel du Palais (☎ 01 39 50 39 29, hotelpalais@ ifrance.com; 6 place Lyautey, Versailles; d €50-55) A warm and well-kept 24-room hotel, very centrally placed across the street from the Versailles-Rive Gauche train station and in front of the local bus station. The bright hallways are more appealing than the rooms, which are inexpensive and very clean but thoroughly bland.

Royal Hôtel (☎ 01 39 50 67 31; www.royalhotel versailles.com; 23 rue Royale, Versailles; d €58-67, tr €85) In the delightful St-Louis neighbourhood, this hotel displays some character and a deep fondness for patterned wallpaper. The smallish rooms are on the verge of being pretty, with an odd mix of bulk furnishings and old-fashioned touches.

FONTAINEBLEAU

The town of Fontainebleau (population 17,811) is known for its elegant Renaissance chateau – one of France's largest royal residences – with splendid furnishings that make it particularly worth visiting. It's much less crowded and pressured than Versailles, and it is surrounded by the beautiful **Forêt de Fontainebleau** (Forest of Fontainebleau), a favourite hunting ground of many French kings and now immensely popular for activities like walking and rock climbing.

Today the lifeblood of Fontainebleau is the international graduate business school **Insead** (www.insead.edu) that brings in around 2000 students each year. The town has also become a popular residence for middle-class French and expatriate English families. Many work in Paris but choose to live here for the safe, healthy living space, or what some locals refer to as Fontainebleau's 'Swiss ambience'. The town is becoming increasingly dynamic – the influx of people and money has been accompanied by an increase in the number of swish cafés, restaurants and bars, as well as cultural events like art exhibitions and concerts.

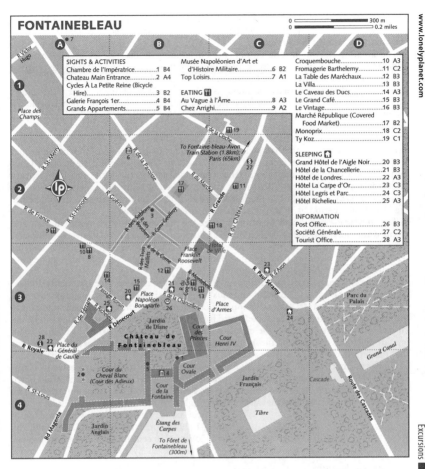

FONTAINEBLEAU

0 ——————— 300 m
0 ——————— 0.2 miles

SIGHTS & ACTIVITIES
Chambre de l'Impératrice.............1 B4
Chateau Main Entrance.................2 A4
Cycles À La Petite Reine (Bicycle
  Hire)......................................3 B2
Galerie François 1er....................4 B4
Grands Appartements...................5 B4

Musée Napoléonien d'Art et
  d'Histoire Militaire...................6 B2
Top Loisirs................................7 A1

EATING
Au Vague à l'Âme........................8 A3
Chez Arrighi..............................9 A2

Croquembouche........................10 A3
Fromagerie Barthelemy................11 C2
La Table des Maréchaux...............12 B3
La Villa...................................13 B3
Le Caveau des Ducs....................14 A3
Le Grand Café...........................15 B3
Le Vintage...............................16 B3
Marché République (Covered
  Food Market)...........................17 B2
Monoprix................................18 C2
Ty Koz...................................19 C1

SLEEPING
Grand Hôtel de l'Aigle Noir........20 B3
Hôtel de la Chancellerie.............21 B3
Hôtel de Londres.......................22 A3
Hôtel La Carpe d'Or...................23 C3
Hôtel Legris et Parc...................24 C3
Hôtel Richelieu.........................25 A3

INFORMATION
Post Office..............................26 B3
Société Générale.......................27 C2
Tourist Office...........................28 A3

The enormous, 1900-room **Château de Fontainebleau** (the list of former tenants or visitors is like a who's who of French royalty) is one of the most beautifully decorated and furnished chateaux in France. Walls and ceilings are richly adorned with wood panelling, gilded carvings, frescoes, tapestries and paintings. The parquet floors are of the finest woods, the fireplaces are decorated with exceptional carvings, and many of the pieces of furniture are originals dating back to the Renaissance.

The first chateau on this site was built in the early 12th century and enlarged by Louis IX a century later. Only a single medieval tower survived the energetic Renaissance-style reconstruction undertaken by François I (r 1515–47), whose superb artisans, many of them brought over from Italy, blended Italian and French styles to create what is known as the First School of Fontainebleau. The *Mona Lisa* once hung here amid other fine artworks of the royal collection.

During the latter half of the 16th century, the chateau was further enlarged by Henri II (r 1547–59), Catherine de Médicis and Henri IV (r 1589–1610), whose Flemish and French artists created the Second School of Fontainebleau. Even Louis XIV got in on the act: it was he who hired Le Nôtre to redesign the gardens.

Fontainebleau, which was not damaged during the Revolution (though its furniture was stolen or destroyed), was beloved and much restored by Napoleon Bonaparte. Napoleon III was another frequent visitor.

During WWII the chateau was turned into a German headquarters. After it was liberated by US General George Patton in 1944, part of the complex served as Allied and then NATO headquarters from 1945 to 1965.

The **Grands Appartements** include a number of outstanding rooms. The spectacular **Chapelle de la Trinité** (Trinity Chapel), with ornamentation dating from the first half of the 17th century, is where Louis XV married Marie Leczinska in 1725 and where the future Napoleon III was christened in 1810. **Galerie François 1er** (François I Gallery), a jewel of Renaissance architecture, was decorated from 1533 to 1540 by Il Rosso, a Florentine follower of Michelangelo. In the wood panelling François I's monogram appears repeatedly along with his emblem, a dragon-like salamander.

The **Salle de Bal** (Ballroom), a 30m-long room dating from the mid-16th century that was also used for receptions and banquets, is renowned for its mythological frescoes, marquetry floor and Italian-inspired coffered ceiling. The large windows afford views of the Cour Ovale (Oval Courtyard) and the gardens. The gilded bed in the 17th- and 18th-century **Chambre de l'Impératrice** (Empress' Bedroom) was never used by Marie-Antoinette, for whom it was built in 1787. The gilding in the **Salle du Trône** (Throne Room), the royal bedroom before the Napoleonic period, is in three shades: gold, green and yellow.

The **Petits Appartements** (Small Apartments) were the private apartments of the emperor and empress and the **Musée Napoléon 1er** (Napoleon I Museum) contains personal effects – uniforms, hats, coats, ornamental swords and knick-knacks – that belonged to Napoleon and his relatives. Neither place has fixed opening hours, and they must be visited with a guide for a separate fee. Ask at the main ticket counter.

As successive monarchs added their own wings to the chateau, five irregularly shaped courtyards were created. The oldest and most interesting is the **Cour Ovale**, no longer oval but U-shaped due to Henri IV's construction work. It incorporates the keep, the sole remnant of the medieval chateau. The largest courtyard is the **Cour du Cheval Blanc** (Courtyard of the White Horse), from where you enter the chateau. Napoleon, about to be exiled to Elba in 1814, bid farewell to his guards from the magnificent 17th-century **double-horseshoe staircase** here. For that reason the courtyard is also called the Cour des Adieux (Farewell Courtyard).

On the northern side of the chateau is the **Jardin de Diane**, a formal garden created by Catherine de Médicis. Le Nôtre's formal, 17th-century **Jardin Français** (French Garden), also known as the Grand Parterre, is east of the **Cour de la Fontaine** (Fountain Courtyard) and the **Étang des Carpes** (Carp Pond). The informal **Jardin Anglais** (English Garden), laid out in 1812, is west of the pond. The **Grand Canal** was excavated in 1609 and predates the canals at Versailles by over half a century. The **Forêt de Fontainebleau**, crisscrossed by paths, begins 500m south of the chateau.

The **Musée Napoléonien d'Art et d'Histoire Militaire** (Napoleonic Museum of Art & Military History), not to be confused with the similarly named museum in the chateau itself, is housed in a 19th-century mansion and has seven rooms filled with military uniforms and weapons. Particularly lovely **gardens** surround the mansion.

The town is surrounded by the magnificent **Forêt de Fontainebleau**, which is hugely popular with walkers and climbers; see the boxed text, opposite.

If you're looking to stop somewhere on the way, the pretty little town of **Barbizon** (around 7km from Fontainebleau) has some lovely art galleries and some sweet hotels, but few social options. It is the birthplace of the 19th-century Barbizon school of landscape painting.

TRANSPORT

Distance from Paris 67km

Direction Southeast

Travel time 35 to 60 minutes by SNCF train

Car Route A6 from Porte d'Orléans, direction Lyon, exit 'Fontainebleau'.

Bus The train station is linked with central Fontainebleau (€1.30), 2km to the southwest, every 10 minutes from about 6am until about 9.30pm (11.30pm on Sunday). The last train back to Paris leaves Fontainebleau a bit after 9.45pm weekdays, just after 10pm on Saturday and sometime after 10.30pm on Sunday.

SNCF Up to 30 daily SNCF commuter trains link Paris' Gare de Lyon with Fontainebleau-Avon station (€7.50). A package (adult/4-9 yr/10-17 yr €20.80/7.70/16) includes return transport from Paris, bus transfers and admission to the chateau.

THE FOREST OF FONTAINEBLEAU

The **Forêt de Fontainebleau**, a 20,000-hectare wood surrounding the town, is one of the loveliest forests in the region. The national walking trails **GR1** and **GR11** are excellent for jogging, walking, cycling and horse riding. For climbers, in particular, the forest is a veritable paradise. Rock climbing enthusiasts have long come to its sandstone ridges, rich in cliffs and overhangs, to hone their skills before setting off for the Alps. The area presents a whole range of difficulties so anyone from bumbling beginners to expert climbers will find their feet. There are different grades marked by colours, with white representing easy climbs (suitable for children) and black representing climbs up and over death-defying boulders. The website http://bleau.info has stacks of information in English on climbing in Fontainebleau.

If you want to give it a go, you can contact **Top Loisirs** (☎ 01 60 74 08 50; www.toploisirs.fr; 16 rue Sylvain Collinet, Fontainebleau) about equipment hire and instruction. Two gorges worth visiting are the **Gorges d'Apremont**, about 7km northwest of Fontainebleau near **Barbizon**, and the **Gorges de Franchard**, a few kilometres south of Gorges d'Apremont. The tourist office sells the comprehensive *Fontainebleau Climbs* (€25), newly translated into English.

The area is covered by IGN's 1:25,000 scale *Forêt de Fontainebleau* map (No 2417OT; €9). The tourist office sells the *Guide des Sentiers de Promenades dans le Massif Forestier de Fontainebleau* (€7.60), whose maps and text (in French) cover almost 20 walks in the forest. It also sells the comprehensive *La Forêt de Fontainebleau* (€12.50), published by the Office National des Forêts (ONF; National Forests Office) which features almost 32 walks.

Information

Office de Tourisme de Pays de Fontainebleau (Tourist Office; ☎ 01 60 74 99 99; www.fontainebleau-tourisme .com; 4 rue Royale, Fontainebleau; 🕓 10am-6pm Mon-Sat, 10am-12.30pm & 3-5pm Sun Apr-Oct, 10am-1pm Sun Nov-Mar). The tourist office, in a converted petrol station a couple of hundred metres west of the chateau, hires out bicycles (half-/full day €15/19). It also offers self-paced audioguide tours (€4.60) of both the palace and the Forêt de Fontaine-bleau in English, with each tour lasting 30 minutes.

Post office (2 rue de la Chancellerie, Fontainebleau; 🕓 8.15am-7pm Mon-Fri, 8.15am-noon Sat)

Société Générale (102 rue Grande, Fontainebleau; 🕓 8.35am-12.30pm & 1.30-5.25pm Mon-Fri, 8.35am-12.30pm & 1.30-4.25pm Sat)

Sights

Château de Fontainebleau (☎ 01 60 71 50 70; www .musee-chateau-fontainebleau.fr in French; Château de Fontainebleau, place Général de Gaulle; adult/under 18/18-25 yr €6.50/free/4.50, 1st Sun of the month for all €4; 🕓 9.30am-6pm Wed-Mon Jun-Sep, 9.30am-5pm Wed-Mon Oct-May) Conducted tours, in English, of the Grands Appartements usually depart at 2.30pm July to September from the staircase near the ticket windows, but check with staff.

Château gardens & courtyards (Château de Fontaine-bleau; admission free; 🕓 9am-7pm May-Sep, 9am-6pm Mar, Apr & Oct, 9am-5pm Nov-Feb)

Cycles À La Petite Reine (☎ 01 60 74 57 57; 32 rue des Sablons, Fontainebleau; hire per hr €5, half-/full day Mon-Fri €10/13, half-/full day Sat & Sun €13/16, week €54; 🕓 9am-7.30pm Mon-Sat, 9am-6pm Sun) This place rents out mountain bikes and requires a deposit (credit card accepted) of €305.

Musée Napoléonien d'Art et d'Histoire Militaire (Napo-leonic Museum of Art & Military History; ☎ 01 60 74 64 89; 88 rue St-Honoré, Fontainebleau; adult/under 12/student & 12-18 yr €3/free/2.30; museum 🕓 2-5.30pm Tue-Sat, gardens 🕓 10am-7pm Mon-Sat mid-Mar–mid-Nov, 10am-5pm Tue-Sat mid-Nov–mid-Mar) A ticket to this museum also allows for entry to the Petits Appartements.

Petits Appartements & Musée Napoléon 1er (Small Apartments & Napoleon I Museum; Château de Fontaine-bleau; adult/under 18/18-25 yr €3/free/2.30)

Top Loisirs (☎ 01 60 74 08 50; www.toploisirs.fr; 16 rue Sylvain Collinet, Fontainebleau)

Eating

Au Vague à l'Âme (☎ 01 60 72 10 32; 39 rue de France, Fontainebleau; crepes & galettes €2.50-9.50, menus lunch €11.50-16, dinner €25 & €35; 🕓 lunch Tue-Sun, dinner to 1am Tue-Sat) This friendly café-restaurant is the place to come for Breton specialities including fresh oysters and an oyster terrine to die for.

Chez Arrighi (☎ 01 64 22 29 43; 53 rue de France, Fontainebleau; menus €16.50-33; 🕓 lunch & dinner to 11pm Tue-Sun) High quality cuisine, including seafood and Corsican specialities, are served here in a traditional if slightly tired-looking setting. You can get a jug of wine for €7 – not to be scoffed at.

Croquembouche (☎ 01 64 22 01 57; 43 rue de France, Fontainebleau; menus lunch €25, €35; 🕓 lunch Fri-Tue, dinner to 10.30pm Thu-Sat, Mon & Tue) Get past the glazed looks and austere décor, as this restaurant has impeccable service and excellent, finely presented cuisine – like beef fillet with foie gras, or delicate fish in refined sauces – as well as some top wines. A place of similar quality in Paris would be considerably more expensive.

La Table des Maréchaux (☎ 01 60 39 55 50; 9 rue Grande, Fontainebleau; starters €13-18, mains €23-25, menu lunch/dinner €28/35 & 40; 🕐 lunch & dinner to 11pm) Situated in the fancy Hôtel Napoléon, this romantic restaurant serves delicious, inventive cuisine: traditional French inspired by foreign flavours and exotic spices. The indoor courtyard with its pretty tables and flowers is a must in summer.

La Villa (☎ 01 01 72 04 05; 10 rue de Montebello, Fontainebleau; starters €8-14, mains €15-18; 🕐 lunch & dinner to 11pm) With its purple-plush furnishings and mood lighting, this restaurant and cocktail lounge is a kind of wannabe version of Paris' swish Costes bars. The trendy food is mainly classic French; the cocktails cost €8.

Le Caveau des Ducs (☎ 01 64 22 05 05; 24 rue de Ferrare, Fontainebleau; salads €13-19, mains €15-23, menus lunch €21, dinner €24-41; 🕐 lunch & dinner) With its exposed beams, red tapestries and intimate stone cellars, not to mention the warm fire in winter, this makes an atmospheric little spot for a meal. The cellar dates from the 17th century. It also has a small terrace outside. At lunch you can get a giant salad with a glass of wine for €13 to €19.

Le Grand Café (☎ 01 64 22 20 32; 33 rue Napoléon Bonaparte, Fontainebleau; mains €9-15; 🕐 7am-1am) This modern café is spacious and airy, with a long welcoming bar and a warm atmosphere. It's a good place for coffee, simple meals and crepes; on weekends food is served all day long.

Le Vintage (☎ 01 60 72 75 13; 8 rue de Montebello, Fontainebleau; light meals & salads €8-11; 🕐 5pm-midnight Mon-Sat, 10.30am-5pm Sun) A barometer of Fontainebleau's increasing pretension, this slick, contemporary-design wine bar has an impressive wine list (available in English) and a good selection of whiskies.

They also offer simple, well-thought *assiettes* (plates) like cheese and *charcuterie* (cured, smoked or processed meat product) platters. If you don't finish your bottle you can take it home with you. Ask about live jazz evenings.

Ty Koz (☎ 01 64 22 00 55; 18 rue de la Cloche, Fontainebleau; crepes & galettes €2.60-10.20; 🕐 lunch & dinner to 10pm) Recently renovated, this little Breton place down a small alleyway north of the centre has excellent crepes and galettes.

CHEAP EATS

Fromagerie Barthelemy (☎ 01 64 22 21 64; 92 rue Grande, Fontainebleau; 🕐 8.30am-12.30pm & 3.30-7.30pm Tue-Thu, 8am-1.30pm & 3.30-7.30pm Fri & Sat, 8.30am-12.30pm Sun) This branch of the famous cheese-mongers in Paris is one of the finest cheese shops in the Île de France.

Marché République (rue des Pins, Fontainebleau; 🕐 8am-1pm Tue, Fri & Sun) Fontainebleau's covered food market is just north of the central pedestrian area.

Monoprix (58 rue Grande, Fontainebleau; 🕐 8.45am-7.45pm Mon-Sat, 9am-1pm Sun) This department store has a supermarket section on the 1st floor.

Sleeping

Fontainebleau has a wide range of accommodation suitable for all budgets but some of its top-end hotels are very fine indeed.

Grand Hôtel de l'Aigle Noir (☎ 01 60 74 60 00; fax 01 60 74 60 01; www.hotelaiglenoir.fr; 27 pl Napoléon Bonaparte, Fontainebleau; d €140-280; 🏊 🖳 🖨 🚹) Recently given an immaculate refurbishment by its ancestral owners, this fancy private mansion has been opposite the chateau since the 17th century. Today it's all rich elegance and international service with a gorgeous pool, grand period furnishings and plush suites.

Hôtel de la Chancellerie (☎ 01 64 22 21 70; hotel.chancellerie@gofornet.com; 1 rue de la Chancellerie, Fontainebleau; s €43, d €53-60) This hotel opposite the post office has 25 plain, old-fashioned but spotless rooms. The walls are somewhat thin. Rates are about €10 more from April to October.

Hôtel de Londres (☎ 01 64 22 20 21; www.hoteldelondres.com; 1 place du Général de Gaulle, Fontainebleau; d €90-138, ste €160) Classy, cosy and beautifully kept, this hotel is attractively furnished in warm reds and royal blues. Many of the rooms here have balconies and gorgeous chateau views. The breakfast room is particularly lovely.

Hôtel La Carpe d'Or (☎ 01 64 22 28 64; fax 01 64 22 39 95; 7 rue d'Avon, Fontainebleau; s €39, d & tw €53) This unremarkable hotel northeast of the place d'Armes has 16 basic but comfortable rooms, but it's perilously close to a tacky nightclub.

Produce inside Fromagerie Barthelemy

Hôtel Legris et Parc (☎ 01 64 22 24 24; legris
.et.parc@wanadoo.fr; 36 rue Paul Séramy, Fontainebleau;
d €90-120; 🏊) Adjacent to the palace park, this lovely
32-room hotel is in a 17th-century residence where Jean
Racine apparently once laid his head. The hotel has a
lovely swimming pool and an excellent restaurant called
L'Éden.

Hôtel Richelieu (☎ 01 64 22 26 46; fax 01 64 23 40 17;
richelieu.bacchus@wanadoo.fr; 4 rue Richelieu, Fontainebleau; s €42-59, d €48-65) Clean and welcoming, though
bland, this 18-room hotel just northwest of the chateau is
part of the Logis de France group. The Bacchus restaurant–
wine bar attached has a very good reputation. Full and half-
board available. Avoid the rooms without windows.

VAUX-LE-VICOMTE

The privately owned **Château de Vaux-le-Vicomte**
and its magnificent gardens 20km north
of Fontainebleau were designed and built
by Le Brun, Le Vau and Le Nôtre between
1656 and 1661 as a precursor to their more
ambitious work at Versailles.

Unfortunately, Vaux-le-Vicomte's beauty
turned out to be the undoing of its owner,
Nicolas Fouquet, Louis XIV's minister of
finance.

It seems that Louis, seething with jeal-
ousy that he had been upstaged at the
chateau's official opening, had Fouquet
thrown into prison, where he died in
1680.

Today visitors can view the interior of
the chateau, including the fabulous **dome,**
the **André Le Nôtre Exhibition** in the chateau's
basement, the delightful formal **gardens** with
elaborate *jeux d'eau* (fountain displays) in
season and the **Musée des Équipages** (Carriage Museum) in the castle stables. A visit by night
when the chateau is lit by 2000 candles is a never-to-be-forgotten experience.

<table>
<tr><td colspan="2">TRANSPORT</td></tr>
<tr><td>Distance from Paris 61km</td></tr>
<tr><td>Direction Southeast</td></tr>
<tr><td>Travel time 60 minutes by car or by RER and taxi</td></tr>
<tr><td>Car Route N6 from Paris and then A5a (direction Melun & exit 'Voisenon'); from Fontainebleau N6 and N36.</td></tr>
<tr><td>RER Line D2 from Paris (€7) to Melun, 6km to the southwest, then taxi (€15 during the day Monday to Saturday and €19 in the evening and on Sunday.) A Chateau bus service is available for one-way/return trips from Melun station for €3.50/7, running Saturday, Sunday and holidays from late March to mid-November. Departure times are 10.10am, 12.10pm, 2.20pm and 3.20pm from Melun, going back from Vaux le Vic at 3.50pm, 5.30pm and 6.25pm</td></tr>
</table>

Sights

Château de Vaux-le-Vicomte (☎ 01 64 14 41 90;
www.vaux-le-vicomte.com; adult/student & child 6-16
yr €12.50/9.90, candlelight visit €15.50/13.40, exhibit,
garden & museum only €7.50; ⌚ 10am-1pm & 2-6pm
Mon-Fri, 10am-6pm Sat & Sun late-Mar–mid-Nov,
candlelight visits 8pm-midnight Fri July & Aug, 8pm-
midnight Sat May-mid-Oct) Audioguides are available
for €2.

Gardens (⌚ 10am-6pm late-Mar–mid-Nov)

Fountain displays (⌚ 3-6pm 2nd & last Sat of month
late-Mar-Oct)

Musée des Équipages (Carriage Museum; ⌚ 10am-1pm &
2-6pm Mon-Fri, 10am-6pm Sat & Sun late-Mar–mid-Nov)

CHANTILLY

The elegant town of Chantilly (population 11,200) is best known for its imposing, but
largely reconstructed chateau surrounded by parkland, gardens, lakes and a vast forest. The
chateau is just over 2km northeast of the train station. The most direct route is to walk along
av de la Plaine des Aigles through a section of the Forêt de Chantilly, but you'll get a better
sense of the town by taking av du Maréchal Joffre and rue de Paris to rue du Connétable,
Chantilly's principal thoroughfare.

The **Château de Chantilly**, which was left in a shambles after the Revolution, is of interest
mainly because of its gardens and a number of superb paintings. It consists of two attached
buildings, which are entered through the same vestibule. The **Petit Château** was built around
1560 for Anne de Montmorency (1493–1567), who served six French kings as *connétable*
(high constable), diplomat and soldier and died while fighting Protestants during the
Counter-Reformation. The attached Renaissance-style **Grand Château**, completely demolished

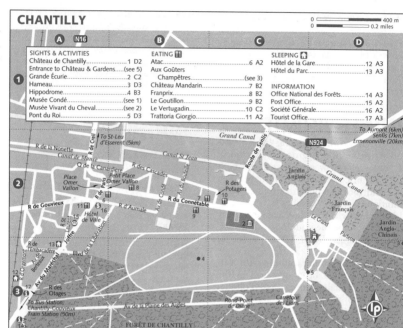

CHANTILLY

0 —————— 400 m
0 —————— 0.2 miles

SIGHTS & ACTIVITIES		EATING 🍴		SLEEPING 🛏️	
Château de Chantilly................1 D2		Atac................................6 A2		Hôtel de la Gare..................12 A3	
Entrance to Château & Gardens......(see 5)		Aux Goûters		Hôtel du Parc....................13 A3	
Grande Écurie...........................2 C2		Champêtres.........................(see 3)			
Hameau.................................3 D3		Château Mandarin...............7 B2		INFORMATION	
Hippodrome.............................4 B3		Franprix...............................8 B2		Office National des Forêts...........14 A3	
Musée Condé..........................(see 1)		Le Goutilon..........................9 B2		Post Office............................15 A2	
Musée Vivant du Cheval...........(see 2)		Le Vertugadin....................10 C2		Société Générale................16 A2	
Pont du Roi.............................5 D3		Trattoria Giorgio................11 A2		Tourist Office........................17 A3	

during the Revolution, was rebuilt by the duke of Aumale, son of King Louis-Philippe, from 1875 to 1885.

The Grand Château, to the right as you enter the vestibule, now contains the **Musée Condé**. Its unremarkable 19th-century rooms feature furnishings, paintings and sculptures haphazardly arranged according to the whims of the duke. He donated the chateau to the Institut de France at the end of the 19th century on the condition that the exhibits were not reorganised and would be open to the public. The most remarkable works are hidden away in a small room called the **Sanctuaire**, including paintings by Raphael, Filippino Lippi and Jean Fouquet.

The Petit Château contains the **Appartements des Princes** (Princes' Suites), which are straight ahead from the entrance. The highlight here is the **Cabinet des Livres**, a repository of 700 manuscripts and over 30,000 volumes, including a Gutenberg Bible and a facsimile of the *Très Riches Heures du Duc de Berry*, an illuminated manuscript dating from the 15th century that illustrates the calendar year for both the peasantry and the nobility. The **chapel**, to the left as you walk into the vestibule, has woodwork and stained-glass windows dating from the mid-16th century and was assembled by the duke of Aumale in 1882.

The chateau's excellent but long-neglected **gardens** were once among the most spectacular in France. The formal **Jardin Français**

TRANSPORT

Distance from Paris 48km

Direction North

Travel time 30/45 minutes by SNCF/RER

Car Route A1 from Paris, exit No 7 'Survilliers-Chantilly'; route N16 from Porte de La Chapelle.

RER Line D1 from Gare de Lyon, Châtelet-Les Halles or Gare du Nord Paris (€7.50) to Chantilly-Gouvieux station

Train Paris' Gare du Nord is linked to Chantilly by SNCF commuter trains that, with RER trains, total almost 40 a day (about 20 on Sunday). The last train back to Paris departs daily just before midnight.

(French Garden), whose flowerbeds, lakes and Grand Canal were laid out by Le Nôtre in the mid-17th century, is northeast of the main building. To the west, the 'wilder' **Jardin Anglais** (English Garden) was begun in 1817. East of the Jardin Français is the rustic **Jardin Anglo-Chinois** (Anglo-Chinese Garden), created in the 1770s. Its foliage and silted-up waterways surround the **Hameau**, a mock village dating from 1774 whose mill and half-timbered buildings inspired the Hameau de la Reine at Versailles. Crème Chantilly – cream beaten with sugar and vanilla and dolloped on everything in France that's sweet and doesn't move – was born here (see the boxed text, below).

The chateau's **Grande Écurie** (stables), built between 1719 and 1740 to house 240 horses and over 400 hounds, are next to Chantilly's famous **Hippodrome** (racecourse), inaugurated in 1834. Today the stables house the **Musée Vivant du Cheval** (Living Horse Museum), whose 30 pampered and spoiled equines live in luxurious wooden stalls built by Louis-Henri de Bourbon (the seventh Prince de Condé). Displays, in 31 rooms, include everything from riding equipment to horse toys to portraits, drawings and sculptures of famous nags. Make sure you stick around for the 30-minute **Présentation Équestre Pédagogique** (Introduction to Dressage), included in the admission price.

South of the chateau is the 6300-hectare **Forêt de Chantilly** (Chantilly Forest), once a royal hunting estate and now crisscrossed by a variety of walking and riding trails. In some areas, straight paths laid out centuries ago meet at multi-angled *carrefours* (crossroads). Long-distance trails that pass through the Forêt de Chantilly include the **GR11**, which links the chateau with the town of **Senlis** (p350) and its wonderful cathedral; the **GR1**, which goes from Luzarches (famed for its cathedral, parts of which date from the 12th century) to Ermenonville; and the **GR12**, which goes northeastward from four lakes known as the Étangs de Commelles to the Forêt d'Halatte.

The area is covered by IGN's 1:25,000 scale map *Forêts de Chantilly, d'Halatte and d'Ermenonville* (No 2412OT; €9). The 1:100,000 scale map *Carte de Découverte des Milieux Naturels et du Patrimoine Bâti* (€6.50), available at the tourist office, indicates sites of interest (eg churches, chateaux, museums and ruins). The **Office National des Forêts** (ONF, National Forests Office) publishes a good walking guide for families called *Promenons-Nous dans les Forêts de Picardie: Chantilly, Halatte & Ermenonville* (€7.50). Mountain bikers may want to pick up a copy of the detailed *Les Cahiers de la Randonnée VTT: Forêts de Chantilly et d'Ermenonville* (€13), available from the tourist office.

Information

Office National des Forêts (ONF, National Forests Office; ☎ 03 44 57 03 88, www.onf.fr in French; 1 av de Sylvie, Chantilly; ✆ 8.30am-noon & 2-5pm Mon-Fri) This office is just southeast of the tourist office. Ask the staff about organised forest walks.

Office de Tourisme de Chantilly (Tourist Office; ☎ 03 44 67 37 37; www.chantilly-tourisme.com; 60 av du Maréchal Joffre, Chantilly; ✆ 9.30am-12.30pm & 1.30-5.30pm Mon-Sat & 10.30am-1.30pm Sun May-Sep, 9.30am-12.30pm & 1.30-5.30pm Mon-Sat Oct-Apr) The tourist office is just round the corner from the train station. Ask the staff for a copy of *Circuit Touristique en Ville*, a pamphlet with a 23-stop walk around town starting from the tourist office.

Post office (26 av du Maréchal Joffre, Chantilly; ✆ 9am-12.15pm & 1.45-6pm Mon-Fri, 9am-12.30pm Sat)

Société Générale (1 av du Maréchal Joffre, Chantilly; ✆ 8.30am-12.15pm & 1.45-5.30pm Mon-Thu, 8.30am-12.15pm & 1.45-6.30pm Fri, 9.30am-3.25pm Sat)

CHÂTEAU DE WHIPPED CREAM

Like every other self-respecting French chateau three centuries ago, the palace at Chantilly had its own *hameau* (hamlet), complete with *laitier* (dairy) where the lady of the household and her guests could play at being milkmaids, as Marie-Antoinette did at Versailles. But the cows at Chantilly's dairy took their job rather more seriously than their fellow bovine actors at other faux dairies, and news of the *crème chantilly* (sweetened whipped cream) served at the hamlet's teas became the talk (and envy) of aristocratic 18th-century Europe. The future Habsburg Emperor Joseph II clandestinely visited this *temple de marbre* (marble temple), as he called it, to try out the white stuff in 1777, and when the Baroness of Oberkirch tasted the goods she cried: 'Never have I eaten such good cream, so appetising, so well prepared.' Today most of the cafés in town will happily serve you some *crème chantilly* – accompanied or simply on its own.

Sights

Château de Chantilly (☎ 03 44 62 62 62; www.chateau dechantilly.com; adult/4-11 yr/student €8/3.50/7; ☯ chateau 10am-5pm Oct-Apr, 10.30am-12.45pm & 2-5pm Mon-Fri & 10.30am-5pm Sat & Sun Nov-Mar, park 10am-8pm Apr-Oct, 10.30am-6pm Nov-Mar) Admission prices range from visits to the park only to a combination ticket covering the chateau, museum, park, canal boat and mini train.

Musée Vivant du Cheval (Living Horse Museum; ☎ 03 44 57 13 13; www.musee-vivantducheval.fr; Grand Écurie, rue du Connétable, Chantilly; adult/child 4-11 yr/12-17 yr €8/5.50/6.50; ☯ 10.30am-6.30pm Mon-Fri & 10.30am-7pm Sat & Sun Apr-Oct, 2-6pm Mon-Fri & 10.30am-6.30pm Sat & Sun Nov-Mar) The Présentation Équestre Pédagogique (Introduction to Dressage) presentation runs at 11.30am, 3.30pm and 5.30pm from April to October, and at 3.30pm Monday to Friday and 11.30am, 3.30pm and 5.15pm Saturday and Sunday from November to March.

Eating

Aux Goûters Champêtres (☎ 03 44 57 46 21; Château de Chantilly; menu lunch/dinner €17.50/28.90 & 34.50; ☯ 11am-7pm Apr-Nov) This fine restaurant in the windmill of the park's *hameau* (hamlet) has local specialities on the menu and is a wonderful place for lunch, particularly during the summer.

Château Mandarin (☎ 03 44 57 00 29; 62 rue du Connétable, Chantilly; starters €3-5.50, mains €6.50-15, menu lunch €12; ☯ lunch & dinner to 10.30pm Tue-Sun) This is a decent Chinese restaurant a short distance west of the Grande Écurie. It also has Thai and Vietnamese dishes.

Le Goutillon (☎ 03 44 58 01 00; 61 rue du Connétable, Chantilly; starters €8-10, mains €15-23; ☯ lunch & dinner to 11pm Mon-Sat) With its red- and white-checked tablecloths, simple wooden tables and classic bistro fare Le Goutillon manages to be typically French without that fake feel. This appealing restaurant serves classics like *terrine de lapin* (rabbit terrine) and beef fillet, with wines to match.

Le Vertugadin (☎ 03 44 57 03 19; 44 rue du Connétable, Chantilly; mains €17-40, menu lunch & dinner €26; ☯ lunch & dinner to 11pm Mon-Sat) This is a very friendly and highly recommended restaurant with excellent *menus* and a walled-in garden that is a delight in summer.

Trattoria Giorgio (☎ 03 44 57 00 48; av du Maréchal Joffre, Chantilly; starters €7-12, pastas €8-12, mains €11.50-19; ☯ lunch & dinner to 11.30pm Tue-Sun) Popular with locals, this very central Italian restaurant is just the ticket for a pizza or more ambitious meal en route to the train station.

CHEAP EATS

Atac (5 petit place Omer Vallon, Chantilly; ☯ 8.30am-7.30pm Mon-Sat) This large supermarket is midway between the train station and the chateau.

Franprix (132 rue du Connétable, Chantilly; ☯ 8.30am-12.30pm & 2.30-7.30pm Tue-Thu, 8.30am-7.30pm Fri & Sat, 8.30am-1pm Sun)

Sleeping

Hôtel de la Gare (☎ 03 44 62 56 90, 06 81 60 16 39; fax 03 44 62 56 99; place de la Gare, Chantilly; s & d €55) This rambling hotel with a dozen rooms opposite the train station is a surprisingly pleasant place with recently renovated, shower-equipped doubles. The only drawback is the Star d'un Star karaoke club that wails from 8pm to 1am (nightly) on the 1st floor.

Hôtel du Parc (☎ 03 44 58 20 00; www.bestwestern.fr; 36 av du Maréchal Joffre, Chantilly; s from €80, d €100-120; ☒ 🖳 🖨) This 57-room place is part of the Best Western chain so you can expect a reasonable standard of service. The rooms have everything you need but are bland and quite expensive; the cheaper rooms face the street.

SENLIS

Just 10km northeast of Chantilly, **Senlis** (population 16,300), is an attractive medieval town of winding cobblestone streets and Gallo-Roman ramparts and towers. It was a royal seat from the time of Clovis to Henri IV and contains an important 12th-century cathedral and four fine museums– the **Musée d'Art et d'Archéologie** (Museum of Art & Archaeology); the **Musée de la Vénerie** (Museum of Venery), with exhibits relating to hunting; the **Musée des Spahis** (Spahi Museum), with displays about the North African cavalry garrisoned in Senlis; and the **Musée de l'Hôtel de Vermandois** (Hotel Vermandois Museum), which looks at the history of Senlis.

The Gothic **Cathédrale de Notre Dame**, which is entered through the south portal, was built between 1150 and 1191. The cathedral is unusually bright, but the stained glass, though original, is generally unexceptional. The magnificent carved stone **Grand Portal** (1170), on the western side facing place du Parvis Notre Dame, has statues and a central relief relating to the life of the Virgin Mary. It is believed to have been the inspiration for the portal at the cathedral in Chartres.

There are no other major sights per se, but Senis is a pretty place and far more charming to wander around than the nearby town of **Chartres** (opposite).

Information

Banque de Picardie (2 rue Bellon; ⊙ 8.45am-12.30pm & 2-5.30pm Mon-Fri, 8.45am-12.30pm & 2-4.30pm Sat) At the corner of rue St-Hailaire, southeast of the cathedral.

Office de Tourisme de Senlis (☎ 03 44 53 06 40; off .tourisme-senlis@wanadoo.fr; place du Parvis Notre Dame; ⊙ 10am-12.30pm & 2-6.15pm Mon-Sat & 10.30am-1pm & 2.30-6.15pm Sun Mar-Oct, 10am-12.30pm & 2-5pm Mon-Sat & 11.15am-1pm & 2.30-5pm Sun Nov-Feb) The tourist office is just opposite (and west of) the cathedral.

Sights

Cathédrale de Notre Dame (place Notre Dame; ⊙ 8am-6pm)

Senlis museums (adult/student & 17-25 yr €4/2; ⊙ 10am-noon & 2-6pm Mon, Thu & Fri, 2-6pm Wed, 11am-1pm & 2-6pm Sat & Sun) One ticket allows entry to the Musée d'Art et d'Archéologie (Museum of Art & Archaeology, ☎ 03 44 32 00 83) at place Notre Dame; the Musée de la Vénerie and Musée des Spahis (☎ 03 44 32 00 81) at place du Parvis Notre Dame; and the Musée de l'Hôtel de Vermandois (☎ 03 44 32 00 82), also at place du Parvis Notre Dame.

Eating & Sleeping

Hostellerie de la Porte Bellon (☎ 03 44 53 03 05; www .portebellon.com; 51 rue Bellon; s & d €61-79) This wonderful 18-room hotel is housed in an 18th-century manor a couple of

www.lonelyplanet.com

hundred metres east of the cathedral. A garden surrounds the property and the restaurant, open for lunch daily and for dinner from 9.30pm Monday to Saturday, is worth a visit in itself (starters are €8.90 to €19, mains go for €17 to €24, lunch *menus* cost €23 and dinner *menus* are €25, €29.50 and €36).

Le Scaramouche (☎ 03 44 53 01 26; 4 place Notre Dame; starters €10-22, mains €14-35, menu lunch/dinner €28/38 & 60; ⊙ lunch & dinner to 10.30pm Thu-Mon) This upmarket restaurant is the best and most central place for a meal while visiting the cathedral or museums.

Market (rue St-Hilaire; ⊙ 8am-1pm Tue & Fri) Surrounding the open-air market southwest of the cathedral are a number of relatively cheap places to eat including pizzerias, creperies, tea salons and cafés.

CHARTRES

The magnificent 13th-century cathedral of Chartres, crowned by two very different spires – one Gothic, the other Romanesque – rises from rich farmland and dominates the medieval town (population 40,250) around its base. The cathedral's varied collection of relics – particularly the Sainte Voile, which is the 'holy veil' said to have been worn by the Virgin Mary when she gave birth to Jesus – attracted many pilgrims during the Middle Ages. These

Portail Royal, Notre Dame (p352) at Chartres

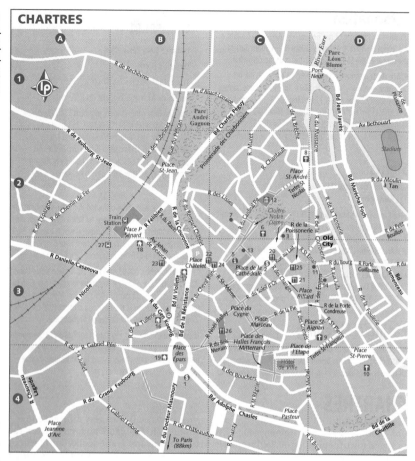

CHARTRES

pilgrims contributed to the building and extending of the cathedral. With its astonishing blue stained glass and other treasures, the cathedral at Chartres is a must-see for any visitor to Paris.

The 130m-long **Cathédrale Notre Dame**, one of the crowning architectural achievements of Western civilisation, was built in the Gothic style during the early 13th century. It was built to replace a Romanesque cathedral that had been devastated, along with much of the town, by fire on the night of 10 June 1194. Because of fundraising among the aristocracy and donated labour from the common folk, construction took only 30 years, resulting in a high degree of architectural unity. It is France's best-preserved medieval cathedral, having been spared post-medieval modifications, the ravages of war and the Reign of Terror (see the boxed text, p355).

All three of the cathedral's entrances to the west, north and south have superbly ornamented triple **portals**, but the west entrance – the **Portail Royal** – is the only one that predates the fire. Carved between 1145 and 1155, its superb statuary, whose features are elongated in the Romanesque style, represent the glory of Christ in the centre, and the Nativity and Ascension to the right and left, respectively. The structure's other main Romanesque feature is the 105m-high **Clocher Vieux** (Old Bell Tower), also called the Tour Sud (South Tower), which was begun in the 1140s. It is the tallest Romanesque steeple still standing.

A visit to the 112m-high **Clocher Neuf** (New Bell Tower), also known as the Tour Nord (North Tower), is well worth the ticket price and the climb up the long spiral stairway. Access is just behind the cathedral bookshop. A 70m-high platform on the flamboyant Gothic spire, built from 1507 to 1513 by Jehan de Beauce after an earlier wooden spire burned down, affords superb views of the three-tiered flying buttresses and the 19th-century copper roof, turned green by verdigris.

The cathedral's 172 extraordinary **stained-glass windows**, almost all of which are 13th-century originals, comprise one of the most important collections of medieval stained glass in Europe. The three most important windows dating from before the 13th century are in the wall above the west entrance, below the rose window. Survivors of the fire of 1194 (they were made around 1150), the windows are renowned for the depth and intensity of their blue tones, which have become known as 'Chartres blue'.

If you want to see more stained glass up close and in more modern guises, trek down the hill from the cathedral's north portal to the **Centre International du Vitrail** (International Stained-Glass Centre), located in a half-timbered former granary.

The cathedral's 110m-long **crypt**, a tombless Romanesque structure built in 1024 around a 9th-century predecessor, is the largest crypt in France. Guided tours in French (with a written English translation) lasting 30 minutes are available year-round.

The most venerated object in the cathedral is the **Sainte Voile** (Holy Veil) relic, which originally formed part of the imperial treasury of Constantinople but was offered to Charlemagne by the Empress Irene when the Holy Roman Emperor proposed marriage to her in AD 802. It has been in Chartres since 876 when Charles the Bald presented it to the town. The cathedral was built because the veil survived the 1194 fire. It is contained in a cathedral-shaped reliquary and is currently displayed in a small side chapel off the eastern aisle.

Chartres' **Musée des Beaux-Arts** (Fine Arts Museum), accessed most easily via the gate next to the cathedral's north portal, is in the former Palais Épiscopal (Bishop's Palace), built in the 17th and 18th centuries. The museum's collections include 16th-century enamels of the Apostles made by Léonard Limosin for François I, paintings from the 16th to 19th centuries and polychromatic wooden sculptures from the Middle Ages.

Chartres' carefully preserved **old town** is northeast and east of the cathedral along the narrow western channel of the River Eure, spanned by a number of footbridges. From rue Cardinal Pie, the stairways called **Tertre St-Nicolas** and **rue Chantault**, the latter lined with medieval houses, lead down to the empty shell of the 12th-century **Collégiale St-André**, a Romanesque collegiate church that closed in 1791 and was damaged in the early 19th century and again during WWII.

Along the river's eastern bank, **rue de la Tannerie** and its extension **rue de la Foulerie** are lined with flower gardens, millraces and the restored remnants of river-side trades: wash houses, tanneries and the like. **Rue aux Juifs** (Street of the Jews) on the western bank has been extensively renovated. Half a block down the hill there's a river-side promenade. Up the hill **rue des Écuyers** has many structures dating from around the 16th century, including a

INFORMATION
BNP Paribas...........................1 B4
Crédit Agricole.......................2 C3
La Crypte...............................3 C2
Post Office.............................4 B3
Tourist Office.........................5 C3

SIGHTS & ACTIVITIES
Cathédrale Notre Dame.............6 C2
Centre International du Vitrail.....7 C2
Clocher Neuf........................(see 6)
Clocher Vieux.......................(see 6)
Collégiale St-André..................8 C2
Crypt...................................(see 3)
Église St-Aignan......................9 D3
Église St-Pierre.....................10 D4
Escalier de la Reine Berthe........11 D3
Musée des Beaux-Arts............12 C2
Portail Royal........................13 D3
Prow-Shaped House...............14 D3

SLEEPING
Auberge de Jeunesse...............15 E2
Hôtel de la Poste...................16 B3
Hôtel du Bœuf Couronné........17 B3
Hôtel Jehan de Beauce...........18 B3
Le Grand Monarque...............19 B4

EATING
Café Serpente.......................20 C3
Covered Market.....................21 C3
La Passacaille.......................22 B3
Le Grill Pélagie.....................23 B3
Le Tripot.............................24 C3
Maison du Saumon et de la
  Truie qui File.....................25 C3
Monoprix.............................26 C3

TRANSPORT
Bus Station..........................27 A3

half-timbered, **prow-shaped house** at No 26 with its upper section supported by beams. At No 35 is the **Escalier de la Reine Berthe** (Queen Bertha's Staircase), a tower-like covered stairwell clinging to a half-timbered house that dates back to the early 16th century.

There are also some old half-timbered houses north of here on **rue du Bourg** and to the west on **rue de la Poissonnerie**; on the latter, look for the magnificent **Maison du Saumon** (Salmon House), also known as the Maison de la Truie qui File (House of the Spinning Sow) at No 10 to No 14. It has carved consoles of the eponymous salmon, the Archangel Gabriel and Mary and Archangel Michael slaying the dragon – and it's now a restaurant (see Eating, opposite).

From **place St-Pierre** you get a good view of the flying buttresses holding up the 12th- and 13th-century **Église St-Pierre**. Once part of a Benedictine monastery founded in the 7th century, it was outside the city walls and thus vulnerable to attack; the fortress-like, pre-Romanesque **bell tower** attached to it was used as a refuge by monks, and dates from around 1000. The fine, brightly coloured **clerestory windows** in the nave, choir and apse date from the early 14th century.

To the northwest, **Église St-Aignan** is interesting for its wooden barrel-vault roof (1625), arcaded nave and painted interior of faded blue and gold floral motifs (c 1870). The stained glass and the Renaissance Chapelle de St-Michel date from the 16th century.

The **Train Touristique de Chartres** makes a 35-minute circuit around the city in the high season.

Information

BNP Paribas (7-9 place des Épars, Chartres; ☽ 8.30am-noon & 1.30-5.35pm Tue, 8.50am-noon & 1.45-5.35pm Wed-Fri, 8.30am-noon & 1.30-4.45pm Sat)

La Crypte (☎ 02 37 21 56 33; 18 Cloître Notre Dame, Chartres; ☽ Apr-Oct) The cathedral-run shop selling religious items and souvenirs.

Office de Tourisme de Chartres (Tourist Office; ☎ 02 37 18 26 26; www.chartres-tourisme.com; place de la Cathédrale, Chartres; ☽ 9am-7pm Mon-Sat & 9.30am-5.30pm Sun Apr-Sep, 10am-6pm Mon-Sat & 10am-1pm & 2.30-4.30pm Sun Oct-Mar) The tourist office, across the square from the cathedral's main entrance, rents out self-paced, 1½-hour English-language audioguide tours (one person/two people €5.50/8.50) of the medieval city.

Post office (place des Épars, Chartres; ☽ 8.30am-7pm Mon-Fri, 8.30am-noon Sat) The main post office is housed in an impressive neo-Gothic building with *fin de siècle* mosaics on the front.

TRANSPORT

Distance from Paris 88km

Direction Southwest

Travel time 55 to 70 minutes by train

Car Route A6 from Paris' Porte d'Orléans (direction Bordeaux-Nantes) then route A10 & A11 (direction Nantes), exit 'Chartres'

SNCF More than 30 SNCF trains a day (20 on Sunday) link Paris' Gare Montparnasse (€12.40) with Chartres, all of which pass through Versailles-Chantiers (€10.10, 45 to 60 minutes). The last train back to Paris leaves Chartres a bit after 9pm weekdays, just before 9pm on Saturday and sometime after 10pm on Sunday.

Sights

Cathédrale Notre Dame (☎ 02 37 21 22 07; www.cathedrale-chartres.com in French; place de la Cathédrale, Chartres; ☽ 8.30am-7.30pm) Hire great English-language audioguide tours (25/45/70 minutes for €3.20/4.20/6.20) from the cathedral shop. Guided tours in French also depart from here (adult/student & under 18/senior €6/3/4, at 10.30am Tuesday to Saturday and 3pm daily from April to October, 2.30pm daily from November to March).

Centre International du Vitrail (International Stained-Glass Centre; ☎ 02 37 21 65 72; www.centre-vitrail.org; 5 rue du Cardinal Pie, Chartres; adult/senior, student & under 18 €4/3; ☽ 9.30am-12.30pm & 1.30-6pm Mon-Fri, 10am-12.30pm & 2.30-6pm Sat & Sun)

Clocher Neuf (New Bell Tower; Cathédrale Notre Dame; adult/under 18/18-25 yr €6.50/free/4.50, admission free on 1st Sun of some months; ☽ 9.30am-noon & 2-5.30pm Mon-Sat & 2-5.30pm Sun May-Aug, 9.30am-noon & 2-4.30pm Mon-Sat & 2-4.30pm Sun Sep-Apr)

Crédit Agricole (1 Cloître Notre Dame, Chartres; ☽ 8.45am-12.30pm & 1.50-5.30pm Tue-Fri, 8.45am-12.30pm & 1.50-4pm Sat)

Crypt (Cathédrale Notre Dame; adult/concession €2.70/2.10; ☽ tours 11am Mon-Sat & 2.15pm, 3.30pm, 4.30pm & 5.15pm daily late-Jun-late-Sep, 11am Mon-Sat & 2.15pm, 3.30pm & 4.30pm daily Apr-late-Jun & late-Sep-Oct, 11am Mon-Sat & 4.15pm Nov-Mar) Thirty-minute guided tours of the crypt in French (with a written English translation) start at La Crypte. At other times they begin at the shop below the North Tower in the cathedral.

Église St-Aignan (place St-Aignan, Chartres; ☽ 9am-noon & 2-6pm)

Église St-Pierre (place St-Pierre, Chartres; ☽ 9am-noon & 2-6pm)

English-language tours (☎ 02 37 28 15 58; millerchartres@aol.com; Cathédrale Notre Dame; adult/senior

& student €10/5; (clock) noon & 2.45pm Mon-Sat Apr-early Nov) The price includes a headset through which you listen to the tour commentary by Chartres expert Malcolm Miller. The Cathedral now requires that headsets be used for all tours.

Musée des Beaux-Arts (Fine Arts Museum; (phone) 02 37 90 45 80; 29 Cloître Notre Dame, Chartres; adult/student & senior €2.70/1.40; (clock) 10am-noon & 2-6pm Mon & Wed-Sat & 2-6pm Sun May-Oct, 10am-noon & 2-5pm Mon & Wed-Sat & 2-5pm Sun Nov-Apr)

Train Touristique de Chartres (Chartres Tourist Train; (phone) 02 37 25 88 50; adult/3-10 yr €5.50/3.20; (clock) 10.30am-6pm Apr-Oct) The train visit lasts 35 minutes. It leaves from in front of the tourist office and cathedral at Place de la Cathedral.

Eating

Café Serpente ((phone) 02 37 21 68 81; 2 Cloître Notre Dame, Chartres; salads & omelettes €5.20-11.50, dishes €13.50-15; (clock) 10am-11pm) This atmospheric brasserie and *salon de thé* (tearoom) is conveniently located opposite the cathedral. It's traditional cuisine with numerous fish dishes, and *tartare de boeuf* (raw beef steak).

La Passacaille ((phone) 02 37 21 52 10; 30 rue Ste-Même, Chartres; starters €4-8, mains €8-14, lunch & dinner menu €14.70; (clock) lunch & dinner to 10.30pm) This welcoming, inexpensive Italian place has particularly good pizzas and fresh pasta.

Le Grill Pélagie ((phone) 02 37 36 07 49; 1 av Jehan de Beauce, Chartres; starters €3.70-7.90, mains €9.90-14.80, lunch & dinner menus €11.50-18.50; (clock) lunch & dinner to 10.30pm Mon-Fri, dinner to 11pm Sat) A popular place specialising in grills and Tex-Mex dishes such as *quesadillas* (€6.50) and *fajitas* (€13.80 to €15.60).

Le Tripot ((phone) 02 37 36 60 11; 11 place Jean Moulin, Chartres; starters €11-19, mains €13.50-24, menu lunch/dinner €15/23, 29 & 38; (clock) lunch Tue-Sat, dinner to 10pm Mon-Sat) This wonderful and well regarded little place just down from the cathedral is one of the best bistros in Chartres.

Maison du Saumon et de la Truie qui File ((phone) 02 37 36 28 00; 10-14 rue de la Poissonnerie, Chartres; starters €9.50-14.50, mains €16-19.50, lunch & dinner menu €19.70; (clock) lunch Tue-Sun, dinner to 11.30pm Tue-Sat) Housed in the medieval house of the same name, this place tries to have something for everyone – Alsatian *choucroute* (sauerkraut with sausage and other prepared meats), Hungarian goulash, Moroccan *tajine*, pirozhki and fish. The result is a little confused, but at least there's something for everyone. Either way the medieval venue is worth the visit.

CHEAP EATS

Covered market (place Billard, Chartres; (clock) 7am-1pm Sat) This market just off rue des Changes south of the cathedral dates from the early 20th century. There are a lot of food shops surrounding it.

SAVED BY RED TAPE

Anyone who has tried to live or work legally in France will know that bureaucracy *à la française* is at best perfect material for a comedy sketch, and at worst a recipe for madness. Yet were it not for administrative bumbling, the magnificent cathedral at Chartres would probably have been destroyed during the French revolution

While antireligious fervour was reaching fever pitch in 1791, the Revolutionaries decided that the cathedral deserved something more radical than mere desecration: demolition. The question was how to accomplish that. To find an answer, they appointed a committee, whose admirably thorough members deliberated for four or five years. By that time the Revolution's fury had been spent, and – to history's great fortune – the plan was shelved.

Monoprix (21 rue Noël Ballay & 10 rue du Bois Merrain, Chartres; (clock) 9am-7.30pm Mon-Sat) This department store with two entrances has a supermarket on the ground floor.

Sleeping

Auberge de Jeunesse ((phone) 02 37 34 27 64; fax 02 37 35 78 85; 23 av Neigre, Chartres; dm €12.15) Reception at this hostel, which is about 1.5km northeast of the train station via blvd Charles Péguy and blvd Jean Jaurès, opens from 2pm to 10pm and curfew is 10.30pm in winter and 11.30pm in summer. To get here from the train station, take bus No 5 (direction Mare aux Moines) to the Rouliers stop. Call ahead as the hostel is sometimes booked out by groups.

Le Grand Monarque ((phone) 02 37 18 15 15; www .bw-grand-monarque.com in French; 22 place des Épars, Chartres; d €115-165, q €235) This three-star hotel is supposedly Chartres' finest, but some of the public areas and the 54 guest rooms now have a frayed look to them.

Hôtel de la Poste ((phone) 02 37 21 04 27; www.hotelposte -chartres.com; 3 rue du Général Koenig, Chartres; d €58-65) This 57-room two-star property just off the place des Épars offers excellent value.

Hôtel du Bœuf Couronné ((phone) 02 37 18 06 06; fax 02 37 21 72 13; 15 place Châtelet, Chartres; s €43, d €55) This cosy, Logis de France–affiliated guesthouse in the centre of everything offers excellent value and has a memorable restaurant (*menu* lunch/dinner €17.95/27; (clock) lunch & dinner to 11pm) with generous *menus*.

Hôtel Jehan de Beauce ((phone) 02 37 21 01 41; www.contact -hotel-chartres.com; 19 av Jehan de Beauce, Chartres; d €55-65) If you're looking for budget accommodation this 46-room hotel has clean, but very Spartan singles, doubles and triples. It's very convenient to the train station.

GIVERNY

This small village (population 544) northwest of Paris and en route to Rouen contains **Maison de Claude Monet,** the home and flower-filled garden of one of the leading impressionist painters and his family from 1883 to 1926. Here Monet painted some of his most famous series of works, including *Décorations des Nymphéas* (Water Lilies). Unfortunately, the hectare of land that Monet owned here has become two distinct areas, cut by the Chemin du Roy, a small railway line that has been converted into what is now the busy D5 road.

The northern area of the property is **Clos Normand,** where Monet's famous pastel pink and green house and the **Atelier des Nymphéas** (Water Lilies studio) stand. These days the studio is the entrance hall, adorned with precise reproductions of his works and ringing with cash-register bells from busy souvenir stands. Outside are the symmetrically laid-out gardens. Visiting the house and gardens is a treat in any season. From early to late spring, daffodils, tulips, rhododendrons, wisteria and irises appear, followed by poppies and lilies. By June, nasturtiums, roses and sweet peas are in blossom. Around September, there are dahlias, sunflowers and hollyhocks.

From the Clos Normand's far corner a tunnel leads under the D5 to the **Jardin d'Eau** (Water Garden). Having bought this piece of land in 1895 after his reputation had been established (and his bank account had swelled), Monet dug a pool, planted water lilies and constructed the famous **Japanese bridge,** which has since been rebuilt. Draped with purple wisteria, the bridge blends into the asymmetrical foreground and background, creating the intimate atmosphere for which the 'Painter of Light' was famous.

The **Musée d'Art Américain** (American Art Museum) contains a fine collection of the works of many of the American impressionist painters who flocked to France in the late 19th and early 20th centuries. It's housed in a modern building about 100m northwest of the Maison de Claude Monet.

TRANSPORT

Distance from Paris 76km

Direction Northwest

Travel time 70 minutes by train to Vernon and then 20 minutes by bus

Car Route A13 from Paris' Port de St-Cloud (direction Rouen), exit No 14 to route N15 (direction Vernon & Giverny).

SNCF From Paris' Gare St-Lazare there are two early-morning trains to Vernon (€11.30) from where Transport Val de Seine buses (☎ 02 32 71 06 39; €2.10) depart for Giverny, 7km to the northwest. There's roughly one train an hour back to Paris between 5pm and 9pm.

Information

Check the excellent Valley of the Impressionists website (www.giverny-art.com). The website www.ville-vernon27.fr has information on Vernon, the town 7km northwest of Giverny.

Office de Tourisme de Vernon (☎ 02 32 51 39 60; tourisme.vernon@wanadoo.fr; 36 rue Carnot, Giverny; ⏰ 9.30am-noon & 2.30-6.30pm Tue-Sat & 10am-noon Sun Apr-Sep, 10am-noon & 2-5pm Tue-Sat Oct-Mar) The closest tourist office to Giverny is in Vernon. If travelling by train you can stop here before carrying on by bus to Giverny.

Sights

Maison de Claude Monet (House of Claude Monet; ☎ 02 32 51 28 21; www.fondation-monet.com; 84 rue Claude Monet, Giverny; adult/7-12 yr/student €5.50/3/4, house €1.50, garden €4; ⏰ 9.30am-6pm Tue-Sun Apr-Oct)

Musée d'Art Américain (American Art Museum; ☎ 02 32 51 94 65; www.maag.org; 99 rue Claude Monet, Giverny; adult/12-18 yr/senior & student €5.50/3/4, audioguide €1; ⏰ 10am-6pm Apr-Oct, 10am-6pm Tue-Sun Nov-Mar)

Eating & Sleeping

Note that many of the restaurants and hotels in town open along with the museum – that is, only between April and October.

Auberge du Vieux Moulin (☎ 02 32 51 46 15; 21 rue de la Falaise, Giverny; salads €12, menus lunch Mon-Fri €15, dinner €24-35; ⏰ lunch Tue-Sun & dinner to 10.30pm Sat Apr-Oct) The lovely little 'Old Mill Inn' a couple of hundred metres east of the Maison de Claude Monet is an excellent place for lunch and has a lovely terrace.

Hôtel La Musardière (☎ 02 32 21 03 18; fax 02 32 21 60 00; 123 rue Claude Monet, Giverny; s & d €55-70) This lovely 10-room hotel evocatively called the 'Idler' and set amid a lovely garden is less than 100m northeast of the Maison de Claude Monet. In summer it has a restaurant, with *menus* for €23 and €35.

Maison de Claude Monet, Giverny (opposite)

AUVERS-SUR-OISE

On 20 May 1890 the painter Vincent van Gogh left a mental asylum in Provence and moved to this small village (population 6940) north of Paris. He came here to reacquaint himself with the light with which he was so familiar in his native Holland, and to be closer to his friend and benefactor Dr Paul Ferdinand Gachet (1828–1909). He set to work immediately, producing at least one painting or sketch every day until his death on 29 July, two months after his arrival.

Today Auvers-sur-Oise is predominantly a shrine to the great impressionist painter, and many sights, including five museums, are related to his short stay and large body of work created here. Foremost is the so-called **Maison de Van Gogh** (van Gogh's House), actually the Auberge Ravoux, where the artist stayed during his 70 days here. Apart from the restaurant **Auberge Ravoux** (p359) on the ground floor, for the most part it's empty. However, there's an excellent video on van Gogh's life and work, and the bedroom in which he fatally wounded himself is strangely moving.

Northwest of the Maison de van Gogh is the **Maison-Atelier de Daubigny,** the house and studio of the artist Charles-François Daubigny (1818–78) – Daubigny began the practice of painting *en plein air* (outside), and his work is considered a precursor to impressionism. The studio was decorated from top to bottom by the artist with some help from the painters Camille Corot (1796–1875) and Honoré Daumier (1808–79). It is positively stunning.

The sprawling 17th-century **Château d'Auvers**, to the west of the Maison-Atelier de Daubigny, has an audiovisual presentation on van Gogh and other impressionists who found

ABSINTHE: SPIRIT OF THE AGE

In its heyday absinthe was akin to the marijuana of the 1960s or the cocaine of '80s. But until it became the drink of choice among artists, artistes and the underclasses (and thus gained in notoriety), absinthe had been a bourgeois favourite, sipped quietly and innocuously in cafés around the land. It was only when the creative world discovered the wormwood-based liqueur and its hallucinogenic qualities that it took off, and everyone from Paul Verlaine, Arthur Rimbaud, Oscar Wilde, Édouard Manet, Edgar Degas, Henri de Toulouse-Lautrec and, of course, Vincent van Gogh wrote about it, painted it and/or drank it. Whether or not it was the *fée verte* (green fairy), as absinthe was known during the *belle époque*, that pushed Van Gogh off the edge is not known; some say he was so poor he couldn't even afford this relatively cheap libation and instead sometimes ate paint containing lead, which may have driven him mad. More than anything else the easy availability and low cost of the spirit led to widespread alcoholism and in 1915, having just entered into war against Germany and its allies, France found it prudent to ban the drink altogether.

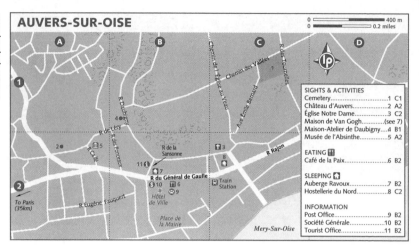

AUVERS-SUR-OISE

0   400 m
0   0.2 miles

SIGHTS & ACTIVITIES
Cemetery...........................1 C1
Château d'Auvers..............2 A2
Église Notre Dame.............3 C2
Maison de Van Gogh............(see 7)
Maison-Atelier de Daubigny....4 B1
Musée de l'Absinthe............5 A2

EATING
Café de la Paix.......................6 B2

SLEEPING
Auberge Ravoux...................7 B2
Hostellerie du Nord...............8 C2

INFORMATION
Post Office...........................9 B2
Société Générale..................10 B2
Tourist Office......................11 B2

their way here at some stage, including Paul Cézanne (1839–1906) and Camille Pissarro (1830–1903). Along the way don't miss the opportunity of visiting the **Musée de l'Absinthe**, the unique absinthe museum that traces the history of the liqueur that could have contributed to van Gogh's downfall (see the boxed text, p357).

A trip to Auvers-sur-Oise should include a visit to the **Église Notre Dame** – subject of van Gogh's *L'Église d'Auvers* (1890) – and the **cemetery** where he is buried beside his brother Théo.

Information

Office de Tourisme d'Auvers-sur-Oise (Tourist Office; ☎ 01 30 36 10 06; www-auvers-sur-oise.com in French; rue de la Sansonne, Auvers-sur-Oise; ⏰ 9.30am-12.30pm & 2-6pm Apr-Oct, 9.30am-12.30pm & 2-5pm Nov-Mar) In the delightful Manoir des Colombières, this office runs an excellent 15-minute video in English and French that helps put in perspective the town's contribution to the impressionist school of art. It also offers guided tours (€5.50) in English and French on Sundays and public holidays between April and October, tours that follow the footsteps of Van Gogh throughout the town.

Post office (place de la Mairie, Auvers-sur-Oise; ⏰ 9am-noon & 2.30-5.30pm Mon-Fri, 9am-noon Sat)

Société Générale (17 rue du Général de Gaulle, Auvers-sur-Oise; ⏰ 9am-noon & 2-5.30pm Mon-Fri, 9am-noon & 2-5pm Sat)

Sights

Note that most places worth seeing in Auvers-sur-Oise are closed in winter.

Cemetery (Chemin des Vallées, Auvers-sur-Oise)

Château d'Auvers (☎ 01 34 48 48 45; www.chateau -auvers.fr; rue de Léry, Auvers-sur-Oise; adult/student & 6-18 yr €10.50/6.50, family €21.50-25.50; ⏰ 10.30am-6pm Tue-Fri & 10.30am-6.30pm Sat & Sun Apr-Sep,

10.30am-4.30pm Tue-Fri & 10.30am-5.30pm Sat & Sun Oct-Dec & mid-Jan–Mar)

Église Notre Dame (rue Daubigny, Auvers-sur-Oise)

Maison-Atelier de Daubigny (☎ 01 34 48 03 03; 61 rue Daubigny, Auvers-sur-Oise; adult/under 12 €5/free; ⏰ 2-6.30pm Thu-Sun early-Apr–early-Nov)

TRANSPORT

Distance from Paris 35km

Direction North

Travel time 70 minutes by train & bus

Car Route A15 from Paris' Porte de Clichy, exit 7 to route N184 (direction Beauvais), exit 'Méry-sur-Oise'.

RER Line A3 from Gare de Lyon or Châtelet-Les Halles (€4.70) to Cergy Préfecture station then bus 95-07 (destination Butry).

SNCF From Gare du Nord or Gare St-Lazare to Pontoise, change to a train heading for Creil and alight at Auvers-sur-Oise. There is a SNCF package (adult/6-9 yr/10-17 yr €15.30/9.70/13.30) that includes return transport from Paris, bus transfers, and admission to the Château d' Auvers. The last train to Paris leaves just after 9pm weekdays and sometime after 10.30pm at the weekend.

Maison de Van Gogh (Auberge Ravoux; ☎ 01 30 36 60 60; 52 rue du Général de Gaulle, Auvers-sur-Oise; adult/under 12/12-18 yr/family €5/free/3/10; ⏰ 10am-6pm Tue-Sun mid-Mar–mid-Nov) Enter from rue de la Sansonne.

Musée de l'Absinthe (☎ 01 30 36 83 26; 44 rue Callé, Auvers-sur-Oise; adult/under 15/student €4.50/free/3.80; ⏰ 1.30-6pm Wed-Fri, 11am-6pm Sat & Sun mid-Jun–mid-Sep, 11am-6pm Sat, Sun & holidays mid-Sep-Nov & Mar–mid-Jun)

Eating & Sleeping

Auberge Ravoux (☎ 01 30 36 60 63; 52 rue du Général de Gaulle, Auvers-sur-Oise; lunch & dinner menus €28/35; ⏰ lunch Tue-Sun & dinner to 9pm Tue-Sat Mar-Nov) What could be a more appropriate way to celebrate the life of Vincent van Gogh than by having lunch or dinner

in the house in which he died? Auberge Ravoux has been a *café d'artistes* (artists' café; or so it claims) since 1876, so it predates van Gogh's fateful sojourn by more than a dozen years.

Café de la Paix (☎ 01 30 36 73 23; 11 rue du Général de Gaulle, Auvers-sur-Oise; starters €9-10, mains €15-16, menus lunch Mon-Fri, €12 dinner daily €16-25; ⏰ 7am-8.30pm Wed-Mon) If the Ravoux is full, head across the road to this cheerful café. Its brasserie fare is very reasonably priced.

Hostellerie du Nord (☎ 01 30 36 70 74; www.hostellerie dunord.fr; 6 rue du Général de Gaulle, Auvers-sur-Oise; s & d €95-125, ste €185; ⏰ 🔇) This lovely inn is housed in a 17th-century building that was one of the first post offices in France. Each of the eight beautifully appointed rooms and suites is named after an artist with a connection to Auvers-sur-Oise. It is open all year.

DISNEYLAND RESORT PARIS

It took almost €4.6 billion and five years of work to turn the beet fields east of the capital into Europe's first Disney theme park, which opened in 1992 amid much fanfare and controversy. Although Disney stockholders were less than thrilled with the park's performance for the first few years, what was originally known as Euro-Disney is now very much in the black, and the many visitors – mostly families with young children – just can't seem to get enough.

Disneyland Resort Paris consists of three main areas: the **Disney Village**, with its five hotels, shops, restaurants and clubs; **Disneyland Park**, with its five theme parks; and **Walt Disney Studios Park**, which brings film, animation and TV production to life. The first two are separated by the RER and TGV train stations; Walt Disney Studios is next to Disneyland Park. Moving walkways whisk visitors to the sights from the far-flung car park.

Disneyland Park is divided into five *pays* (lands). **Main Street, USA**, just inside the main entrance and behind Disneyland Hotel, is a spotless avenue reminiscent of Norman Rockwell's idealised small-town America c 1900, complete with larger-than-life Disney characters let loose among the crowds. **Frontierland**, which adjoins Main Street, USA, is a re-creation of the 'rugged, untamed American West'.

Adventureland, evoking the Arabian Nights and the wilds of Africa (among other exotic lands that are portrayed in Disney films), is home to Pirates of the Caribbean, as well as to Indiana Jones and the Temple of Peril, which is a roller coaster that spirals through a hair-raising 360 degrees – in reverse! **Fantasyland** brings classic fairy-tale characters such as Sleeping Beauty, Pinocchio, Peter Pan and Snow White to life; you'll also find 'It's a Small World' here. **Discovery**eryland features a dozen high-tech attractions and rides (including Space Mountain and Orbitron) and futuristic films at Videopolis that pay homage to Leonardo da Vinci, George Lucas and – just for a bit of local colour – Jules Verne. In 2006 a new, interactive **Buzz Lightyear** attraction opened.

Walt Disney Studios, which opened in March 2002, has a sound stage, a production backlot and animation studios that help illustrate up close how films, TV programs and cartoons are produced.

Be prepared to queue up for rides and shows – in the warm months the lines can get very long.

TRANSPORT

Distance from Paris 32km

Direction East

Travel time 35 to 40 minutes by RER

Car Route A4 from Porte de Bercy, direction Metz-Nancy and exit No 14.

RER Line A4 to Marne-la-Vallée/Chessy, Disneyland's RER station, from central Paris (€6.40). Trains run every 15 minutes or so, with the last train back to Paris at about 12.20am.

Sights

Disneyland Resort Paris (☎ 08 25 30 60 30; from the UK 0 87 05 03 03 05, from the USA 407-WDISNEY or 407-934 7639; www.disneylandparis.com); **Disneyland Park** (Apr-Oct adult/3-11 yr €42/34; ☺ 9am-8pm except from 10am Mon-Fri early-May-mid-Jun & Sep-Mar, 9am-11pm early-Jul-Aug); **Walt Disney Studios Park** (Apr-Oct adult/3-11 yr €42/34; ☺ 9am-6pm late-Jun-early-Sep, 10am-6pm Mon-Fri & 9am-6pm Sat & Sun early-Sep-late-Jun) One-day admission fees include unlimited access to all rides and activities in *either* Disneyland Park or Walt Disney Studios Park. Those who opt for the latter, however, can also enter Disneyland Park three hours before it closes. Multiple-day passes are also available: a Passe-Partout (adult/child €52/43) allows entry to both parks for one day, while a Hopper Ticket (per day adult/child €52/43) allows you to enter and leave both parks as often as you like over a number of days – these days need not be consecutive but must be used within one year. Fees change from season to season and there are always a multitude of special offers and accommodation/transport packages available at any one time.

Eating & Sleeping

There are 50 restaurants at Disneyland Paris, including venues like Silver Spur Steakhouse in Frontierland and Annette's Diner in Disney Village. Depending on the restaurant, most have adult *menus* for between €20 and €30 and a children's *menu* for around €10. Disneyland Park restaurant hours change according to the season; those in Disney Village are open from 11am or 11.30am to about midnight daily. You are not allowed to picnic inside the theme park.

Each of the resort's six hotels (central booking ☎ 01 60 30 60 30; fax 01 64 74 59 20) has its own all-American theme, reflected in the design, décor, restaurants and entertainment. All of the rooms have two double beds (or, in the case of Hôtel Cheyenne, one double bed and a set of bunk beds) and can sleep up to four people. Free shuttle buses link the hotels with the parks.

Rates are highest during the following periods: July and August and around Christmas; on Friday and Saturday nights and during holiday periods from April to October; and on Saturday nights from mid-February to March. The cheapest rates are available on most weeknights (ie Sunday to Thursday or, sometimes, Friday) from January to mid-February, from mid-May to June, for most of September, and from November to mid-December. As for the park, prices vary greatly; most guests stay as part of a package.

Disneyland Hôtel (d per person €258-599; ♿) This 496-room property at the entrance to the two parks bills itself as a 'lavish Victorian fantasy' and is the pinnacle of Disneyland Resort Paris accommodation.

Hôtel Cheyenne (d per person €105-230; ♿) The 14 timber-framed buildings of this 1000-room hotel – each with its own hokey name – are arranged to resemble a Wild West frontier town.

Hôtel Santa Fe (d per person €69-180; ♿) This 1000-room hotel, which offers the most affordable accommodation in the resort itself, has an American Southwest style.

PARC ASTÉRIX

An alternative to Disneyland Resort Paris (p359), **Parc Astérix** is just beyond Roissy Charles de Gaulle airport. Like Disneyland, it's divided into a number of 'regions' – the Village of the Gauls, the Roman Empire, Ancient Greece, the Middle Ages, Old Paris etc. There are lots of rides, including a hair-raising roller coaster called Tonnère de Zeus (Zeus' Thunder) and the Oxygénarium flume. The Three Musketeers also figure prominently.

Information

Parc Astérix (☎ 08 91 67 67 11; www.parcasterix.com; 1-day pass adult/3-11 yr €34/24, 2-day pass adult/3-11 yr €65/45; ☺ 10am-6pm Apr, 10am-6pm Tue-Thu & 9.30am-7pm Sat & Sun May–mid-Jul, 9.30am-7pm mid-Jul–Aug, 10am-6pm Wed, Sat & Sun Sep–early-Oct) Tickets including admission and all transport to/from the park (adult/3-11 yr €40/26.20) are available at most RER and SNCF stations in central Paris.

TRANSPORT

Distance from Paris 36km

Direction Northeast

Travel time 50 to 60 minutes by RER & bus

Car Route A1, Parc Astérix exit between exit Nos 7 and 8.

RER Line B3 from Châtelet or Gare du Nord to Aéroport Roissy Charles de Gaulle 1 train station, then take the Courriers Île-de-France bus (adult/3-11 yr €5.80/4.40 return); the bus leaves every half-hour from 9.30am to 6.30pm, returning from the park every half-hour from 4.30pm to 7pm or 8pm.

Excursions

PARC ASTÉRIX

Transport

Transport

As one of the most visited destinations on earth, most roads lead to Paris. Almost all major (and minor) airlines fly through it, and it is thoroughly integrated into the train and bus routes of France and greater Europe. As for getting around, the metro system is extremely efficient, if somewhat stinky. But the best way to get around Paris is to walk – unless you're really pressed for time or it's raining. With the city sights spread across a distance no greater than 10km, most major places of interest can be reached and navigated by foot. Indeed, often metro stops are only a five minute walk apart from each other. Buses are a scenic option but are slowed by traffic, and getting to know the different routes takes much practice even for residents. Biking and rollerblading are also great ways to get around. With such beautiful surrounds, getting from A to B is a historical and aesthetic feast in itself. And, of course, a culinary one!

Flights, tours and rail tickets can be booked online at www.lonelyplanet.com /travel_services.

AIR
Airlines

Almost all international airlines go through Paris. The Aéroports de Paris website (www.adp.fr) has information on flights, routes and carriers.

Aer Lingus (EI; ☎ 01 70 20 00 72; www.aerlingus.com)

Air Canada (AC; ☎ 08 25 88 08 81; www.aircanada.com)

Air France (AF; ☎ 08 20 82 08 20, arrivals & departures 08 92 68 10 48; www.airfrance.com)

Air New Zealand (NZ; ☎ 01 40 53 82 23; www.airnz.com)

British Airways (BA; ☎ 08 25 82 54 00; www.british -airways.com)

British Midland (BD; ☎ 01 41 91 87 04; www.flybmi.com)

Continental Airlines (CO; ☎ 01 42 99 09 01, 01 71 23 03 35; www.continental.com)

Delta Air Lines (DL; ☎ 08 00 35 40 80; www.delta.com)

Easyjet (U2; ☎ 08 25 08 25 08; www.easyjet.com)

KLM (KL; ☎ 08 90 71 07 10; www.klm.com)

Lufthansa Airlines (LH; ☎ 08 26 10 33 34; www .lufthansa.com)

CLIMATE CHANGE & TRAVEL

Climate change is a serious threat to the ecosystems that humans rely upon, and air travel is the fastest-growing contributor to the problem. Lonely Planet regards travel, overall, as a global benefit, but believes we all have a responsibility to limit our personal impact on global warming.

Flying & Climate Change

Pretty much every form of motorised travel generates CO_2 (the main cause of human-induced climate change) but planes are far and away the worst offenders, not just because of the sheer distances they allow us to travel, but because they release greenhouse gases high into the atmosphere. The statistics are frightening: two people taking a return flight between Europe and the US will contribute as much to climate change as an average household's gas and electricity consumption over a whole year.

Carbon Offset Schemes

Climatecare.org and other websites use 'carbon calculators' that allow travellers to offset the level of greenhouse gases they are responsible for with financial contributions to sustainable travel schemes that reduce global warming – including projects in India, Honduras, Kazakhstan and Uganda.

Lonely Planet, together with Rough Guides and other concerned partners in the travel industry, support the carbon offset scheme run by climatecare.org. Lonely Planet offsets all of its staff and author travel.

For more information check out our website: www.lonelyplanet.com.

Northwest Airlines (NW; ☎ 08 90 71 07 10; www.nwa.com)

Qantas Airways (QF; ☎ 08 20 82 05 00; www.qantas.com)

Ryanair (FR; ☎ 08 92 68 20 73; www.ryanair.com)

Scandinavian Airlines (SAS; ☎ 08 20 32 53 35; www.scandinavian.net)

Singapore Airlines (SQ; ☎ 08 21 23 03 80; www.singaporeair.com)

Thai Airways International (TG; ☎ 01 44 20 70 80; www.thaiair.com)

United Airlines (UA; ☎ 08 10 72 72 72; www.united.com)

US Airways (US; ☎ 08 10 63 22 22; www.usairways.com)

Virgin Atlantic (VS; ☎ in UK 44 87 05 74 77 47; www.virgin-atlantic.com)

As well as airline websites, there are a number of efficient online resources for buying good-value plane tickets. Some of the best include the following:

Anyway (www.anyway.fr in French)

Bargain Holidays (www.bargainholidays.com)

Cheap Flights (www.cheapflights.co.uk)

easyvols (www.easyvols.com in French)

ebookers (www.ebookers.com)

e-mondial (www.e-mondial.com in French)

Go Voyages (www.govoyages.com in French)

Last Minute (www.lastminute.com)

Opodo (www.opodo.com)

Travelocity (www.travelocity.com)

Voyages SNCF (www.voyages-sncf.com in French)

Airports

Paris has two main international airports: Aéroport d'Orly and Aéroport Roissy Charles de Gaulle. A third airport at Beauvais handles flights by some charter companies and Ryanair.

AÉROPORT D'ORLY

The older and smaller of Paris' two major airports, **Orly** (ORY; Map pp422–3; ☎ 01 49 75 15 15, flight info 08 92 68 15 15; www.adp.fr) is 18km south of the city. Air France and some other international carriers (eg Iberia and TAP Air Portugal) use Orly Terminal-Ouest (the west terminal). Free shuttle bus services link Orly Terminal-Sud

(south terminal) and Orly Terminal-Ouest, as well as the carparks and the RER C station Pont de Rungis-Aéroport d'Orly (see below). The Orlyval automatic metro links both terminals and connects with the RER B (see below).

The following are the public transport options to/from Orly airport. Apart from RATP bus 183, all services call at both terminals. Tickets for the bus services are sold on board. Children aged two to 11 are usually half price.

Air France Bus 1 (☎ 08 92 35 08 20; www.cars-airfrance.com in French; one way/return €8/12; ⏰ 6am-11pm both directions) This *navette* (shuttle bus) runs every 15 minutes to/from the eastern side of Gare Montparnasse (Map pp434–5; 30-45 minutes) as well as Aérogare des Invalides (Map pp434–5; 30-45 minutes) in the 7e. On your way into the city, you can ask to get off at metro Porte d'Orléans (Map pp422–3) or metro Duroc (Map pp434–5).

Jetbus (☎ 01 69 01 00 09; one way/return €5.50/9.20; ⏰ 6.43am-10.49pm from Orly, 6.15am-10.15am from Paris) Jetbus runs every 15 to 25 minutes to/from metro Villejuif Louis Aragon (Map pp422–3; 55 minutes), which is a bit south of the 13e on the city's southern fringe. From there a regular metro/bus ticket will get you into the centre of Paris.

Noctilien Night bus (☎ 08 92 68 77 14, 08 92 68 41 14 in English; ticket €5.60; ⏰ 12.30am-5.30pm) Part of the RATP's night service, Noctilien bus 31 links Gare de Lyon (Map pp446–7), Place d'Italie (Map p448) and Gare d'Austerlitz (Map pp446–7) in Paris with Orly-Sud, running every hour and take around 45 minutes to an hour to reach Orly.

Orlybus (☎ 08 92 68 77 14; ticket €5.80; ⏰ 6am-11.30pm from Orly, 5.35am-11pm from Paris) This RATP bus runs every 15 to 20 minutes to/from metro Denfert-Rochereau (Map pp422–3; 30 minutes) in the 14e, and makes several stops in the eastern 14e in each direction.

RATP Bus 183 (☎ 08 92 68 77 14; ticket €1.40 or 1 metro/bus ticket; ⏰ 5.35am-8.35pm each direction) This is a slow public bus that links Orly-Sud (only) with metro Porte de Choisy (Map pp422–3; one hour), at the southern edge of the 13e. It runs every 35 minutes.

RER B and Orlyval (☎ 08 92 68 77 14; to Paris €9.05; ⏰ 6am-11pm each direction) From the airport, take the Orlyval automatic rail and connect with the RER B station Antony. To get to Paris take RER B4 north (35 to 40 minutes to Châtelet, every four to 12 minutes). Orlyval tickets are valid for the subsequent RER and metro journey.

RER C and shuttle (☎ 08 90 36 10 10; to/from Paris €5.65; ⏰ 5.35am-11.30pm from Orly, 5.06am-12am to Orly) From the airport take an airport shuttle bus (every 15 to 30 minutes) to the RER station Pont de Rungis-Aéroport d'Orly. From there the RER C2 train crosses Paris (50 minutes to Gare d'Austerlitz). A ticket remains valid for the subsequent metro journey. Coming from Paris be sure to get the shuttle at Pont de Rungis that goes to the correct terminal.

Along with public transport the following private options are available, though some shuttle bus services are reported to be less than reliable so leave plenty of time:

Allô Shuttle (☎ 01 34 29 00 80; www.alloshuttle.com) Various shuttle services provide door-to-door transfers for about €26 per single person (€17 per person for two or more). Book in advance and allow for numerous pick-ups and drop-offs.

Paris Airports Service (☎ 01 55 98 10 80; www.paris airportservice.com)

Shuttle Van PariShuttle (☎ 08 00 69 96 99; www .parishuttle.com)

Taxi Trips to/from central Paris and Orly will cost about €40 to €45 and take around 30 minutes; see p369 for taxi phone numbers.

World Shuttle (☎ 01 46 80 14 67; www.world -shuttles.com)

Transport between Aéroport Roissy Charles De Gaulle and Aéroport Orly is offered by the following services:

Air France bus 3 (☎ 08 92 35 08 20; www.cars-airfrance .com in French; ticket €16; ☼ 6am-10.30pm) This bus runs between Orly and Roissy Charles de Gaulle (one hour, every 30 minutes) and is free for Air France passengers making flight connections.

RER B and Orlyval (☎ 08 90 36 10 10; ticket €16.90; ☼ 6am-11pm each direction) The RER line B connects the stations CG1 and CDG2 at Roissy-Charles de Gaulle with Antony station. From here the Orlyval automatic train links with the two terminals at Orly airport. The trip between the airports takes one hour and trains run every four to 15 minutes.

Taxi The fare from one airport to the other should cost around €56. Count on at least one hour's travel time.

AÉROPORT ROISSY CHARLES DE GAULLE

Thirty kilometres northeast of Paris in the suburb of Roissy, **Roissy Charles de Gaulle** (CDG; ☎ 01 48 62 22 80, 08 92 68 15 15; www.adp.fr) consists of three terminals, appropriately named Aérogares 1, 2 and 3. Aérogares 1 and 2 are used by international and domestic carriers. Aérogare 3 is used mainly by charter companies.

Roissy Charles de Gaulle has two train stations: Aéroport Charles de Gaulle 1 (CDG1) and the sleek Aéroport Charles de Gaulle 2 (CDG2). Both are served by commuter trains on RER line B3. A free shuttle bus links all of the terminals with the train stations.

There are various public transport options for travel between Aéroport Roissy Charles de Gaulle and Paris. Tickets for the bus services are sold on board. Children aged two to 11 are usually half price.

Air France bus 2 (☎ 08 92 35 08 20; www.cars-airfrance .com in French; one way/return €12/18; ☼ 5.45am-11pm each direction) Links the airport every 15 minutes with two locations on the Right Bank: near the Arc de Triomphe just outside 2 av Carnot, 17e (Map pp426–7; 35-50 minutes) and the Palais des Congrès de Paris, 17e (Map pp426–7; 35-50 minutes).

Air France bus 4 (☎ 08 92 35 08 20; www.cars-airfrance .com in French; one way/return €12/18; ☼ 7am-9pm each direction) Links the airport every 30 minutes with Gare de Lyon (Map pp446–7; 45-55 minutes) and Gare Montparnasse (Map pp434–5; 45-55 minutes).

Noctilien Night bus (☎ 08 92 68 77 14, 08 92 68 41 14 in English; ticket €7; ☼ 12.30am-5.30pm) Part of the RATP's night service, Noctilien buses 121 (linking Montparnasse, Châtelet, Gare du Nord) and 140 (linking Gare du Nord and Gare de l'Est) go to Roissy-Charles de Gaulle every hour.

RATP Bus 350 (☎ 08 92 68 77 14; ticket €4.20 or 3 metro/bus tickets; ☼ 5.45am-7pm each direction) Links Aérogares 1 and 2 with Gare de l'Est (Map pp428–9; one hour, every 30 minutes) and Gare du Nord (Map pp428–9; one hour, every 30 minutes).

RATP Bus 351 (☎ 08 92 68 77 14; ticket €4.20 or 3 metro/bus tickets; ☼ 7am-9.30pm from the airport, 8.30am-8.20pm from Paris) Links the eastern side of place de la Nation (Map pp422–3) with Roissy-Charles de Gaulle (55 minutes, every 30 minutes).

RER B (☎ 08 90 36 10 10; ticket €8; ☼ 4.56am-12.15am from Paris Nord, 4.56am-11.56pm from the airport) RER line B3 links CDG1 and CDG2 with the city (30 minutes; every four to 15 minutes). To get to the airport take any RER line B train whose four-letter destination code begins with E (eg EIRE) and a shuttle bus (every five to eight minutes) will take you to the correct terminal. Regular metro ticket windows can't always sell RER tickets to the airport so you may have to buy one at the RER station where you board.

Roissybus 352 (☎ 08 92 68 77 14; ticket €8.40; ☼ 5.45am-11pm from Paris, 6am-11pm from the airport) This direct public bus links from several points in both terminals with rue Scribe behind the Palais Garnier in the 9e (Map pp426–7; 60 minutes, every 15 to 20 minutes).

In addition to the public transport options you can use the following:

Shuttle Van The four companies in the Orly section (p363) will take you from Roissy Charles de Gaulle to your hotel for around €25 for a single person, or €17 for two or more people. Book in advance.

Taxi Trips to/from the city centre cost from €40 to €55, depending on the traffic and time of day.

For transport options between Aéroport Roissy Charles De Gaulle and Aéroport Orly see opposite.

AÉROPORT PARIS-BEAUVAIS

Eighty kilometres north of Paris, the **Aéroport Paris-Beauvais** (BVA; ☎ 03 44 11 46 86, flight information ☎ 08 92 68 20 66-5; www .aeroportbeauvais.com) is used by charter companies and Ryanair for its discount European flights, including those between Paris and Dublin, Shannon and Glasgow.

Express Bus (☎ 08 92 68 20 64; ticket €16.90; ☼ 8.05am to 10.40pm from Beauvais, 5.45am-8.05pm from Paris) Leaves Parking Pershing (Map pp426–7), just west of the Palais des Congrès de Paris, three hours before each Ryanair departure (you can board up to 15 minutes before) and leaves the airport 20 to 30 minutes after each arrival, dropping passengers off just south of the Palais des Congrès on Place de la Porte Maillot (Map pp426–7). The trip takes one to 1¼ hours. Tickets can be purchased from Ryanair (☎ 03 44 11 41 41) at the airport or from a kiosk in the carpark, or online (http:// ticket.aeroportbeauvais.com).

Taxi Trips between central Paris and Beauvais cost €110 during the day and €150 at night and all day Sunday.

BICYCLE

For detailed information on where and how to cycle in Paris, see p275. For information on guided bicycle tours in Paris, see p95.

BICYCLES ON PUBLIC TRANSPORT

Bicycles are not allowed on the metro except on line 1 on Sunday and public holidays. You can, however, take your bicycle to the suburbs on some RER lines on weekdays before 6.30am, between 9am and 4.30pm, after 7pm, and all day on the weekend and on public holidays. More lenient rules apply to SNCF commuter services. Contact SNCF (p369) for details.

BOAT

Batobus (☎ 0 825 05 01 01, 01 44 11 33 99; www.batobus.com; adult/child 2-6 1-day pass €11/5, 2-day pass €13/6; ☼ 10am-7pm Oct-May, 10am-9pm Jun-Sep), a fleet of five glassed-in trimarans, docks at small piers along the Seine. As you can jump on and off at will, Batobus can be used as a form of transport. Tickets are available at each stop, as well as at tourist offices. A special offer with **Paris l'Open Tour** (p96) allows two days unlimited travel on Batobus boats and Open Tour buses for adult/child €39/18 from Batobus locations. The boats depart every 25 minutes from the following locations:

Champs-Élysées (Map pp426–7; Port des Champs-Élysées, 8e; Ⓜ Champs-Élysées Clemenceau)

Eiffel Tower (Map pp434–5; Port de la Bourdonnais, 7e; Ⓜ Champ de Mars-Tour Eiffel)

Hôtel de Ville (Map pp436–7; quai de l'Hôtel de Ville, 4e; Ⓜ Hôtel de Ville)

Jardin des Plantes (Map pp444–5; quai St-Bernard, 5e; Ⓜ Jussieu)

Musée d'Orsay (Map pp434–5; quai de Solférino, 7e; Ⓜ Musée d'Orsay)

Musée du Louvre (Map pp436–7; quai du Louvre, 1er; Ⓜ Palais Royal-Musée du Louvre)

Notre Dame (Map pp436–7; quai Montebello, 5e; Ⓜ St-Michel)

St-Germain des Prés (Map pp436–7; quai Malaquais, 6e; Ⓜ St-Germain des Prés)

For pleasure cruises on the Seine, Canal St-Martin and Canal de l'Ourcq, see p95.

BUS
Local

Paris' bus system, which is operated by the Régie Autonome des Transports Parisians (RATP; see p369), runs from 5.45am to 8.30pm Monday to Saturday; after that another 20 lines continue until 12.30am. Services are drastically reduced on Sunday and public holidays when buses run from 7am to 8.30pm. Among many *service en soirée* (evening service) routes – distinct from the Noctilien overnight services described on p366 – are: number 26 between the Gare St-Lazare and Cours de Vincennes via Gare du Nord and Gare de l'Est; number 38 linking Gare du Nord, Châtelet and Porte d'Orléans via blvd St-Michel; number 92 from Gare

Montparnasse to place Charles de Gaulle and back via Alma Marceau; and number 95 between Porte de Montmartre and Porte de Vanves via Opéra and St-Germain. The same fares and conditions apply on evening routes as for regular daytime services. Most evening routes finish at around midnight.

Night Buses

Night buses pick up the traffic after the last metro (around 1am). Buses depart hourly from 12.30am to 5.30pm. The RATP runs 27 night buses on its improved **Noctilien network** (www.noctilien.fr has information, maps and itineraries in English), in partnership with the SNCF which runs an additional eight lines, including direct or semi-direct services out to the suburbs. The services (formerly called Noctambus) pass through the main *gares* (train stations) and cross the major axes of the city before leading out to the suburbs. Many go through Châtelet (rue de Rivoli and blvd Sébastopol). Look for blue N or Noctilien signs at bus stops. There are two circular lines within Paris (the N01 and N02) that link four main train stations, St-Lazare, Gare de l'Est, Gare de Lyon, Montparnasse (but not Châtelet), as well as popular nightspots Bastille, the Champs-Élysées, Pigalle and St-Germain.

The buses are equipped with security surveillance systems linked to local police, and RATP staff members are posted at major points to help passengers. Do remain alert, however, and watch your bags and pockets – especially on weekends when the post-drinking crowd circulates.

Noctilien services are free if you have a Carte Orange, Mobilis or Paris Visite pass (p368) for the zones in which you are travelling. Otherwise you pay a certain number of standard €1.40 metro tickets, depending on the length of your journey: the driver can sell you tickets and will explain how many you need to get to your destination.

Tickets & Fares

Short bus rides (ie one or two bus zones) cost one metro/bus ticket (€1.40); longer rides require two tickets. Transfers to other buses or the metro are not allowed on the same ticket. Travel to the suburbs costs up to three tickets, depending on the zone. Special tickets valid only on the bus can be purchased from the driver.

Whatever kind of single-journey ticket you have, you must *oblitérer* (cancel) it in the *composteur* (cancelling machine) next to the driver. If you have a Carte Orange, Mobilis or Paris Visite pass (p368), just flash it at the driver when you board. Do *not* cancel the magnetic coupon that accompanies your pass.

Long Distance

Eurolines (Map pp444–5; ☎ 01 43 54 11 99, 08 92 89 90 91; www.eurolines.fr; 55 rue St-Jacques, 5e; ◷ 9.30am-6.30pm Mon-Fri, 10am-1pm & 2-6pm Sat; Ⓜ Cluny-La Sorbonne), an association of more than 30 national and private bus companies that links Paris with points all over Western and Central Europe, Scandinavia and Morocco, can organise ticket reservations and sales. The **Gare Routière Internationale de Paris-Galliéni** (Map pp422–3; ☎ 08 92 89 90 91; 28 av du Général de Gaulle; Ⓜ Gallieni), the city's international bus terminal, is in the inner suburb of Bagnolet.

CAR & MOTORCYCLE

The easiest way to turn a stay in Paris into an uninterrupted series of hassles is to drive. If driving the car doesn't destroy your holiday sense of spontaneity, parking the thing certainly will. But while driving in Paris is nerve-wracking, it's not impossible – except for the faint-hearted or indecisive. The fastest way to get across the city is usually via the blvd Périphérique (Map pp422–3), the ring road that encircles the city.

Hire

You can get a small car (eg a Renault Twingo) for one day, with 250km mileage but without insurance, from around €71 with Budget. Most of the larger companies listed below have offices throughout Paris and at airports and main train stations. Several are represented at **Aérogare des Invalides** (Map pp434–5; Ⓜ Invalides) in the 7e.

Avis (☎ 08 02 05 05 05; www.avis.fr)

Budget (☎ 08 25 00 35 64; www.budget.fr in French)

Europcar (☎ 08 25 35 83 58; www.europcar.fr in French)

Hertz (☎ 08 25 86 18 61, 01 55 31 93 21; www.hertz.fr)

Smaller agencies often offer more attractive deals. For example, Rent A Car Système has an economy-class car from €39 per 24-hour day for 100km (0.18c for additional kilometres), €90 for a weekend with 500km and €199 for seven days with 800km.

The companies listed here offer reasonable rates and have several branches throughout Paris. A wider selection is in the *Yellow Pages* under 'Location d'Automobiles: Tourisme et Utilitaires'. It's a good idea to reserve at least three days ahead, especially for holiday weekends and during the summer.

ADA (☎ 08 25 16 91 69; www.ada.fr in French) ADA has a dozen branches in Paris including **8e arrondissement** (Map pp426–7; ☎ 01 42 93 65 13; 72 rue de Rome, 8e; Ⓜ Rome) and **11e arrondissement** (Map pp428–9; ☎ 01 48 06 58 13; 34 av de la République, 11e; Ⓜ Parmentier).

easyCar (www.easycar.com) Britain's budget car-rental agency rents out mini Mercedes from €13 a day plus extras, and Smart cars (from €8) from branches at main train stations including **Montparnasse** (Map pp434–5; Parking Gaîté, 33 rue du Commandant René Mouchotte, 15e; Ⓜ Gaîté). Branches are in underground car parks and are fully automated systems; you must book in advance and fill in all the forms online on location.

Rent A Car Système (☎ 08 91 70 02 00; www.rentacar .fr) Rent A Car has 16 outlets in Paris, including **Louvre-Pyramides** (Map pp426–7; ☎ 01 42 96 95 95; 15 rue Pyramides, 1er; Ⓜ Pyramides), **Bercy** (Map p449; ☎ 01 43 45 98 99; 79 rue de Bercy, 12e; Ⓜ Bercy) and **16e arrondissement** (Map pp422–3; ☎ 01 42 88 40 04; 84 av de Versailles, 16e; Ⓜ Mirabeau).

If you've got the urge to look like you've just stepped into (or out of) a black-and-white French film from the 1950s, a motor scooter will fit the bill perfectly.

Free Scoot (Map pp428–9; ☎ 01 44 93 04 03; www .free-scoot.com; 144 blvd Voltaire, 11e; Ⓨ 9am-1pm & 2-7pm Mon-Fri; Ⓜ Voltaire) Rents out 50cc scooters per day/24-hour day/weekend/week from €30/35/75/145, and 125cc scooters for €45/55/110/245. Prices include third-party insurance as well as two helmets, locks, raingear and gloves. To rent a 50cc scooter you must be at least 21 and leave a credit card deposit of €1300. For a 125cc one, the minimum age is 23 and the deposit is €1600. There's also a branch in the **5e arrondissement** (Map pp444–5; ☎ 01 44 07 06 72; 63 quai de la Tournelle, 5e; Ⓜ Maubert Mutualité).

Parking
In many parts of Paris you have to pay €1.50 to €2 an hour to park your car on the street. Municipal parking garages usually charge €4 an hour and between €20 and €25 for 24 hours.

Parking fines are €11 to €35, depending on the offence and its gravity, and parking attendants dispense them with great abandon. You pay them by purchasing a *timbre amende* (fine stamp) for the amount written on the ticket from any *tabac* (tobacconist), affixing the stamp to the preaddressed coupon and dropping it in a letter box.

METRO & RER NETWORKS
Paris' underground network, which is run by the RATP (Régie Autonome des Transports Parisians), consists of two separate but linked systems: the Métropolitain, known as the *métro*, with 14 lines and 372 stations; and the Réseau Express Régional (RER), a network of suburban lines (designated A to E and then numbered) that pass through the city centre. When giving the names of stations in this book, the term 'metro' is used to cover both the Métropolitain and the RER system within Paris proper.

Information
Metro maps of various sizes and degrees of detail are available for free at metro ticket windows. RATP *Paris 1* provides plans of metro, RER, bus and tram routes in central Paris; *Paris 2* superimposes the same over street maps; and *Île-de-France 3* covers the area around Paris. *Touristes: Grand Plan Touristique* combines all three and adds tourist information.

For information on the metro, RER and bus systems, contact **RATP** (☎ 08 92 68 77 14 in French, ☎ 08 92 68 41 14 in English; www.ratp.fr; Ⓨ 6am-9pm). The RATP website has itineraries and route information in English (in the 'international passengers' section) and traffic information (French only).

Metro
Each metro train is known by the name of its terminus. On maps and plans each line has a different colour and number (from one to 14); Parisians usually refer to the line number.

Signs in metro and RER stations indicate the way to the correct platform for your line. The *direction* signs on each platform indicate the terminus. On lines that split into several branches (like lines 3, 7 and 13), the terminus of each train is indicated on the cars with backlit panels, and often on the increasingly common electronic signs on each platform giving the number of minutes until the next train.

Signs marked *correspondance* (transfer) show how to reach connecting trains. At stations with many intersecting lines, like Châtelet and Montparnasse Bienvenüe walking from one train to the next can take a long time.

Different station exits are indicated by white-on-blue *sortie* (exit) signs. You can get your bearings by checking the *plan du quartier* (neighbourhood maps) posted at exits.

Each line has its own schedule, but trains usually start at around 5.30am with the last train beginning its run between 12.35am and 1am.

RER

The RER is faster than the metro but the stops are much further apart. Some attractions, particularly those on the Left Bank (eg the Musée d'Orsay, Eiffel Tower and Panthéon), can be reached far more conveniently by the RER than by metro.

RER lines are known by an alphanumeric combination – the letter (A to E) refers to the line, the number to the spur it will follow somewhere out in the suburbs. As a rule of thumb, even-numbered RER lines head for Paris' southern or eastern suburbs while odd-numbered ones go north or west. All trains whose four-letter codes (indicated both on the train and on the lightboard) begin with the same letter share the same terminus. Stations served are usually indicated on electronic destination boards above the platform.

TICKETS & FARES

The same RATP tickets are valid on the metro, the RER (for travel within the city limits), buses, trams and the Montmartre funicular. They cost €1.40 if bought individually and €10.70 (€5.35 for children four to 11) for a *carnet* (book) of 10. Tickets are sold at all metro stations, though not always at every entrance. Ticket windows and vending machines accept most credit cards.

One metro/bus ticket lets you travel between any two metro stations for a period of two hours, no matter how many transfers are required. You can also use it on the RER for travel within zone 1. However, a single

ticket cannot be used to transfer from the metro to a bus, from a bus to the metro or between buses.

Always keep your ticket until you exit from your station; you may be stopped by a *contrôleur* (ticket inspector) and will have to pay a fine (€25 to €45 on the spot), if you don't have a valid ticket.

TRAVEL PASSES

The cheapest and easiest way to use public transport in Paris is to get a Carte Orange, a combined metro, RER and bus pass whose accompanying magnetic coupon comes in weekly and monthly versions. You can get tickets for travel in two to eight urban and suburban zones but, unless you'll be using the suburban commuter lines extensively, the basic ticket valid for zones 1 and 2 should be sufficient.

A weekly Carte Orange (*coupon hebdomadaire*) costs €15.70 for zones 1 and 2, and is valid from Monday to Sunday. It can be purchased from the previous Thursday until Wednesday; from Thursday weekly tickets are available for the following week only. Even if you'll only be in Paris for three or four days, it may work out cheaper than buying *carnets* and it will certainly cost less than buying a daily Mobilis or Paris Visite pass (opposite). The Carte Orange monthly ticket (*coupon mensuel*; €51.70 for zones 1 and 2) begins on the first day of each calendar month; you can buy one from the 20th of the preceding month. Both are on sale in metro and RER stations from 6.30am to 10pm and at certain bus terminals. You can also buy your Carte Orange coupon from vending machines and, if you have a French postal address, on the RATP website (www.ratp.fr).

When buying a Carte Orange for the first time, take a passport-size photograph (four photos cost €4 at photo booths in most stations) to any metro or RER ticket window. Request a Carte Orange (which is free) and the kind of coupon (weekly or monthly) you'd like. To prevent tickets from being used by more than one person, you must write your *nom* (surname)and *prénom* (first name) on the Carte Orange, and the number of your Carte Orange on the weekly or monthly coupon you've bought.

The Navigo system, somewhat like London's Oyster cards, provides you with a refillable monthly or yearly unlimited pass that you can recharge at Navigo machines. You can swipe these tickets over the electronic panel as you go through the turnstiles. Ask at the ticket counter for a form. Navigo cards cannot be recharged for periods of less than one month.

TOURIST PASSES

The Mobilis and Paris Visite passes are valid on the metro, RER, SNCF's suburban lines (right), buses, night buses, trams and the Montmartre funicular railway. No photo is needed but write your card number on the ticket. The passes can be purchased at larger metro and RER stations, SNCF offices in Paris, and the airports.

The Mobilis card coupon allows unlimited travel for one day in two to eight zones (€5.20 to €18.30). It is available at all metro, RER and SNCF stations in the Paris region. Compare this with the cost of a *carnet* if you are just travelling in central Paris.

Paris Visite allows unlimited travel (including to airports) as well as discounted entry to certain museums and other discounts and bonuses. Passes are valid for either three, five or eight zones. The zone 1 to 3 pass costs €8.55/13.70/18.25/26.65 for one/two/three/five days. Children four to 11 pay €4.55/6.85/9.15/13.70.

TAXI

The *prise en charge* (flagfall) is €2. Within the city limits, it costs €0.77 per kilometre for travel between 7am and 7pm Monday to Saturday (*Tarif A*; white light on meter). At night (7pm to 7am), on Sundays and in the inner suburbs the rate is €1.09 per km (*Tarif B*; orange light on meter). Travel in the outer suburbs is at *Tarif C*, €1.31 per kilometre. There's a €2.60 surcharge for taking a fourth passenger, but drivers often refuse for insurance reasons. The first piece of baggage is free; additional pieces over 5kg cost €1 extra.

The number of taxi licenses is limited in Paris so it can be hard to find one, especially after 1am. Some 'freelance' (illegal) taxis have emerged but are not organised (like minicabs are in London) and there are no guarantees on price or safety.

Radio-dispatched taxi companies, on call 24 hours, include:

Abeille Radio Taxi (☎ 01 42 70 00 42)

Alpha Taxis (☎ 01 45 85 85 85)

ASTC (☎ 01 42 88 02 02)

Taxis Bleus (☎ 01 42 60 61 40)

Taxis G7 (☎ 01 47 39 47 39)

Taxis-Radio étoile (☎ 01 42 70 41 41)

TRAIN

Suburban

The RER and the commuter lines of the **SNCF** (Société' Nationale des Chemins de Fer; ☎ 08 91 36 20 20, 08 91 67 68 69 for timetables; www.sncf.fr) serve suburban destinations outside the city limits (ie zones 2 to 8). Purchase your ticket *before* you board the train or you won't be able to get out of the station when you arrive. You are not allowed to pay the additional fare when you get there.

If you are issued with a full-sized SNCF ticket for travel to the suburbs, validate it in one of the time-stamp pillars *before* you board the train. You may also be given a *contremarque magnétique* (magnetic ticket) to get through any metro/RER-type turnstiles on the way to/from the platform. If you are travelling on a multizone Carte Orange, Paris Visite or Mobilis pass, do *not* punch the magnetic coupon in one of the time-stamp machines. Most but not all RER/SNCF tickets purchased in the suburbs for travel to the city allow you to continue your journey by metro. For some destinations, tickets can be purchased at any metro ticket window; for others you have to go to an RER station on the line you need to buy a ticket.

Mainline & International

Paris has six major train stations, each of which has its own metro station: Gare d'Austerlitz (13e), Gare de l'Est (10e), Gare de Lyon (12e), Gare du Nord (10e), Gare Montparnasse (15e) and Gare St-Lazare (8e). Each station handles passenger traffic to different parts of France and the rest of Europe. Information for **SNCF mainline services** (☎ 36 35 or 08 92 35 35 35 from outside France; www.sncf.com) is available by phone or Internet.

Main stations have left-luggage offices or lockers (*consignes*). They cost €4/7.50/9.50 for 48 hours for a medium/large/extra large bag. After that it costs €5 a day. Most left-luggage offices and lockers are open from 6am to 11pm.

TRAM & FUNICULAR

Paris has two tram lines: T1 links the northern suburb of St-Denis with Noisy le Sec on RER line E2 via metro Bobigny Pablo Picasso on metro line No 5; T2 runs south along the Seine from La Défense to the Issy Val de Seine RER station on line C. However, the majority of visitors are unlikely to make use of either. The national and Île de France governments have undertaken an ambitious scheme to extend these lines around Paris over the next decade so that eventually they will completely encircle Paris about 5km outside the Périphérique. A new line through the 13e, 14e and 15e is scheduled to open late 2006, though again it will be of limited use to visitors or anyone staying in central Paris. The T3 tramway traces a curve around the southern edge of Paris. It leads from Point to Garigliano in the 15e, through Porte de Versailles (where it links with the T2), Porte d'Orleans, Porte d'Italie and up to Porte d'Ivry. Normal metro tickets and passes remain valid here and function in the same way as on the buses. You can buy tickets at automatic machines at each stop.

One form of transport that most travellers will use is the Montmartre funicular, which whisks visitors up the southern slope of Butte de Montmartre from square Willette (Ⓜ Anvers) to Sacré Cœur.

TRAVEL AGENTS

You'll find travel agencies everywhere in Paris but the following are among the largest and offer the best service (if not always deals):

Forum Voyages (www.forum-voyages.fr in French; ☉ 9.30am-7pm Mon-Sat) Has nine outlets in Paris, including branches at **Opéra** (Map pp428–9; ☎ 01 42 61 39 12; 11 av de l'Opéra, 1er; Ⓜ Pyramides) and **St-Germain** (Map pp434–5; ☎ 01 45 44 38 61; 1 rue Cassette, 6e; Ⓜ St-Sulpice).

Latin Nouvelles Frontières (☎ 08 25 00 08 25; www .nouvelles-frontieres.fr in French; ☉ 9am-7pm Mon-Sat) Has 22 outlets around the city, including **Opéra** (Map pp428–9; ☎ 01 42 61 02 62; 13 av de l'Opéra, 1er; Ⓜ Pyramides) and **Odéon** (Map pp436–7; ☎ 01 43 25 71 35; 116 blvd St-Germain, 6e; Ⓜ Odéon)

OTU Voyages (☎ 08 20 81 78 17; www.otu.fr in French) There's a branch opposite the Centre Pompidou plus one at **Luxembourg** (Map pp436–7; ☎ 01 44 41 38 50; 39 av Georges Bernanos, 5e; ☉ 9am-6.30pm Mon-Fri, 10am-noon & 1.15-5pm Sat; Ⓜ Port Royal)

Voyageurs du Monde (Map pp428–9; ☎ 01 49 26 07 14, 08 92 23 56 56; www.vdm.com in French; 55 rue Ste-Anne, 2e; ☉ 9.30am-7pm Mon-Sat; Ⓜ Pyramides or Quatre-Septembre) 'World Travellers' is an enormous agency with more than 10 departments dealing with different destinations. There's also a good **travel bookshop** (☎ 01 42 86 17 38; ☉ 9.30am-7pm Mon-Sat) downstairs. The agency has its own **restaurant** (see p182) as well as a **shop & exhibition centre** (☎ 01 42 86 16 25; ☉ 9.30am-7pm Mon-Sat; 50 rue Ste-Anne) opposite.

Directory

Directory

ACCOMMODATION

The accommodation options in this guide are listed alphabetically by area for mid- and top-range hotels, followed by a separate 'cheap sleeps' section. When budgeting for your trip remember that hotel rates often rise in April and stay at that level till at least September. There are often some bargains to be had during the late autumn (say, November) and winter months (January and February).

For details on accommodation types and costs in Paris see p304 and p306. For information on long-term rentals, see p307.

Booking Services

The Paris Convention & Visitors Bureau (Office de Tourisme et de Congrès de Paris), particularly the Gare du Nord branch (p386) can find you a place to stay for the night of the day you stop by and will make the booking for free. The only catch is that you have to use a credit card to make the booking. Be warned: the queues can be very long in the high season.

A number of travel agencies (p370) can also book reasonably priced accommodation. The student travel agency **OTU Voyages** (Map pp436–7; ☎ 01 40 29 12 22, 01 55 82 32 32; www.otu.fr in French; 119 rue St-Martin, 4e; 🕙 9.30am-6.30pm Mon-Fri, 10am-6pm Sat; Ⓜ Rambuteau), directly across the huge *parvis* (square) from the Centre Pompidou, can *always* find you accommodation, even at the height of summer. You pay for the accommodation plus a finder's fee of €15, and the staff will then give you a voucher to take to the hotel. Prices for singles cost around €35, doubles start at about €40. Again, be prepared for long queues (and waits) in the high season.

An agency that arranges B&B stays in Paris and gets good reviews from readers is **Alcôve & Agapes** (☎ 01 44 85 06 05; www .bed-and-breakfast-in-paris.com), meaning 'alcoves and feasts'. Expect to pay anything from €60 to €195 for a double and most hosts will expect you to stay a minimum of three or four nights.

BUSINESS HOURS

Small businesses are open daily, except Sunday and sometimes Monday. Hours are usually 9am or 10am to 6.30pm or 7pm, usually with a midday break from 1pm to 2pm or 2.30pm.

Banks usually open from 8am or 9am to between 11.30am and 1pm, and then 1.30pm or 2pm to 4.30pm or 5pm, Monday to Friday or Tuesday to Saturday. Exchange services may end 30 minutes before closing time.

Most post offices open 8am to 7pm weekdays and 8am or 9am till noon on Saturday.

Supermarkets open Monday to Saturday, though a few open on Sunday morning as well. Small food shops are mostly closed on Sunday and often Monday too, so Saturday afternoon may be your last chance to stock up on certain types of food (eg cheese) until Tuesday.

Restaurants keep the most convoluted hours of any business in Paris; for details see p176.

Most museums are closed one day a week: usually Monday or Tuesday. Some museums have a weekly *nocturne* in which they stay open until as late as 10pm one night a week, including the Louvre (Wednesday and Friday) and the Musée d'Orsay (Thursday).

CHILDREN

Paris abounds in places that will delight children, and there is always a special child's entry rate to paying attractions (though eligibility ages vary). Visits can be designed around a stop (or picnic) at the places listed here; more details are in the Sights chapter. For details about theme parks in the area, see p360 and p359.

Children's Playgrounds (Map pp446–7; Port de Plaisance de Paris-Arsenal, 4e; Ⓜ Bastille); Jardin du Luxembourg (Map pp444–5; 6e; Ⓜ Luxembourg); Square Willette (Map p432; Montmartre, 18e; Ⓜ Anvers)

Cité des Sciences et de l'Industrie (Map pp422–3; Parc de la Villette, 19e; Ⓜ Porte de La Villette) Including the Géode and Cinaxe.

Eiffel Tower (Map pp434–5; Parc du Champ de Mars, 7e; Ⓜ Champ de Mars-Tour Eiffel)

Exploradôme (Map pp422–3; Jardin d'Acclimatation; Bois de Boulogne; Ⓜ Les Sablons)

Jardin des Enfants aux Halles (Map pp436–7; Fnac Forum des Halles, 1er; Ⓜ Les Halles) Playground and games centre.

Ménagerie du Jardin des Plantes (Map pp444–5; Jardin des Plantes, 5e; Ⓜ Jussieu or Gare d'Austerlitz) Near the Musée National d'Histoire Naturelle.

Palais de la Découverte (Map pp426–7; Champs-Élysées, 8e; Ⓜ Champs-Élysées Clemenceau).

Parc Zoologique de Paris (Map pp422–3; Bois de Vincennes; Ⓜ Porte Dorée) Parc Floral de Paris is beyond the zoo, also in Bois de Vincennes.

Lonely Planet's *Travel with Children* by Cathy Lanigan includes all sorts of useful advice for those travelling with their little ones. If you read French, the newspaper *Libération* (p19) produces a supplement every other month called *Paris Mômes* (Paris Kids; www .parismomes.fr) with listings and other information aimed at kids up to age 12.

An excellent website is www.babygoes2 .com with both general background and practical information, suggested trips and airline links.

Baby-sitting

L'Officiel des Spectacles (€0.35), the weekly entertainment magazine that appears on newsstands every Wednesday, lists *gardes d'enfants* (baby-sitters) available in Paris.

Au Paradis des Petits (☎ 01 43 65 58 58) From €6.70 per hour (€9.20 subscription fee).

Baby Sitting Services (☎ 01 46 21 33 16) From €6.80 per hour (€11.90 subscription), €60 for 10 hours or one day.

Étudiants de l'Institut Catholique (Map pp434–5; ☎ 01 44 39 60 24; 21 rue d'Assas, 6e; Ⓜ Rennes) From €7 per hour (plus €2 for each session).

CLIMATE

The Paris basin lies midway between coastal Brittany and mountainous Alsace and is affected by both climates. The Île de France region records among the nation's lowest annual precipitation (about 610mm), but rainfall is erratic; you're just as likely to be caught in a heavy spring shower or an autumn downpour as in a sudden summer cloudburst. Paris' average yearly temperature is just under 11°C (3°C in January,

19°C in July), but the mercury sometimes drops below zero in winter and can climb to the mid-30s in the middle of summer.

You can find out the weather forecast in French for the Paris area by calling ☎ 0 892 680 275. The national forecast can be heard on ☎ 0 899 701 234 in French or ☎ 0 899 701 111 in one of 11 different languages. Call charges for either number are €1.35 then €0.35 per minute. The summary can also be read for free on the website of Météo France (www.meteofrance.com).

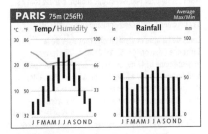

COURSES
Cooking

What better place to discover the secrets of *la cuisine française* than in Paris, the capital of gastronomy? Courses are available at different levels and lengths of time and the cost of tuition varies widely. One of the most popular – and affordable – for beginners is the **Cours de Cuisine Françoise Meunier** (Map pp428–9; ☎ 01 40 26 14 00; www.fmeunier.com; 2nd fl, 7 rue Paul Lelong, 2e; Ⓜ Bourse), which offers three-hour courses (adult/12-14 yr €100/60) at 10.30am from Wednesday to Friday and at the same time on Saturday once a month (see website for exact dates). 'Carnets' of five/20 courses cost €440/1700.

Other major cooking schools in Paris include the following:

École Le Cordon Bleu (Map pp434–5; ☎ 01 53 68 22 50; www.cordonbleu.edu; 8 rue Léon Delhomme, 15e; Ⓜ Vaugirard or Convention) Dating back to 1895, the Cordon Bleu school has professional courses as well as one-day 'gourmet sessions' (€142) on subjects like petits fours and terrines, and a four-day course (€889) on French regional cuisine.

École Ritz Escoffier (Map pp426–7; ☎ 01 43 16 30 50; www.ritzparis.com; 38 rue Cambon, 1er; Ⓜ Concorde) This prestigious cooking school is in what is arguably Paris' finest hotel – but you enter from the rear. A four-hour Saturday themed workshop (truffles, sea scallops, asparagus, Easter lamb etc) costs €125; a three-day introductory course in summer is €530.

Language

All manner of French-language courses, lasting from two weeks to a full academic year, are available in Paris, and many places begin new courses every month or so.

Alliance Française (Map pp434–5; ☎ 01 42 84 90 00; www.alliancefr.org; 101 blvd Raspail, 6e; ⏰ 8.30am-6pm Mon-Fri; Ⓜ St-Placide) French courses (minimum two weeks) at all levels begin every fortnight; registration (€55) takes place five days before. *Intensif* courses meet for four hours a day, start at 8.30am and 1.30pm and cost €350/640 for two weeks/one month; *extensif* courses involve two hours of class a day, have six starting times a day between 8.30am and 8pm and cost €190/320.

Cours de Langue et Civilisation Françaises de la Sorbonne (Map pp444–5; ☎ 01 40 46 22 11; www.ccfs-sorbonne.fr; 47 rue des Écoles, 5e; ⏰ 11am-4pm Mon-Fri; Ⓜ Cluny-La Sorbonne or Maubert Mutualité) The Sorbonne's prestigious French Language and Civilisation Course has courses for all levels. A four-week summer course starts at €490, while 20 hours a week of lectures and tutorials costs €1250 per semester. Instructors take a very academic (though solid) approach to language teaching; don't expect to learn how to haggle in a market or cuss about road hogs even after a year here.

Eurocentres (Map pp436–7; ☎ 01 40 46 72 00; www.eurocentres.com; 13 passage Dauphine, 6e; ⏰ 8.15am-6pm Mon-Fri; Ⓜ Odéon) Intensive courses lasting two/four weeks with 10 to 13 participants cost from €660/1272. New courses begin every two, three or four weeks.

Institut Parisien de Langue et de Civilisation Françaises (Map pp426–7; ☎ 01 40 56 09 53; www.institut-parisien.com; 29 rue de Lisbonne, 8e; ⏰ 8.30am-5pm Mon-Fri; Ⓜ Monceau) Four-week courses with a maximum of 12 students per class cost €131/197/262/328 for 10/15/20/25 hours a week plus enrolment (€40) and exam (€15) fees.

Langue Onze (Map pp428–9; ☎ 01 43 38 22 87; www.langueonzeparis.com; 15 rue Gambey, 11e; Ⓜ Parmentier; ⏰ 11am-5pm Mon-Fri) This small, independent language school gets good reviews from readers. Two-/four-week intensive courses of four hours' instruction a day are €375/595 and evening classes (four hours a week) start at €175 a month. Classes have a maximum of nine students.

CUSTOMS

Duty-free shopping within the EU was abolished in 1999; you cannot, for example, buy tax-free goods in, say, France and take them to the UK. However, you can still enter an EU country with duty-free items from countries *outside* the EU (eg Australia, the USA).

The usual allowances apply to duty-free goods purchased at airports or on ferries originating outside the EU: 200 cigarettes, 50 normal cigars, 100 small cigars or 250g of loose tobacco; 2L of still wine and 1L of spirits of 22% or less, or 2L of fortified wine of 22% or less; 100mL of perfume; 250cc of eau de toilette; and other duty-free goods to the value of €175.

Do not confuse these with *duty-paid* items (including alcohol and tobacco) bought at normal shops and supermarkets in another EU country (eg Spain or Germany) and brought into France, where certain goods might be more expensive. Here allowances are generous: 800 cigarettes, 200 cigars, 400 small cigars or 1kg of loose tobacco; and 10L of spirits (more than 22% alcohol by volume), 20L of fortified wine or aperitif, 90L of wine or 110L of beer.

DISCOUNT CARDS

Museums, the SNCF (Société Nationale des Chemins de Fer; national rail service), ferry companies and other institutions give discounts to those aged under 26 (ie holders of the International Youth Travel Card, IYTC), students with an International Student Identity Card (ISIC; age limits may apply) and *le troisième age* (usually those aged over 60). Look for the words *tarif réduit* (reduced rate) or *demi-tarif* (half-price tariff) and then ask if you qualify. Under-18s get an even wider range of discounts, including free admission to the government-run *musées nationaux* (national museums) and everyone gets to see the permanent collections of most city-run museums for free. Some 18 museums are free on the first Sunday of every month, though not necessarily year-round. For specifics, see p125.

The **Carte Musées-Monuments** (Museums Monuments Card; ☎ 01 44 61 96 60; 1-/3-/5-day €18/36/54) is valid for entry to three dozen venues in Paris – including the Louvre, Centre Pompidou and Musée d'Orsay – and another 22 in the Île de France, including parts of the chateaux at Versailles, Fontaine and Chantilly (see p336). The pass is available from the participating venues as well as branches of the Paris Convention & Visitors Bureau (p386), Fnac outlets (p259), RATP (Régie Autonome des Transports Parisiens) information desks and major metro stations.

ELECTRICITY

France runs on 220V at 50Hz AC. Plugs are the standard European type with two round pins. French outlets often have an earth (ground) pin; you may have to buy a French adapter to use a two-pin European plug. The best place for adapters and other electrical goods is the Bazar de l'Hôtel de Ville (BHV; p287) department store near Hôtel de Ville or any branch of the electronics chain **Darty** (www.darty.fr in French; 10am-7.30pm Mon-Sat), which has a **République branch** (Map pp428–9; 01 42 79 79 31; 1 av de la République, 11e; M République) and a **Ternes branch** (Map pp426–7; 01 42 79 79 30; 8 av des Ternes, 17e; M Ternes).

EMBASSIES & CONSULATES

French Embassies & Consulates

Almost all of the French embassies and consulates listed below have information posted on the Internet at www.france.diplomatie.fr.

Australia embassy (02-6216 0100; www.ambafrance-au.org; 6 Perth Ave, Yarralumla, ACT 26000); consulate (02-9261 5779; www.consulfrance-sydney.org; 20th fl, St Martin's Tower, 31 Market St, Sydney, NSW 2000)

Belgium embassy (02-548 8700; www.ambafrance-be.org; 65 rue Ducale, 1000 Brussels); consulate (02-229 8500; www.consulfrance-bruxelles.be; 12a place de Louvain, 1000 Brussels)

Canada embassy (613-789 1795; www.ambafrance-ca.org; 42 Sussex Drive, Ottawa, Ont K1M 2C9); consulate (416-925 8041; www.consulfrance-toronto.org; Suite 2200, 2 Bloor St East, Toronto, Ont M4W 1A8)

Germany embassy (030-590 03 90 00; www.ambafrance-de.org; Parizer Platz 5, 10117 Berlin); consulate (069-795 09 60; www.consulatfrance.de/francfort; 60325 Frankfurt am Main)

Ireland embassy (01-277 5000; www.ambafrance-ie.org; 36 Ailesbury Rd, Ballsbridge, Dublin 4)

Italy embassy (06-686 01 302; www.ambafrance-it.org; Piazza Farnese 67, 00186 Rome); consulate (06-686 011; www.france-italia.it/consulat.rome; Via Giulia 251, 00186 Rome)

Netherlands embassy (070-312 58 00; www.ambafrance-nl.org; Smidsplein 1, 2514 BT The Hague); consulate (020-530 69 69; www.consulfrance-amsterdam.org; Vijzelgracht 2, 1000 HR Amsterdam)

New Zealand embassy (04-384 2555; www.ambafrance-nz.org; 13th fl, Rural Bank Building, 34-42 Manners St, Wellington)

South Africa embassy Apr-Jan (012-425 1600; www.ambafrance-za.org; 250 Melk St, New Muckleneuk, 0181 Pretoria); embassy Feb-Mar (021-422 1338; www.ambafrance-za.org; 78 Queen Victoria St, 8001 Cape Town)

Spain embassy (91-423 8900; www.ambafrance-es.org; Calle de Salustiano Olozaga 9, 28001 Madrid); consulate (93-270 3000; www.consulfrance-barcelone.org; Ronda Universitad 22b, 08007 Barcelona)

Switzerland embassy (031-359 2111; www.ambafrance-ch.org; Schlosshaldenstrasse 46, 3006 Berne); consulate (01-268 8585; www.consulatfrance-zurich.org; Signaustrasse 1, 8008 Zürich)

UK embassy (020-7073 1000; www.ambafrance-uk.org; 58 Knightsbridge, London SW1X 7JT); consulate (020-7073 1200; www.consulfrance-londres.org, 21 Cromwell Rd, London SW7 2EN)

USA embassy (202-944 6000; www.ambafrance-us.org; 4101 Reservoir Rd NW, Washington, DC 20007); consulate (212-606 3600; www.consulfrance-newyork.org; 934 Fifth Ave, New York, NY 10021)

Embassies & Consulates in Paris

It's important to realise what your own embassy – the embassy of the country of which you are a citizen – can and cannot do to help you if you're in trouble. In general, it won't be much help if the trouble you're in is even remotely your own fault. Remember that you are bound by French law while visiting Paris. Your embassy will not be sympathetic if you commit a crime locally, even if such actions are legal in your own country.

In genuine emergencies you might get some assistance, but only if other channels have been exhausted. For example, if you need to get home urgently, a free ticket home is exceedingly unlikely – the embassy would expect you to have insurance. If you have all your money and documents stolen, it might assist with getting a new passport, but a loan for onward travel is usually out of the question.

The following is a list of selected embassies and consulates in Paris. For a more complete list, consult the *Pages Jaunes* (Yellow Pages; www.pagesjaunes.fr) under 'Ambassades et Consulats' or the website of the tourist office (www.parisinfo.com).

Australia embassy (Map pp434–5; 01 40 59 33 00; 4 rue Jean Rey, 15e; M Bir Hakeim)

Belgium embassy (Map pp426–7; 01 44 09 39 39; 9 rue de Tilsitt, 17e; M Charles de Gaulle-Étoile)

Canada embassy (Map pp426–7; ☎ 01 44 43 29 00; 35 av Montaigne, 8e; Ⓜ Franklin D Roosevelt)

Germany embassy (Map pp426–7; ☎ 01 53 83 45 00; 13-15 av Franklin D Roosevelt, 8e; Ⓜ Franklin D Roosevelt); consulate (Map pp426–7; ☎ 01 53 83 46 40; 28 rue Marbeau, 16e; Ⓜ Porte Maillot)

Ireland embassy (Map pp426–7; ☎ 01 44 17 67 00; 4 rue Rude, 16e; Ⓜ Argentine)

Italy embassy (Map pp434–5; ☎ 01 49 54 03 00; 47-51 rue de Varenne, 7e; Ⓜ Rue du Bac); consulate (Map pp422–3; ☎ 01 44 30 47 00; 5 blvd Émile Augier, 16e; Ⓜ La Muette)

Netherlands embassy (Map pp434–5; ☎ 01 40 62 33 00; 7 rue Eblé, 7e; Ⓜ St-François Xavier)

New Zealand embassy (Map pp426–7; ☎ 01 45 01 43 43; 7ter rue Léonard de Vinci, 16e; Ⓜ Victor Hugo)

South Africa embassy (Map pp434–5; ☎ 01 45 55 92 37; 59 quai d'Orsay, 7e; Ⓜ Invalides)

Spain embassy (Map pp426–7; ☎ 01 44 43 18 00; 22 av Marceau, 8e; Ⓜ Alma-Marceau)

Switzerland embassy (Map pp434–5; ☎ 01 49 55 67 00; 142 rue de Grenelle, 7e; Ⓜ Varenne); consulate (Map pp434–5; ☎ 01 45 66 00 80; 13 rue du Laos, 15e)

UK embassy (Map pp426–7; ☎ 01 44 51 31 00; 35 rue du Faubourg St-Honoré, 8e; Ⓜ Concorde); consulate (Map pp426–7; ☎ 01 44 51 31 02; 18bis rue d'Anjou, 8e; Ⓜ Concorde)

USA embassy (Map pp426–7; ☎ 01 43 12 22 22; 2 av Gabriel, 8e; Ⓜ Concorde); consulate (Map pp426–7; ☎ 0 810 264 626; 2 rue St-Florentin, 1er; Ⓜ Concorde)

EMERGENCY

The following numbers are to be dialled in an emergency. See p380 for hospitals with 24-hour accident and emergency departments.

Ambulance (SAMU; ☎ 15)

EU-wide emergency hotline (☎ 112)

Fire brigade (☎ 18)

Police (☎ 17)

Rape crisis hotline (☎ 0 800 05 95 95)

Urgences Médicales de Paris (Paris Medical Emergencies; ☎ 01 53 94 94 94)

SOS Médecins (☎ 01 47 07 77 77, 24-hr house calls 0 820 33 24 24; www.sosmedecins.fr)

SOS Helpline (☎ 01 47 23 80 80; ☻ in English 3-11pm)

Lost Property

All objects found anywhere in Paris – except those picked up on trains or in train stations –

are brought to the city's **Bureau des Objets Trouvés** (Lost Property Office; Map pp422–3; ☎ 0 821 002 525; 36 rue des Morillons, 15e; ☻ 8.30am-5pm Mon, Wed & Fri, 8.30am-8pm Tue & Thu; Ⓜ Convention), which is run by the Préfecture de Police. Since telephone enquiries are impossible, the only way to find out if a lost item has been located is to go there and fill in the forms.

Items lost on the metro are held by station agents (☎ 0 892 98 77 14; ☻ 7am-9pm Mon-Fri, 9am-5.15pm Sat & Sun) for three days, before being sent to the Bureau des Objets Trouvés. Anything found on trains or stations is taken to the lost-property office (usually attached to the left-luggage office) of the relevant station. Phone enquiries (in French) are possible:

Gare d'Austerlitz (☎ 01 53 60 71 98)

Gare de l'Est (☎ 01 40 18 88 73)

Gare de Lyon (☎ 01 53 33 67 22)

Gare du Nord (☎ 01 55 31 58 40)

Gare Montparnasse (☎ 01 40 48 14 24)

Gare St-Lazare (☎ 01 53 42 05 57)

GAY & LESBIAN TRAVELLERS

Paris is home to thriving gay and lesbian communities, and same-sex couples are a common sight on its streets, especially in the Marais district of the 4e. In 1999 the government enacted PACS (Pacte Civile de Solidarité) legislation, designed to give homosexual couples some of the legal protection (eg inheritance) it extends to married heterosexuals (though it falls well short of the laws now codified in Spain and the UK). In May 2001 Paris elected Bertrand Delanoë, the first openly gay mayor of a European capital.

Information & Organisations

Most of France's major gay organisations are based in Paris. If you require a more complete list pick up a copy of *Genres*, an almost-annual listing gay, lesbian, bisexual and transsexual organisations, at the Centre Gai et Lesbien de Paris Île de France (Gay and Lesbian Centre; opposite).

Act Up-Paris (☎ 01 48 06 16 74, 01 48 06 13 89; www .actupparis.org) Public meetings are held every Tuesday at 7.30pm at the **École des Beaux-Arts** (Map pp436–7; Amphithéâtre des Loges, 14-16 rue Bonaparte, 6e; Ⓜ St-Germain des Prés).

Association des Médecins Gais (☎ 01 48 05 81 71; www.medecins-gays.org in French) The Association of Gay Doctors, based at the Centre Gai et Lesbien, deals with gay-related health issues. Telephone advice on physical-health issues is available from 6pm to 8pm on Wednesday and 2pm to 4pm on Saturday. For counselling call between 8.30pm and 10.30pm Thursday or Sunday.

Centre Gai et Lesbien de Paris Île de France (CGL, Gay & Lesbian Centre; Map pp440–1; ☎ 01 43 57 21 47, 01 43 57 27 93; www.cglparis.org; 3 rue Keller, 11e; ⏱ 4-8pm Mon-Sat; Ⓜ Ledru Rollin) This is your single best source of information in Paris. The large library of books and periodicals (mostly in French) is open from 6pm to 8pm on Tuesday and 4pm to 6pm Thursday and Friday.

Écoute Gaie (☎ 0 810 81 10 57; www.france.qrd.org /assocs/ecoute-gaie in French; ⏱ 6-10pm Mon-Thu) Established in 1982, this is the oldest hotline for gays and lesbians in Paris.

SOS Homophobie (☎ 0 810 10 81 35; www.france.qrd .org/assocs/sos in French; ⏱ 6-10pm Mon & Fri, 8-10pm Tue-Thu & Sun, 2-4pm Sat) This hotline takes anonymous calls concerning discriminatory acts against gays and lesbians.

Publications & Websites

Têtu (www.tetu.com in French; €5) is a general-interest national magazine for gays and lesbians available monthly at newsstands everywhere. Be on the look-out for the bimonthlies *illico* (www.e-llico .com) and *2X* (www.2xparis.fr), which have interviews and articles (in French) and listings of gay clubs, bars, associations and personal classifieds. They're available free at most gay venues. The monthly magazine *Lesbia* (☎ 01 43 48 89 54; €4), established in 1989, looks at women's is-sues and gives a rundown of what's hap-pening around the country.

The following guidebooks list pubs, res-taurants, clubs, beaches, saunas, sex shops and cruising areas; they are available from Les Mots à la Bouche bookshop (p289).

Dyke Guide: Le Guide Lesbien (€12) The essential French-language guide for girls on the go in France and Paris.

Le Petit Futé Paris Gay & Lesbien (€14) A French-language guide that goes well beyond pursuits hedon-istic, with political, cultural, religious and health listings along with bars and restaurants. Highly recommended.

Paris Gayment (€6; www.parigramme.com) A French-language, 110-page sourcebook from the ones behind *Paris Est à Nous* and contains just about every address of interest to 'girls who love girls and boys who love boys and their friends'.

Spartacus International Gay Guide (€28.95, US$32.95; www.spartacusworld.com) A male-only guide to just about every country in the world world with more than 100 pages devoted to France and 40 pages on Paris.

Among some of the better gay and lesbian websites are the following:

Adventice (www.adventice.com) This is the oldest free gay site in French but its cultural, err, bent is now almost totally commercial.

Dyke Planet (www.dykeplanet.com in French) The best French-language website for gay women.

Gay France (www.gayfrance.fr in French) Lots and lots of male-to-male chat and classifieds.

La France Gaie & Lesbienne (www.france.qrd.org) 'Queer resources directory' for gays and lesbians.

HOLIDAYS
Public Holidays

There is at least one holiday a month in France and, in some years, up to four in the month of May alone. Be aware, though, that unlike in the USA or UK, where public holidays usually fall on (or are shifted to) a Monday, in France a *jour férié* (public holiday) is celebrated strictly on the day on which it falls. Thus if May Day falls on a Saturday or Sunday, no provision is made for an extra day off.

The following holidays are observed in Paris:

New Year's Day (Jour de l'An) 1 January

Easter Sunday (Pâques) Late March/April

Easter Monday (Lundi de Pâques) Late March/April

May Day (Fête du Travail) 1 May

Victory in Europe Day (Victoire 1945) 8 May

Ascension Thursday (L'Ascension) May (celebrated on the 40th day after Easter)

Pentecost/Whit Sunday (Pentecôte) Mid-May to mid-June (7th Sunday after Easter)

Whit Monday (Lundi de Pentecôte) Mid-May to mid-June (7th Monday after Easter)

Bastille Day/National Day (Le Quatorze Juillet/Fête Nationale) 14 July

Assumption Day (L'Assomption) 15 August

All Saints' Day (La Toussaint) 1 November

Armistice Day/Remembrance Day (Le Onze Novembre) 11 November

Christmas (Noël) 25 December

School Holidays

France is divided into three zones when it comes to school holidays and you'll see maps designating Zone A (coloured yellow), Zone B (blue) and Zone C (red) everywhere. Paris and southwestern France are Zone C.

Exact dates vary from year to year but school holidays generally fall as follows:

Autumn A 13-day holiday, it usually runs from about 20 October to a day or two after La Toussaint (All Saint's Day).

Christmas & New Year About 20 December to 4 January.

Winter Runs from about 10 February to 10 March, with pupils in each of the three zones off for overlapping 15-day periods.

Spring Begins a week before Easter and lasts a month, which also means pupils have overlapping 15-day holidays.

Summer Nationwide summer holidays lasts from the end of June or very early July until the start of September.

INSURANCE

A travel insurance policy to cover theft, loss and medical problems is a good idea. Some policies offer lower and higher medical-expense options; the higher ones are chiefly for countries such as the USA, which have extremely high medical costs. There is a wide variety of policies available, so check the small print. EU citizens on public-health insurance schemes should note that they're generally covered by reciprocal arrangements in France.

Some policies specifically exclude 'dangerous activities', which can include scuba diving, motorcycling, even trekking. A locally acquired motorcycle licence is not valid under some policies.

You may prefer a policy which pays doctors or hospitals directly rather than you having to pay on the spot and then claim it back later. If you have to claim later make sure you keep all documentation. Some policies ask you to call back (reverse charges) to a centre in your home country where an immediate assessment of your problem can be made. Ensure that your policy covers ambulances or an emergency flight home.

Paying for your airline ticket with a credit card often provides limited travel accident insurance, and you may be able to reclaim the payment if the operator doesn't deliver. Ask your credit card company what it's prepared to cover.

INTERNET ACCESS

You'll find phonecard-operated Internet terminals known as Netanoo (www.net anoo.com in French) in certain phone boxes (booths) throughout Paris. A 120-unit *télécarte* gets you about two hours' connection while a 50-unit one is worth about 50 minutes online.

Wi-fi is widely available at midrange and top-end hotels in Paris and occasionally in public spaces such as train stations and tourist offices.

Paris is awash in Internet cafés, and you'll find at least one in your immediate neighbourhood. Among the biggest, best and/or most central are:

Cyber C@fe (Map pp444–5; ☎ /fax 01 43 26 01 79; 42 rue Descartes, 5e; per 10/30/60 min €1/2/3, per 5/10 hr €10/20; ⏱ 10.30am-12.30am; Ⓜ Cardinal Lemoine or Place Monge) Very centrally located in the Latin Quarter.

Cyber Cube (Map pp434–5; ☎ 01 56 80 08 08; www .cybercube.fr; 9 rue d'Odessa, 14e; per 1 min €0.15, per 5/10 hr €30/40; ⏱ 10am-10pm; Ⓜ Montparnasse Bien-venüe) One of three branches; expensive but convenient to Gare Montparnasse.

Cyber Squ@re (Map pp428–9; ☎ 01 48 87 82 36; info@cybersquare-paris.com; 1 place de la République; per 5/15/30/60 min €0.75/2.30/3.80/6, per 10/20 hr €45/76; ⏱ 10am-8pm Mon-Sat; Ⓜ République) This small but convivial place on two levels is entered from passage Vendôme.

Cybercafé Latin (Map pp434–5; ☎ /fax 01 42 22 01 18; 35bis rue de Fleurus, 6e; per 20/30/60 min €1.50/2.20/4, per 5/10/20 hr €16/29/53; ⏱ 9.30am-8.30pm Mon-Fri, 1-7.30pm Sat; Ⓜ St-Placide) Just west of the Jardin du Luxembourg.

Netvision (Map pp436–7; ☎ 01 43 25 13 90; netprod@hotmail.com; 10 Gît le Cœur, 6e; per 15/30 min €1.50/3; ⏱ 10am-8pm; Ⓜ St-Michel) This is on a quiet street just west of the blvd St-Michel and south of the river.

Taxiphone Internet (Map pp432; ☎ 01 42 59 64 14; 2 rue de La Vieuville, 18e; per 10/20/30/60 min €1/2/3/4, per 5 hr €10; ⏱ 9am-10pm; Ⓜ Abbesses) One of the few Internet cafés in high-rent Montmartre (at least that we could find).

Toonet – The Cyber Space (Map pp440–1; ☎ 01 58 30 97 37; 74 rue de Charonne, 11e; per 1/5/15/30hr €5/16/30/45; ⏱ 10.30am-9pm Mon-Sat; Ⓜ Charonne or Ledru Rollin)

Web 46 (Map pp436–7; ☎ 01 40 27 02 89, fax 01 40 27 03 89; 46 rue du Roi de Sicile, 4e; per 15/30/60 min €2.50/4/7, per 5 hr €29; ⏱ 10am-midnight Mon-Fri, 10am-9pm Sat, noon-midnight Sun; Ⓜ St-Paul) A very pleasant, very well run café in the heart of the Marais.

XS Arena Luxembourg (Map pp444–5; ☎ 01 43 44 55 55; www.xsarena.com; 17 rue Soufflot, 5e; per 1/2/3/4/5 hr €3/6/8/10/11; ⊙ 24hr; Ⓜ Luxembourg) This branch of a minichain of Internet cafés is bright, buzzy and open round the clock, with a huge branch at Les Halles (Map pp436–7; ☎ 01 40 13 02 60; 31 blvd de Sébastopol, 1er; ⊙ 24hr; Ⓜ Les Halles).

LAUNDRY

There's a *laverie libre-service* (self-service laundrette) around every corner in Paris; your hotel or hostel can point you to one in the neighbourhood. Machines usually cost €3.20 to €4 for a small load (3.5kg to 7kg) and €5.80 to €7 for a larger one (10kg to 16kg). Drying costs €1 for 10 minutes. Some laundrettes have self-service *nettoyage à sec* (dry-cleaning) machines.

Change machines are sometimes out of order or refuse to accept notes; come prepared with change for the *séchoirs* (dryers) as well as the *lessive* (laundry powder) and *javel* (bleach) dispensers. Usually you put coins into a *monnayeur central* (central control box) – not the machine itself – and push a button that corresponds to the number of the washer or dryer you wish to operate.

The control boxes are sometimes programmed to deactivate the machines 30 minutes to an hour before closing time (laundrettes are usually open from between 6.30am and 7.30am to 10pm).

Among centrally located self-service laundrettes are the following:

C'Clean Laverie (Map pp428–9; 18 rue Jean-Pierre Timbaud, 11e; Ⓜ Oberkampf)

Julice Laverie 56 rue de Seine, 6e (Map pp436–7; Ⓜ Mabillon); 22 rue des Grands Augustins, 6e (Map pp436–7; Ⓜ St-André des Arts)

Laverie Libre Service 7 rue Jean-Jacques Rousseau, 1er (Map pp436–7; Ⓜ Louvre-Rivoli) Near the BVJ Paris-Louvre hostel; 35 rue Ste-Croix la Bretonnerie, 4e (Map pp436–7; Ⓜ Hôtel de Ville); 25 rue des Rosiers, 4e (Map pp436–7; Ⓜ St-Paul); 216 rue St-Jacques, 5e (Map pp444–5; Ⓜ Luxembourg) Three blocks southwest of the Panthéon; 63 rue Monge, 5e (Map pp444–5; Ⓜ Place Monge) South of the Arènes de Lutèce; 14 rue de la Corderie, 3e (Map pp428–9; Ⓜ République or Temple); 94 rue du Dessous des Berges, 12e (Map p449; Ⓜ Bibliothèque); 92 rue des Martyrs, 18e (Map p432; Ⓜ Abbesses); 4 rue Burq, 18e (Map p432; Ⓜ Blanche) West of the Butte de Montmartre.

Laverie Libre Service Primus 40 rue du Roi de Sicile, 4e (Map pp436–7; Ⓜ St-Paul); 83 rue Jean-Pierre Timbaud, 11e (Map pp428–9; Ⓜ Couronnes)

Laverie Miele Libre Service (Map pp440–1; 4 rue de Lappe, 11e; Ⓜ Bastille)

Laverie SBS (Map pp428–9; 6 rue des Petites Écuries, 10e; Ⓜ Château d'Eau)

Le Bateau Lavoir (Map pp444–5; 1 rue Thouin, 5e; Ⓜ Cardinal Lemoine) Near place de la Contrescarpe.

Salon Lavoir Sidec (Map p432; 28 rue des Trois Frères, 18e; Ⓜ Abbesses)

LEGAL MATTERS
Drink Driving

As elsewhere in the EU, the laws in France are very tough when it comes to drinking and driving, and for many years the slogan has been: '*Boire ou conduire, il faut choisir*' (roughly 'To drive or to booze, you have to choose'). The acceptable blood-alcohol limit is 0.05%, and drivers exceeding this amount face fines of up to €4500 (or a maximum of two years in jail). Licences can also be immediately suspended. If you cause an accident while driving drunk, the fine could be increased to €30,000.

The Police

Thanks to the Napoleonic Code on which the French legal system is based, the police can search anyone they want to at any time – whether or not there is probable cause.

France has two separate police forces. The Police Nationale, under the command of departmental prefects (and, in Paris, the Préfet de Police), includes the Police de l'Air et des Frontières (PAF; the border police). The Gendarmerie Nationale, a paramilitary force under the control of the Ministry of Defence, handles airports, borders and so on. During times of crisis (eg a wave of terrorist attacks), the army may be called in to patrol public places.

The dreaded Compagnies Républicaines de Sécurité (CRS) – riot-police heavies to be avoided at all costs – are part of the Police Nationale. You often see hundreds of them, each bigger and butcher than the next and armed with the latest riot gear, at marches or demonstrations. Police with shoulder patches reading 'Police Municipale' are under the control of the local mayor.

The American concept of neighbourhood cops walking their beat or the British bobby giving directions does not exist whatsoever in France; police here are to

Directory

LAUNDRY

maintain order, not mingle. If asked a direct question, a French policeman or policewoman will be correct and helpful but not much more; assisting tourists is not part of their job description. If the police stop you for any reason, be polite and remain calm. They have wide powers of search and seizure and, if they take a dislike to you, they may choose to use them all. Be aware that the police can, without any particular reason, decide to examine your passport, visa, *carte de séjour* (residence permit) and so on. Do not challenge them; this is not America or Britain.

French police are very strict about security. Do not leave baggage unattended; they are quite serious when they warn that suspicious objects will be summarily blown up. Your bags will be inspected and you will have to pass through security gates not only at airports but also at many public buildings (including certain museums and galleries) throughout the city. If asked to open your bag or backpack for inspection, please do so willingly – it's for your own safety ultimately.

MAPS

Many Parisians swear by *Paris par Arrondissement* (€23.50), which has a double-page hand-drawn street plan of each arrondissement. Some find it confusing, though it does list the nearest metro station with each street name in the index. More user-friendly is L'Indispensable's *Paris Practique par Arrondissement* (€4.90), a pocket-sized atlas with a larger format. The same publisher's larger *Le Petit Parisien* (€6.50) has three maps for each arrondissement showing streets, metro lines and bus routes. Lonely Planet's *Paris City Map* is handy, laminated and has four plans that cover the more popular parts of town, a street index and a metro map.

The best place to find a full selection of maps is the Espace IGN (p296).

MEDICAL SERVICES
Hospitals

There are some 50 *assistance publique* (public health service) hospitals in Paris. If you need an ambulance, call ☎ 15; the EU-wide emergency number (with English speakers) is ☎ 112. For emergency treatment, call

Urgences Médicales de Paris (☎ 01 53 94 94 94) or SOS Médecins (☎ 01 47 07 77 77 or 0 820 332 424). Both offer 24-hour house calls.

Hospitals in Paris include:

American Hospital of Paris (Map pp422–3; ☎ 01 46 41 25 25; www.american-hospital.org; 63 blvd Victor Hugo, 92200 Neuilly-sur-Seine; M Pont de Levallois Bécon) Offers emergency 24-hour medical and dental care.

Hertford British Hospital (Map pp422–3; ☎ 01 46 39 22 22; www.british-hospital.org; 3 rue Barbès, 92300 Levallois-Perret; M Anatole France) A less-expensive English-speaking option than the American Hospital.

Hôtel Dieu (Map pp436–7; ☎ 01 42 34 82 34; www .aphp.fr; 1 place du Parvis Notre Dame, 4e; M Cité) One of the city's main government-run public hospitals (Assistance Publique Hôpitaux de Paris); after 8pm use the emergency entrance on rue de la Cité.

Dental Care

For emergency dental care contact either of the following:

Hôpital de la Pitié-Salpêtrière (Map pp446–7; ☎ 01 42 16 00 00; rue Bruant, 13e; M Chevaleret) The only dental hospital with extended hours – from 6am to 10.30pm. After 5.30pm use the emergency entrance at 83 blvd de l'Hôpital, 13e (M St-Marcel)

SOS Dentaire (Map pp444–5; ☎ 01 43 36 36 00, 01 43 37 51 00; 87 blvd de Port Royal, 13e; M Port Royal) A private dental office that offers services when most dentists are off-duty (8pm to 11pm weekdays, 9.45am to 11pm weekends).

METRIC SYSTEM

France uses the metric system, which was invented by the French Academy of Sciences after the Revolution and adopted by the French government in 1795. The metric system replaced a confusing welter of traditional units of measurement that lacked all logical basis and made conversion complicated and commerce chaotic. For a conversion chart, see inside the front cover.

MONEY

The euro (abbreviated € and pronounced *eu*-roh in French) is the national currency of France and, at present, 11 of the 25 other member-states of the EU (Austria, Belgium, Finland, Germany, Greece, Ireland, Italy, Luxembourg, Netherlands, Portugal and Spain). One euro is divided into 100 cents (*centimes* in French). There are seven euro notes in different colours and sizes; they come in denominations of €5, €10, €20, €50, €100, €200 and €500. The designs on the recto (generic windows or portals) and verso (imaginary bridges, map of the EU) are exactly the same in all 12 countries and symbolise openness and cooperation.

The eight coins in circulation are in denominations of €1 and €2, then one, two, five, 10, 20 and 50 cents. The 'head' side of the coin, on which the denomination is shown, is identical throughout the euro zone; the 'tail' side is specific to each member-state, though euro coins can be used anywhere that accepts euros, of course. In France the €1 (silver centre with brassy ring) and €2 (brassy centre with silver ring) coins portray the tree of liberty; the 10, 20 and 50 cent coins (all brass) have *la Semeuse* ('the Sower'), a recurring theme in the history of the French franc; and the one, two and five cent coins (all copper) portray Marianne, the symbol of the French Republic.

Exchange rates are given in the Quick Reference section on the inside front cover of this book. The latest rates are available on websites such as www.oanda .com/convert/classic and www.xe.com. For a broader view of the local economy and costs in Paris, see p21.

ATMs

You'll find an ATM, which is known as a DAB (*distributeur automatique de billets*) or *point d'argent* in French, linked to the Cirrus, Maestro, Visa or MasterCard networks, virtually on every corner. Those without a local bank account should know that there is nearly always a transaction surcharge of €3 (or more!) for cash withdrawals. You should contact your bank to find out how much this is before using ATMs too freely.

Changing Money

In general, cash is not a very good way to carry money. Not only can it be stolen, but in France it doesn't usually offer the best exchange rates. What's more, in recent years ATMs and the euro have virtually wiped out *bureaux de change* and even centrally located banks rarely offer exchange services these days.

That said, some banks, post offices and *bureaux de change* pay up to 2.5% or more for travellers cheques, more than making

up for the 1% commission usually charged when buying the cheques in the first place.

Post offices that have a Banque Postale can offer the best exchange rates, and they accept banknotes in various currencies as well as travellers cheques issued by Amex or Visa. The commission for travellers cheques is 1.5% (minimum €5) and for cash €5.

Commercial banks usually charge a similar amount per foreign-currency transaction. For example BNP Paribas charges €5.70 for cash while Société Générale takes €5.40. The rates charged on travellers cheques vary but neither BNP Paribas or Société Générale charge a fee to change travellers cheques in euros.

In Paris, *bureaux de change* are faster and easier, open longer hours and give better rates than most banks. It's best to familiarise yourself with the rates offered by the post office and compare them with those on offer at *bureaux de change*, which are not generally allowed to charge commissions. A survey conducted when we were updating this book in Paris showed *bureaux de change* charging anything between 6% and 13% plus €3 or €4 on cash transactions and 6% to just under 10% (plus €3) to change travellers cheques.

Among some of the better *bureaux de change* are the following (generally open between 10am and 6pm):

Best Change (Map pp436–7; ☎ 01 42 21 46 05; 21 rue du Roule, 1er; Ⓜ Louvre Rivoli) Three blocks southwest of Forum des Halles.

Bureau de Change (Map pp426–7; ☎ 01 42 25 38 14; 25 av des Champs-Élysées, 8e; Ⓜ Franklin D Roosevelt) In the centre of Paris' most popular shopping street.

European Exchange Office (Map p432; ☎ 01 42 52 67 19; 6 rue Yvonne Le Tac, 18e; Ⓜ Abbesses) A few steps from the Abbesses metro station.

Le Change du Louvre (Map pp436–7; ☎ 01 42 97 27 28; 151 rue St-Honoré, 1er; Ⓜ Palais Royal-Musée du Louvre) This moneychanger is on the northern side of Le Louvre des Antiquaires (p285).

Société Touristique de Services (STS; Map pp436–7; ☎ 01 43 54 76 55; 2 place St-Michel, 6e; Ⓜ St-Michel) A *bureau de change* in the heart of the Latin Quarter.

Travelex (Map p432; ☎ 01 42 57 05 10; 82-86 blvd de Clichy, 18e; Ⓜ Blanche) Next to the landmark Moulin Rouge.

Credit Cards

In Paris, Visa/Carte Bleue is the widely accepted credit card, followed by MasterCard (Eurocard). Amex cards can be useful at more upmarket establishments and allow you to get cash at some ATMs. In general, all three cards can be used for train travel, restaurant meals and cash advances.

When you get a cash advance on your Visa or MasterCard account, your issuer charges a transaction fee, which can be very high; check with your card issuer before leaving home. Also, many banks charge a commission of 4% (minimum around €6) for an advance.

Call the following numbers if your card is lost or stolen. It may be impossible to get a lost Visa or MasterCard reissued until you get home so two different credit cards are generally safer than one.

Amex (☎ 01 47 77 72 00)

Diners Club (☎ 0 810 31 419)

MasterCard/Eurocard (☎ 0 800 90 23 90, 01 45 67 84 84)

Visa/Carte Bleue (☎ 0 892 70 57 05)

Travellers Cheques

The most flexible travellers cheques are issued by American Express (in US dollars or euros) and Visa, as they can be changed at many post offices.

Amex offices don't charge commission on their own travellers cheques (though they charge about 4% on other brands). If your Amex travellers cheques are lost or stolen in Paris, call ☎ 0 800 90 86 00 (24-hour, toll-free). Reimbursements can be made at the main **American Express** (Map pp426–7; ☎ 01 47 77 79 50; www.americanexpress.fr; 11 rue Scribe, 9e; 🕒 9am-5.30 to 6.30 Mon-Sat; Ⓜ Auber or Opéra).

See Changing Money, p381, for information on fees charged for cashing travellers cheques.

NEWSPAPERS & MAGAZINES

Among English-language newspapers widely available in Paris are the *International Herald Tribune* (€2), which is edited in Paris and has very good coverage of both French and international news; the *Guardian* and the more compact *European Guardian*; the *Financial Times*; the *Times of London*; and the colourful (if lightweight) *USA Today*. English-language news weeklies that are widely available include *Newsweek*, *Time* and the *Economist*. For information about the French-language press, see p19.

The Paris-based *Fusac* (*France USA Contacts*), a freebie issued every fortnight, consists of hundreds of ads placed by companies and individuals. To place an ad, contact **Fusac** (Map pp422–3; ☎ 01 56 53 54 54; www.fusac.fr; 26 rue Bénard, 14e; Ⓜ Alésia or Pernety). It is distributed free at Paris' English-language bookshops, Anglophone embassies and the **American Church** (Map pp434–5; ☎ 01 40 62 05 00; www.acparis.org; 65 quai d'Orsay, 7e; reception 🕒 9am-noon & 1-10.30pm Mon-Sat, 9am-2pm & 3-7pm Sun; Ⓜ Pont de l'Alma or Invalides), which functions as a kind of community centre for English speakers and is an excellent source of information on au pair work, short-term accommodation etc. A new free monthly worth a second look is *The Paris Times* (www.theparistimes.com).

PHARMACIES

Pharmacies with extended hours include:

Pharmacie Bader (Map pp436–7; ☎ 01 43 26 92 66; 12 blvd St-Michel, 5e; 🕒 9am-9pm; Ⓜ St-Michel)

Pharmacie des Champs (Map pp426–7; ☎ 01 45 62 02 41; Galerie des Champs, 84 av des Champs-Élysées, 8e; 🕒 24hr; Ⓜ George V)

Pharmacie des Halles (Map pp436–7; ☎ 01 42 72 03 23; 10 blvd de Sébastopol, 4e; 🕒 9am-midnight Mon-Sat, 9am-10pm Sun; Ⓜ Châtelet)

Pharmacie Européenne (Map pp426–7; ☎ 01 48 74 65 18; 6 place de Clichy, 17e; 🕒 24hr; Ⓜ Place de Clichy)

PHOTOGRAPHY

Kodak and Fuji colour-print film is available in supermarkets, Photo Station shops and certain Fnac stores, but it is relatively expensive compared with a lot of other countries so it might pay to stock up before you leave home. Developing a 24-exposure film costs from €9 but can be almost twice that if you want your photos in a hurry. For slides (*diapositives*) avoid Kodachrome: it's difficult to process quickly in France and may not be handled correctly.

A good companion when snapping on the streets is *Travel Photography: A Guide to Taking Better Pictures* by Richard I'Anson.

PLACES OF WORSHIP

The following places offer services in English. For a more comprehensive list of churches and other places of worship, check the *Pages Jaunes* (Yellow Pages; www.pagesjaunes.fr).

Adath Shalom Synagogue (Map pp434–5; ☎ 01 45 67 97 96; www.adathshalom.org; 8 rue George Bernard Shaw, 15e; Ⓜ Dupleix) Conservative Jewish.

American Cathedral in Paris (Map pp426–7; ☎ 01 53 23 84 00; www.americancathedral.org; 23 av George V, 8e; Ⓜ George V) Anglican/Episcopal.

American Church in Paris (Map pp434–5; ☎ 01 40 62 05 00; www.acparis.org; 65 quai d'Orsay, 7e; Ⓜ Pont de l'Alma or Invalides) Nondenominational Protestant.

Church of Jesus Christ of the Latter Day Saints (Map pp422–3; ☎ 01 42 45 29 29; 64-66 rue de Romainville, 19e; Ⓜ Porte des Lilas) Mormon.

First Church of Christ Scientist (Map p448; ☎ 01 47 07 26 60; 36 blvd St-Jacques, 14e; Ⓜ St-Jacques) Christian Scientist.

Mosquée de Paris (Map pp444–5; ☎ 01 45 35 97 33; www.mosquee-de-paris.org in French; 39 rue Geoffroy St-Hilaire, 5e; Ⓜ Censier Daubenton or Place Monge) Muslim.

St Joseph's Catholic Church (Map pp426–7; ☎ 01 42 27 28 56; www.stjoeparis.org; 50 av Hoche, 8e; Ⓜ Charles de Gaulle-Étoile) Roman Catholic.

Sri Manikar Vinayakar Temple (Map pp428–9; ☎ 01 40 34 21 89; 72 rue Philippe de Girard, 18e; Ⓜ La Chapelle or Marx Dormoy) Hindu.

POST

Most post offices *(bureaux de poste)* in Paris are open from 8am to 7pm weekdays and 8am or 9am till noon on Saturday. *Tabacs* (tobacconists) usually sell postage stamps.

The **main post office** (Map pp436–7; ☎ 01 40 28 76 00; www.laposte.fr; 52 rue du Louvre, 1er; 🕑 24hr; Ⓜ Sentier or Les Halles), five blocks north of the eastern end of the Musée du Louvre, is open round the clock, but only for basic services such as sending letters and picking up poste restante mail (windows five to seven; €0.53 per letter). Other services, including currency exchange, are available only during regular opening hours. Be prepared for long queues after 7pm and at the weekend. Poste restante mail not specifically addressed to a particular branch post office will be delivered here. There is a one-hour closure from 6.20am to 7.20am Monday to Saturday and from 6am to 7am on Sunday.

Postal Codes

Each arrondissement has its own five-digit postcode, formed by prefixing the number of the arrondissement with '750' or '7500' (eg 75001 for the 1er arrondissement, 75019

for the 19e). The only exception is the 16e, which has two postcodes: 75016 and 75116. All mail to addresses in France *must* include the postcode. Cedex (*Courrier d'Entreprise à Distribution Exceptionelle*) simply means that mail sent to that address is collected at the post office rather than delivered to the door.

Postal Rates

Domestic letters weighing up to 20/50g cost €0.53/0.82. Postcards and letters up to 20/40/60g sent within the EU cost €0.55/1/1.20; €0.75/1.60/1.95 to the rest of Europe and Africa; and €0.90/1.80/2.40 to North America, Asia and Australasia.

RADIO

You can pick up a mixture of the BBC World Service and BBC for Europe in Paris on 648 kHz AM. The Voice of America (VOA) is on 1197 kHz AM and 96.9 MHz FM. You can pick up an hour of Radio France Internationale (RFI) news in English three times a day (7am, 2.30pm and 4.30pm) on 738 kHz AM.

Pocket-sized short-wave radios and the Internet make it easy to keep abreast of world news in English wherever you are. The BBC World Service can be heard on 6195 kHz, 9410 kHz and 12095 kHz (a good daytime frequency), depending on the time of day. BBC Radio 4 broadcasts on 198 kHz LW, and carries BBC World Service programming in the wee hours of the morning. The VOA broadcasts in English at various times of the day on 7170 kHz, 9535 kHz, 9760 kHz, 9770 kHz, 11805 kHz, 15205 kHz and 15255 kHz.

The following are some of the more popular French-language radio stations:

France Info (105.5 MHz FM; www.radiofrance.fr/chaines /france-info) Operates 24-hour, all-news radio.

France Inter (87.8 MHz FM, 738 kHz AM; www.radiofrance .fr/chaines/france-inter) France's official international station.

Paris Jazz (88.2, 98.1 MHz FM; www.comfm.com/live /radio/parisjazz) Jazz and blues.

Paris Live Radio (963 kHz AM; www.parislive.fm) English-language station with news, music, community information etc.

Radio FG (98.2 MHz FM; www.radiofg.com) The station for House, techno, garage, trance, club news and gigs.

Radio Nova (101.5 MHz FM; www.novaplanet.com) Latino, clubs, modern beats.

SAFETY

In general, Paris is a safe city and random street assaults are rare. The so-called Ville Lumière (City of Light) is generally well lit, and there's no reason not to use the metro before it stops running at some time between 12.30am and just past 1am. As you'll notice, women *do* travel alone on the metro late at night in most areas, though not all who do so report feeling 100% comfortable.

Metro stations that are best avoided late at night include: Châtelet-Les Halles and its seemingly endless corridors; Château Rouge in Montmartre; Gare du Nord; Strasbourg St-Denis; Réaumur Sébastopol; and Montparnasse Bienvenüe. *Bornes d'alarme* (alarm boxes) are located in the centre of each metro/RER platform and in some station corridors.

Nonviolent crime such as pickpocketing and thefts from handbags and packs is a problem wherever there are crowds, especially packs of tourists. Places to be particularly careful include Montmartre (especially around Sacré Cœur); Pigalle; the areas around Forum des Halles and the Centre Pompidou; the Latin Quarter (especially the rectangle bounded by rue St-Jacques, blvd St-Germain, blvd St-Michel and quai St-Michel); below the Eiffel Tower; and anywhere on the metro during rush hour. Take the usual precautions: don't carry more money than you need, and keep your credit cards, passport and other documents in a concealed pouch, a hotel safe or a safe-deposit box.

TAXES & REFUNDS

France's value-added tax (VAT) is known as TVA *(taxe sur la valeur ajoutée)* and is 19.6% on most goods except medicine and books, for which it's 5.5%. Prices that include TVA are often marked TTC *(toutes taxes comprises*; literally 'all taxes included').

If you're not an EU resident, you can get a TVA refund provided that: you're aged over 15; you'll be spending less than six months in France; you purchase goods worth at least €175 at a single shop on the same day (not more than 10 of the same item); the goods fit into your luggage; you are taking the goods out of France three months after purchase; and the shop offers *vente en détaxe* (duty-free sales).

Present a passport at the time of purchase and ask for a *bordereau de vente à l'exportation* (export sales invoice) to be signed by the retailer and yourself. Most shops will refund less than the full amount (about 14%) to which you are entitled, in order to cover the time and expense involved in the refund procedure.

As you leave France or another EU country, have all three pages of the *bordereau* validated by the country's customs officials at the airport or at the border. Customs officials will take one sheet and hand you two. You must post one copy (the green one) back to the shop and retain the third (pink) sheet for your records. Once the shop where you made your purchase receives its stamped copy, it will send you a *virement* (fund transfer) in the form you have requested. Be prepared for a wait of up to three months.

If you're flying out of Orly or Roissy Charles de Gaulle, certain shops can arrange for you to receive your refund as you're leaving the country. You must make such arrangements at the time of purchase.

For more information contact the customs information centre (☎ 0 825 30 82 63; www .douane.minefi.gouv.fr).

TELEPHONE
Domestic Calls

There are no area codes in France – you always dial the 10-digit number. Paris numbers always start with ☎ 01.

Until 2005 the sole domestic *service des renseignements* (directory enquiries or assistance) was operated by France Télécom. Now more than two-dozen operators offer the service on six-digit numbers starting with 118 (France Télécom, for example, uses ☎ 118 710, 118 711 and 712). For a complete listing in French consult www .allo118.com.

Note that while numbers beginning with ☎ 0 800, 0 804, 0 805 and 0809 are toll-free in France, other numbers beginning with '8' are not. A number starting with ☎ 0 810, 0 811, 0 819 or 0 860) is charged at local rates while one beginning with ☎ 0 820, 0 821, 0 870 or 0 871 can cost €0.12 per minute, or even €0.15 if the prefix numbers are ☎ 0 825, 0 826, 0 884 or 0 890. The ubiquitous ☎ 0 892 numbers are always billed at an expensive €1.35 for connection then €0.34

per minute whenever you call. Prices can be even higher when calling from a mobile phone.

International Calls

France's country code is ☎ 33. To call a number in Paris from outside France, dial your country's international access code (usually ☎ 00 but exceptions include ☎ 011 from the USA and ☎ 001 from Hong Kong), then ☎ 33 and then the local number, omitting the first '0'.

To call abroad from Paris, dial France's international access code (☎ 00), the country code (see below), the area code (usually without the initial '0', if there is one) and the local number. International Direct Dial (IDD) calls to almost anywhere in the world can be placed from public telephones.

For international directory enquiries, dial ☎ 3212 but it's an expensive service. Instead consult the phone book on the Internet (www.pagejaunes.fr).

Selected Country Codes

Australia	☎ 61
Belgium	☎ 32
Canada	☎ 1
Germany	☎ 49
Ireland	☎ 353
Italy	☎ 39
Netherlands	☎ 31
New Zealand	☎ 64
South Africa	☎ 27
Spain	☎ 34
Switzerland	☎ 41
UK	☎ 44
USA	☎ 1

Mobile Phones

France uses GSM 900/1800, which is compatible with the rest of Europe and Australia but not with the North American GSM 1900 (though many North Americans now have GSM 1900/900 phones that do work in France) or the totally different system in Japan. If you have a GSM phone, check with your service provider about using it in France, and beware of calls being routed internationally, which can make a 'local' call very expensive indeed.

Orange/France Telecom (☎ 0 800 47 14 71 or ☎ +33 1 41 43 79 40 outside France; www

.orange.fr) has a €79 package that includes a basic Nokia mobile phone, a local phone number and 10 minutes of prepaid call time. For more time, you can buy a prepaid Mobicarte recharge card (€10 to €100) from *tabacs* (tobacconist) and other places you'd buy a *télécarte* (phonecard); Mobicartes from €30 offer extra talk time (€5 bonus for €30, €10 bonus for €40, up to €50 extra for €100). If you don't mind changing your telephone number to a French one during your visit, you can also buy a local SIM card for your mobile (provided it's not blocked) for €30 (plus 10 minutes' talk time) and recharge with Mobicartes as you go along.

Phonecards

All public phones can receive both domestic and international calls. If you want someone to call you back, just give them France's country code and the 10-digit number, usually written after the words 'Ici le...' or 'No d'appel' on the tariff sheet or on a little sign inside the phone box. Remind them to drop the '0' of the initial '01' of the number. When there's an incoming call, the words '*décrochez – appel arrive*' (pick up receiver – incoming call) will appear in the LCD window.

Public telephones in Paris require a *télécarte* (phonecard; €7.50/14.50 for 50/120 calling units), which can be purchased at post offices, *tabacs*, supermarkets, SNCF ticket windows, metro stations and anywhere you see a blue sticker reading '*télécarte en vente ici*' (phonecard for sale here).

You can buy prepaid phonecards in France that are up to 60% cheaper for calling abroad than the standard *télécarte*. Euro-Latina, Eureka and Iradium Europe are said to offer the best value. They're usually available in denominations of up to €15 from *tabacs*, newsagents, phone shops and other sales points, especially in ethnic areas such as rue du Faubourg St-Denis (10e), Chinatown (13e) and Belleville (19e and 20e). In general they're valid for two months but the ones offering the most minutes for the least euros can expire in just a week.

TELEVISION

Midrange and top-end hotels usually offer English-language cable and satellite TV, including CNN, BBC Prime, Sky and other networks. Canal+ sometimes screens non-dubbed English-language films.

A variety of TV listings are sold at newsstands, including *Télérama* (€1.60), which includes a supplement of the best films of the month. Foreign films that are shown in their original language with subtitles are marked 'VO' *(version originale)*.

TIME

France uses the 24-hour clock in most case, with the hours usually separated from the minutes by a lower-case 'h'. Thus, 15h30 is 3.30pm, 00h30 is 12.30am and so on.

France is on Central European Time, which is one hour ahead of (ie later than) GMT. During daylight-saving time, which runs from the last Sunday in March to the last Sunday in October, France is two hours ahead of GMT.

Without taking daylight-saving time into account, when it's noon in Paris it's 11pm in Auckland, 11am in London, 6am in New York, 3am in San Francisco and 9pm in Sydney.

TIPPING

French law requires that restaurant, café and hotel bills include a service charge (usually 12% to 15%); for more information, see p177. In taxis, the usual procedure is to round up to the nearest €0.50 or €1 regardless of the fare.

TOILETS

Public toilets in Paris are signposted *toilettes* or *WC*. The tan-coloured, self-cleaning cylindrical toilets you see on Parisian pavements are open 24 hours and did cost €0.40 until the spring of 2006 when the city made them all free.

If you are not a paying customer, café-owners do not appreciate you using their facilities. If you are desperate, try a fast-food place, major department store or even a big hotel. There are public toilets (€0.40 or free) in front of Notre Dame cathedral, near the Arc de Triomphe, east down the steps at Sacré Cœur, at the northwestern entrance to the Jardins des Tuileries and in a few metro stations. Check out the wonderful Art Nouveau public toilets, built in 1905, below place de la Madeleine, 8e (Map pp426–7). As ludicrous as it may sound, 'opening' hours at these public toilets are usually 10am till noon and 1pm to 6pm –

the attendant requiring an hour's lunch break, of course.

In older cafés and bars, you may find a *toilette à la turque* (Turkish-style toilet), which is what the French call a squat toilet.

TOURIST INFORMATION

The main branch of the **Paris Convention & Visitors Bureau** (Office de Tourisme et de Congrès de Paris; Map pp426–7; ☎ 0 892 68 30 00; www.parisinfo.com; 25-27 rue des Pyramides, 1er; ☻ 9am-7.30pm Jun-Oct, 10am-7pm Mon-Sat & 11am-7pm Sun Nov-May, closed May Day; Ⓜ Pyramides) is about 500m northwest of the Louvre.

The bureau also maintains five centres and kiosks elsewhere in Paris, listed below (telephone numbers and websites are the same as for the main office). For details of the area around Paris, contact **Espace du Tourisme d'Île de France**, p335.

Anvers (Map p432; opp 72 blvd Rochechouart, 18e; ☻ 10am-6pm, closed Christmas Day, New Year's Day & May Day; Ⓜ Anvers)

Eiffel Tower (Map pp434–5; Parc du Champ de Mars, 7e; ☻ 11am-6.40pm 25 Mar-Oct; Ⓜ Champ de Mars-Tour Eiffel) In a kiosk between the Nord and Est Pillars beneath the Eiffel Tower.

Gare de Lyon (Map pp446–7; Hall d'Arrivée, 20 blvd Diderot, 12e; ☻ 8am-6pm Mon-Sat, closed May Day) In the arrivals hall for mainline trains.

Gare du Nord (Map pp428–9; 18 rue de Dunkerque, 10e; ☻ 8am-6pm, closed Christmas Day, New Year's Day & May Day; Ⓜ Gare du Nord) Under the glass roof of the Île de France departure and arrival area at the eastern end of the station.

Opéra-Grands Magasins (Map pp426–7; 11 rue Scribe, 9e; ☻ 9am-6.30pm Mon-Sat, closed Christmas Day, New Year's Day and May Day; Ⓜ Auber or Opéra) In the same building as American Express.

Syndicate d'Initiative de Montmartre (Map p432; 21 place du Tertre, 18e; ☻ 10am-7pm; Ⓜ Abbesses) This locally run tourist office and shop is in Montmartre's most picturesque square and open year-round.

These information offices are beyond central Paris, at La Défense and St-Denis:

Espace Info-Défense (Map p155; ☎ 01 47 74 84 24; www.ladefense.fr in French; 15 place de la Défense; ☻ 10am-6pm Mon-Sat Apr-Sep, 9.30am-5.30pm Mon-Sat Oct-Mar; Ⓜ La Défense Grande Arche) La Défense's tourist office has reams of free information, including the useful *Discover La Défense* brochure, details on cultural activities and sells somewhat dated guides to the area's monumental art (€2.30), architecture (€5.40) and history (€6.10). A better bet is the *La Défense* DVD (€10).

Le Kiosk (Map p157; ☎ 01 48 13 06 07; 6 place de la Légion d'Honneur; ◷ 11am-6pm Mon-Fri, 10am-1pm Sat; Ⓜ Basilique de St-Denis) This office has information about festivals and other cultural events, such as the **Banlieues Bleues** (☎ 01 49 22 10 10; www.banlieues bleus.org) jazz and blues festival in March and April and the **Festival de St-Denis** (www.festival-saint-denis.fr) from late May to late June.

Office de Tourisme de St-Denis Plaine Commune (Map p157; ☎ 01 55 87 08 70; www.saint-denis-tourisme .com in French; 1 rue de la République; ◷ 9.30am-1pm & 2-6pm Mon-Sat, 10am-2pm Sun Nov-Mar, 10am-1pm & 2-4pm Sun Apr-Oct; Ⓜ Basilique de St-Denis) The helpful tourist office is 100m west of the basilica.

Lonely Planet's website (www.lonelyplanet .com) is a good start for many of Paris' more useful links. Other good English-language websites about Paris (and France) include:

French Government Tourism Office (www.francetourism .com) Official tourism site with all manner of information on and about travel in France and lots on Paris.

Mairie de Paris (www.paris.fr) Statistics and city information direct from the Hôtel de Ville.

Paris Pages (www.paris.org) Good links to museums and cultural events.

Paris Convention & Visitors Bureau (Office de Tourisme et de Congrès; www.parisinfo.com) Super site with more links than you'll ever need.

TRAVELLERS WITH DISABILITIES

Paris is not particularly well equipped for *les handicapés* (disabled people): kerb ramps are few and far between, older public facilities and bottom-end hotels usually lack lifts, and the metro, dating back more than a century, is inaccessible for those in a wheelchair *(fauteuil roulant)*. But efforts are being made and in 2001 the tourist office launched its 'Tourisme & Handicap' initiative in which museums, cultural attractions, hotels and restaurants that provided access or special assistance or facilities for those with physical, mental, visual and/or hearing disabilities would display a special logo at their entrances. For a list of the places qualifying, see the tourist office's website (www.parisinfo.com).

Information & Organisations

The SNCF has made many of its train carriages more accessible to people with physical disabilities. A traveller in a wheelchair can travel in both the TGV (*train à grande vitesse*; high-speed train) and in the 1st-class carriage with a 2nd-class ticket on mainline trains provided they make a reservation by phone or at a train station at least a few hours before departure. Details are available in the SNCF booklet *Le Mémento du Voyageur Handicapé*. Contact **SNCF Accessibilité Service** (☎ 0 800 15 47 53; www.voyages-sncf .com/voyageurs_handicapes in French) for advice on planning your journey.

For information on accessibility to all forms of public transport in the Paris region, get a copy of the *Guide Practique à l'Usage des Personnes à Mobilité Réduite* from the **Syndicat des Transports d'Île de France** (☎ 01 47 53 28 00; www.stif-idf.fr). Other useful sources of information are **RATP Mission Accessibilité** (RATP Mission for Accessibility; ☎ 01 49 28 18 84; mission. accessibilite@ratp.fr), a group set up to improve access on all forms of public transport in the Paris region, and **Info Mobi** (☎ 0 810 64 64 64; www.infomobi.com).

Access in Paris by Gordon Crouch and Ben Roberts, a 245-page guide to the French capital for the disabled, last appeared in 1997, but it was being updated at the time of research and should be available from **Access Project** (www.accessinparis.org; 39 Bradley Gardens, West Ealing, London W13 8HE, UK) by the time you read this.

The following organisations can provide information to disabled travellers:

Association des Paralysées de France (APF; ☎ 01 53 80 92 97; www.apf.asso.fr in French; 13 place de Rungis, 75013 Paris) Brochures on wheelchair access and accommodation throughout France, including Paris.

Groupement pour l'Insertion des Personnes Handicapées Physiques (GIHP; ☎ 01 43 95 66 36; www.gihp national.org in French; 10 rue Georges de Porto Riche, 75014 Paris) Provides special vehicles outfitted for people in wheelchairs for use within the city.

VISAS

There are no entry requirements for nationals of EU countries. Citizens of Australia, the USA, Canada and New Zealand do not need visas to visit France for up to three months. Except for people from a handful of other European countries (including

Switzerland), everyone, including citizens of South Africa, needs a 'Schengen Visa', named after the Schengen Agreement that abolished passport controls between Austria, Belgium, Denmark, Finland, France, Germany, Greece, Italy, Luxembourg, the Netherlands, Portugal, Spain and Sweden and was later ratified by the non-EU governments of Norway and Iceland. A visa for any of these countries should be valid throughout the Schengen area, but it pays to double check with the embassy or consulate of each country you intend to visit.

Visa fees depend on the current exchange rate but transit and the various types of short-stay (up to 90 days) visas all cost €35, while a long-stay visa allowing stays of more than 90 days costs €99. You will need: your passport (valid for a period of three months beyond the date of your departure from France); a return ticket; proof of sufficient funds to support yourself; proof of prearranged accommodation; a recent passport-sized photo; and the visa fee in cash payable in local currency.

If all the forms are in order, your visa will usually be issued on the spot. You can also apply for a French visa after arriving in Europe – the fee is the same, but you may not have to produce a return ticket. If you enter France overland, your visa may not be checked at the border, but major problems can arise if the authorities discover that you don't have one later on (for example, at the airport as you leave the country).

Carte de Séjour

If you are issued a long-stay visa valid for six months or longer, you should apply for a carte de séjour (residence permit) within eight days of your arrival in France. Students must apply in person for a carte de séjour at the **Centre des Étudiants Étrangers** (Foreign Student Centre; Map pp434–5; ☎ 01 53 71 51 68 information; 13 rue Miollis, 15e; ☺ 8.35am-4.30pm Mon-Thu, 8.35am-4pm Fri; Ⓜ Cambronne or Ségur). Arrive early – the queues can be mammoth.

Those holding a passport from one of the original EU member-states and seeking to take up residence in France no longer need to acquire a carte de séjour; their passport or national ID card is sufficient. Citizens of any one of the 10 so-called accession countries that joined the EU in 2004 who wish to stay permanently should apply to the

Service Étranger (Foreign Service) office in Salle Nord Est, which is on the ground floor next to escalier F (stairway F) in the Préfecture de Police (below).

Foreigners with non-EU passports must go to one of two offices, depending on the arrondissement in which they're living or staying. The offices are open from 9am to 4.30pm Monday to Thursday and from 9am to 4pm on Friday. The office that deals with 1er to 10e and 15e to 18e Arrondissements is **Hôtel de Police** (Map pp426–7; ☎ 01 44 90 37 17; 19-21 rue Truffaut, 17e; Ⓜ Place de Clichy or La Fourche); for 11e to 14e and 19e to 20e Arrondissements go to **Hôtel de Police** (Map pp434–5; ☎ 01 53 74 14 06; 114-116 av du Maine, 14e; Ⓜ Gaîté).

Long-Stay & Student

If you would like to work, study or stay in France for longer than three months, apply to the French embassy or consulate nearest to you for the appropriate long séjour (long-stay) visa. For details of au pair visas, which must be arranged before you leave home (unless you're an EU resident), see opposite.

Unless you hold an EU passport, it's extremely difficult to get a visa that will allow you to work in France. For any sort of long-stay visa, begin the paperwork in your home country several months before you plan to leave. Applications cannot usually be made in a third country nor can tourist visas be turned into student visas after you arrive in France. People with student visas can apply for permission to work part-time; enquire at your place of study.

Visa Extensions

Tourist visas cannot be extended except in emergencies (such as medical problems). If you have an urgent problem, you should call the Service Étranger (Foreign Service) at the **Préfecture de Police** (Map pp436–7; ☎ 01 53 71 51 68; www.prefecture-police-paris .interieur.gouv.fr in French; 1 place Louis Lépine, 4e; ☺ 8.35am-4.45pm Mon-Thu, 8.35am-4.15pm Fri; Ⓜ Cité) for guidance.

If you don't need a visa to visit France, you'll almost certainly qualify for another automatic three-month stay if you take the train to, say, Geneva or Brussels and then re-enter France. The fewer recent French entry stamps you have in your passport the easier this is likely to be.

If you needed a visa the first time around, one way to extend your stay is to go to a French consulate in a neighbouring country and apply for another one there.

WOMEN TRAVELLERS

In 1923 French women obtained the right to – wait for it – open their own mail; the right to vote didn't come till 1945 during De Gaulle's short-lived postwar government and until 1964 a woman still needed her husband's permission to open a bank account or get a passport. It was in such an environment that Simone de Beauvoir wrote *Le Deuxième Sexe* (The Second Sex) in 1949.

Younger French women especially are quite outspoken and emancipated but self-confidence has yet to translate into equality in the workplace, where women are passed over for senior and management positions in favour of their male colleagues.

Women attract more unwanted attention than men, but female travellers need not walk around Paris in fear: people are rarely assaulted on the street. However, the French seem to have given relatively little thought to sexual harassment (*harcèlement sexuel*), and many men still think that to stare suavely at a passing woman is to pay her a flattering compliment.

Information & Organisations

France's women's movement flourished as in other countries in the late 1960s and early 1970s, but by the mid-'80s had become moribund. For reasons that have more to do with French society than anything else, few women's groups function as the kind of supportive social institutions that exist in the USA, the UK and Australia.

La Maison des Femmes de Paris (Map pp446–7; ☎ 01 43 43 41 13; http://maisondesfemmes .free.fr in French; 163 rue de Charenton, 12e; ☒ office 9am-7pm Mon-Fri; Ⓜ Reuilly Diderot) is a meeting place for women of all ages and nationalities, with events, workshops and exhibitions scheduled throughout the week.

France's national rape-crisis hotline (☎ 0 800 05 95 95; ☒ 10am-7pm Mon-Fri) can be reached toll-free from any telephone, without using a phonecard. It's run by a group called Collectif Féministe contre le Viol (Feminist Collective Against Rape; CFCV; www.cfcv.asso.fr).

In an emergency, you can always call the police (☎ 17). Medical, psychological and legal services are available to those referred by the police at the Service Médico-Judiciaire (☎ 01 42 34 86 78; ☒ 24hr) of the Hôtel Dieu (p380).

WORK

Although there are strict laws preventing non-EU nationals from being employed in France, it's increasingly possible to work 'in the black' (ie without the legally required documents). Au pair work is popular and can be done legally even by non-EU nationals.

For practical information on employment in Paris and France, consider picking up the recently updated *Live and Work in France* by Victoria Pybus or *Living and Working in France: A Survival Handbook* by David Hampshire.

To work legally in France you need a *carte de séjour* (opposite): getting one is almost impossible if you aren't a citizen of the EU, unless you are a full-time student.

Non-EU nationals cannot work legally unless they obtain an *autorisation de travail* (work permit) before arriving in France. This is no easy matter, as a prospective employer has to convince the authorities that there is no French person – or other EU national, for that matter – who can do the job being offered to you.

Au Pair Work

Under the au pair system, single people aged 18 to about 27 can live with a French family and receive lodging, full board and some pocket money in exchange for taking care of the kids, babysitting, doing light housework and perhaps teaching English to the children. Most families prefer young women, but some positions are also available for men. Many families want au pairs who are native English-speakers; knowing at least some French may be a prerequisite. For practical information, pick up the recently updated *Au Pair and Nanny's Guide to Working Abroad* by Susan Griffith and Sharon Legg.

By law, au pairs must have one full day off a week. Some families may provide metro passes. The family must also pay for French social security, which covers about 70% of medical expenses (get supplementary insurance if you are not an EU citizen).

Residents of the EU can easily arrange for an au pair job and a *carte de séjour* after arriving in France. Non-EU nationals who decide to look for au pair work after entering the country cannot do so legally and won't be covered by the protections provided for under French law.

Check the bulletin boards at the American Church (p382) as well as *FUSAC* (p382) for job ads. In the latter, you'll find au pair work listed under 'Childcare Positions'.

Doing Business

If you are going to Paris on business, it's a good idea to contact one of the main commercial offices or your embassy's trade office in Paris before you leave home, to establish contacts and make appointments. These include the following:

American Chamber of Commerce (Map pp426–7; ☎ 01 56 43 45 67; www.amchamfrance.org; 156 blvd Haussmann, 75008 Paris)

Australian Trade Commission (Map pp434–5; ☎ 01 40 59 33 85; www.austrade.gov.au; 4 rue Jean Rey, 75015 Paris)

Canadian Government Department of Commercial & Economic Affairs (Map pp426–7; ☎ 01 44 43 29 00; www.amb-canada.fr; 35 av Montaigne, 75008 Paris)

Chambre de Commerce et d'Industrie de Paris (CCIP; ☎ 01 53 40 46 00; www.ccip.fr) Check website for appropriate address.

France-Canada Chamber of Commerce (Map pp434–5; ☎ 01 43 59 32 38; www.ccfc-france-canada.com in French; 5 rue Constantine, 75007 Paris)

Franco-British Chamber of Commerce & Industry (Map pp426–7; ☎ 01 53 30 81 30; www.francobritishchamber .com; 31 rue Boissy d'Anglas, 75008 Paris)

Irish Embassy Trade Office (Map pp426–7; ☎ 01 44 17 67 04; paris@dfa.ie; 4 rue Rude, 75016 Paris)

New Zealand Embassy Trade Office (Map pp426–7; ☎ 01 45 01 43 10; paris@nzte.govt.nz; 7ter rue Léonard de Vinci, 75116 Paris)

UK Embassy Trade Office (Map pp426–7; ☎ 01 44 51 34 56; www.amb-grandebretagne.fr; 35 rue du Faubourg St-Honoré, 75008 Paris)

US Embassy Trade Office (Map pp426–7; ☎ 01 43 12 23 83; www.buyusa.gov/france/en; 2 av Gabriel, 75008 Paris)

If you are looking to set up a business in France and need a temporary office or secretarial assistance, contact the following:

Copy-Top (www.copytop.com in French) This chain is useful for photocopying, printing etc and has more than two-dozen outlets in central Paris, including 87 blvd Voltaire, 11e (Map pp440–1; ☎ 01 48 05 80 84; ⏰ 8.30am-6pm Mon-Fri; Ⓜ Voltaire) and 52 blvd du Montparnasse, 15e (Map pp434–5; ☎ 01 42 22 80 58; ⏰ 8.30am-6pm Mon-Fri; Ⓜ Montparnasse Bienvenüe).

NewWorks (☎ 01 72 74 24 00; www.newworks.net in French) This *service bureau* chain can supply most of your office and secretarial needs and can serve as your temporary office. There are four branches, including Opéra (Map pp426–7; ☎ 01 72 74 24 44; 12 rue Auber, 9e; ⏰ 8.30am-7pm Mon-Fri; Ⓜ Auber or Havre-Caumartin) and Champs-Élysées (Map pp426–7; ☎ 01 72 74 24 54; 10 rue du Colisée, 8e; ⏰ 8.30am-7pm Mon-Fri; Ⓜ Franklin D Roosevelt).

Job-Seeking

The fortnightly *FUSAC* (p382) is an excellent source for job-seekers; check out the classified ads under 'Employment & Careers'.

The following agencies might be of some assistance.

Agence Nationale pour l'Emploi (National Employment Agency; ANPE; www.anpe.fr in French) France's national employment service has lists of job openings and branches throughout the city. The following assists those residing in the 1er, 4e and 12e arrondissements: **ANPE Hôtel de Ville** (Map pp436–7; ☎ 01 42 71 24 68; 20bis rue Ste-Croix de la Bretonnerie, 4e; ⏰ 9am-5pm Mon-Wed & Fri, 9am-6pm Thu; Ⓜ Hôtel de Ville)

Centres d'Information et de Documentation Jeunesse (Youth Information and Documentation Centres; www.cidj .com in French) CIDJ offices have information on housing, professional training and educational options, and notice boards with work possibilities. Its **Paris headquarters** (Map pp434–5; ☎ 0 825 090 630, 01 44 49 12 00; 101 quai Branly, 15e; ⏰ 10am-6pm Mon-Fri, 9.30am-1pm Sat; Ⓜ Champ de Mars-Tour Eiffel) is a short distance southwest of the Eiffel Tower.

Language

Language

It's true – anyone can speak another language. Don't worry if you haven't studied languages before or that you studied a language at school for years and can't remember any of it. It doesn't even matter if you failed English grammar. After all, that's never affected your ability to speak English! And this is the key to picking up a language in another country. You just need to start speaking.

Learn a few key phrases before you go. Write them on pieces of paper and stick them on the fridge, by the bed or even on the computer – anywhere that you'll see them often.

You'll find that locals appreciate travellers trying their language, no matter how muddled you may think you sound. So don't just stand there, say something! If you want to learn more French than we've included here, pick up a copy of Lonely Planet's comprehensive but user-friendly *French Phrasebook*.

SOCIAL
Be Polite!

Politeness pays dividends in Parisian daily life and the easiest way to make a good impression on Parisian merchants is always to say *Bonjour Monsieur/Madame/Mademoiselle* when you enter a shop, and *Merci Monsieur/Madame/Mademoiselle, au revoir* when you leave. *Monsieur* means 'sir' and can be used with any adult male. *Madame* is used where 'Mrs' or 'Ma'am' would apply in English. Officially, *Mademoiselle* (Miss) relates to unmarried women, but it's much more common to use *Madame* – unless of course you know the person's marital status! Similarly, if you want help or need to interrupt someone, approach them with *Excusez-moi, Monsieur/Madame/Mademoiselle*.

Meeting People

Hello.
Bonjour/Salut. (polite/informal)
Goodbye.
Au revoir/Salut. (polite/informal)
Please.
S'il vous plaît.
Thank you (very much).
Merci (beaucoup).
Yes/No.
Oui/Non.
Do you speak English?
Parlez-vous anglais?
Do you understand (me)?
Est-ce que vous (me) comprenez?

Yes, I understand.
Oui, je comprends.
No, I don't understand.
Non, je ne comprends pas.

Could you please ...?
Pourriez-vous ..., s'il vous plaît?
  repeat that   répéter
  speak more   parler plus lentement
  slowly
  write it down   l'écrire

Going Out

What's on ...?
Qu'est-ce qu'on joue ...?
  locally   dans le coin
  this weekend   ce week-end
  today   aujourd'hui
  tonight   ce soir

Where are the ...?
Où sont les ...?
  clubs   clubs/boîtes
  gay venues   boîtes gaies
  places to eat   restaurants
  pubs   pubs

Is there a local entertainment guide?
Y a-t-il un programme des spectacles?

PRACTICAL
Question Words

Who?   Qui?
Which?   Quel/Quelle? (m/f)

When?	Quand?
Where?	Où?
How?	Comment?

Numbers & Amounts

0	zéro
1	un
2	deux
3	trois
4	quatre
5	cinq
6	six
7	sept
8	huit
9	neuf
10	dix
11	onze
12	douze
13	treize
14	quatorze
15	quinze
16	seize
17	dix-sept
18	dix-huit
19	dix-neuf
20	vingt
21	vingt et un
22	vingt deux
30	trente
40	quarante
50	cinquante
60	soixante
70	soixante-dix
80	quatre-vingts
90	quatre-vingt-dix
100	cent
1000	mille
2000	deux mille

Days

Monday	lundi
Tuesday	mardi
Wednesday	mercredi
Thursday	jeudi
Friday	vendredi
Saturday	samedi
Sunday	dimanche

Banking

I'd like to ...
Je voudrais ...

cash a cheque	encaisser un chèque
change money	changer de l'argent
change some	changer des chèques
travellers cheques	de voyage

Where's the nearest ...?
Où est ... le plus prochain?

ATM	le guichet automatique
foreign exchange office	le bureau de change

Post

Where is the post office?
Où est le bureau de poste?

I want to send a ...
Je voudrais envoyer ...

fax	un fax
letter	une lettre
parcel	un colis
postcard	une carte postale

I want to buy ...
Je voudrais acheter ...

an aerogram	un aérogramme
an envelope	une enveloppe
a stamp	un timbre

Phones & Mobiles

I want to buy a phone card.
Je voudrais acheter une carte téléphonique.
I want to make a call (to Australia/to Rome).
Je veux téléphoner (en Australie/à Rome).
I want to make a reverse-charge/collect call.
Je veux téléphoner avec préavis en PCV.
('PCV' is pronounced 'pay say vay')

Where can I find a/an ...?
Où est-ce quee je peux trouver ...?
I'd like a/an ...
Je voudrais ...

adaptor plug	une prise multiple
charger for my phone	un chargeur pour mon portable
mobile/cell phone for hire	louer un portable
prepaid mobile/ cell phone	un portable pré-payé
SIM card for your network	une carte SIM pour le réseau

Internet

Where's the local Internet café?
Où est le cybercafé du coin?

I'd like to ...
Je voudrais ...

check my email	consulter mon courrier électronique
get online	me connecter à l'internet

Transport

What time does the ... leave?
À quelle heure part ...?

bus	le bus
ferry	le bateau
plane	l'avion
train	le train

What time's the ... bus?
Le ... bus passe à quelle heure?

first	premier
last	dernier
next	prochain

Are you free? (taxi)
Vous êtes libre?
Please put the meter on.
Mettez le compteur, s'il vous plaît?
How much is it to ...?
C'est combien pour aller à ...?
Please take me to (this address).
Conduisez-moi à (cette adresse), s'il vous plaît.

FOOD

breakfast	le petit déjeuner
lunch	le déjeuner
dinner	le dîner
snack	un casse-croûte
eat	manger
drink	boire

Can you recommend a ...
Est-ce que vous pouvez me conseiller un ...

bar/pub	bar/pub
café	café
restaurant	un restaurant

Is service/cover charge included in the bill?
Le service est compris?

For more detailed information on food and dining out, see p47.

EMERGENCIES

It's an emergency!
C'est urgent!
Could you please help me/us?
Este-ce que vous pourriez m'aider/nous aider, s'il vous plaît?
Call the police/a doctor/an ambulance!
Appelez la police/un médecin/une ambulance!
Where's the police station?
Où est le commissariat (de police)?

HEALTH

Where's the nearest ...?
Où est ... le/la plus prochain/e? (m/f)

chemist (night)	la pharmacie (de nuit)
dentist	le dentiste
doctor	le médecin
hospital	l'hôpital (m)

I need a doctor (who speaks English).
J'ai besoin d'un médecin (qui parle anglais).

Symptoms

I have (a) ...
J'ai ...

diarrhoea	la diarrhée
fever	de la fièvre
headache	mal à la tête
pain	une douleur

GLOSSARY

(m) indicates masculine gender, (f) feminine gender, (pl) plural and (adj) adjective

arrondissement (m) – one of 20 administrative divisions in Paris; abbreviated on street signs as 1er (1st arrondissement), 2e or 2ème (2nd) etc
auberge (de jeunesse) (f) – (youth) hostel

banlieues (f pl) – suburbs
belle époque (f) – 'beautiful age'; era of elegance and gaiety characterising fashionable Parisian life roughly from 1870 to 1914
billeterie (f) – ticket office or window
bon vivant – a person who enjoys good food and drink
boulangerie (f) – bakery

boules (f pl) – a game played with heavy metal balls on a sandy pitch; also called *pétanque*
brasserie (f) – 'brewery'; a restaurant that usually serves food all day long
brioche (f) – small roll or cake, sometimes made with nuts, currants or candied fruits
bureau de change (m) – currency exchange bureau
bureau des objets trouvés (m) – lost and found bureau, lost property office

cacher (adj) – kosher
café du quartier (m) – neighbourhood café
carnet (m) – a book of (usually) 10 bus, tram, metro or other tickets sold at a reduced rate
carrefour (m) – crossroads, intersection

carte (f) – card; menu; map
carte de séjour (f) – residence permit
chambre d'hôte (f) – private room, usually bed and breakfast
chanson française (f) – 'French song'; traditional musical genre where lyrics are paramount
chansonnier (m) – cabaret singer
charcuterie (f) – a variety of pork products that are cured, smoked or processed, including sausages, hams, pâtés and rillettes; shop selling these products
cimetière (m) – cemetery
cour (f) – courtyard
crêpe (f) – 'crepe'; a large, paper-thin pancake served with various fillings, both savoury and sweet

demi (m) – half; 330mL glass of beer
département (m) – administrative division of France
digestif (m) – 'digestive'; a drink served after a meal

eau (f) – water
église (f) – church
épicerie (f) – small grocery store
escalier (m) – stairway
espace (f) – space; outlet
exposition universelle (f) – world exhibition

forêt (f) – forest
formule or **formule rapide** (f) – similar to a *menu* but allows choice of whichever two of three courses you want (eg starter and main course or main course and dessert)
fromagerie (f) – cheese shop
fumoir (f) – smoking room or chamber

galerie (f) – gallery; covered shopping arcade (also called *passage*)
galette (f) – a pancake or flat pastry, with a variety of (usually savoury) fillings; see also *crêpe*
gare or **gare SNCF** (f) – railway station
gare routière (f) – bus station
grand projet (m) – huge, public edifice erected by a government or politician generally in a bid to immortalise themselves
Grands Boulevards (m pl) – 'Great Boulevards'; the eight contiguous broad thoroughfares that stretch from place de la Madeleine eastwards to the place de la République
gratin (m) – dish cooked in the oven and browned with breadcrumbs or cheese

halles (f pl) – covered food market
hameau (m) – hamlet
hammam (m) – steam room, Turkish bath
haute cuisine (f) – 'high cuisine'; classic French style of cooking typified by elaborately prepared multicourse meals
hôtel de ville (m) – city or town hall
hôtel particulier (m) – private mansion

intra-muros – 'within the walls' (Latin); refers to central Paris

jardin (m) – garden
kir (m) – white wine sweetened with a blackcurrant (or other) liqueur

laverie (f) – laundrette
libre-service – self-service
lycée (m) – secondary school

mairie (f) – city or town hall
marché (m) – market
marché aux puces (m) – flea market
menu (m) – fixed-price meal with two or more courses; see *formule*
musée (m) – museum
musette (f) – accordion music

nocturne (f) – late night opening at a museum, department store etc

palais de justice (m) – law courts
parc (m) – park
parvis (m) – square in front of a church or public building
passage couvert (m) – covered shopping arcade (also called *galerie*)
pastis (m) – an aniseed-flavoured aperitif mixed with water
pâté (m) – potted meat; a thickish paste, often of pork, cooked in a ceramic dish and served cold (similar to ter-rine)
pâtisserie (f) – cakes and pastries; shop selling these products
pelouse (f) – lawn
pétanque (f) – see *boules*
pied-noir (m) – 'black foot'; French colonial born in Algeria
place (f) – square or plaza
plan du quartier (m) – map of nearby streets (hung on the wall near metro exits)
plat du jour (m) – daily special in a restaurant
poissonnerie (f) – fishmonger, fish shop
pont (m) – bridge
port (m) – harbour, port
port de plaisance (m) – boat harbour or marina
porte (f) – door; gate in a city wall
pourboire (m) – tip
préfecture (f) – prefecture; capital city of a *département*
produits biologique – organic food

quai (m) – quay
quartier (m) – quarter, district, neighbourhood

raï – a type of Algerian popular music
RATP – Régie Autonome des Transports Parisiens; Paris' public transport system
RER – Réseau Express Regional; Paris' suburban train network
résidence (f) – 'residence'; hotel usually intended for long-term stays
rillettes (f pl) – shredded potted meat or fish

rive (f) – bank of a river
rond point (m) – roundabout
rue (f) – street or road

salle (f) – hall; room
salon de thé (m) – tearoom
séance (f) – performance or screening (film)
SNCF – Société Nationale de Chemins de Fer; France's national railway organisation
soldes (m pl) – sale, the sales
sono mondiale (f) – world music
spectacle (m) – performance, play or theatrical show

square (m) – public garden

tabac (m) – tobacconist (which also sells bus tickets, phonecards etc)
tartine (f) – a slice of bread with any topping or garnish
télécarte (f) – phonecard
TGV – train à grande vitesse; high-speed train
tour (f) – tower
traiteur (m) – caterer, delicatessen

vélo (m) – bicycle
vin de table (m) – table wine
voie (f) – way; railway platform

Behind the Scenes

THE LONELY PLANET STORY

The story begins with a classic travel adventure: Tony and Maureen Wheeler's 1972 journey across Europe and Asia to Australia. There was no useful information about the overland trail then, so Tony and Maureen published the first Lonely Planet guidebook to meet a growing need.

From a kitchen table, Lonely Planet has grown to become the largest independent travel publisher in the world, with offices in Melbourne (Australia), Oakland (USA) and London (UK). Today Lonely Planet guidebooks cover the globe. There is an ever-growing list of books and information in a variety of media. Some things haven't changed. The main aim is still to make it possible for adventurous travellers to get out there – to explore and better understand the world.

At Lonely Planet we believe travellers can make a positive contribution to the countries they visit – if they respect their host communities and spend their money wisely. Every year 5% of company profit is donated to charities around the world.

THIS BOOK

This guidebook was commissioned in Lonely Planet's London office, and produced by the following:

Commissioning Editors Meg Worby, Judith Bamber, Tashi Wheeler

Coordinating Editor Holly Alexander

Coordinating Cartographer Simon Tillema

Coordinating Layout Designer Jessica Rose

Managing Cartographer Mark Griffiths

Assisting Editors Elizabeth Anglin, Sasha Baskett, Janice Bird, Yvonne Byron, Gennifer Ciavarra, Barbara Delissen, Joanne Newell, Lauren Rollheiser, Laura Stansfeld

Assisting Cartographers Emma McNicol, Malisa Plesa

Assisting Layout Designers Laura Jane, Cara Smith, Wibowo Rusli

Cover Designer Marika Kozak

Colour Designer Jessica Rose

Project Manager Nancy Ianni

Language Content Coordinator Quentin Frayne

Thanks to Melanie Dankel, Sally Darmody, Tasmin Mc-Naughton, Kate McDonald, Trent Paton, Stephanie Pearson, Gabbi Stefanos, Celia Wood & The Boys in the Bubble (LPI)

Cover photographs Woman with Umbrella, Louvre, Paris, France, Leanne Pedersen/Masterfile (top); View down a spiral staircase, Leanne Pedersen/Photolibrary (bottom)

Internal photographs by Lonely Planet Images and Jean-Bernard Carillet except for the following: p2 (#1, #2 & #5), p84 (#1 & #3), p85 (#1), p86 (#3), p87 (#3 & #4), p88 (#2), p89 (#2), p90 (#4), p139 (#1), p140 (#4), p142 (#1), p144 (#1), p146 (#2), 195 (#2), p202 (#2), p8, p14, p30, p39, p55, p58, p102, p123, p154, p166, p176, p193, p211, p279, p283, p304, p315, p324 & p346 Jonathan Smith; p199 (#3) Ann Cecil; p83 (#1) & p86 (#2) Juliet Coombe; p87 (#2) Olivier Cirendini; p196 (#2) Elliot Daniel; p89 (#4) & p196 (#4) Greg Elms; p139 (#3) John Hay; p89 (#3) Dan Herrick; p139 (#2) Mark Honan; p90 (#3) & p141 (#3) Dennis Johnson; p195 (#1) Izzet Keribar; p2 (#3) & p195 (#3) Richard I'Anson; p83 (#3) Regis Martin; p145 (#3) Doug McKinlay; p84 (#2) & p197 (#1) Martin Moos; p200 (#4) & p201 (#3) Russell Mountford; p90 (#2) Richard Nebesky; p198 (#2) Stephen Saks; p199 (#2) Neil Setchfield; p88 (#1) Witold Skrypczak; p83 (#4) Jan Stromme; p145 (#1), p198 (#1) & p201 (#1) Barbara Van Zanten; p198 (#3) Brent Winebrenner; p199 (#1), p351 & p357 Christopher Wood; p140 (#2) & p141 (#1) Bruce Yuan-Yue Bi. All images are copyright of the photographer unless otherwise indicated. Many of the images in this guide are available for licensing from Lonely Planet Images: www.lonelyplanetimages.com.

THANKS

STEVE FALLON

A number of people helped in the updating of Paris, in particular resident Brenda Turnnidge, who provided invaluable support and insider's information with her usual efficiency and enthusiasm. Thanks too to Zahia Hafs, Caroline Guilleminot and Olivier Cirendini for assistance, ideas, hospitality and/or a few laughs along the way. Special thanks and a hat tip to Holly Alexander and her team at LP in Melbourne for hurrying up the editing process as I travelled the Mali-Slovenia Express at breakneck speed. Much appreciated. As always, I'd like to dedicate my share of Paris to my Partner (now with a capital – and legal – 'P') Michael Rothschild.

Finally, to all the wonderful and infuriating Parisians I met along the way this time round – elegant and stylish, cultured and entertaining, bitchy and attitudinous *à l'extrême – merci encore une fois*. You're just what the world needs more of.

ANNABEL HART

Thanks to everyone at LP, and to Steve Fallon, for their patience and hard work. Big thanks to my fellow bar-crawlers, clubbing co-pilots, shopping advisors and friends: Jules, Karo, Seb, Lina, Marie, Olivier, Christophe and Antoine. Thanks to Zahia for all her encouragement. Particular thanks to Estelle, my fashion consultant, and Annabelle for her cultural insights and invaluable last-minute assistance. Bisous to my whole *'boîte à copains'* in Paris, especially Claire, Arno and Julien; I will be missing you by now.

OUR READERS

Many thanks to the travellers who used the last edition and wrote to us with helpful hints, useful advice and interesting anecdotes:

Susan Alexander, Christine Alexanian, Lillian Anekwe, Garry Aslanyan, Simon Ball, Kate Black, Nicola Brew, Wendy Brown, Kerrie Buckley, Eddie Buglass, Amanda Burke, Maria Bursey, Graham Button, Christian Byhahn, Kenny Campbell, Nikitas Chondroyannos, Romani Claudia, Greta Cleghorn, Krista Coleman, Andrew Cosgrave, David Cruden, Vicky & Steffan Davies, Catherine Demayo, Mary Beth Deyoung, Laura & Ami Diner, Jeffrey Dorfman, Benjamin Dyson, Heather Ebbott, Oyvind Ellingsen, Brian Engel, Agincic Erzana, Craig Falls, Lea Feng, Stan Fletcher, Brian Floca, Elliott Forsyth, Margaret Frey, Jacqueline Gilmartin, Estelle Green, Miriam Greenbaum, Debbie Guest, Melanie Hall, Kristal Hargraves, Nancy Heaton, Meinoud Hehenkamp, Jim Hendrickson, Moritz Herrmann, Evan Hirsch, Adam Hobill, Cecile Hubert, John & Joan Hunter, Paula Ijzerman, Ajay Jain, Beth Jensen, Dustin Johnson, Suzanne Johnson, Victoria Johnson, Barry Johnston, Patricia Kaddar, Dawn Keremitsis, Nigel King, Mary Ellen Kitler, Richard Koehl, Joelle Kohn, Tonko Lacmanovic, Jenni le Comte, Richard Libby, Nana Lim, Ynyr Lloyd, Lydia Loriente, Peter MacLean, Maria Sanchez, Trevor Mazzucchelli, Craig McGrath, Laura Mentch, Fergus Mitchell, Tina Mizgalski, David Murphy, Namrata Nandan, Mark Nunez, Stephanos Papadopoulos, Kirk Preston, Karlmarx Rajangam, Jason Ramer, Loren Ransley, Jessie Reeves, Denise Reich, Stephane Reynolds, P Robertson, Anne & Peter Rolston, Janice Rossen, Anna Rowe, Ginny Seers, Cindy Shurtleff, Jas Singh, Neha Singhal, Jacalyn Soo, Ian Southwell, Jenny Storti, Patricia Sykes, Balazs Szanto, Yoong Heng Tan, Bill Thames, Caroline Topp, Barbara Toussaint, Edward Tsui, Julie Un, Rosa Williams, Matthew Wilner-Reid, Keefe Wong, John Worzencraft, Andrew Young

ACKNOWLEDGMENTS

Many thanks to the following for the use of their content:
Paris Metro Map © 2006 RATP

Notes

Notes

Notes

Notes

Notes

Notes

Index

See also separate indexes for Eating (p416), Drinking (p415), Shopping (p417) and Sleeping (p418).

Index

Index

000 map pages
000 photographs

Index

SHOPPING

SLEEPING

Index

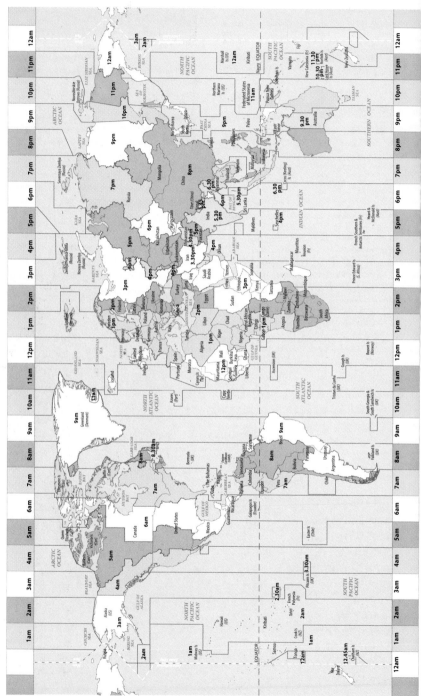

MAP LEGEND

ROUTES

Tollway	Mall/Steps
Freeway	Tunnel
Primary Road	Walking Tour
Secondary Road	Walking Tour Detour
Tertiary Road	Walking Trail
Lane	Walking Path
One-Way Street	Pedestrian Overpass

TRANSPORT

Ferry	Rail
Metro	Rail (Underground)

HYDROGRAPHY

River, Creek	Water

BOUNDARIES

Ancient Wall	Arrondissement

AREA FEATURES

Area of Interest	Forest
Building, Featured	Land
Building, Information	Mall
Building, Other	Park
Building, Transport	Sports
Cemetery, Christian	

POPULATION

✪ CAPITAL (NATIONAL)	◉ CAPITAL (STATE)
● Large City	● Medium City
● Small City	● Town, Village

SYMBOLS

Sights/Activities
- Castle, Fortress
- Christian
- Islamic
- Jewish
- Monument
- Museum, Gallery
- Other Site
- Ruin
- Swimming Pool
- Winery, Vineyard
- Zoo, Bird Sanctuary

Eating
- Eating

Drinking
- Café
- Drinking

Entertainment
- Entertainment

Shopping
- Shopping

Transport
- Airport, Airfield
- Bus Station
- Funicular
- Other Site
- Parking Area
- Taxi Rank

Sleeping
- Sleeping
- Camping

Information
- Bank, ATM
- Embassy/Consulate
- Hospital, Medical
- Information
- Internet Facilities
- Other Site
- Police Station
- Post Office, GPO
- Telephone
- Toilets

Maps

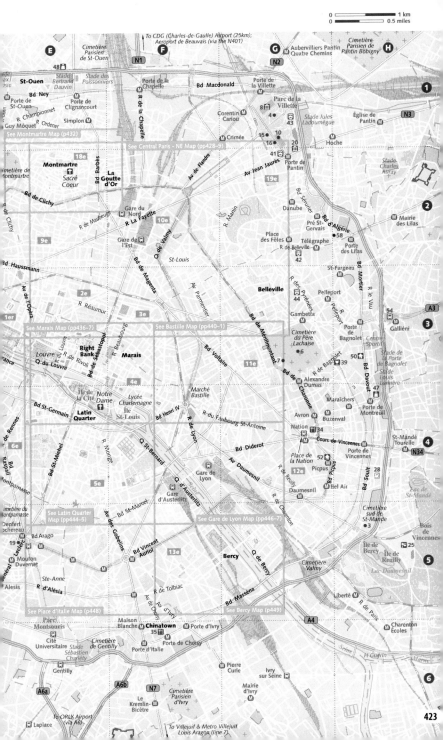

GREATER PARIS (pp422–3)

CENTRAL PARIS - NW (pp426–7)

CENTRAL PARIS – NW

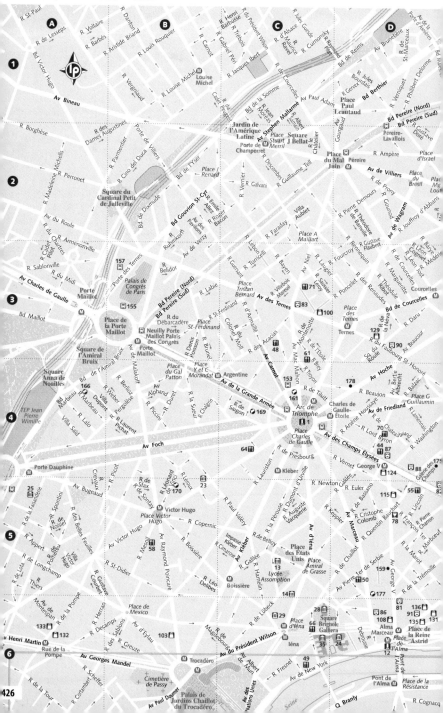

CENTRAL PARIS – NE

CENTRAL PARIS - NE (pp428–9)

CENTRAL PARIS - NE (pp428–9)

MONTMARTRE

0 _____ 200 m
0 _____ 0.1 miles

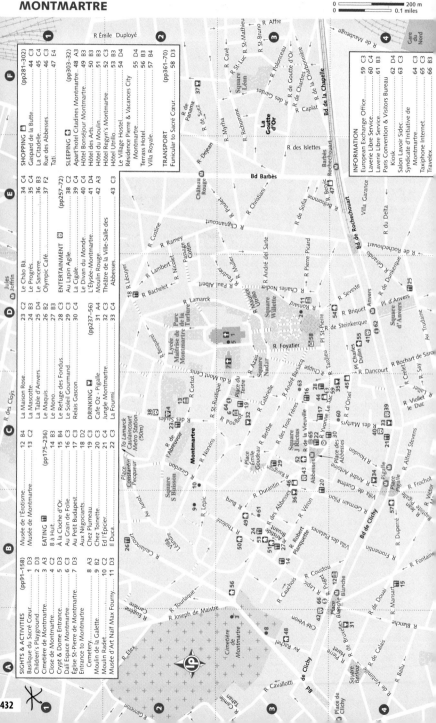

CENTRAL PARIS - SW (pp434–5)

CENTRAL PARIS – SW

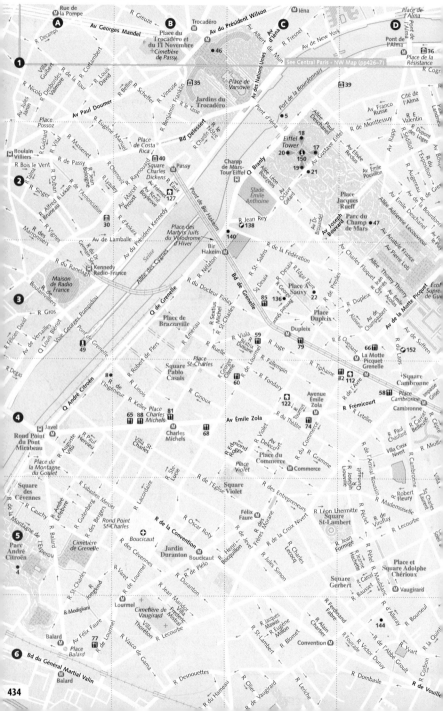

See Central Paris - NW Map (pp426–7)

434

101 Blvd Raspail   530

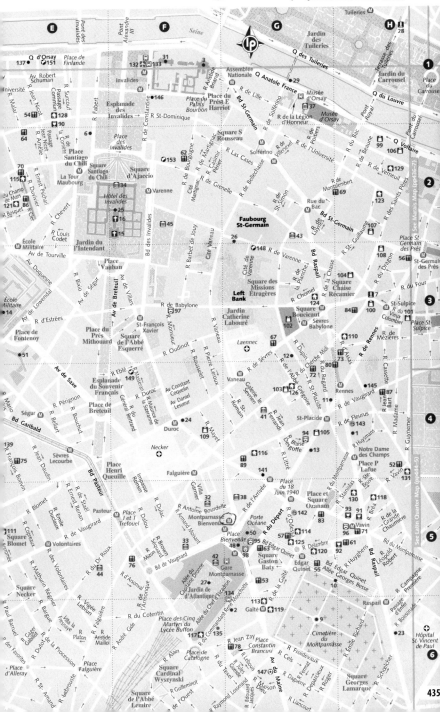

400 m
0   0.2 miles

435

MARAIS

Av de l'Opéra

R des Pyramides
75

R d'Argenteuil

R de l'Echelle

R de Montpensier

R Molière

Jardin
du Palais
Royal
14

Banque
de
France

R Hérold

Hôtel
des Postes
312

R Montorgueil
Market

R Étienne Marcel

R de Rivoli

56

R de Valois

R de Rohan

Palais
Royal
61

180
179

Place du
Palais
Royal
182
235

R St-Honoré

Place des
Bons Enfants

R des Bons Enfants

R de Coquillière

R Coq Héron

216

R Jean Jacques Rousseau

R Croix des Petits Champs

R du Pélican

J J Rousseau

Place des
Deux-Ecus
155
254

197
196

R du Jour

240
198
17

R Montmartre

Les
Halles
62

Place
René
Cassin
63

R Rambuteau

76

Jardin
du
Carrousel

303
211

Place du
Palais Royal
Musée du
Louvre

38
82
261
120
123
309
311
11
115

7

Place
du
Carrousel
3
2
40

84

R de Marengo

R de l'Oratoire

R Bailleul
242
87

97

Place M
Quentin

R des Halles

R Berge

Place
M de
Navarre

301
106

Cour
Napoléon
32

Jardin
de
l'Oratoire

57

Cour
Carrée

Jardin
de
l'Infante

157
R Perrault
246

R de Rivoli

Forum
des
Halls
31

Musée du
Louvre

R de l'Amiral de Coligny

Place
du
Louvre
19
275

225
B Baillet
224
222

R Boucher

R du Roule

R des Déchargeurs
192

Châtelet

Pont de Carrousel

Q du Louvre
294

R de l'Arbre Sec

R de la Monnaie
R du Pont Neuf

Pont
Neuf

R St-Germain l'Auxerrois

R des Bourdonnais

R Bertin Poirée

R des Deux Boules
96

Deux
Boules

R des Lavandières

Châtel

Seine

Q Malaquais
293

Pont Neuf

Av Victoria

178
Châtel

Q de la Mégisserie

R des Saints-Pères

R Bonaparte

Place de
l'Institut
6
39

Q de Conti

Square
du Vert
Galant
71

34
174

Place
du Pont
Neuf

274

Place
Dauphine

Q de l'Horloge

Ile
de
la Cité

Q au
Change

R des Beaux Arts
302
285

51

Q des Orfèvres

68

12

R de Seine

R Visconti

249

259
284

265

R Jacob

152
186

263
191

R de Nevers

R Guénégaud

149

R Dauphine

253
93

R des Grands Augustins

67

R de Lutèce

Bd du Palais

R St-Michel

317

280
266

R Jacob

Jacques
Callot

Passage
Dauphine
27

R de
Nesle

R Christine
276

R des Grands Augustins

Q des Grands Augustins

Place de
Furstemberg
59

R de Buci

74
105
91

100

305
109
208
162
85

279
128

77

Ande
Mazet

306

R Commerce St-André

314
291

289
83

318
St-Michel
St-Michel

Pont St-Michel

St-Michel—
Notre Dame

137
117

Place St-
Germain
des Prés
143
161

Square
Desruelles

St-Germain
des Prés
239

R Gozlin

248
126

R du Four

Mabillon

R de l'Abbaye

R de l'Ancienne
Comédie

Cour du
Commerce St-André

R St-André des Arts
86
R Suger

Place
St-Michel

St-Michel—
Notre Dame

St-Michel
Place
St-André
des Arts

R de la Huchette

183

R de Rennes

R des Ciseaux

112
146
127

R Clément

R Grégoire de Tours

228
15

124
169

R de Seine

R André

R Mazarine

R Séguier

R de Savoie
236

R de l'Éperon

R du Jardinet

R Hautefeuille

R Danton

R Mignon
271

315
270

R St-Séverin

R de la
Parcheminerie

135
24
273

210
156

R de Canettes
213

147
113
155
172

Marché
St-Germain
99

R des
Quatre Vents
269

Carrefour
de l'Odéon

Bd St-Germain

R Serpente

R de la Harpe

R St-Jacques

199

250
144

212

R St-Sulpice

247

R de Tournon

R de Condé

R de l'Odéon

Odéon

35
58

131
290

30

Bd St-Michel

Cluny—
La Sorbonne

R St-Julien
le Pauve

R Dante

200

Place
St-Sulpice
29
25

154
238

R de l'École de Médecine

R Monsieur le Prince

R Pierre
Sarrazin

R Boutebrie

R de Cluny

436

See Latin Quarter Map (pp444–5)

MARAIS (pp436-7)

BASTILLE

See Marais Map (pp436–7)

See Gare de Lyon Map (pp446–7)

BASTILLE (pp440–1)

LATIN QUARTER (pp444–5)

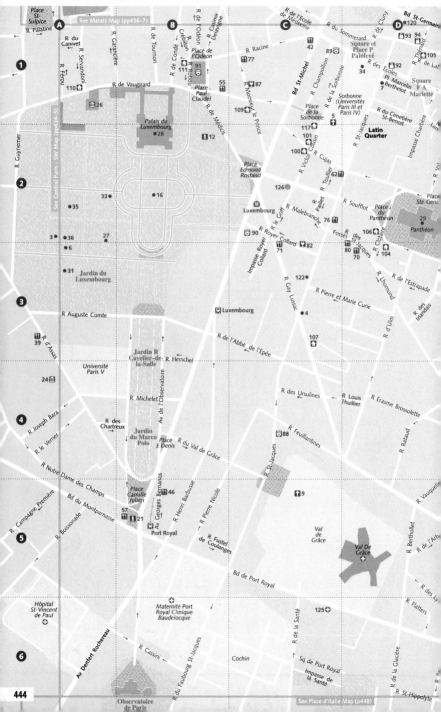

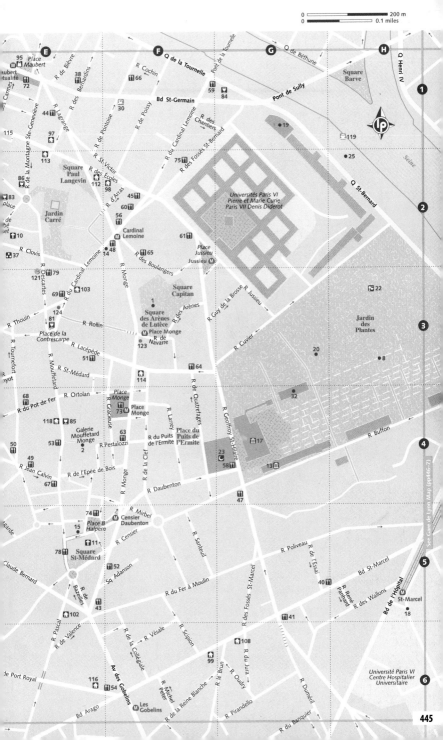

R de Sully
Bd Morland
Bd Morland
R de Schomberg
R l'Arsenal
R Crillon
R de Brissac
R Mornay
Bd Bourdon
R Jules César
Bd de la Bastille
R Biscornet
R Lacuée
R Émilio Castelar
R de Lyon
R Moreau
Cité du Chêne Vert
R Traversière
R de Prague
R Charles Baudei
Promenade Plantée
16
14
R de Bercy
Av Ledru Rollin
R d'Austerlitz
R Crémieux
R Parrot
R Michel Chasles
R Abel
R Legraverend
R Émile Gilbert
Bd Diderot
Gare de Lyon
R Hector Malot
26
31
Gare de Lyon
Pont Morland
Quai de la Rapée
Sq Georges Lesage
Pl Mazas
● 5
R Audubon
Q St-Bernard
Pont d'Austerlitz
Voie Mazas
R Traversière
R Van Gogh
Q de la Rapée
Jardin des Plantes
R Buffon
六 6
Gare d'Austerlitz
Cour d'Arrivée
● 3
Cour Départ
● 4
9
Pont Charles de Gaulle
Gare d'Austerlitz
R de Bercy
R Villi
Seine
Square Marie Curie
Q d'Austerlitz
R Fulton
R Bellièvre
R Giffard
Pont de Bercy
La Pitié–Salpêtrière
✛ 29
R Edmond Flamand
Bd Vincent Auriol
Quai de la Gare
Q de la Gare
George Balanchine
Université Paris VI Centre Hospitalier Universitaire
Jardin J Joyce

See Latin Quarter Map (pp444–5)

28

A B C D
1 2 3 4 5 6

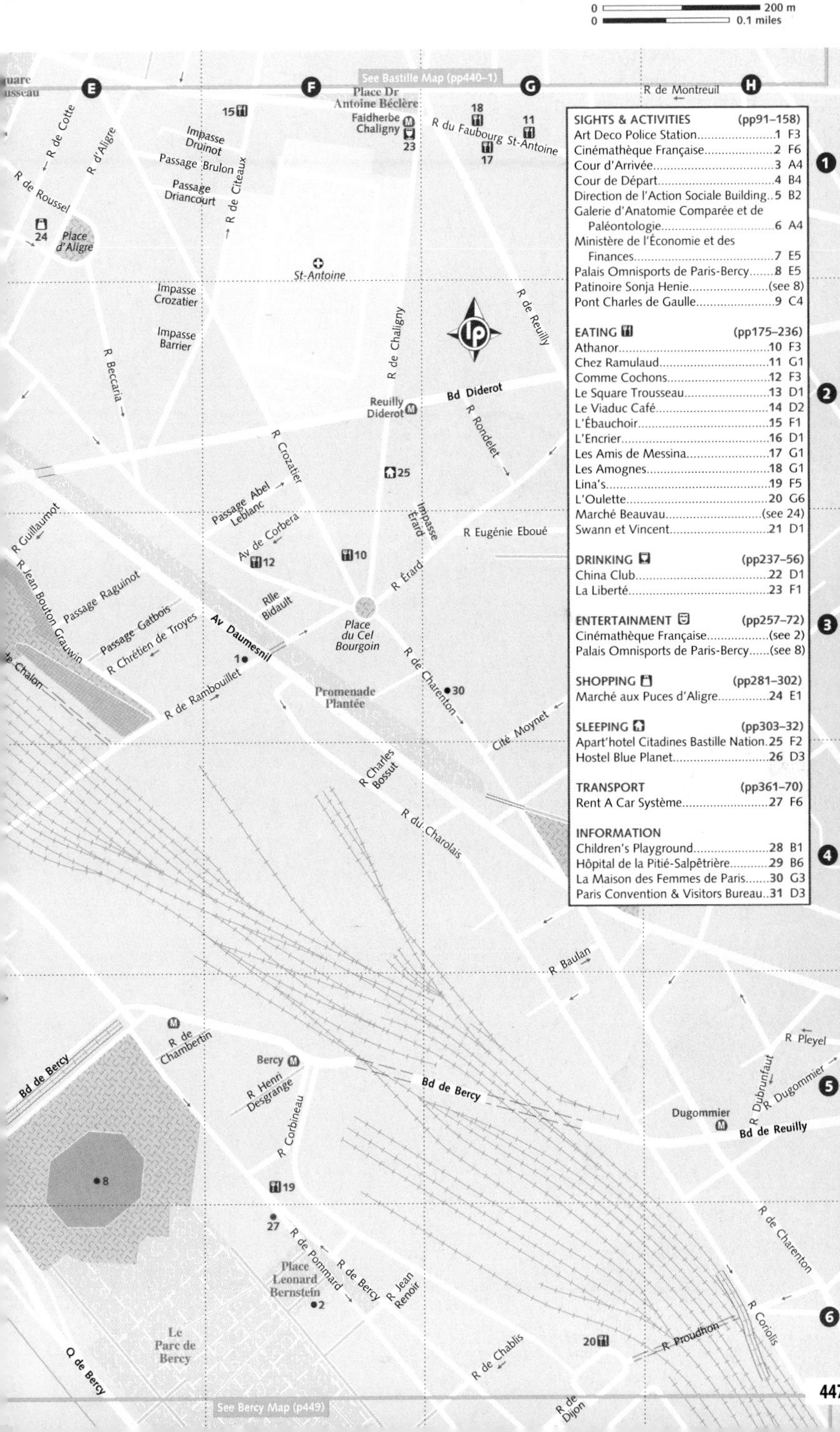

0 200 m
0 0.1 miles
See Bastille Map (pp440–1)
E
F
G
H
R de Montreuil
Place Dr Antoine Béclère
Faidherbe Chaligny
R du Faubourg St-Antoine
R de Cotte
R d'Aligre
R de Roussel
Impasse Druinot
Passage Brulon
Passage Driancourt
R de Cîteaux
Place d'Aligre
St-Antoine
Impasse Crozatier
Impasse Barrier
R Beccaria
R de Chaligny
R de Reuilly
Reuilly Diderot
Bd Diderot
R Rondelet
R Crozatier
Passage Abel Leblanc
Av de Corbera
Impasse Érard
R Eugénie Eboué
R Guillaumot
R Jean Bouton
Passage Raguinot
Passage Gatbois
R Chrétien de Troyes
Grauwin
Av Daumesnil
Rlle Bidault
R Érard
Place du Cel Bourgoin
R de Charenton
R de Rambouillet
Promenade Plantée
Cité Moynet
R Charles Bossut
R du Charolais
R Baulan
R Pleyel
R Dubrunfaut
R Dugommier
Dugommier
Bd de Reuilly
Bd de Bercy
R de Chambertin
Bercy
R Henri Desgrange
R Corbineau
R de Pommard
R de Bercy
R Jean Renoir
Place Leonard Bernstein
Le Parc de Bercy
Q de Bercy
R de Chablis
R Proudhon
R de Charenton
R Coriolis
R de Dijon
See Bercy Map (p449)

SIGHTS & ACTIVITIES (pp91–158)
Art Deco Police Station....1 F3
Cinémathèque Française....2 F6
Cour d'Arrivée....3 A4
Cour de Départ....4 B4
Direction de l'Action Sociale Building..5 B2
Galerie d'Anatomie Comparée et de Paléontologie....6 A4
Ministère de l'Économie et des Finances....7 E5
Palais Omnisports de Paris-Bercy....8 E5
Patinoire Sonja Henie....(see 8)
Pont Charles de Gaulle....9 C4

EATING (pp175–236)
Athanor....10 F3
Chez Ramulaud....11 G1
Comme Cochons....12 F3
Le Square Trousseau....13 D1
Le Viaduc Café....14 D2
L'Ébauchoir....15 F1
L'Encrier....16 D1
Les Amis de Messina....17 G1
Les Amognes....18 G1
Lina's....19 F5
L'Oulette....20 G6
Marché Beauvau....(see 24)
Swann et Vincent....21 D1

DRINKING (pp237–56)
China Club....22 D1
La Liberté....23 F1

ENTERTAINMENT (pp257–72)
Cinémathèque Française....(see 2)
Palais Omnisports de Paris-Bercy....(see 8)

SHOPPING (pp281–302)
Marché aux Puces d'Aligre....24 E1

SLEEPING (pp303–32)
Apart'hotel Citadines Bastille Nation.25 F2
Hostel Blue Planet....26 D3

TRANSPORT (pp361–70)
Rent A Car Système....27 F6

INFORMATION
Children's Playground....28 B1
Hôpital de la Pitié-Salpêtrière....29 B6
La Maison des Femmes de Paris....30 G3
Paris Convention & Visitors Bureau..31 D3

0 — 400 m
0 — 0.2 miles

See Bercy Map (p449)

SIGHTS & ACTIVITIES	(pp91–158)
Catacombes	1 A1
Manufacture des Gobelins	2 E1
Piscine de la Butte aux Cailles	3 D3

EATING	(pp175–236)
Chez Gladines	4 D3
L'Avant-Goût	5 E2
Le Temps des Cérises	6 D3

DRINKING	(pp237–56)
Le Merle Moqueur	7 D3

SLEEPING	(pp303–32)
Hôtel des Beaux-Arts	8 F3
Hôtel La Manufacture	9 E2

INFORMATION	
First Church of Christ Scientist	10 B2

BERCY

0 ————————————————— 400 m
0 ————————————————— 0.2 miles

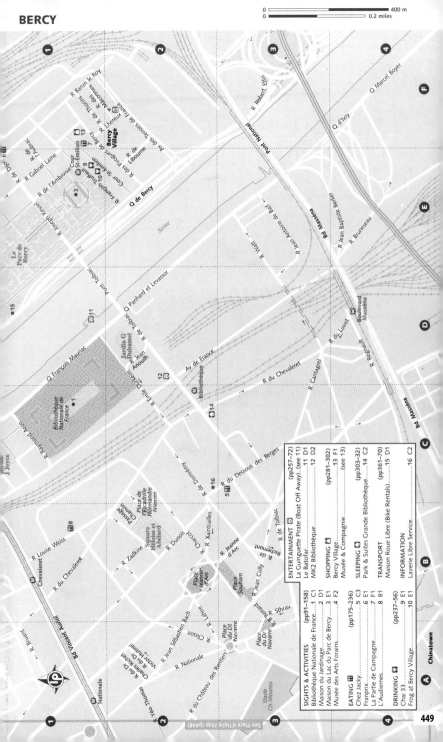

R Baron le Roy
R des Maisonnettes
R de Thorins
R Lheureux
R de Libourne
R de Dijon
R Gabriel Lamé
R de l'Ambroise
R François Truffaut
R Joseph Kessel
J Joyce
Q François Mauriac
R Raymond Aron

Bercy Village
Av des Terroirs de France
Q de Bercy
Cour St-Emilion
Cour St-Emilion
Le Parc de Bercy
Seine
Pont de Tolbiac

Jardin G Duhamel
R Jean Anouilh
R Emile Durkheim
Bibliothèque
Av de France
R du Chevaleret
R de Domrémy

Bibliothèque Nationale de France

R Robert Etlin
R Marcel Boyer
Q d'Ivry
Pont National
Bd Masséna
R Jean Antoine de Baïf
R Watt
R Jean Baptiste Berlier
R Bruneseau
R du Loiret
R Cantagrel
R Renault
Boulevard Masséna
Bd Masséna

R Louise Weiss
R du Chevaleret
Chevaleret
R Zadkine
Passage Thuré
Place de l'Escadrille Normandie Niemen
Square Héloïse et Abélard
R Dunois
R Chevet
R Xaintrailles
R Jeanne d'Arc
Place Jeanne d'Arc
Place Souham
R Jean Colly
R de Richemont
R de Tolbiac
R du Dessous des Berges
R Yves Toudic
R du Dr Charles Richet
Bd Vincent Auriol
R du Dr Victor Hutinel
R Jean Sébastien Bach
R Clisson
R Nationale
R du Château des Rentiers
R B Sthrau
Place du Dr Navarre
Stade Ch Moureu
Nationale
Chinatown

See Place d'Italie Map (p448)

Legend

SIGHTS & ACTIVITIES	**(pp91–158)**
Bibliothèque Nationale de France	1 C1
Maison du Jardinage	2 D1
Maison du Lac du Parc de Bercy	3 E1
Musée des Arts Forains	4 F2
EATING	**(pp175–236)**
Chez Jacky	5 C3
Franprix	6 E1
La Partie de Campagne	7 F1
L'Audiernes	8 B1
DRINKING	**(pp237–56)**
Chai 33	9 E1
Frog at Bercy Village	10 E1
ENTERTAINMENT	
La Guinguette Pirate (Boat Off Away)	(see 11)
Le Batofar	11 D1
MK2 Bibliothèque	12 D2
SHOPPING	**(pp281–302)**
Bercy Village	13 F1
Musée & Compagnie	(see 13)
SLEEPING	**(pp303–32)**
Park & Suites Grande Bibliothèque	14 C2
TRANSPORT	**(pp361–70)**
Maison Roue Libre (Bike Rentals)	15 D1
INFORMATION	
Laverie Libre Service	16 C2

METRO MAP

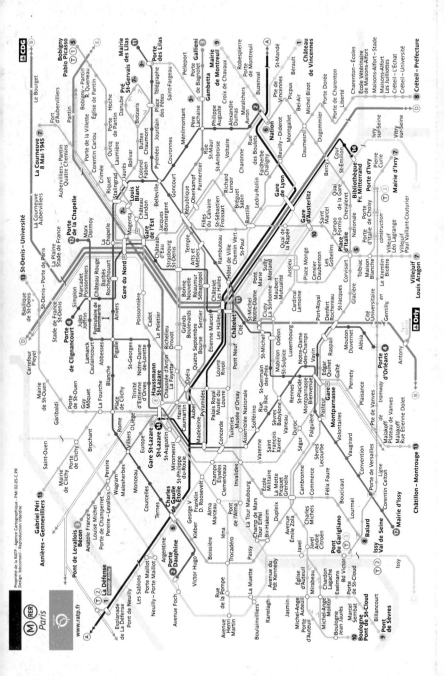